# THE ANCIENT EGYPTIAN PYRAMID TEXTS

TRANSLATED INTO ENGLISH

BY

R. O. FAULKNER
D.LIT., F.S.A.

A Digireads.com Book
Digireads.com Publishing
16212 Riggs Rd
Stilwell, KS, 66085

The Ancient Egyptian Pyramid Texts
By R. O. Faulkner
ISBN: 1-4209-2934-8



Please visit *www.digireads.com*

# PREFACE

THE Pyramid Texts of Ancient Egypt were carved on the walls of the pyramids of King Wenis of the end of the Fifth Dynasty and of the rulers of the Sixth Dynasty, and constitute the oldest *corpus* of Egyptian religious and funerary literature now extant. Furthermore, they are the least corrupt of all such collections of funerary texts, and are of fundamental importance to the student of Egyptian religion. Despite the comparative rarity of corruptions, however, the Pyramid Texts provide problems and difficulties of their own. They include very ancient texts among those which were nearly contemporary with the pyramids in which they were inscribed, imposing on the modern reader problems of grammar and vocabulary; the orthography is apt to be unusual; and there are many mythological and other allusions of which the purport is obscure to the translator of today. The first attempt at translation goes back to 1882, when, in vol. iii of the *Recueil de travaux relatifs à la philologie et l'archéologie égyptiennes et assyriennes*, Maspero began a series of printed hieroglyphic texts and accompanying translations from each pyramid in turn; this was a remarkable achievement when it is realized how little at that time was known of Egyptian grammar and vocabulary. These articles were later collected in one volume and published in 1894 under the title *Les Inscriptions des pyramides de Saqqarah*. In 1910 there appeared the standard edition by Sethe of the hieroglyphic texts, in which they are grouped into *Sprüche* —here called 'Utterances', often abbreviated to 'Utt.'—and the corresponding passages from the different pyramids are displayed in parallel in numbered sections, an arrangement essential to a satisfactory study of the inscriptions. This publication by Sethe consists of two volumes of hieroglyphic texts and two slimmer ones of *Kritischer Apparat*, etc., and it will remain the indispensable source for students of these ancient texts. In 1912 Breasted, using Sethe's text, incorporated very many quotations thence in his *Development of Religion and Thought in Ancient Egypt*; in 1923 Speleers published in French a translation and index in his *Textes des pyramides égyptiennes*; Sethe's German translation and commentary appeared posthumously over a period of some thirty years under the title *Übersetzung und Kommentar zu den altägyptischen Pyramidentexten*, while in 1952 Mercer published an English version in four volumes. Piankoff has recently published a study of the Pyramid of Unas in the Bollinger Series, but it came to my notice too late to be utilized here.

In these circumstances it might well be asked why a fresh translation should be foisted on the public when several versions using Sethe's text already exist. The answer is that in the last half-century great advances have been made in our knowledge of Ancient Egyptian, thanks largely to the labours of Gunn, Gardiner, and Edel; a second reason is the bulk and cost of the more recent publications. Sethe's *Übersetzung und Kommentar* is not only very bulky, consisting of six (undated) volumes, but is also exceedingly costly and is still incomplete; his original manuscript as available to his posthumous editors stopped short at Utt. 582 and did not include Utt. 1–212, which consist largely of ritual formulae. Further, Sethe's copy as handed over dates back something like forty years, and its editors themselves remark that if the author had lived to complete his work and revise it, undoubtedly he would have made many alterations, though even in its imperfect state Sethe's translation is an indispensable tool for all future students of these texts. Speleers's one-volume translation of 1923 is now outdated, though the vocabulary-index is of value, while Mercer's version does not represent current knowledge of Ancient Egyptian, and Piankoff's study refers to only one pyramid out of six. Further, since Sethe's original publication of the text, more material has come to light which has enabled many lacunae to be filled and more texts to be added.

In preparing the present translation I have attempted not only to bring to bear on the Egyptian text our current knowledge of grammar and lexicography, but also to produce a work which will be usable by both philologists and students of ancient religion, which will be of modest bulk, and, above all, which will cost as little as circumstances permit. The notes on the translations have therefore been reduced to the bare minimum; when in doubt the scholar in Ancient Egyptian will in most cases be able to consult Sethe's books, while the student of religion will not be interested in lengthy philological discussion. For similar reasons I have refrained from dilating on the literary or religious aspects of the texts.

The text upon which this translation is based is, of course, that of Sethe, embodying the corrections noted in his 'Nachträge' and *Kritischer Apparat*; in the cases of lacunae, often extensive, where all sources are lacking in the original edition, these have been filled as far as possible from the texts later published by Jéquier in *Le Monument funéraire de Pepi II*, vol. i, pls. 1 ff. and *Les Pyramides des reines Neit et Apouit*, pls. 7 ff., hereinafter cited as JPII and Nt respectively and quoted by line-number. Jéquier's *La Pyramide d'Aba* (cited as Aba) has been used but sparely; the pyramid in question is later than the end of the Sixth Dynasty and is not entirely in accord with the original canon. The texts used for the purpose of completing and extending Sethe's edition are appended in a second supplementary volume, except that in cases of minor extent the relevant passages are quoted in my notes.

The idiom in which the present translation is couched is on the whole that of modern English. To a generation of students and scholars not brought up on the Book of Common Prayer and the Authorized Version of the Bible, an idiom based on Tudor or Jacobean English is alien and conveys a sense of unreality and artificiality. I have therefore dispensed with the pronouns 'thou', 'thy', 'thee', 'ye' and have employed the current 'you', 'your', and have dropped such verbal inflexions as 'makest', 'maketh', 'didst'. On the other hand, I have retained a very few archaisms such as, for example, 'behold', which to my mind is more expressive of the original than 'see', 'look', and which should not disturb the modern reader, even if the linguistic purist does not approve. The cartouches of the royal dead have been rendered simply as 'King' or 'the King'; to write 'King W.T.M.N' and the like is ugly and clumsy, while 'King X' is not much better. Confining myself to the simple title has the advantage of stressing the fact that these texts have in origin no personal application to one particular king, but are chosen out of an existing *corpus*. In arranging the translation I have not split it up into short sentences corresponding to the numbered sections of Sethe's text as did Sethe himself and Mercer; I have reproduced the prose passages in a continuous text and have confined short lines to poetical texts and 'litanies', the section numbers being noted in the margin in all cases. My hope is that this procedure will not only make the translation easier to read but will also give some notion of the literary character of a text. Whether my judgement has always been sound in these matters is for the critics to decide.

Some other points of translation call for mention. One such point is my treatment of the word *kꜣ*, on which see Gardiner in *JEA* 36, 7, n. 2; Greven, *Der Ka in Theologie und Königskult des Alten Reiches*; and my review in *JEA* 41, 141. Rather than follow the custom usual among translators of simply transcribing the word as *ka* and thus avoiding committal, I have ventured to translate it into English as 'double' in those cases, much in the majority, where it appears to be an entity in its own right in association with the dead king, but I have not hesitated to use the terms 'spirit', 'essence', or 'power' where these seem to be the real sense. Another problem is posed by the term *Dꜣt*, translated in this book as 'Netherworld'; in this case it must be remembered that to the early Egyptians it embraced not only the world beneath the earth but also part of the visible sky, see Sethe's discussion in *Komm.* i, 49 ff. 'Netherworld', therefore, though the nearest equivalent in English, is not always to be taken at the foot of the letter.

One of the great difficulties in translating the Pyramid Texts, as in a lesser degree with all but purely formal Egyptian texts, is the ambiguity of the written language and also our imperfect knowledge of it. The rules of grammar are well defined so far as they go, but within those rules a doubt must often remain, for example, as to whether a given sentence is to be understood as a statement or as a wish; in such cases a translator can render a passage only as he himself feels it. In vol. 9 of the *Journal of Egyptian Archaeology*, when introducing his translation of *The Eloquent Peasant*, Sir Alan Gardiner referred to this problem, and on p. 6 he wrote: 'The only basis we have for preferring one rendering to another, when once the exigencies of grammar and dictionary have been satisfied—and these leave a large margin for divergencies—is an intuitive appreciation of the trend of the ancient writer's mind.' Without doubt many of the divergencies between Sethe's translation and my own arise from just this necessity of personal interpretation, and it is well that differences of opinion should be ventilated, so that other workers in this field may be made aware of the possibilities and perhaps be enabled to decide between them.

In order to arrive at the basic form of the Utterances, they have been translated with the pronoun of the 1st person instead of the king's name wherever there has been warrant for doing so; it is certain that in many cases the original composition was deemed to have been spoken by the dead king. In every case the grounds for this treatment, except in those texts where the reason is obvious, have been stated in the notes to the translations, and many Utterances gain considerably in life and force thereby.

Apart from the very great debt I owe to Sethe's publications, I have had valuable suggestions from Mr. C. H. S. Spaull, who read a considerable portion of the typescript and raised a number of points, and from Mr. H. S. Smith, Reader in Egyptology at University College, London, with whom I have had a number of fruitful discussions on various points of Egyptian religion. I must also express my deep gratitude to the Delegates of the Oxford University Press, for undertaking the publication of this book, and to the Council of the British Academy, and the Sir Alan Gardiner Settlement for Egyptological Purposes, for their generous financial subventions towards the cost of printing.

# CONTENTS

# ABBREVIATIONS

| | |
|---|---|
| Abubakr, *Kronen* | A. el M. J. Abubakr, *Untersuchungen über die ägyptischen Kronen.* |
| *Adm.* | *The Admonitions of an Egyptian Sage.* |
| *AEO* | A. H. Gardiner, *Ancient Egyptian Onomastica.* |
| *Äg. Stud.* | *Ägyptologische Studien*, ed. O. Firchow (*Festschrift* in honour of H. Grapow). |
| Allen | T. G. Allen, *Horus in the Pyramid Texts.* |
| *Amenemhēt* | N. de G. Davies and A. H. Gardiner, *The Tomb of Amenemhēt.* |
| *Amun* | K. Sethe, *Amun und die acht Urgötter von Hermopolis.* |
| *Ann. Serv.* | *Annales du Service des antiquités de l'Égypte.* |
| *BD* | E. A. W. Budge, *The Book of the Dead*, 1898 edition, Text volume. |
| *BH* | P. E. Newberry, *Beni Hasan.* |
| *Bibl. Or.* | *Bibliotheca Orientalis.* |
| *BIFAO* | *Bulletin de l'Institut français d'archéologie orientale du Caire.* |
| *Book of Hours* | R. O. Faulkner, *An Ancient Egyptian Book of Hours.* |
| Breasted, *Development* | J. H. Breasted, *Development of Religion and Thought in Ancient Egypt.* |
| Brit. Mus. | British Museum. |
| Cairo | Musée du Caire. |
| *Ch. B.* | A. H. Gardiner, *Hieratic Papyri in the British Museum. Third Series: Chester Beatty Gift.* |
| *Concise Dict.* | R. O. Faulkner, *A Concise Dictionary of Middle Egyptian.* |
| *CT* | A. de Buck, *The Egyptian Coffin Texts.* |
| *D. el B.* | E. Naville, *The Temple of Deir el Bahari.* |
| Dav. *Ptah.* | N. de G. Davies, *The Mastaba of Ptahhetep and Akhethetep.* |
| *Dict. géogr.* | H. Gauthier, *Dictionnaire des noms géographiques contenus dans les textes hiéroglyphiques.* |
| *Dram. Texte* | K. Sethe, *Dramatische Texte zu altaegyptischen Mysterienspielen.* |
| *Dream-book* | Chester Beatty Papyrus No. III. |
| *Eb.* | Ebers Medical Papyrus. |
| Edel | E. Edel, *Altägyptische Grammatik.* |
| *Ex Oriente Lux* | *Jaarbericht van het vooraziatisch-egyptisch Genootschap Ex Oriente Lux.* |
| *Frises* | G. Jéquier, *Les Frises d'objets des sarcophages du Moyen Empire.* |
| Gardiner | A. H. Gardiner, *Egyptian Grammar*, 3rd edition. |
| *Gîza* | H. Junker, *Gîza.* |
| *GNS* | A. H. Gardiner, *Notes on the Story of Sinuhe.* |
| *Hamm.* | J. Couyat and P. Montet, *Les Inscriptions hiéroglyphiques et hiératiques du Ouadi Hammamat.* |
| *Hatnub* | R. Anthes, *Die Felsenschriften von Hatnub.* |
| *Herdsm.* | *The Story of the Herdsman.* |
| *Ḥeḳanakhte* | T. G. H. James, *The Ḥeḳanakhte Papers and other Early Middle Kingdom Documents.* |

| | |
|---|---|
| *Ikhekhi* | T. G. H. James, *The Mastaba of Khentika called Ikhekhi.* |
| *JEA* | *Journal of Egyptian Archaeology.* |
| *JNES* | *Journal of Near Eastern Studies.* |
| JPII | G. Jéquier, *Le Monument funéraire de Pepi II*, hieroglyphic text quoted by line-number. |
| *Komm.* | K. Sethe, *Übersetzung und Kommentar zu den altägyptischen Pyramidentexten.* |
| *L. Eg. Misc.* | R. A. Caminos, *Late Egyptian Miscellanies.* |
| Lanzone, *Mitologia* | R. V. Lanzone, *Dizionario di mitologia egiziana.* |
| *Leb.* | A. Erman, *Gespräch eines Lebensmüden mit seiner Seele, P. Berlin 3024*, re-edited by R. O. Faulkner, *JEA* 42, 21 ff. |
| *Les.* | K. Sethe, *Aegyptische Lesestücke zum Gebrauch in akademischen Unterricht.* |
| *Med. Habu* | *Medinet Habu*, edited by the Oriental Institute of Chicago University. |
| *Meir* | A. M. Blackman, *The Rock Tombs of Meir.* |
| *Minerals* | J. R. Harris, *Lexicographical Studies in Ancient Egyptian Minerals.* |
| Nt | G. Jéquier, *Les Pyramides des reines Neit et Apouit*, hieroglyphic text quoted by line-number. |
| *Neit* | Printed text of last, quoted by page-number. |
| *Paheri* | J. J. Tylor and F. Ll. Griffith, *The Tomb of Paheri at El Kab*, bound up with E. Naville, *Ahnas el Medineh.* |
| *Peas.* | *The Story of the Eloquent Peasant.* |
| *Prisse* | The Prisse Papyrus, edited by Z. Žába, *Les Maximes de Ptahhotep.* |
| *PSBA* | *Proceedings of the Society of Biblical Archaeology.* |
| *Ptah.* (*E.R.A.*) | R. F. E. Paget and A. A. Pirie, *The Tomb of Ptah-hetep*, second part of J. E. Quibell, *The Ramesseum.* |
| *Pyr.* | K. Sethe, *Die altaegyptischen Pyramidentexte.* |
| *RB* | A. de Buck, *Egyptian Reading-book.* |
| *Religion and Thought* | J. H. Breasted, *Development of Religion and Thought in Ancient Egypt.* |
| *Rev. d'Ég.* | *Revue d'Égyptologie.* |
| *Saqq. Mast.* | M. A. Murray, *Saqqara Mastabas.* |
| *Sh. S.* | *The Story of the Shipwrecked Sailor.* |
| *Sin.* | *The Story of Sinuhe.* |
| *Stud. Griff.* | *Studies presented to F. Ll. Griffith on his Seventieth Birthday.* |
| *Syntax* | B. Gunn, *Studies in Egyptian Syntax.* |
| *Ti* | G. Steindorff, *Das Grab des Ti.* |
| *Urgeschichte* | K. Sethe, *Urgeschichte und älteste Religion der Ägypter.* |
| *Urk.* i | —— *Urkunden des alten Reichs.* |
| *Urk.* iv | —— and W. Helck, *Urkunden der 18. Dynastie.* |
| *Urk.* v | H. Grapow, *Religiöse Urkunden. Ausgewählte Texte des Totenbuches.* |
| *Wb.* | A. Erman and H. Grapow, *Wörterbuch der aegyptischen Sprache.* |
| *Westc.* | *Westcar Papyrus.* |
| *Zahlen* | K. Sethe, *Von Zahlen und Zahlworten bei den alten Ägypten.* |
| *ZÄS* | *Zeitschrift für ägyptische Sprache und Altertumskunde.* |

## NOTE TO READERS

Square brackets [ ] denote a restored passage.

Square brackets with dots [. . .] denote a lacuna.

Angle brackets ⟨ ⟩ denote words or suffixes omitted in the original.

Round brackets ( ) denote English words supplied to bring out the sense.

Dots . . . not in brackets indicate that a word or words are untranslatable.

# TRANSLATIONS AND NOTES

*The sarcophagus texts*

## Utterance 1

Recitation by Nūt, the greatly beneficent: The King is my eldest son who split open my womb; he is my beloved, with whom I am well pleased. § 1

## Utterance 2

Recitation by Gēb: The King is my bodily son [. . .]

## Utterance 3

Recitation by Nūt the great who dwells in the Lower Mansion:[1] The King is my beloved son, my first-born[2] upon the throne of Gēb, with whom he[3] is well pleased, and he has given to him his heritage in the presence of the Great Ennead. All the gods are in joy, and they say: How goodly is the King! His father Gēb is pleased with him. § 2 § 3

1. A shrine in Ōn, *Dict. géogr.* iv, 121. Ōn (Heliopolis) is discussed in *AEO* ii, 144* ff.
2. Cf. *Dram. Texte*, 29.
3. Gēb.

## Utterance 4

Recitation by Nūt: O King, I have given[1] to you your sister Isis, that she may lay hold of you and give to you your heart for your body.

1. Or 'I give', synchronous present, cf. *Syntax*, 69 ff.

## Utterance 5

Recitation by Nūt: O King, I have given to you your sister Nephthys, that she may lay hold of you and give to you your heart for your body.

## Utterance 6

Recitation by Nūt the Great Fruitful One:[1] The King my son is my beloved; I have given to him the two horizons[2] that he may have power in them as Ḥarakhti. All the gods say: It is the truth that the King is your best-beloved among your children; watch over him eternally. § 4

1. *Nḫbt wrt*, cf. *Wb.* ii, 309, 1.

2. Dual; shown not to be sing. by *ỉm·sn*, while the plural is ruled out by the fact that to the Egyptians there were only two horizons, i.e. the places where the sun rises and sets.

## Utterance 7

§ 5 Recitation by Nūt the great[1] who dwells in the Mansion of *Snỉt*:[2] The King is my son of my desire; I have given to him the Netherworld[3] that he may preside over it as Horus who presides over the Netherworld. All the gods say: Your father Shu knows that you love the King more than your mother Tefēnet.[4]

1. The *n* of *ỉn* 'by' is misplaced.
2. A shrine in Ōn, cf. *Wb.* iv, 503, 6; *Dict. géogr.* iv, 134.
3. On *Dɜt*, here translated by 'Netherworld', cf. *Komm.* i, 49 ff.
4. Misspelt *Tftn*.

§§ 6–8 Utt. 8–10 consist solely of royal protocols and are not translated.

## Utterance 11

(§ 8) Recitation by Nūt: I enfold your beauty within this soul[1] of mine for all life, permanence, dominion and health for the King—may he live for ever!

1. The 'soul' of Nūt here is the coffin bearing her name which encloses the body of the king. Although not actually carved on a sarcophagus, this text belongs to the sarcophagus group of Utterances.

*Restoration of the corpse and presentation of food and water*

## Utterance 12

§ 9 *Lost*

## Utterance 13

I[1] give you your head, I fasten your head to the bones for you.

1. Introductory *ḏd mdw* is omitted henceforward from the translation when it is no more than a formal rubric.

## Utterance 14

I give him his eyes, that he may be content—a *ḥtp*-offering.

## Utterance 15

Gēb has given you your eyes, that you may be content [. . .]

## Utterance 16

[. . .] the Eye of Horus—water, a *nmst*-jar. §10

## Utterance 17

O Thoth, put for him his head on him—water, a *ds*-jar.

## Utterance 18

He has brought it for him—water, a drinking cup.

## Utterance 19

*Lost*

### *The Ritual of Opening the Mouth*

## Utterance 20

O King, I have come in search of you, for I am Horus; I have struck your §11
mouth for you, for I am your beloved son; I have split open your mouth for
you.[1] [I announce him to his mother when she laments him, I announce §12
him to her who was joined to him. Your mouth is in good order(?), for I have
adjusted your mouth] to your bones [for you]. Recite four times: O Osiris
the King, I split open your mouth for you with the . . .[1] of the Eye of Horus
—1 foreleg.

1. *Ḥpḫ*, meaning obscure. Pun on *ḫpš* 'foreleg'.

## Utterance 21

[Your mouth is in good order(?), for I split open your mouth for you, I split §13
open your eyes for you. O King, I open your mouth for you] with the adze of Wepwawet, [I split open your mouth for you][1] with the adze of iron which spilt open the mouths of the gods. O Horus, open the mouth of this King! [O Horus, split open the mouth of this King! Horus has opened the mouth of this King, Horus has split open the mouth of this King] with that wherewith he split open the mouth of his father, with that wherewith he split open the

§ 14 mouth of Osiris,[1] with the iron which issued from Seth, with the adze [of iron which split open the mouths of the gods. The King's mouth is split open with it, and he goes and himself[2] speaks with the Great Ennead in the Mansion of the Prince which is in] Ōn,[3] and he assumes the *Wrrt*-crown before Horus, Lord of Patricians.[4]

1. For Sethe's amended restorations see *Pyr.* iii, 1. On *nwt Wp-wrwt* cf. *Meir*, iii, p. 28, n. 2.
2. With *ḏt* 'self' compare the later *ḥrw* 'self'. Cf. Edel, § 176.
3. Cf. *Dict. géogr.* iv, 127.
4. On the *pꜥt* cf. *AEO* i, 98* ff.

## Utterance 22

§ 15 O Osiris the King, I bring to you your son whom you love, who will split open your mouth.

## Utterance 23

*A libation spell*

§ 16 O Osiris, take away all those who hate the King[1] and who speak evilly against his name. O Thoth, hasten, take away him who is harmful to[2] Osiris, and carry off him who speaks evilly against the King's name; put him in your hand. Recite four times: Do not let go[3] of him! Beware lest you let go of him! —Pour water.

1. So the original text.
2. *Sw* 'be harmful', 'dangerous', again in §§ 611*b*; 646*d*; 1335*b*; 1336*b*; 1931*c*; cf. also *irt Ḥr swit* 'the endangered Eye of Horus', § 600*c*; in the sense of 'bad' of smell, § 1790*b*; see *Komm.* iii, 135.
3. On the construction cf. Edel, § 1104.

## Utterance 24

O Thoth, hasten, take the King's foe[1] to Osiris.

1. Read *Ḏḥwty iz iṯ ḫft(y) n Nt* . . ., Nt 68.

## Utterance 25

§ 17 Someone has gone with his double,[1]
Horus has gone with his double,
Seth has gone with his double,
Thoth has gone with his double,

*Dwn-ꜥnwy* has gone with his double,[2]
Osiris has gone with his double,
*Ḫnt-ỉrty* has gone with his double,
You also having gone[3] with your double.
O King, the arm of your double is in front of you! § 18
O King, the arm of your double is behind you!
O King, the foot of your double is in front of you!
O King, the foot of your double is behind you![4]

O Osiris the King, I give to you the Eye of Horus, that your face may be provided with it; the perfume[5] of the Eye of Horus is diffused over you—incense and fire.

1. Cf. §§ 826. 1431, where, however, the preposition is *ḥr*. On the translation of *kꜣ* see the Preface.
2. The first four gods belong to the cardinal points, cf. *JEA* 36, 9. On the reading *Dwn-ꜥnwy* here cf. ibid. 10.
3. [hieroglyph] is old perfective 2nd sing.; cf. *Komm.* iv, 79. For *ḏdk* 'also' cf. *Dram. Texte*, 53; Edel, §§ 111. 180.
4. This jingle may mean that the king's double strides along at his side, arms and legs swinging back and forth.
5. W 77 inserts *ḏd mdw zp 4* before this sentence; W 5*a* places it in the final rubric.

*Title to Utterances* 26–8, *see* § 1644*a*

A ball of incense.

## Utterance 26[1]

O Horus who is[2] Osiris the King, take the Eye of Horus to yourself, even the § 19
Eye of Horus which he has diffused abroad by means of its perfume.

1. Cf. Utt. 449. 621.
2. Regarding *ỉmy* as of equivalence; 'who is in' gives poor sense.

## Utterance 27

O Osiris the King, take the Eye of Horus and provide yourself with its perfume.

## Utterance 28

O Osiris the King, Horus has given you his Eye; provide[1] your face with it.

1. Imperative with reinforcing dative; a direction to the deceased is needed.

*Title to Utterances* 29 *and* 598, *cf.* § 1644*b*

Dried incense.

## Utterance 29

§ 20 O King, I have come and I bring to you the Eye of Horus. May you provide
your face with it, that it may cleanse you, its perfume being on you. The
perfume of the Eye of Horus is on this King, it removes your efflux and
§ 21 protects you from the sweat(?)[1] of the hand of Seth.| O Osiris the King,
may the intact Eye of Horus belong(?) to you,[2] the Eye of Horus being intact,
intact!

1. Lit. 'flood', but determined with drops of fluid.
2. On *nḫḫ* (*n·k*) *ḥr·k* see *Komm.* i, 160 f.

## Utterance 30

O Horus who is Osiris the King, you are provided with the Eye of Horus; take[1] it.

1. Certainly *mi* 'take', despite the det. Λ.

## Utterance 31

O Osiris the King, Horus has filled you with his complete Eye.

## Utterance 32

§ 22 This cold water of yours, O Osiris, this cold water of yours, O King, has
gone forth to your son, has gone forth to Horus. I have come and I bring to
you the Eye of Horus, that your heart may be refreshed possessing it; I bring
§ 23 it to you under your sandals.| Take the efflux which issued from you; your
heart will not be inert, possessing it. Recite four times: Take what comes forth
at the voice to you[1]—cold water and two pellets of natron.[2]

1. This is a well-known crux. At first glance it would appear as if *pr* exceptionally had transitive sense, but in § 488*b* Sethe translates the same expression as 'die ihr hervorgekommen seid auf die Stimme', explaining the construction as 'altertümliche Anwendung des Beziehungskasus anstelle eines präpositionellen Ausdrucks', *Komm.* ii, 322 f.

2. So W 10*a*; varr. W 32*a* 'Giving cold water of the Northland'; W 78*a* 'Cold water and two pellets'; W 346*a* 'Giving cold water'; N 260 'Give cold water of the Northland ( *sic*)'; N 347 'Two pellets of natron and cold water'. Cf. *Giza* iii, 103 f.

## Utterance 33

O King, take this cold water of yours,[1] for you have coolness with Horus § 24
in your name of Him who issued from cold water; take the efflux which issued from you. Horus has caused the gods[2] to assemble for you at the place[3] where you have gone, Horus has caused the Children of Horus to muster for you at the place where you drowned.[4] ¹O Osiris the King, take § 25
your natron that you may be divine, for Nūt has caused you to be a god to your foe in your name of God; Ḥar-renpi recognizes you, you being young in your name of Fresh Water.[5]

1. Cf. Utt. 423.
2. Var. N 563 'your gods', with certainly an error for ; read 'all the gods'.
3. Var. *bw nb* 'every place'.
4. The sense of *mḥ* is clear, cf. § 615*d*.
5. Read , cf. 767*a*.

## Utterance 34

*Zmln, zmln*[1] which splits open your mouth![2] O King, taste its taste in front § 2
of them of the God's Booth. What Horus spits out is *zmln*, what Seth spits out is *zmln*, what reconciles[3] the Two Gods is *zmln*. Recite four times: You are purified in the company of the Followers of Horus—Upper Egyptian natron of Nekheb, 5 pellets.

1. The context shows that *zmln* is a substantive, not an adverb or particle as *Wb.* iii, 453, 6 suggests; it is something that can be spat out, and apparently a pleasant substance which can calm the quarrelling gods. In *ZÄS* 47, 125 Blackman suggested 'cream'.
2. N interpolates 'natron, 1 pellet' after each sentence.
3. For *t(w)t ib* 'reconcile' cf. *twt ib·f ḥnꜥ·i* 'he is in accord with me', *Leb.* 40. See also § 488*a*.

## Utterance 35

Your purification is the purification of Horus,[1] your purification is the puri- § 27
fication of Seth, your purification is the purification of Thoth, your purification is the purification of *Dwn-ꜥnwy*,[2] and your purification is also[3] among them; your mouth is the mouth of a sucking calf[4] on the day it was born—Lower Egyptian natron of *Št-pt*,[5] 5 pellets.

1. Purification, not censing, is the meaning here, since natron is the substance presented.
2. See Utt. 25, n. 2.
3. On *ḏdk(t)* see Utt. 25, n. 3.
4. The king's mouth is as pure and uncontaminated as that of a sucking calf. For this expression cf. 'sucking calf', Louvre C 17.
5. *Št-pt*, later *Šrt-pt*, finally *Šrp*, was in the Wādi Natrūn, cf. *Dict. géogr.* v, 143; *Komm.* iii, 87.

## Utterance 36

§ 28 Your purification[1] is the purification of Horus, your purification is the purification of Seth, your purification is the purification of Thoth, your purification is the purification of *Dwn-ʿnwy*, your purification is the purification of your double, your purification is the purification of your purification,[2] and
§ 29 this purification of yours also[3] is among your brethren the gods.| Your purification is upon your mouth; may you cleanse all your bones, and may you provide what appertains to you. O Osiris, I give to you the Eye of Horus that your face may be provided with it, it being suffused[4]—incense, 1 pellet.

1. Here 'censing' also is a permisisble translation, since the offering is incense.

2. Presumably so, as this sentence appears to follow the model of what precedes, *nṯr·k*+*nṯr*+ genitive. The sense must be that the king is doubly purified.

3. See Utt. 25, n. 3. Note the position of *pn*, separated from its noun.

4. i.e. the face, which is suffused with the perfume; *pḏpḏ*, being masculine, cannot refer to the Eye of Horus.

## Utterance 37

§ 30 O King, I fasten for you your jaws which were divided—*psš-kf*.[1]

1. An instrument for 'opening the mouth'.

## Utterance 38

O Osiris the King, I split open your mouth for you—god's iron of Upper Egypt, 1 ingot; god's iron of Lower Egypt, 1 ingot.

*Ritual of Offering; the preliminary repast*

## Utterance 39

§ 31 O King, take the Eye of Horus for which he goes; I bring it to you and I put it in your mouth for you—*zrw*[1] of Upper Egypt and *zrw* of Lower Egypt.

1. An unknown substance.

## Utterance 40

O King, take the *šḫk* of Osiris—*šḫk*.[1]

1. Meaning unknown.

## Utterance 41

Take the tip of Horus' own breast,[1] take what is for your mouth—milk, 1 jar. § 32

1. For the doubling of the *n* in *mnḏ* see also *smn(n)*, § 1482*b*.

## Utterance 42

Take the breast of your sister Isis the milk-provider(?),[1] which you shall take to your mouth—an empty *mnzꜣ*-jar.

1. Meaning uncertain, but cf. *Wb.* i, 475, 5. The translation 'protectress', loc. cit. 8, is not excluded, but in this context is less likely.

## Utterance 43

Take the two Eyes of Horus, the black and the white; take them to your § 33
forehead that they may illumine your face—the lifting up of a white jar and a black jar.[1]

1. Var. 'a *ḥꜣṯs*-jar of white *mnw*-stone, the right eye; a *ḥꜣṯs*-jar of black *mnw*-stone, the left eye'.

## Utterance 44

Rēꜥ in the sky is gracious to you, and he conciliates the Two Lords for you. § 34
'Night'[1] is gracious to you, the Two Ladies are gracious to you. Graciousness is what has been brought to you,[2] graciousness is what you see, graciousness is what you hear, graciousness is in front of you, graciousness is behind you, graciousness is your portion—a fresh *pꜣt*-cake.

1. 'Night' is in antithesis to Rēꜥ, sun, just as the Two Ladies are in antithesis to the Two Lords. The sense of the Utterance must be that day and night, god and goddess combine to bestow their favours on the king.
2. Emend *ỉnt nt·k* into *ỉn(y)t n·k*, passive participle+dative.

## Utterance 45

O Osiris the King, take the white teeth of Horus, which shall furnish your § 35
mouth—5 bunches of onions.

## Utterance 46

Recite four times: A boon which the King grants to the double of the King. O Osiris the King, take the Eye of Horus, your *pꜣt*-cake, that you may eat—a *pꜣt*-cake of the offering.[1]

1. Var. a 'fresh *pꜣt*-cake'.

## Utterance 47

§ 36 O Osiris the King, take the Eye of Horus which was wrested from Seth and which you shall take to your mouth, with which you shall split open your mouth—wine, a *hꜣts*-jar of white *mnw*-stone.

## Utterance 48

O Osiris the King, your mouth is split open with that of which you have full measure[1]—wine, a *hꜣts*-jar of black *mnw*-stone.

1. With *mḥt îm·k* compare *mḥ m* 'full measure of', *Peas.* R35. The king's mouth is opened to take a full draught of wine.

## Utterance 49

§ 37 O Osiris the King, take the ferment(?) which issued from you—beer, a *ḥnt*-bowl of black *mnw*-stone.

## Utterance 50

O Rēʿ, if you dawn in the sky,[1] you dawn for the King, lord of all things; if all things belong to[2] yourself, then all things will belong to the double of the King, all things will belong to himself—the lifting up before him of a sanctified offering.[3]

1. Lit. 'your dawning is in the sky'.
2. — is *n(y)*, genitival adjective used predicatively, cf. Gardiner, § 114, 2, but here with nominal subject.
3. So N; W omits *fꜣt ḫft ḥr·f*.

## Utterance 51

§ 38 O King, take the Eye of Horus which you shall taste—a *dpt*-cake.

## Utterance 52

O you who are put under the earth and are in darkness![1]—an *ꜣḥ*-cake.

1. Cf. *Dram. Texte*, 214. The allusion is to the king in his tomb-chamber.

## Utterance 53

O King, take the Eye of Horus that you may be embraced[1]—*zḫn*-meat.[2]

1. Cf. *Dram. Texte*, 233. 'Sought out' is also a possible translation.
2. Cf. *AEO* ii, 253* f.

## Utterance 54

O King, take the Eye of Horus, which was wrested from Seth and saved for § 39
you; your mouth is split open with it—beer,[1] a *ḥnt*-bowl of white *mnw*-stone.

1. So N, the better reading, cf. § 39*c*; W has 'wine'.

## Utterance 55

O King, take the ferment(?) which issued from Osiris—beer, a *ḥnt*-bowl of black *mnw*-stone.

## Utterance 56

O King, take the Eye of Horus, rescued for you; it will never escape from § 40
you—beer, an iron *ḥnt*-bowl.

## Utterance 57

O King, take the Eye of Horus, provide yourself with it—beer, a *ḥnt*-bowl of *ḥtm*-material.

### *Presentation of weapons, garments, and insignia*

## Utterance 57A

Bring the two Eyes of Horus—a *iwnt*-bow.[1] § 40+1

1. The Utterances numbered here 57A–S, Utt. 58–70 of Sethe's text, and those numbered below 71–71I, form in Nt, 283–328 a continuous offering-text which has been translated in full. For the hieroglyphic text see the Supplement, pp. 1–7.

## Utterance 57B

Take that wherewith they have . . .[1]—arrows(?).[2] § 40+2

1. *Bḫr·n·sn*, meaning unknown; the context suggests that 'shot' may be a possibility.
2. *Ḫrtỉ* may be a metathesis of *ḫrỉt* 'arrows', *Frises*, 216.

## Utterance 57C

Take them, namely what I give you—*rḏ*-bowstring(s). § 40+3

## Utterance 57D

He has put them on the ground—*nw-rḏ*-bowstring(s).[1] § 40+4

1. Cf. *Frises*, 227, n. 1; see also Utt. 71G, n. 4.

## Utterance 57E

§ 40+5 O Osiris [the King],[1] I bring to you the two Eyes of Horus—a *iwnt*-bow.[2]

1. The fact that Nt is a queen is ignored in the translations, as, with rare exceptions, it is in the hieroglyphic text; these Utterances are of general application to dead kings, and their use for the benefit of queens appears to have been an innovation.
2. Virtually a repetition of Utt. 57A.

## Utterance 57F

§ 40+6 [. . .] Seth—a *pḏt*-bow.

## Utterance 57G

§ 40+7 I give [. . .] the heart of Seth—[. . .].

## Utterance 57H

§ 40+8 [. . .]—[. . .]-bowstring (?).

## Utterance 57I

§ 40+9 [. . .] which their lord grasped—[. . .].

## Utterance 57J

§ 40+10 [O Osiris] the King, I bring to you the two Eyes of Horus which dilate the heart [. . .]—[. . .].

## Utterance 57K

§ 40+11 O Osiris the King, take[1] the Eye of Horus, prevent it from being consumed.

1. For  the facsimile has .

## Utterance 57L

§ 40+12 O Osiris the King, take the Eye of Horus which he has made hale—a kilt (called) 'Horus is high'.[1]

1. This rubric covers both Utterances 57K and 57L. The signs after the name of the offering read , which I can interpret only as an epithet of the garment, on which see *Frises*, 18.

## Utterance 57M

O Osiris the King, take the Eye of Horus and prevent him[1] from destroying it—a belt.[2] § 40+13

1. Seth.
2. *'Idr*, cf. *Frises*, 23 f.

## Utterance 57N

O Osiris the King, take possession of the sole Eye of Horus—a *wꜥtt*-tail.[1] § 40+14

1. Part of the royal insignia, cf. *Frises*, 110.

## Utterance 57O

O Osiris the King, take the Eye of Horus which ⟨he⟩ rescued[1] from Seth when he snatched it—a *ḫbzt*-tail. § 40+15

1. In writing *nḥm* 'rescue' the publication has □ for ◡ as again in Nt, ll. 301. 304, a very common confusion in the facsimile of Nt. For the missing suffix cf. locc. citt.

## Utterance 57P

O Osiris the King, take the Eye of Horus which was guarded from Gēb—a stool(?).[1] § 40+16

1. [hieroglyphs]; the translation is a guess based on the determinative.

## Utterance 57Q

O Osiris the King, take the Eye of Horus on account of which Seth has rejoiced—a *mṯpn*(*t*)-dagger.[1] § 40+17

1. Cf. *Frises*, 200; Jéquier, *Neit*, p. 26, thinks to see ◠ under □.

## Utterance 57R

O Osiris the King, take the Eye of Horus which he has wrested(?)[1] from Seth—a *mꜣgsw*-dagger. § 40+18

1. Read *mꜣgst·n·f*; probably a word deliberately coined for the pun.

## Utterance 57S

O Osiris the King, receive the Eye of Horus which he rescued from Seth when ⟨he⟩ snatched it—a *ḫbzt*-tail. § 40+19

1. A repetition of § 40+15; the suffix of *ḥnp·n·f* has been omitted.

## Utterance 58

§ 41 O Osiris the King, take the Eye of Horus by means of which he has danced[1]—a tailed loin-cloth.

1. We return here to Sethe's edition. The text translated is that of Nt, 302, where the words following *irt Ḥr* read 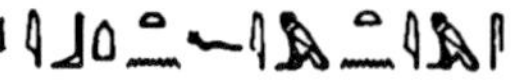; *im·tn* after *ibꜣt·n·f* is surely an error.

## Utterance 59

O Osiris the King, take the Eye of Horus, recognize(?) it[1]—a cloak.[2]

1. Cf. Nt, 303, which after *irt Ḥr* reads ; the initial 𓇋 appears to be prothetic *i* of the imperative of a causative niphʿal formation from the stem *sꜣꜣ* 'be wise'.
2. Read *s(ꜣ)ꜣt*; in § 2044*a* it is clearly a fringed garment.

## Utterance 59A

O Osiris the King, take the Eye of Horus which he saved from Seth when he snatched ⟨it⟩[1]—a *ḥbzt*-tail.

1. Cf. Nt, 304. A repetition of § 40+15, +19; at end read *ḥnp⟨·n⟩·f ⟨sy⟩*.

## Utterance 60

§ 42 [. . .] upon the Eye of Horus[1]—six-weave god's linen.

1. Nt, 305 has a different text, though the final rubric agrees. Nt, 305 reads: 'O Osiris the King, I give it (masc.) to you through(?) him; his heart is watchful for you.'

## Utterance 61

O Osiris the King, take the foreleg of Seth which Horus has torn off[1]—four-weave god's linen.

1. Cf. Nt, 306.

## Utterances 62, 62A

§ 43 O Osiris the King, take the water which is in the Eye of Horus, do not let go of it. O Osiris the King, take the Eye of Horus, the water in which Thoth has seen[1]—a *ḥrs*-sceptre, a *ḏbꜣ*-sceptre and a mace.

1. Cf. Nt, 307–8.

## Utterance 63

[O Osiris the King, I conduct you to your son] Horus; put him within § 44
yourself. [I am Isis; go behind me, O Osiris the King]—a *mḫn*-mace, a *iȝr*-mace, and a *ḥrs*-sceptre.[1]

1. Not in Nt. For the restoration of the latter part of the Utterance cf. *Pyr.* iii, 5.

## Utterance 64

O Osiris the King, you are secluded(?) because of him;[1] behold, you have § 45
brought him to naught[2]—a *ḏsr*-mace.

1. Cf. Nt, 309. The translation of *ḏsr* depends on the notion of privacy inherent in this stem; presumably the king is shut off from his enemy Seth, to whom the pronoun here and in the next clause undoubtedly refers.
2. For the sense of *ip* cf. P. Bremner-Rhind, 28, 15; 30, 2.

## Utterance 65

O Osiris the King, may you love ⟨him⟩, for he is Horus[1]—a *ḥrs*-sceptre.

1. Cf. Nt, 310, which omits *sw* before *swt* by haplography.

## Utterance 66

O Osiris the King, make the Eye of Horus come back to you[1]—a *ḫt-sḫt*- § 46
sceptre.

1. Cf. Nt, 311.

## Utterance 67

O Osiris the King, let not your face be blind(?),[1] for I place it[2] in your hand for you, even that which they . . .[3] for you—a *iwnw-ḥrs*-sceptre.

1. Cf. *Komm.* iii, 190–1. Nt, 312 has the var. .
2. The sceptre.
3. For *ndsds* see also § 1204*d*, but its meaning is unknown. Nt, 312 has 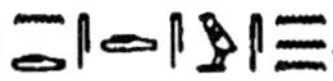.

## Utterance 68

O Osiris the King, take the water which is in the Eye of Horus. O King, fill § 47
your hand with the *ḥrs*-sceptre, provide yourself with the *ḥrs*-sceptre, that it may equip you as a god. Do not let go of it! Beware lest you let go of it!—a *ḥrs*-sceptre.[1]

1. Cf. Nt, 313–15.

## Utterance 69

§ 48 O Osiris the King, take the finger of Seth which causes the white Eye of Horus to see—a *smꜣ*-staff.[1]

1. Cf. Nt, 316.

## Utterance 70

O Osiris the King, take the white Eye of Horus which illumines the tip of the finger of Seth—2 lumps of electrum.[1]

1. Cf. Nt, 317. For Utt. 71–71I we are entirely dependent on Nt, see the Supplement, pp. 6–7.

## Utterance 71

§ 49 O Osiris the King, lay hold of the . . .[1] of your foe—a *ḏꜥm*-sceptre.

1. *ꜥfꜥ*, meaning unknown.

## Utterance 71A

§ 49+1 O Osiris the King, let him not be far from you—a *wꜣs*-sceptre.[1]

1. Cf. Edel, § 1104(*bb*); 'him' presumably refers to Horus.

## Utterance 71B

§ 49+2 O Osiris the King, be holy, be holy[1] upon his fingers—a forked staff.

1. Hortative old perfective. The sense 'be secluded' is also possible.

## Utterance 71C

§ 49+3 O Osiris the King, live, live—a pendant.

## Utterance 71D

§ 49+4 O Osiris the King, take the Eye of Horus which hung from the hands of his children—a flail.

## Utterance 71E

§ 49+5 O Osiris the King, take the hand of Nephthys(?),[1] prevent her from putting it on them[2]—a crook.

1. Reading doubtful; the facsimile has a small o in place of 𓂋.
2. The followers of Seth?

## Utterance 71F

Slay that evil one(?)[1]—a *pḏ-ʿḥʿ*-mantlet.[2] O Thoth, bring it—a . . . mantlet.[3] § 49+6

1. Again in Utt. 71I; the word may be connected with *ʿḥʿ* 'unlucky', 'evil' in the calendars.
2. Cf. Gardiner, Sign-list, T 13, n. 2; *Frises*, 224.
3. Reading doubtful.

## Utterance 71G

O Thoth, bring it—a *ḏbʿ-nṯr*-mantlet.[1] Take[2] it and put it under you, for it is § 49+7 yours[3]—a *nw-rḏ*-bowstring and a *gn*(?)-mantlet.[4]

1. Cf. Gardiner, loc. cit.
2. A confusion of *m* 'take' and *ímí* 'give'; the former is meant.
3. Taking the independent pronoun *ṯwt* in its possessive sense.
4. *Nw-rḏ gn*(?) corresponds to the *nw-n-nṯr* of Gardiner, loc. cit. For *nw-rḏ* see also § 40+4.

## Utterance 71H

O Osiris the King, lay hold of him.[1] Hasten with Osiris the King.[2] I am § 49+8 Gēb; O Thoth, bring him, that slayer(?)[3]—a *íry-nṯr*-mantlet.

1. 'Him' presumably refers to the 'slayer(?)' just to be mentioned.
2. Apparently a direction to the officiant.
3. *Pḏ* may represent the simplex of the niphʿal formation *npḏ* 'slay', *Concise Dict.* 130; see also § 49+9. The use of the demonstrative *pf* seems to imply that *pḏ* is someone or something objectionable.

## Utterance 71I

That [slayer(?)], this evil one(?); slay(?)[1] this King's foe, that this King may § 49+9 arise—a *pḏ-ʿḥʿ*-mantlet.

1. See n. 2 above.

*Presentation of unguents*

The anointing.

## Utterance 72

Recite four times:[1] O Osiris the King, I have filled your eye for you ⟨with⟩[2] § 50 the ointment—festival perfume.

1. W places this rubric at the end of the speech.
2. Read ⟨*m*⟩ *mḏt*; the two *m*'s have been merged by haplography.

## Utterance 73

O Osiris the King, take the ferment(?) which is in his face[1]—*ḥknw*-oil.

1. The pronoun presumably refers to Horus.

## Utterance 74

§ 51 O Osiris the King, take the Eye of Horus on account of which he suffered(?)[1] —*sfṯ*-oil.

1. *Wb.* iv, 118, 5 translates *sfkk* with 'jem. bestrafen o.a. (mit *n* des Dativs)', presumably on the assumption that the suffix *·f* refers to Seth, but it seems to me that a better sense is obtained by regarding the suffix as referring to Horus and the verb as describing the suffering undergone by Horus when his eye was torn out, in which case *ỉsfkkt·n·f* will be a relative form.

## Utterance 75

O Osiris the King, take the Eye of Horus, which he has protected—*nẖmn*-oil.

## Utterance 76

O Osiris the King, take the Eye of Horus, wherewith he has brought and supported[1] the gods—*twꜣwt*-oil.

1. W omits *twꜣwt·n·f*.

## Utterance 77

§ 52 Ointment, Ointment, where are you?[1] O you who should be on the brow of Horus, where are you? If you are on the brow of Horus,[2] I will put you on the brow of this King, that you may give pleasure to him who has you,
§ 53 that you may make a spirit of him who has you, that you may cause him to have power in his body, and that you may put the dread of him in the eyes of all[3] the spirits who shall look at him and everyone[3] who shall hear his name—first quality pine-oil.

1. *Ṯn ỉ·wn·ṯ* is a crux. I am not convinced by 'arise and open' of Speleers and Mercer, which seems to me unfitted to the context, but the only alternative I can suggest is the question 'where are you?' For the position of the interrogative *ṯn* at the head of the sentence cf. *ṯn sw* 'where is he?', *CT* iii, 51*f.*; *ṯn sw pr* 'whence is he who has come forth?', *CT* ii, 292*a*, the latter quoted by Edel, § 1012 and by Gardiner, § 503, 4; see also below, §§ 671*a*, 681*a*. On the analogy of these passages we would expect the question to read *ṯn ṯm* (for the ancient pronoun cf. § 52*b*) but there is perhaps no absolute objection to the substitution of *ỉ·wn·ṯ* 'you are' for the pronoun; we may have here an attempt to avoid an assonance or just possibly a survival of an obsolete usage.
2. W omits 'the brow of'.
3. W has 𓎡 for 𓎟.

## Utterance 78

O Osiris the King, I bring to you the Eye of Horus, which he has taken to your brow—first quality Libyan oil. § 54

*Presentation of eye-paint*

Lift up before him.

## Utterance 79

Recite four times: O Osiris the King, I paint an uninjured Eye of Horus on your face for you—green eye-paint, 1 bag.[1]

1. *Msdmt* 'black eye-paint' belongs after § 55*d* in the N-text.

## Utterance 80

O Horus who is this Osiris the King, take the uninjured Eye of Horus. O § 55
Horus who is this Osiris the King, I paint it on your face for you, for Horus painted his uninjured Eye. O King, I attach your eyes to your face for you intact, so that you may see with them—black eye-paint, 1 bag.

## Utterance 81

*Hymn for awakening the king, adapted to presentation of napkins*

May you[1] awake in peace! § 56
May Tait awake in peace!
May Taitet awake in peace!
⟨May⟩ the Eye of Horus which is in Dep ⟨awake⟩ in peace!
May the Eye of Horus which is in the Mansions of the *Nt*-crown awake in peace!

O you who receive the working women(?) and who adorn the Great One of the carrying-chair,[2] | cause the Two Lands to bow to this King even as they § 57
bow to Horus; cause the Two Lands to dread this King even as they dread Seth; sit in front of this King as his god, open his path at the head of the spirits, that he may stand at the head of the spirits as Anubis who presides over the Westerners. Recite four times:[3] Forward, forward to Osiris!—2 napkins.

1. Feminine.
2. Cf. Utt. 438, n. 2.
3. N only.

*Presentation of the morning meal*

## Utterance 82

§ 58 It is Thoth who brings himself with it;[1] he has come forth with the Eye of Horus—an offering-table.[2]

1. N inserts 'an offering-table'.
2. Var. N: 'Give the invocation-offering.

## Utterance 83

Give[1] him the Eye of Horus, that he may be satisfied with it. O come with the King's boon!

1. 𓏙 probably imperative.

## Utterance 84

§ 59 O Osiris the King, take the Eye of Horus with which he has been satisfied—the King's boon, the King's boon.

*Title to Utterances* 85–92

Placing the offering-table on the ground.

## Utterance 85

O Osiris the King, take the Eye of Horus and be satisfied with it—a 'Broad-Hall' offering.

## Utterance 86

Cause it to turn back[1] to you. Sit down now; the King's invocation-offering.

1. Imperative with reinforcing dative.

## Utterance 87

§ 60 O Osiris the King, take the Eye of Horus and absorb it into your mouth—the morning meal.

## Utterance 88

O Osiris the King, take the Eye of Horus, prevent him[1] from trampling[2] it—a *tw*-loaf.

1. Seth.
2. Cf. *Wb.* v, 237, 10–12.

## Utterance 89

O Osiris the King, take the Eye of Horus which he[1] has pulled out—a *itḥ*-loaf.

1. Seth.

## Utterance 90

O Osiris the King, take the Eye of Horus, for little is that which Seth has § 61
eaten of it—a jar of strong ale.[1]

1. Cf. *L. Eg. Misc.* 425.

## Utterance 91

O Osiris the King, take the Eye of Horus which they have reft(?) from him[1]—a jar of *ḫnms*-drink.

1. *Iḫḫmt·n·sn r·f*, see also § 89*c*; the translation is conjectural.

## Utterance 92

O Osiris the King, take the Eye of Horus, I lift it to your face for you—the lifting up of a *ḥnt*-bowl of bread.

*Title to Utterance* 93

The lifting up before him.

## Utterance 93

Lift up your face, O Osiris; lift up your face, O King, whose spirit goes! § 62
Lift up your face, O King, be strong and effective; look at that which issued
from you, the faeces(?) which were formed(?)[1] thereby.[1] Wash yourself, split § 63
open your mouth by means of the Eye of Horus, invoke your double as Osiris, that he may protect you from all wrath of the dead. O King, take this bread of yours which is[2] the Eye of Horus.—Set down on the ground before him.

1. A figurative use of *sḫt* 'weave'? The sense of the passage is doubtful.
2. *Imy* of equivalence.

*Title to Utterances* 94–6

§ 64 Give a meal.

### Utterance 94

O Osiris the King, take the Eye of Horus with which you have refreshed(?) yourself[1]—a *šns*-loaf.

1. Cf. *Wb.* ii, 338, 20.

### Utterance 95

I provide you with the ferment(?) which issued from you[1]—a jar of beer.

1. W adds 'four times' and further inserts a Postscript to Utt. 94–5: 'a meal, 1 loaf and 1 beer-jar' (§ 64*a*).

### Utterance 96

O Osiris the King, take the full equivalent[1] of the Eye of Horus—a *swt*-joint.

1. Read *isw twt*.

*Title to Utterances* 97–9

§ 65 Place at his left hand.

### Utterance 97

O Osiris the King, this is this Eye of Horus which he has demanded from Seth.

### Utterance 98

O Osiris the King, Horus has put his Eye into your hand for you.

### Utterance 99

§ 66 O Osiris the King, I give to you the Eye of Horus; give me[1] your hand that I may give it to you.

1. Imperative *imi n*(·*i*).

*Postscript to Utterances* 97–9

*Hꜣṯr*[1]

1. Meaning unknown.

*Heading to Utterances 100–2*

Place in his left hand. § 67

### Utterance 100

O Osiris the King, he has smitten(?) another,[1] but I have loved you and I am [your] protector [. . .].

1. Feminine.

### Utterance 101

O Osiris the King, she who protects you has come; take possession of the Eye of Horus [. . .].

### Utterance 102

I am Horus, O Osiris the King [. . .] give me your hand [. . .] take possession § 68
of [. . .].

*The Postscript is lost*

*Title to Utterances 103 ff.*

Place in his left hand.[1]

1. Cf. JPII, 389.

### Utterances 103 ff.

*Fragments of twelve short Utterances corresponding to Sethe's Utt.* 103–5 *are recorded in JPII,* 390 *ff., but none of them is sufficiently well preserved to provide an intelligible text.*

*Title to Utterances* 106–7, *cf.* § 1644*c*

A bow.

### Utterance 106

*Presentation of sandals*

O King, I am your son, I am Horus; I have come and I bring to you Horus' § 69
own Eyes; seize them and join them to yourself.[1] I have joined them to § 70
you and have united them to you, for they are complete. Horus [has put]

them on this King's feet that they may guide [this] King [to the firmament, to Horus, to the sky, to the] great [god, and that they may protect] this King
§ 71 from all his foes.[1] [O King, I bring to you the two Eyes of] Horus which expand his heart; join [them to yourself, lay hold of them].

## Utterance 107

*Lost*

## Utterance 108

72 O Osiris the King, absorb the water which is in it[1]—a bowl of water.

1. The Eye of Horus. This Utterance and the next represent the cleansing of the mouth with water and natron before the ritual meal. Up to Utt. 171, N (and T from Utt. 142) add after each formula: 'Recite four times: For the King the lifting up four times.'

## Utterance 109

O Osiris the King, take the Eye of Horus which purifies his mouth—2 bowls of *bd*-natron.

*Presentation of the repast*

## Utterance 110

O Osiris the King, take the Eye of Horus, absorb it into your mouth—the morning meal.[1]

1. Cf. § 60*a*.

## Utterance 111

§ 73 O Osiris the King, take the Eye of Horus which Seth has trampled[1]—a *tw*-loaf.[2]

1. § 60*b* has *ḫw n·k tỉ·f s(ỉ)* 'prevent him from trampling it'.
2. Var. '2 *tw*-loaves'.

## Utterance 112

O Osiris the King, take the Eye of Horus which he has pulled out—a *ỉtḥ*-loaf.[1]

1. Cf. § 60*c*.

## Utterance 113

O Osiris the King, take that which should be on you—2 *ḥṯ*-loaves.

## Utterance 114

O Osiris the King, I bring to you that which resembles(?)[1] your face—2 *nḥr*- § 74
loaves.

1. Cf. Utt. 606, n. 5.

## Utterance 115

O Osiris the King, I have set your eye in place—4 *dpt*-loaves.

## Utterance 116

O Osiris the King, take the Eye of Horus and prevent him from suffering because of it—4 *pzn*-loaves.

## Utterance 117

O Osiris the King, receive what should be on you—4 *šns*-loaves. § 75

## Utterance 118

O Osiris the King, take your eye, take possession of it—4 *imy-tꜣ*-loaves.

## Utterance 119

O Osiris the King, take the Eye of Horus which he has baked(?)[1]—4 *ḫnfw*- § 76
loaves.

1. *Ḫnft·n·f* again § 95*a*; perhaps connected with *ḫnfyt* 'fire', *Wb.* iii, 291, 15.

## Utterance 120

O Osiris the King, take the Eye of Horus, do not let it spring up(?)—4 *ḥbnnt*-loaves.

## Utterance 121

O Osiris the King, take the Eye of Horus which he has pulled out—4 *ḳmḥ*- § 77
loaves.[1]

1. As §§ 60*c*; 73*c*, but with a different offering.

## Utterance 122

O Osiris the King, take the Eye of Horus which I put in your mouth for you—your 4 *ỉdtt*-loaves.[1]

1. 'Your' in W only; N shows  to be a det. only.

## Utterance 123

§ 78 O Osiris the King, take the Eye of Horus, your *pꜣt*-cake, that you may eat—4 *pꜣt*-loaves.[1]

1. Cf. § 35*b. c.*

## Utterance 124

O Osiris the King, take the Eye of Horus which he has pulled out[1]—4 pieces of roast meat.

1. Cf. §§ 60*c*; 73*c*; 77*a*, but again with a different offering.

## Utterance 125

§ 79 O Osiris the King, I bring to you his sound white teeth—4 bunches of onions.[1]

1. Cf. § 35*a*.

## Utterance 126

O Osiris the King, take the . . .[1] of the Eye of Horus—a foreleg.

1. *Ḥpẖ*; cf. § 12*c*.

## Utterance 127

§ 80 O Osiris the King, dance! Gēb will not do wrong to his rightful heir[1]—a hind-leg (of beef).

1. Lit. 'his heir who inherits'.

## Utterance 128

O Osiris the King, take the Eye of Horus that you may be sought out[1]—a *zẖn*-joint.

1. Or 'embraced'; the verb *zẖn* carries both meanings.

## Utterance 129

O Osiris the King, take the full equivalent of the Eye of Horus—a *swt*-joint.[1] § 81

1. Cf. § 64*d*.

## Utterance 130

O Osiris the King, take those who rebelled against you—4 ribs.

## Utterance 131

O Osiris the King, take your . . .[1]—a roast joint. § 82

1. *Isšnw·k*, meaning unknown.

## Utterance 132

O Osiris the King, take the Eye of Horus, go to it—a liver.

## Utterance 133

O Osiris the King, take the Eye of Horus for which he goes—a spleen. § 83

## Utterance 134

O Osiris the King, take the Eye of Horus which is in front of him—a *ḥꜥ*-joint.

## Utterance 135

O Osiris the King, take the Eye of Horus which is in front of Seth—meat § 84
of the forepart.

## Utterance 136

O Osiris the King, take the severed(?)[1] heads of the followers of Seth—a *r*-bird.[2]

1. Cf. *Wb.* iv, 192, 10; in W the det. of the offering is a dressed and decapitated bird.
2. Identified with *Anser anser*, cf. *Bibl. Or.* 21, 32.

## Utterance 137

O Osiris the King, take the end(?) of this heart—a *ṯ(rp)*-bird.[1] § 85

1. *Anser albifrons*, loc. cit.

## Utterance 138

O Osiris the King, take the Eye of Horus which he has brought—a duck.

## Utterance 139

§ 86 O Osiris the King, take those who have come, for they are pacified[1]—a *s(r)*-bird[2].

1. Reading *ỉ·srf·sn* with W rather than *sỉrf·sn* of T, which appears to be a *vox nihili.* According to *Wb.* iv, 197, *srf* in the sense of 'pacify' does not occur until late times, but 'warm', which seems the only alternative, is meaningless here.
2. A breed of goose, *Bibl. Or.* 21, 32.

## Utterance 140

O Osiris the King, take the Eye of Horus; prevent him from having pain in it—a pigeon.

## Utterance 141

O Osiris the King, take the Eye of Horus which he has pulled out—a *zỉf*-loaf.[1]

1. Cf. §§ 60*c*; 73*c*; 77*a*; 78*c*.

## Utterance 142

§ 87 O Osiris the King, take the Eye of Horus, for it will not be sundered from you—2 *šˁt*-cakes.

## Utterance 143

O Osiris the King, the Eye of Horus is allotted[1] to you—2 *npꜣt*-cakes.[2]

1. Read *sỉp* or possibly *ỉ·s(ỉ)p*, passive *sḏm·f*.
2. Var. N *pꜣt*.

## Utterance 144

§ 88 O Osiris the King, take the Eye of Horus, the water in which he has squeezed out—2 *mzt*-cakes.

## Utterance 145

O Osiris the King, take the Eye of Horus, for little is that which Seth has eaten of it—2 bowls of strong ale.[1]

1. Cf. § 61*a*.

## Utterance 146

O Osiris the King, take the eye of Horus; they have come . . .[1] by means of § 89
it—2 bowls of sacred milk.

1. *Tsšnwn*; old perfective 3rd plur. of a verb of unknown meaning.

## Utterance 147

O Osiris the King, take the Eye of Horus which they have reft(?) from him—2 bowls of *ḫnms*-drink.[1]

1. Cf. § 61*b*. The sign ⲁ in W is borrowed from *ḫm* 'not know'.

## Utterance 148

O Osiris the King, provide yourself with the ferment(?) which issued from § 90
you—2 bowls of beer.[1]

1. Cf. §§ 37*a*; 39*c*.

## Utterance 149

O Osiris the King, provide yourself with the ferment(?) which issued from you—2 bowls of *sḫpt*-drink.

## Utterance 150

O Osiris the King, provide yourself with the ferment(?) which issued from you—2 bowls of *pḫ(ꜣ)*-drink.

## Utterance 151

O Osiris the King, provide yourself with the ferment(?) which issued from § 91
you—2 bowls of Nubian beer.

## Utterance 152

O Osiris the King, take the breast of Horus which they offer[1]—2 bowls of figs.

1. Early form of *drp*, *Wb.* v, 418, 2.

## Utterance 153

§ 92 O Osiris the King, your mouth is split open by means of it[1]—2 bowls of Lower Egyptian wine.

1. The fem. Eye of Horus, not the masc. *mnḏ* 'breast' of § 91*c*.

## Utterance 154

O Osiris the King, take the Eye of Horus which they have spat out; prevent him[1] from swallowing it—2 jars of *ꜥbš*-wine.

1. Seth.

## Utterance 155

§ 93 O Osiris the King, take the pupil which is in the Eye of Horus, for your mouth is split open by means of it—2 bowls of *ỉmt*-wine.

## Utterance 156

O Osiris the King, take the Eye of Horus which he has fished up, for your mouth is split open by means of it—2 bowls of *ḥꜣmw*-wine.

## Utterance 157

§ 94 O Osiris the King, take the Eye of Horus; it will not be loosed[1] from you—2 bowls of *snw*-wine.

1. for *snỉ* 'loose' cf. § 1100*d*.

## Utterance 158

O Osiris the King, take the Eye of Horus when it springs up(?)[1]—2 bowls of *ḥbnnt*-loaves.

1. A formation with prefixed *ḥ* of the reduplicated stem *bnbn*, itself derived from the simplex *wbn* 'rise'. Compare Utt. 120.

## Utterance 159

O Osiris the King, take the Eye of Horus which he has baked(?)[1]—2 bowls of *ḫnfw*-loaves. § 95

1. Cf. § 76*a*.

## Utterance 160

O Osiris the King, take the Eye of Horus which he has rescued from Seth—2 bowls of *išd*-fruit.

## Utterance 161

O Osiris the King, take the white Eye of Horus and prevent him[1] from wearing[2] it—2 bowls of white *sšt*-fruit. § 96

1. Seth.
2. As a diadem, cf. *Dram. Texte*, 155.

## Utterance 162

O Osiris the King, take the green Eye of Horus and prevent him from wearing it—2 bowls of green *sšt*-fruit.

## Utterance 163

O Osiris the King, take the Eye of Horus and prevent him from tearing it out—2 bowls of bruised(?) wheat. § 97

## Utterance 164

O Osiris the King, take the Eye of Horus and prevent him from tearing it out—2 bowls of bruised(?) barley.

## Utterance 165

O Osiris the King, take the Eye of Horus, . . .[1] it—2 bowls of *bꜣ(bꜣ)t*. § 98

1. *Ꜥ̓snbꜣbꜣ*, apparently an imperative with pronominal object; meaning unknown.

## Utterance 166

O Osiris the King, take the Eye of Horus which they[1] have licked—2 bowls of zizyphus-fruit.

1. The followers of Seth?

## Utterance 167

§ 99 O Osiris the King, open your eyes that you may see with them—2 bowls of zizyphus-bread.

## Utterance 168

O Osiris the King, take the Eye of Horus and prevent him[1] from entrapping it—2 bowls of carob beans.

1. Seth.

## Utterance 169

§ 100 O Osiris the King, take the sweet Eye of Horus, make it come back to you[1]—2 bowls of all kinds of sweets.

1. Taking *sḥt* literally, as in § 46*a*. Sethe, discussing the same expression in *Komm.* iii, 101–2 = § 591*c*, translates it as 'führe es dir zu Gemüte', but the baldly literal rendering seems fully to meet the case.

## Utterance 170

O Osiris the King, take the Eye of Horus, allot it to yourself[1]—2 bowls of all kinds of fresh vegetables.[2]

1. Cf. § 591*c*.
2. *Rnpwt* often means 'yearly sustenance', and Junker, *Gîza* iii, 111 ff. so translates it in the present context, but here the basic meaning of 'fresh vegetables' is more appropriate; this is an item on a menu, not an allusion to income.

## Utterance 171

O Osiris the King, may ⟨the Eye of Horus⟩ belong(?) to you, to you—a *ḥnkt*-offering.

### *Heading to Utterance* 172

§ 101 Recite four times: a meal is offered to the King.

## Utterance 172

A boon which the King and Gēb grant to this King; there is given to you every offering and every oblation which you can desire, whereby it will be well with you before the god for ever and ever.

## Utterance 173

O Osiris the King, Horus has come that he may join you, for you are his father—ʿ*bt*-grain.

## Utterance 174

Betake yourself to Gēb—2 bowls of *bzn*-grain.

## Utterance 175

Gēb has given you your eyes, that you may be content—a table of offerings. § 102

## Utterance 176

O Osiris the King, you are his[1] double—a *ḳḥꜣ*-loaf.

1. Gēb's.

## Utterance 177

Take the eyes of this great one, O Osiris the King—2 *t-wr*-loaves. § 103

## Utterance 178

Be content with them—2 'Broad-Hall' offerings.

## Utterance 179

Your face is content because of Horus, for you are his father—a *ḥtpnt*-loaf.

## Utterance 180

Take the pupil of the Eye of Horus, . . . it[1]—I give Horus to you[2]—2 bowls of § 104
*bꜣ(bꜣ)t*.

1. Read *nbꜣbꜣ s(y)*. Cf. § 98*a*; here the verb has neither the *s*-prefix not the prothetic *i*.
2. In this formula *di·n·(i)* is to be understood as Gunn's synchronous present, see his *Syntax*, chap. vii.

## Utterance 181

Take the pupil of the Eye of Horus which they have licked—I give Horus to you—2 bowls of zizyphus-fruit.

## Utterance 182

§ 105 Take the Eye of Horus which he has entrapped—I give [Horus] to you—2 bowls of carob beans.

## Utterance 183

Take the ferment(?) which issued from Osiris—2 jars of *ḥbt*-drink.

## Utterance 184

§ 106 O Osiris the King, take the water which is in you—I give Horus to you—[2(?)] jars of *ṯnm*-beer.[1]

1. Later *tnmw*, cf. *JEA* 13, 189.

## Utterance 185

Take the Eye of Horus and split open your mouth with it—[2(?)] bowls of Lower Egyptian wine.

## Utterance 186

§ 107 O Osiris the King, take the green Eye of Horus of which he has taken possession—I give Horus to you—[2(?)] bowls of new bread.

## Utterance 187

Take the Eye of Horus when it springs up(?)[1]—I give Horus to you—2 bowls of *ḥbn(n)t*-loaves.

1. Cf. § 94*a*.

## Utterance 188

§ 108 Take the Eye of Horus which he has baked(?)—I give Horus to you—2 bowls of *ḫnfw*-loaves.[1]

1. Cf. §§ 76*a*; 95*a*; note the peculiar writings of *ḫnf*.

## Utterance 189

Take the white Eye of Horus which he has worn[1]—I give Horus to you—2 bowls of white *sšt*-fruit.

1. Cf. § 96*a*.

## Utterance 190

Take the green Eye of Horus which he has worn—I give Horus to you—[2] bowls of green *sšt*-fruit.

## Utterance 191

Take the Eye of Horus which was allotted to him—I give Horus to you— § 109
[2 bowls of] *npꜣt*-cakes.

## Utterance 192

Take the Eye of Horus which he has torn out—I give Horus to you—[2] bowls of bruised(?) corn.

## Utterance 193

O Osiris the King, take the Eye of Horus whereof I make offering to you[1]— § 110
2 bowls of figs.

1. For *dꜣp* cf. Utt. 152, n. 1.

## Utterance 194

O Osiris the King, this Eye of Horus is sweet; make it come back to you[1]—2 § 111
bowls of all kinds of sweets.

1. Cf. Utt. 169, n. 1.

## Utterance 195

Allot it to yourself—2 bowls of all kinds of fresh vegetables.[1]

1. Cf. Utt. 170, n. 1.

## Utterance 196

May ⟨the Eye of Horus⟩ belong(?) to you—2 *ḥnkt*-offerings. § 112

## Utterance 197

§ 113 O Osiris the King, this Eye of Horus is strong, I give[1] it to you that you may be strong[2] and that your foe may fear you; the morning bread is in its due time.[3]

1. Read , cf. *Pyr.* iii, 9.
2. Read *lmlm·k*, cf. §§ 249*b*; 614*c*; 782*b*, with var. .
3. Read *t dwꜣ m ḏr·f*, compare  Nt, 759–60 = § 1929, which speaks against Sethe's proposal to read *m ḏr·f m tr·f* loc. cit., as do the varr.  Saqqara tomb of *Skwsḫt* and  Saqqara tomb of *Ỉpi zꜣ Ḥwtḥr*, both quoted in a letter from Gunn to Wainwright, and shown to me by the latter many years ago. The entry  *t* 'zerstampfen' of *Wb.* v, 211 is to be deleted; the group reads *t dwꜣ* 'morning bread' or less probably 'bread of worship'. In the tomb of *Skwsḫt* quoted above the name of *Dwꜣ-mwt·f* is written . Nt, 281 has the same reading as § 113*b* in this phrase.

## Utterance 198

§ 114 O Osiris the King, Horus has filled you completely with his Eye, with the oblation.

## Utterance 199

§ 115 O Osiris the King, turn yourself on account of this bread of yours, accept it from me. Recite four times: May the Eye of Horus belong(?) to you—the reversion[1] of the god's offering.

1. Cf. *JEA* 24, 83 ff.

## Utterance 200

*The king is censed*

§ 116 Hail to you, Incense! Hail to you, Brother of the God![1] Hail to you, Marrow[2] (?) which is in the limbs of Horus! Be great, my father,[3] extend yourself in your name of 'Pellet'.[4] May your perfume be on the King, may your savour(?) be on the King; O Eye of Horus, be high and great[5] on the King—incense.

1. Pun on *sn nṯr* 'brother of the god' and *snṯr* 'incense'.
2. *Mn wr*, lit. 'great firmness'.
3. The incense.
4. Pun on *pḏ* 'extend' and *pꜣḏ* 'pellet'.
5. i.e. be well diffused.

*Further Utterances connected with food*

## Utterance 201

O my father the King,[1] take the Eye of Horus, the *pȝt*-cake of the gods, for § 117
they feed thereon.

1. The king's son as officiant addresses his dead father.

## Utterance 202

O my father the King, take the ferment(?) which issued from Osiris.

## Utterance 203

O Osiris the King, take it, the Eye of Horus, to yourself.

## Utterance 204

Rejoice, O you who hoe(?)![1] Lift up the hearts of those who tore(?)[2] the breast, § 118
for they have swallowed the bright Eye of Horus which is in Ōn. O little
finger of the King, pull out this which is in the navel of Osiris.⌉ The King § 119
will not thirst, he will not hunger, the King will not be sad(?), for it is the arms of Ḥa which drive away his hunger, say(?) they who are filled,[3] say(?) they whose hearts are filled.

1. Perhaps imperf. participle of a verb *ḥnn* 'hoe', cf. the noun with that meaning. *Ḥnn* 'tear up' documents, § 954*b*, is probably the same stem.
2. With their nails (⌐) in grief? The word is otherwise unknown, and my translation is a guess. *Pace* Mercer, it has nothing to do with *ṯzi* 'lift up'.
3. Regarding *mḥy* as perf. passive participle.

## Utterance 205

O you who are over the baked foods, O you who are concerned with the § 120
supplies of drink,[1] the King is committed to Fetket the butler of Rēʿ, for Rēʿ himself has committed him to him, and Rēʿ commits him to him who is over the catering for this year. They[2] seize and give to him, they grasp and
give to him barley, emmer, bread, and beer,⌉ because what belongs to the King, § 121
it is his father who gives to him, it is Rēʿ who gives to him barley, emmer, bread, and beer, because he is the Great Bull who smote Kenzet,[3] because the King is he who is at the quintet of meals in the Mansion. The trio (of meals)

§ 122 is in the sky with Rēʿ and the pair is on earth with the Two Enneads,[1] for he belongs to the looser, and it is he who looses; he belongs to the seer, and it
§ 123 is he who sees. O Rēʿ, it is better with him today than yesterday.[1] The King has copulated with Mowet,[4] the King has kissed Shuset,[5] the King has joined with Nekhebut,[6] the King has copulated with the Beauteous One, for his dread is the lack of food and drink(?).[7] Assuredly it is the Beauteous One who cares for the King, she gives bread to the King and she treats him well today.

1. Lit. 'flood', the liquid counterpart to *sṯḥw*.
2. The beings invoked at the beginning of the Utterance.
3. A region of Nubia, cf. *Dict. géogr.* v, 205.
4. Semen personified as a goddess?
5. Meaning unknown.
6. Fruitfulness personified? Cf. *nḫbt* as an epithet of Nūt in § 4*a*.
7. *Nr* could be the noun *nr(w)* 'fear' or the verb *nr* with the same meaning; there appears to be a play on words here, for in § 123*d*, where the object is a person, *nr n* seems to mean 'care for', cf. *nri* 'protect', *Concise Dict.* 134. *Tbtb* is apparently a kind of grain, and in *D. el B.* 110 *šsšs* appears to be a liquid.

## Utterance 206

*A variant of the last*

(123) O you who are over the baked foods, O you who are concerned with the supplies of drink, commit the King to Fetket the butler of Rēʿ, that he may commit the King to Rēʿ himself, and that Rēʿ may commit the King to those who are over the catering. When he bites he gives to the King, and when he sips[1] he gives to the King, and the King lies down in good health every day.

1. *Ndb* in M and N and *ndbdb* in T and P, cf. 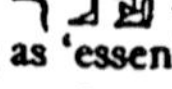 *Paheri*, 7. By reason of the dets. 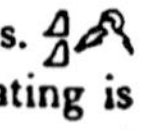 of *ndbdb* in P, *Wb*. ii, 368, 12 gives the meaning as 'essen', but this is surely wrong; eating is already represented by *psḥ* 'bite' in the preceding clause, and a word for drinking is wanted here. For the exact meaning 'sip' cf. *Paheri*, 7 cited above, where at a feast a waiter says to a lady guest: *Swr, m ir ndb, m·t nn iw·i r wḏḥ·t* 'Drink, don't sip! Look, I won't wait for you!'

## Utterance 207

§ 124 A meal for me, O butcher! A meal for me, O butcher! A meal, O you who are in the Eye of Rēʿ! A meal for me, O fowler who is in the Eye of the God! O butler, bring water and light the fire, for the calf of leg is with the roast meat—4 handfuls of water.

## Utterance 208

*A variant of the last*

A meal for me, O Atum! A meal for me, O Atum! A meal for me, O you who (124)
are in the Eye of the Bark of the God! The calf of leg is with the roast meat—
4 handfuls of water.

## Utterance 209

If Want flourishes, the King cannot take his meal; if the King flourishes, § 125
Want cannot take *his* meal. May the eastern porters regularly bring this bread
of yours.

## Utterance 210

Awake, O *Wpiw*![1] Be high, O Thoth![2] Awake, you sleepers! Rouse up, you § 126
dwellers in Kenzet, who are before the Great Egret who went up from the
cultivation and the Wepwawet-jackal which emerged from the tamarisk- § 127
bush.[3] | My[4] mouth is pure, the Two Enneads cense[5] me, and pure indeed is
this tongue which is in my mouth.[6] What I detest is faeces,[7] I reject urine,[8]
I detest my own detestableness. | What I detest is these two, and I will never § 128
eat the detestableness of these two, just as Seth rejected the poison(?).[9] O
you two Companions[10] who cross the sky, who are Rēʿ and Thoth,[11] take me[12]
with you, | that I may eat of what you eat, that I may drink of what you drink, § 129
that I may live on what you live on, that I may sit on what you sit on, that
I may be strong through that whereby you are strong, that I may sail in that
in which you sail. | My booth is plaited with rushes,[13] my drink-supply is in § 130
the Field of Offerings, my food-offerings are among you, you gods, my water
is wine like that of Rēʿ, and I go round the sky like Rēʿ, I traverse the sky like
Thoth.

1. A jackal-god, cf. *Komm.* iii, 349.
2. i.e. arise from being supine.
3. These expressions refer to the dead king, cf. *Dram. Texte*, 31. For *ḥȝp* 'cultivation', W has *ḥp*, probably in error.
4. For the 1st person see n. 7 below.
5. Cf. *Dram. Texte*, 206.
6. So W and T. *Wn* of M and N is due to confusion between † and +.
7. For the 1st person cf. *CT* iii, 79*h* ff.; 80*a*; 84*c* ff.; 85*a* ff.

8. For *twr* 'reject' cf. §§ 577*d*; 1830*d*.
9. Taking *mt* to be a writing of *mtwt*; 'poison' would fit the context.
10. So W and T; M and N 'you two companions of his' (i.e. 'mine').
11. Sun and Moon.
12. Imperative with reflexive dative.
13. Var. N: 'in the Field of Rushes'.

## Utterance 211

§ 131 My[1] detestation is hunger, and I will never eat it. My detestation is thirst, and
I will never drink it. It is indeed I who will give bread to those who exist, for
my foster-mother is Iat,[2] and it is she who nourishes me, it is indeed she
§ 132 who bore me. | I was conceived in the night, I was born in the night, I belong
to those who are in the suite of Rēʿ, who are before the Morning Star. I was
conceived in the Abyss, I was born in the Abyss; I have come and I have
brought to you the bread which I found there.

1. For the 1st person see above, Utt. 210, n. 7.
2. A milk-goddess; for *ỉtt* 'milk' cf. *Gîza* i, 124.

## Utterance 212

§ 133 The Eye of Horus drips upon the bush of . . .,[1] the Foremost of the Westerners comes for me[2] and has brought provisions to Horus who presides over the Houses. What he lives on, I live on; what he eats of, I eat of; what he drinks of, I drink of; my meal is the calf of leg and the roast meat.

1. *Ḏnw*, an unidentified plant.
2. Probably another case of original 1st person; the suffix of the 3rd person in the text has no antecedent, and looks as if it had been inserted automatically by the ancient editor.

## Utterance 213

§ 134 O King,[1] you have not departed dead,[2] you have departed alive; sit upon
the throne of Osiris, your sceptre in your hand, that you may give orders to
the living; your lotus-bud sceptre in your hand, that you may give orders to
§ 135 those whose seats are hidden.[3] | Your arm(s) are Atum, your shoulders are
Atum, your belly is Atum, your back is Atum, your hinder-parts are Atum,
your legs are Atum, your face is Anubis. The Mounds[4] of Horus serve you,
the Mounds of Seth serve you.

1. Sethe's translation and commentary begin here.

2. On the translation of the words *n im·n·k is* as a negative present perfect, contrary to the usual rule, see *Komm.* i, 2; according to Sethe, it is the presence of the particle *is* which indicates this exception.

3. i.e. the dead.

4. i.e. the respective realms of the gods in terms of the 'tells' on which human settlements so often stand.

## Utterance 214

*The king goes to the sky*

O King, beware of the lake![1]—recite four times. The messengers of your double come for you,[2] the messengers of your father come for you, the messengers of Rēʿ come for you,| so go after your sun and cleanse yourself, for your bones are those of the divine falcons who are in the sky. May you be beside the god, may you depart and ascend to your son,[3] may you fetter(?)[4] anyone who shall speak evilly against your name.| Go up, for Gēb has committed him to a low estate in his town so that he may flee and sink down weary.[5] But you shall bathe in the starry firmament, you shall descend upon the iron bands on the arms of Horus in his name of Him who is in the *Ḥnw*-bark.| The sun-folk[6] shall call out to you, for the Imperishable Stars have raised you aloft. Ascend to the place where your father is, to the place where Gēb is, that he may give you that which is on the brow of Horus,[7] so that you may have a soul thereby and power thereby and that you may be at the head of the Westerners thereby.

§ 136 § 137 § 138 § 139

1. Read *zꜣ kw š*, cf. *Komm.* i, 6. Cf. Utt. 500, n. 3, which shows why the lake is dangerous.

2. So rather than Sethe's 'zu dir', cf. *Stud. Griff.* 57.

3. Sethe has 'überlasse dein Haus deinem Sohn', but *pr* 'house' is not usually so written; the M.K. text quoted by Sethe, ibid. 10, may well be a later emendation. The king as Osiris is adjured to join his son and protector Horus, cf. §§ 138*c*; 139*c*.

4. Sethe has 'deiner Erzeugung', reading *nt(y) ṯt·k*, cf. *Komm.* i, 11, but the absence of the *m* of predication puts this out of court. More probably we should read *nṯṯt·k*, a transitive verb with *mdwty·fy* as object; it may possibly be synonymous with or a miswriting of *nṯṯ* 'fetter', *Wb.* ii, 367, 2. Sethe's misunderstanding of *nṯṯt·k* affects his translation of what follows. For *rn n W* we should certainly read *rn·k*, the scribe having mechanically substituted the king's name for the suffix.

5. Understanding *nn* as the verb for 'be weary'; all this is the fate of the evil-speaker.

6. On the *ḥnmmt* see *AEO* i, 98* ff.; Iversen, *Fragments of a Hieroglyphic Dictionary*, 22.

7. The royal uraeus.

## Utterance 215

*The king ascends to the sky as a star*

§ 140 O King, your messengers go, your heralds run to your father, to Atum. O Atum, raise him up to you, enclose him within your arms.

§ 141 There is no star-god who has no companion, have you your companion?[1] Look at me![2] You have seen the shapes of the children of their fathers, who know their speech, the Imperishable Stars; see now those who are in the
§ 142 Castle, who are Horus and Seth. Spit on the face of Horus for him,[3] that you may remove the injury which is on him; pick up the testicles of Seth, that you may remove his mutilation;[4] that one is born for you, this one is conceived for you.

§ 143 You are born, O Horus, in your name[5] of Him at whom the earth quakes; ⟨you are conceived, O Seth, in this your name of⟩ Him at whom the sky trembles.[6] If this one has no mutilation and if that one has no injury—and *vice versa*—then you will have no injury and you will have no mutilation.

§ 144 You are born, O Horus, for Osiris, and you have more renown[7] than he, you have more power than he. You are conceived, O Seth, for Gēb, and you
§ 145 have more renown than he, you have more power than he. There is no seed of a god which passes away at his word(?),[8] and you shall not pass away at his word(?). Rēʿ-Atum will not give you to Osiris,[9] and he shall not claim your heart[10] nor have power over your heart.[11] Rēʿ-Atum will not give you to Horus,
§ 146 and he shall not claim your heart nor have power over your heart. O Osiris, you shall never have power over him, nor shall your son have power over him; O Horus, you shall never have power over him, nor shall your father have
§ 147 power over him.[12] 'You belong, O So-and-so, to this god', said the Twin Children of Atum. 'Raise yourself', say they, 'in your name of God, and come into being, an Atum to every god.'[13]

§ 148 Your head is Horus of the Netherworld, O Imperishable.
Your face is *Mḫnt-irty*, O Imperishable.
Your ears are the Twin Children of Atum, O Imperishable.
Your eyes are the Twin Children of Atum, O Imperishable.
Your nose is the Jackal,[14] O Imperishable.
Your teeth are Sopd, O Imperishable,
§ 149 Your hands are Ḥapy and Duamūtef—
You demand that you ascend to the sky and you shall ascend—
Your feet are 'Imsety and Ḳebḥsenuf—
You demand that you descend to the Lower Sky and you shall descend—

Your members are the Twin Children of Atum, O Imperishable.
You shall not perish and your double shall not perish,
For *you* are a double.

1. Sethe translates the second sentence as a virtual question, 'soll ich dein Gefährte sein,' but a better sense seems to be obtained by reading *ỉn ⟨n·⟩k rmnwty·k* 'Have you your companion?', with successive *n*'s reduced to one by haplography. In my view Atum is demanding of the king his qualifications for admission to the celestial hierarchy, his 'companion' being his *ka*, here representing the essence of kingship. Cf. *JNES* 25, 153 ff., where I discuss all the Pyr. material concerning the relationship of the king and the stars.

2. Reading with Sethe as an imperative, *mꜣꜣ wỉ*.

3. Spitting on what is injured is a well-known folk-remedy. Note the abnormal position of the dative, on which see *Komm.* i, 27.

4. 𓇋𓇋𓇋 is the later .

5. Emending *rn·f* into *rn·k* with Sethe. The text of §§ 144 ff. is confusedly worded, for Horus and Seth are sometimes addressed as separate deities and sometimes jointly in the singular, when the two together embody the king.

6. For the emendation, which here seems certain, cf. *Komm*, i, 28 f.

7. *Bꜣ* here seems to be the equivalent of the later *bꜣw* 'power', 'fame'; Sethe has 'du bist ruhmvoller geworden'.

8. 𓇋 in *n ỉ·f* is here regarded as meaning 'speech', 'word', a possibility which Sethe considers but rejects, *Komm.* i, 32. I doubt the likelihood of his alternative *nỉ·f* 'ein zu ihm Gehöriger', of which he himself is by no means certain.

9. *N dỉ* here and in § 145*c* seems to me to be more a promise for the future than, as Sethe considers it, an already completed action. In support of my view I cite a passage in a similar context *n rdỉ·n⟨·ỉ⟩ sw n Wsỉr* 'I will never give him to Osiris', Nt, 488. 799 = §§ 1945–6. Sethe, in referring to this latter passage, seems to have overlooked the significance of *n sḏm·n·f* as a negative universal, described by him always as 'die Gunn'sche Regel', cf. *Komm.* i, 33 ff.

10. *Ỉb.* For *ỉp* 'claim' see Utt. 535, n. 13.

11. *Ḥꜣty.*

12. I have translated the text as it stands, rejecting Sethe's extensive emendations, loc. cit. I find it hard to believe in the probability of such considerable omissions from the text.

13. Hardly 'so wirst du wie Atum' as Sethe, which would require *m* after *ḫpr*. 'Atum' appears to be in apposition to the suffix in *ḫpr·k* and so to be applied to the king, while the direct genitive in *Ỉtm nṯr nb* is best translated into English as 'to'; the king assumes the rank of the supreme deity and is not like Atum but *is* Atum.

14. Or 'Wepwawet'.

## Utterance 216

*The king as a star fades at dawn with the other stars*

I have come to you, O Nephthys; § 150
I have come to you, O Night-bark;
I have come to you, O *Mꜣꜥ-ḥr-ṯrwt*;

I have come to you, O *Msḫ3t-k3w*;
Remember me.[1]
§ 151 Orion is swallowed up[2] by the Netherworld,[3]
Pure and living in the horizon.
Sothis is swallowed up by the Netherworld,
Pure and living in the horizon.[4]
I am swallowed up by the Netherworld,
Pure and living in the horizon.
It is well with me and with them,[5]
It is pleasant for me and for them,
Within the arms of my father,
Within the arms of Atum.

1. *Sḫ3·ṯn* is optative *sḏm·f*, the plural suffix of the 2nd person referring to all the beings previously invoked. The object of the verb should be emended into the 1st person to agree with what has gone before.

2. Lit. 'encircled'.

3. The stars vanish at dawn.

4. Despite the lack of concord of gender, I believe, *contra* Sethe, *Komm.* i, 48, that *wʿb ʿnḫ* here is on exactly the same footing as in the other two instances and that both verbs are in the old perfective; in a triple repetition of the phrase, the scribe has ignored the discrepancy of gender in the case of Sothis.

5. Sethe 'ihretwegen'.

## Utterance 217

*The king joins the sun-god*

§ 152 O Rēʿ-Atum, this King comes to you, an imperishable spirit, lord of the affairs(?)[1] of the place of the four pillars;[2] your son comes to you, this King comes to you. May you[3] traverse the sky, being united in the darkness; may you rise in the horizon, in the place where it is well with you.

§ 153 O Seth and Nephthys, go and proclaim to the gods of Upper Egypt and their spirits: 'This King comes indeed, an imperishable spirit. If he wishes you to die, you will die; if he wishes you to live, you will live.'

§ 154 O Rēʿ-Atum, this King comes to you, an imperishable spirit, lord of the affairs(?) of the place of the four pillars; your son comes to you, this King comes to you. May you traverse the sky, being united in the darkness; may you rise in the horizon, in the place where it is well with you.

§ 155 O Osiris and Isis, go and proclaim to the gods of Lower Egypt and their spirits: 'This King comes indeed, an imperishable spirit, as one to be worshipped, who is in charge of the Nile. Worship him, you spirits who are in the waters! Whom he wishes to live will live; whom he wishes to die will die.'

O Rēʿ-Atum, this King comes to you, an imperishable spirit, lord of the § 156
affairs(?) of the place of the four pillars; your son comes to you, this King comes to you. May you traverse the sky, being united in the darkness; may you rise in the horizon, in the place where it is well with you.

O Thoth, go and proclaim to the western gods and their spirits: 'This King § 157
comes indeed, an imperishable spirit, adorned with Anubis on the neck,[4] who presides over the Western Height. He claims hearts, he has power over hearts. Whom he wishes to live will live; whom he wishes to die will die.'

O Rēʿ-Atum, this King comes to you, an imperishable spirit, lord of the § 158
affairs(?) of the place of the four pillars; your son comes to you, this King comes to you. May you traverse the sky, being united in the darkness; may you rise in the horizon, in the place where it is well with you.

O *Dwn-ʿnwy*,[5] go and proclaim to the eastern souls and their spirits: § 159
'This King comes indeed, an imperishable spirit. Whom he wishes to live will live; whom he wishes to die will die.'

O Rēʿ-Atum, your son comes to you, the King comes to you; raise him up, § 160
enclose him in your embrace, for he is the son of your body for ever.

1. See, however, *Komm.* i, 56.
2. 'The four pillars' represent the four cardinal points, as do Seth, Osiris, Thoth, and *Dwn-ʿnwy*. On the last-named see n. 5 below.
3. The plural pronouns refer to Rēʿ-Atum and the king.
4. Cf. the collar worn by *Skrḫʿbḥw* in *Saqq. Mast.* i, 1.
5. For the identification of the god as *Dwn-ʿnwy* rather than as Horus, cf. *JEA* 36, 9 f.

## Utterance 218

*The king assumes authority in the Beyond*

O Osiris, this King comes indeed, importuning(?) the Nine,[1] an imperishable § 161
spirit; he claims hearts, he takes away powers and bestows powers. Every grant(?) of his is what compels (to duty) him whom he has summoned to his side,[2] (even) him who has appealed to him, and there is none who shall
escape;! he shall have no bread, his double shall have no bread, and his bread § 162
shall come to an end for him. Gēb has spoken the pronouncement of the Ennead: 'A falcon when he takes possession', say they: 'Behold,[3] you have a soul and you are mighty.'

This King comes indeed, importuning(?) the Nine, an imperishable § 163
spirit, who surpasses you,[4] who is like you, who is more weary than you,

who is greater than you, who is more hale than you, who shouts more loudly than you, and your time yonder is no more.[5] See what Seth and Thoth have
§ 164 done, your two brothers who do not know how to mourn you.[1] O Isis and Nephthys, come together, come together! Unite, unite!

This King comes indeed, importuning(?) the Nine, an imperishable spirit, and the Westerners who are on earth belong to this King.

§ 165 This King comes indeed, importuning(?) the Nine, an imperishable spirit, and the Easterners who are on earth belong to this King.

This King comes indeed, importuning(?) the Nine, an imperishable spirit,[1]
§ 166 and the Southerners who are on earth belong to this King.

This King comes indeed, importuning(?) the Nine, an imperishable spirit, and the Northerners who are on earth belong to this King.

This King comes indeed, importuning(?) the Nine, an imperishable spirit, and those who are in the Lower Sky belong to this King.

This King comes indeed, importuning(?) the Nine, an imperishable spirit.

1. The Nine Gods or the Nine Bows? More probably perhaps the former, though Sethe thinks otherwise. The translation of *ẖwrr* is doubtful; Sethe has 'überdrüssig(?)'.

2. Lit. 'him whom he has sided (*rmn*) to himself'.

3. *M kw* or *mk* ⟨*k*⟩*w*, not *mk w*(*i*).

4. Osiris.

5. Lit. 'has stilled'. The king takes over the role of Osiris as king of the dead.

## Utterance 219

*The king is identified with Osiris*

§ 167 O Atum, this one here is your son Osiris whom you have caused to be restored that he may live. If he lives, this King will live; if he does not die, this King will not die; if he is not destroyed, this King will not be destroyed; if he does not mourn, this King will not mourn; if he mourns, this King will mourn.[1]

§ 168 O Shu, this one here is your son Osiris whom you have caused to be restored that he may live; if he lives, this King will live, *etc.*

§ 169 O Tefēnet, this one here is your son Osiris whom you have caused to be restored that he may live; if he lives, this King will live, *etc.*

§ 170 O Gēb, this one here is your son Osiris whom you have caused to be restored that he may live; if he lives, this King will live, *etc.*

§ 171 O Nūt, this one here is your son Osiris whom you have caused to be restored that he may live; if he lives, this King will live, *etc.*

O Isis, this one here is your brother Osiris, whom you have caused to be § 172
restored that he may live; if he lives, this King will live, *etc.*

O Seth, this one here is your brother Osiris, who has been caused to be § 173
restored that he may live and punish you; if he lives, this King will live, *etc.*

O Nephthys, this one here is your brother Osiris, whom you have caused § 174
to be restored that he may live; if he lives, this King will live, *etc.*

O Thoth, this one here is your brother Osiris, who has been caused to be § 175
restored that he may live and punish you; if he lives, this King will live, *etc.*

O Horus, this one here is your father Osiris, whom you have caused to be § 176
restored that he may live; if he lives, this King will live, *etc.*

O Great Ennead, this one here is Osiris, whom you have caused to be § 177
restored that he may live; if he lives, this King will live, *etc.*

O Lesser Ennead, this one here is Osiris, whom you have caused to be § 178
restored that he may live; if he lives, this King will live, *etc.*

O City(?),[2] this one here is your son Osiris, of whom you have said: § 179
'Someone is reborn to your father.[3] Wipe his mouth for him, for his mouth has been split open by his beloved son Horus and his members have been
numbered by the gods.'| If he lives, this King will live, *etc.* § 180

In your name of Dweller in Ōn, who endures long in his necropolis. If he § 181
lives, this King will live, *etc.*

In your name of Dweller in ʿAndjet,[4] headman of his nomes. If he lives, § 182
this King will live, *etc.*

In your name of Dweller in the Mansion of Selḳet, a contented spirit. If § 183
he lives, this King will live, *etc.*

In your name of Dweller in the God's Booth, who is in the censing, who § 184
is in the coffer,[5] in the chest,[6] in the sack. If he lives, this King will live, *etc.*

In your name of Him who is in the Castle of the Mace[7] of *pꜣꜥr* wood. § 185
If he lives, this King will live, *etc.*

In your name of Dweller in Orion, with a season in the sky and a season § 186
on earth. O Osiris, turn your face and look on this King, for your seed which
issued from you is effective.| If he lives, this King will live, *etc.* § 187

In your name of Dweller in Dep. Your hand is about the meal, your daugh- § 188
ter; provide yourself with it. If he lives, this King will live, *etc.*

In your name of Dweller in the Mansion of the Greatest of Bulls. Your § 189
hand is about the meal, your daughter; provide yourself with it. If he lives, this King will live, *etc.*

In your name of Dweller in Unu of the South. Your hand is about the meal, § 190
your daughter; provide yourself with it. If he lives, this King will live, *etc.*

§ 191 In your name of Dweller in Unu of the North. Your hand is about the meal, your daughter; provide yourself with it. If he lives, this King will live, *etc.*

§ 192 In your name of Dweller in the City of Lakes.[8] What you have eaten is an Eye, and your belly is rounded out with it; your son Horus has released it[9] for you that you may live by means of it. If he lives, this King will live, *etc.*

§ 193 Your body is the body of this King, your flesh is the flesh of this King, your bones are the bones of this King; when you go, this King goes (also), and when this King goes, you go (also).

1. For *nhp* 'mourn' cf. *ZÄS* 47, 163. Sethe translates the verb as 'richten', suggesting a connexion with *hp* 'law', cf. *Komm.* i, 85, but no verb *nhp* with this meaning is known to *Wb.*
2. Cf. *Komm.* i, 87 f.; the 'City' is either the tomb of Osiris or *Nnt* 'the Lower Sky', but the absence of the det. ⊏⊐ speaks against the latter alternative. The sections which follow are all addressed to Osiris in various aspects.
3. The suffix is plural, possibly in reference to the company of the dead.
4. Cf. *AEO* ii, 176* ff.
5. Cf. *Wb.* v, 437, 17.
6. Ibid. 404, 15.
7. So rather than 'White Castle'; the object within ▯ or ▯ seems always to be a noun.
8. Or 'nomes', but the absence of the fem. ending speaks against this alternative.
9. From himself, for the Eye is his.

## Utterances 220 and 221

*These two Utterances, which are translated here as one, are closely connected, being part of the ritual accorded to the crown of Lower Egypt. First comes the opening of the shrine containing the crown; secondly an address by the officiating priest to the crown as goddess; thirdly a prayer by the king to the crown which clearly was originally in the 1st person; and finally the crown's reply to the king's prayer.*

*The opening of the shrine*

§ 194 The doors of the horizon are opened, its bolts are drawn back.

*The speech by the priest to the crown thus revealed*

He[1] has come to you, O *Nt*-crown; he has come to you, O Fiery Serpent; he has come to you, O Great One; he has come to you, O Great of Magic,
§ 195 being pure for you and fearing you.[1] May you be pleased with him, may you be pleased with his purity, and may you be pleased with his speech which he says to you. How kindly is your face, for you are content, renewed, and

rejuvenated, even as the father of the gods fashioned you. He has come to you, O Great of Magic, for he is Horus encircled with the protection of his Eye, O Great of Magic.

*The king's prayer*

Ho *Nt*-crown![2] Ho *'Inl*-crown! Ho Great Crown! Ho Crown great of magic! § 196
Ho Fiery Serpent![1] Grant that the dread of me be like the dread of you; § 197
grant that the fear of me be like the fear of you; grant that the acclaim of me be like the acclaim of you; grant that the love of me be like the love of you. Set my *ʿbȝ*-sceptre at the head of the living, [set] my [*sḫm*-sceptre] at the
head of the spirits,[3] and grant that my sword prevail over my foes.[1] Ho *'Inl*- § 198
crown! If you have gone forth from me, so have I gone forth from you.

*The deified crown replies*

If Ikhet the Great has borne you, Ikhet the Serpent has adorned you;
If Ikhet the Serpent has borne you, Ikhet the Great has adorned you,[4]
Because you are Horus encircled with the protection of his Eye.

1. i.e. the king.
2. Here begins Utt. 221.
3. N and Nt (l. 569) reverse the order of the sceptres.
4. Sethe's restoration is confirmed by Nt, 570.

## Utterance 222

*The king joins the sun-god*

*The officiating priest addresses the king*

Stand upon it, this earth which issued from Atum, this spittle[1] which issued § 199
from Khoprer; come into being upon it, be exalted upon it, so that your father may see you, so that Rēʿ may see you.

*The king speaks*[2]

I have come to you, my father, I have come to you, O Rēʿ. § 200
I have come to you, my father, I have come to you, O *Ndl*.[3]
I have come to you, my father, I have come to you, O *Pndn*.
I have come to you, my father, I have come to you, O *Dndn*.
I have come to you, my father, I have come to you, O Great Wild Bull. § 201
I have come to you, my father, I have come to you, O Great Float-user.[4]
I have come to you, my father, I have come to you, O Sopd.

I have come to you, my father, I have come to you, O Sharp of Teeth.[5]
§ 202 Grant that I may seize the sky and take possession of the horizon.
Grant that I may rule the Nine and provide for the Ennead.
Place the crook in my hand, that the head of Lower and Upper Egypt may be bowed.
§ 203 I charge my opponent and stand up,
The great headman in my great waters.[6]
Nephthys has favoured me,
And I have captured my opponent.

*The priest speaks*

§ 204 Provide yourself[7] with the Great of Magic, (even) Seth dwelling in Nūbet, Lord of Upper Egypt;[8] nothing is lost to you,[9] nothing has ceased(?)[10] for you; behold, you are more renowned and more powerful than the gods of
§ 205 Upper Egypt and their spirits.| O you whom the Pregnant One ejected,[11] you have terminated(?)[12] the night, being equipped as Seth who broke forth violently,[13] (even) you whom Isis has favoured.

§ 206 Equip yourself as Horus, being young; indeed nothing is lost to you, nothing has ceased(?)[14] for you; behold, you are more renowned and more
§ 207 powerful than the northern gods and their spirits.| Cast off[15] your impurity for Atum in Ōn and go down[16] with him; assign[17] the needs(?) of the Lower Sky and succeed to the thrones of the Abyss(?).[18] May you come into being with your father Atum, may you go up on high with your father Atum, may you rise with your father Atum, may (your) needs(?) be loosed from
§ 208 you, your head being under the care of(?)[19] the Lady of Ōn.[20] | Go up, open your way by means of the bones of Shu,[21] the embrace of your mother Nūt will enfold you. Be pure in the horizon and get rid of your impurity in the Lakes of Shu.

§ 209 Ascend and descend; descend with Rēʿ, sink into darkness with *Ndi.*
Ascend and descend; ascend with Rēʿ, rise with the Great Float-user.[22]
§ 210 Ascend and descend; descend with Nephthys, sink into darkness with the Night-bark.
Ascend and descend; ascend with Isis, rise with the Day-bark.

§ 211 May you have power in your body, for you have no hindrance; you are born for Horus, you are conceived for Seth. Be pure in the Western nome, receive your purification in the Heliopolitan nome with your father, with Atum.|
§ 212 Come into being, go up on high, and it will be well with you, it will be pleasant for you in the embrace of your father, in the embrace of Atum.|

O Atum, raise this King up to you, enclose him within your embrace, for he is your son of your body for ever. § 213

1. Cf. Nt, 571. § 199 is spoken by the officiant.

2. This 'litany' appears to be a speech by the king following on the priestly summons; hence the translation in the 1st person, which is made necessary by the 2nd person of the priest's speech. Sethe's restored  is confirmed by JPII, 719+9.

3. This and the two following strophes end in obscure aliases of the sun-god; *Dndn* may perhaps mean 'Wanderer', cf. *Komm.* i, 125; v, 156.

4. See n. 22 below.

5. Epithet of Sopd.

6. For *wrw* see also § 1728*a*.

7. As against Sethe, who translates *ḫtm·ty n·k ṯw* as 'du hast dich ausgestattet', a hortative old perfective with reinforcing dative gives a better sense, for it is pointless to tell the king what he has done, since presumably he is aware of his own actions; advice as to what he should do is much more to the point. Further, for Sethe's version we would expect *i·k ḫtm·ty*, assuming a transitive use of the old perfective.

8. The king is identified with Seth as representing the kingship of Upper Egypt; cf. also § 205*b*. On Nūbet, Ombos, cf. *AEO* ii, 28* f.

9. The construction is *n* + subjectless passive *sḏm·ty*.

10. Perhaps a writing with prothetic *i* of *ꜣb* 'cease'. Sethe translates similarly, but considers *i* to be part of the parent stem, cf. *Komm.* i, 134.

11. In birth.

12. Cf. *Komm.* i, 137.

13. At birth. The restoration *ibib* is confirmed by JPII, 719+12.

14. Reading confirmed by loc. cit.; Nt, 577.

15. Optative *sḏm·f*.

16. Reading confirmed by JPII, 719+13; Nt, 578.

17. For this sense of *wḏꜥ* cf. *GNS* 69.

18. *Nhw* apparently for *Nw*.

19. Lit. 'belongs to'.

20. Taking *iwnt* to be a fem. adjective 'belonging to Ōn', as does Sethe. *Iwnt* 'Dendera' hardly comes into question here.

21. Clouds or morning mist?

22. On reed-floats (*zḫn*) as a means of transport cf. *Religion and Thought*, 109, n. 1. In §§ 209*c* and 455*a* Sethe translates *zḫn-wr* as 'das grosse Schwimmer-Floss', but it seems to me that it is the user of the float rather than the float itself who is invoked here and above in § 201*b*, as also in § 455*a*. This implies that we should recognize the nisba form *zḫn(y)* 'he of the float' in these two cases.

## Utterance 223

*Provision of food for the king*

Awake! Turn yourself about! So shout I.[1] O King, stand up and sit down to § 214
a thousand of bread, a thousand of beer, roast meat of your rib-joints from

§ 215 the slaughter-house, and *ith*-bread from the Broad Hall.[2] | The god is provided with a god's offering, the King is provided with this bread of his. Come[3] to your soul, O Osiris, O soul among the spirits, mighty in your places, whom the Ennead protect in the Mansion of the Prince.

§[216 O King, raise yourself up to me, betake yourself to me, do not be far from me, for the tomb is your barrier against me.[4] I give you the Eye of Horus,

§ 217 I have allotted it to you; may it belong(?) to you.[1] O King, arise, receive this your bread from my hand. O King, I will be a helper to you.[5]

1. Cf. § 1491*a*.

2. Cf. § 2194*c*.

3. Hortative old perfective. Sethe's 'du bist gekommen' would require *i·k ii·t(y)* and also suits the context less well.

4. Reading *m ḥr ir·i ix imḏr·k ir·i*; Sethe would attach the final *r* in W to the following *di·n* of the next line. The king is urged to leave the tomb.

5. Reading *wnn⟨·i⟩ ⟨n·⟩k* with omission of the suffix 1st sing. and haplography of successive *n*'s. Sethe's 'ich bin dir' would require *iw⟨·i⟩ n·k*.

### Heading to Utterance 224

§ 218 Recite four times: Offering is made to him[1] in all his dignities wherever he may be.

1. Read *wdn ⟨n·⟩f*. For the Postscript to this Utterance in § 218*b*, see after the main text.

## Utterance 224

### *The king becomes the universal governor*

(218) Rouse yourself, O King! Turn yourself about, O King! Go,[1] that you may govern the Mounds of Horus; go, that you may govern the Mounds of Seth;

§ 219 go, that you may govern the Mounds of Osiris.[1] A boon which the King

§ 220 grants in all your dignities[1] wherever you may be:[2]—May your lotus-bud sceptre be at the head of the living, may your staff be at the head of the spirits as Anubis who presides over the Westerners, as ꜥAndjety who presides over the eastern nomes.

1. Surely imperative with reinforcing dative rather than *sḏm·n·f* as Sethe.

2. So W; after 'in all your dignities' T. M. N interpolate 'your garment is the leopard-skin, your garment is the kilt; may you walk in your sandals, may you slaughter (read *rḫs·k*) an ox, may you go in the *Wꜥḏ-ꜥn* bark in all your dignities . . .'.

### *Postscript to Utterance 224 (§ 218b)*

A boon which Gēb grants in all your dignities wherever you may be.

### *Epilogue to Utterance 224, also used by T as an Introduction*

How happy is your condition! Your spirit, O King, is among your brothers § 221
the gods. How changed it is, how changed it is![1] Protect[2] your children[3] and
beware of this boundary of yours which is on earth. Recite four times:[4]
Clothe your body, that you may come[5] to them.

1. Read *nš w(i) s(y)*, the pronoun referring back to *ḫrt·k*; cf. *Komm.* i, 170.
2. Sethe regards *nḏ* as a participle, but the prothetic *i* in W hints at the imperative, which makes good sense.
3. N: 'your son', with 𓎟 for 𓎡.
4. So all texts except W, which has *zp 4* at the end of the Utterance.
5. Prospective *sḏm·f*.

## Utterance 225

### *A variant of Utterance 224*

Rouse yourself,[1] O King! Turn yourself about, O King! Go,[2] that you may § 222
govern the Mounds of Horus, that you may govern the Mounds of Seth and
address the Mounds of Osiris.

A boon which the King grants, that your son be on your throne. Your § 223
garment is the leopard-skin, your garment is the kilt; may you walk in your
sandals, may you slaughter an ox,[1] may you go in the *Wrḏ-rn* bark wherever § 224
you may be in all your dignities, with your lotus-bud sceptre at the head of the
living and your[3] staff at the head of the spirits. The old man goes that he
may protect his son.[4] Clothe[5] your body that you may come to me; [may the
Eye of Horus] belong(?) to you.

1. 𓊃 for 𓊃𓅭.
2. See Utt. 224, n. 1.
3. 𓎟 for 𓎡.
4. Perhaps to be emended into *i·šm smsw i·nḏ·k zꜣ·k* 'Go, old man, that you may protect your son', cf. *Komm.* i, 172.
5. Hortative old perfective.

### *A series of spells against snakes and other noxious creatures*

## Utterance 226

One snake is enveloped by another when is enveloped the toothless calf § 225
which came forth from the pasture.[1] O earth, swallow up what went forth

§ 226 from you; O monster,[2] lie down, crawl away.| The Majesty of the Pelican has fallen into the water; O snake, turn round, for Rēʿ sees you.

1. Cf. *JEA* 36, 64.

2. *Ḥkꜣw*, translated as 'monster', has det. [hieroglyph] §§ 433*b*; 435*b*; [hieroglyph] 245*b*; [hieroglyph] *CT* iii, 396*e*; for the related adjective 'monstrous', used of a she-ass, cf. § 523*b*. See *Komm.* i, 177.

## Utterance 227

§ 227 The head of the great black bull is cut off. O *hpnw*-snake, I say this against you; O god-repelling scorpion,[1] I say this against you. Turn round, slide into the earth,[2] for I say this against you.

1. Read *ḫsr-nṯr* with scorpion det.

2. — is an error for —; cf. *Komm.* i, 184.

## Utterance 228

§ 228 One face falls on another,[1] one face beholds another; the particoloured knife, black and green, has gone forth thereat[2] and it has swallowed for itself that which it has licked.

1. Here *ḥr* 'face' probably has the secondary sense of 'glance', cf. its use to express sight, *Concise Dict.* 174, s.v. *ḥr* (2), and § 238*a* below.

2. *R·s*; Sethe translates as 'dagegen' and comments 'drückt die Gegenwehr aus', *Komm.* i, 187. Mr. Spaull suggests that the colours of the knife may be those shown by an obsidian blade when flashed in the sun.

## Utterance 229

§ 229 This here is the fingernail of Atum which is (pressed) on the spine[1] of *Nḥbw-kꜣw*, and which stilled the turmoil in Unu; fall down, crawl away!

1. *Ṯz bkꜣw*, lit. 'the knot of the vertebrae'; see also § 409*b*. *Nḥbw-kꜣw* is a serpent deity, cf. *JEA* 21, 41 ff.

## Utterance 230

§ 230 Your poison-fangs(?) be in the earth, your ribs be in the hole! Pour out the water[1] while the Two Kites stand by; your mouth is closed by the instrument of punishment,[2] and the mouth of the instrument of punishment is closed by Mafdet. He who has been made weary(?) is bitten by the *nʿw*-serpent.|

§ 231 O Rēʿ, I[3] have bitten the earth, I have bitten Gēb, I have bitten the father

of him who bit me. It is this person who has bitten me, I did not bite him;[1] it was he who came against me, I did not go against him, (he bit me) at the § 232
second instant of seeing me,[4] at the second instant of looking at me. If you bite me, I will cause you to be alone; if you (only) look at me, I will permit (you to have) your companion.

The male serpent is bitten by the female serpent, the female serpent is § 233
bitten by the male serpent; the sky is enchanted, the earth is enchanted, the Male who protects[5] the plebs is enchanted,[1] the god whose head is blind is § 234
enchanted, and you yourself are enchanted, O you scorpion here! These are the two knots of Elephantine which are in the mouth of Osiris, which were knotted for Horus on the spine.[6]

1. i.e. the poison of scorpion or snake.
2. Cf. *Komm.* i, 195.
3. The 1st person must surely be original here, since these spells are meant to be uttered by the deceased himself against the dangers he meets on his way, as in Utt. 227 above.
4. Cf. op. cit. 197.
5. Lit. 'behind'; for the sense cf. *ḥꜣy* 'protector', *Concise Dict.* 161.
6. Cf. *Komm.* i, 201 f.

## Utterance 231

Your bone is a harpoon and you are harpooned; the (hostile) hearts are held § 235
off(?), the bowmen who are in the . . .[1] are felled. That is Ḥemen!

1. *Mtꜣ* or *mtꜣ-st*, meaning unknown.

## Utterance 232

. . . his mother, his mother . . . the desert(?) is washed for me(?). Do not § 236
fail to know me.[1]

1. All utterly obscure, and Sethe does not translate. Wilke's attempt (*ZÄS* 67, 127) to regard this as a rain-spell hardly carries conviction in the context of a series of spells against snakes and scorpions, which in view of its obscurity is the only real clue we have to its purpose.

## Utterance 233

Fall, O serpent which came forth from the earth! Fall, O flame which came § 237
forth from the Abyss! Fall down, crawl away!

## Utterance 234

§ 238 My eye[1] is on you, O you who are on your coils;[2] get down, O you who are on your spine, you who are in your *nṯwt*-bush. Turn back because of me,[3] you (serpent) rejoicing in[4] two faces.

1. Lit. 'face', cf. Utt. 228, n. 1.
2. Sethe translates as 'du der auf seinen Eingeweiden liegt', but the det. suggests to me rather that a coiled snake is envisaged; the word *rlt* appears not to be known elsewhere. The suffix *·f* is fully in accord with Egyptian usage, but must be rendered in English by the 2nd person.
3. Surely so rather than Sethe's 'weiche zurück vor der (Schlange)'.
4. *Ḥknt* is taken to be old perfective 2nd sing.; *ḥkn m* is the exact equivalent of the colloquial English expression 'rejoicing in' = possessing.

## Utterance 235

§ 239 . . .[1] you have copulated with the two female guardians of the threshold[2] of the door . . .

1. Untranslatable at both beginning and end.
2. Cf. *Komm.* i, 213 f. I have, however, translated *rt* as 'threshold' in preference to Sethe's 'Thürflügel-Angelsteine' because as written the word shows no indication of dual number.

## Utterance 236

§ 240 . . . *Ss* son of *Ḥlfgt* is your name.

## Utterance 237

§ 241 O spittle which has come to naught(?), which is in the dust(?), which has fled into your mother's house:[1] O monster, lie down!

1. This rendering differs from Sethe's, but is none the less a guess; 'spittle', i.e. poison, is apparently used of a snake on the basis of *pars pro toto*; the snake is rendered powerless and lies in the dust. On this view of the spell, 'your (lit. 'his') mother's house' will be the snake's hole.

## Utterance 238

§ 242 Your father's bread is yours, O *Ỉkl-nhy*,[1] your own bread belongs to your father and you, O *Ỉkl-nhy*. A gold collar and *ḥknw*-oil, O *Ḫʿy-tꜣw*;[2] this one here is your bull, the strong one on account of whose actions men act.

1. A serpent.
2. For a variant of the latter part of this Utterance see Utt. 282. For the god *Ḫʿy-tꜣw* cf. §§ 423*c*; 518*d*.

## Utterance 239

The White Crown goes forth, having swallowed the Great One,[1] the tongue § 243
of the White Crown gulped down the Great One, but the tongue was not seen.

1. Fem. The text is a cry of triumph of Upper over Lower Egypt; the fact that Lower Egypt was represented by the cobra led to its secondary use as a spell against snakes.

## Utterance 240

The serpent is in the sky, the centipede of Horus is on earth. The ox-herd is § 244
Horus when he treads; I[1] have trodden in the path[2] of Horus, and what I do not know, he does not know.[3] My eye is on you,[1] O you who are in your § 245
*nꜣwt*-bush, and you are dragged off,[4] O you who are in your cavern, O cooking-pot of Horus[5] which pervades[6] the earth. O monster, crawl away.[7]

1. So also Sethe. The 1st person is certainly original, see § 244*c* (T).
2. Read *zbnt*, cf. *Komm.* i, 223. Sethe translates as 'Spazierplatz'.
3. Cf. Edel, § 1095, though I translate somewhat differently. *Rḫ·f* of T is to be preferred; 'he' is Horus.
4. Old perfective 2nd sing. On the writing of *sṯꜣ* cf. *JEA* 42, 31, 11.
5. The snake, apparently thought of as the contents of the pot.
6. *Ḫtt* appears to be an adjective qualifying *ḫnft*; Sethe's 'schlüpf in die Erde' demands a preposition which is not present.
7. The end of this Utterance is a puzzle.  is apparently a vocative;  looks like the imperative *imi* 'give' or 'place'. According to Nt, 708 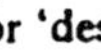 is not the word for 'desert' as Sethe thought, but the determinative of *hiw* 'monster' as in §§ 433. 435, while by all analogy *zbn* should be an imperative and not the object of *imi*. I suggest that *imi* has been inserted in error; Nt, 708 does not show it, and without it a perfectly good sense is obtained.

## Utterance 241

O you expectoration of a wall, you vomit of a brick,[1] what comes out of your § 246
mouth is turned back against yourself.[2]

1. Opprobrious allusions to the snake or other vermin crawling out of a crevice in a wall.
2. The creature falls a victim to its own poison.

## Utterance 242

The flame is extinguished, no light is found in the house of him who possesses § 247
Nūbet. The biting snake pervades[1] the house of him whom it would bite, and it dwells in it.

1. Sethe translates as 'eingeschlichen hat' with the preposition 'in', but no such sense of the verb *ḫtḫt* is otherwise known; it seems preferable to regard it as the compound preposition of Gardiner, § 178 and to translate it with 'is throughout', 'pervades'.

## Utterance 243

§ 248 Two *ḥts*-sceptres and two *ḥts*-sceptres belong to the two *ḏmꜥ*-cords—twice—like the bread which is withheld(?) from you. Are you really here? Are you really there? O slave, be off(?).

## Utterance 244

§ 249 O [Osiris the King], here is this Eye [of Horus]; [take] it, that you may be strong[1] and that he[2] may fear you—break the red jars.

1. Read *(i)m(i)m* 'be strong', cf. §§ 614*c*; 782*b*.
2. The snake.

## Utterance 245

*The king joins the stars*

*The king speaks*

§ 250 I[1] come to you, O Nūt, I come to you, O Nūt, I have cast my father to the earth,[2] I have left Horus behind me, my wings have grown into those of a falcon, my two plumes are those of a sacred falcon, my soul has brought me and its magic has equipped me.

*The sky-goddess speaks*

§ 251 Open up[3] your place in the sky among the stars of the sky, for you are the Lone Star,[4] the companion of Ḥu; look down upon Osiris[5] when he governs the spirits, for you stand[6] far off from him, you are not among them and you shall not be among them.[7]

1. As Sethe has seen, the suffix of the 2nd person in the speech by the goddess shows that the king's speech must originally have been in the 1st person.
2. Sethe considers this to refer to the burial of the king's father.
3. Optative *sḏm·f*, lit. 'may you split open'.
4. Cf. *JNES*, 25, 160 f.
5. i.e. 'look down upon' from above. Osiris rules in the Netherworld, far below the starry sky where the king now takes his place.
6. Note the archaic construction of old independent pronoun + old perfective.
7. The spirits whom Osiris rules.

## Utterance 246

*The king is a ruler in the Beyond*

§ 252 See among whom this King stands,[1] the horns on his head being those of two wild bulls, for you[2] are a black ram, the son of a black ewe (*sic*), whom a

white ewe bore, whom the four teats(?)[3] suckled.| The blue-eyed Horus comes § 253
against you,[4] beware of the red-eyed Horus, violent of power, whose might[5]
none can withstand! His messengers go, his couriers run, they bear tidings to
Him whose arm is raised in the East[6] of the going[7] | of this One in you,[8] of § 254
whom *Dwn-ʿnwy* says:[9] 'He shall give orders to the fathers of the gods.'

The gods are silent before you, the Ennead have put their hands on their
mouths, before this One in you, of whom *Dwn-ʿnwy* says: 'He shall give
orders to the fathers of the gods.'| Stand at the doors of the horizon, open § 255
the doors of the firmament, that you may stand at the head of them[10] like
Gēb at the head of his Ennead. They go in and they smite down ill, they
come forth and lift up their faces,| and they see you as Min at the head of § 256
the Two Conclaves.[11] Someone stands behind you, your brother stands
behind you, your relative[12] stands behind you, and you shall not perish, you
shall not come to an end, but your name shall endure(?)[13] among men and your
name shall come into being among the gods.

1. The fem. ending in the relative form *ʿḥʿt* presumably refers to the ewes mentioned below. The imperative 'see' is addressed generally to the denizens of the Beyond. Note the adverbial use of *m-ʿb*.

2. This pronoun must refer to the king himself, though the abrupt change of person is curious; as Sethe points out, *Komm.* i, 243, it is characteristic of this Utterance. From § 254*a* on, the suffix ·*k* can refer only to the king.

3. *Wꜣpt*; the translation 'teats' was suggested by Gunn.

4. Plural, addressed to the celestial onlookers.

5. *Bꜣ*, singular, used as a synonym of the more familiar *bꜣw*.

6. Sethe, *Komm.* i, 245, equates this being with Rēʿ, but the upraised arm also suits Min, with whom the king is identified in § 256*a*.

7. Taking *ỉmt* to be infinitive. Sethe translates somewhat differently.

8. From here on the king is regularly addressed in the 2nd person, cf. n. 2 above.

9. Relative form, cf. § 254*c*.

10. The gods.

11. On the *ỉtrty* cf. *JEA* 30, 27 f.

12. So Gunn and Sethe.

13. See *Komm.* i, 160 f., 250.

## Utterance 247

### *The officiant addresses the king*

Your son Horus has acted on your behalf,[1] and the Great Ones tremble when § 257
they see the sword which is in your hand when you ascend from the Nether-
world.| Hail to you, O Wise One! Gēb has created you, the Ennead has § 258

borne you, Horus is pleased with his father, Atum is pleased with his years, the gods of East and West are pleased with the Great One[2] who came into being in the arms of Her who bore the god.

§ 259 O King, O King, see![3] O King, O King, behold! O King, O King, hear!
§ 260 O King, O King, be yonder! | O King, O King, raise yourself on to your side and do my command. O you who hate sleep but who were made limp, arise, O you who were in Nedit! Your good bread is prepared in Pe, take your
§ 261 power in Ōn, | for it is Horus who commanded that men help his father. As for the Lord of Storm, the slavering[4] of Seth is forbidden(?) to him. He[5] raises you up, and it is he who will raise up Atum.

1. Sethe has 'Worte sprechen, das dir dein Sohn Horus gethan hat', which to my mind misses the point of the passage. I take *ḏd mdw* to be merely the usual introductory rubric and *ir·n* to be the narrative *sḏm·n·f* form in the common idiom *ir n* 'act on behalf of', 'help', which is what Horus did for his dead father.

2. Fem., referred by Sethe to a newly risen star.

3. It seems that we have here a series of imperatives, the dead king being called upon to re-exercise his bodily senses and to rise again, though Sethe favoured participles, in part as alternative possibilities, *Komm.* i, 256, because of the non-geminated forms *m͗* and *wn*; but to my mind the sense demands imperatives; for M.E. non-geminated forms cf. Gardiner, § 336.

4. *Isd*; possibly heavy rain is envisaged.

5. Horus.

## Utterance 248

*The king becomes a star*

§ 262 The King is a great one, the King has issued from between the thighs of the Ennead. The King was conceived by Sakhmet, and it was Shezmētet who
§ 263 bore the King, | a star brilliant[1] and far-travelling, who brings distant products[2] to Rēʿ daily. The King has come to his throne which is upon the Two Ladies[3] and the King appears as a star.

1. Lit. 'sharp of brow' or 'visage'.

2. For *in ḫrt* 'bring products', cf. *Urk.* i, 123, 17; 141, 11.

3. i.e. they support the throne. Sethe, however, explains *tpt* rather differently, cf. *Komm.* i, 261 f.

## Utterance 249

*The king is a flower in the sun-god's hand*

§ 264 O you two fighters,[1] tell the Noble One, whoever he may be,[2] that I am[3] this *zšzš*-flower which sprang up from the earth. My hand is cleansed by him
§ 265 who prepared my throne, | and I am at the nose of the Great Power;[4] I have

come into the Island of Fire, I have set Right in it in the place of Wrong, and I am on my way to the linen garments[5] which the uraei guard on the night of the great flood which came forth from the Great One.[6] | I appear as § 266
Nefertem, as the lotus-bloom which is at the nose of Rēʿ; he will issue from the horizon daily and the gods will be cleansed at the sight of him.

1. A pair of celestial gate-wardens, according to *Komm.* i, 26, but it is possible that Horus and Seth, the two typical foes, may have been envisaged. For the sing. *ḥrw* cf. *CT* ii, 223*e*.

2. For this translation of *m rn·f pw* cf. 'until they have found your thief *n rn·f* whoever he may be' *Wenamūn*, 1, 19–20, with *n* for older *m*. Demotic instances of this expression are cited by Gardiner, *Late-Egyptian Stories*, 62a, at bottom. For *m rn·k pw* with the same meaning see § 1724*a*.

3. For the 1st person cf. *Komm.* i, 265; the king is speaking of himself.

4. In the king's avatar as a flower.

5. Regarding *r* as a preposition, lit. 'I am toward (= bound for) the linen garments'. The objections to Sethe's 'N ist der Hüter der Wäsche', taking *r* to stand for *ỉry*, are (1) that the *sšrw* already have guardians, namely uraei, and (2) that *sšrw* means 'linen' in general rather than 'washing', cf. *BIFAO* 30, 171 ff. *Sšrw* appears to mean linen garments which the uraei guard, and which the king makes for.

6. Fem., in reference to the sky.

## Utterance 250

### *The king is announced by Sia*

This is the King who is over the spirits, who unites hearts—so says[1] he who is § 267
in charge of wisdom, being great,[2] and who bears the god's book, (even) Sia[3] who is at the right hand of Rēʿ.

### *The king declares himself to be Sia*

I have come to my throne[4] which is over the spirits, I unite hearts, O you who are in charge of wisdom, being great. I become Sia who bears the god's book, who is at the right hand of Rēʿ. | O you who are protected by my hand, § 268
it is I who say what is in the heart of the Great One[5] in the Festival of Red Linen. I, even I, am Sia who is at the right hand of Rēʿ, the haughty one(?)[6] who presides over the Cavern of the Abyss.

1. *N* for *ỉn* 'so says'.

2. Old perfective 3rd masc. sing.; in § 267*c* we have the 2nd sing. in identical context.

3. The personification of intelligence and understanding.

4. Following Sethe in the use of the 1st person.

5. A goddess, cf. *Komm.* i, 274.

6. For *snk-ỉb* cf. *Urk.* vii, 10, 14, where it is considered to be a bad quality in a local magnate; but it might be considered not inappropriate in a king.

## Utterance 251

*The king departs to join the sun-god*

§ 269 O you who are over the hours, who are before Rēʿ, prepare a way for me[1] so
§ 270 that I may pass within the patrol of those with warlike faces,| for I am bound for this throne of mine, (even I) the pre-eminent of thrones who am behind the great god,[2] whose head is set in place, who has assumed a sharp strong horn as one who bears a sharp knife which cuts throats. That which removes trouble from before the Bull, which causes those who are in darkness to
§ 271 quake,[3] is the strong horn which is behind the great god.| I have subdued those who are to be punished, I have smitten their foreheads, and I am not opposed in the horizon.

1. For the 1st person cf. *Komm.* i, 276.
2. Cf. *Pyr.*, vol. iii, p. 16.
3. *Sʿhd* 'cause to quake' is the causative of *ʿhd* 'palpitate', *GNS* 30.

## Utterance 252

*The king becomes the supreme deity*

§ 272 Lift up your faces, you gods who are in the Netherworld, for the King has come that you may see him, he having become the great god. The King is
§ 273 ushered in with trembling, the King is robed.| Guard yourselves, all of you,[1] for the King governs men, the King judges the living within the domain of Rēʿ,[2] the King speaks to this pure region in which he has made his dwelling
§ 274 with Him who judged between the two gods.[3] | The King has power on his head, the King wields the sceptre and he[4] shows respect to the King. The King sits with those who row the bark of Rēʿ, the King commands what is good and he[5] does it, for the King is the great god.

1. The translation by Sethe, 'der euch allesamt geehrt hat', seems entirely to miss the sense, which is not that the king honours the gods, but that they are called upon to beware of his power and be subject to him, since he himself is the supreme god. I take *mk* to be the imperative of *mkì* 'guard', 'protect'.
2. i.e. all the cosmos.
3. i.e. Thoth.
4. Thoth.
5. Rēʿ.

## Utterance 253

*The king is cleansed in the Field of Rushes*

§ 275 Someone has bathed in the Field of Rushes,[1]

Rēʿ has bathed in the Field of Rushes.
Someone has bathed in the Field of Rushes,
This King has bathed in the Field of Rushes.
This King's hand[2] is in Rēʿ's hand.
O Nūt, take his hand!
O Shu, lift him up!
O Shu, lift him up!

1. On this 'litany' see *Komm.* i, 290 ff.
2. So W; T has  'diploma' twice in § 275*e*, surely in error.

## Utterance 254

*The king arrives in the sky*[1]

*The king's advent is announced*

The Great One[2] has been censed[3] for the Bull of Nekhen, and the fiery blast is against you who are behind the shrine.[4] O great god whose name is unknown, a meal is (set) in place for the Sole Lord. § 276

*The king threatens a general cataclysm if a place is not made for him*

O Lord of the horizon, make ready a place for me, for if you fail to make ready a place for me, I will lay a curse on my father Gēb, and the earth will speak no more, Gēb will be unable to protect(?) himself, | and whoever I find in my way, I will devour him piecemeal(?). The *ḥnt*-pelican will prophesy, the *psḏt*-pelican will go up, the Great One[5] will arise, the Enneads will speak, the earth being entirely dammed up;[6] | the borders[7] will be joined together, the river-banks will unite, the roads will be impassable to travellers,[8] the slopes[9] will be destroyed for those who would go up. § 277 § 278 § 279

*Speeches by different deities*

'Set the rope aright, cross the Milky Way(?),[10] smite the ball in the meadow of Apis![11] | Oho! Your fields are in fear,[12] you *iȝd*-star, before the Pillar of the Stars,[13] for they have seen the Pillar of Kenzet, the Bull of the sky,[14] and the Ox-herd[15] is overwhelmed before him.[16] | Ho! Fear and tremble, you violent ones who are on the storm-cloud of the sky! He split open the earth by means of what he knew on the day when he wished to come thence'[17]—⌈so says *Wr-skȝt* who dwells in the Netherworld. § 280 § 281 § 282

Behold, she comes to meet you,[18] does the Beautiful West, meeting you with her lovely tresses, and she says: 'Here comes he whom I have borne,[19]⌉

§ 283 whose horn is upstanding, the eye-painted Pillar, the Bull of the sky! Your
§ 284 shape is notable;[20] pass in peace,| for I have protected you'—so says the Beautiful West to the King.

'Go, row to the Field of Offerings and travel to Him who is on his *ḳꜣt*-plant'
§ 285 —|so says *Ḫnty-mnỉt·f*. 'You sink into the earth to your thickness, to your middle, to your full span(?), you see Rēʿ in his fetters, you praise Rēʿ in his loosing from fetters by means of the amulet of the Great One which is in its
§ 286 red linen,| and the Lord of Peace will give you his hand.'[21]

*Speech by the king*

O you female apes who cut off heads, I will escape safely from you; I have affixed my head to my neck, and my neck is on my trunk in this my name of Affixer-of-heads, by means of which I affixed the head of Apis on that day
§ 287 when the ox was lassoed.| Those whom I have caused ⟨to eat⟩, they eat ⟨their food, those whom I have caused to⟩ drink,[22] they drink of their water-flood;
§ 288 so will I be honoured there by those who see me.| The Serpent of Praise on her sceptre[23] is my Tefēnet[24] whom Shu supports, she makes spacious my place in Busiris,[25] in Mendes,[26] and in Djedut,[27] she sets up my two standards
§ 289 in front of the Great Ones,| she excavates a pool for me in the Field of Rushes, she confirms my land in the two Fields of Offerings, and I give judgement in
§ 290 the heavens[28] between the two Contestants,| for my power is the power of the Eye of *Tbỉ*,[29] my strength is the strength of the Eye of *Tbỉ*. I have protected myself from those who would do this against me, who would take away my
§ 291 food from me,| who when it was in being would take my supper from me and who when it was in being would take the breath from my nose and who would bring to an end[30] my days of life. I am stronger than they, having
§ 292 reappeared upon my shore;| their hearts fall to my fingers, their entrails are for the denizens of the sky,[31] their blood is for the denizens of the earth.[32] Their heirs are (doomed) to poverty, their houses to conflagration, and their
§ 293 courtyards to the high Nile.| But I am happy, happy, for I am the Unique One, the Bull of the sky, I have crushed those who would do this against me
§ 294 and have annihilated their survivors.| That which appertains to my throne, which I have taken and lifted up, is this which my father Shu gave me in the presence of Seth.[33]

1. Contrary to Sethe's view that there are ten different strata to be detected in this Utterance, it seems to me that it falls into four parts: (1) a brief announcement of the king's advent in the sky; (2) a speech by the king uttering dire threats of a general cataclysm if his way is not made clear; (3) speeches by *Wr-skꜣt*, the Beautiful West, and *Ḫnty-mnỉt·f*; (4) a long speech by the

king, the four parts making a connected whole. The translation of the king's speech in the 1st person rests on §§ 282*b* ff., where the king is addressed in the 2nd person. Cf. *Komm.* i, 334. 348.

2. Fem., possibly the royal crown, but in this context hardly that of Lower Egypt as apparently in § 295*d*. Sethe suggests that the uraeus serpent may be meant, *Komm.* i, 304 f.

3. *ỉdy* is passive *sḏm·f*, cf. *Syntax*, 75 ff.

4. So rather than 'round about' ('um') as Sethe; see my notes on P. Bremner-Rhind, 4, 6 = *JEA* 22, 134–5.

5. Masculine.

6. Old perfective + 'complementary infinitive', lit. 'dammed up a damming'.

7. i.e. the cliffs bordering the Nile valley; cf. *Komm.* i, 314.

8. Lit. 'those who pass'.

9. Or 'stairways', but a natural feature would fit the context better. Possibly the gentle rise from the level of the river to the foot of the cliffs may be envisaged.

10. Cf. *Komm.* i, 315.

11. These three imperatives, addressed to the king, may well be part of the speech of *Wr-skȝt*, named in § 282*a*.

12. Cf. *Komm.* i, 316–17. The speaker now turns to address the dwellers in the sky.

13. The dead king.

14. Again the king. Cf. *Komm.* i, 317–18.

15. A star or constellation?

16. Cf. *Komm.* i, 318 f.

17. The king has broken out of his tomb by means of his knowledge of magic.

18. A speech to the king, probably by the previously mentioned *Wr-skȝt*, announcing the arrival of the goddess of the West.

19. T unnecessarily appends *r T pn*, perhaps in anticipation of § 284*a*.

20. *Ṯnỉ*, lit. 'distinguishable' from all others.

21. Cf. *Komm.* i, 323 f. Sethe would separate these words from the preceding speech of *Ḫnty-mnỉt·f*, but no other speaker is named, so it would seem that they are a continuation of the foregoing. As Sethe points out, we have here an allusion to the burial of a king in the days when he was simply interred in the earth, while 'Rēʿ in his fetters' refers to the temporary obliteration of the sun each night, being released from his bonds each morning.

22. Restoration of obvious omissions, cf. *Komm.* i, 331 f.

23. Cf. *Komm.* i, 333 f.

24. Dual in T; Sethe suggests that the editor of this text may have misunderstood his copy in the 1st person.

25. Busiris, cf. *AEO* ii, 176* ff.

26. For *Ḏdwt* see also § 350*c*; it is probably identical with *Ḏdỉt* 'necropolis of Ōn', §§ 181. 964. 1046.

27. Mendes, cf. *AEO* ii, 150* ff.

28. Conceived of as *Mḥt-wrt* the celestial cow, originally the celestial waterway; the name means 'Great Flood'.

29. According to Sethe the sun is meant.

30. Read *sỉʿ* with T; its later equivalent *sʿr* occurs in the same sense *CT* i, 158*d*, *sʿḥʿ* of W being an error. Cf. *Komm.* i, 340.

31. The carrion birds.
32. The carnivorous animals.
33. So W; T is much more verbose but adds nothing essential.

## Utterance 255

*A variant of the last*

§ 295 The horizon[1] is censed for Horus of Nekhen;[2] a meal for the Lords! The
horizon is censed for Horus of Nekhen, and the flame of its blast is against
you who are behind the shrine, the outburst of its blast is against you who
have raised up the Great One.[3]
§ 296 The horizon is censed for Horus of Nekhen; a meal for the Lords! O you
§ 297 hateful one, hateful of character and hateful of shape,| remove yourself from
your place and lay your insignia of rank on the ground for me,[4] for if you do
not remove yourself from your place or lay your insignia of rank on the ground
for me, then I will come, my face being that of this Great One,[5] the Lord of
§ 298 power who is strong through the injury which was done to him;[6] | I will put
flame in my eye, and it will encompass you and set storm among the doers of
§ 299 (evil) deeds, and its (fiery) outburst among these primeval ones.| I will
smite away the arms of Shu which support the sky and I will thrust my
§ 300 shoulder into that rampart on which you lean.| The Great One indeed will
rise within his shrine and lay his insignia on the ground for me, for I have
assumed authority and have power through understanding.

1. *ꜣḫt* 'horizon' is clearly an error for *ı͗ḫt* 'uraeus', cf. *Komm.* i, 349.
2. Cf. *Dict. géogr.* iii, 99.
3. Fem.; according to *Komm.* i, 350 the allusion is to the crown of Lower Egypt, but in T the word is plural.
4. This Utterance, like the last, was doubtless originally in the 1st person, cf. ibid. 348.
5. Masculine.
6. 'The Lord of power' is Horus. The translation follows W; T has 'what was injured in him'.

## Utterance 256

*The dead king assumes his royal heritage*

§ 301 I[1] have succeeded to Gēb, I have succeeded to Gēb; I have succeeded to
Atum, I am on the throne of Horus the first-born, and his Eye is my strength,
§ 302 I am protected from what was done against him,| the flaming blast of my
uraeus is that of Ernūtet[2] who is upon me. I have set the fear of me in their[3]
§ 303 hearts by making strife[4] with them.| The gods have looked on in nudity[5] and

bow to me in adoration. Row me, O mother of mine; tow me, O abode of mine; make fast(?)[6] your cable.

1. For the 1st person cf. *dmỉ⟨·ỉ⟩* in W, § 303*c*, which the editor has omitted to alter to the 3rd person.
2. A cobra-goddess acting as the royal uraeus.
3. 'Their' refers to the king's enemies.
4. Cf. *ḥꜣꜥyt* in *Concise Dict.* 162; Sethe translates by 'Blutbad'.
5. A token of awe and respect; cf. *Komm.* i, 358.
6. Cf. ibid. 359 f., but the interpretation of *hy* as an interjection suits the context ill, however  (W) be understood, and I suggest that 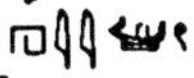 (T) may be a verb in the imperative, perhaps an order that the tow-rope be made fast.

## Utterance 257

*The king is identified with the sun*

There is tumult in the sky; 'We see something new', say the primeval gods. § 304
O you Ennead, Horus is in the sunlight, the possessors of forms make salutation to him, all the Two Enneads serve him,[1] for he sits on the throne § 305
of the Lord of All. The King takes possession of the sky, he cleaves its iron;[1] the King is conducted ⟨on⟩[2] the roads to Khoprer,[1] the King rests in life in § 306
the West, and the dwellers in the Netherworld attend him. The King shines anew in the East, and he who settled the dispute will come[3] to him bowing. Make salutation, you gods, to the King, who is older than the Great One, to whom belongs[4] power on his throne;[1] the King assumes authority, eternity is § 307
brought to him and understanding is established at his feet for him. Rejoice[5] at the King, for he has taken possession of the horizon.

1. i.e. the visible canopy of sky.
2. *Sšm(w)* is passive *sḏm·f*, but a preposition has been omitted before *wꜣwt*. Cf. *Komm.* i, 367.
3. Sethe's 'zu ihm kommt' does not account for the *t* in *ỉwt*; probably it is prospective *sḏm·f*, though the *sḏmt·f* form is not absolutely excluded.
4. Sethe's interpretation of *ỉn sw* as 'so sagt er' is impossible, for *ỉn* 'so says' takes a suffix pronoun like any other verb; *ỉn sw* is surely a variant of *n-sw* 'to him belongs' (not here 'he belongs to'), cf. *n-ṯw s(y)* 'it belongs to you', § 2033. On the variant text of T see *Komm.* i, 370 f.
5. W appears to have borrowed the det. of *hny* from *hy* 'make fast(?)' a rope in the preceding Utterance.

## Utterance 258

*The king leaves the earth for the sky*

The King is Osiris in a dust-devil,[1] earth is his detestation, and the King § 308
will not enter into Gēb lest he perish and lest he sleep in his mansion upon

earth; his bones are made strong,[2] his ills are removed. The King has become pure through the Eye of Horus, his ill is removed by the two Kites of Osiris,
§309 the King has shed his efflux to the earth in Ḳūṣ.[3] | It is his sister the Lady of Pe who laments him, for the King is bound for the sky, the King is bound for the sky on the wind, on the wind! He will not be excluded, and there is nothing through which he can be excluded; there will be no session on him in the Tribunal of the God, for the King is unique(?),[4] the eldest of the gods. |
§310 His bread-offering is up above with Rēʿ, his meal[5] is in the Abyss, for the King is one who goes to and fro; he comes and goes with Rēʿ and he has
§311 occupied his mansions.[6] | The King bestows powers and takes away powers, he imposes an obstacle and removes an obstacle,[7] and the King spends day and night propitiating the Two Adzes[8] in Unu; his foot shall not be opposed nor his desire frustrated.

1. The king ascends to the sky in a whirlwind of dust. Cf. § 309*b* and *Komm.* i, 37.
2. So T rightly; W has *sḏ* 'broken', which is the exact contrary of the sense intended; the king is as whole as he was in life. Cf. also § 312*d*.
3. Cf. *AEO* ii, 27* f.
4. Lit. 'upon his one(-ness)'.
5. For *ʿ3bt* 'meal' cf. *CT* iii, 1*a*; 60*a*.
6. Cf. *BD* 127, 9; 131, 1; 398, 5.
7. Cf. *Ann. Serv.* 27, 227. The sense is that the king controls all movement.
8. i.e. the two combatants in Unu (cf. § 229*b*), who apparently fought with adzes.

## Utterance 259

*A variant of the last*

§312 This King is Osiris in a dust-devil; earth is this King's detestation, and he will not enter into Gēb lest this King perish and lest he sleep in his mansion on earth. This King's bones are made strong, his ills are removed, this King has become pure through the Eye of Horus, his ill is removed by the Two
§313 Kites of Osiris, this King has dropped his cords[1] to the earth in Ḳūṣ. | It is the King's sister the Lady of Pe[2] who laments him, the Two Attendants who mourned for Osiris have mourned for him. This King is bound for the sky, this King is bound for the sky with Shu and Rēʿ, and this King will not be excluded, for there is none who will exclude; this King is on his own foot, he the eldest of the gods, and there will be no session on this King in the
§314 Tribunal of the God. | This King's bread-offering is up above with Rēʿ, this King's meal is in the Abyss, for this King is one who goes to and fro, this King goes with Rēʿ, this King comes with Rēʿ, he has occupied his mansions, |

he imposes an obstacle and he removes an obstacle, he bestows powers and § 315
he takes away powers; this King spends day and night getting rid of the Two Adzes in Unu,[3] and this King's foot shall not be opposed nor shall his desire be frustrated.

1. *Sic*, error for *rḏw* 'efflux', cf. § 308*f*.
2. Cf. *AEO* ii, 188* ff.
3. Cf. Utt. 258, n. 8.

## Utterance 260

*The king claims his rights as Horus*

O Gēb, Bull of the sky, I[1] am Horus, my father's heir. I have gone and re- § 316
turned, the fourth of these four gods who have brought water, who have administered purification, who have rejoiced in the strength of their fathers; I desire to be vindicated by what I have done.[1] I the orphan have had judge- § 317
ment with the orphaness,[2] the Two Truths have judged, though a witness was lacking.[3] The Two Truths have commanded that the thrones of Gēb shall revert to me, so that I may raise myself to what I have desired.[1] My § 318
limbs which were in concealment are reunited, and I join those who are in the Abyss, I put a stop to the affair in Ōn,[4] for I go forth today in the real form of a living spirit,[1] that I may break up the fight and cut off the turbulent § 319
ones.[5] I come forth, the guardian of justice, that I may bring it, it being with me; the wrathful ones bustle about for me and those who are in the Abyss assign life to me.

My refuge is my Eye, my protection is my Eye, my strength is my Eye, § 320
my power is my Eye.[1] O you southern, northern, western, and eastern gods, § 321
honour me and fear me, for I have seated myself in the awning(?) of the Two Courtyards, and that fiery snake the *ḏnn*-serpent would have burnt you, striking to your hearts.[1] O you who would come against me in obstruction, § 322
come to me, come to me (as friends), for I am the *alter ego* of my father, the blossom of my mother.[1] I detest travelling in darkness, for then I cannot see, § 323
but fall upside down; I go forth today that I may bring justice, for it is with me, and I will not be given over to your flame, you gods.

1. For the original 1st person cf. the writing  § 317*c* where the doubled [hieroglyph] shows that the 3rd person is secondary. Sethe, *Komm.* i, 393, would exclude the 1st person from the beginning of the Utterance on what to me seem insufficient grounds. In his view the division between the two parts of this text falls at § 321.
2. Cf. ibid. 398 ff.
3. Cf. ibid. 400.

4. i.e. the fight between Horus and Seth, cf. *CT* i, 19*c*–20*a*, where it is vividly described: 'The earth was torn up when the Rivals fought, and their feet scooped out the Pool of the God which is in Ōn.' Sethe was clearly unaware of this passage.

5. Sethe has 'den Streit bestrafen'; both renderings are tenable.

## Utterance 261

*The king becomes a flash of lightning*

§ 324 The King is a heart-tosser(?),[1] the favourite son of Shu, long-extended,[2]
fierce of brilliance;[3] the King is a flame (moving) before the wind to the end
of the sky and to the end of the earth when the hand of the lightning is
§ 325 voided of the King.| The King travels the air and traverses the earth, he
§ 326 kisses the *Nt*-crown, (even he) whom the god cast forth.[4] | Those who are
in the firmament(?)[5] open their arms to him, the King stands on the eastern
side of the celestial vault, there is brought to him a way of ascent to the sky,[6]
and it is he who performs the errand of the storm.

1. Who makes the heart leap with fright as does a blinding flash; the translation is due to Sethe.
2. Lit. 'stretched out a stretching', participle + 'complementary infinitive'.
3. Read *ıзb iḫw*.
4. As a lightning flash.
5. *Wmwnyt*; Sethe has 'Laubdach(?)', cf. *Komm.* ii, 5 f.
6. i.e. the storm-clouds on which the dead king rides. Sethe translates slightly differently.

## Utterance 262

*The gods are prayed to recognize the king*

§ 327 Be not unaware of me,[1] O God;
If you know me, I will know you.
⟨Be not unaware of me, O God;
Of me it is said: 'He who has perished.'⟩[2]
§ 328 Be not unaware of me, O Rēʿ;
If you know me, I will know you.
Be not unaware of me, O Rēʿ;
Of me it is said: 'Greatest of all who have been completely destroyed.'[3]
§ 329 Be not unaware of me, O Thoth;
If you know me, I will know you.
Be not unaware of me, O Thoth;
Of me it is said: 'He who rests alone.'

Be not unaware of me, O Ḥar-Sopd; § 330
If you know me, I will know you.
Be not unaware of me, O Ḥar-Sopd;
Of me it is said; 'Miserable One.'[4]
Be not unaware of me, O Dweller in the Netherworld; § 331
If you know me, I will know you.
Be not unaware of me, O Dweller in the Netherworld;
Of me it is said: 'He who wakes healthy.'
Be not unaware of me, O Bull of the sky; § 332
If you know me, I will know you.
Be not unaware of me, O Bull of the sky;
Of me it is said: 'This star ⟨of the Lower Sky⟩.'[5]

Behold, I have come; behold, I have come; behold, I have gone up on high,[6] § 333
but I have not come of myself;[7] there was brought a message which came for
me.[8] | I have passed by my house of Danger(?),[9] the striking power of the § 334
Great Lake has missed me, my fare for the Great Ferry-boat has not been
taken,[10] the Castle of the Mace of the Great Ones will not oppose me on the
Street of Stars(?).[11] | Behold, I have reached the height of heaven,[12] I have § 335
seen the Viper[13] in the Night-bark, and it is I who row in it;[14] I have recog-
nized the Uraeus in the Day-bark,[15] and it is I who baled it out;| the sun-folk § 336
have testified concerning me,[16] the hailstorms of the sky have taken me, and
they raise me up to Rēʿ.[17]

1. For the 1st person cf. *Komm.* ii, 9. The translation follows Sethe in adhering to the W text, supplemented in places from TP, a version which in general appears to be the product of indifferent editing. A much damaged text from N, preserved in JPII, 709 + 26–36, belongs to the TP recension.

2. W has suffered corruption here; on the analogy of subsequent verses 327*b–c* should have read *m ḫm W nṯr ḏd ir⟨·i⟩ sk* 'be not unaware of me, O God; of me it is said: "He who has perished."' For § 327*a–c* TP has 'be not unaware of me, O God, for I know you; do not let me be unaware of you, O God, for I know you; of me it is said: "He who has perished"', and so *pari passu* for the rest of this 'litany'. Apart from this corruption, the text of W is superior.

3. For *ir·k* of W read *ir⟨·i⟩* with T, and so throughout. At the end of the clause, W adds *tm* 'completely'.

4. *Ḳsn*; var. T: *rs wḏ3* 'he who wakes healthy'. In § 331*c* the position is reversed.

5. So T; W has *nḫḫ pn* only.

6. Var. T: 'behold I have gone up on high, behold I have come.'

7. Cf. Utt. 213, n. 2.

8. Var. T: 'it was your messages which fetched me, the god's word raised me up.'

9. Cf. *Komm.* ii, 17 f. P reads: 'to the appearance of the upper road'. In WT read perhaps *pr b3*, lit. 'house of the soul', which in §§ 1930–1 is a dangerous place which must be avoided.

10. Var. T: 'T has crossed over in the Great Ferry-boat, and no fare has been taken in it.'

11. The suffix of *ḥsf·n·f* in W is superfluous and is lacking in T, which has the variant spelling *ḥsb*. *Msḳt sḥdw* 'street of stars(?)' is doubtless the Milky Way; cf. *Komm.* ii, 20.

12. T adds: 'the sun-folk have seen me'.

13. *Ḏt*; the suffix is superfluous, cf. § 336*a* (T). The specific term 'viper' may or may not be taxonomically correct, but a more specific term than 'serpent' is needed to distinguish it from the uraeus serpent shortly to be named.

14. Sethe translates as 'NN. ist es, da in ihr erfahren ist'. There is nothing to choose between the two versions.

15. Var. T: 'the Day-bark summons me.' What remains of P agrees with W.

16. Var. T: 'I have seen the Viper in the Night-bark, I recognize the Uraeus in the Day-bark.'

17. Var. T: 'the god has summoned me by name, he drives away the hailstones by means of them (*sic*), and I mount up to Rēʿ.'

## Utterance 263

*The king ferries over the sky to Reʿ*[1]

§ 337 The reed-floats of the sky are set in place for Rēʿ
That he may cross on them to the horizon.
The reed-floats of the sky are set in place for Ḥarakhti
That Ḥarakhti may cross on them to Rēʿ.
The reed-floats of the sky are set in place for me[2]
That I may cross on them to the horizon, to Rēʿ.
The reed-floats of the sky are set in place for me
That I may cross on them to Ḥarakhti and to Rēʿ.

§ 338 It is well with me and my double, I live with my double, my panther-skin
is on me, my sceptre is in my arm, my baton is in my hand, and I rule(?)[3] for
§ 339 myself those who have gone to it.[4] | They bring to me these four spirits, the
Elders who are at the head of the wearers of the side-lock, who stand in the
§ 340 eastern side of the sky and who lean on their staffs,[5] | that they may tell my
good name to Rēʿ and announce me to *Nḥbw-kꜣw*, so that my entry may be
greeted. The Fields of Rushes are filled (with water), and I ferry across on
§ 341 the Winding Waterway; | I am ferried over to the eastern side of the horizon,
I am ferried over to the eastern side of the sky, and my sister is Sothis, my
offspring is the dawn-light.[6]

1. On the many Utterances concerned with the reed-floats see *Komm.* ii, 27 ff.

2. See Utt. 266, n. 1.

3. Sethe's 'er macht sich dienstbar (oder gehorsam)' is quite unconvincing, despite his discussion in *Komm.* ii, 39; the king's role in the Beyond is to rule, not to obey, 'those who

have gone to it'. Whatever may be the precise meaning of *nhn*, the context demands that it should refer to authority assumed by the dead king; it can hardly be connected with the late verb *nhn* 'sich stützen auf etw.', *Wb.* ii. 286, 5. Note the preservation of the original suffix ·*i* of the 1st person before ·*f* of the 3rd person.

4. Scil. the Beyond; the expression *zì r·s* refers to the dead.

5. *Ḏrm* is better translated 'staff' rather than 'sceptre', seeing that one can lean on it, and indeed its form is that of a staff.

6. Read *msṯwt·f dwȝt*. *Msṯwt* is the feminine of *msṯw* 'offspring'; the dawn-light (*dwȝt*) is born of the union of the king with his sister Sothis. In §§ 357. 929. 935. 1707 the (masculine) offspring is *nṯr-dwȝ* 'the Morning Star'. The present reading may be due to a scribal emendation, the copyist confusing *dwȝ* and *dȝt*; on the other hand it may have been an intentional variant from the more usual *nṯr-dwȝ*.

## Utterance 264

*A variant of Utterance* 263

The reed-floats of the sky are set down for Horus § 342
That he may cross on them to the horizon, to Ḥarakhti.
The reed-floats of the sky are set down for me[1]
That I may cross on them to the horizon, to Ḥarakhti.
The reed-floats of the sky are set down for Shezemty
That he may cross on them to the horizon, to Ḥarakhti.
The reed-floats of the sky are set down for me
That I may cross on them to the horizon, to Ḥarakhti.
The Nurse-canal is opened, § 343
The Winding Waterway is flooded,
The Fields of Rushes are filled with water,
And I am ferried over thereon to yonder eastern side of the sky, § 344
To the place where the gods fashioned me,
Wherein I was born, new and young.
When there comes this time of the morrow, § 345
The time of the fifth day,
The time of the sixth day,
The time of the seventh day,
The time of the eighth day,
Summons is made to me by Rēʿ, § 346
A meal is given to me by *Nḥbw-kȝw*
As Horus, as the horizon-dweller,
When comes this time of the morrow,

The time of the third day,
The time of the fourth day.

§ 347 Lo, I stand up as this star which is on the underside of the sky, I give
§ 348 judgement as a god, having tried cases as a magistrate.[1] I have summoned
them,[2] and these four gods who stand at the staffs of the sky[3] bring them to
me that they may tell my name to Rēʿ and announce my name to Ḥarakhti:[1]
§ 349 'He[4] has come to you, he has come to you that he may loosen the bandages
and cast off the bonds.'

§ 350 He[5] has saved me from Kherty, he will never give me to Osiris, for I have
not died the death,[6] I possess a spirit in the horizon and stability in Djedut.

1. Cf. Utt. 266, n. 1.
2. The king's celestial attendants? The plural suffix has no antecedent.
3. The gods of the four cardinal points.
4. The speech of the attendants announcing the king's arrival.
5. Presumably Rēʿ.
6. Cf. Utt. 213, n. 2.

## Utterance 265

*Another variant of Utterance* 263

§ 351 The reed-floats of the sky are set in place for Rēʿ
That he may cross on them to the horizon, to Ḥarakhti.
The reed-floats of the sky are set in place for Ḥarakhti
That he may cross on them to the horizon, to Rēʿ.
The reed-floats of the sky are set in place for me myself[1]
That I may cross on them to the horizon, to Rēʿ and to Ḥarakhti.
§ 352 The Nurse-canal is opened,
The Winding Waterway is flooded,
The Fields of Rushes[2] are filled,
§ 353 That I may be ferried over to the eastern side of the sky,
To the place where the gods were born,
And I was born there with them
As Horus, as the horizon-dweller.
§ 354 I am vindicated;
Rejoice over me, rejoice over my double!
§ 355 They[3] summon me
And they bring to me these four who pass by, wearers of the side-lock,
Who stand by their staffs on the eastern side of the sky,
§ 356 That they may tell my name, that of the good one, to Rēʿ,

And that they may announce my name, that of the good one, to *Nḥbw-kꜣw*.
I am vindicated;
Rejoice over me, rejoice over my double!
My sister is Sothis, my offspring is the Morning Star,[4] § 357
I am on the under-side of the sky with Rēʿ.
I am vindicated;
Rejoice over me, rejoice over my double!

1. Cf. Utt. 266, n. 1.
2. *Ḏꜣrw* is clearly a sculptor's misreading of *iꜣrw*, cf. §§ 340c; 343b; 359a.
3. Again the unspecified attendants, cf. Utt. 264, n. 2.
4. Cf. *JNES* 25, 159.

## Utterance 266

*Another variant of Utterance* 263

The reed-floats of the sky are set in place for Rēʿ § 358
That Rēʿ may cross on them to the horizon, to Ḥarakhti.
The reed-floats of the sky are set in place for me[1]
That I may cross on them to the horizon, to Ḥarakhti.
The reed-floats of the sky are set in place for Ḥarakhti
That Ḥarakhti may cross on them to the horizon, to Rēʿ.
The reed-floats of the sky are set in place for me
That I may cross on them to the horizon, to Rēʿ.
The Nurse-canal is opened, § 359
The Field of Rushes is filled,
The Winding Waterway is flooded,
That I may be ferried over thereon to the horizon, to Ḥarakhti. § 360
Bring[2] to me these four brethren who pass by, wearers of the side-lock,
Who sit by their staffs in the eastern side of the sky;
Tell[3] my good name to *Nḥbw-kꜣw*; § 361
Rejoice over me, rejoice over my double,
For I am vindicated and my double is vindicated before God!
Rēʿ has [taken(?)] me to himself, to the sky, to the eastern side of the sky; § 362
As this Horus, as the dweller in the Netherworld,
As this star which illumines the sky.[4]
My sister is Sothis, [. . .] § 363
Never (again) will the sky be void of me,
Never (again) will the earth be void of me

By the command of [. . .]
Bring this to me[5]
And I will be your third in Ōn.[6]

1. The ending ꜣꜣ in *ḏꜣy* in § 358*h* points to the presence of the suffix 1st singular, suggesting that these 'reed-float' texts were originally in the 1st person, as were also the 'ferry-boat' texts. See also *Komm.* ii, 29.

2. Imperative with reinforcing particle *m*.

3. Read *ḏd·in sw[t]*.

4. Cf. *JNES* 25, 153.

5. The regular expression used when the dead man demands a ferry-boat, not only in the *Pyr.* but also later, cf. *Urk.* v, 147 ff., where it is obvious that the deceased himself is speaking.

6. i.e. a third to Rēʿ and Ḥarakhti.

## Utterance 267

*An address to Osiris and another to Rēʿ*

§ 364 You have your heart, O Osiris; you have your legs, O Osiris; you have your arms, O Osiris; (so too) my[1] heart is my own, my legs are my own, my arms
§ 365 are my own.ˡ A stairway to the sky is set up for me that I may ascend on it to the sky, and I ascend on the smoke of the great censing.
§ 366 I fly up as a bird and alight as a beetle; I fly up as a bird and alight as a
§ 367 beetle on the empty throne which is in your bark, O Rēʿ.[2] ˡ Stand up, remove yourself, O you who do not know the Thicket of Reeds, that I may sit in
§ 368 your place and row over the sky in your bark, O Rēʿ,ˡ that I may push off from the land in your bark, O Rēʿ. When you ascend from the horizon, my sceptre will be in my hand as one who rows your bark, O Rēʿ.
§ 369 You mount up to the sky, you are far from the earth, far from wife and kilt.[3]

1. For the 1st person cf. *Komm.* ii, 83.

2. Var. 'the bark of Rēʿ'.

3. Spoken by Rēʿ to the king, who is now removed from earthly matters. 'Kilt' here signifies the royal office.

## Utterance 268

*The king is crowned and enthroned in the Beyond*

§ 370 This King washes himself when Rēʿ appears, the Great Ennead shines forth,
§ 371 and He of Ombos is high at the head of the Conclave.ˡ This King takes over the nobles as a limb in himself, this King takes hold of the *Wrrt*-crown from the hands of the Two Enneads.

Isis nurses him, Nephthys suckles him,[1] Horus accepts him beside him,[1] § 372
he purifies this King in the Jackal Lake,[2] he cleanses this King's double in
the Lake of the Netherworld,[3] he wipes over the flesh of this King's double
and of his own by means of that which is on the shoulders of Rēʿ in the
horizon,[4] which he receives[1] when the Two Lands shine again and he clears § 373
the vision of the gods.[5] He conducts this King's double and his own to the
Great Mansion, and courts are made for him, the *ḥmꜣṯt*[6] is knit up for him,[1]
and the King guides the Imperishable Stars. He ferries across to the Fields § 374
of Rushes, and those who are in the horizon row him, those who are in the
firmament convey him.[1] This King is omnipotent,[7] and his arms do not fail; § 375
this King is pre-eminent, for his double has reached him.

1. Lit. 'at his two fingers'. N has: 'Horus accepts N, may he live for ever [. . .].'
2. Cf. *Dict. géogr.* v, 127.
3. Cf. ibid. 128.
4. According to Sethe the dawn-wind is meant.
5. i.e. they can see again after the darkness of the night.
6. Possibly the curl on the Red Crown, cf. Abubakr, *Kronen*, 53.
7. Lit. 'potent a potency'.

## Utterance 269

*A censing prayer*

The fire is laid, the fire shines; § 376
The incense is laid on the fire, the incense shines.
Your perfume comes to me, O Incense;
May my perfume come to you, O Incense.
Your perfume comes to me, you gods; § 377
May my perfume come to you, you gods.
May I be with you, you gods;
May you be with me, you gods.
May I live with you, you gods;
May you live with me, you gods.
I love you, you gods; 378
May you love me, you gods.[1]

*The king ascends to the sky*

Here comes the *pꜣḳ*, here comes the *pꜣḏ*[2]
Which issued from the knee of Horus!

§ 379 Here comes the ascender, here comes the ascender!
Here comes the climber, here comes the climber!
Here comes he who flew up, here comes he who flew up![3]
I ascend upon the thighs of Isis,
I climb up upon the thighs of Nephthys,
§ 380 My father Atum seizes my hand for me,
And he assigns me to those excellent and wise gods,
The Imperishable Stars.

*A prayer to the hippopotamus-goddess Ipy*

§ 381 O my mother Ipy, give me this breast of yours, that I may apply it to my
§ 382 mouth and suck this your white, gleaming, sweet milk.[1] As for yonder land
in which I walk, I will neither thirst nor hunger in it for ever.

1. The inclusion of the dependent pronoun of the 1st person in the P-text is clear evidence that this prayer was spoken by the king.

2. Terms for disks or pellets of incense; *pꜣḏ* here is a pun on the word for 'knee-cap'.

3. All these expressions are the king's description of himself.

## Utterance 270

*A summons to the celestial ferryman*

§ 383 Awake in peace!
O *Ḥr·f-ḥꜣ·f* in peace!
O *Mꜣ-ḥꜣ·f* in peace!
O Ferryman of the sky in peace!
O Ferryman of Nūt in peace!
O Ferryman of the gods in peace!

§ 384 I[1] have come to you that you may ferry me across in this ferry-boat in which
§ 385 you ferry the gods.[1] I have come to his[2] side (*gs*) just as the god came to his
§ 386 side; I have come to his side (*smꜣ*)[3] just as the god came to his side.[1] There
is no one living who makes accusation against me,[4] there is no one dead who
makes accusation against me, there is no duck[5] which makes accusation
§ 387 against me, there is no ox which makes accusation against me.[1] If you do not
ferry me over, I will leap up and put myself on the wing of Thoth, and *he* will
ferry me over to yonder side.[6]

1. For the 1st person in 'ferryman' texts cf. Utt. 266, nn. 1, 5; see also n. 4 below.

2. The ferryman's; for 'side' we have *gs* here and *smꜣ* in § 385*c*; W spells *gs* in the first instance with a superfluous *s*. Although Egyptian makes a distinction between *gs* and *smꜣ*, in contexts such as this it is not really possible to do so in English. See also n. 3 below.

3. In 385*b* P interpolates: 'I have come to his side (*smꜣ*) just as the god came to his side (*gs*)', a superfluous anticipation of § 385*c*.

4. *Ir·y* in M and N (§ 386*a*. *b*) is clear evidence that this text was originally in the 1st person.

5. Cf. Gardiner, Sign-list, G39; the duck here represents the birds and the ox represents the land-animals.

6. P adds 'of the horizon' with direct (!) genitive.

## Utterance 271

### *An 'ascension' text*

I[1] have inundated the land which came forth from the lake, I have torn out the papyrus-plant, I have satisfied the Two Lands, I have united the Two Lands, I have joined my mother the Great Wild Cow.| O my mother, the Wild Cow[2] which is upon the Mountain of Pasture and upon the Mountain of the *zḥzḥ*-bird,[3] the two *ḏd*-pillars stand, though the broken rubble(?)[4] has fallen,| and I ascend on this ladder which my father Rēʿ made for me. Horus and Seth take hold of my hands and take me to the Netherworld.| O you who were winked at, beware of him to whom command has been given; O you to whom command has been given, beware of him who was winked at.[5] The face of the god is open to me,[6] and I sit on the great throne beside the god. § 388 § 389 § 390 § 391

1. For the 1st person cf. *Komm.* ii, 122.

2. *Smꜣt ḥmt* literally and rather tautologically means 'female Wild Cow', not 'Wildkuh und Frau' as Sethe; cf. *ꜥꜣt ḥm(t) hiwt* 'monstrous she-ass', § 523*b*, and the later *st-ḥmt* (ⲥϩⲓⲙⲉ) 'woman'.

3. On the *ḏw smy* and the *ḏw zḥzḥ* cf. *Komm.* ii, 125 f.

4. Cf. ibid. 127.

5. Cf. ibid. 130 f.

6. i.e. the god views the king with favour. N has the exact opposite: 'the king opens the face of the god.'

## Utterance 272

### *The king demands admission to the Beyond*

'O Height which is not sharpened,[1] Portal of the Abyss, I[2] have come to you; let this be opened to me.' § 392

'Is the King the little one yonder?'[3]

'I am at the head of the Followers of Rēʿ, I am not at the head of the gods who make disturbance.'[4]

1. i.e. which has no summit peak; a flat-topped gateway is envisaged.

2. For the 1st person cf. *Komm.* ii, 132.
3. A virtual question (Gardiner, § 491) spoken by the portal, cf. *Komm.* ii, 134 f.
4. The king's reply. On *tḫtḫ* see Utt. 607, n. 3.

## Utterances 273–4

*The king hunts and eats the gods*

§ 393 The sky is overcast,[1]
The stars are darkened,
The celestial expanses[2] quiver,
The bones of the earth-gods tremble,
The planets(?) are stilled,[3]
§ 394 For they have seen the King appearing in power[4]
As a god who lives on his fathers
And feeds on his mothers;
The King is a master of wisdom
Whose mother knows not his name.
§ 395 The glory of the King is in the sky,
His power[5] is in the horizon
Like his father Atum who begot him.
He begot the King,
And the King is mightier than he.
§ 396 The King's powers are about him,
His *ḥmwst*[6] are under his feet,
His gods[7] are upon him,
His uraei are on the crown of his head,
The King's guiding-serpent is on his brow,
Even that which sees the soul,
Efficient for burning(?);[8]
The King's neck is on his trunk.
§ 397 The King is the Bull of the sky,
Who conquers(?) at will,[9]
Who lives on the being of every god,
Who eats their entrails(?),
Even of those who come with their bodies full of magic
From the Island of Fire.
§ 398 The King is one equipped,
Who assembles his spirits;

The King has appeared as this Great One,
A possessor of helpers;
He sits with his back to Gēb,[10]
For it is the King who will give judgement[11] § 399
In company with Him whose name is hidden
On that day of slaying the Oldest Ones.
The King is a possessor of offerings who knots the cord
And who himself prepares his meal;
The King is one who eats men and lives on the gods, § 400
A possessor of porters who dispatches messages;
It is Grasper-of-topknots who is(?) Keḥau[12] § 401
Who lassoes them for the King;
It is the Serpent with raised head
Who guards them for him
And restrains them for him;
It is He who is over the reddening(?)[13]
Who binds them for him;
It is Khons who slew the lords § 402
Who strangles them for the King[14]
And extracts for him what is in their bodies,
For he is the messenger whom the King sends to restrain.
It is Shezmu[15] who cuts them up for the King § 403
And who cooks for him a portion of them
On his evening hearth-stones;
It is the King who eats their magic
And gulps down their spirits;
Their big ones are for his morning meal, § 404
Their middle-sized ones are for his evening meal,
Their little ones are for his night meal,
Their old men and their old women are for his incense-burning;
It is the Great Ones[16] in the north of the sky § 405
Who set the fire for him
To the cauldrons containing them
With the thighs of their oldest ones.
Those who are in the sky serve the King, § 406
And the hearth-stones are wiped over[17] for him
With the feet of their women.
He has travelled around the whole of the two skies,[18]

He has circumambulated the Two Banks[19]
§ 407 For the King is a great Power
Who has power over the Powers;
The King is a sacred image,
The most sacred of the sacred images[20] of the Great One,
And whomsoever he finds in his way,
Him he devours piecemeal(?).
The King's place is at the head
Of all the august ones who are in the horizon,
§ 408 For the King is a god,
Older than the oldest.
Thousands serve him,
Hundreds offer to him,
There is given to him a warrant as Great Power
By Orion, father of the gods.
§ 409 The King has appeared again in the sky,
He is crowned as Lord of the horizon;
He has broken[21] the back-bones
And has taken the hearts of the gods;
§ 410 He has eaten the Red Crown,
He has swallowed the Green One.[22]
The King feeds on the lungs of the Wise Ones,[23]
And is satisfied with living on hearts and their magic;
§ 411 The King revolts against licking the *sbšw*[24]
Which are in the Red Crown.
He enjoys himself when their[25] magic is in his belly;
The King's dignities shall not be taken away from him,
For he has swallowed the intelligence of every god.
§ 412 The King's lifetime is eternity,
His limit is everlastingness
In this his dignity of:
'If he wishes, he does;
If he dislikes, he does not',[26]
Even he who is at the limits of the horizon for ever and ever.
§ 413 Lo, their souls are in the King's belly,
Their spirits are in the King's possession
As the surplus of his meal out of(?) the gods[27]
Which is cooked for the King out of their bones.

Lo, their souls are in the King's possession,
Their shades are (removed) from their owners,
While the King is this one who ever appears and endures,[28] § 414
And the doers of (ill) deeds have no power to destroy
The favourite place[29] of the King among those who live in this land
For ever and ever.

1. *Gp* is *sḏm·f*, not old perfective as Sethe thought; the fact that the subject follows the verb is conclusive as to the verb-form.

2. For *pḏwt* 'celestial expanses' cf. §§ 801*b*; 1004*b*; 1443*a* (sing.); 1486*a*; 1490*b*. The word is a derivative of *pḏ* 'extend', *Concise Dict.* 97.

3. Sethe is surely right in reading *gr r·sn*, rather than *grr·sn* as I did in *JEA* 10, 99; nor do I now believe that *gnmw* has anything to do with Coptic ϭιnλλογτ 'Pleiades'. The precise meaning of the word remains obscure; since it clearly refers to moving objects (Sethe 'die Bewegungen') in a celestial context, I suggest that its meaning may be 'planets'.

4. *Bꜣ*, old perfective of *bꜣ* 'be a soul', 'have power'; cf. the noun *bꜣw* 'power'; so also Sethe. In § 253*c* the noun *bꜣ* certainly means 'power' or 'might'.

5. *Wsr·f.*

6. The *ḥmwst* is the feminine counterpart of the *kꜣ*, cf. *Dram. Texte*, 62 f.; *Komm.* ii, 148. An appropriate equivalent in English is lacking.

7. Sethe interprets 'gods' as protecting deities hovering over the king, but the use of the preposition *tp* rather than *ḥr* suggests that 'gods' may refer to the sacred insignia worn on the king's person, which would undoubtedly have been deemed to possess amuletic protective power.

8. A difficult passage; my version relies largely on that of Sethe. The soul seen by the serpent is presumably that of an enemy of the king.

9. I adhere to my original translation, where I took *nhd* to be a nipḥʿal formation from *hd* 'attack', *JEA* 10, 99. Sethe reads *nh d m ib* 'der (einst) Mangel litt und in sein Herz gab (zu leben)', cf. *Komm.* ii, 150; this interpretation seems out of accord with what one would expect of the Bull of the sky, where aggression would be more appropriate to the present context.

10. i.e. in front of Gēb, acting as his surrogate. Sethe has 'gegen (d.i. Seite an Seite mit) Geb', cf. *Komm.* ii, 153, but the literal translation makes good sense.

11. The future tense is enforced both by the construction with *sḏm·f* and by the sense; judgement will take place on a day now to be named.

12. Gardiner, *JEA* 37, 31, translates this passage rather differently.

13. So Sethe, who recalls *Mꜣʿ-ḥr-ṯrwt* of § 150*b*. Presumably the 'reddening' is the blood of the victims.

14. Following T; the W text uses the future construction *in* + noun + *sḏm·f*.

15. The god of the oil- and wine-press.

16. So W; *ʿꜣtyw* of T looks like a corruption: Sethe has 'Die aus Mineral bestehenden'. The allusion is to the Circumpolar Stars.

17. Sethe 'zusammengestellt', cf. *Komm.* ii, 163, but I question whether *isr* can bear this meaning.

18. i.e. of the upper world and of the Netherworld.

19. Egypt.

20. The present translation differs both from my own in *JEA* 10, 98 and from Sethe's, cf. *Komm.* ii, 165. The construction of *ꜥšm ꜥšmw*, lit. 'a sacred image of the sacred images', is parallel to that of Gardiner, § 97, 2nd example.

21. Despite the determinative ⸺, *ḥsb* here surely has its basic meaning 'break' rather than its secondary significance of 'count', 'reckon' (*Komm.* ii, 168), which fits the context much less well.

22. A reference to the conquest of Lower Egypt. 'The Green One' may be a reference to Wadjet, tutelary serpent-goddess of the northern kingdom, though Sethe thought it might be the name of a crown.

23. Sethe translates as 'den Lungen, die weise sind', regarding the lungs as the seat of wisdom (*Komm.* ii, 168), but gives no evidence for this view.

24. Sethe connects *sbšw* with the curl in front of the Red Crown, but *sbšw* is plural; at least it is clearly a part of the crown which is objectionable to him who would devour it.

25. Referring to the 'hearts' of § 410*c*.

26. On this passage see Gardiner, *JEA* 33, 99.

27. Sethe: 'durch seine Zukost zu den Göttern'. It is clear from what follows that the preparation of soup is envisaged.

28. The participles *ḫꜥ* and *ỉmn* are doubled.

29. The royal pyramid, see *Komm.* ii, 175.

## Utterance 275

*The king goes to the horizon*

§ 415 The King has come to you, you falcons, for your Horus-mansions[1] are
§ 416 barred(?)[2] to the King.| His *mꜥrḳ*[3] is on his hinder parts, of the hide(?)[4] of a baboon; the King opens the double doors, the King attains the limit of the horizon, the King has laid his *msdt*[5] there on the ground, and the King becomes the Great One who is in Shedet.[6]

1. Reading *ḥwt-Ḥr·ṯn* with honorific transposition of *Ḥr*. It is hard to accept Sethe's suggestion, *Komm.* ii, 176, that *Ḥr* may be a particle.

2. Cf. loc. cit.

3. A garment, cf. ibid. 177. The derivation of this noun from *ꜥrḳ* 'bent' suggests that it may be a kilt or girdle 'bent' round the waist.

4. Cf. loc. cit.

5. Also a garment, cf. ibid. 178. The word is derived, as Sethe has seen, either from *sd* 'tail' or from *sd* 'clothe', more probably perhaps the latter, and the context suggests that the garment may have been something in the nature of a cloak.

6. Cf. *AEO* ii, 116* f.

*Here begins a series of spells against snakes and other dangerous creatures*

## Utterance 276

§ 417 Do against yourself what you can do against yourself, you *zkzk*-snake(?) who are in your hole(?), you hindrance!

## Utterance 277

Horus fell because of his Eye, the Bull[1] crawled away because of his testicles; Fall! Crawl away! § 418

1. Var. 'Seth'. A corrupt version in Nt, 712.

## Utterance 278

Babi[1] stands up, having met *Ḫnt-ḥm* whom the spittle protects(?), whom this one[2] protects(?), (even) he the very well beloved. May the *wfꜣ*-snake be got rid of; cause me to be protected.[3] § 419

1. On this god see Derchain in *Rev. d'Ég.* 9, 23 ff.; *ZÄS* 90, 22 ff.
2. The rare independent use of *tn*.
3. For the 1st person in these spells cf. Utt. 230, n. 3.

## Utterance 279

O King, I(?) have stamped down(?) the mud of the canals, and Thoth is my champion when it is dark, is dark(?).[1] § 420

1. A spell against the crocodile by night?

## Utterance 280

O Evil-doer, Evil-doer![1] O you who creep, you who creep! Your face[2] be behind you! Beware of the Great Door![3] § 421

1. For this translation of *irty* cf. *irr* 'evil-doer', *Peas.* B1, 193. Cf. also Utt. 380.
2. An order to turn back. JPII, 1055 + 61 has *ʿwy·k* for *ḥr·k*.
3. The entrance to the tomb.

## Utterance 281

*Untranslatable.* § 422

## Utterance 282

O ... this is your ...[1] for me a gold collar and *ḥknw*-oil. O *Ḥʿy-tꜣw*, *ḥknw*-oil! This is your bull, the strong one against whom this was done. § 423

1. Untranslatable. This spell is a variant of Utt. 238.

## Utterance 283

§ 424 Indeed I dart this left thumb-nail of mine against you, I strike a blow[1] with it on behalf of Min and the *iklw*. O you who are wont to rob, do not rob.

1. Sethe 'ich gebe ein Zeichen', but *sḫt* means 'to strike a blow', not merely to make an offensive gesture. A corrupt version of this Utt. is in Nt, 713–14.

## Utterance 284

§ 425 He whom Atum has bitten has filled my mouth,[1] and he coils up.[2] The centipede is smitten by Him of the Mansion, and He of the Mansion is smitten by the centipede. That lion is within this lion, and I fight the two bulls within the ibis.[3]

1. i.e. to be eaten.
2. JPII, 1055 + 59 has ; the rest is lost. Nt, 713 follows N, but adds 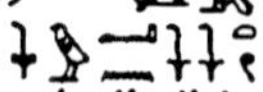 and stops.
3. Sethe thinks that the 'bulls' are scorpions which the ibis has eaten, *Komm.* ii, 193, but the spell is most obscure. For the 1st person cf. *ʿḥꜣ·i* in P.

## Utterance 285[1]

§ 426 Your two drops of poison are on the way to your poison-sacs:[2] spit them out at once(?), they[3] being filled(?) with water. O you winker who wears a fillet, O *Sšꜣw*, rain,[4] that the serpent may become rotten(?) and that the throat of my heart[5] may be clean . . .[6] the lion is endangered(?) in the water and the throat of this[7] heart of mine is lengthened(?).

1. A very obscure spell, cf. *Komm.* ii, 194 ff. A corrupt version of § 426*a* in Nt, 714.
2. Or 'fangs', lit. 'bowls'. The snake is ordered to get rid of its venom.
3. The sacs.
4. A noun referring to what is wanted from *Sšꜣw*.
5. The wind-pipe.
6. Sethe's interpretation is so conjectural that I cannot accept it and have left *iḫti ibnw* untranslated. The following *sw* I tentatively connect with *sw(w)* 'harmful', 'dangerous', 'be endangered', Utt. 23, n. 2.
7. *Ity* at the end of the spell I take to be an early form of the fem. demonstr. adj. *tw*, qualifying *ḥtt* in the compound *ḥtt-ib*.

## Utterance 286

§ 427 *An incomprehensible spell which makes mention of the Nt-crowns; they are praised (ḥz) and raised up (nṯz).*

## Utterance 287

O you who ... your mother,[1] O you who ... your mother, are you really here, are you really here? O lion, be off! § 428

1. Lit. 'his'.

## Utterance 288

O *hkl*-snake, O *hkrt*-snake, go with your face on the path! O eye of mine, do not look at him! You shall not effect your errand against me; be off! Out of it! § 429

## Utterance 289

The bull falls[1] to the *sḏḥ*-snake and the *sḏḥ*-snake falls to the bull. Fall! Crawl away! § 430

1. Certainly *sḏm·f*, despite Sethe's preference for the old perfective; the word-order, with the subject following the verb, is conclusive on this point. In § 2254*a* (Supplement, p. 76) 'bull-snake' is substituted for 'bull'.

## Utterance 290

One face falls on another, the black[1] knife goes forth against it,[2] and it[3] has swallowed for itself. One face falls on another, the black knife goes forth against it, and it has taken for itself. § 431

1. W: *nm ꜣb km* 'black-mottled knife'. Cf. Utt. 228.
2. Fem., referring to the unnamed target of the spell.
3. Masc., referring to the knife.

## Utterance 291

Your honour is removed, O white ...,[1] by him who came forth from the *fnṯ*-snake. Your honour is taken away, O white ..., by him who came forth from the *fnṯ*-snake. § 432

1. I am not convinced by Sethe's interpretation of *bꜣꜣ* as 'hole', despite the det. and his ingenious argument that 'white' here means 'empty'; if the Egyptian meant 'empty' he had an ordinary word (*šw*) at his disposal, and a hole can neither have 'honour' nor be 'white'.

## Utterance 292

*Incomprehensible.* § 433

## Utterance 293

§ 434 Get back, you hidden snake; hide yourself, do not let me see you. Get back,
you hidden snake; hide yourself,[1] do not come to the place where I am, that
§ 435 I may not pronounce against you this your name of *Nmi* son of *Nmit*.[1] The
Majesty of the Pelican falls into the Nile; run away, run away! O monster,
lie down!

1. This repetition omitted in W.

## Utterance 294

§ 436 I am Horus who came forth from the acacia, who came forth from the acacia,
to whom it was commanded: 'Beware of the lion!'; to whom the command
§ 437 went forth: 'Beware of the lion!'[1] I have come forth from my *ḏnit*-jar after
having spent the night in my *ḏnit*-jar,[1] and I will appear in the morning.
I have come forth from my *ḏnit*-jar, having spent the night in my *ḏnit*-jar,
and I will appear in the morning.

1. An allusion to immersion during embalming?

## Utterance 295

§ 438 Mafdet leaps at the neck of the *in-dt·f*-snake, she does it again at the neck of the serpent with raised head.[1] Who is he who will survive? It is I who will survive.

1. Mafdet here appears in the role of a mongoose.

## Utterance 296

§ 439 O *ṯtw*-snake, whither? You shall not move, but shall stand still for me, for I am Gēb. O *hmṯ*-snake, brother of the *hmṯt*-snake, shall your father . . . die?[1]

1. For the interpretation of the last clause as a virtual question, cf. *Komm.* ii, 218; the meaning of *ḏ''mhw* is not known. Another text of this spell, in the 1st person, is in Nt, 708–9.

## Utterance 297

§ 440 My hand has come upon you, the avenger(?) is this which has come upon
you, (even) Mafdet, pre-eminent in the Mansion of Life; she strikes you
§ 441 on your face, she scratches you on your eyes,[1] so that you fall into your
faeces and crawl into your urine. Fall! Lie down! Crawl away, for your
mother Nūt sees you!

## Utterance 298

Rēʿ arises, his uraeus upon him, against this snake which came forth from § 442
the earth and which is under my fingers. He will cut off your (*sic*) head with
this knife which is in the hand of Mafdet who dwells in the Mansion of Life.[1]
He will draw out those things which are in your mouth,[2] he will draw off § 443
your poison with these four cords which belong to[3] the sandals of Osiris.
O monster, lie down! O bull, crawl away!

1. So Nt, 710, which again has the original 1st person for the king.
2. The snake's poison fangs.
3. Lit. 'which are behind', i.e. in the service of. The allusion appears to be to the cords which bound the sandals of Osiris on his feet.

## Utterance 299

The serpent is in the sky, the centipede of Horus is on earth. Horus has(?) § 444
sandals[1] when he treads down the Lord of the Mansion, the Bull of the
Cavern.[2] O *Šnṯ*-snake, I will not be opposed![3] My sycamore is his sycamore,
my refuge is his refuge, and whomsoever I shall find in my way, him I will
devour piecemeal(?).

1. Lit. 'sandals of Horus'.
2. i.e. the snake in its hole.
3. Note the suffix 1st sing. in W.

## Utterance 300

*A 'ferryman' text*

O Kherty of Nezat,[1] ferryman of the *Ỉḳht*-bark which Khnum made, bring me § 445
this,[2] for I am Sokar of Rostau,[3] I am bound for the place where dwells Sokar
who presides over *Pḏw-š*.[4] This is our brother(?)[5] who brings this[6] for these
. . .[7] of the desert.

1. A locality of unknown situation, *Dict. géogr.* iii, 101.
2. The ferry-boat; cf. *Urk.* v, 147 ff., where the 1st person is clear.
3. Cf. *Dict. géogr.* iii, 127.
4. Cf. *Komm.* ii, 228 f; another instance *Book of Hours*, 2, 3.
5. Cf. *Komm.* ii, 229 ff.; apparently 'our' refers to the king and Sokar, *ỉpw* referring to the ferryman, but the passage remains obscure.
6. The ferry-boat, cf. n. 2 above.
7. Cf. *Komm.* ii, 230 ff., but I find it difficult to accept 'Brückenjoche(?)' as a translation of *mỉḏw*, though I have no alternative to offer.

## Utterance 301

*An address to the primeval gods*

§ 446 You have your offering-bread, O Niu and Nēnet,
You two protectors(?)[1] of the gods
Who protect the gods with your[2] shadow.
You have your offering-bread, O Amūn and Amaunet,
You two protectors(?) of the gods
Who protect the gods with your shadow.
§ 447 You have your offering-bread, O Atum and Ruti,
Who yourselves created your godheads and your persons.
O Shu[3] and Tefēnet who made the gods,
Who begot the gods and established the gods:
§ 448 Tell your father
That the King[4] has given you your offering-loaves,
That the King has propitiated you with your dues.[5]
You shall not hinder the King when he crosses to him[6] at the horizon,
§ 449 For the King knows him and knows his name;
'Eternal' is his name; 'The Eternal, Lord of the Year' is his name.
The Ready Fighter,[7] Horus who is over the stars of the sky
Is he who brings Rēʿ to life every day;
§ 450 He refashions the King and brings the King to life every day.

*The king presents unguent*

The King has come to you, O Horus of Shat;[8] The King has come to you, O
§ 451 Horus of Shezmet;[9] the King has come to you, O Horus of the East.˺ Behold,
the King brings to you your great left Eye in a healed condition(?);[10] accept it
from the King intact, with its water in it intact, with its blood in it intact, and
§ 452 with ⟨its⟩ ducts(?)[11] in it intact.˺ Ascend for it and take it in this your name
of '*ꜣḳs*-ornament of the god'; mount up to it in this your name of Rēʿ;˺
§ 453 put it on your brow in this its name of 'Brow-unguent'; delight in it in this
§ 454 its name of 'Willow';˺ gleam with it among the gods in this its name of
'She who gleams'; be joyful by means of it in this its name of '*Ḥknw*-oil',
for Ernūtet loves you.

*Address to the rising sun*

§ 455 Arise, O great float-user,[12] as Wepwawet, filled with your power, having
gone up from the horizon! Take the *Wrrt*-crown from the great and mighty
§ 456 talkers(?)[13] who preside over Libya˺ and (from) Sobk, Lord of Bakhu.[14] You

shall travel to your fields, you shall cross the interior of your *ksbt*-woods, your nose shall snuff the sweet savours of Shezmet, you shall raise up the King's double for him at his side, even as this wig(?)[15] of yours mounted up to you.[1]
Cleanse the King, make the King bright in this your Jackal-lake, O Jackal, § 457
in which you cleansed the gods. You have power, you have effectiveness, O Horus, Lord of the green stone! Four times—Two green falcons.

1. Sethe translates *mḫnmty* as 'Quellen (? Ursprünge)', cf. *Komm.* ii, 237 f., but this fits ill with the context. Since *ḫnmty* (= *ḫnmty*) in the next clause is admittedly a participle (rather than a relative form) of *ḫnm* 'protect', there seems no reason why the same root-meaning should not underlie the dual noun *mḫnmty*; compare *m ḫnmt* 'in the protection of', § 1962*b*, which in fact could stand for ⟨*m*⟩ *mḫnmt* with the two *m*'s merged by haplography.

2. The original has the 3rd person, in accord with Egyptian usage.

3. *P(w)* must indicate the vocative, in view of the 2nd person in § 448*a*; thus Sethe's 'Schu ist das und Tefnut' must be discarded.

4. The 1st person may well have been original, as Sethe thought, but his argument for it in *Komm.* ii, 240, based on *Pyr.* iii, 24, is open to question. The ancient emendation to which he refers may have been due to a sculptor's error in the word-order. In view of this doubt, the translation has not been transposed into the 1st person.

5. *Ṯwt·ṯn* is the independent pronoun 2nd masc. sing. used as a noun substantive with a possessive suffix, lit. 'your belonging-to-you', cf. loc. cit.

6. The 'father' referred to in § 448*a*.

7. *Mʿḥꜣ ʿ* (or *mḥ*), lit 'fighter with the arm'.

8. Cf. *Dict. géogr.* v, 110.

9. Cf. ibid. 146.

10. So rather than 'Heilerin' as Sethe; the following phrases point to the Eye having been healed rather than acting as healer.

11. For *ḥtw* Sethe has 'Atem', which does not seem to make sense here. However, he rightly connects the word with *ḥtyt* 'throat', cf. *Komm.* ii, 244, and I suggest that ducts or vessels ('throats'?) for conveying the fluids of the eye may be what is meant.

12. See Utt. 222, n. 22.

13. Sethe's translation of *ꜣʿʿw* as 'Quellenorten' is open to question, and I have tentatively connected it with the verb *ꜣʿʿ* 'jabber'. A description of persons rather than places is required.

14. Cf. *AEO* i, 118.*

15. Cf. *Komm.* ii, 249 f.

## Utterance 302

### *The king becomes a star*

The sky is clear, Sothis lives,[1] because I[2] am a living one, the son of Sothis,[3] § 458
and the Two Enneads have cleansed themselves for me in Ursa Major, the imperishable. My house in the sky will not perish, my throne on earth will

§ 459 not be destroyed,[1] for men hide, the gods fly away. Sothis has caused me to fly up to the sky into the company of my brethren the gods, Nūt the great
§ 460 has uncovered her arms for me,[4] | the Two Souls who are at the head of the Souls of Ōn,[5] who attend on Rēʿ,[6] have bowed themselves, even they who spend the night making this mourning for the god.[7]

*The king flies to the sky like a bird*

§ 461 My seat is with you, O Rēʿ, and I will not give it to anyone else;| I will ascend to the sky to you, O Rēʿ, for my face is that of falcons, my wings are those of ducks, my talons are the fangs of Him of the Cerastes-Mountain.|
§ 462 There is no word against me on earth among men, there is no accusation in the sky among the gods, for I have annulled the word against me, which I
§ 463 destroyed in order to mount up to the sky.| Wepwawet has caused me to fly up to the sky among my brethren the gods. I use my arms as a goose, I flap my wings as a kite; the flier flies, O men, I fly away from you.

1. i.e. is visible.
2. For the 1st person cf. *Komm.* ii, 254.
3. i.e. is also a star.
4. i.e. has thrown back her cloak and extended her arms in welcome.
5. The Two Souls are probably Isis and Nephthys, cf. *Komm.* ii, 259.
6. *Ḥr tp Rʿ*; hardly 'unter dem Tagesanfang' as Sethe, compare the common *ḥry tp nsw* 'one who attends the king'.
7. Presumably for Osiris.

## Utterance 303

*The king ferries over to the sky*

§ 464 'O you western gods, eastern gods, southern gods, and northern gods! These four pure reed-floats which you set down for Osiris when he ascended to the
§ 465 sky,| so that he might ferry over to the firmament with his son Horus beside him so that he might bring him up and cause him to appear as a great god in the firmament—set them down for me!'[1]

§ 466 'Are you Horus, son of Osiris? Are you the god, the eldest one, the son of Ḥatḥōr? Are you the seed of Gēb?'[2]

§ 467 'Osiris has commanded[3] me to appear as the counterpart of Horus, and these four spirits who are in Ōn have written (it) on the record of the two great gods who are in the firmament.'[4]

1. The 1st person was certainly original here, because the king and the gods are addressing each other directly, cf. *Komm.* ii, 268 f.

2. The gods demand the king's credentials. Sethe, ibid. 269, is certainly right in interpreting these sentences as virtual questions; for instances from Middle Egyptian cf. Gardiner, § 491.

3. The king replies; here again the context demands the 1st person.

4. According to Sethe, ibid. 270, these are Ḥu and Sia.

## Utterance 304

*The king climbs to the sky on a ladder*

'Hail to you, daughter of Anubis, who is at the windows of the sky, the companion of Thoth, who is at the uprights of the ladder! Open my way that I may pass.[1] § 468

Hail to you, Ostrich which is on the bank of the Winding Waterway! Open my way that I may pass. § 469

Hail to you, Bull of Rēʿ who has four horns, a horn of yours in the west, a horn of yours in the east, a horn of yours in the south, and a horn of yours in the north! Bend down this western horn of yours for me that I may pass.' § 470

'Are you a pure Westerner?'[2] § 471

'I have come forth from Falcon City.[3]

Hail to you, Field of Offerings, and hail to the herbs which are in you, even my herbs which are in you!'[4]

'Pleasant is the purity which is in me.'[5]

1. As Sethe has seen, the 1st person was certainly original; in § 471 the king is addressed directly in the 2nd person.

2. Cf. Utt. 303, n. 2. The Bull questions the king.

3. Presumably the royal residence on earth.

4. i.e. the benefits to be found in the field. Sethe's translation of *sm* as 'Verehrungswürden', *Komm.* ii, 277 f., in this context yields but poor sense.

5. The Field's reply to the king's greeting. The W text seems superior to that of T, which has *imy·ṯ* as if the king were still speaking.

## Utterance 305

*The king climbs to the sky on a ladder*

A ladder is knotted together by Rēʿ before Osiris, a ladder is knotted together by Horus before his father Osiris when he goes to his spirit, one of them being on this side and one of them being on that side, while I am between them.[1] § 472

'Are you a god whose places are pure?' § 473

'I have come forth[2] from a pure (place).'[3]

'Stand up, O King', says Horus. 'Sit down, O King', says Seth. 'Take his hand,'[4] says Rēʿ.

*A general funerary text*

§ 474 The spirit is bound for the sky, the corpse is bound for the earth, and what
men receive when they are buried is its thousand of bread and its thousand
§ 475 of beer upon the altar of the Foremost of the Westerners.| Poor[5] is the heir
who has no document, so he[6] writes with a big finger and does not write with
a little finger.

1. I do not entirely agree with Sethe's subdivision of this Utterance, *Komm.* ii, 281. In my view § 472*d* belongs to the 'ladder' passage, the king standing between the gods who help him up, while § 473 describes the questioning and welcome when the king reaches the sky and is a natural sequel to § 472, so that the two are best taken together. On the other hand, as Sethe truly remarks, §§ 474–5 constitute a general funerary text quite distinct from what has gone before.
2. Read *pr(·i)*, *sḏm·f* form 1 sing.; the king replies to the question.
3. Perhaps alluding to the place of embalmment.
4. N wrongly: 'your hand'.
5. N has corrupted *ḥwr* into *wrš*, which makes no sense. Cf. Cairo 58030, 6, 5.
6. Cf. *Komm.* ii, 287; the king's name is substituted in error for the pronoun *·f*.

## Utterance 306

*An 'ascension' text*

§ 476 'How lovely to see! How pleasing to behold!' say they, namely the gods,
§ 477 when this god ascends to the sky, when you[1] ascend to the sky| with your
power upon you, your terror about you, and your magic at your feet. Gēb
has acted on your behalf in accordance with the manner in which things
§ 478 should be done for you.| There come to you the gods the Souls of Pe, the
gods the Souls of Nekhen, the gods who are in the sky, and the gods who are
§ 479 on earth. They make supports for you upon their arms;| may you ascend to
the sky and mount up on it in this its name of 'Ladder'. 'The sky is given to
§ 480 you, the earth is given to you', says Atum;| it is Gēb who speaks about it:
'The Mounds of my realm[2] are the Mounds of Horus and the Mounds of
Seth, and the Fields of Rushes worship you in this your name of *Dwȝw* as
§ 481 Sopd who is under his *ksbt*-trees.| Has he[3] slain you or has his heart said that
you shall die because of him? Behold, you have become the enduring Bull of
the wild bulls against him. Endure, endure,[4] O enduring Bull, that you may
be enduring at the head of them and at the head of the spirits for ever.'

1. This Utterance appears originally to have been addressed to the king in the 2nd person, cf. §§ 478*b* (MN); 479*a*; 480*c* ff.; *Komm.* ii, 290.

2. Lit. '⟨my⟩ mound', but the translation 'realm' seems unavoidable.

3. Presumably Seth.

4. Sethe: 'es bleibt, es bleibt', but an imperative seems needed here, and the prothetic *i* points in the same direction.

## Utterance 307

*The king declares his right to join the gods*

An Ōnite (character) is in me,[1] O God; your Ōnite (character) is in me, O God;[2] an Ōnite (character) is in me, O Rēʿ; your Ōnite (character) is in me, O Rēʿ. My mother is an Ōnite, my father is an Ōnite,[1] and I myself am an Ōnite, born in Ōn when Rēʿ was ruler of the Two Enneads and the ruler of the plebs was Nefertem, (even I) who have no equal, the heir of my father Gēb.[1] As for any god who shall thrust out his arm[3] when my face turns to you that I may worship you and call upon you on my body, O God, on my nose, O God:[4] he shall have no bread, he shall have no offering-loaf in the company of his brethren the gods;[1] he shall not send (a messenger), he shall not overleap the path(?)[5] in the company of his brethren the gods, the doors of the Night-bark shall not be opened to him, the doors of the Day-bark shall not be opened to him, he shall not be judged as a citizen,[6] the doors of Her who provides(?) shall not be opened to him.[7]

§ 482

§ 483

§ 484

§ 485

I have come for you, for I am the wild bull of the wild grassland,[8] the great-faced bull which came out of Ōn; I have come for you, a wild bull of the wild grassland, for I am he who always fashioned you and will continue to fashion you.[9] § 486

1. On the rendering in the 1st person see *Komm.* ii, 308.

2. See ibid. 309 f.

3. To hold off the king.

4. So rather than 'wegen seiner Person . . . wegen seiner Nase' as Sethe; the king is lying prostrate in worship.

5. See Sethe, ibid. 315, but can *ibt* bear the meaning he gives it? 'In der Brunst(?)' would require a preposition, and the det. ⇆ of *ibt* in § 1321*c* does not support his suggestion.

6. i.e. he will be treated as a stranger.

7. Cf. *Komm.* ii, 317; however, a better sense is obtained by translating *ḥtmwt* as 'provider', implying that the offending being is to be deprived of food, compare § 484*d*. For *ḥtmwt* cf. also § 1329*a*.

8. Sethe has 'Steppe'.

9. On *ḏrt* cf. *Komm.* ii, 319; Edel, § 753*c*; here the particle implies continuity in the past as well as in the future.

## Utterance 308

*The king greets the gods*

§ 487 Hail to you, Horus in the Horite Mounds!
Hail to you, Seth in the Sethite Mounds!
Hail to you, Iaru in the Field of Rushes!
§ 488 Hail to you, you Two who are reconciled,[1]
You two daughters of the four gods who preside over the Great Mansion,
You who come forth at the voice to me,[2] being naked,[3]
§ 489 For I have looked on you as Horus looked on Isis,[4]
I have looked on you as the Snake looked on the Scorpion,[5]
I have looked on you as Sobk looked on Neith,[6]
I have looked on you as Seth looked on the Two who are reconciled.

1. Cf. Utt. 34, n. 3.
2. Cf. Utt. 32, n. 1; *Komm.* ii, 322 f. For the 1st person cf. ibid. 321.
3. The 'nakedness' applies to the readiness of the daughters of the gods to suckle the king.
4. The four final strophes all allude to the son–mother relationship.
5. Lit. 'as *Nḥbw-kꜣw* looked on *Srḳt*'.
6. For Neith as nurse of crocodiles cf. Lanzone, *Mitologia*, pl. 175, 3; *PSBA* 35, 50; Metternich Stela, register XIII (much conventionalized).

## Utterance 309

*The king as secretary to the sun-god*

§ 490 I am[1] the *ḏḥꜣt*[2] of the gods who is behind the Mansion of Rēꜥ, born of 'Prayer-
§ 491 of-the gods'[3] who is in the bow of the bark of Rēꜥ. I sit before him,[1] I open his boxes, I break open his edicts, I seal his dispatches, I send out his messengers who do not grow weary, and I do what he says to me.

1. For the 1st person cf. *Komm.* ii, 326.
2. Meaning unknown; see loc. cit., though the suggested connection with *dḥꜣ* 'straw' seems far-fetched.
3. Personified as a goddess; cf. ibid. 327 f.; Sethe would equate her with Māꜥet.

## Utterance 310

*The gods are warned not to curse the king*

§ 492 If I[1] be cursed,[2] then will Atum be cursed;
If I be reviled,[3] then will Atum be reviled;
If I be smitten, then will Atum be smitten;
If I be hindered on this road, then will Atum be hindered,

For I am Horus, § 493
I have come following my father,
I have come following Osiris.

*The king summons the celestial ferryman*

'O you whose vision is in his face and whose vision is in the back of his head,[1] bring this to me!' § 494

'Which ferry-boat shall be brought to you?'

'Bring me "It-flies-and-alights".'[4]

1. Cf. *Komm.* ii, 329.
2. Sethe: 'bezaubert', but cf. *Sin.* B 74; § 1501*b*.
3. Sethe: 'bekampft', but cf. *Hatnub*, 10, 5; *RB* 118, 11.
4. The name of the boat.

## Utterance 311

*The king requests recognition by the sun-god*

See me,[1] O Rēʿ; recognize me, O Rēʿ. I belong to those that know you, so § 495
know me.[2] If my lord ascends, I will not forget the boon which is given;
She who excludes whomsoever she should exclude[3] opens the doors of the § 496
horizon at the ascent of the Day-bark.

I know the Hall of the Baldachin in the middle of the Platform of the
Zenith(?) from which you go forth when you go aboard the Night-bark; § 497
commend me—*four times repeated*—to the four blustering winds which are about you, which see with two faces,[4] who contend with fierce roaring(?)[5]
with those who are to be in trouble, with those whom they would destroy. § 498
May they not make opposition when I turn to you, when I come to you and § 499
tell you this name of yours of 'Great Flood which came forth from the Great One'. I will not be blind if you put me in darkness, I will not be deaf even
though I do not hear your voice; take me with you, with you, (even I) who § 500
drive away storms for you, who dispel the clouds for you, and who break up the hail for you. I will make for you praise on praise, I will make for you adoration on adoration; may you set me over the Vulture-goddess.

1. The remains of an older text on the wall of the tomb confirm the 1st person; on the abnormal word-order see *Komm.* ii, 335.

2. The older text apparently had *irḫ·k(wi)* 'I know that . . .' followed by the conditional clause of § 495*c*, but it seems not improbable that the archetypal reading may have been *irḫ·k w(i)* 'may you know me', and that this was later misunderstood as the old perfective 1st sing. (this latter certainly correctly in § 496*b*).

3. Cf. *Komm.* ii, 336 f.

4. Cf. ibid. 339. According to Sethe the 'two faces' refer to the two aspects of the winds, gentle and destructive.

5. *Mr* at the beginning of § 498*a* is an adjective qualifying *wtwt*, where the final *t* is clearly radical; *mdw ḥnʿ* is well known in the sense of 'contend with'.

## Utterance 312

*A food-spell*

§ 501 There flies the bread, there continues to fly the bread, to my mansions, the Mansions of the *Nt*-crown.

## Utterance 313

*The sky is opened to the king*

§ 502 The phallus of Babi is drawn back,[1] the doors of the sky are opened, the King has opened [the doors of the sky][2] because of the furnace-heat which is
§ 503 beneath what the gods pour out.[1] What Horus lets slip(?), what Horus lets slip(?), the King lets slip(?) there into this furnace-heat which is beneath what the gods pour out.[3] They make a road for the King that the King may pass on it, for the King is Horus.

1. Emending *nn* into *ḥnn* 'phallus' as *Komm.* ii, 345, where a Middle Kingdom version from Lisht is quoted; the word is used figuratively for a door-bolt.

2. Sethe continues to follow the Lisht text, but the sense thus obtained seems indifferent; certainly his proposed restoration *Ḥr zp 2* is to be discarded. I suggest that we should read *twn ʿrwy pt twn W* [*ʿrwy pt*] . . . as in Sethe's edition of the text, passing over *Ḥr zp 2*.

3. Cf. *Komm.* ii, 346 f., but the whole passage is utterly obscure.

## Utterance 314

*A protective spell*

§ 504 Get back, O Long-horn, doomed to slaughter,[1] on whose vertex are the fingers of the Earth-god. Fall down! Crawl away!

1. *Ngı*, lit. 'one to be broken', is a pun on *ng* 'long-horn'. *Komm.* ii, 348 calls this spell a 'Zaubertext zur Besänftigung eines Schlachtrindes' but the imperative *zbn* 'crawl away' points to a snake—the horned cerastes?—rather than a bull being the object of the spell.

## Utterance 315

*The king greets the celestial baboons*

Here am I,[1] O *ỉꜥn*-baboon, O hyaena, O *pꜣṯṯ*-baboon; my death is at my own desire, my honour is upon me, I make acclamation[2] and rejoicing(?), and I will sit among you, O . . .[3] § 505

1. Lit. 'It is I'; on the 1st person see *Komm.* ii, 349.
2. Cf. ibid. 350 f.
3. *Ḥꜥꜣtyw*, meaning unknown; cf. ibid. 351.

## Utterance 316

*The king demands admittance to the sky*

O *Ḥmỉ*, O *Sḥd*-star, I[1] will never give you my magic, for I sit side by side with Her who is holy in Ōn.[2] Take me to the sky! § 506

1. In all probability this spell was supposed to be spoken by the king himself.
2. Perhaps a reference to the Heliopolitan Ennead, cf. *Komm.* ii, 352 f.

## Utterance 317

*The king becomes the crocodile-god Sobk*

I[1] have come today[2] from out of the waters of the flood; I am Sobk, green of § 507
plume,[3] watchful of face, raised of brow, the raging one who came forth
from the shank and tail of the Great One[4] who is in the sunshine.[1] I have § 508
come to my waterways which are in the bank[5] of the flood of the Great
Inundation,[6] to the place of contentment, green of fields, which is in the
horizon.[1] I make green the herbage which is on the banks of the horizon, § 509
that I may bring[7] greenness to the Eye of the Great One[8] who dwells in the
field. I take my seat which is in the horizon,[1] I appear as Sobk son of Neith, § 510
I eat with my mouth, I urinate and copulate with my phallus, I am the
owner of seed[9] who takes women from their husbands whenever[10] he wishes,
according to his desire.

1. Cf. *Komm.* ii, 355.
2. Or 'here', cf. *Ḥeḳanakhte*, pp. 111 f.
3. Probably figurative for the greenish hide of the crocodile.
4. Feminine, possibly an avatar of Neith, cf. Utt. 308, n. 6 and § 510*a* below.
5. Sethe, *Komm.* ii, 357, translates *ỉdb* as 'Land', but the more usual 'Ufer' fits the context. In § 508*a* the reference is to riparian land on the edge of the flood and in § 509*a* to the edges of the horizon-region; here the use of the dual is significant.
6. The sky according to Sethe.

7. *ỉnt* is prospective *sḏm·f* in a clause of purpose.
8. Feminine.
9. Read *nb mtwt*, cf. *Komm.* ii, 361.
10. On *r-st* see loc. cit.

## Utterance 318

*This Utterance exists in three versions, one in W and two in T. It falls into three parts: (1) the king appears as a serpent; (2) he receives myrrh (not in Tᵃ); and (3) he becomes ruler over the gods.*

### *The W-text*

§ 511 [The King is a serpent, the Bull who leads],[1] who swallowed his seven uraei and his seven neck-vertebrae came into being, [who gives orders] to the seven Enneads which hear the word of the monarch.

§ 512 The King has come that he may inhale myrrh, that the King may accept myrrh, for his nostrils(?) are (full) of myrrh, his finger-nail is (full) of myrrh.[2]

The King takes away your power,[3] you gods; serve the King when he confers[4] your powers.

### *The first T-text*

§ 511 The King is a serpent who was irritated(?) and who swallowed the seven uraei and his seven neck-vertebrae came into being, who gives orders to his seven Bows and who gives orders to the monarch (*sic*).[5] The Pelican[6] is the King's mother and the King is her son.

§ 512 The King has come that he may accept a finger-nail-(full) of myrrh, myrrh being on the nail.

The King has come that he may take away your power, you gods; the King turns round[7] when he has conferred your powers.

### *The second T-text*

§ 511 The King is a serpent, the Bull of the Ennead, who swallowed his seven uraei so that they might become his seven neck-vertebrae, and the Enneads are those who were aforetime, who heard the affairs of Him who was.[8]

§ 512 The King has come that he may destroy your power and confer your powers.[9]

1. Cf. *Komm.* ii, 366 f.
2. § 512*a. b* apparently indicates that the king takes myrrh to his nostrils as a snuff-taker inhales snuff, from a little heap on finger- or thumb-nail.

3. Sethe has 'euren Hals', but despite *Komm.* ii, 373 it makes poor sense, whereas the translation 'power' fits the context well. The objection that *wsrt* must have a different meaning from *wsr* in T[2] can be countered easily by quoting *nfr* (noun) and *nfrt*, both of which can mean 'goodness', 'kindness'.

4. *Sḏmt·f* form, as against *sḏm·n·f* or *sḏm·f* in the T texts.

5. See n. 8 below.

6. Cf. *Komm.* ii, 371.

7. *Sic*; probably we should emend into *pḥr n* 'serve' as in W.

8. It is obvious that the ancient copyists themselves did not understand this Utterance, and in attempting to edit it they have made it even more incomprehensible. Both T[1] and T[2] are thoroughly garbled at this point. The W-text is at least intelligible.

9. T[2] has forgotten to mention the gods to whom the plural suffixes refer.

## Utterance 319

*The king is identified with the sun-god*

The King is the Bull with radiance in the midst of his eye, the King's § 513
mouth is hale through the fiery blast and the King's head through the horns of the Lord of Upper Egypt,[1] the King controls[2] the god, the King has power over the Ennead, the King makes lapis-lazuli grow, the King makes the *twn*-plant of Upper Egypt sprout up.

The King has tied the cords of the *šmšmt*-plant, the King has united the § 514
heavens, the King has power over the southern and northern lands and the gods who were aforetime, the King has built the city of the god in accordance with its proper due,[3] for the King is the third at his accession.[4]

1. Sethe questions the genitival relationship of *wpt* and *nb šmꜥ*, and would regard the latter as in apposition to the King's name, *Komm.* ii, 377.

2. Cf. ibid. 377–8.

3. Sethe: 'ihren Belangen', ibid. 381.

4. Cf. ibid. 382. Gardiner's article 'The Baptism of Pharaoh' in *JEA* 36, 3 ff. makes it probable that Horus and either Seth or Thoth were the other two members of the triad.

## Utterance 320

*The king becomes a star*

The King has cleared the night, the King has dispatched the hours;[1] the § 515
Powers appear and ennoble the King as Babi. The King is the son of one who is unknown;[2] she bore the King to Him whose face is yellow, Lord of

§ 516 the night skies.[3] | Humble(?)[4] yourselves, you lords; hide yourselves, you common folk, from before the King, for the King is Babi, Lord of the night sky, Bull of the baboons[5] who lives on those who do not know him.[6]

1. i.e. has brought the time-marking stars into view in a clear sky; for this sense of *ḏsr* compare *ḏsr pt ḥꜥꜥ ꜣḫtyw* 'the sky is cleared and the horizon-dwellers rejoice', *CT* i, 223*a*; similarly in the sense of 'clearing' a road, ibid. 223*e*; *Hamm.* 114, 11; *Les.* 71, 16.

2. Feminine; apparently implying that the King's mother was a mysterious being. Sethe, who interprets *iḫmt* as an active participle, takes the view that it was the king's mother 'who did not know' how great her son was to be, cf. *Komm.* ii, 384.

3. For *ḳnl* 'yellow' and its derivatives cf. *Concise Dict.* 280. Sethe strangely translates *ḳnl ḥr* as 'dem mit dem tüchtigen Gesicht' and takes it to refer to Gēb, while he thinks that the 'Lord of the night skies' may be Orion. To me it seems possible that *ḳnl ḥr nb ìsnwt* may be a description of Canopus, which is yellowish in colour and which, as the second brightest star in the sky, might well be called 'Lord of the night skies'; it is visible throughout Egypt. On the other hand, while the king is born to the 'Lord of the night skies', in § 516*b* he himself is said to be 'Babi, Lord of the night sky'; there seems to have been some confusion over this title, but it may be significant that in § 516*b* *ìsꜣt* is singular. On the translation of this word as 'night sky' cf. *ZÄS* 86, 111.

4. So guessed by Sethe, *Komm.* ii, 386; certainly *wr* 'great' does not fit the context.

5. Cf. *Rev. d'Ég.* 9, 26.

6. Lit. 'his unknowing ones'.

## Utterance 321

*An 'ascension' text*

§ 517 O you the back of whose head is behind him,[1] bring to the King the . . .[2] which was on the back of Osiris, so that the King may ascend on it to the sky and that the King may escort Rēꜥ[3] in the sky.

1. i.e. looks straight ahead, in contrast to the celestial ferryman *Mꜣ-ḥꜣ·f* 'he who looks behind him'.

2. *Sfrt-ḥtpt*, whatever it may be, is clearly a means of ascent to the sky, cf. *Komm.* ii, 387, where the *ḥtpt* element is translated by 'Mahl'.

3. Cf. ibid. 387 f. To the references for *stp zꜣ* 'escort' add those quoted in *Concise Dict.* 254.

## Utterance 322

*Another 'ascension' text*

§ 518 The sky is opened, the earth is opened, the doors of *Sꜣt(y)*[1] are opened for Horus, the lotus-doors[2] are thrown open for Seth. Turn yourself about for me,[3] O you who are in your fortress; I have passed by you as Atum, I am *Ḥꜥy-tꜣw*[4] who dwells in Lebanon.

1. Cf. *Komm.* ii, 389.
2. For *išbt* 'lotus' cf. § 1164.
3. For the 1st person cf. the older P-text in § 518*c.d.*
4. For this god cf. *Komm.* ii, 391.

## Utterance 323

### *A 'lustration' text*

*The King speaks:* I[1] have bathed with Rēʿ in the Lake of Rushes. § 519
*The priest replies:* Horus will rub your flesh, O King; Thoth will rub your feet.[2] O Shu, raise up[3] the King; O Nūt, give your hand to the King.

1. The context demands the 1st person, for the king is addressed in the 2nd person in what follows.
2. On the pairing of Horus and Thoth cf. *JEA* 36, 8 ff.
3. Imperative in TP; *sḏm·f* in M. The former is the better reading, see the next clause, which is imperative in all versions.

## Utterance 324

### *The king comes to Horus as a healer*

*The King speaks:* Hail to you, door-keeper of Horus at the gate[1] of Osiris![2] § 520
Tell my[3] name here(?)[4] to Horus,| for I have come[5] with hair-spittle for this § 521
hair of his,[6] which is ill at [the beginning of] the months[7] and which is bald at the beginning of the half-months.[8]

*The door-keeper speaks:* May you heal him with magic [. . .][9] who is among the gods, into his pristine state.[10]

*The King speaks:* Hail to you,[11] immortal she-hippopotamus![12] [Have] § 522
you [come] against me as an immortal she-hippopotamus? I have wrenched away[13] one of the two sceptres of Horus from you [and have struck(?)] you with it.[14]

Hail to you, you [monstrous] she-ass! Have you come against me as a § 523
monstrous[15] she-ass? I have struck you with the tail [which grows(?)][16] in the Lake of Osiris.

Hail to you, Khnum, being driven off! May you refashion me,[17] for you are § 524
that *ʿmʿ*-plant of mine which my foot [treads down(?)], which cannot spring up again(?) at my toes. You are one of the two pillars of the Great Mansion.[18]

1. *Ir ʿrrwt* is supplied from Nt, 818.
2. Nt substitutes her own name.
3. As Sethe has seen, the context demands the 1st person.
4. In the lacuna read *m nw* with Nt, 818.

5. The Nt-text ends here, breaking off in mid-sentence.

6. Spitting is a means of healing in folk-medicine, cf. *JEA* 16, 171, n. 4.

7. The new moons.

8. The full moons.

9. There is no positive evidence for Sethe's suggested restoration of the lacuna as *ir·n·k n wr*, cf. *Komm.* ii, 400.

10. Lit. 'his primal state of his being'.

11. Here begin the healing spells.

12. *Nḥḥwt* appears to be an adjective in the feminine derived from *nḥḥ* 'eternity'.

13. For the sense given to *zẖz* cf. its meanings of 'tear out' an eye, § 97*a* and 'pull up' plants, Dav. *Ptah.* ii, 13. The connection, if any, with *zẖz* 'run' is quite obscure.

14. *Komm.* ii, 403 f. points out that § 522*d* is an obvious blunder and should be ignored. It has therefore been omitted from the translation.

15. *Hiwt* 'monstrous' is an adjective derived from *hiw* 'monster'; cf. Utt. 226, n. 2.

16. *Sd* 'tail' is apparently a metaphor for a plant (bulrush, simulating the tufted tail of an ass?) which grows in the said lake; the sign at the end of the lacuna suggests *rd* 'grow'. Cf. *Komm.* ii, 404 f.

17. On this strange sentence see ibid. 405 f. For *iḳd·f* read *iḳd·k*.

18. The relevance of this sentence, and indeed of the entire 'Khnum' passage, to the preceding context is quite obscure.

## Utterance 325

### *A 'lustration' text*

§ 525 The doors of the sky [are opened],
The doors of the firmament are thrown open at dawn for Horus of the Gods.
He goes up into the Field of Rushes,
He bathes in the Field of Rushes.[1]
§ 526 The doors of the sky are opened,
The doors of the firmament are thrown open at dawn for Ḥarakhti.
He goes up into the Field of Rushes,
He bathes in the Field of Rushes.
§ 527 The doors of the sky are opened,
The doors of the firmament are thrown open at dawn for Horus of the East.
He goes up into the Field of Rushes,
He bathes in the Field of Rushes.
§ 528 The doors of the sky are opened,
The doors of the firmament are thrown open at dawn for Horus of Shezmet.
He goes up into the Field of Rushes,
He bathes in the Field of Rushes.
§ 529 The doors of the sky are opened,

The doors of the firmament are thrown open at dawn for me myself.
I go up into the Field of Rushes,
I bathe in the Field of Rushes.

I am pure, I take to myself my iron bones, [I] stretch out [for myself] my § 530
imperishable limbs which are in the womb of my mother Nūt.[1] O Rēʿ, give § 531
me your hand, for Shu takes me to be 'Companion of Shu', and I have sucked the milk of the two black cows, the nurses of the Souls of Ōn.

O *Hpꜣt*, press(?) on the womb of the sky with the power of the seed of the § 532
god which is in it.[2] Behold me, I am the seed of the god which is in it.

O *Hpꜣt*, *Hnny*, *Zmnnw*, I am pure, I have taken my god's-kilt, and I § 533
establish myself there[3] as a god like them.

O *Hpꜣt*, *Hnny*, *Zmnnw*, take me[4] that I may dwell among you.

1. For other versions of this text see Utt. 479. 563. Sethe, *Komm.* ii, 419, sees indications of the 1st person in § 533*b*, and the Utterance has been translated accordingly.

2. Cf. *Komm.* ii, 416 ff. I believe, however, that *iṯꜣp* is an imperative with prothetic *i*. Sethe translates *iṯꜣp r* as 'drückend war es für', but that would require the dependent pronoun *sw* after the supposed adjective or participle *iṯꜣp*, and the prothetic *i* is not accounted for. Sethe's comparison with the construction adjectival predicate + dative (Gardiner, § 141) in my opinion is not valid. For *ṯꜣp* see also § 1416*c*.

3. Var. M: 'I am established', passive *sḏm·f*.

4. Var. *sḏꜣ M*; for *sḏꜣ* 'conduct' cf. §§ 1217*a*; 1418*b*; 1429*a*; *CT* iii, 254*a*. For this invocation see also §§ 1418*b*; 1420*b*.

## Utterance 326

### *An 'ascension' text*

O you golden collar, the well-beloved of Horus, which puts the finishing § 534
touch to the breast,[1] which is on the neck of Rēʿ: if you are bound for the sky, the King is bound for the sky.

1. Lit. 'front'; obviously not 'brow' here.

## Utterance 327

### *The king is fed*

The messenger of Horus loves me[1] and has brought his eye; the messenger § 535
of Seth loves me and has brought his testicles; the messenger of Thoth loves
me and has brought his arm,[2] | and the Two Enneads have trembled at them. § 536
These are indeed my messengers whom I love and who will bring me to a meal, and they *will* bring[3] me to a meal.

1. Sethe translates the opening words as 'Bote des Horus, der von ihm gewünscht wurde, war T', but this would require the perfective passive participle (*mry·f*), whereas the N-text shows unmistakably that the king's name is not the predicate of a non-verbal sentence but the object of a *sḏm·f* form. I find it hard to accept Sethe's arguments, *Komm.* iii, 3 ff.; it seems to me that a better sense is obtained if *ỉnw Ḥr* 'messenger of Horus', var. *ỉn n Ḥr* 'he who brings to Horus' be regarded as subject in anticipatory emphasis before the *sḏm·f* form *mr·f*; Horus, Seth, and Thoth in turn present to the king those parts of their bodies which will help him most. However, Sethe is certainly right in his view that the 1st person is original in reference to the king; note *ỉnw w(ỉ)* in § 536*b*.

2. N only.

3. Regarding *ỉnt·sn* as the prospective *sḏm·f*, emphasizing the prospective participle *ỉnw* in § 536*b*.

## Utterance 328

*The king becomes a star*

§ 537 I am a holy one who is in the forefront, who lifts the brow, a star to whom the gods bow, at whom the Two Enneads tremble, and it is my hand which will raise me up.[1]

1. Cf. *Komm.* iii, 8 ff. Here the four Utterances concerned are translated consecutively; for the 1st person cf. ibid. 13, where N is shown to have preserved it.

## Utterance 329

*A variant of the last*

§ 538 I am a holy one who is in the forefront, who lifts the brow, a star to whom the gods bow, at whom the Two Enneads tremble. This face of mine sees my uplifting, I am a nose which breathes.

## Utterance 330

*An 'ascension' text*

§ 539 I ascend to the sky upon the *šdšd*[1] which is in the space which separates(?);[2] her sandal[3] is grasped by ⟨my(?)⟩ uplifted hand.

1. The bolster-like protuberance on the front of the cult-standard of Wepwawet, cf. *Komm.* iii, 11.

2. *Scil.* sky and earth; Sethe has 'das in der Scheidung war'.

3. i.e. of the sky-goddess, cf. Sethe, ibid. 12. N omits the suffix in *ṯbwt·s*, as if the sandal were the king's.

## Utterance 331

*A variant of the last*

I ascend to the sky upon the *šdšd* which is in the space which separates(?), § 540
and I grasp[1] her sandal. I am a nose which breathes, this face of mine sees my uplifting.

1. Cf. Utt. 330, n. 3. The 1st person is indicated by the absence of suffixes after *nḏr* in § 540*b* and after *ḥr* 'face' in § 540*d* (N).

## Utterance 332

*An 'ascension' text*

I am[1] this one who escaped from the coiled serpent,[2] I have ascended in a § 541
blast of fire, having turned myself about. The two skies go to me, the two earths come to me,[3] I have trodden on the green *ḳꜣd*-plant which is under the feet of Gēb, I have travelled[4] the roads of Nūt.

1. For the 1st person cf. *Komm.* iii, 14.
2. Sethe translates *mḥn* by 'Schlangentopf-Brettspiel', as if escape had been won in a game on this board, but a better sense is obtained by regarding *mḥn* as referring to an actual coiled serpent hostile to the king: for the meaning of the word cf. *Urk.* iv, 951, 10; *BD* 287, 8; 446, 12. The det.  would then be due to a reminiscence of the 'coiled-serpent' game *mḥn*.
3. Sethe: 'NN ist (davon) gegangen, O Himmel, O Himmel, NN ist (wieder) gekommen, O Erde, O Erde'; but an act of homage by sky and earth is more probable; the duals would then refer to sky and earth in their eastern and western aspects.
4. Lit. 'trampled'.

## Utterance 333

*A 'lustration' text*

I have[1] cleansed myself upon the earth-hill whereon Rēʿ cleansed himself, I § 542
place the stairway(?), I set up the ladder, and those who are in the West[2] grasp my hand.

1. The 1st person is original, cf. *Komm.* iii, 18 and § 542*c*, older P-text.
2. *Imyw wrt* is translated by Sethe as 'die welche in der Grossen (d. h. dem Himmel) ist', but to me it seems more likely that we have here a derivative of *imy-wrt* 'West', *Concise Dict.* 18.

## Utterance 334

*The king greets the sun-god*[1]

Hail to you, Rēʿ, you who traverse the sky and cross Nūt, having traversed the § 543
Winding Waterway. I have grasped your tail[2] for myself, for I am a god and

§ 544 the son of a god,[1] I am a flower which has issued from the Nile(?),[3] a golden flower which has issued from Iseion.[4] I have traversed Pe, I have crossed
§ 545 *Knmwt*;[5] | I have traversed Pe as Kherty who presides over Nezat, I have crossed *Knmwt* as Shezmu who is in his oil-press bark. May the god desire that I be more alive than Fetket.[6]

1. Sethe would date this text to the time of the predynastic Kingdom of Buto, *Komm.* iii, 22.

2. i.e. of Rēʿ in bull-shape. For the 1st person cf. ibid. 21 (§ 543*c*), as indeed the context appears to demand.

3. Cf. ibid. 22.

4. Cf. *Dict. géogr.* iii, 107.

5. Op. cit. v, 204.

6. Sethe: 'dass N lebe wie der *Ftkt* lebt', but the translation of *ir* as 'wie' is questionable; it is more likely to be comparative, the king is to have a better living than Fetket, butler of Rēʿ in §§ 120*b*; 123*g*.

## Utterance 335

### *An 'ascension' text*

§ 546 How happy are those who see me[1] adorned with my fillet from the brow of Rēʿ! My kilt which is on me is Ḥatḥōr, my plume is a falcon's plume, and indeed I will ascend to the sky among my brethren the gods.

1. *Mꜣꜣw* is perfective active participle. For the 1st person see *sšd·i* next following in three texts out of four.

## Utterance 336

### *An address to the sun-god*

§ 547 Hail to you, Bull of bulls, when you rise![1] I[2] grasp you by your tail, I grip you by the root of your tail(?)[3] when you rise, a great one[4] being behind you and a great one being before you.

§ 548 Hail to you, greatest of the gods! Receive me, for I belong to you,[5] and your heart is glad. As for my corpse,[6] it is rejuvenated.[7]

1. Lit. 'act the ascending one', referring to sunrise. *Prrw* is perfective active participle.

2. The 1st person is probably original, for it is surely the king, and not an officiant, who is addressing the sun-bull. See also n. 5 below.

3. The det. ○ of *wbnw* may imply not only the usual det. of *wbn* but also proximity to the anus; the word seems to mean the 'root' of the tail, which rises (*wbn*) from the hindquarters of the animal.

4. Feminine.

5. I question Sethe's 'du gehörst zu ihm'. I suspect that the original reading of T was *n·k w(i)* and that when the dependent pronoun was changed by the ancient editor into *sw* the *w* after *n·k* was retained in error. It is clear that later editors did not understand this phrase in T, for in P it is changed into *di·k ˁnḫ·f* 'that you may let him live', while M and N omit it entirely. *Iw* after *išp* in M is probably an unerased object-pronoun 'me'.

6. Var. P: 'flesh and bones'.

7. *Nḫnw* is a passive participle used as nominal predicate with *pw*, lit. 'it is what is rejuvenated'.

## Utterance 337

*An 'ascension' text*

The sky thunders, the earth quakes, because of the dread of you, O Osiris, § 549
when you ascend. | O you milch-cows who are here,[1] you nursing cows who § 550
are here, go round about him, beweep him, lament him, mourn him when he ascends and goes to the sky among his brethren the gods.

1. *Imywt nn*, lit. 'who are in this', with an unusual writing of the fem. plur. of *imy*.

*Here begins a series of food-spells*

## Utterance 338

O Hunger, do not come for me;[1] go to the Abyss, depart to the flood! I am § 551
satisfied, I am not hungry by means of this *kmḥw*-bread of Horus which I have eaten, which my chief woman has prepared for me, and I am satisfied thereby,
I assume my (normal) condition thereby.[2] | I will not be thirsty by reason of § 552
Shu, I will not be hungry by reason of Tefênet; Ḥapy, Duamūtef, Ḳebḥsenuf, and Imsety will expel this hunger which is in my belly and this thirst which is on my lips.

1. The 1st person is probable here and in the Utterances which follow; so also *Komm.* iii, 36.
2. The sculptor of T has misread *zp·f* as *ti pn*.

## Utterance 339

My hunger is from the hand of Shu, my thirst is from the hand of Tefēnet, § 553
but I live on the morning-bread which comes in due season. I live on that whereon Shu lives, I eat of that whereof Tefēnet eats.

## Utterance 340

§ 554 I have come to you, you Old One; may you turn back to me as the east wind is turned back behind the west wind; may you come[1] to me as the north wind comes after the south wind. Recitation: Set down.[2]

1. A clear example of the independent use of the prospective *sḏm·f* form *iwt·f*, here used to express the optative; in the next clause we have the outwardly similar *sḏmt·f* form following a preposition.
2. *Scil.* the offering which is to be made.

## Utterance 341

§ 555 The vision of Horus is cleared by the Earth-god, and the vision of the Earth-god is cleared by Horus.[1] Plenty has put her hands on me, and my hands have enclosed the bird-catch. Whatever[2] the Fen-goddess makes belongs to her son 'Bird-catch', and I eat with him today.

1. i.e. the two gods are revealed to each other. Horus here probably means the king, and the passage may possibly refer to his resurrection from the tomb.
2. Note *nb* after *irt* instead of *nbt*.

## Utterance 342

§ 556 Here am[1] I, O Isis; here am I, O *ꜣsbt*;[2] here am I, O Nephthys. Come that you[3] may see your son; the nome of the Black Bull serves me, the *Wrrt*-
§ 557 crown serves me.[1] My bag is (made) from a *twn*-plant, my basket is (made) from a *nnt*-plant, and I have come carrying what is wished for and given.

1. Lit. 'this is'.
2. Not 'the flaming one', which would be *ꜣzbt*, cf. *ꜣzb* 'fierce' of radiance, § 324*b*.
3. Sing.; the three goddesses are regarded as one.

## Utterance 343

§ 558 Here comes the feeble one;[1] the brazier burns, the servers stand up, and a meal is given to me.

1. i.e. the king, limp in death and needing sustenance.

## Utterance 344

§ 559 Hail to you, Great Flood, butler of the gods, leader of the sun-folk! May you propitiate men and gods for me, that they may give me every meal.

## Utterance 345

O Werkaf, butler of Horus, Master of the hall of Rēʿ, Elder of the palace[1] of Ptaḥ, give me a sufficiency, that I may eat according to your giving. § 560

1. Sethe: 'Küchenältester'. In any case, Werkaf is regarded here as the official in charge of the issue of food.

## Utterance 346

The spirits are in Pe, the spirits are indeed[1] in Pe, the spirits will continue § 561
to be in Pe, and my[2] spirit is in Pe. The flame is red, the Beetle is alive,[3] and
men are glad;[4] a meal for me, you butchers![5] | It is[6] what you give, my § 562
mistress, even the love of me and help for me;[7] it is what you give, my mistress, help for me and kindness to[8] me in the company[9] of the gods.[10]

1. Collocation of particles *is* and *ỉ*. *Contra* Edel, § 858*a*, I regard *is* as an enclitic at the end of the second clause.
2. For the 1st person cf. *Komm.* iii, 55.
3. Cf. §§ 570; 697*a*, with Sethe's remarks ibid. 56 f. As against Sethe, however, I take *dšr* and *ʿnḫ* as adjectival predicates; his suggestion of a comparison, 'rot wie(?) die Flamme, lebend wie(?) der Kafergott', would require a preposition *mỉ* or *m* before the nouns. His interpretation of the symbolism, as referring to the continuing life of the king, is, however, surely correct.
4. Impersonal *sḏm·tw* followed by complementary infinitive.
5. Var. 'servants'.
6. Omission of neuter suffix, cf. Gardiner, § 123.
7. Lit. 'of'; Sethe translates *smw* as 'Verehrung', but cf. *Concise Dict.* 225.
8. Lit. 'of'.
9. Lit. 'body'.
10. Var. 'all the gods'.

## Utterance 347

The King's[1] mouth is as incense, the King's lips are as myrrh. Descend, O § 563
King, into the field of your double, to the Field of Offerings. [. . . of] the
King is on . . .,[2] the King's meal is like that of the ship of the god. | The life § 564
of the King is more than a year, the King's food-offerings are more than the Nile. O double of the King, bring (something) so that the King may eat with you.

1. The 3rd person apparently is original, as being a statement by the officiant, who in § 563*b* and again in § 564*b* addresses the king directly. The alternative with the 1st person would imply a dialogue between king and priest, which seems improbable here.
2. *Nʿrt* is an untranslatable hapax. N omits this clause.

## Utterance 348[1]

§ 565 Hail to you, Great Flood, butler of the gods, leader of the sun-folk! Make the gods gracious to me that they may make me flourishing, love me, and make me hale.[2]

1. Cf. Utt. 344.
2. N erroneously *ṯn* instead of *sn* in the last clause.

## Utterance 349[1]

§ 566 O Werkaf, butler of Horus, Master of the Hall of Rēʿ, Elder of the Palace of Ptaḥ, give me a sufficiency that I may eat according as you give, (even) a sufficiency of my meat.

1. Cf. Utt. 345.

## Utterance 350

*The king flourishes as a growing plant*

§ 567 O you who stride out greatly,[1] strewing green-stone, malachite, turquoise of(?)[2] the stars, if you are green, then will the King be green, (even as) a living rush is green.

1. A female being. For *ii* cf. also *CT* i, 284*a*; 285*b*.
2. Sethe: '(als)'.

## Utterance 351

*The king is reborn*

§ 568 A vulture has become pregnant [with] the King in the night at your horn, O contentious(?) cow. If you are green, then will the King be green, (even as) a living rush is green.

## Utterance 352

*A conflation of the two previous Utterances*

§ 569 A vulture has become pregnant with the King in the night at your horn, O contentious(?) cow. Your papyrus-plant is the green of the turquoise[1] of the stars, your papyrus-plant is the green of the King, (even as) a living rush is green, and the King is green with you.

1. *Sic.* A reference to *iʒmt* may have been omitted.

## Utterance 353

*The king is alive*

I have come from[1] Pe, and the flame is red, the Beetle is alive.[2] § 570

1. Or: 'into', but cf. *Komm.* iii, 69 f. For the 1st person cf. Utt. 346 and Sethe's restoration of T.
2. Cf. Utt. 346, n. 3. Var. P: 'redder than the flame, more alive than the Beetle'.

## Utterance 354[1]

*A food-spell*

A meal for me, O butcher! A meal for me, O Pillar! [. . . O butler], present water! [. . .]. § 571

1. Cf. Utt. 207.

## Utterance 355

*Title*

The doors of the sky are opened. § 572

*A 'resurrection' text*

O King, your head is knit to your bones for you, and your bones are knit to your head for you. The doors of the sky are opened to you, the great bolts are drawn back for you, the brick is drawn out of the great tomb for you.[1]
Your face is that of a jackal, your tail is that of a lion, you sit on this throne § 573
of yours and give orders to the spirits. You come to me, you come to me,
indeed you come to me as Horus who protects his father Osiris,[1] and I am § 574
your *wt-Inpw* priest.[1] You set your arm over the land, while your ready fighter[2] is in the Great Mound, and you go to and fro in it among the spirits. Stand up, raise yourself up like Osiris.

1. Cf. *Dram. Texte*, 29; *Komm.* iii, 74 f.
2. Cf. *Komm.* iii, 75, but the prefixed *m* suggests that *mꜥḥ* is a noun rather than a verb; cf. § 449*b*, where this expression is an epithet of Horus.

## Utterance 356

*Horus and Gēb support the king against Seth*

O King, Horus has come that he may seek you, he has caused Thoth to turn § 575
back the followers of Seth for you, and he has brought them to you altogether,[1]

§ 576 he has driven back the heart of Seth[1] for you, for you are greater than he.[2] You have gone forth in front of him, your nature is superior to his; Gēb has
§ 577 seen your nature and has set you in your place.| Gēb has brought your two sisters to your side for you, namely Isis and Nephthys; Horus has caused the gods to join you, so that they may be brotherly to you in your name of
§ 578 '*Snwt*-shrines',[3] and not reject[4] you in your name of 'Two Conclaves'.| He has caused the gods to protect you, and Gēb has put his sandal on the head of your foe, who flinches from you. Your son Horus has smitten him, he has
§ 579 wrested his Eye from him and has given it to you;| you have a soul by means of it, you have power by means of it at the head of the spirits. Horus has caused you to lay hold of your foes, and there is none of them who shall escape
§ 580 from you.| Horus indeed has a soul, and he recognizes his father in you in your name of 'Soul of the King's litter(?)';[5] Nūt has placed you as a god to Seth in your name of 'God'; your mother Nūt has spread herself over you
§ 581 in her name of *Št-pt*;[6] | Horus has laid hold of Seth and has set him under you on your behalf so that he may lift you up and quake beneath you as the
§ 582 earth quakes, you being holier than he in your name of 'Sacred Land'.| Horus has caused you to examine him[7] in his inmost parts, lest he escape from you; he has caused you to lay hold of him with your hand, lest he get away from you.

O Osiris the King, Horus has protected you, he has acted on behalf of his spirit in you, so that you[8] may be content in your name of 'Contented Spirit'.

1. i.e. has made him afraid.
2. Seth.
3. Pun on *snsn* 'be brotherly'; cf. *Dram. Texte*, 234 f.
4. For *twr* 'reject' cf. Utt. 210, n. 8.
5. Cf. *Komm.* iii, 86. It seems possible to me, however, that the original reading may have been *bꜣ rpt ỉty* 'soul of the litter of the king', with honorific transposition in the script of the last two words; certainly the king could be regarded as the 'soul' of his litter when he occupied it. The writing *bꜣty rpt* quoted by Sethe from the Osireion might well be due to a misunderstanding of the original hieroglyphic group.
6. See Utt. 35, n. 5.
7. Seth.
8. N wrongly 'he'.

## Utterance 357

*The gods help the king*

§ 583 O Osiris the King,[1] Gēb has given you your eyes, that you may be content with the eyes of this Great One in you; Gēb has caused that Horus give

them to you, so that you may be pleased with them.| Isis and Nephthys have § 584
seen and found you, Horus has reassembled you, Horus has caused Isis and
Nephthys to protect you, they have given you to Horus and he is pleased
with you.| It goes well with Horus in your company in your name of 'Horizon § 585
from which Rēʿ goes forth'; in your embrace in your name of 'Inmate of the
Palace'. You have closed your arms about him, about him, and his bones are
in due order(?),[2] his heart is proud.

O Osiris the King, mount up to Horus, betake yourself to him, do not be § 586
far from him.| Horus has come that he may recognize you; he has smitten § 587
Seth for you bound, and you are his fate(?).[3] Horus has driven him off for
you, for you are greater than he;[4] | he swims bearing you;[5] he lifts up one who § 588
is greater than he in you, and his followers have seen you, that your strength
is greater than his, so that they cannot thwart[6] you.| Horus comes and § 589
recognizes his father in you, you being young in your name of 'Fresh Water';[7]
Horus has split open your mouth for you.

O King, do not languish,[8] do not groan, for Gēb has brought Horus to § 590
you that he may claim their[9] hearts for you; he has brought all the gods to
you at once, and there is none of them who can escape from him.| Horus has § 591
protected you, and he will not fail to protect you;[10] Horus has wrested his
Eye from Seth and has given it to you, (even) this his sweet Eye. Make it
come back[11] to you, assign it to yourself, and may it belong(?) to you.| Isis § 592
has reassembled you,[12] the heart of Horus is glad about you in this your
name of 'Foremost of the Westerners', and it is Horus who will make good
what Seth has done to you.

1. Before the invocation of the king the $P^2$ text inserts: 'It is Horus and Gēb who give a boon to the Osiris King P.' Cf. Sethe's remarks *Komm.* v, 170 f.

2. Sethe: 'sich dehnen', 'strecken', op. cit. iii, 96.

3. i.e. of Seth. For the sense here given to *kꜣ* cf. *JEA* 36, 7, n. 2; to the references quoted there for *kꜣ* = 'fortune' add *kꜣ pw nsw* 'the king is fortune' or 'fate', *Les.* 68, 19.

4. Var. $P^2$: 'your foe'.

5. Var. T: 'you swim bearing him', a strange reversal of the true order of the pronouns; M has both suffixes *·f* and *·k* after *nb*.

6. For *ḫꜣ(y)* 'thwart' cf. *CT* i, 154*c*, quoted by Sethe, *Komm.* iii, 98, as B3Bo 335.

7. Cf. §§ 25*c*; 767*a* for this pun on *rnp* 'young'.

8. For *gꜣ* 'languish' cf. *Peas.* B1, 100.

9. The followers of Seth.

10. For *n ḏd·n nḏ·f* 'he will never fail to protect you' cf. also §§ 618*b*; 1797*b* (in 1st person). The exact significance of *ḏd·n*, apparently a verb in the *sḏm·n·f* with a *sḏm·f* form as subject, is by no means clear, but there can be little doubt as to the meaning of the sentence.

11. Cf. Utt. 169, n. 1.

12. The P-text inserts 'it is Horus who will make good what Seth has done to you' and omits it from § 592*c*.

## Utterance 358

*The dead king is freed from his wrappings*

§ 593 O First-born of Shu,[1] your knotted bonds are loosed by[2] the two Lords of the Abyss.

1. So T; var. N: 'O King, you are the first-born of Shu'.
2. Or 'so say'.

## Utterance 359

*The king crosses to the Beyond*

§ 594 Horus has cried out because of his Eye, Seth has cried out because of his testicles, and there leaps up the Eye of Horus, who had fallen on yonder side of the Winding Waterway, so that it may protect itself from Seth. Thoth saw it on yonder side of the Winding Waterway when the Eye of Horus leapt up on yonder side of the Winding Waterway and fell on Thoth's wing
§ 595 on yonder side of the Winding Waterway.| O you gods who cross over on the wing of Thoth to yonder side of the Winding Waterway, to the eastern side
§ 596 of the sky, in order to dispute with Seth about this Eye of Horus:| I will cross[1] with you upon the wing of Thoth to yonder side of the Winding Waterway, to the eastern side of the sky, and I will dispute with Seth about this Eye of Horus.

§ 597 Awake in peace, O *M*ꜣ-*ḥ*ꜣ*·f*, in peace!
Awake in peace, O you who are in the sky, in peace!

O Ferryman of the Winding Waterway, tell my name to Rēʿ, announce me
§ 598 to Rēʿ,| for I am bound for yonder distant castle of the owners of doubles who worship Rēʿ there in the Mounds of Horus and the Mounds of Seth as their god of those who have gone to their doubles.

§ 599 O Rēʿ, commend me to *M*ꜣ-*ḥ*ꜣ*·f*, the ferryman of the Winding Waterway, so that he may bring me his ferry-boat which belongs to the Winding Waterway, in which he ferries the gods to yonder side of the Winding Waterway,
§ 600 to the eastern side of the sky,| so that he may ferry me over to yonder side of the Winding Waterway, to the eastern side of the sky, for I am seeking
§ 601 the endangered[2] Eye of Horus,| I am bound for the numbering of fingers.[3]

My face is washed by the gods,[4] male and female; Imsety, Ḥapy, Duamūtef, and Ḳebḥsenuf are ⟨at⟩[5] my right side, on which is Horus[6] who

smote *Ḏndrw* in front of his two pillars;[7] Nephthys and *Ḫnt-n-irty* are ⟨at⟩[8] my left side, on which is Seth.[1] I am recognized by my throne,[9] my oar[10] § 602
has remembered me; I have found my throne empty in the hold of the golden bark of Rēʿ.

1. The invocation of the ferryman in § 597 indicates that this summons was spoken by the king himself, as were all the 'ferryman' texts, and the preoccupation of §§ 594–601 with ferrying suggests that the same applies to the whole.

2. See Utt. 23, n. 2.

3. Cf. *ZÄS* 57, 72.

4. N corruptly: 'the faces of the gods are washed'.

5. The preposition *r* has been omitted.

6. Sethe: 'welche Horus ist', identifying the king with Horus, but cf. Griffiths, 'in which Horus is,' in *JEA* 28, 66. It is more likely that Horus and Seth (§ 601*f*) would be standing on either side of the king than that he would be identified with each in turn.

7. Sethe: 'der vor seinen beiden Papyrus-szeptern ist', taking *ḫnt* to be the adjective rather than the preposition.

8. See n. 5 above.

9. Var. P: 'his throne has recognized him'.

10. T has no suffix after *mʿwḥ* 'oar', which again speaks for the 1st person. Cf. *Komm.* iii, 107 f.

## Utterance 360

### *A variant of Utterance 272*

O Height which is not sharpened,[1] gate of the sky, I am[2] Shu who came forth § 603
from Atum. O Nu, let these (gates) be opened for me, for behold I have come, a god-like soul.

1. Cf. Utt. 272, n. 1.

2. Cf. Utt. 272, n. 2.

## Utterance 361

### *The king is to be admitted to the sky*

Nu has commended the King[1] to Atum, the Open-armed has commended § 604
the King to Shu, that he may cause[2] yonder doors of the sky to be opened for the King, barring[3] (ordinary) folk who have no name. Grasp the King by his hand and take the King to the sky, that he may not die on earth among men.

1. The imperatives of § 604*e*, apparently addressed to Shu, seem to indicate that it was not the king himself but the officiant who uttered this spell.

2. N has the imperative here.

3. On the sense given to *ḫr* cf. *Komm.* iii, 121, though Sethe's interpretation of *Westcar*, 7, 17 does not hold. In that passage *ḫr iꜣwt* starts a new sentence: 'Now old age is . . .', as he himself has seen in *Les.* 29, 18.

## Utterance 362

*Atum (here = the sun at night) is prayed to summon the king to his side so that the latter may kindle a light for him*

§ 605 O my[1] father, O my father in darkness! O my father Atum in darkness!
§ 606 Fetch me to your side,| so that I may kindle a light for you and that I may
protect you, even as Nu protected these four goddesses on the day when they
protected the throne, namely Isis, Nephthys, Neith, and Selḳet-ḥetu.[2]

1. For the 1st person cf. *Komm.* iii, 123.
2. i.e. the four goddesses who guard the sarcophagus and Canopic chests of the king, cf. Fox, *Tutankhamun's Treasure*, pls. 26, 42, 43, with accompanying text.

## Utterance 363

*The king crosses the river of death*

§ 607 O Way of Horus, make ready your tent for me,[1] make ready your arms for
me. O Rēʿ, come and ferry me over to yonder side even as you ferried over
§ 608 your attendant Weneg whom you love.| If you set your hand to the West, you
will set your hand on me; if you set your hand to the East, you will set your
hand on me, just as you did for the *bnty*-ape your eldest son.

1. Probably spoken by the king himself, as the reference to ferrying suggests.

*A series of four 'resurrection' texts*

## Utterance 364

§ 609 O Osiris the King, stand up! Horus comes and claims you from the gods, for
Horus has loved you, he has provided you with his Eye,[1] Horus has attached
§ 610 his Eye to you;| Horus has split open your eye for you that you may see with
it, the gods have knit up your face for you, for they have loved you, Isis and
Nephthys have made you hale, and Horus is not far from you, for you are
§ 611 his essence.| May your face be well-disposed to him; hasten, receive the
word of Horus, with which you will be well pleased. Listen to Horus, for it
will not be harmful to you; he has caused the gods to serve you.

§ 612 O Osiris the King, awake! Gēb brings Horus to you and he recognizes
§ 613 you; Horus has found you, and it will go well with him through you.| Horus
has caused the gods to mount up to you, he has given them to you that they

may make you glad.[2] Horus has set you in front of the gods and has caused you to take possession of all that is yours.[3] Horus has attached himself to you and he will never part from you.| Horus has revived you in this your name § 614
of ʿAndjeti, Horus has given you his strong Eye; he has given[4] it to you that you may be strong[5] and that every foe of yours may fear you. Horus has completely filled you with his Eye in this its name of 'God's Oblation'.| Horus § 615
has assembled the gods for you, and they will never escape from you in the place where you have gone. Horus has mustered the gods for you, and they will never escape from you in the place where you drowned.| Nephthys has § 616
collected all your members for you in this her name of 'Seshat, Lady of Builders'. ⟨She⟩[6] has made them hale for you, you having been given to your mother Nūt in her name of 'Sarcophagus',[7] she has embraced you in her name of 'Coffin', and you have been brought to her in her name of 'Tomb'.|
Horus has reassembled your members for you, and he will not let you perish; § 617
he has put you together, and nothing shall be disturbed[8] in you; Horus has set you up, and there shall be no unsteadiness(?).

O Osiris the King, lift up your heart, be proud, open your mouth, for § 618
Horus has protected you and he will not fail to protect you.[9] | O Osiris the § 619
King, you are a mighty god, and there is no god like you. Horus has given you his children that they may bear you up;| he has given you all the gods that § 620
they may serve you, and that you may have power over them; Horus has lifted you up in his name of '*Ḥnw*-bark'; he bears you up in your name of Sokar.| Live,[10] that you may go to and fro every day; be a spirit in your name § 621
of 'Horizon from which Rēʿ goes up'; be strong, be effective, be a soul, and have power for ever and ever.

1. *M irt·f* only in T.
2. Lit. 'illumine your face'.
3. Cf. *Komm.* iii, 137. Sethe's translation of *nbt* as 'the Lady' is open to question, since that word is invariably part of a direct genitive, 'the Lady of . . .'; here *nbt* is surely the adjective 'every', qualifying *ṯwt* 'what is yours' in the sense of 'crown'. This latter word, as Gunn suggested, appears to be a specialized use of the independent pronoun *ṯwt* in its possessive sense, 'what is yours', the crown being exclusively the possession of the monarch.
4. Read *d·n⟨·f⟩ n·k*; for the omission of the subject-suffix see also § 616*c*.
5. *Ỉmim·k*, cf. Utt. 244, n. 1.
6. Suffix *·s* omitted, see n. 4 above.
7. The interior of the lid of the sarcophagus, as a simulacrum of the sky, was sacred to the sky-goddess Nūt.
8. *Sḏm·n·ty* form used impersonally; cf. also § 1610*b*.
9. See Utt. 357, n. 10.
10. Hortative old perfective.

## Utterance 365

§ 622 Raise yourself, O King; run, you who are greatly strong. You shall sit at
the head of the gods, you shall do this which Osiris did in the Mansion of
the Prince[1] which is in Ōn. Receive your dignity, for your foot will not be
§ 623 obstructed in the sky, you will not be opposed on earth,| for you are a spirit
whom Nūt bore, whom Nephthys suckled, and they put you together. Arise
§ 624 in your strength and do what formerly you used to do,| for you are more
spirit-like than all the spirits. You shall go[2] to Pe and find him whom you
will meet there;[3] you shall return to Nekhen and find him whom you will
§ 625 meet there;| you shall do what Osiris did, for you are he who is upon his
throne. Arise, O spirit, greatly strong, adorned as a great wild bull; you will
not be opposed in any place where you walk, your foot will not be obstructed
in any place where you desire to be.

1. Var. T: 'the Mansion of the Wand' or 'Mast'.
2. Shown to be future by the prospective *sḏm·f* form *iwt·f* in § 624*c*.
3. Sethe interprets *ḥsf·k im* in a hostile sense, as rightly in § 625*c*, but here it seems to me that the dead king is merely being directed to visit the gods whom he will meet in the cities named. It is improbable that the deities in the great religious centres of Pe and Nekhen would be hostile to the king.

## Utterance 366

§ 626 O Osiris the King, arise, lift yourself up! Your mother Nūt has borne you,
Gēb has wiped your mouth for you, the Great Ennead protects you and has
§ 627 put for you your foe[1] under you;| 'Carry one who is greater than you' say
they to him in your name of 'Palace of the Great Saw'. 'Lift up him who is
§ 628 greater than you' say they in your name of 'Thinite Nome'.| Your two sisters
Isis and Nephthys come to you that they may make you hale, and you are
complete and great in your name of 'Wall of the Bitter Lakes', you are hale
§ 629 and great in your name of 'Sea';| behold, you are great and round[2] in ⟨your
name of⟩ 'Ocean'; behold, you are circular and round as the circle which
surrounds the *Ḥ3w-nbwt*;[3] behold, you are round and great as the *Šn-ʿ3-sk*.[4]|
§ 630 Isis and Nephthys have waited[5] for you in Asyūṭ because their lord is in you
in your name of 'Lord of Asyūṭ', and because their god is in you in your name
§ 631 of 'God';| they praise you lest you be far from them in your name of 'Sacred
§ 632 Beard'; they join you lest you be angry in your name of '*Ḏndrw*-bark'.| Your
sister Isis comes to you rejoicing for love of you. You have placed her on your
phallus and your seed issues into her, she being ready as Sothis, and Ḥar-
§ 633 Sopd has come forth from you as Horus who is in Sothis.| It is well with you

through him in his[6] name of 'Spirit who is in the *Ḏndrw*-bark', and he protects you in his name of Horus, the son who protects his father.

1. The plural *ḫftyw* of T is clearly a slip, as is shown by the suffix 3rd sing. in § 627*a*.
2. The description of the king as 'great and round' here and as 'circular and round' below seems to be the Egyptian way of saying that the king's authority and power are all-embracing and universal.
3. Cf. *AEO* i, 206*; *BIFAO* 46, 125; 48, 107; *ZÄS* 81, 11.
4. Cf. *Dict. géogr.* v, 138.
5. Sethe translates *zı·n* as 'begrüsst haben', although in *Komm.* iii, 169 he admits the possibility of the meaning 'wait for'. The latter suits the context better and accounts for the pre-preposition *n*. Cf. also § 757*a*.
6. P wrongly *rn·k*; this epithet and the next refer to Horus.

## Utterance 367

O Osiris the King, Gēb brings Horus to you that he may protect you and bring to you the hearts of the gods; may you neither languish nor groan. Horus has given to you his Eye that you may take possession of the *Wrrt*-crown by means of it at the head of the gods.[1] Horus has reassembled your limbs and he has put you together, and nothing in you shall be disturbed.[1] Thoth has laid hold of your foe for you, he having been decapitated together with those who are in his following, and he[2] will have no mercy on him.

§ 634
§ 635

1. Cf. Utt. 364, n. 8.
2. Thoth.

## Utterance 368

### *The king is protected*

O Osiris the King, this is Horus in your embrace, and he protects you; it is well with him again with you in your name of 'Horizon from which Rēʿ goes forth'.[1] Clasp[2] your arms about him, about him, and he will not escape from you.[1] Horus will not let you perish, for Horus has set your foe under your feet for you; may you live, for Horus has given you his children that they may go beneath you and none of them will turn back when they carry you.[1] Your mother Nūt has spread herself over you in her name of *Št-pt*, she has caused you to be a god to your foe in your name of 'God', she will protect you from all things evil in her name of 'Great Well',[3] for you are the greatest of her children.[1] Gēb is gracious to you; he has loved you and protected you, he has given you your head, he has caused Thoth to reassemble you so that what was on you[4] comes to an end.

§ 636
§ 637
§ 638
§ 639

1. So T; P and M have written *im·k* for *im·s* and so have made the epithet unintelligible.
2. Imperative with reflexive dative rather than *sḏm·n·f* as Sethe.
3. Sethe: 'Sieb', *Komm.* iii, 185 f.
4. Presumably the signs of death and decay.

## Utterance 369

### *Horus restores the king*

§ 640 O Osiris the King, stand up! Horus has caused you to stand up, for Gēb has caused Horus to see his father in you in your name of 'Mansion of the
§ 641 Monarch'.[1] Horus has given you the gods, he has caused them to go up to you that they may make you glad; Horus has given you his Eye that you may see
§ 642 with it.[1] Horus has set for you your foe under you that he may lift you up; do not let go of him. You shall come[1] to your (former) condition, for the gods
§ 643 have knit together your face for you.[1] Horus has split open your eye for you that you may see with it in its name of 'Opener of Roads'; your foe is smitten by the children of Horus, they have made bloody his beating, they have
§ 644 punished him, he having been driven off, and his smell is evil.[1] Horus has struck your mouth for you,[2] he has adjusted your mouth to your bones for you, Horus has split open your mouth for you, and it is your well-beloved son who has re-set your eyes for you.[3] Horus will not let your face be sightless(?)[4] in your name of 'Horus at the head of his people'.

1. Prospective *sḏm·f*.
2. Cf. 11*b* ff.
3. Note the rare construction *in* + noun + *sḏm·n·f*.
4. So Sethe.

## Utterance 370

### *As last*

§ 645 O Osiris the King, Horus has caused the gods to join you and to be brotherly to you in your name of '*Snwt*-shrines'. Go up to Horus, betake yourself to
§ 646 him, do not be far from him in your name of 'Sky'.[1] Horus has attached himself to you and he will never part from you, for he has made you live. Run, receive his word and be pleased with it; listen to him, for it will not harm
§ 647 you.[1] He has brought to you all the gods at once and there is none of them who will escape from him. Horus has attached himself to his children; join yourself with those of his body, for they have loved you. Horus has acted on behalf of his spirit in you so that you may be content in your name of 'Contented Spirit'.

## Utterance 371

*As before*

O Osiris the King, Horus has placed you in the hearts of the gods, he has § 648
caused you to take possession of all that is yours.[1] Horus has found you, and
it goes well with him through you. Go up against your foe, for you are greater
than he in your name of '*Pr-wr*-shrine'.| Horus has caused him to lift you § 649
up in your name of 'Great lifted one'. He has saved you from your foe, he
has protected you as one who is to be protected in due season, Gēb has seen
your nature and has set you in your place.| Horus has stretched out for you § 650
your foe under you, for you are older[2] than he, you have come forth[3] before
him. You are the father of Horus who begot him in your name of 'Begetter',
and Horus is glad at you in your name of 'Foremost of the Westerners'.

1. Cf. Utt. 364, n. 3.
2. Read *wt·ty*, old perfective.
3. From the womb.

## Utterance 372

*As before*

O Osiris the King, awake! Horus has caused Thoth to bring your foe to you, § 651
he[1] has set you on his[2] back that he may not thwart you; take your place upon
him,| go up and sit on him, do not let him escape from you. Go down, being § 652
holier than he, and set danger against him.| Horus has cut off the strong arms § 653
of your foes and Horus has brought them to you cut up, Horus has driven
off their doubles from them . . .[3] in your name of '*Nzr-mš*-bull'.[4]

1. Thoth.
2. The foe = Seth.
3. Sethe: 'damit du mächtig(?) seist durch das, was dein Herz mit ihnen thun(?) wird', cf. *Komm.* iii, 200, but his translation is conjectural, and I feel unable to accept it, even though I have no alternative to suggest.
4. Varr. *Nzr-m-rš*, *Nz-mš*.

## Utterance 373

*A 'resurrection' text*

Oho! Oho! Raise yourself, O King; receive your head, collect your bones, § 654
gather your limbs together, throw off the earth from your flesh,| receive your § 655
bread which does not grow mouldy and your beer which does not grow sour,
and stand at the doors which keep out the plebs. *Ḫnty-mnwt·f* comes out to

§ 656 you and grasps your hand, he takes you to the sky, to your father Gēb.[1] He is joyful at meeting you, he sets his hands on you, he kisses you and caresses you, he sets you at the head of the spirits, the Imperishable Stars. Those whose seats are hidden worship you, the Great Ones care for you, the
§ 657 Watchers wait upon you.[1] Barley is threshed for you, emmer is reaped for you, and offering thereof is made at your monthly festivals, offering thereof is made at your half-monthly festivals, being what was commanded to be done for you by your father Gēb. Rise up, O King, for you have not died!

## Utterance 374

*The king travels the Beyond unhindered*

§ 658 Be great,[1] O King! Ferry over, O King! May your name be notified to Osiris. Your foot is great, your foot is mighty, so traverse the Great Bed;[2] you will [not] be seized by the earth-gods, you will not be opposed by the starry
§ 659 sky.[1] The doors of the sky will be opened to you that you may go out from them as Horus and as the jackal beside him who hides(?)[3] his shape from his foes, [for] there is no father of yours among men who could beget you, for there is no mother of yours among men who could bear you.[4]

1. *Wrt* and *ḏ*ꜣ*t* are hortative old perfectives.
2. i.e. the sky, according to Sethe.
3. Cf. *Komm.* iii, 211.
4. Cf. *Syntax*, 35.

*Utterances* 375–99 *are concerned with spells against snakes and other dangers*

## Utterance 375

§ 660 *Tšy* protects the King, *Tšy* looses the King.[1] Bring your message, you porter of *Tšy*, bring your pleasant(?) message,[2] you porter of *Tšy*. May you not come against the King, the son of a great one, you knife of the castrator![3]

1. Or: 'He who protects *Tšy* is the King', etc. That is Sethe's view, cf. *Komm.* iii, 213 f., but since all this group of spells is intended for the *king's* protection, I have adopted the alternative possibility. Exceptionally for this class of spell, the 3rd person seems to be original here. Who *Tšy* is remains obscure.
2. Cf. ibid. 214 f.
3. The danger against which the Utterance is directed.

## Utterance 376

O knife of the castrator, O shining one, shining one, *Wnty*, *Wnty*![1] O sailor(?)[2] who uses[3] his garments for the Day-bark![4] § 661

1. A *nomen divi* of doubtful meaning. Sethe, on somewhat slender grounds, translates the word as 'Triumphator', *Komm.* iii, 217. The epithet 'shining' could be applied to a glittering knife-blade, but hardly 'triumphant', at least in this context.

2. Sethe restores  after *nf* and translates as 'Schiffer', but the relationship of this clause to what precedes remains obscure.

3. So Sethe.

4. Here the Utterance breaks off short, the continuation not having been recorded. On account of the mention of the solar bark, Sethe regards the extant portion as an invocation of the sun-god; perhaps to prevent use of the surgical knife on the king, as in the preceding Utterance.

## Utterance 377

May you be shut up(?)[1] in your name of 'Fortress', may you be overturned in § 662
your name of *Ἰgrt*, because you are the *hpłw*-snake who is on his belly, who lives on the hearts of those gods who are in Ōn. Get back! Take yourself off from it!

1. Sethe: 'du sollst landen', seeing in *mnni* a geminated form of *mni* (*mini*) 'moor', Coptic ⲙⲟⲟⲛⲉ, *Komm.* iii, 218. Geminated forms of *mni*, however, do not seem to occur elsewhere, and it is not impossible that we have here a verb *mnni* 'shut up', 'imprison' cognate with *mnnw* 'fortress', which likewise is often written with two medial *n*'s, cf. *Concise Dict.* 109.

## Utterance 378

O Snake in the sky! O Centipede on earth! The sandal of Horus is what § 663
tramples the *nḫi*-snake underfoot, the *nḫi*-snake of[1] Horus the young child
with his finger in his mouth,ǀ and I am[2] Horus the young child with his § 664
finger in his mouth. It is dangerous[3] for me, so I have trodden on you; be
wise about me(?) and I will not tread on you,ǀ for you are the mysterious § 665
and invisible one of whom the gods speak; because you are one who has no legs, because you are one who has no arms, with which you could walk after
your brethren the gods.ǀ O you two who are feeble, are feeble(?), O you two § 666
who are lifted up, lifted up(?), who make the *mtt*-cord of the god, beware of me and I will beware of you.

1. i.e. which endangered.

2. For the 1st person cf. *Komm.* iii, 221 f.; these anti-vermin texts are nearly all spoken by the king.

3. So Sethe.

## Utterance 379

§ 667 Your water is in the sky, your thousands are on earth . . .[1]

1. The interpretation of these words is doubtful, cf. *Komm.* iii, 227. The final *isy-ḥ* is untranslatable.

## Utterance 380

§ 668 O Evil-doer, Evil-doer! O Creeper, Creeper![1] Your foot be behind you![2] Beware of the Twice Great!

1. Cf. Utt. 280 with n. 1.
2. i.e. 'turn back'.

## Utterance 381

§ 669 The great centipede goes down, having cursed Him of the Mansion, and He of the Mansion is cursed by the centipede.[1]

1. Cf. § 425*c*.

## Utterance 382

§ 670 O *ikrw*-snake, O *ikrt*-snake, be far from me, (even I) who am in . . .[1] Horus goes round about in pursuit of his Eye. O wandering snake, plough up the earth.[2]

1. *Ḏrʿmw.*
2. To make a hole for itself and so get out of the way? Sethe, *Komm.* iii, 231, interprets this as referring to the interment of the royal corpse, quoting § 285*a*, which, however, is in a different context.

## Utterance 383

§ 671 O *ṯtw*-snake, *ṯtw* snake, where are you going?[1] Attend on me, for I am . . .[2] your father is dead . . .[2] The Majesty of the Pelican has fallen into the Nile here.[3] O you who are in . . .,[4] come here!

1. On the position of the interrogative word cf. Utt. 77, n. 1. A related text is Utt. 296.
2. *Ḏrʿmw.*
3. Cf. §§ 226*a*; 435*a*; 680*a*. On *pn* 'this' in the sense of 'here' cf. *Komm.* iii, 232.
4. *Hpnn.*

## Utterance 384

This hand of mine which comes against you is the hand of the Great Fetterer[1] § 672
who dwells in the Mansion of Life. He whom she grips will not live; he whom she strikes, his head will not remain affixed. Fall! Crawl away!

1. An epithet of Mafdet, cf. § 677*d*.

## Utterance 385

Rēʿ appears against you, Horus draws his nine bows against this spirit which § 673
has come out of the earth with head cut off and tail truncated, (namely) the *ḏsr*-snake *Ddi* son of Selḳet-ḥetu.[1] Turn yourself about, turn over, . . .[1] O § 674
*ḥfnw*-snake, O *ḥfnnt*-snake,[1] listen to me,[2] listen to the earth, listen to your § 675
father Gēb; if you do not listen to me, you will hear my brand which will be(?) on your head.[3] O *srtw*-snake, lie down![1] Leap up, O earth-god, and grasp § 676
him! Slink into the earth, make straight(?) your tail;[4] if I use my arm against you, you will die, and if my arm destroys you, you will not live.[1] 'My waterway § 677
is your waterway', says Shu. Shu stands upon your fetters; turn yourself about, turn yourself over, for my fingers which are on you are the fingers of Mafdet who dwells in the Mansion of Life.[1] May you be spat upon; fall, turn § 678
back, turn over! Horus has felled you and you will not live; Seth has cut you up and you will not rise up.

1. Sethe translates *ʿḥb dti n·k im·f* as 'damit man dir vergebe(?) in Bezug auf ihnen (dem Toten)', but this is conjectural, cf. *Komm.* iii, 236 f., and it seems preferable to admit ignorance of the meaning of this clause.
2. The absence of a nominal antecedent to the suffix *·f* indicates that the 1st person is original here, as Sethe has noted in his discussion of the preceding passage.
3. i.e. will hear the hissing of the hot metal as it burns the skin.
4. Spoken by the king rather than the earth-god and addressed to the snake, which cannot retreat into its hole until its tail is in line with its body.

## Utterance 386

I have come to you, O corrupt one(?),[1] and you shall pass me in *R-Pšny*.[2] § 679
If you drive me away, I will drive you away. Horus fell because of his Eye, Seth suffered because of his testicles. O Serpent whose head is raised, who is in the *nзwt*-bushes, fall down, crawl away!

1. Sethe suggests a connection with *iwtyw* 'corruption', *Urk.* v, 76, 9.
2. Cf. *Dict. géogr.* ii, 152, s.v. *pchnou.*

## Utterance 387

§ 680 The Great One has fallen, the Majesty of the Pelican has fallen. O monster, lie down!

## Utterance 388

§ 681 Where is[1] Horus, who escaped from the *šnṯ*-snake? Behold me, I am Horus who escaped from the *šnṯ*-snake and ran. No messenger has been given to him,[2] his boy has been taken from him. As for the snake 'Festal of phallus',[3] Horus has shattered his mouth with the sole of his foot.

1. Sethe: 'erhoben ist'. I have taken *ỉn* to be the interrogative as in § 671*a*; it seems that a better sense is obtained thus.
2. The snake.
3. Cf. *Komm.* iii, 246 f. My view of *ḥb*, however, is different from that of Sethe, which would require *ḥb m ḥnn*; the -det. is probably but a reminiscence of *ḥb* 'catch' of fish or fowl which has found its way into the homophone *ḥb* 'festal'. The epithet may imply that the snake was somewhat short and thick, like e.g. the puff-adder.

## Utterance 389

§ 682 My eye[1] is on you, O you who are in your cavern! Drag yourself off,[2] O you god in it, from before me! I am the Great Maiden; he whom I see will not live; he on whom my eye falls, his head will not remain in place. O *srỉw*-snake, crawl away! O you who are in the *nꜥwt*-bush, turn over!

1. Lit. 'my face'. For the 1st person see *Komm.* iii, 248.
2. Read *sṯꜣ ṯw*, loc. cit.

## Utterance 390

*In part a purification text, in part a snake-spell*

§ 683 The King is pure, his double is pure. How hale is the King! How hale is the King! Horus is hale of his body. [How hale is] the King! How hale is the King! Seth is hale of his body and the King is hale of his body between you (*sic*).

*The snake-spell*

§ 684 'I am[1] he who draws the bowstring as Horus and who pulls the cord as Osiris.'

§ 685 'That man has gone and this man has come. Are you Horus?'[2]
'Down on your face! Be turned upside down!'[3]

'Are you Seth?'

'Down on your face! Be dragged off! This foot of mine [which I put on you] is the foot of Mafdet; this hand of mine which I lay on you is the hand of Mafdet who dwells in the Mansion of Life.[1] I strike you on your face so that § 686
your venom may fail [. . .] your jaw. O *siw*-snake, lie down! O *nʿw*-snake, crawl away!'

1. The king addresses the snake, who questions him.
2. The snake speaks.
3. The king replies.

## Utterance 391

To be spoken twice: On your side! Lie down![1] Turn back, turn back! Out § 687
of it, out of it![2] [O *Tšy*, release] me,[3] protect me.

Your affair is settled,[4] your testament is valid(?),[5] what is before you is in good order.[6]

1. Hortative old perfective; so also *ḫtt* (for *ḫt·ty*) next following.
2. Cf. § 429*c*.
3. Cf. *Komm.* iii, 258.
4. Reply to the king's appeal; lit. 'your affair is cool'.
5. *Ỉlt* = *ỉ(w)r·t(y)*, lit. 'is pregnant', cf. ibid. 259.
6. Lit. 'is at peace'.

## Utterance 392

My water is in the sky, my fledgelings are on earth, my heart is . . .[1] § 688

1. Cf. Utt. 379. The meaning of *sk* in *sk ib* is obscure; Sethe's 'traurig(?)' seems no more than a conjecture.

## Utterance 393

Your sycamore be your grain, your grain be your sycamore! Your tail be on § 689
your[1] mouth, O *šnṯ*-snake! Turn, turn yourself about, O Great Bull! [. . .] the Great One, whom he has cursed, escapes. O *sꜣ-tꜣ*-snake, beware of the earth! O *sꜣ-tꜣ*-snake, beware of the . . .![2]

1. Read *r·k*.
2. Cf. *Komm.* iii, 263.

## Utterance 394

§ 690 Lion is behind lion in(?) life; the two bulls are (now) an ibis.[1]

1. Cf. § 425*d. e.* Perhaps 'are in the ibis'.

## Utterance 395

§ 691 To be spoken twice: Earth! Beware of the earth, O *sꜣ-tꜣ*-snake, beware of the . . .![1] Beware of your father whom Osiris begot; O *sꜣ-tꜣ*-snake, beware of the . . .!

1. Cf. § 689*d.*

## Utterance 396

§ 692 O *ṯꜣrf*-snake, here is(?) the smell of drawing (the plough over) the earth.[1]

1. Cf. *Komm.* iii, 265 f.

## Utterance 397

You are . . .[1] [. . .] drown him, drown him![2] O Shu, your arms be about me!

1. *Dꜥꜥmw.*
2. See Utt. 666, n. 9.

## Utterance 398

§ 693 O hacker up of the earth who hacks up the earth, do not hack up the earth! Beware of foes! I am conceived by . . .,[1] I am born of . . .,[1] it is . . .[1] who has gone to my mother with me.[2]

1. *Dꜥꜥmw.* The 1st person is confirmed by *Komm.* iii, 267.
2. For the sense of *im* here cf. *JEA* 25, 166; 39, 20. 31.

## Utterance 399

§ 694 Your water is in the sky, your fledgelings are on earth . . .[1]

1. Cf. Utt. 392.

## Utterance 400

### *A food-spell*

§ 695 The Eye of Horus drips upon the bush of *ḏnw.*[1] O you double Horus who presides over the houses, Lord of provisions, Great One in Ōn, give the

King bread, give the King beer, make rich provision for the King,[1] make rich provision for the King's offering-table, richly provide the King's shambles. If the King be hungry, the Double Lion will be hungry; if the King be thirsty, Nekhbet will be thirsty. O Goddess of the *ḥdn*-plant, O Goddess of the *ḥdn*-plant, do not use the smell of your *ḥdn*-plant against the King; you shall not use the smell of your *ḥdn*-plant against the King.[2] § 696

1. Cf. § 133*a*. One would expect this text to have been originally in the 1st person, but there is no positive evidence for it.

2. The *ḥdn* was certainly a plant of offensive smell, since a broom made from it was used in the rite of 'Removing the footprints' to make the tomb untenable by evil spirits; cf. *Amenemḥēt*, p. 93.

## Utterance 401

*The king is alive*

I[1] have come from Pe, redder than fire, more alive than the Beetle; I have seen the Great Serpent, I have received the Great Serpent, my glance falls on the Great Serpent. Authority has bowed his head to me, and I cross his canal with my serpent behind me. § 697

1. For the 1st person cf. Utt. 353.

## Utterance 402

*The king becomes the new-born sun*

My[1] seat with Gēb is made spacious, my star is set on high with Rēʿ, I travel to and fro in the Fields of Offerings, for I am that Eye of Rēʿ which spends the night and is conceived and born every day. § 698

1. For the 1st person cf. *Komm.* iii, 277 f.

## Utterance 403

*A prayer that the king be provided for*

O you whose *ʿꜣb*-tree is green, § 699
Who are upon your field:
O Opener of the Flower
Who are upon your sycamore:
O Gleaming of Banks who are upon your *imꜣ*-tree,
O Lord of Green Fields, § 700
Today(?) is joyous shouting(?)!

The King will always[1] be among you,
The King will go forth in your company(?),
The King will live on what you live on.

§ 701 O you Bulls of Atum, make the King sturdy, strengthen(?) the King more than the *Nt*-crown which is on him, more than the flood which is on his lap, more than the dates which are in his fist.

1. On *ḏrt* cf. Edel, § 753*c*.

## Utterance 404

*The king associates with the gods of Lower Egypt*

§ 702 The King capers(?) with you, O Caperer(?)—repeat four times—who are over the offices of Wedjōyet; the King is greater than Horus of the Red One, the Red Crown which is upon Rēʿ, the King's green eye-paint consists of the papyrus-head of your eye which is in the heat(?), and the King is sturdy with you.[1]

1. It is not clear whether the suffixes of the 2nd person refer to Horus or to Rēʿ; Sethe, *Komm.* iii, 289, thinks the latter.

## Utterance 405

*The king is the eye of the sun-god*

§§ 703–4 O Rēʿ! O *Wꜣḫty, Wꜣḫty*! O *Pndty, Pndty*! I[1] am you and you are I.[1] Rejoice at me and rejoice at my double, for if you shine in me, I will shine in you; make me hale and I will make you hale; make me flourish and I will make you
§ 705 flourish,[1] for I am that eye of yours which is on the horns of Ḥatḥōr, which turns back[2] the years from me; I spend the night and am conceived and born every day.

1. For the 1st person cf. *Komm.* iii, 290.
2. The second *ínnt* is probably a 'complementary infinitive'.

## Utterance 406

*The sun-god is invoked for food*

§ 706 Hail to you, O Rēʿ, in your life and in your beauty,[1] in your thrones, in your
§ 707 . . .[2] Bring me[3] the milk of Isis, the flood of Nephthys, the overspill of the lake, the surge of the sea, life, prosperity, health, happiness, bread, beer,
§ 708 clothing, and food, that I may live thereby.[1] May the Brewers obey me,[4] being long (at work) by day and content with me at night; I partake[5] of the
§ 709 meal when they have satisfied themselves.[1] May I see you when you go forth

as Thoth, when a waterway is prepared for the Bark of Rēʿ to his fields which are in *Ỉꜣsw*;[6] may you rush on(?)[7] as one who is at the head of his Chaos-gods.[8]

1. So N; T employs the stem *nfr* twice over with presumably slightly different meaning.
2. *Sꜣwy* is identified by Sethe with  (*Concise Dict.* 209) and translated by him as 'gold two-thirds fine', cf. also his *Zahlen*, 95 f.; but Harris, *Minerals*, 38 disputes this. Certainly a mention of precious metal here fits the context but ill, unless possibly in the sense of gold collars.
3. For the 1st person cf. *Komm.* iii, 295.
4. In T read *sḏm n⟨·i⟩*, and in § 708*b* *ḥtp n⟨·i⟩* in both texts.
5. Read *smꜣ⟨·i⟩*.
6. A part of the sky, cf. *Komm.* iii, 303.
7. For *gwꜣ* 'rush on', cf. loc. cit.
8. T: *ḥyw·f*; N: *ḥḥw·f*. For my translation 'Chaos-gods', following N, cf. *Ex Oriente Lux*, 18 (1964), 268 f.

## Utterance 407

*The king takes his place in the Beyond*

I purify myself,[1] I assume my pure throne which is in the sky, I will endure § 710
and my goodly thrones will endure, I assume my pure seat which is in the
bow of the Bark of Rēʿ.[1] It is the sailors who row Rēʿ, and it is they who will § 711
row me; it is the sailors who convey Rēʿ round about the horizon, and it is
they who will convey me round about the horizon.[1] My mouth is split open § 712
for me, my nose is broken open for me, my ears are unstopped for me, I will
give judgement and I will judge between contestants,[1] I will give orders to § 713
one who is greater than I. Rēʿ purifies me and protects me from what might
be evilly done against me.

1. P 139. 140 are unmistakably in the 1st person.

## Utterance 408

*The king takes part in the regular festivals*

I am born in the night;[1] come, for I am born. O you two who conceive by § 714
day, rouse(?)[2] yourselves that you may give birth to me[3] who am in the egg.[4]
[1]Since you have borne me, therefore you will have to bring me up.[5] I am glad § 715
over Him who presides over the Netherworld, the gods are glad over me
when they see me rejuvenated,[1] for the festal meal of the sixth day of the § 716

month is for my breakfast, the festal meal of the seventh day is for my supper, cows in suck[6] are slaughtered for me at the *Wꜣg*-festival. What is desired, of which (some) is given, is what I give,[7] for I am the Bull of Ōn.

1. Originally in the 1st person, see the older text of P. T appears to have been slightly corrupted.

2. Sethe: 'damit ihr langmütig seiet', but it is doubtful if *rw* can bear this meaning; for *rw* 'rouse' cf. *JEA* 17, 23.

3. P omits this clause.

4. On *swḥt* cf. *Komm.* iii, 315.

5. *Sk ꜣ* consists of the non-enclitic particle *sk* and the enclitic *ꜣ*. As Sethe has seen, the repetition of this collocation implies an initial circumstance and a necessary consequence; the use of the *sḏm·n·f* form in *snḫ·n·ṯn* is probably dictated by the desire to retain strict parallelism between the two clauses.

6. For *sbnt* cf. 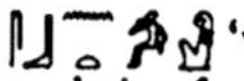 'woman who gives suck', *Peas.* B2, 120.

7. Imperfective relative form with omission of the feminine ending.

## Utterance 409

### *A food-spell*

§ 717 The King is the Bull of the Ennead,[1] possessor of five meals, three in the sky and two on earth; it is the Night- and Day-barks which convey this to
§ 718 the King from the *nḫn*-shrine[2] of the god.[1] Filth is the King's detestation, he rejects urine[3] and will not drink it, the King lives on the tree of sweet things and the censing which is on earth.

1. Despite the determinative, *psḏt* here is certainly the word for 'Ennead', cf. *Komm.* iii, 324 f.

2. On *nḫn nṯr* cf. *Rev. d'Ég.* 17, 194.

3. The lacuna is completed by JPII, 1055+53.

## Utterance 410

### *An address to the ḏd-pillar*

§ 719 O you of Busiris, O *ḏd*-pillar which is in *Grgw-bꜣ·f*,[1] may the King be[2] your . . .,[3] may the King always be your . . .;[3] the King finds you seated on the tower of Khaty on which the gods sit; the owners of doubles are bound[4] for him, there come [. . .].

1. Cf. *Dict. géogr.* v, 218.

2. The use of *wn* instead of *iw* shows that this clause cannot be translated as a present indicative as does Sethe; *wn* is probably prospective *sḏm·f* with optative meaning.

3. The meaning of *wrwt* is not known.

4. For *nwḥ* 'bind' someone see *CT* ii, 54*j*; *Urk.* iv, 612, 14; Sethe has 'zu dem die Herren von *Kꜣ*'s gezogen werden'.

## Utterance 411

*Apparently a fragment of a 'ferryman' text*

[. . .] bring this to me, place me [. . .]. § 720

## Utterance 412

*A 'resurrection' text*

The Great One falls upon his side, He who is in Nedit quivers, his head is § 721
lifted by Rēʿ; he detests sleep, he hates inertness. |

O flesh of the King, do not decay, do not rot, do not smell unpleasant. § 722
Your foot will not be overpassed, your stride will not be overstridden, you
shall not tread on the corruption of Osiris. | You shall reach the sky as Orion, § 723
your soul shall be as effective as Sothis; have power, having power; be strong,
having strength; may your soul stand among the gods as Horus who dwells
in *ʾIrw*.[2] | May the terror of you come into being in the hearts of the gods like § 724
the *Nt*-crown which is on the King of Lower Egypt, like the *Mizwt*-crown
which is on the King of Upper Egypt, like the tress which is on the vertex
of the *Mnṯw*-tribesmen. You shall lay hold of the hand of the Imperishable
Stars, | your bones shall not perish, your flesh shall not sicken, O King, your § 725
members shall not be far from you, because you are one of the gods.

Pe sails upstream to you, Nekhen sails downstream to you, | the Mourning- § 726
Woman calls to you, the *imi-ḫnt* priests are vested for you, there is a welcome
for you, O King, by your father, there is a welcome for you by Rēʿ. | The § 727
doors of the sky are opened for you, the doors of the starry sky are thrown
open for you, for you have gone down[3] as a jackal of Upper Egypt, as Anubis
who is on his belly, as *Wpiw* who is pre-eminent in Ōn.

The Great Maiden who dwells in Ōn has placed for you her hands on you, § 728
because there is no mother of yours among men who could bear you, because
there is no father of yours among men who could beget you.[4] | Your mother § 729
is the great wild cow who dwells in Nekheb,[5] white of head-cloth, long of
plumes, and pendulous of breasts; she suckles you and will not wean you. |
Remove yourself from upon your left side, put yourself[6] upon your right side, § 730
for your seats among the gods endure and Rēʿ leans on you with his arm.
Your scent is as their scent, your sweat is as the sweat of the Two Enneads, |
you appear in the royal hood, your hand grasps the sceptre, your fist grips § 731
on the mace; stand at the head of the Conclaves, judge the gods, | for you § 732
belong to the stars who surround Rēʿ, who are before the Morning Star,
you are born in your months as the moon, Rēʿ leans upon you in the horizon, |

§ 733 the Imperishable Stars follow you. Make yourself ready until Rēʿ comes, that you may be pure when you ascend to Rēʿ, and the sky will not be devoid of you for ever.

1. For an elaborate subdivision of this Utterance into its elements cf. *Komm.* iii, 337 f. It is certainly clear that the Osirian fragment which opens the Utterance (§ 721) is an interpolation into a speech otherwise addressed to the deceased.
2. Cf. *Dict. géogr.* i, 92.
3. Into the tomb?
4. Cf. *Syntax*, 35 f.
5. Cf. *AEO* ii, 8*.
6. So N; T less well: 'sit'.

## Utterance 413

*As last*

§ 734 Raise yourself, O King! You have your water, you have your inundation, you have your milk which is from the breasts of Mother Isis. Raise yourself,
§ 735 you child of Horus,[1] child who is in *Ḏbʿwt-P*,[2] as Seth who is in *Ḥnḥnt*.[3]! This Great One spends the night fast asleep; awake, O King, raise yourself, receive
§ 736 your head, gather your bones together, shake off your dust,! and sit on your iron throne, so that you may eat the foreleg, devour the haunch, and partake of your rib-joints in the sky in company with the gods.

1. Sethe: 'dich erheben die Kinder des Horus', but in view of the direct imperative 'raise yourself' in §§ 734*a* and 735*b*, it seems likely that *ṯs ṯw* here is also an imperative and that *ms Ḥr* is a vocative used of the king.
2. Cf. *Komm.* iii, 363–4.
3. Hypselis(?). Cf. ibid. 364–5.

*A series of Utterances concerning the royal attire* (*Utterances* 414–18)

## Utterance 414

*The king is summoned to clothe himself*

§ 737 O King, take your bright tunic, take your cloak upon you, be clad in the Eye of Horus which is in Weaving-town, that it may make a shout for you before the gods, that it may make your cognizance before the gods, that you may assume the *Wrrt*-crown by means of it before the gods, and that you may assume the *Wrrt*-crown by means of it before Horus Lord of Patricians.

## Utterance 415

*A prayer to the goddess of weaving*

Hail to you, Tait, who are upon the lip of the Great Lagoon, who reconciled § 738
the god to his brother! Do you exist, or do you not? Will you exist or will
you not?[1] Guard the King's head, lest it become loose; gather together the § 739
King's bones, lest they become loose, and put the love of the King into the
body of every god who shall see him.

1. Cf. *Komm.* iii, 373. The interpretation as virtual questions seems to me the more probable solution of the puzzle.

## Utterance 416

*A garment is presented*

This is an intact garment which Horus made for his father Osiris. § 740

## Utterance 417

*The king is clothed*

While(?) the Great One sleeps upon his mother Nūt, your mother Tait clothes § 741
you, she lifts you up to the sky in this her name of 'Kite'. He whom she has found[1] is her Horus; here is your Horus, O Isis; take his hand to Rēʿ at the horizon.

1. Lit. 'the found one whom she has found'.

## Utterance 418

*An address to the sacred unguent*

Hail to you, Unguent! Hail to you who are on the brow of Horus, which § 742
Horus has placed on the vertex of his father Osiris! I place you on the vertex of my father the King[1] just as Horus placed you on the vertex of his father Osiris.

1. Following M and N, cf. *Komm.* iii, 378. The king's son is speaking as the chief officiant at the funeral, as in the next Utterance.

## Utterance 419

*The king is addressed by his son on the occasion of his funeral*

Hail to you, my father,[1] on this your day when you stand before Rēʿ when § 743
he ascends from the East and when you are clad with this your dignity which

is among the spirits! Arms are linked for you, feet dance for you, hands are
§ 744 waved[2] for you.| Isis has grasped your hand and she inducts you into the baldachin. The land is covered(?),[3] the mourners wail.

§ 745 A boon which Anubis, Foremost of the Westerners, grants! Your thousand of bread, your thousand of beer, your thousand of ointment, your thousand of
§ 746 alabaster, your thousand of clothing, your thousand of cattle!| The goose is decapitated for you, the *ṯrp*-bird is slaughtered for you, Horus has dispelled the evil which was on you in your four days, Seth has annulled what he did against you in your eight days.

§ 747 The doors are opened because of those whose seats are hidden; arise,
§ 748 remove your earth, shake off your dust, raise yourself,| that you may travel in company with the spirits, for your wings are those of a falcon, your gleam(?) is that of a star, the night-demon(?)[4] will not bend over you, your heart (*ib*)
§ 749 will not be taken away, your heart (*ḥꜣty*) will not be carried off.| You are a great one with intact *Wrrt*-crown; may you provide yourself with your iron members. Cross the sky to the Field of Rushes, make your abode in the Field of Offerings among the Imperishable Stars, the followers of Osiris.

1. The M-text is followed; T has the 3rd person, which is clearly secondary here.
2. See also § 1366*b*; *CT* i, 272*d*; used of stamping feet § 2014*a*.
3. Lit. 'adorned', 'clad', perhaps in allusion to funeral garb.
4. On *ḫrwty* see *Komm.* iii, 387. I suggest, however, a derivation from *ḫrwy* 'night' with some such meaning as 'ghost', 'afrit'.

## Utterance 420

### *The king is purified*

§ 750 O King, be pure! Cense yourself for Rēʿ! How fair is your purity! . . .[1] . . . yourself among the gods . . . . . . yourself among the people of the God's Booth . . .

1. The rest of this Utterance consists largely of plays on the stem *zmn*, of doubtful meaning. The word does not appear to have any connection with *zmn* 'dwell', §§ 533*e*; 1418*b*; 1420*b*.

## Utterance 421

### *An 'ascension' text*

§ 751 O my father the King, may you climb and mount the sunshine, for to you belongs the half-light which is on the pole(?) of the sky.

## Utterance 422

*The king becomes a spirit*

O King, go, that you may be a spirit and have power as a god, as the successor § 752
of Osiris;| you have your soul within you, you have your power about you, § 753
you have your *Wrrt*-crown upon you, you have your *Mizwt*-crown upon
your shoulder. Your face is before you, worship of you is before you,| the § 754
followers of the god are behind you, the nobles of the god are in front of you.
They recite: 'The god comes, the god comes, this King comes on the throne
of Osiris, the spirit who is from Nedit comes, the Power who is in the Thinite
nome.'| Isis speaks to you, Nephthys calls to you, the spirits come to you § 755
bowing and they kiss the earth at your feet because of the dread of you, O
King, in the towns of Sia.| Ascend to your mother Nūt; she will take your § 756
hand and give you a road to the horizon, to the place where Rēʿ is. The doors
of the sky are opened to you, the doors of the firmament are thrown open
to you,| and you will find Rēʿ standing as he waits for you; he will take your § 757
hand for you and guide you to the two Conclaves of the sky, he will set you on
the throne of Osiris.

O King, the Eye of Horus comes to you, it addresses you; your soul which § 758
is among the gods comes to you, your power which is among the spirits comes
to you. The son has protected his father, Horus has protected Osiris, Horus
has protected this King from his foes.| May you arise, O King, protected and § 759
provided as a god, equipped with the form of Osiris upon the throne of the
Foremost of the Westerners; may you do what he was wont to do among the
spirits, the Imperishable Stars;| may your son succeed to your throne § 760
equipped with your form, and may he do what formerly you were wont to
do in the presence of the Foremost of the Living, in accordance with what
Rēʿ the great god commanded.| May he cultivate barley, may he cultivate § 761
emmer, may he present you therewith.

O King, there is given to you what is yours[1] by Rēʿ; may you speak of § 762
yourself when you have received the form of a god; may you be great thereby
with the gods who preside over the Lake.

O King, may your soul stand among the gods and among the spirits, for § 763
it is fear of you which is on their hearts.

O King, succeed to your throne at the head of the living, for it is the dread
of you which is on their hearts.| May your name live upon earth, may your § 764
name endure(?)[2] upon earth, for you shall not perish, nor shall you be
destroyed for ever and ever.

1. Between *rdi n·k* and *ir(y)·k* T inserts *ꜥnḫ wꜣs nb ḏt n·k*.
2. Cf. *Komm.* i, 160 f., 250; iii, 412.

## Utterance 423

*A text from the Ritual of Offering*[1]

§ 765 O King, receive this your cold water, for you have coolness with Horus in your name of 'Him who issued from cold water'. Receive your natron that you may be divine, for Nūt has caused you to be a god to your foe in your
§ 766 name of 'God'.[1] Receive the efflux which issued from you, for Horus has caused the gods to assemble for you in the place where you went. Receive the efflux which issued from you, for Horus has caused his children to muster
§ 767 for you in the place where you drowned.[1] Ḥar-renpi recognizes you, you being youthful in this your name of 'Fresh Water'. Horus is a soul and he recognizes his father in you in his name of 'Horus of the Soul-of-the-King litter'.

1. Cf. Utt. 33.

## Utterance 424

*A miscellany of short spells*

§ 768 O King, such is your going and these movements of yours, they are the
§ 769 going of Horus in this going of his, in these movements of his.[1] His couriers run, his heralds hurry, they announce him to the Holy One in the East.

O King, your arms are those of *Wpiw*, your face is that of Wepwawet.

§ 770 O King, a boon which the King grants, that you occupy the Mounds of Horus, that you travel about the Mounds of Seth, that you sit on your iron throne and judge their affairs at the head of the Great Ennead which is in Ōn.

§ 771 O King, *Mḫnt-n-irty* will guard you,[1] (even he) your herdsman who looks after your calves.

O King, . . .[2] will guard you more than the spirits.

§ 772 O King, be aware, take this god's-offering of yours with which you are
§ 773 content every day,[1] a thousand of bread, a thousand of beer, a thousand of

oxen, a thousand of fowl, a thousand of all sweet things, a thousand of every kind of clothing.

O King, you have your water, you have your inundation, you have your *bzn*-grain, which have been brought to you by your brother the Old One. § 774

1. Sethe: 'hüte dich vor', but I do not agree with his comment in *Komm.* iii, 420; if the god is in charge of the king's calves, surely he would also guard their owner; why should the king be expected to beware of his herdsman?

2. Meaning unknown. On *zꜣ ṯw* see n. 1 above.

## Utterance 425

*The king is protected and fed*

O Osiris the King, may you be protected! I give[1] to you all the gods, their heritages, their provisions, and all their possessions, for you have not died. § 775

1. The *sḏm·n·f* form of three texts out of four is to be explained by Gardiner, § 414, 5 (Gunn's 'synchronous present', *Syntax*, ch. 7).

## Utterance 426

*The king assumes the kingship*

O Osiris the King, appear[1] as King of Upper and Lower Egypt, because you have power over the gods and their spirits. § 776

1. *Ḫꜥ n·k* is construed as imperative with reinforcing dative; the objection to Sethe's 'du bist erscheinen' is that there is no point in telling the king that he has appeared, for he would naturally be aware of the fact.

*Here follows a series of addresses to the sky-goddess Nūt*

## Utterance 427

'O Nūt, spread yourself over your son Osiris the King that you may conceal him from Seth; protect him, O Nūt. Have you come that you may conceal your son?'[1] § 777

'I have indeed come that I may protect this great one.'

1. A virtual question, answered in the next clause. P erroneously repeats the suffix of the 2nd person after *iw·n* and *ḫnm* in Nūt's reply.

## Utterance 428

§ 778 O Nūt, fall over your son Osiris the King, protect him, O Great Protectress, (even) this great one who is among your children.

## Utterance 429

§ 779 Thus says Gēb:[1] O Nūt, it is well with you; power was yours in the womb of your mother Tefēnet before you were born, that you might protect this King,[2] for he has not died.

1. P only; M and Nt (405) omit *in Gb.*
2. P inserts *m ꜥnḫ wis* after the king's name; interpolations of this kind are not rare in P, but are not part of the original text and have been ignored in the translations.

## Utterance 430

§ 780 You are violent, moving about in your mother's womb in your (*sic*) name of Nūt.

## Utterance 431

§ 781 You are the daughter, mighty in her mother, who appeared as a bee;[1] make the King a spirit within yourself, for he has not died.

1. Hardly 'King of Lower Egypt' in this context.

## Utterance 432

§ 782 O Great One[1] who came into being in the sky, you have achieved power,[2] you have achieved strength,[3] and have filled every place with your beauty; the entire land is yours. Take possession of it, for you have enclosed the earth and all things within your embrace, and you have set this King as an Imperishable Star who is in you.

1. Nūt is addressed.
2. On *n* before *sḫm* and *lmlm*, cf. *Komm.* iii, 435; Edel, § 843.
3. In N read *n lmlm* with P. M; there has been confusion with *nmnm* 'quiver'.

## Utterance 433

§ 783 I have made you fruitful(?)[1] by means of Gēb in your name of 'Sky', for I have joined[2] the entire land to you everywhere.

1. On *n* before *pnd* see Utt. 432, n. 2. The pronoun 'you' is feminine, referring to Nūt.
2. Var. M. N: 'Gēb has joined'.

## Utterance 434

Be far from the earth, for to you belongs(?)[1] the head of your father § 784
Shu; be powerful by means of it, for he has loved you and has set himself under you and (under) all things.[2] | You have taken to yourself every god who § 785
possesses his bark, that you may install(?)[3] them in the starry sky, lest they depart from you as stars. Do not let this King be far from you in your name of 'Sky'.

1. Assuming that *n·ṯ* is a possessive dative, perhaps the predecessor of *n·k ỉmy* 'to you belongs' with following subject (Gardiner, § 114, 4). I find it hard to accept Sethe's suggestion, *Komm.* iii, 44), that *nṯ* may be verbal.
2. Meaning all that is in the sky?
3. Lit. 'be-star', reading *sbꜣ* with Sethe rather than *sk* (P). The sky-goddess is making sure that the gods as stars shine in *her* sky.

## Utterance 435

I am Nūt the granary(?), I have called on the name of Osiris the King.[1] § 786

1. After *msnṯt* read *nỉs·k(wỉ) rn Wsỉr P*. Then follows the titulary of King Phiops I.

## Utterance 436

### *A 'lustration' text*

*The title:* Giving cold water.[1] § 788

You have your water, you have your flood, the fluid which issued from the god, the exudation which issued from Osiris. Your hands have been washed, your ears have been opened. | This mighty one has been made a spirit for the § 789
benefit of(?) his soul. Wash yourself so that your double may wash himself and that your double may sit and eat bread with you without cessation for ever and ever. | This going of yours is that of the successor of Osiris,[2] your § 790
face[3] is in front of you,[4] worship of you is before you, | and it is pleasing § 791
to your nose on account of the perfume of *Ỉḫt-wtt*; to your feet when they tread out your festival measure; to your teeth and your nails when your biscuits(?)[5] are broken.

May you ferry over by means of the Great Bull, the Pillar of the Serpent- § 792
nome, to the Fields of Rēʿ which he loves. Raise yourself, O King, for you have not died.

1. M only.

2. The particle *is* (miswritten in P) fulfils the function normally borne by the *m* of predication. Compare *sty is Wsir* in § 1358*a*.

3. P incorrectly *sr·k* for *ḥr·k*.

4. i.e. you look straight ahead.

5. Sethe: 'Kuchenscheiben'.

## Utterance 437

*A 'resurrection' text*

§ 793 Awake for Horus! Arise against Seth! Raise yourself as Osiris, as a spirit, the
§ 794 son of Gēb, his first-born! You arise as Anubis who is on the baldachin,[1] the Ennead tremble at you, the three-day festival[1] is celebrated for you, you are pure for the New Moon, your appearing is for the monthly festival, the Great Mooring-post[2] calls to you as to Him who stands up and cannot tire, who dwells in Abydos.

§ 795 O earth, hear this which the gods have said! Rēʿ speaks, he makes a spirit of this King, who receives his spirit-form in front of the gods as Horus son of Osiris; he gives him his spirit which is among the Watchers of Pe, he ennobles him as a god who is among the Watchers of Nekhen.

§ 796 The earth speaks: The doors of the earth-god are opened for you, the doors of Gēb are thrown open for you, you come forth at the voice of Anubis, he
§ 797 makes a spirit of you like Thoth,[1] you judge the gods, you set bounds to the celestial expanses between the Two Wands in this your spiritualized state
§ 798 which Anubis commanded.[1] If you walk, Horus will walk; if you speak, Seth will speak; betake yourself to the waterway, fare upstream to the Thinite
§ 799 nome, and traverse Abydos.[1] The celestial portal to the horizon is opened to you, and the gods are joyful at meeting you; they take you to the sky with
§ 800 your soul, you having been endowed with a soul through them.[1] You will ascend to the sky as Horus upon the *šdšd* of the sky in this dignity of yours which issued from the mouth of Rēʿ as Horus who is at the head of the spirits,
§ 801 you being seated upon your iron throne.[1] May you remove yourself to the sky, for the roads of the celestial expanses which lead up to Horus are cleared
§ 802 for you. Seth is brotherly toward you as the Great One of Ōn,[1] for you have traversed the Winding Waterway in the north of the sky as a star crossing the sea which is beneath the sky. The Netherworld has grasped your hand
§ 803 at the place where Orion is,[1] the Bull of the Sky has given you his hand, and you eat of the food of the gods whereof they eat, the savour of *Ddwn* is on you, (even) of the youth of Upper Egypt who came out of Nubia; he

gives you the incense wherewith the gods are censed.[1] The two daughters § 804
of the King of Lower Egypt, his first-born, the two Great Ladies,[3] bore you, Rēʿ has summoned you from the zenith(?) of the sky as Horus who presides over his thigh-offerings, *Sꜣṯwty* Lord of *Sbwt*,[4] as the Jackal, the Governor of the Bows,[5] as Anubis who presides over the Pure Land.[1] He sets you as § 805
the Morning Star in the middle of the Field of Rushes, you being seated on your throne. Your amputated parts are raised up by the Double Crown, Lord of the Bows, your abundance is in the Field of the Gods, whereon they feed.[1] You have your spiritualization, you have your messengers, you § 806
have your intelligence, you have your earth-attackers(?).[6]

A boon which the King grants, a boon which Anubis grants, your thousand of the young of oryx from the highlands; they come to you with bowed head.

A boon which the King grants, a boon which Anubis grants, your thousand § 807
of bread, your thousand of beer, your thousand of *t-wr*-bread which came forth from the Broad Hall, your thousand of all sweet things, your thousand of oxen, your thousand of everything which you eat and on which you set your heart;[1] the *imꜣ*-tree serves you, the zizyphus-tree bends its head to you, being § 808
what Anubis has done for you.

1. *Tp* here, as in *tp-ꜣbd* 'monthly festival', *tp-tr* 'seasonal festival', appears to be a prefix implying regular recurrence; whether it implies in this case a festival lasting three days or one which was celebrated every three days, is not altogether clear. Cf. *JEA* 38, 21, n. 2.

2. Either Isis or Nephthys, cf. *Komm.* iv, 17.

3. Sethe translates this passage rather differently, see his remarks ibid. 30 ff.

4. An unidentified locality named only here and in § 1015.

5. *Pḏwt* here probably refers to foreign peoples, not to the celestial expanses as before; the passage recalls the design 'jackal over nine bows' of the seal of the administration of the royal necropolis at Thebes. Cf. *Ex Oriente Lux*, no. 19 (1965–6), 393 ff.

6. Cf. also § 959*b* and *Komm.* iv, 249.

## Utterance 438

*The king is acclaimed as an immortal*

Oho! Oho! I will make it for you, this shout of acclaim, O my father, because § 809
you have no human fathers and you have no human mothers; your father is the Great Wild Bull, your mother is the Maiden.[1] Live the life, for you have § 810
not died the death, just as Horus who presides over Khem[1] lives. The Great Cavern of Ōn is opened to him,[1] (even he) the Great One of the litter, the § 811
Great One of the carrying-chair[2] of the Foremost of the Westerners. They give you water at the monthly festivals and at the half-monthly festivals, and

you give to the great ones, you lead the lesser ones; yours are the rib-pieces from upon the slaughter-block of the Foremost of the Westerners in accordance with your translation[3] to the possessors of veneration.

1. The Greek Letopolis, modern Ausîm, *AEO* ii, 165*.

2. Grdseloff, *Ann. Serv.* 42, 115 ff., translates *wr ḥts* and *wr ʿ* as 'pédagogue des princesses' and 'des princes' respectively, but such a rendering is completely inappropriate in this context. To my mind 'the Great One of' the litter or carrying-chair is its occupant. The same comment applies to § 892*c* below.

3. [hieroglyphs], var. [hieroglyphs], is to be read *swnn*, infinitive of the causative of *wnn* 'be'; lit. 'according to your being caused to be one belonging to the lords of veneration'. Cf. *Komm.* iv, 46.

## Utterance 439

### *The king is identified with the goddess Satis*

§ 812 I am Satis who takes possession of the Two Lands, the Burning One who receives her two shores; I[1] have gone up to the sky and found Rēʿ standing
§ 813 that I might meet him;[1] I will seat[2] myself beside him, and Rēʿ will not permit that I put myself on the ground, for he knows that I am greater than he,[3] I am more spirit-like[4] than the spirits, I am superior to the superior
§ 814 ones,[5] I am more enduring than the enduring ones,[1] I have triumphed over *Nbt-ḥtp*, I have stood up in the north of the sky and also of the earth,[6] and I have taken possession of the Two Lands as King.[7]

1. The suffix 1st sing. is preserved in P before the cartouche.

2. The endings in *ḥmsy*, var. *ḥmsw*, suggest the prospective *sḏm·f*, and the interpretation as a future tense is confirmed by the use of *n sḏm·n·f* in § 813*b*.

3. Following P; M reads: 'he knows that M is greater than he, for M is great', while N elaborates this into: 'he knows that N is his eldest son, for this N is greater than any god'; for [hieroglyph] at the end read [hieroglyph].

4. *Wnn* here expresses an enduring state in present time. N uses the adjectival predicate *ʿḫ* followed by the particle *wnnt*, a different way of saying the same thing.

5. For this sense of *iḳr* cf. *Prisse* 5, 11 = *Äg. Stud.* 82.

6. Var. P: 'with him'.

7. Var. P: 'as king of the gods'.

## Utterance 440

### *The king is not to be excluded from the sky*

§ 815 If[1] you wish to live, O Horus in charge of your staff[2] of justice, then you shall not close the doors of the sky, you shall not slam shut its door-leaves before[3] you have taken the King's double to the sky, to the nobles of the

god,[4] to those whom the god loves,[1] who lean on their staffs, the guardians § 816
of Upper Egypt, clad in red linen,[5] who live on figs, who drink wine, who are anointed with unguent. He[6] shall speak on the King's behalf to the great god, he shall conduct the King to the great god.

1. Cf. *Komm.* iv, 55. This *ỉn* may well be the origin of Late Egyptian *ỉnn* 'if', cf. Černý in *JEA* 27, 108–9; it appears to be derived from the interrogative use of *ỉn*.
2. For *mʿnḫt* 'staff' cf. *CT* iii, 371*b*; 377*d*; Nt, 692 has .
3. For this sense of *ḏr* cf. *Gîza*, iii, 93.
4. In § 815*c–d* read *ḥr ỉpsw nṯr* with Sethe; N has *n rḫw nṯr* 'to those who know the god', and Nt, 693 follows suit.
5. P. M insert after the ideogram; in § 2261*d* (Utt. 736 in Supplement) we have the writings N, 1055+45; Nt, 693. See also *Komm.* iv, 58.
6. The King's double.

## Utterance 441

### *An offering-spell*

The earth is hacked up, the offering is presented[1] to you before you. May § 817
you go on that road whereon the gods go.[1] Turn yourself about that you may § 818
see this offering which the King has made for you, which the Foremost of the Westerners has made for you; may you go to those northern gods the Imperishable Stars.

1. Sethe: 'gebrochen', but this makes poor sense. The meaning given to *sḳr* depends not only on the present passage (see also §§ 978*c*; 1120*c*; 1323*c*; 1326*a*), but is shown unmistakably *sḳr t-ḥḏ* 'presenting white bread', *D. el B.* ii, 29.

## Utterance 442

### *The dead king becomes a star*

This Great One has fallen on his side,[1] he who is in Nedit is felled. Your § 819
hand is taken by Rēʿ, your head is lifted up by the Two Enneads. Behold, he
has come as Orion, behold, Osiris has come as Orion,[1] Lord of Wine in the § 820
*Wꜣg*-festival. 'My beautiful one!' said his mother; 'My heir!' said his father (of) him whom the sky conceived and the dawn-light bore. O King, the sky
conceives you with Orion, the dawn-light bears you with Orion.[1] He who § 821
lives, lives by the command of the gods, and you live. You will regularly ascend with Orion from the eastern region of the sky, you will regularly
descend with Orion into the western region of the sky,[1] your[2] third is Sothis § 822

pure of thrones, and it is she[3] who will guide you both on the goodly roads which are in the sky in the Field of Rushes.

1. 𓍿𓇋, var. 𓍿, is a writing of the enclitic *tr* > *ty*, cf. Edel, § 842.
2. The suffix is the dual *ṯn*(*y*), referring to the king and Orion, with whom Sothis makes a third.
3. Note the rare independent pronoun *stt* in a participial statement.

*Four Utterances concerned with the sky-goddess Nūt*

## Utterance 443

§ 823 O Nūt, the eyes have gone forth[1] from your head, you have carried off Horus and his greatly-magical, you have carried off Seth and his greatly-magical. O Nūt, you have mustered your children in your name of Lady[2] of Ōn. Assign this King to life, lest he perish.

1. The *n* before *pr·n* in M. N is a particle, cf. Edel, § 843.
2. Sethe: 'Sänfte', but this makes indifferent sense; for *rpwt* > *rpyt* as the presiding 'Lady' or goddess of a place, cf. § 207*e*; *CT* i, 183*i*. See further *JEA* 31, 108 ff.

## Utterance 444

§ 824 O Nūt, you have appeared as a bee;[1] you have power over the gods, their doubles, their heritages, their provisions, and all their possessions. O Nūt, cause the King to be restored, that he may live.

1. See Utt. 431, n. 1.

## Utterance 445

O Nūt, if you live, then the King will live.

## Utterance 446

§ 825 O King, your mother Nūt spreads herself over you that she may conceal you from all things evil, for she has protected you from all things evil, and you are the greatest of her children.

## Utterance 447

*The king departs to the Beyond*

§ 826 Someone has gone to his double, Osiris has gone to his double, Seth has gone to his double, *Mḫnt-irty* has gone to his double, you also have gone to your
§ 827 double.[1] | O King, someone comes, so you will not lack; your mother comes, so

you will not lack; Nūt, so you will not lack; the Great Protectress, so you will not lack; the Protectress of the frightened, so you will not lack.[1] She will § 828
protect you, she will prevent you from lacking, she will give you your head, she will reassemble your bones for you, she will join together your members for you,[2] she will bring[3] your heart into your body for you,[1] so that you § 829
may be at the head of those who are at your feet and give orders to those who follow after you, that you may perpetuate your house after you, and prevent your children from mourning. Your purity is the purity of the gods who have gone to their doubles,[4] your purity is the purity of the gods who have departed, so that they may not suffer(?).[5]

1. [hieroglyphs] old perfective 2nd sing.; *ḏd·k* 'you also', cf. *Dram. Texte*, 53; Edel, § 180.
2. N only.
3. *Int·s*, prospective *sḏm·f*.
4. Not in P.
5. *Nwḏ*; *Wb.* ii, 226, 12, 'Art schlechtes Schicksal'; cf. also *Komm.* iv, 85.

## Utterance 448

*A prayer to Thoth*

O Thoth, reassemble me,[1] that what is on me may cease to be.[2] § 830

1. Probably originally in the 1st person, cf. *Komm.* iv, 85.
2. P adds: 'O Thoth, give him (me) the Eye of Horus.'

## Utterance 449

*An offering formula*

O Horus who is[1] Osiris the King, take to yourself the Eye of Horus. § 831

1. Cf. Utt. 26, n. 2.

## Utterance 450

*A variant of Utterance* 447

Someone has gone to his double, Osiris has gone to his double, Seth has gone § 832
to his double, *Ḫnt-irty* has gone to his double, the King has gone to his double.[1] O King, you have departed that you may live, you have not departed § 833
that you may die; you have departed that you may be a spirit at the head of the spirits, that you may have power at the head of the living. Have a soul, having a soul; be strong, being strong.[1] Someone comes, so you will not lack; § 834
your mother comes to you, so you will not lack; Nūt comes to you, so you will

not lack; the Great Protectress comes to you, so you will not lack; the Protec-
§ 835 tress of the frightened, so you will not lack.[1] She will protect you, she will prevent you from lacking, she will give you your head, she will reassemble your bones for you, she will join together your members for you, she will bring
§ 836 your heart into your body for you,[1] that you may be at the head of those who are at your feet, that you may give orders to those who are in your presence, that you may perpetuate your house after you,[2] and that you may prevent your children from mourning. Your purity is the purity of the gods, the Lords of affairs who have gone to their doubles.

1. P omits.
2. P omits.

## Utterance 451

*A 'purification' text*

§ 837 O King, awake! Raise yourself! Stand up, that you may be pure and that your double may be pure, that your soul may be pure, that your power may
§ 838 be pure.[1] Your mother comes to you, Nūt comes to you, the Great Protectress comes to you that she may cleanse you, O King; that she may protect you, O King; and that she may prevent you from lacking.

§ 839 O King, may you be pure, may your double be pure, may your power which is among the spirits be pure, may your soul which is among the gods be pure.

§ 840 'O King, gather your bones together and take your head', says Gēb. 'He will remove the evil which is on you, O King', says Atum.

## Utterance 452

*A variant of the last*

§ 841 O King, stand up, that you may be pure and that your double may be pure,
§ 842 for Horus has cleansed you with cold water.[1] Your purity is the purity of Shu; your purity is the purity of Tefēnet; your purity is the purity of the four house-spirits when they rejoice in Pe.

Be pure! Your mother Nūt the Great Protectress purifies you, she protects
§ 843 you.[1] 'Take your head, gather your bones together', says Gēb. 'The evil which is on this King is destroyed, the evil which was on him is brought to an end', says Atum.

1. Sethe: 'Himmel', which yields a poorer sense. The determinative  in P is due to confusion with the homophonous word for 'sky'.

## Utterance 453

*The king is clothed*

O King, stand up, don the Eye of Horus, receive it upon yourself, that it may § 844
be joined to you and joined to your flesh;[1] that you may go forth in it, that § 845
the gods may see you clad in it. 'Take the great *Wrrt*-crown', says the Great Ennead of Ōn.

O King, live! The Eye of Horus is brought to you, and it will not be far § 846
from you for ever.

## Utterance 454

*The king embraces all lands in his authority*

O King, you have enclosed every god within your arms, their lands and all § 847
their possessions. O King, you are great and round[1] as the circle which surrounds the *Ḥ3w-nbwt*.

1. See Utt. 366, n. 2.

## Utterance 455

*A 'purification' text*

The canals are filled, the waterways are flooded by means of the purification § 848
which issued from Osiris. O you *sm*-priest, you patrician, you ten great ones
of the Palace, you ten great ones of Ōn,[1] you Great Ennead, sit down and see § 849
the purification of my father this King as one purified with *zmn* and with
natron,[1] the saliva which issued from the mouth of Horus, the spittle which § 850
issued from the mouth of Seth, wherewith Horus is purified, wherewith the evil which was on him, which Seth did against him, is cast out on the ground; wherewith Seth is purified, and the evil which was on him, which Horus
did against him, is cast out on the ground;[1] wherewith this King is purified, § 851
and the evil which was on him is cast out on the ground, being what *Nwt·k-nw*[1] did against you (*sic*) in company with your spirits.

1. An incomprehensible expression, inconclusively discussed by Sethe in *Komm.* iv, 109 ff.

## Utterance 456

*Praise of the sun-god*

Hail to you, Great One, son of a Great One! The roof(?) of the *Pr-wr* is torn § 852
off(?)[1] for you, the *Pr-nzr* serves[2] you, the apertures of the sky-windows are opened for you, the movements of the sunshine are released for you.[3]

§ 853 Hail to you, Unique One, who daily endures! Horus comes, the Far-strider comes, he who has power over the horizon comes, (even) he who has power over the gods.

§ 854 Hail to you, Soul who are in your blood,[4] Unique One of whom your father spoke, Wise One of whom the gods spoke, who takes his place at the zenith of the sky,[5] in the place where you are content. You traverse the sky in your striding, you include Lower and Upper Egypt within your journeyings;⌉
§ 855 whoever really knows it, this utterance of Rēʿ, and recites them, these spells of Ḥarakhti, he shall be the familiar of Rēʿ, he shall be the companion of
§ 856 Ḥarakhti.⌉ The King knows it, this utterance of Rēʿ, the King recites them, these spells of Ḥarakhti, and the King will be the familiar of Rēʿ, the King will be the companion of Ḥarakhti, and the King's hand will be held in the sky among the Followers of Rēʿ.

1. For *zḫz* with the sense of 'violent removal' cf. Utt. 324, n. 13; is the roof torn off to admit the sunshine? If *srw* does indeed mean 'roof' (cf. *JEA* 42, 57), then *zḫz* cannot mean 'run', despite the determinative 𓂻 in M. Sethe translates as 'Für dich läuft der *śrw* des *prj-wr*' without reaching any conclusion as to the meaning of *srw*.

2. For *rw(t) n* 'serve' cf. *Les.* 75, 18; *BD* 494, 7.

3. For the interpretation of *wn* and *snfḫḫ* as passives cf. § 1078*a–d*. *Wn·k* in 852*d* (N) is a miswriting of *wn n·k*, with the two successive *n*'s reduced to one by haplography.

4. Sethe, doubtless rightly, sees in this phrase an allusion to the reddened sun and sky at dawn.

5. Sethe, *Komm.* iv, 117, sees in *wpt pt* an allusion to the separation of sky and earth, but the writing of N speaks definitely of the 'top of the sky', i.e. the zenith, in contrast to the blood-red dawn. For *wpt* clearly in the sense of 'zenith' cf. *Urk.* iv, 1542, 13.

## Utterance 457

*The king is renewed*

§ 857 The fields are content, the irrigation ditches are flooded for this King today. There has been given to him his power thereby, there has been given to him his might thereby.

§ 858 Raise yourself, O King, receive your water, gather together your bones,
§ 859 stand on your feet, being a spirit at the head of the spirits;⌉ raise yourself to this bread of yours which knows no mouldiness and your beer which knows no sourness, that you may have a soul thereby, that you may be effective thereby, that you may be powerful thereby, and that you may give some to him who is in your presence. O King, you are a spirit and your survivor is a spirit.

## Utterance 458

*A spell apparently akin to Utterance 437*

[. . .]| the herdsman waits on you, the New Moon festival is celebrated for you, §§ 860–1
the monthly festival is celebrated for you, the half-monthly festival comes into being for you, the sixth-day festival is celebrated for you, [. . .] comes into being [for you]. [. . .]| hands are given to you, the dance goes down to §§ 862–3
you, the Great Mooring-post[1] speaks to you [. . .].

1. Cf. *Komm.* iv, 17.

## Utterance 459

*The king is restored to life*

O King, receive this pure water of yours which issued from Elephantine,[1] § 864
your water from Elephantine, your *bd*-natron from *Ỉrw*,[2] your *ḥzmn*-natron from the Oxyrhynchite nome,[3] your incense from Nubia.| May you sit on § 865
your iron throne, your forepart being that of a jackal and your hinder part being that of a falcon; may you devour the haunch from upon the slaughter-block of Osiris and rib-pieces from upon the slaughter-block of Seth.| Your bread is the god's bread which is in the Broad Hall; may you strike with the § 866
*ꜥbꜣ*-sceptre, may you govern with the *ỉꜣt*-sceptre, may you give orders to the gods, may you grasp for yourself the hand of the Imperishable Stars,| may you ascend from the Thinite nome, may you descend into the Great § 867
Valley.[4] Stand up! Raise yourself!

1. Cf. *AEO* ii, 2* ff.
2. Cf. *Komm.* iv, 128; perhaps identical with *Ỉrw* determined with [hieroglyph] in § 723*c*.
3. Cf. *Dict. géogr.* i, 175.
4. Cf. *Komm.* iv, 132.

## Utterance 460

*As the last*

O King, your cool water[1] is the great flood which issued from you. § 868

Be silent that you[2] may hear it, this word which the King speaks.| His § 869
power is at the head of the spirits, his might is at the head of the living, he sits beside the Foremost of the Westerners.

Your[3] *pzn*-bread is from the Broad Hall, your rib-pieces are from upon the slaughter-block of the god.| O King, raise yourself, receive this warm bread § 870 of yours and this warm beer of yours which went forth from your house, which are given to you.

1. Following M.
2. Plural, referring to the officiants and mourners.
3. The king is addressed.

## Utterance 461

*The king becomes a star*

§ 871 O King, may you ascend as the Morning Star, may you be rowed as the Lake-dweller,[1] may those who are in the Abyss be afraid of you, may you
§ 872 give orders to the spirits.ˡ Isis cries out to you, Nephthys calls to you, the Great Mooring-post removes (any) impediment for you as (for) Osiris in his suffering.

O you of the Abyss, O you of the Abyss, beware of the Great Lake![2]
§ 873 ˡSit on this your iron throne, give commands to those whose seats are hidden. The doors of the sky are opened for you, the doors of the firmament are thrown open for you, that you may travel by boat to the Field of Rushes,ˡ
§ 874 that you may cultivate barley, that you may reap emmer and prepare your sustenance therefrom like Horus the son of Atum.

1. *Ḥnty* looks like a nisba of *ḥnt* 'swampy lake'; N has the obscure variant *ḥtrty*.
2. See Utt. 466, n. 3.

## Utterance 462

*A 'resurrection' text*

§ 875 O King, mighty in waking and great in sleeping, for whom sweetness is sweet, raise yourself, O King, for you have not died.

## Utterance 463

*The king is the Lone Star*

§ 876 The doors of the sky are opened for you, the doors of the firmament are thrown open for you, (even) those[1] which keep out the plebs. The Mooring-post cries(?)[2] to you, the sun-folk call to you, the Imperishable Stars wait on you.[1] Your wind is incense, your north wind is smoke, you are great in the Thinite nome, you are this Lone Star which comes forth from the east of the sky, and who will never surrender himself to Horus of the Netherworld. § 877

1. A rare independent use of the plural demonstrative *ipw*; cf. *Komm.* iv, 143.
2. Cf. loc. cit.

## Utterance 464

*Appendix to the above*

O you who are high exalted among the Imperishable Stars, you shall never perish. § 878

## Utterance 465

*The king demands a place in the Beyond*

O you gods of the horizon who are in the limit of the sky, if you wish that Atum should live, that you should smear on oil, that you should don clothing § 879
and receive your *pſḳ*-cakes,[1] then take my hand and place me in the Field of Offerings, for you have caused me to be a spirit among the spirits, you have caused me to have might among the gods. I will make for you a mighty § 880
food-offering and a great oblation,[1] I will traverse the sky, I will lead those who are in the settlements, I will take possession of the *Wrrt*-crown therein like Horus son of Atum. § 881

1. The king is speaking; for the 1st person in what follows cf. *Komm.* iv, 146. On *in* 'if' see Utt. 440, n. 1.

## Utterance 466

*The king becomes a star*

O King, you are this great star, the companion of Orion,[1] who traverses the § 882
sky with Orion, who navigates the Netherworld with Osiris;[1] you ascend § 883
from the east of the sky, being renewed at your due season and rejuvenated at your due time. The sky has borne you with Orion, the year has put a fillet
on you[2] with Osiris,[1] hands have been given to you, the dance has gone down § 884
to you, a food-offering is given to you, the Great Mooring-post cries out to you as (to) Osiris in his suffering.

O King, navigate and arrive, but beware of the Great Lake![3] § 885

1. Procyon? Hardly Sirius, which is always the fem. *Spdt*, Sothis.
2. Ornament of a young child. Cf. *Komm.* iv, 151.

3. For the danger of the Great Lake, cf. § 334*a*; the same warning in §§ 872*d*; 1752*c*. On the other hand, in § 1203*b* it appears to be well-disposed to the deceased, while in § 1930*c* it seems merely something to be overpassed.

## Utterance 467

### *An 'ascension' text*

§ 886 O[1] Rēʿ, as for this which you said, O Rēʿ, 'O for a son!', for you are royal,[2]
O Rēʿ, 'he having a soul and being mighty and strong, active of arms and
§ 887 far-striding':| here am I,[3] O Rēʿ; I am your son, I am a soul, I am strong,
I am mighty, active of arms and far-striding.
§ 888 I shine in the East like Rēʿ, I travel in the West like Khoprer, I live on
what Horus Lord of the sky lives on by decree of Horus Lord of the sky.
§ 889 I am pure, O Rēʿ,| I go down to my seat, I take my oar, I row Rēʿ when
traversing the sky, (even I) a star of gold, the flash[4] of the Bull of the sunshine; a spear of gold which appertains to Him who traverses the sky.
§ 890 Someone flies up, I fly up from you, O men; I am not for the earth, I am
§ 891 for the sky.| O you local god of mine, my double is beside you, for I have
soared to the sky as a heron, I have kissed the sky as a falcon, I have reached
§ 892 the sky as a locust[5] which hides(?) the sun.| I have not opposed the King,[6]
I have not succoured Bastet,[7] I will not act the dancer(?)[8] as the great one
of the carrying-chair.[9]
§ 893 Is there a son of Rēʿ who will prepare his place? Then I will prepare my
place. Is there a son of Rēʿ who will be hale? Then will I be hale. (Or) one
who will be hungry? Then will I be hungry.

1. On the interjection *wy* cf. Edel, § 864; it occurs also in *CT* ii, 211*a*.

2. *Ỉt(y)* in *ỉt ṯw* can be only a predicative adjective 'royal' derived from *ỉt(y)* 'king', because it has a dependent pronoun as subject. It can hardly be a 'temporaler Zustandsatz' as Sethe thought (*Komm.* iv, 154), as that would require the *sḏm·f* form of the adjective-verb, in this case **ỉt·k*; it appears to give the reason why Rēʿ wanted a son. For a similar wish by the sun-god, see Utt. 691 (Supplement, p. 51).

3. Emend probably into *mk w(ỉ) ỉr⟨·ỉ⟩* as § 2121*a*.

4. *Sšd*, cf. *Concise Dict.* 249; *JEA* 53, 41; the determinative [hieroglyph] is taken over from the homophone *sšd* 'fillet'.

5. Var. P: 'as Ḥarakhti'.

6. The successor to the throne?

7. Sethe: 'hat nicht die Bastet (zu sehr) verehrt', but it is doubtful if the stem *sm* can ever mean 'verehren'. Its usual sense is 'help', 'succour', *Concise Dict.* 225; since the context requires that a bad action be denied, we must conclude that in any way to assist the dangerous feline Bastet was highly undesirable. For an entirely different tradition cf. § 1111*a*.

8. On *ihꜣbw* 'dancers' cf. *Dram. Texte*, 123; *JEA* 32, 19; in *BD* 74, 3 it is determined with . Sethe's translation 'nicht giebt es einen *ihꜣbw* den NN gethan hat' is grammatically inadmissible; his version would require *n* (= M.E. *nn*) *ihꜣbw ir(w)·n NN*.

9. Cf. Utt. 438, n. 2.

## Utterance 468

*A collection of short spells*

If[1] the Great One spends the day with his double, this Great One having slept with his double, then will this King spend the day with his double,[1] this King having slept with his double. If this Great One awakes, then will this King awake, the gods will awake, the Powers will rouse up. § 894

O King, raise yourself, stand up! The Great Ennead which is in Ōn has assigned you to your great throne, that you may sit, O King, at the head of the Ennead as Gēb, chiefest of the gods, as Osiris at the head of the Powers, and as Horus, Lord of men and gods. § 895

O King, whose form is as mysterious as that of Anubis, receive your jackal-face. The Herdsman waits upon you, (even you) who are at the head of the Conclaves as Anubis who presides over the God's Booth, and you make[1] the Followers of Horus content. May Horus protect you, O King, may Horus make you content with the offering with him. O King, may your heart be content with it in the monthly festival and in the half-monthly festival; may the rejoicing woman rejoice at you as (at) Anubis who presides over the God's Booth;[1] may Isis cry out to you, may Nephthys call to you as Horus who protects his father Osiris. The son has protected his father, Horus has protected this King.[1] As Osiris lives, as the spirit who is in Nedit lives, so does this King live. O King, may your name live at the head of the living; may you be a spirit, O King, at the head of the spirits; may you have power at the head of the Powers. § 896 § 897 § 898 § 899

O King, the dread of you is the intact Eye of Horus, (namely) the White Crown, the serpent-goddess who is in Nekheb; may she set the dread of you, O King, in the eyes of all the gods, in the eyes of the spirits the Imperishable Stars, and those whose seats are hidden; in the eyes of everything which shall see you and shall hear your name. § 900

O King, I provide you with the Eye of Horus, the Red Crown rich in power and many-natured, that it may protect you, O King, just as it protects Horus;[1] may it set your power, O King, at the head of the Two Enneads as § 901 § 902

the two serpent-goddesses who are on your brow, that they may raise you
up,[2] O King; that they may guide you to your mother Nūt that she may take
§ 903 your hand.| May you not languish, may you not groan, may you not suffer(?).
Horus has caused you to be a spirit at the head of the spirits and to have
power at the head of the living. How good it is, what Horus has done for this
King, for this spirit whom a god fashioned, whom two gods fashioned!

§ 904 O King, be a soul like the Souls of Ōn! Be a soul like the Souls of Nekhen! Be a soul like the Souls of Pe! Be a soul like a living star at the head of its brethren!

§ 905 O King, I am Thoth.[3] A boon which the King grants: There is given to you your bread and your beer and these two *pꜣḏ*-balls[4] of yours which came forth from Horus who is in the Broad Hall, that he may make your heart content thereby, O King, for ever and ever.

1. The repetition of *wrš* in two parallel clauses suggests the protasis and apodosis of a conditional sentence; so too *rs* . . . *rs* in § 894*c*.
2. N omits the suffix after *ṯz*.
3. Var. 'Horus'.
4. Of incense.

## Utterance 469

*The king joins the solar bark*

§ 906 I[1] am pure, I take my oar to myself, I occupy my seat, I sit in the bow of the
ship of the Two Enneads, I row Rēʿ to the West, and he establishes my seat
§ 907 above the owners of doubles, he records[2] me above the living.| The doors of
*Bꜣ-kꜣ*[3] which is in the firmament are opened for me, the doors of iron which
are in the starry sky are thrown open for me, and I go through them; my
§ 908 leopard-skin is on me, my sceptre is in my hand,| I am hale and also my flesh,
it goes well with me and with my name; I live and also my double. It dispels
the evil which is before me, it removes the evil which is behind me, as with
the throwsticks of Him who presides over Khem, which remove the evil
§ 909 which is before him and dispel the evil which is behind him.| I see[4] what the
*nḫḫ*-stars[5] do, because so fair is their shape; it is well for me with them and
it is well for them. I am a *nḫḫ*-star, the companion of a *nḫḫ*-star,[6] I become
a *nḫḫ*-star,[7] and I will not suffer(?) for ever.

1. For the 1st person cf. § 909*a*. *c* and *Komm*. iv, 180.
2. *Zš m*, lit. 'writes as'.
3. An unknown region of the sky, cf. *Komm*. iv, 182.

4. The suffix 1st sing. persists in *mꜣ·i*.

5. Cf. § 332*c*.

6. Cf. *Komm.* iv, 186.

7. *Nḫḫ* here is a denominative verb derived from the similar word for 'star', construed with 'complementary infinitive'.

## Utterance 470

### *A collection of spells*

I know[1] my mother, I have not forgotten my mother the White Crown, § 910
splendid and stout, dwelling in Nekheb, Lady of the *Pr-wr*, Lady of the Land of Pastures(?),[2] Lady of the Secret Land, Lady of the Field of Fishers, Lady of the Valley of the Blessed.[3]

'O Ruddy One, O Red Crown, O Lady of the lands of Dep, O my mother,' § 911
say I,[4] 'give me your breast that I may suck from it', say I.[5]

'O my son,' says she,[6] 'take my breast and suck it,' says she, 'that you may § 912
live,' says she,[7] 'and be little (again)', says she.⌉ 'You shall ascend to the sky § 913
as do falcons, your feathers being those of ducks', says she.

O *Hḏhḏ*,[8] bring me this,[9] for I am the Great Wild Bull.

'O Bull of Offerings, bend down your horn and let me pass', say I. § 914

'Where are you going?'[10]

'I am going to the sky[11] that I may see my father, that I may see Rēʿ', say I.[12] § 915

'To the High Mounds or to the Mounds of Seth?'

'The High Mounds will pass me on to the Mounds of Seth, to yonder tall § 916
sycamore in the east of the sky, quivering (of leaves)(?), on which the gods sit,⌉ because I am a living[13] falcon who explores the firmament; because I am § 917
the great steering-oar which conveys the . . .[14] of the sky; because I am one great of pace[15] and far-striding.

I have bathed in the Field of Rushes, I am clothed in the Field of Khoprer, § 918
and I find Rēʿ there.⌉ When Rēʿ ascends in the East, he will find me there;[16] § 919
when Rēʿ comes to the West, he will find me there; (as for) the fair place[17] in which Rēʿ walks, he will find me there.

1. For the 1st person cf. *Komm.* iv, 189.

2. *Tꜣ sml*; the latter word is perhaps a variant of *sm* 'pastures', etc., *Concise Dict.* 225. Sethe has 'des verehrungswürdigen Land', following his regular mistranslation of *sm*.

3. For *ḥtptyw* cf. *D. el B.* iv, 114, determined with 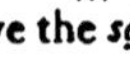.

4. P has *i·ky*, old perfective 1st sing.; P and M have the *sḏm·n·f* form *kw·n* in the 3rd person. On this and the following passages cf. *JEA* 21, 177 ff.

5. N only.
6. *ỉ·t(y)*, old perfective 3rd sing.
7. P only.
8. A brief invocation of the celestial ferryman, cf. *Komm.* iv, 193.
9. The ferry-boat.
10. The bull questions the king. The suffix *·f* in *sḏr·f* (P) is an obvious error for *·k*.
11. P, as often, unnecessarily adds *n ꜥnḫ wꜣs nb* 'for all life and dominion'. Such interpolations are ignored in the translation.
12. *ỉ·k* for *ỉ·ky*, cf. n. 4 above.
13. Var. 'content'.
14. *Ḫꜣtnwy*, dual noun of unknown meaning.
15. Lit. 'sole' of foot.
16. Var. 'in the horizon'.
17. Lit. apparently 'place of goodness'.

## Utterance 471

*An 'ascension' text*

§ 920 I am[1] the essence of a god, the son of a god,[2] the messenger of a god; I have come that I may bathe in the Field of Rushes and that I may go down to the
§ 921 Field of Kenzet.| The Followers of Horus cleanse me, they bathe me, they dry me, they recite for me 'The Spell for Him who is on the Right Way', they
§ 922 recite for me 'The Spell of Him who ascends',| and I ascend to the sky. I will[3] go aboard this bark of Rēꜥ, it is I who will command on my own account
§ 923 those gods who row him.| Every god will rejoice at meeting me just at they rejoice at meeting Rēꜥ when he ascends from the eastern side of the sky in peace, in peace.

1. Cf. *Komm.* iv, 199.
2. N only.
3. Future time is confirmed by *in* + noun + *sḏm·f* in the next sentence (P).

## Utterance 472

*A 'ferryman' text*

§ 924 The sky quivers, the earth quakes before me, for I[1] am a magician, I possess
§ 925 magic.| I have come that I may glorify Orion, that I may set Osiris at the head, that I may set the gods upon their thrones. O *Mꜣ-ḥꜣ·f*, Bull of the gods, bring me this[2] and set me on yonder side.

1. The 1st person is regular in 'ferryman' texts. See also *Komm.* iv, 204.
2. The ferry-boat.

## Utterance 473

*The king crosses the celestial river*

The reed-floats of the sky are set down for Rēʿ by the Day-bark § 926
That Rēʿ may cross on them to Ḥarakhti at the horizon.
The reed-floats of the sky are set down for Ḥarakhti by the Night-bark
That Ḥarakhti may cross on them to Rēʿ at the horizon.
The reed-floats of the sky are brought down to me[1] by the Day-bark § 927
That I may go up on them to Rēʿ at the horizon.
The reed-floats of the sky are brought down to me by the Night-bark
That I may go up on them to Ḥarakhti at the horizon.

I go up on this eastern side of the sky where the gods were born, and I am § 928
born as Horus, as Him of the horizon;| I am vindicated and my double is § 929
vindicated; Sothis is my sister, the Morning Star is my offspring.| I have § 930
found the spirits with their mouths equipped, who sit on the shores of the Lake of *Sḥsḥ*, the drinking-bowl[2] of the spirit whose mouth is an owner of equipment.[3]

'Who are you?',[4] say they to me, say the spirits with their mouths equipped.

'I am a spirit with his mouth equipped.'

'How has this happened to you', say they to me, say the spirits with their § 931
mouths equipped, 'that you have come to this place more noble than any place?'

'I have come[5] to this place more noble than any place (because): § 932
'The reed-floats of the sky were set down for Rēʿ by the Day-bark
'That Rēʿ might cross on them to Ḥarakhti at the horizon.
'The reed-floats of the sky were set down for Ḥarakhti by the Night-bark
'That Ḥarakhti might cross on them to Rēʿ at the horizon.
'The reed-floats of the sky were brought down to me by the Day-bark
'That I might go up on them to Rēʿ at the horizon.
'The reed-floats of the sky were brought down to me by the Night-bark § 933
'That I might go up on them to Ḥarakhti at the horizon.

'I go up on this eastern side of the sky where the gods were born, and I am § 934
born as Horus, as Him of the horizon;| I am vindicated and my double is § 935
vindicated, so acclaim me and acclaim my double, for Sothis is my sister, the
Morning Star is my offspring.| I will come with you and wander with you § 936
in the Field of Rushes; I will serve as herdsman with you[6] in the Field of
Turquoise;| I will eat of what you eat, I will live on what you live on, I will § 937
be clad in that with which you are clad, I will be anointed with that with

which you are anointed, I will take water with you from the Nurse-canal, the drinking-bowl of the spirit whose mouth is the owner of equipment.'[7]

§ 938 I sit at the head of the Great Conclave and give orders to the spirit whose mouth is the owner of equipment; I sit on the bank of the Lake of *Sḥsḥ* and I give orders to the spirit whose mouth is the owner of equipment.

1. For the 1st person cf. Utt. 266, n. 1; confirmed in the present instance by *shꜣ n⟨·i⟩* in § 927*c* (P).
2. The aforesaid lake; a similar figure in § 937*f*.
3. i.e. who can say all the spells necessary for survival in the Beyond; a curious variant of the commoner *ꜣḫw m r·sn ꜥpr*, e.g. §§ 930*a*. *c*.
4. Cf. de Buck in *Archiv Orientální*, 20, 397 ff.; emend into *in m tr·k*.
5. The king's reply to the last question consists in part of a repetition of §§ 926–9, and continues to the end of § 937.
6. Var. P: 'like your herdsman'.
7. The king's long speech ends here; § 938 is a sort of general summing up of the situation addressed to the world at large.

## Utterance 474

### *A variant of Utterance 306*

§ 939 'How lovely to see!' says she, namely Isis; 'How pleasing to behold!' says
§ 940 she, namely Nephthys, to my father,[1] to the King,| when he ascends to the sky among the stars, among the Imperishable Stars. His power is on him,
§ 941 his terror is about him, his magic is at his feet,| and he goes thereby to his mother Nūt, he ascends[2] upon her in this her name of 'Ladder'. 'I[3] bring to you the gods who are in the sky, I[4] assemble for you the gods who are on
§ 942 earth, that you may be with them and walk arm-in-arm[5] with them.| I bring to you the Souls of Pe, I assemble for you the Souls of Nekhen, and all are yours'—so says Gēb, who has conferred with Atum about this which he has
§ 943 done.| 'The Fields of Rushes, the Mounds of Horus, the Mounds of Seth, all are yours'—so says Gēb, who has conferred with Atum about this which
§ 944 he has done.| 'He[6] has come against you and has said that he will kill you,[7] but he will not kill you; it is you who will kill him,[8] you will make yourself firm against him as the firmest of the Wild Bulls.'

§ 945 Recite four times:[9] O King, long endure![10] You are long enduring!

1. P exceptionally has the writing .
2. Var. M: *iḳ·k*. It may have been that this Utterance was originally in the 2nd person, but the suffix in M may possibly be an anticipation of the speech of Gēb to the king which starts in § 941*c*.

3. The texts show some confusion of persons here. *In·i* of P is correct, for Gēb is speaking to the king, and all texts have this reading in § 942*a*; M has *in·s*, as if it were Nūt who is to do the bringing, while N appears to read *in·sn*, though there is no plural antecedent. Sethe takes *in·i* to be the passive *sḏm·f*, but it seems to me more likely to stand for 'I bring' on the part of Gēb.

4. The plural suffix in *dmḏ·sn* is certainly faulty; read *dmḏ*⟨*·i*⟩ as in § 942*a*.

5. *Ḥr ᶜwy·sn*.

6. Seth, against Osiris embodied in the king. Probably a continuation of Gēb's speech.

7. A rare instance of *oratio obliqua*.

8. Var. P: 'his foe'.

9. A ritual direction to the officiant.

10. Hortative old perfective.

## Utterance 475

### *A 'ferryman' text*

Ahoy, Ferryman! Bring this to Horus, bring his Eye; bring this to Seth, bring § 946
his testicles!| There leaps up the Eye of Horus who fell in the east side of § 947
the sky,[1] and I[2] will leap up with it, I will travel[3] in the east side of the
sky,| I will go and escort Rēᶜ in the place of the gods who have gone to their § 948
doubles, who live in the Mounds of Horus and who live in the Mounds of
Seth.| Behold, I have come and gone, for I have reached the height of the § 949
sky, and I have not been opposed by the Great Ones of the Castle of the
Mace, who are on the Milky Way(?).| The Day-bark is summoned for me, § 950
and I am he who bales it out, for Rēᶜ has set me as a possessor of life and
dominion.[4]

1. Compare *Urk.* v, 146, 17–147, 4.
2. The king is speaking, as in all 'ferryman' texts. Surprisingly M has the 2nd person.
3. So P; N has 'stand' for 'travel'; M has *ḫr* 'fall' again in the 2nd person, reverting to the 3rd from § 948*a* on.
4. So P; M has 'at the head of the eternal ones' (*ḏtyw*), which Sethe, *Komm.* iv, 234 suggests may be a corruption of *Ḏtit* a vulture-goddess, cf. § 500*d*.

## Utterance 476

### *A series of short spells*

The sky is pure for Rēᶜ, the earth is pure for Horus, every god who is between § 951
them cleanses me,[1] and I worship the god.

§ 952 O Keeper of the Way, Warden of the Great Portal, bear witness concerning me[2] to these two great and mighty gods, because I am Weneg, son of Rēʿ, who supports the sky, who guides the earth and judges the gods.

§ 953 I sit among you, you stars of the Netherworld; may you support me like Rēʿ and serve me like Horus;[3] raise me up on high[4] like Wepwawet and love me like Min.

§ 954 Scribe, scribe, smash your palette, break your pens, tear up your rolls![1]
§ 955 O Rēʿ, expel him from his place and set me in his place, that I may be fortunate, bearing the staff. O Rēʿ, expel him from his place and set me in his place,[5] for I am he.

1. It is almost certainly the king who is speaking here, and the same is probably true of the other parts of this Utterance; in § 955*b* the M and N texts are certainly in the 1st person.

2. *Rṯ* in P is quite obscure. It could possibly be a misreading of the hieratic writing of the enclitic *rr*.

3. P omits *mi Ḥr*.

4. P omits.

5. P omits these two clauses.

## Utterance 477

*Osiris is raised from the dead*

§ 956 The sky reels, the earth quakes, Horus comes, Thoth appears, they raise Osiris from upon his side and make him stand up in front of the Two Enneads.[1]
§ 957 Remember, Seth, and put in your heart this word which Gēb spoke, this threat which the gods made against you in the Mansion of the Prince in Ōn
§ 958 because you threw Osiris to the earth,[1] when you said, O Seth: 'I have never done this to him', so that you might have power thereby, having been
§ 959 saved, and that you might prevail over Horus;[1] when you said, O Seth: 'It was he who attacked me', when there came into being this his name of 'Earth-attacker(?)';[1] when you said, O Seth: 'It was he who kicked me', when there came into being this his name of Orion, long of leg and lengthy of stride, who presides over Upper Egypt.
§ 960 Raise yourself, O Osiris, for Seth has raised himself, he has heard the threat of the gods who spoke about the god's father.[2] Isis has your arm, O
§ 961 Osiris; Nephthys has your hand, so go between them.[1] The sky is given to you, the earth is given to you, and the Field of Rushes, the Mounds of Horus, and the Mounds of Seth; the towns are given to you and the nomes assembled for you by Atum,[3] and he who speaks about it is Gēb.

*The king serves Osiris*

Sharpen your knife, O Thoth, which is keen and cutting, which removes § 962
heads and cuts out hearts! | He will remove the heads and cut out the hearts § 963
of those who would oppose themselves to me[4] when I come to you, Osiris,
and of those who would drive me off when I come to you, Osiris.[5] | I have § 964
come to you, my lord,[6] I have come to you, Osiris; I will wipe your face,
I will clothe you with the clothing of a god, I will do you priestly service in
Djedit. | It is Sothis your beloved daughter who prepares yearly sustenance § 965
for you in this her name of 'Year' and who guides me when I come to you.

I have come to you, my lord, I have come to you, Osiris; I will wipe your § 966
face, I will clothe you with the clothing of a god, I will do you priestly service in *Ỉꜣdỉ*, I will eat[7] a limb from your foe, I will carve it for Osiris, I will put it in front of the carvers.

I have come to you, my lord, I have come to you, Osiris; I will wipe your § 967
face, I will clothe you with the clothing of a god, I will do for you this which Gēb commanded me to do for you. I will make firm your hand over the living, I will lift up your hand bearing the *wꜣs*-staff.

I have come to you, my lord, I have come to you, Osiris. I will wipe your § 968
face, I will clothe you with the clothing of a god, I will do you priestly
service. | It is your son Horus whom you begot who has removed me from[8] § 969
the head of the dead and has put me among the gods, being divine.[9] | Their § 970
water is my water, their bread is my bread, their purity is my purity; what Horus did for Osiris, he will do for me.

1. Cf. *Komm.* iv, 249.
2. i.e. Osiris, father of Horus.
3. Sethe: 'sagt Atum', which is equally possible.
4. For the 1st person cf. ibid. 255.
5. N has *dr·f tpw* 'he removes the heads' at the beginning of § 963*c*; in § 963*d* P alone has *dỉ·f n·k ꜥnḫ wꜣs* 'he gives you life and dominion'.
6. Var. P: 'Lord of the Sky', see also § 966*a*.
7. Var. P: *stm* 'destroy'.
8. Var. P: 'who has not placed me at'.
9. Following P. Var. N: 'he has placed me at the head of his divine spirits'.

## Utterance 478

*Invocation of the ladder to the sky*

Hail to you, Ladder of the God! Hail to you, Ladder of Seth! Stand up, § 971
Ladder of the God! Stand up, Ladder of Seth! Stand up, Ladder of Horus,

which was made for Osiris that he might ascend on it to the sky and escort
§ 972 Rēʿ!| You[1] have come seeking your brother Osiris, for his brother Seth has
§ 973 thrown him down on his side in yonder side of *Gḥsty*.[2] | Horus comes with his
power upon him and turns his face to his father Gēb: I am[3] your son, I am
§ 974 Horus;| you begot me just as you begot the god, the Lord of the ladder. You
have given to him[4] the ladder of the god, you have given to him the ladder of
§ 975 Seth, that he[5] may ascend on it to the sky and escort Rēʿ.| Now let the ladder
of the god be given to me, let the ladder of Seth be given to me, that I may
ascend on it to the sky and escort Rēʿ as a divine guardian(?)[6] of those who
have gone to their doubles.

§ 976 The Eye of Horus gleams(?)[7] upon the wing of Thoth on the left-hand side
of the ladder of the god. O men, a serpent is bound for the sky, but I am
the Eye of Horus; its foot is obstructed in every place where it is, but I take
§ 977 my departure as the Eye of Horus.| Desire that I should come among you,
O my brethren the gods; rejoice at meeting me, O my brethren the gods, just
as Horus rejoiced at meeting his Eye when his Eye was given to him in the
§ 978 presence of his father Gēb.| As for any spirit or any god who shall stretch
out his arm against me when I ascend to the sky upon the ladder of the god,
the earth shall not be hacked up for him, an offering shall not be presented[8]
to him, he shall not cross to the evening meal in Ōn, he shall not cross to
§ 979 the morning meal in Ōn.| He who shall see and he who shall hear shall guard
and protect(?)[9] himself when I[10] ascend to the sky upon the ladder of the god;
§ 980 for I appear as the uraeus which is on the vertex of Seth.| As for any spirit or
any god who will help me[11] ⟨when I ascend to the sky⟩[12] on the ladder of the
god:[13] my bones are assembled for me, my limbs are gathered together for
me, and I leap up to the sky into the presence of the god the Lord of the ladder.

1. The suffix 2nd fem. sing. refers to the ladder, here equated with Isis.

2. Cf. *AEO* ii, 9*.

3. Horus in the person of the king speaks. For the 1st person cf. *Komm.* iv, 264 and § 979*c* (M. N).

4. Osiris.

5. P wrongly: 'that the king may ascend'; the suffix in N. M refers to Osiris.

6. The meaning of *tl* is not known, and my suggestion is a pure guess.

7. Translation uncertain, cf. *Komm.* iv, 265.

8. On the sense of *sḳr* here, cf. Utt. 441, n. 1.

9. If I understand him aright, Sethe regards *ḥwn* as a *sḏm·n·f* form, cf. *Komm.* iv, 267 f., but that in two parallel verb-forms one should be *sḏm·f* and one *sḏm·n·f* seems highly unlikely, especially as they appear to have their subjects in common. I therefore have taken *ḥwn* to be a *sḏm·f* form like *zii*, though the meaning assigned to it is a guess.

10. The suffix here must refer to the king, for only he is climbing the ladder.

11. Lit. 'his arm shall be for me'.

12. Sethe's emendation ⟨*pr·f ir pt*⟩ before *ḥr mȝkt* seems certain.

13. There appears to be an ancient omission here also. Just as in § 978 whoever opposes the king will suffer penalties, so here in § 980 we would expect a mention of the benefits to accrue to those who help the king. Sethe would transfer the passage relating to the restoration of the king's body back to § 975, but this seems unnecessary on the assumption of a previous textual omission.

## Utterance 479

*A 'lustration' text*

The doors of the sky are opened, § 981
The doors of the firmament are thrown open for Horus of the Gods;
He goes forth at dawn and bathes[1] in the Field of Rushes.
The doors of the sky are opened, § 982
The doors of the firmament are thrown open for Horus of the East;
He goes forth at dawn and bathes in the Field of Rushes.
The doors of the sky are opened, § 983
The doors of the firmament are thrown open for Horus of Shezmet;
He goes forth at dawn and bathes in the Field of Rushes.
The doors of the sky are opened, § 984
The doors of the firmament are thrown open for Osiris;
He goes forth at dawn and bathes in the Field of Rushes.
The doors of the sky are opened, § 985
The doors of the firmament are thrown open for me;[2]
I go forth at dawn and bathe in the Field of Rushes.

Someone[3] goes forth at dawn and bathes in the Field of Rushes. § 986
Horus of the Gods goes forth at dawn and bathes in the Field of Rushes.
Someone goes forth at dawn and bathes in the Field of Rushes. § 987
Horus of Shezmet goes forth at dawn and bathes in the Field of Rushes.
Someone goes forth at dawn and bathes in the Field of Rushes. § 988
Osiris goes forth at dawn and bathes in the Field of Rushes.
Someone goes forth at dawn and bathes in the Field of Rushes. § 989
I go forth at dawn and bathe in the Field of Rushes.

O Rēʿ, make the womb of Nūt pregnant with the seed of the spirit which is § 990
in her. May the earth be high under my feet, may Tefēnet grasp my hand. It
is Sokar who will purify me, it is Rēʿ who will give me his hand.[1] May I be § 991

pre-eminent at the head of the Ennead, may I take my place which is in the firmament. O *Hnny, Hnny*, O *Ỉpꜣṯy, Ỉpꜣṯy*, take me with you.

1. The texts vary between *wꜥb·f* 'he bathes' and *wꜥb n·f* 'he becomes clean' (construction of Gardiner, § 141). The latter predominates, but in the closely related Utt. 325 and 563 *wꜥb·f* is consistent throughout, so that is the reading adopted here.

2. Although this Utterance shows no outward indication of the 1st person, Utt. 325 does appear to have been originally so composed, so that the 1st person has been used in the translation here also.

3. The interjection *ỉỉ* is used as a reader's direction to indicate an alternative version of the preceding recitation and is not susceptible of translation into English.

## Utterance 480

*Another version of Utterance* 306

§ 992 How lovely to see, how uplifting to behold, when this god ascends to the sky
just as Atum, father of the King,[1] ascends to the sky! His soul is upon him,
§ 993 his magic is about him, the dread of him is at his feet.| He has brought the
cities to the King, he has gathered the nomes together for the King, he has
joined together the *msmw*-lands[2] for the King—that is what Gēb, chiefest of
§ 994 the gods, said about it.| The Mounds of Horus, the Mounds of Seth, the
Field of Rushes, they worship this King as *Dwꜣw*, as *Ỉꜣḥs* who presides over
Upper Egypt, as *Ddwn* who presides over Nubia, as Sopd who is under his
§ 995 *ksbt*-trees.| They lift up the ladder for the King, they erect the ladder for the
King, they raise the ladder for the King. Come,[3] O ladder (*mꜣḳt*), come, O
§ 996 ladder (*pꜣḳt*), may there come your name which the gods have spoken.| He
who ascends comes, he who ascends comes![4] He who climbs comes, he who
climbs comes! He who is lifted up comes, he who is lifted up comes! The
King ascends upon the thighs of Isis, the King climbs upon the thighs of
§ 997 Nephthys,| the King's father Atum grasps the King's hand and sets the King
§ 998 at the head of yonder gods who are excellent, wise, and imperishable.[5] | Behold
this which has been said to you, you gods, lest the King be not at your head;
behold, the King is established at your head as the enduring bull of the Wild
Bulls.

1. So N; P has 'father Atum'. The translation 'father of Atum' is excluded here by the fact that Atum was self-generated.

2. The meaning of *msmw* is not known.

3. 𓇋 is shown to be an imperative addressed to the ladder by the suffix 2nd fem. sing. in *ỉỉ rn·ṯ*.

4. The participial epithets are masculine and therefore must refer to the king.

5. i.e. the Imperishable Stars, see also § 380*b*.

## Utterance 481

*A summons to the ferryman*

O *Iww*[1] *Ḥr·f-ḥ3·f*, ferry me[2] across! The reed-floats of the sky are set in place, § 999
that I may cross by means of them to Rēʿ at the horizon.

The reed-floats of the sky are set in place for Rēʿ, that he[3] may cross by § 1000
means of them to Horus of the Gods at the horizon.

The reed-floats of the sky are set in place for me, that I may cross by means of them to Rēʿ at the horizon.

I ferry across in order that I may stand on the east side of the sky in its northern region among the Imperishable Stars, who stand at their staffs and sit(?)[4] at their East;| I will stand among them, for the Moon is my brother, § 1001
the Morning Star is my offspring; put your hand on me, that I may live.

1. A name or epithet of the ferryman, translated by Sethe as 'Wachtelklage(?)'.
2. In the 1st person as in all ferryman texts; cf. *Komm.* iv, 282; *ḏ3y* in §§ 999*b* (N). 1000*b* (P) appears to preserve the original suffix ·*i*.
3. P wrongly has the king's name; the suffix in N. M refers to Rēʿ.
4. On *ḥdw* cf. *Komm.* iv, 284 f.

## Utterance 482

*The king is summoned to take food*

O my father the King, raise yourself upon your left side, place yourself upon § 1002
your right side for this fresh water which I have given[1] to you.

O my father the King, raise yourself upon your left side, place yourself § 1003
upon your right side for this warm bread which I have made for you.

*A 'resurrection' text*

O my father the King, the doors of the sky are opened for you, the doors of § 1004
the celestial expanses are thrown open for you. The gods of Pe are full of sorrow, and they come to Osiris at the sound of the outcry of Isis and Nephthys.| The Souls of Pe clash (sticks)[2] for you, they smite their flesh for § 1005
you, they clap their hands for you, they tug their side-locks for you, and they say to Osiris:| 'Go and come, wake up and sleep, for you are enduring in life!| § 1006
Stand up and see this, stand up and hear this which your son has done for § 1007
you, which Horus has done for you. He smites him who smote you, he binds him who bound you,| he sets him under your[3] eldest daughter who is in § 1008
*Ḳdm*.[4] Your eldest sister is she who gathered up your flesh, who closed[5] your hands, who sought you and found you on your side on the river-bank of

§ 1009 Nedit,[1] so that mourning might cease in the Two Conclaves. 'O you gods,' speak to him, fetch him.

§ 1010 You shall ascend to the sky, you shall become Wepwawet,[1] your son Horus will lead you on the celestial ways; the sky is given to you, the earth is given to you, the Field of Rushes is given to you in company with these two great gods who come out of Ōn.

1. Gunn, *Syntax*, 73 translates as 'am giving', but the rendering as a present perfect is indicated by *ir·n·i* in § 1003*c*, which can hardly be understood as 'which I am making'; the officiant could offer only bread already made.

2. In § 2014*a* this verb is used of clapping hands. Here apparently it is used pregnantly without expressed object, but note the determinative. The intransitive meaning 'dance' seems out of place in this context.

3. So N, as also § 1977*d*; P. M have 'his'.

4. An unknown locality, cf. *Komm.* iv, 291 f.

5. Sethe translates *ḳfnt ḏrwt·k* as 'die deine Hände aufgelesen hat', but with some doubts. He does not quote an occurrence of this stem with the determinative  in the sense of 'bend' the arms in respect, § 1213*b*. In the present instance the determinative has the form , as if the stem meant 'bend over', and I would suggest that the goddess has 'bent over', i.e. closed the hands of Osiris lying limply open in death, and by so doing has restored their natural functions.  of § 1213*b* could conceivably be due to a misunderstanding of a hieratic .

## Utterance 483

### *A 'resurrection' text*

§ 1011 The libation is poured and Wepwawet is on high. Wake up, you sleepers!

§ 1012 Rouse up, you watchers! Wake up, Horus![1] Raise yourself, Osiris the King, you first-born son of Gēb, at whom the Great Ennead tremble! May you be pure at the monthly festival, may you be manifest at the New Moon, may the three-day festival be celebrated for you. The Great Mooring-post calls

§ 1013 to you as to Him who stands up and cannot tire, who dwells in Abydos.[1] O earth, hear this which Gēb said when he spiritualized Osiris as a god; the watchers of Pe install him, the watchers of Nekhen ennoble him as Sokar who presides over *Pḏw-š*[1], (as) Horus, Ḥa, and Ḥemen.

§ 1014 The earth speaks, the gate of the earth-god[2] is open, the doors of Gēb are

§ 1015 opened for you in your presence and your speech goes up to Anubis,[1] your dignity which came forth from the mouth of Anubis is that of Horus *Ḫnty-mnwt·f*, of *Sꜣṯwty* Lord of *Sbwt*, of the Jackal of Upper Egypt, and of the Governor of the Great Ennead.

§ 1016 May you remove yourself to the sky upon your iron throne, may you cross the lake, may your face be . . .[3] in the north of the sky, may Rēʿ summon

you from the zenith(?) of the sky; may you mount up to the god and may Seth[4] be brotherly to you;| may the savour of *Ddwn*, the youth of Upper § 1017
Egypt, be on you and may he give to you his pure incense which he burned for the gods at the birth of the twin daughters of the King of Lower Egypt who are upon the Lord of the Great One.[5]| May you have abundance of § 1018
green herbs whereof the children of Gēb had abundance,[6] may your amputated parts be raised up, having power over the Bows.

A boon which Anubis grants: the *imꜣ*-tree shall serve you, the zizyphus- § 1019
tree shall bow its head to you, you shall circumambulate the sky like *Zwnṯw*.[7]

1. Cf. Utt. 300, n. 4.
2. Var. P: 'the Netherworld'.
3. *Ḫrwi*, meaning unknown.
4. Var. P: 'Horus'.
5. Compare § 804*a*.
6. A curious writing of *bꜣḫḫw* in P and M.
7. See *Komm.* iv, 301.

## Utterance 484

### *An 'ascension' text*

I am[1] the Great One[2] who ascends to the sky [. . .| '. . .] in peace' says she. §§ 1020–1
'My son the King has come in peace', says she, namely Nūt, 'without any whip having fallen on his back, without anything evil having fallen on his hands;[3] I will not allow him to fall, I will not allow him to slip.'[4]

I am[5] the primeval hill of the land in the midst of the sea, whose hand no § 1022
earthlings have grasped, and no earthlings have grasped [my] hand [. . .] earthlings; Shu presses down the earth under [my(?)] feet [. . .]| that is what § 1023
he has done.[6] He separates me from my brother ʿAnti and reunites me with my brother ʿAfti;[7]| his name lives because of natron, and he is divine. I live § 1024
on what he lives on, on the *t-wr*-loaf behind the god. I am a breaker of commands, a breaker of commands who is at your feet, you gods.

1. For the original 1st person cf. *sn·i*, § 1023*b*.
2. Or possibly 'the swallow'.
3. Cf. *JEA* 34, 28.
4. For *znbꜣ* 'slip' cf. also § 1536*a*; *CT* ii, 118*d. e.*
5. The king speaks.
6. On the construction with *ḥm pw* cf. Edel, § 840.
7. See n. 1 above.

## Utterance 485

*Another 'ascension' text*

§ 1025 [The doors of the sky] are opened [for you, the doors of the firmament are
§ 1026 thrown open for you . . . the Mansion of] Horus which is in the sky.¹ As for any god who will take me[1] to the sky, may he live and endure; bulls shall be slaughtered for him, forelegs shall be cut off for him, and he shall ascend to the
§ 1027 Mansion of Horus which is in the sky;¹ but as for any god who will not take me to the sky, he shall not have honour, he shall not possess a leopard-skin, he shall not taste *pꜣḳ*-bread, and he shall not ascend to the Mansion of Horus
§ 1028 which is in the sky on that day when judgement is made ¹ [. . .].

1. For the 1st person see Utt. 484 and 485A, texts of similar purport.

## Utterance 485A

*As last*

§ 1029 [. . . I have come to you, my father,] I [have come][1] to you, O Rēʿ, a calf of
§ 1030 gold born of the sky, a fatted calf of gold which *Ḥzꜣt* created.¹ O Horus, take me with you, living and enduring; O Horus, do not leave me boatless. I have come to you, my father, I have come to you, O Gēb; may you give
§ 1031 me your hand, so that I may ascend to the sky to my mother Nūt¹ [. . .].

1. For the restorations and the 1st person cf. *Komm.* iv, 310 f.

## Utterance 485B

*The dead Osiris is sought and found*

§ 1032 [. . .] the Two Enneads have [found] a protector who is at his side, the Two Enneads have not found someone who lags behind him. Gēb comes with his
§ 1033 power upon him and his yellow eyes(?)[1] in his face¹ that he may smite you[2] and examine the lands in search of Osiris, and he has found him thrown down upon his side in *Gḥsty*. O Osiris, stand up for your father Gēb that he may
§§ 1034–5 protect you from Seth;¹ Nu [. . .¹ I have protected] Osiris from his brother Seth, I am[3] he who bound his legs and bound his arms and who threw him down on his side in *Tꜣ-rw*.[4]

1. According to Sethe, yellow with glaring rage.
2. Plural, referring presumably to beings named in the lacuna of § 1031.
3. Apparently Gēb is speaking.
4. An unknown locality.

## Utterance 485C

*An 'ascension' text*

O Horus who is upon the *šdšd*, give me[1] your hand that I may ascend to the § 1036
sky, to Nūt. ⟨O Nūt,⟩ set your hand on me with life and dominion, that you may assemble my bones and collect my members.| May you gather together § 1037
my bones at(?) [. . . there is no limb of mine][2] devoid of God.| May I ascend § 1038
and lift myself up to the sky as the great star in the midst of the East.

1. Probably originally in the 1st person, cf. Utt. 485, n. 1.
2. Cf. *Komm.* iv, 316 f.

## Utterance 486

*Address to the waters of the Nile*

Hail to you, you waters which Shu brought, which the two sources lifted up, § 1039
in which Gēb bathed his limbs. Hearts (*ἰbw*) were pervaded with fear, hearts
(*ḥꜣtyw*) were pervaded with terror | when I[1] was born in the Abyss before the § 1040
sky existed, before the earth existed, before that which was to be made firm existed, before turmoil existed, before that fear which arose on account of the Eye of Horus existed.

*The king claims to be of the company of the gods*

I am[2] one of this great company which was born aforetime in Ōn,[3] who shall § 1041
not be arrested because of a king, nor cited to the magistrates; who shall be
neither executed nor found guilty.| Such am I; I shall be neither executed, § 1042
nor arrested because of a king, nor cited to the magistrates, my foes shall not
be triumphant.| I shall not be poor, my nails shall not grow long, the bones § 1043
in me shall not be broken.

*The king is rescued from water and from earth*

If I[4] go down into the water, Osiris will lift me up, the Two Enneads will § 1044
support me, Rēᶜ will put his hand on me wherever the god is.

If I go down into the earth, Gēb will lift me up, the Two Enneads will § 1045
support me, Rēᶜ will put his hand on me wherever the god is.

1. The suffix of the 1st person is preserved in N; read *ἰ·msw·ἰ*.
2. Sethe: 'wohl urspr. 1. Person', *Komm.* iv, 318.
3. i.e. the Great Ennead of Heliopolis.
4. Here also the 1st person is almost certainly original.

## Utterance 487

*An offering-spell*

§ 1046 O my father the King, be a spirit in the horizon, be enduring in Djedit; may
§ 1047 you give orders at the head of the living for ever.[1] Rise up on your left side, put yourself on your right side, and receive this your bread which I have given[1] to you, for I am your son and heir.

1. Cf. Utt. 482, n. 1.

## Utterance 488

*An 'ascension' text*

§ 1048 O King, free course is given to you by Horus, you flash[1] as the Lone Star in the midst of the sky; you have grown wings as a great-breasted falcon, as a
§ 1049 hawk seen in the evening traversing the sky.[1] May you cross the firmament by the waterway of Rēʿ-Ḥarakhti, may Nūt put her hands on you [. . .].

1. Sethe translates *sšd* as 'geschmückt', which does not well suit a reference to a star. I suggest *sšd* 'flash', see Utt. 467, n. 4; so also § 1490.

## Utterance 489

§ 1050–1 If you wish that I[1] should speak [. . .] who sees *Inw* [. . .] opened are(?) [. . .][1] is seen the command(?) [. . .].

1. Traces of an older text which presumably had the 1st person; see Sethe's edition of the text. On *in* 'if' cf. Utt. 440, n. 1.

## Utterance 490

§§ 1052–4 Words spoken to [. . .][1] I am[1] [your] ox-herd [. . .][1] since you two have borne me [. . .].

1. See the older text.

## Utterance 491

*An 'ascension' text*

§ 1055 If I[1] die, [my] double will have power,[2] [for I am the third of those two gods
§ 1056 who ascend to the sky as a pair of falcons, and I ascend on their wings;[1] who descend to the earth][3] as a pair of serpents, and I descend on [their] coils[4] [. . .].

1. For the 1st person see Sethe's original text.
2. Compare *CT* iii, 20*b*.
3. Cf. *Komm.* iv, 328 f.
4. Cf. *CT* iii, 24*a*–*b*.

## Utterance 491A

*An offering-spell*

I am[1] he who knelt in the Abyss, I am he who sat down in [. . . ˡ . . . Horus gives me this bread of his][2] with which he satisfied the plebs, and I eat of it with them. §§ 1057–8

1. For the 1st person see § 1058*b*.
2. For the restoration cf. *Komm.* iv, 329.

## Utterance 492

*Entirely lost*

*Here follow four food-spells*

## Utterance 493[1]

Hail to you who are in control of abundance, who guard provisions, who sit § 1059
in front of the Green Field beside the Lord of the sunlight: may you cause me[2] to eat of the grain[3] which grew there, like Osiris[4] on the Great Flood. It is He who sees with his face who causes (something) to come in to me[5] with Him who eats with his mouth. Those who are in charge of the gifts of the elder gods,ˡ they induct me into abundance, they induct [me into pro- § 1060
visions],[6] (even) the two who preside over[7] the food-offerings of the Field of Rushes; I eat with my mouth like Him with parted hair,ˡ and I defecate § 1061
with my hinder parts like Selḳet. I give food-offerings and share provisions like Him who is tall of plumes, who dwells in the Field of Rushes. Breath is in my nose and semen is in my phallus[8] like Him who is invisible(?) of shape in the midst of the sunshine.ˡ I have seen Nu, I appear upon my road; § 1062
praise is given to me, I am great because of my power, and at the sixth-day festival in *Ḫr-ꜥḥꜣ*[9] I eat of the pregnant cow like those who are in Ōn.

1. See the Supplement, pp. 8–9.
2. For the 1st person cf. § 1061*b* and *Komm.* iv, 331.
3. *Npl*, cf. *Komm.* iv, 331.
4. Cf. JPII, 1055+48.
5. Read *in Mꜣ-m-ḥr·f sꜥḳ n·i*, cf. loc. cit.
6. Var. Nt: 'they induct this Nt into abundance and provisions'.
7. For *ḫntt* read the dual *ḫnty*, cf. *Komm.* iv, 333.
8. Var. Nt: 'breath is in Nt's nostril and urine is in his phallus (*sic*).' Nt is a woman.
9. Cf. *AEO* ii, 131* ff.

## Utterance 494

§ 1063 Someone sits to eat bread, Rēʿ sits to eat bread, water is given by the Two Enneads, [and the flood] stands [on the river-banks. O Flood, I have come to you that you may give me bread when I am hungry and give me beer when I am thirsty].[1]

1. Sethe, *Komm.* iv, 336, emends his original text. From his translation it appears that his revised version should read: *ʿḥʿ rf ỉgb ḥr wḏbw. ỉgb, ỉỉ·n·ỉ ḫr·k dỉ·k n·ỉ t tw·ỉ ḥḳr·kwỉ dỉ·k n·ỉ ḥnḳt tw·ỉ ỉb·kwỉ*, using the M.K. texts *CT* iii, 17*a*–*c* + 19*a*–*d*.

## Utterance 495

§ 1064 O Great Ennead which is in Ōn, Mistress of the Enneads, may my[1] possessions be in front of the Conclave, for my two meals are in [the *ḏdbt*-shrine, my three meals are in the horizon[2] . . .].

1. See the older text.
2. Cf. *Komm.* iv, 338.

## Utterance 496

§ 1065 Hail to you, Food! Hail to you, Abundance! Hail to you, Grain! Hail to you, Flour! Hail to you, you gods [who lay a meal before Rēʿ, who . . . with food, who are on the Great Flood! I shall eat of that which Rēʿ bites, being seated
§ 1066 on the throne of the sunlight].[1] | I am[2] a man of Dendera, I have come from Dendera[3] with Shu behind me, Tefēnet before me, and Wepwawet clad(?)[4] at my right hand. They cause [that Field of Offerings of Rēʿ] to nourish[5] [me, so that I eat after(?) they have been gathered together for me like those who preside over the Ennead, who live on the Great Flood].

1. On the restoration in this Utterance see *Komm.* iv, 339 ff.; *CT* iii, 63*b*–64*g*.
2. See the older text.
3. Cf. *AEO* ii, 30*.
4. A conjecture. For other views cf. *Komm.* iv, 340 f.
5. For *sḫm* read *sʿnḫ*, ibid. 341.

## Utterance 497

### *A 'resurrection' text*

§ 1067 [O King, stand up][1] and sit down, throw off the earth which is on you! Get rid of these two arms behind you, namely Seth! The Eye of Horus will come to you at the ten-day festival while you yearn(?) after it [. . .].

1. Restored from § 1068*b*.

## Utterance 498

*As last*

Awake, Osiris! awake, O King! Stand up and sit down, throw off the earth § 1068
which is on you! I come and give you [the Eye of] Horus; may it belong(?) to you [. . .][1] this joint[1] which is in the Broad Hall. Go up and take this bread § 1069
of yours from me.

O Osiris the King, I am your son whom you begot, and I come with [. . .].

1. Read *ỉswt* ⟨*t*⟩*n*.

## Utterance 499

*A spell to ward off a foe*

Get you back, . . . you who cannot(?) . . . . The door-bolt is drawn back, so § 1070
beware! Stand up by means of my knife.[1]

1. Read *ds·ỉ*, cf. JPII, 1055+57, an otherwise somewhat corrupt version. The prick of the king's knife causes the foe to rise up. Possibly a noxious creature such as a snake or a scorpion is envisaged.

## Utterance 500

*As last*

O you heart yonder, O your heart yonder,[1] get you gone, get you gone! Get § 1071
back, you great hidden one who issued from a hidden limb! See, O man,[2] and beware of the Lake of (the Evil-)doer![3]

1. Sethe translates *ỉb ỉm* as a statement, 'ein Herz ist da', but to me it seems more likely to be a vocative, the repeated *ỉb ỉm* introducing the repeated imperative *ḫtḫt ỉm*. To what specific menace *ỉb ỉm* refers remains obscure.
2. Sethe: 'ein Mann sieht es', but the text lacks an object to *mꜣ*, and an imperative followed by a vocative gives better sense; it is the deceased who is now being addressed. For the non-geminated imperative *mꜣ* cf. Edel, § 601; Gardiner, § 336.
3. Read *zꜣꜣ ṯw š ỉr(w)*, cf. JPII, 1055+58. For this pregnant use of *ỉrỉ* cf. *ỉrwt* 'evil deeds', § 298*a*; *ỉrr* 'evil-doer', *Peas.* B1, 193.

## Utterance 501

*A food-spell*

[. . .] there are provided(?) for me three meals, one [in] the sky and two on § 1072
earth, power [. . .].

*The fragmentary traces recorded in Sethe's edition of the text under Utt.* 502 *belong to Utterances preserved in JPII and Nt, which have been copied in the Supplement, pp.* 10–11 *and numbered* 502 *and* 502A–C. *No additional text of Utt.* 502D (§ 1077) *has been found.*

## Utterance 502[1]

*A serpent-spell*

§ 1073 O *Htty*, *Htty*, you who go on your four coils, wake up, come and lie down in your house . . .[2] O Monster, lie down!

1. Supplement, p. 10.
2. *Wnt* is obscure. It may be the old perfective 2nd sing. *wn·t(y)* 'while you exist', but this is far from certain.

## Utterance 502A[1]

*Sothis is active*

§ 1074 Sothis goes forth[2] clad in her brightness(?),[3] she censes[4] the bright ones(?)[5] who are among them.[6] The striking powers of the city are quiet,[7] the region is content. I have prepared a road that I may pass on it(?),[8] namely(?) what Meref[9] foretold in Ōn.

1. Supplement, p. 10.
2. N has *pr*, Nt *spr*; the former is the better reading.
3. Lit. 'sharpness', perhaps in allusion to the outstanding brilliance of the star.
4. N has *ld*, Nt *sld*; again the former is the better reading.
5. *Spdw*, determined with △△△ in N, ▵▵▵ in Nt, ▵ being perhaps a misreading of △. The meaning of the word is doubtful.
6. It is obscure to what the suffix *·sn* can refer unless vaguely to the gods or stars in general; after *lmy[w]* the text is preserved only in Nt.
7. *Igr* is parallel to *hrt* and appears to be the old perfective 3rd plur. with loss of the old fem. ending. From this point on the text is obscure, and I translate the words without understanding the sense.
8. The fem. suffix *·s* is required after *lm*, but the space in the facsimile and the trace of the sign there shown can fit only *·f*.
9. This deity occurs also in *CT* i, 45*a* in the form *Imrf*, again associated with Ōn.

## Utterance 502B

§ 1075 *Untranslatable. The text is from JPII,* 1055+66, *Supplement, p.* 11.

## Utterance 502C[1]

[. . .] ⟨the sky⟩[2] is complete, the earth is complete, the caverns are complete, and what is in them is complete before these four gods in their goings forth of . . .[3] § 1076

1. Supplement, p. 11.
2. The beginning of the Utterance is lost. The first *tmm* lacks a subject, but the context shows that *pt* 'sky' should be supplied.
3. Entirely obscure.

## Utterance 502D

Come [. . .].[1] § 1077

1. No text has been found to complete this Utterance.

## Utterance 503

*An 'ascension' text*

The sky is opened, the earth is opened, the apertures of the celestial windows § 1078
are opened, the movements of the Abyss are revealed(?),[1] the movements of
the sunlight are released, by that One who endures every day.| This one § 1079
who is before me speaks to me[2] when I ascend to the sky, I am anointed with
unguent and clad in fine linen. I seat myself upon (the throne) 'She who
preserves Justice'.| I am back to back with those gods in the north of the sky, § 1080
the Imperishable Stars; (therefore) I will not perish—the Inexhaustibles,
(therefore) I will not become exhausted[3]—who cannot be dragged out (of the
water),[4] (therefore) I will not be dragged out.| When Montju is high,[5] I will § 1081
be high with him; when Montju runs, I will run with him.

1. Lit. 'opened'.
2. For the 1st person see the older text. Sethe's translation 'Ich sage mir dies vor mir her' makes poor sense; *nw tp-ʿw·l* is surely the subject of *ḏd*. Why should the king speak to himself? Rather is he greeted by 'this one' on his arrival in heaven.
3. i.e. by swimming in the celestial waters, cf. *Komm.* iv, 350.
4. Cf. loc. cit.
5. Sethe plausibly suggests that *Mnṯw* here may be the name of a star.

## Utterance 504

*The king is purified*

The sky is pregnant of wine,[1] Nūt has given birth to her daughter the dawn- § 1082
light, and I[2] raise myself indeed; my third is Sothis, pure of seats.| I have § 1083

bathed in the Lakes of the Worshipping Women, I have purified myself in the Lakes of the Jackals.

*He demands a clear road to the sky*

§ 1084 O Thorn-bush, remove yourself from my road,| so that I may take for myself the southern region of the Field of Rushes. The *Mꜣꜥ*-canal is opened, the Winding Waterway is flooded.

The reed-floats of the sky are set down for Horus
That he may cross to Rēꜥ at the horizon.
§ 1085 The reed-floats of the sky are set down for the Horizon-dweller
That he may cross to Rēꜥ at the horizon.
The reed-floats of the sky are set down for Horus of Shezmet
That he may cross to Rēꜥ at the horizon.
The reed-floats of the sky are set down for Horus of the East
That he may cross to Rēꜥ at the horizon.
§ 1086 The reed-floats of the sky are set down for me,
For I am Horus of the Gods
And I will cross indeed to Rēꜥ at the horizon.

§ 1087 I take to myself my throne which is in the Field of Rushes,[3] | and I descend to the southern region of the Field of Offerings.

*The king worships the gods*

I am a great one, the son of a great one, I issue from between the thighs of the Two Enneads, I have worshipped Rēꜥ, I have worshipped Horus of the
§ 1088 East,[4] I have worshipped Ḥarakhti,| and he is girt with his kilt; if he is pleased with me, he will be pleased with Horus who is on his tongue; if he is pleased with Horus who is on his tongue, he will be pleased with me.

1. i.e. is red at dawn.
2. For the 1st person see the older text of P.
3. § 1086*c* continues § 1084*a*, §§ 1084*b*–6*b* being a lengthy interpolation.
4. M and N omit.

## Utterance 505

*An 'ascension' text*

§ 1089 I have[1] gone up in Pe to the Souls of Pe, I am girt with the girdle[2] of Horus, I am clad with the garment of Thoth, Isis is before me and Nephthys is

behind me,⌉ Wepwawet opens a way for me, Shu lifts me up, the Souls of Ōn § 1090
set up a stairway for me in order to reach the Above, and Nūt puts her hand on me just as she did for Osiris on the day when he died.

*A 'ferryman' text*

'O *Ḥr·f-ḥ3·f*, ferry me over to the Field of Rushes.' § 1091

'Whence have you come?'

'I have come from *ỉw3rt*,[3] my companion(?) is the serpent which came forth
from the god, the uraeus which came forth from Rēʿ.⌉ Ferry me over and put § 1092
me down at the Field of Rushes; these four spirits who are with me are Ḥapy, Duamūtef, Imsety, and Ḳebḥsenuf, two on one side and two on the other.⌉
I am the steering-oar;[4] when I find the Two Enneads, they will give me § 1093
their hands, and I will sit between them to give judgement; I will give orders to whomsoever I may have found there.'

1. See the older text of P.
2. See Utt. 535, n. 12.
3. Unknown locality, cf. *Komm.* iv, 365.
4. Note the exceptional use of the *m* of predication after an independent pronoun in § 1093*a* (older text of P). The M-text strangely puts this sentence into the 2nd person.

## Utterance 506

*The king is various entities*

I am[1] *Zṯty*; I am *Zty-zty*; I am the *Zw-zw* water;[2] I am *Zwnṯw*, the coffer of § 1094
the sky;⌉ I am the double-maker,[3] the spirit of the Kings of Lower Egypt; § 1095
I am the creator who created this land;[4] I am he who . . .[5] the Two Lands; I am he who quivers(?); I am he who will quiver(?);[6] I am Praise; I am
Majesty; I am *B3t* with her two faces;⌉ I am one who is saved,[7] and I have § 1096
saved myself from all things evil.

I am a she-jackal,[8] I am jackal-like; I am Ḥapy; I am Duamūtef; I am § 1097
Imsety; I am Ḳebḥsenuf;⌉ I am *Dwn-ʿnwy*; I am these great gods who § 1098
preside over the Lake; I am a living soul with bearded(?) face, who endowed
his head with divinity,[9] who saved himself and removed himself⌉ from those § 1099
who disturb Her who does what has to be done when She who does what has to be done, and who commands what has to be commanded[10], is at rest; I will help him who does what is good and I will make command on behalf of him who commands what is good.

My lips are the Two Enneads; I am the Great Word; I am one who is § 1100
loosed; I am one who ought to be loosed, and I am loosed from all things evil.

§ 1101 O men and gods, your arms under me! Lift me up, raise me to the sky, just as the arms of Shu are under the sky when he raises it. To the sky! To the sky! To the great throne among the gods!

1. For the 1st person see the oldest text of P.
2. These three names are quite obscure; for *Zwnṯ(w)* next following see §§ 1019; 1152; 1250.
3. Read *irw-kꜣ*, cf. *Komm.* iv, 370.
4. For the meaning of *imn* here cf. *Ḫnmw imn ḥnmmt* 'Khnum who created the sun-folk', Brit. Mus. 826, 10 = *RB* 114, 4. Sethe has not understood this passage.
5. *Ṯmi*, meaning unknown.
6. *Ḳrḳr* is used of the 'quivering(?)' of a tree, § 916*b*. As Sethe remarks, *Komm.* iv, 371, its significance as a characteristic of the king is not clear.
7. Var. 'who saved himself'.
8. *Wnšt* is translated by Sethe as 'Wölfin', but the wolf was not indigenous to Egypt; a species of jackal must be meant. The jackal-gods Anubis and Wepwawet are sometimes erroneously described as 'wolves'.
9. For *ʿšm* as a verb cf. § 1378*c*; *CT* iii, 367*d*.
10. *Ir·ty* and *wḏ·ty* are prospective passive participles, as also *sn·ty* in 1100*c*; cf. *Syntax*, 26 ff.

## Utterance 507

*An 'ascension' text*

§ 1102 O *Iḥmty*,[1] say to him who has that he who has not is here.[2] The *Bʿn*-canal is
opened, the Field of Rushes is flooded, the Winding Waterway is full of
§ 1103 water;| the reed-floats of the sky are set down for Horus that he may cross
on them to Rēʿ; the reed-floats of the sky are set down for Rēʿ that he may
§ 1104 cross on them to Ḥarakhti.| He[3] commends me[4] to my father the moon, for
my offspring is the Morning Star; he commends me to these four children
§ 1105 who sit on the east side of the sky,| he commends me to these four children
who sit on the east side of the sky,[5] to these four black-haired children who
§ 1106 sit in the shade of the Tower of *Ḳꜣty*.[6] | My father is great, my father is great,
and I will be a 'my-father-is-great'.[7]

1. On *Iḥmty* cf. *Komm.* v, 2; who this being may be remains obscure.
2. Sethe regards *ḏd n* as a *sḏm·n·f* form with *nty n·f* as subject and *ʿꜣ* as the word for 'door', translating as 'Gesagt hat einer, dem gehörte was ist, für den es schlechterdings keinen Thürflügel gab'. To me it seems more likely that *ḏd* is imperative with following dative *n nty n·f*, and that *ʿꜣ*, var. *ʿꜣn*, is the adverb 'here', the determinative ▭ being merely phonetic; the final *n* in the N-text can be accounted for by the affinity between *ꜣ* and *n*, as in the well-known instance of the writing *mꜣn* for *mꜣ(ꜣ)* 'see'. *Iḥmty* is announcing to a god (*nty n·f* 'him who has') the arrival of the dead king (*iwty n·f* 'he who has not'), *ntt* being the conjunction 'that'. The king is represented as appealing *in forma pauperis*, having been stripped of everything by death.

3. Presumably Ḥarakhti or Rēʿ.

4. See the older text of P.

5. § 1105*a–b* is apparently a dittograph. M and N omit *i·wḏ* + object in § 1104*c* and in § 1105*a* apparently interpret the verb as a passive.

6. Cf. § 719*b*, where, however, the name of the tower is not *Ḳꜣty* but *Ḥꜣty*.

7. Apparently so, but cf. § 719*b*, where we have the obscure *wn T m wrwt·k, wnn T m wrwt·k*.

## Utterance 508

*As last*

Someone ascends, I[1] ascend; the Mistress of Dep rejoices and she who dwells § 1107
in Nekheb is glad on that day on which I ascend to my place, O Rēʿ.[2] | I have § 1108
laid down for myself this sunshine of yours as a stairway under my feet on
which I will ascend to that mother of mine, the living uraeus which should
be upon me, O Rēʿ.[3] | She will have compassion on me and will give me her § 1109
breast that I may suck it; 'My son,' says she, 'take this breast of mine and
suck it', says she; 'turn about, O you who have not yet come to the number
of your days.'[4]

The sky thunders, the earth quakes, the gods of Ōn tremble at the sound of § 1110
the offering in my presence. | My mother Bastet has nursed me, she who § 1111
dwells in Nekheb has brought me up; she who dwells in Dep has put her
hands on me, and | behold, I have come; behold, I have come, behold, I have § 1112
gone up on high,[5] I will make[6] for myself my meal[7] of the figs and of wine
which are in the vineyard of the god; | the butcher of what is under his § 1113
finger(s) makes a meal for me from it....[8]

My sweat is the sweat of Horus, my odour is the odour of Horus. | To the § 1114
sky![9] To the sky among the gods who shall ascend![10] I am bound for the sky
among the gods who shall ascend! 'My brother is here at my side here', | says § 1115
Gēb; he grasps me by my hand and guides me into the gateways of the sky.
The god is in my seat, the god is happy in my seat, | and Satis has cleansed § 1116
me with her four jars from Elephantine.

'Ho, whence[11] have you come, my son?'

'My father,[12] I have come to the Ennead which is in the sky that I may propitiate it with its bread.'

'Ho, whence have you come, my son?' § 1117

'My father, I have come to the Ennead which is on earth that I may propitiate it with its bread.'

'Ho, whence have you come, my son?'

'My father, I have come to the *Ḏndḏndr*-bark[13] ⟨...⟩.'

§ 1118 'Ho, whence have you come, my son?'
'My father, I have come to these two mothers of mine, the two vultures
§ 1119 long of hair and pendent of breasts who are on the Mountain of *Sḥsḥ*,| that
they may extend their breasts to my mouth and never wean me.'

1. See the older text of P, which shows the old perfective *prỉ·k(ỉ)*.

2. Sethe: 'anstelle des Rēʿ', but the suffix of the 2nd person in *ỉꜣḫw·k* in § 1108*a* shows that 'Rēʿ' must be a vocative.

3. So rather than 'which is upon Rēʿ', for the sun-god is still being addressed, so that we would expect a vocative here also.

4. I question Sethe's interpretation of § 1109*c*. *Mḏr* I take to be an imperative 'turn about' = show movement to demonstrate that you are still alive; for *mḏr* 'turn' cf. §§ 484*b*; 498*b*; 1953*c*–4*a* = Nt 787; *CT* i, 183*c*.

5. Var. P: 'come for life and dominion'.

6. *Ỉry* is prospective *sḏm·f*; the editor of P has changed the *n* of the reflexive dative *n·ỉ* into *·f* but has forgotten to erase the suffix *·ỉ*.

7. *Ḥsmnw* 'meal'—Sethe: 'Reinigungsmahl'—occurs again as  in Leyden V6, 15.

8. § 1113*b* is untranslatable.

9. Sethe reads *ỉry pt* 'zum Himmel gehört', but more probably we have here an exclamation *ỉr pt* 'To the sky!' as in § 1101*d*; the following 'I am bound for the sky' confirms this supposition.

10. Read *prwtyw*, apparently a formation akin to *wpwtyw* 'messengers', *kꜣwtyw* 'workmen', *ʿḥwtyw* 'cultivators', though a plural prospective participle is a possibility not entirely to be excluded.

11. *Sic*, though the son never answers his father's question, but instead states the purpose of his coming.

12. The text is wrongly divided here; *ỉt·ỉ* belongs to § 1116*d*, etc., cf. *Komm.* v, 16 f.

13. A variant of the *Ḏndrw*-bark, §§ 631. 633. 1637. The clause giving the purpose of the king's coming has been omitted.

## Utterance 509

*The king ascends to the sky in an earthquake*

§ 1120 The sky thunders, the earth quakes, Gēb quivers, the two domains of the god
§ 1121 roar, the earth is hacked up, and the offering is presented before me.[1] | I
ascend to the sky, I cross over the iron (firmament), I traverse the *Ḥꜣsw*-
§ 1122 water, I demolish the ramparts of Shu;| I ascend to the sky, my wing-
feathers[2] are those of a great bird. My entrails have been washed by Anubis,
and the encircling of Horus and the embalming of Osiris have been carried
§ 1123 out in Abydos.[3] | I ascend to the sky among the Imperishable Stars, my sister
is Sothis, my guide is the Morning Star, and they grasp my hand at the Field
§ 1124 of Offerings.| I sit on this iron throne of mine, the faces of which are those
§ 1125 of lions,[4] and its feet are the hooves of the Great Wild Bull.| I stand in my

empty place which is between the two great gods, my papyrus-shaped sceptre in my hand.| I will lift up my hand to the sun-folk, and the gods will come[5] § 1126
bowing, with the two great gods watchful beside them;| they will find me § 1127
among the Two Enneads, doing judgement. 'He is the magistrate of all magistrates', say they of me, and they have installed me among the Two Enneads.

1. For *skr* 'present' an offering, cf. Utt. 441, n. 1; for the 1st person see the oldest text of P. The insertion of *ꜥnḫ ḏd* or *n ꜥnḫ wꜣs* at the end of sentences, a usage peculiar to P, has been ignored, as elsewhere.

2. This translation of *tpt ḏnḥw* is due to Gunn.

3. Cf. *Komm.* v, 23. The 'encircling' of Horus may refer to his walking round and round his father's body affixing the funeral wrappings.

4. Perhaps referring to lion-masks on the arms of the throne.

5. *Iwt* is the prospective *sḏm·f* form of this verb; cf. also §§ 306*c*; 554*c*; 624*c*; 642*c*.

## Utterance 510

### *A miscellany of spells*

It is not I[1] who asks that he may see you in this form of yours which has § 1128
come into being for you; O Osiris, someone asks[2] that he may see you in this form of yours which has come into being for you;| it is your son who asks § 1129
that he may see you in this form of yours which has come into being for you; it is Horus who asks that he may see you in this form of yours which has come into being for you,| in accordance with what you said: 'There are § 1130
assembled for me these likenesses(?)[3] which are[4] like the fledgeling swallows which are under the river-bank'; in accordance with what you said: 'A loving son comes in the form of a *zꜣ-mr·f*-priest'.| They[5] row Horus, they row Horus § 1131
in the procession of Horus on the Great Flood.

The doors of the sky are opened, § 1132
The doors of the firmament are thrown open
For Horus of the East at dawn,
That he may go down and bathe in the Field of Rushes.
The doors of the sky are opened, § 1133
The doors of the firmament are thrown open
For me at dawn,
That I may go down and bathe in the Field of Rushes.
The doors of the sky are opened, § 1134
The doors of the firmament are thrown open

For Horus of the Netherworld at dawn,
That he may go down and bathe in the Field of Rushes.
§ 1135 The doors of the sky are opened,
The doors of the firmament are thrown open
For me at dawn,
That I may go down and bathe in the Field of Rushes.
§ 1136 The doors of the sky are opened,
The doors of the firmament are thrown open
For Horus of Shezmet at dawn,
That he may go down and bathe in the Field of Rushes.
§ 1137 The doors of the sky are opened,
The doors of the firmament are thrown open
For me at dawn,
That I may go down and bathe in the Field of Rushes.

§ 1138 The earth is hacked up for me, the oblation is offered for me;[6] I appear
as King, my dignity is mine, my throne is mine; I cross the *Ptrty*-water, I
§ 1139 travel the Winding Waterway,| *Imtt* grasps my hand for herself at her shrine,
at her secret place which the god made for her, because I am pure, the son
§ 1140 of a pure one,| and I am purified with these four *nmst*-jars of mine which are
filled to the brim from the Canal of the God in Iseion, which possesses the
breath of Isis the Great, and Isis the Great dries ⟨me⟩[7] as Horus.

§ 1141 'Let him come, for he is pure': so says the priest of Rēʿ concerning me to
the door-keeper of the firmament, and he announces me to those four gods
§ 1142 who are upon the Canal of Kenzet.| They prepare my right way to my father
Gēb,[8] they prepare my right way to Rēʿ, for my boundary-stones are not, my
land-marks cannot be found, while Gēb, with one arm to the sky and the
§ 1143 other to the earth, announces me to Rēʿ.| I govern the gods for him, I command the god's bark for him.

§ 1144 I take possession of the sky, its pillars and its stars.| The gods come to
me bowing, the spirits serve me because of my power; they have broken their
§ 1145 staffs and smashed their weapons,| because I am a great one, the son of a
great one, whom Nūt bore. My strength is the strength of Seth of Nūbet; I
§ 1146 am the Great Wild Bull who went forth as Foremost of the Westerners;| I am
the flowing fluid, I have issued from the creating of the waters; I am a snake[9]
multitudinous of coils; I am the scribe of the god's book, who says what is
§ 1147 and brings about what is not;| I am this head-band of red colour which went

forth from *Ỉḫt* the great; I am this Eye of Horus which is stronger than men
and mightier than the gods.| Horus lifts me up, Seth raises me; I will[10] make § 1148
an offering, I will pour out a star, I will propitiate the two gods who are
contented and propitiate the two gods who are discontented.

1. Cf. the older text of P.
2. *Dbḥ* is taken to be subjectless *sḏm·f*; the absence of introductory *in* precludes regarding it as a participle as in the subsequent clauses.
3. Sethe: 'Versammelt auch mir zu diesen Einheiten'; cf. *Komm.* v, 32 f. The meaning of the second *twt*, however, is doubtful.
4. As Sethe points out, *nty* is sing. to agree with *nn*.
5. 'They' presumably refers to the 'likenesses(?)' mentioned above.
6. On *sḳr* cf. Utt. 441, n. 1.
7. Cf. *Komm.* v, 39.
8. Var. 'for Osiris King P'.
9. Var. *Nḥbw-kɜw*.
10. *Ỉry* of the older text of P looks like a prospective *sḏm·f*, cf. *iry·i m* 'what shall I do?', *Adm.* 2, 9. For *iry* > *ir* M has *iy* 'come'.

## Utterance 511

*The king goes to the sky in an earthquake*

Gēb laughs, Nūt shouts for joy[1] before me[2] when I ascend to the sky.| The §§ 1149–50
sky thunders[3] for me, the earth quakes for me, the hail-storm is burst apart[4]
for me, and I roar as does Seth.| Those who are in charge of the parts[5] of the § 1151
sky open the celestial doors for me, and I stand on the air,[6] the stars are
darkened for me with the fan of the god's water-jars.[7] | I traverse the sky § 1152
like *Zwnṯw*, a third to Sothis, pure of thrones. I have bathed in the pools of
the morning,| and the Cow who traverses the waters prepares my fair roads § 1153
and guides me to the Great Throne which the gods made, which Horus made
and which Thoth brought into being.| Isis conceives me, Nephthys begets § 1154
me, and I sit on the Great Throne which the gods have made.| *Dwɜw* will § 1155
come[8] to me rejoicing and the gods in homage(?); the Horizon-dwellers
will come to me on their faces and the Imperishable Stars bowing down;| I § 1156
will receive the offering-stone and dedicate the altar, I will hold up the sky
with life and support the earth with joy; this right hand of mine will support
the sky with a *wɜs*-staff, and this left hand of mine will support the earth with
joy.| I will find a fare for myself, (because) the Summoner, the gate-keeper of § 1157
Osiris, detests a crossing without payment(?) being made to him.[9] | I will take § 1158

for myself my breath of life, I will breathe in joy for myself, I will be inundated with god's-offerings, I will snuff the wind for myself, I will have
§ 1159 abundance of the north wind, I will be content among the gods.[1] I will be as effective as *Spd-wr*, I will preside at the head of the Two Conclaves, I will
§ 1160 smite with a sceptre and rule with a staff,[1] I will set a record of myself among men and the love of me among the gods. It is said: 'Say that which is, do not
§ 1161 say that which is not,[1] for the god detests falsity(?) of words.' I am protected, so may you not name me, for I am your son, I am your heir.[10]

1. The shaking of Gēb's laughter is the quaking of the earth, while Nūt's shouts of joy represent the thunder; the phenomena are described more explicitly in § 1150*a–b*.

2. Cf. the oldest text of P.

3. Lit. 'shouts'.

4. Hardly 'dispel' here; it must be the down-rush of hail which is meant.

5. Lit. 'limbs', 'members'.

6. Lit. 'on Shu', the air-god.

7. Cf. *Paheri*, 3, right, where a man fans jars to keep them cool. The figure of speech stands for the clouds and wind which precede a rain-storm and chill the air.

8. *Iwt* is prospective *sḏm·f*, cf. Utt. 509, n. 5.

9. The translation of § 1157 is difficult. I have taken *gmm·i* to be a *sḏm·f* form and *nisw iry-rꜣ Wsir* to be the subject in anticipatory emphasis of § 1157*c*. For Sethe's discussion cf. *Komm.* v, 55 f.

10. The suffix only in P[1].

## Utterance 512

*Speeches by the dead king's son*

§ 1162 My[1] father has remade his heart, the other having been removed for him because it objected to(?)[2] his ascending to the sky when he had waded in the waters of the Winding Waterway.

§ 1163 Anubis comes and meets you[1] and Gēb gives you his hand, O my father, (even) he who guards the earth and rules the spirits. I weep deeply, O my father.[3]

§ 1164 Oho! Raise yourself, my father, receive these your four pleasant *nmst*-jars;[4] bathe in the Jackal Lake, be cleansed in the Lake of the Netherworld,
§ 1165 be purified on top of your lotus-flower in the Field of Rushes.[1] Traverse the sky, make your abode in the Field of Offerings among the gods who have
§ 1166 gone to their doubles. Sit upon your iron throne,[1] take your mace and your sceptre, that you may lead those who are in the Abyss, give orders to the
§ 1167 gods, and set a spirit in its spirit-state.[1] Run your course, row over your

waterway like Rēʿ on the banks of the sky. O my father, raise yourself, go in your spirit-state.

1. Cf. the older text of P. According to *Komm.* v, 60, § 1162 refers to the removal of the heart from the corpse and its replacement by a substitute.
2. On *ḫꜣk·f ỉr pr·f ỉr pt* see ibid. 61.
3. Apparently an allusion to the embalming and funeral of the king.
4. A 'lustration' text.

## Utterance 513

*As last*

My[1] father ascends to the sky among the gods who are in the sky; he stands § 1168
at the Great Polar Region and learns the speech of the sun-folk.

Rēʿ finds you on the banks of the sky as a waterway-traveller who is in § 1169
the sky: 'Welcome, O you who have arrived', say the gods.[1] He sets his hand § 1170
on you at the zenith(?) of the sky; 'Welcome, O you who know your place', say
the Ennead.

Be pure; occupy your seat in the Bark of Rēʿ, row over the sky and mount § 1171
up to the distant ones; row with the Imperishable Stars, navigate with the
Unwearying Stars,[1] receive the freight of the Night-bark. § 1172

May you become a spirit which is in the Netherworld, may you live of that
pleasant life whereof the Lord of the Horizon lives,[1] (even) the Great Flood § 1173
which is in the sky. 'Who has done this for you?'[2] say the gods who serve
Atum.[1] 'It is one greater than I who has done this for me, (even) he who is § 1174
north of the waterway, the end of the sky. He has heard my appeal, he has done what I said, and I have removed myself[3] from the Tribunal of the Magistrates of the Abyss at the head of the Great Ennead.'

1. Cf. the oldest text.
2. Cf. Edel, § 842.
3. Sethe's restorations are confirmed by JPII, 1261+18. For *ỉṯ ḏt* cf. §§ 1098*d*; 1484*c*.

## Utterance 514

Endure(?) [. . .], endure(?), O Tadpole; this [. . .] who presides over Khem § 1175
with his life-amulets on his neck. Your (fem.) seat [belongs to] your son, [your (masc.)] seat belongs to your son, and Gēb has summoned(?) [. . .].

## Utterance 515

*The king is to be ferried across and fed*

§ 1176 O sounding-poles[1] of Horus, O wings of Thoth, ferry me across, do not leave
§ 1177 me[2] boatless.| Give me bread, give me beer, from this your bread of eternity,
§ 1178 from this your beer of everlasting,| for I am he who belongs to the two obelisks of Rēꜥ which are on earth, and I belong to the two sphinxes of Rēꜥ which are in the sky.

*The king serves Rēꜥ*

§ 1179 I go on the reed-floats of the sky which are before Rēꜥ, bearing this jar of Rēꜥ's cold water which cleanses Upper Egypt before Rēꜥ when he goes up
§ 1180 from his horizon.| I am bound for the Field of Life, the abode of Rēꜥ in the firmament, I have found the Celestial Serpent,[3] the daughter of Anubis, who met me with these four *nmst*-jars of hers with which the heart of the
§ 1181 great god was refreshed on that day of awakening,| and she refreshes therewith
§ 1182 my heart for me for life; she cleanses me, she censes me.| I receive my meal[4] from what is in the granary of the great god, I am clothed by the Imperishable Stars, I preside at the head of the Two Conclaves, and I sit in the seat of those who are equipped with (good) reputation.

1. For *smꜥ* cf. *CT* i, 267*f*; v, 147*a*.
2. Cf. the older text of M: also § 1181*a* (P).
3. Assuming a derivation from *ḳbḥw* 'firmament'.
4. *St* here is the prefix of *Concise Dict.* 206–7.

*Here begins a series of 'ferryman' texts*

## Utterance 516

§ 1183 O Trembler, ferryman of the Field of *pꜣꜥt*-land, I am[1] your ox-herd who is
§ 1184 in charge of your birth-place(?),| I am your potter upon earth who broke the
§ 1185 egg(?)[2] when Nūt was born.| I have come and have brought to you this mansion of yours which I built for you on that night when you were born,
§ 1186 on the day of your birth-place(?); it is a beer-jar (*sic!*).| You are a foundling who is ignorant of his father and does not know his mother; may I not name
§ 1187 you to those who do not know you, so that they may know you?| Ferry me over speedily to the landing-place of that field which the gods made, on which the gods carouse on those their days of annual festivals.

1. Texts summoning the ferryman were all originally in the 1st person.
2. Cf. *Komm.* v, 77 f.

## Utterance 517

O you who ferry over the righteous boatless as the ferryman of the Field of § 1188
Rushes, I am deemed righteous in the sky and on earth, I am deemed righteous in this Island of Earth to which I have swum and arrived, which is between the thighs of Nūt. | I am that pygmy of 'the dances of god' who diverts § 1189
the god in front of his great throne. This is what you have heard in the houses and overheard on the streets on that day when you were summoned[1] to hear orders.

Behold the two who are upon the throne of the great god and who summon § 1190
me; they are Prosperity and Health. | Ferry me over to the Field of the Beauti- § 1191
ful Throne of the great god in which he does what has to be done among the blessed ones; he commends them to food-spirits[2] and assigns them to the catch of fowl, | and it is I whom he commends to food-spirits and he assigns § 1192
me to the catch of fowl.

1. P, in the 3rd person, has 𓈖𓇋𓈖 for 𓈖𓇋𓇋.
2. Clearly not 'doubles' here; perhaps to be connected with the later word *kʒw* 'food', cf. *Komm.* v, 84 f.

## Utterance 518

O *Iw*, ferryman of the Field of Offerings, bring this[1] to me, for it is I who § 1193
go and it is I who come, | (even I) a son of the Day-bark whom it bore in face § 1194
of the earth in an unblemished birth by which the Two Lands live, upon that right side of Osiris.

I am the herald of the year, O Osiris; behold, I have come on business of § 1195
your father Gēb; in peace are the affairs of the year.[2] | I have gone down with § 1196
the Two Enneads into the cool waters,[3] I am the plumb-line of the Two Enneads by means of which the Field of Offerings was founded.[4] | I found § 1197
the gods standing wrapped in their garments with their white sandals on their feet; they threw off their sandals on the ground and discarded their garments; 'We were not happy until you came down', said they. 'I speak to you, I have § 1198
made you enduring(?);[5] "Causeway of Happiness" is the name of this causeway north of the Field of Offerings.'

Stand up, Osiris, and commend me to those who are in charge of the § 1199
Causeway of Happiness north of the Field of Offerings just as you commended Horus to Isis on that day on which you made her pregnant. | May they let me § 1200
eat of the fields and drink from the pools within the Field of Offerings.

1. i.e. the ferry-boat.
2. Much expanded in M and N.
3. Hardly 'the sky' as Sethe; one does not descend heavenwards. This seems to be a reference to bathing.
4. Var. P: 'I am the potter of the Two Enneads who founded the Field of Offerings.'
5. The king's reply to the greeting of the gods? The translation is by no means certain, and Sethe's version differs from mine. I read the passage as *ḏd(·i) n·ṯn i·smn·n(·i) ṯn*.

## Utterance 519

*A 'ferryman' text, with others*

§ 1201 O *Ḥr·f-ḥȝ·f*, gate-keeper of Osiris, say to Osiris: 'Let me fetch for the King
this boat of yours in which your pure ones are ferried across in order to
obtain for you the cold water at the (polar) quarter of the Imperishable
§ 1202 Stars',| so that I may ferry across in it together with that head-band of green
and of red cloth which has been woven from the Eye of Horus in order to
§ 1203 bandage therewith that finger of Osiris which has become diseased.[1] | I walk
quite unhindered, for the ordinance of the Great Lake protects me.

The doors of the sky-windows are opened, the doors of the Lower *Ȝȝt* are thrown open; O you Two Enneads, take me with you to the Field of Offerings, in accordance with my translation to a 'Blessed One'.[2]

§ 1204 I smite with my sceptre, I rule with my staff, and I lead the servants of
Rēʿ. Pour cold water, O earth! Burn incense, O Gēb! . . .,[3] you Two Enneads! |
§ 1205 I am a soul who will pass among you, you gods.

The *pȝʿt*-land is opened up, the *pȝʿt*-land is filled with water, the Field of
§ 1206 Rushes is inundated, the Field of Offerings is filled with water,| and they go
to these four youths who stand on the east side of the sky. They bind together
for Rēʿ the two reed-floats on which Rēʿ goes to his horizon; they bind
together for me[4] the two reed-floats on which I go to the horizon, to Rēʿ.

§ 1207 O Morning Star, Horus of the Netherworld, divine Falcon, *wȝḏȝḏ*-bird
whom the sky bore: Hail to you with these your four contented faces which
see Her who is in Kenzet and which dispel the storm for the sake of(?) peace;|
§ 1208 give me these your two fingers which you gave to the Beautiful, the daughter
of the great god, when the sky was separated from the earth, when the gods
§ 1209 ascended to the sky,| you having a soul and appearing in the front of your
boat of 770 cubits which the gods of Pe bound together for you, which the
§ 1210 eastern gods built for you. Take me with you in the cabin of your boat,| for

I am the son of the Beetle, born in *Ḥtpt*[5] under the tresses of (the goddess of) *ỉw·s-ʿꜣ·s*-town,[6] north of Ōn, who[7] ascended from the vertex of Gēb.

I am this one who was between the thighs of *Ḫnt-ỉrty* on that night when § 1211
I flattened[8] bread and on that day of cutting off the heads of the mottled snakes.[9]| Take this favourite harpoon of yours, your staff which penetrates § 1212
the waterways, whose barbs are the lightnings of Rēʿ, whose points are the claws of Mafdet, wherewith I cut off the heads of the adversaries who are in the Field of Offerings.

I have gone down upon the sea; bow your head and bend down your arm, § 1213
O sea! These are they whom Nūt bore, who have gone down upon you with their garlands on their heads and their garlands of the *ỉb*-tree at their throats,| § 1214
who make green the *Nt*-crowns of the canals of the Field of Offerings for Isis the Great, who tied on the fillet in Chemmis when she brought her loin-cloth and burnt incense before her son Horus the young child,| that he might cross § 1215
the earth on his white sandals and go to see his father Osiris.

I have opened up my way among those who possess a catch of fowl, I have conversed with the owners of doubles,| I have gone to the great island in the § 1216
midst of the Field of Offerings on which the swallow-gods alight; the swallows are the Imperishable Stars. They will give me this staff of life on which they live, and I[10] will have life thereby at once.

You[11] shall take me with you to your great field which you have laid down(?) § 1217
with the help(?) of the gods, and what you eat at night when they are bright is the fullness of the God of Food.[12]| I will eat of what you eat, I will drink of § 1218
what you drink, and you will give satiety to me at the pole, at that which is the foremost of its flagstaffs.[13]| You will cause me to sit because of my § 1219
righteousness and I will stand up because of my blessedness; I will stand up when I have taken possession of my blessedness in your presence, just as Horus took possession of his father's house from his father's brother Seth in the presence of Gēb.| You shall set me to be a magistrate among the spirits, § 1220
the Imperishable Stars in the north of the sky, who rule over offerings and protect the reaped corn, who cause this to go down to the chiefest of the food-spirits[14] who are in the sky.

1. *Zỉ mr*; cf. colloquial English 'go sick'.
2. Cf. Utt. 439, n. 2.
3. The meaning of *ndsds* is quite uncertain, Sethe, *Komm.* v, 102 f., suggests 'erschrickt' or 'sich demütigt', but neither of these meanings seems to fit the previous occurrence of this word in § 46*c*.

4. The 1st person is preserved in § 1206e (N), which adds: 'I am King N', and in § 1206f (N).

5. Cf. *AEO* ii, 137*.

6. Named after and identified with the goddess *Ỉw·s-ˁ3·s*.

7. The said goddess.

8. *Zšp*; cf. *Komm.* v, 110 f. The determinative, however, appears to be not a knife-blade but a curved utensil with a handle which was rocked over the dough to flatten it, after the manner of a rolling-pin. The same word and determinative are used of polishing furniture in *Ti*, 132. 133, which seems conclusive against the interpretation of the determinative as a knife. N has the suffix of the 1st person after *zšp*.

9. Cf. *JEA* 29, 36 (33). In *CT* i, 14*d* we find that the heads of the presumably decapitated snakes have been 'knit on' (*ṯs*) by the deceased to himself or herself in Ōn.

10. P curiously has the plural ·*ṯn* 'you'.

11. An unnamed god, probably Rēʿ.

12. Reading *wnmt·k m ḫrw ỉ·ḥḏ·sn* as subject and *m mḥt m Ḥw* as adverbial predicate with *m* of predication; the suffix in *ỉ·ḥḏ·sn* refers to the gods as stars. *Ỉ·ḥḏ·s t3* of M and N is clearly a corruption and makes no sense as it stands. *Ḥw* here is not the god of authoritative utterance but his namesake who presides over food.

13. The determinative of *kwt* clearly represents a pole with cords or stays attached. Sethe takes *ḫntt smwt* to be an alternative name or epithet of the pole and translates as 'die vor ihren Schwestern ist'. In view of the context and the determinatives I have taken *smwt* to be the homophonous word for 'flagstaffs', *Concise Dict.* 230; in either case the sense is that the *kwt* is the most important of all poles.

14. See Utt. 517, n. 2.

## Utterance 520

### *Another 'ferryman' text*

§ 1221 O you four who are at the head of the lock-wearers, as your locks are on your foreheads, as your locks are on your temples, as your locks are on the backs
§ 1222 of your heads, on the top[1] of your heads being dancing tresses,[2] | bring me this ferry-boat, bring me this carrying-boat! It is *Ḥkrr* who ferries them across ⟨to⟩ me in company with *M3-ḥ3·f*. I will cross to that side on which are the
§ 1223 Imperishable Stars, that I may be among them. | If you delay to ferry me over in this ferry-boat, I will tell your names to men whom I know, to everyone,[3] and I will pluck out those dancing tresses which are on the top of your heads like lotus-buds in the swamp-gardens.

1. Lit. 'in the middle of'.

2. Lit. 'dancers'.

3. Cf. *tmw* 'everyone', *Concise Dict.* 299; Sethe's 'denen, die das nicht tun (d. h. kennen)' or Edel's 'die nicht (kennenden)', § 1124, are not convincing, for it is questionable whether such an independent use of the negative verb is possible. The presence of ⌒ can be accounted for by the fact that the negative verb *tm* and *tmw* 'everyone' are virtual homophones.

## Utterance 521

*The king calls for a gift*

Cross the lake, O Bringer![1] Cross the lake, O Bringer! Is it a goose? Then bring it. Is it a duck? Then bring it. Is it a long-horn? Then bring it. § 1224

*The king soars skyward*

May you soar skyward as a *ꜥḥꜥw*-bird,[2] may you fly up[3] as a *it-ḥrꜣw*-bird[4] and go to your fathers who are foremost in *Pḏw-š*.[5] | May there be brought to you this bread of yours which cannot grow mouldy and this beer of yours which cannot turn sour. May you eat this your sole bread alone; you will not give it to whoever (comes) after you, for you have taken it from the *knmt*-bird.[6] § 1225 § 1226

1. I question both of Sethe's alternatives; to me it seems that we have here imperatives spoken by the king to the 'bringer'.

2. A series of wishes on the king's behalf. In P *ꜥḥꜥw* is determined with a heron; this text also has the 3rd person instead of the 2nd.

3. Sethe has connected *ittt·k* with a supposed word *it* 'reed-leaf', but better sense can be obtained by regarding it as a miswriting of *i͟t͟t*, var. *itt*, 'fly up', *Concise Dict.* 34. Mercer translates as 'thou fliest low(?)'.

4. Lit. 'father-of-children-bird', determined in P and N with a heron.

5. A locality sacred to Sokar.

6. It is not quite certain whether *nḥm·n·k* (the suffix is missing in P) is in the affirmative or whether it should be regarded as dependent upon the negation in § 1226*d*. In the translation I have taken the former view. In N *knmt* has the skin-determinative proper to an animal.

## Utterance 522

*A 'ferryman' and other short texts*

O *Mꜣ-ḥꜣ·f*, O *Ḥr·f-ḥꜣ·f*,[1] behold, I have come and have brought to you this re-knit Eye of Horus which was in the Field of Strife;[2] bring me this boat which Khnum built. § 1227

O Ḥapy, Imsety, Duamūtef, Ḳebḥsenuf, bring me this boat which Khnum built, which is in this waterway of the *ḥtm*-bird.[3] § 1228

O Swallower, open the way for me! O storm-snake(?), open the way for me! O Vulture, open the way for me![4] § 1229

Hail to you, Beautiful, in peace! If you love me, I will love you. I rebuff you, O Evil; if you avoid me, I will avoid you.[5] § 1230

1. M omits.

2. Var. P: 'Field of the Rower', clearly a misunderstanding of *ḫnnw* 'strife' in M and N.

3. Var. P: 'the Winding Waterway'.

4. So P: var. M. N: 'Remove yourself from my road'.

5. 𓈖𓇋 is a variant of *nỉ* 'drive away', 'rebuff', etc., *Concise Dict.* 125. In § 1230*d* the sense seems to be 'avoid' rather than 'rebuff'; here the scribe of P has not understood his original and has emended it into *n ỉṯ·ṯ P pn, n ỉṯ ṯn P pn* 'if you do not take this P, this P will not take you'.

## Utterance 523

*A prayer for the king*

§ 1231 May the sky make the sunlight strong for you, may you rise up to the sky as
the Eye of Rēʻ, may you stand at that left Eye of Horus by means of which the
§ 1232 speech of the gods is heard.[1] Stand up[1] at the head of the spirits as Horus
stood at the head of the living; stand up at the head of the spirits[2] as Osiris
stood at the head of the spirits.

1. Hortative old perfective.
2. P adds in apposition: 'the Imperishable Stars'.

## Utterance 524

*A text concerning the Eye of Horus*

§ 1233 I am[1] cleansed with the purification which Horus performed for his Eye;
I am Thoth who protects you,[2] I am not Seth who carried it off; rejoice, you
§ 1234 gods! Be joyful, you Enneads![1] O Horus, meet[3] me, for I wear the White
Crown, the Eye of Horus wherewith one is strong. Be joyful, you gods, over
§ 1235 me when I ascend;[1] my face is that of a jackal, my arms are those of a falcon,
my wing-feathers are those of Thoth, and Gēb causes me to fly up to the
§ 1236 sky that I may take the Eye of Horus to him.[1] I have removed your boundary,
you dead, I have overstepped your[4] landmarks, you obstructors who are under
the hand of Osiris. I have blocked the roads of Seth, I have escaped the
§ 1237 messengers of Osiris,[1] and there is no god who can lay hold on me, there is
no adversary who can oppose himself to my road, for I am Thoth, the
mightiest of the gods.

§ 1238 Atum summons me to the sky,[5] and I take the Eye of Horus to him.[1] I am
the son of Khnum, and there is no evil which I have done. Long may this
§ 1239 word be in your sight, O Rēʻ; hear it, O Bull of the Ennead![1] Open up my

road, make my seat spacious at the head of the gods, that I may take the Eye of Horus to him and that I may cause to be reknit for him that which went forth from his head.[1] I will cause him to see with both his intact eyes, by § 1240
means of which he will make his foes pass away.

Horus has taken possession of his Eye and has given it to me.[1] My savour § 1241
is the savour of a god, the savour of the Eye of Horus is on my flesh, and I am pre-eminent possessing it; I sit on your great throne, you gods, and I am side by side with Atum between the Two Wands.[1] I am he who prevents § 1242
the gods from becoming weary in seeking the Eye of Horus; I searched for it in Pe, I found it in Ōn, I took it from the head of Seth in that place where they fought.[1] O Horus, stretch out your arm to me; O Horus, take your Eye; § 1243
may it go forth to you, may it go forth to you when I come to you.[6] May the Eye of Horus come to you with me, upon me for ever.

1. For the 1st person cf. § 1234*c*.
2. Fem., therefore it must refer to the Eye.
3. Hortative old perfective.
4. ⇐ here and in § 2247*c* (Supplement, p. 73) must be an error for [hieroglyph]; cf. *Komm.* v, 138.
5. *N ʿnḫ* is an addition peculiar to P and not part of the basic text. It is therefore omitted in the translation.
6. See n. 5 above.

## Utterance 525

*An 'ascension' text*

Rēʿ is cleansed for you, Horus is adorned for you, inability to see(?)[1] comes § 1244
to an end, sleepiness is dispelled before the being of the god, the son of the god, and the messenger of the god.[1] Go down into the Canal of Kenzet,[2] § 1245
bathe in the Field of Rushes, for the Followers of Horus will cleanse you, they will recite for you the 'Spell for Him Who Ascends', they will recite for you (the 'Spell for) Him Who Travels'.[3]

Go aboard this bark of Rēʿ which the gods row; rise up, for they will § 1246
rejoice at meeting you just as they rejoice at meeting Rēʿ when he ascends in the east, having been lifted up, lifted up.

1. i.e. in the darkness of night; for the meaning given to *nḫrw* cf. *Komm.* v, 144.
2. Read *mr Knzty*, cf. § 1141*c*.
3. Var. P: 'Him who is lifted up' (*ṯwtw*). Throughout this Utterance I have followed M. N in preference to P.

## Utterance 526

*A variant of Utterance 323*

§ 1247 I have[1] bathed in the Lake of Rushes in which Rēʿ bathed; O Horus, rub my back; O Thoth, rub my feet; O Shu,[2] take me to the sky; O Nūt, give me your hand.

1. For the 1st person cf. Utt. 323, n. 1; here the king himself speaks throughout, without the intervention of a priest.
2. Var. P: 'my feet are the feet of Shu'.

## Utterance 527

*The creation of Shu and Tefēnet*

§ 1248 Atum is he who (once) came into being,[1] who masturbated[2] in Ōn. He took his phallus in his grasp that he might create orgasm by means of it, and so
§ 1249 were born the twins Shu and Tefēnet.| May they put the King[3] between them and set the King among the gods in front of the Field of Offerings. Recite four times: May the King ascend to the sky, may the King descend to the earth.

1. i.e. the primeval god who evolved from the Chaos. The use of *pw* in P shows that we have here a sentence with nominal predicate; *ḫpr*, as Sethe points out, is a participle. N has misunderstood this sentence and has emended *ḫpr* 'who came into being' into *Ḫprr* 'the Beetle', the young sun.
2. On the etymology of *msꜣw* see *Komm.* v, 148.
3. It is probable that this text was originally in the 1st person, but there is no definite indication to that effect.

## Utterance 528

*A 'ferrying' text*

§ 1250 O *Zwnṯw*, you who cross the sky nine times a night, take my hand[1] and ferry me over this waterway; may I go aboard this bark of the god in which the
§ 1251 company of the Ennead rows, and may I be rowed in it.| I will recite[2] for you the 'Spell of the Natron-god', I will recite for you the 'Spell of the Incense-god', for the Incense-god[3] stands at the head of the Great Ennead and the Natron-god sits at the head of the Great Conclave.

1. So P; var. M. N: *smꜣ* 'scalp', 'top-knot'.
2. Prospective *sḏm·f*; P has been left in the 1st person.
3. P omits.

## Utterance 529

*An appeal to the celestial janitor*

O Gate-keeper of the sky, act against that messenger of the god[1] who comes out! If he comes out of this western gate of the sky, use(?)[2] for him this southern gate of the sky; if he comes out of this eastern gate of the sky, use(?) for him this northern gate of the sky. § 1252

1. P omits.
2. *In* here can hardly have its literal meaning 'bring', although Sethe so translates it, and I tentatively suggest the rarer sense 'use', cf. § 696*f*. It may be that the janitor is to 'use', i.e. open, another gate so that the messenger may be induced to return by it before he can harm the deceased.

## Utterance 530

*An 'ascension' text*

Hail to the Ladder which the Souls of Pe and the Souls of Nekhen have erected and gilded! Set your hand on me[1] that I may sit between the two great gods, that my seats may be pre-eminent, that my hand may be taken at the Field of Offerings, and that I may sit among the stars which are in the sky. § 1253

1. Despite the lack of direct evidence, it is virtually certain that the king himself is addressing the ladder. For the 1st person in a somewhat similar text, cf. Utt. 478, n. 3.

## Utterance 531

*A 'ferrying' text*

O you two kites[1] who are on the wings of Thoth, you two who are on the crown of the head of the Wanderer,[2] bring me this[3] and set me on yonder side, for I am on an errand for Horus as one who must have free passage.[4] § 1254

1. A designation commonly applied to Isis and Nephthys in their role of mourners at a funeral.
2. Cf. *Komm.* v, 156.
3. The ferry-boat.
4. Cf. ibid. 157.

## Utterance 532

*An Osirian text*

The *ḏd*-pillar of the Day-bark is released for its lord, the *ḏd*-pillar of the Day-bark is released for its protector. Isis comes and Nephthys comes, one of them from the west and one of them from the east, one of them as a § 1255

§ 1256 'screecher',[1] one of them as a kite; | they have found Osiris, his brother
Seth having laid him low in Nedit; when Osiris[2] said 'Get away from me',
§ 1257 when his name became Sokar.| They prevent you (*sic*) from rotting in accord-
ance with this your name of Anubis; they prevent your putrefaction from
dripping to the ground[3] in accordance with this your name of 'Jackal of Upper
Egypt'; they prevent the smell of your corpse from becoming foul in accord-
§ 1258 ance with this your name of Horus of *Ḥꜣty*.| They prevent Horus of the East
from putrefying; they prevent Horus Lord of Patricians from putrefying;
they prevent Horus of the Netherworld from putrefying; they prevent Horus
Lord of the Two Lands from putrefying, and Seth will never be free from
carrying you, O Osiris.

§ 1259 Wake up for Horus, stand up against Seth; raise yourself, O Osiris, first-
§ 1260 born son of Gēb, at whom the Two Enneads tremble.| The Herdsman waits
on you, the festival of the New Moon is celebrated for you, so that you may
appear at the monthly festival. Fare southward to the lake, cross over the
§ 1261 sea,| for you are he who stands untiring in the midst of Abydos; be a spirit
in the horizon, be long-enduring in Mendes.

§ 1262 Your hand is taken by the Souls of Ōn, your hand is grasped by Rēꜥ, your
head is raised by the Two Enneads, and they have set you, O Osiris, at the
head of the Conclave of the Souls of Ōn. Live, live and raise yourself!

1. A falcon or similar raptor; for *ḥꜣ* 'screech' of falcon, cf. *CT* i, 73*d*–74*a*; of kite, 74*e*. After *ḥꜣt* 'screecher' P inserts: 'Nephthys comes'.

2. In P the cartouche is regularly appended to the name of Osiris from here on; in N it appears in other contexts in §§ 1260*b*, 1261*c*, where it is not found in P; only in § 1262*b* do both texts have the cartouche. It has therefore been assumed that the insertion of the cartouche is secondary, and it has been ignored in the translation.

3. P has *ꜥꜣ* 'door' for *tꜣ* 'ground', doubtless through a misreading of a hieratic copy.

## Utterance 533

§ 1263 [. . .] which issued from [. . .]. The King is the blood[1] which issued from Rēꜥ,
the sweat which issued from Isis.

1. On *ṯr* cf. *Minerals*, 154.

## Utterance 534

### *A spell for the king's tomb*

§ 1264 Thus says Horus: A boon which Gēb grants! May there be benefited(?)[1] the
tomb[2] of him whom Horus respects and Seth protects.

May there be benefited(?) the tomb of him whom Osiris respects and Kherty protects.

May there be benefited(?) the tomb of him whom Isis respects and Nephthys protects, (even) the tomb of the chieftain whom *Mḫnt-ỉrty* respects and Thoth protects. § 1265

May there be benefited(?) the tomb of him whom the slayers respect and those who are among the old ones(?)[3] protect.

I have come[4] and I have installed(?) this house of mine. The hall of this is purer than the firmament, the door which is on it is two opposing bulls(?),[5] and its lock is two evil eyes. § 1266

May Osiris not come[6] with this his evil coming; do not open your arms to him:[7] 'Go southward, go to Nedit; go northward, go to *ʿdꜣ*!'[8] § 1267

May Horus not come with this his evil coming; do not open your arms to him, but let there be said to him[9] this his name of 'Blind of . . .'.[10] 'Go to *ʿnpt*;[11] go northward, go to Iseion!'[12] § 1268

May Seth not come with this his evil coming; do not open your arms to him, but let there be said to him this his name of 'Hare'. 'Go to the Mountains of Blackness(?);[13] go northward, go to *Ḥnt*!'[14] § 1269

If *Ḫnt-ỉrty* comes with this his evil coming, do not open your arms to him, but let there be said to him this his name of 'Spittle'. 'Go to *Ddnw*,[15] you will be found in a trembling condition for them (*sic*); go northwards, go to Khem!' § 1270

If Thoth comes with this his evil coming, do not open your arms to him, but let there be said to him his name of 'Motherless'. 'Go, go southward to Gebelēn(?);[16] go to Pe, to the Abode of Thoth!' § 1271

If Isis comes with this her evil coming, do not open your arms to her, but let there be said to her her name of 'Extensively corrupt'. 'Go southward, go to the Houses of *Mꜣnw*;[17] go northward, go to *Ḥdbt*,[18] to the place where you were beaten!' § 1272

If Nephthys comes with this her evil coming, let there be said to her this her name of 'Imitation woman who has no vagina'. 'Go to the Mansions of Selḳet,[19] to that place where you were beaten (on) your hinder-parts!'[20] § 1273

If the slayers come with those who are among the old ones(?), let there be said to them[21] this their name of 'Blind of . . .'.[22] 'Go to [. . .]!' § 1274

If I come[23] with my double, the mouths of the gods will be opened and will request that I descend to [the Lower Sky, and I will descend] to the place where the gods are. § 1275

§ 1276 If I come with my double, open your arms to me; the mouths of the gods will be opened and will request that I ascend to the sky, and I will ascend.
§ 1277 I have come as *Wpiw*.

A boon which Gēb and Atum grant: that this pyramid and temple be installed for me and for my double, and that this pyramid and temple be
§ 1278 enclosed for me and for my double. This Eye of Horus is pure; may it belong(?) to me.

As for anyone who shall lay a finger on this pyramid and this temple which belong to me and to my double, he will have laid his finger on the Mansion of Horus in the firmament, he will have offended(?)[24] the Lady of the Mansion[25]
§ 1279 everywhere(?) [. . .] Gēb;[26] his affair will be judged by the Ennead and he will be nowhere and his house will be nowhere; he will be one proscribed, one who eats himself.

1. The meaning of *iḥm* is not certain; Sethe translates it by 'begünstige(?)'.

2. Sethe takes *ḥrt* to be the word for 'sky', but the context shows that the homophonous word for 'tomb' is what we have here.

3. Sethe: 'die, welche in Huldigung sind', cf. *Komm.* v, 175.

4. Note the 1st person in *iw·n(·i)* and *wdn·n(·i)*; the king is speaking.

5. i.e. on the leaves of the door, facing outward. *Ḥtn* appears to be a word for 'bull' with the dual ending omitted as superfluous and *ḥns* is the old perfective 3rd (dual) of a verb meaning 'move in two directions', *JEA* 41, 13 with n. 5.

6. The negation *im* must be expressing a negative wish here, cf. Gardiner, §§ 342. 345; Sethe, *Komm.* v, 177 f. regards it as introducing a 'Finalsatz' and translates it with 'damit . . . nicht', but this would require *tm*, cf. Gardiner, § 347.

7. Note the abnormal position of the dative; on permissible exceptions to the usual word-order cf. Gardiner, § 507. An officiant now appears to be addressing the dead king. This section bars off from the king as hostile all the deities of the Osirian circle. It is clearly of different origin from what precedes.

8. The god is told to take himself off. The location of *ꜥḏꜣ* is not known. Cf. *Komm.* v, 180.

9. On the non-enclitic particle *kw* see Edel, § 858*d*, but the following *iḏḏ·t(y)* is surely optative passive *sḏm·ty·f*. The god is not merely unwelcome but is to be insulted, cf. especially §§ 1272*b*; 1273*b*.

10. *Šꜣrw*, meaning unknown.

11. Mendes(?), cf. *Dict. géogr.* i, 147.

12. *Nṯr(w)*, op. cit. iii, 107.

13. Location unknown.

14. A var. of *Ḥnḥnt*, Hypselis(?); cf. *Komm.* iii, 364–5; v, 182.

15. Location unknown.

16. Cf. *AEO* ii, 20*.

17. Location unknown; according to *Komm.* v, 185 not to be confused with *Pr-mꜣnw* of the Nitocris Stela.

18. Location unknown.

19. Location unknown.

20. Sethe translates *ʿnnt(y)* with 'Vogelbeinen', relying on the shape of the determinatives, but this makes poor sense; rather does the word appear to be a synonym of the more usual *pḥwy*. Read probably *hy·t im* ⟨*m*⟩ *ʿnnty·t*.

21. On *s* for *sn* cf. *JEA* 16, 64 (5); the omission of *n* here, however, may be merely a scribal blunder.

22. *Šnw*; cf. n. 10 above.

23. The king speaks.

24. *Šꜣs* used transitively, lit. 'tread on'; cf. English 'tread on the toes of' in the sense of 'annoy'.

25. Cf. *Komm.* v, 191; Sethe's 'Hausherrin' rather than 'Nephthys' is surely right in this context.

26. Sethe: 'die Stätte, die sich Geb erdacht hat', loc. cit., but the restoration seems somewhat speculative.

## Utterance 535

*An Osirian text adapted for the king*

Thus said Isis and Nephthys:[1] The 'screecher'[2] comes, the kite comes, § 1280
namely Isis and Nephthys; they have come seeking their brother Osiris,
seeking their brother the King | . . .[3] Weep for your brother, O Isis; weep for § 1281
your brother, O Nephthys; weep for your brother! Isis sits down with her
hands on her head,| Nephthys has grasped the tips of her breasts because of § 1282
their brother the King, who crouches[4] on his belly, an Osiris in his danger(?),
an Anubis foremost of grip(?).| You shall have no putrefaction, O King; you § 1283
shall have no sweat, O King; you shall have no efflux, O King; you shall
have no dust, O King.| O *Ḥꜣt(y)* son of *Ḥꜣt(y)*,[5] *Nmny* who came out of *Mnt*,[6] § 1284
you have been cut up(?) into three (parts) in these your four days and your
eight nights.[7] | The starry sky serves your celestial serpent[8] whom you love; § 1285
your orphan comes to the front,[9] you are at the head of those who are foremost,[10] orphans are orphaned for you(?).[11] You have relieved Horus of his
girdle,[12] so that he may punish the followers of Seth.| Seize them, remove § 1286
their heads, cut off their limbs, disembowel them, cut out their hearts, drink
of their blood,| and claim[13] their hearts in this your name of Anubis Claimer § 1287
of hearts! Your eyes have been given to you as your two uraei because you
are Wepwawet who is on his standard and Anubis who presides over the
God's Booth.

O King, you preside over the houses of the Great Ones who are in Ōn; § 1288
the spirits fear you, and also the Imperishable Stars; the dead fall on their

§ 1289 faces before you, you have seized hold of the sun-folk.¦ O First-born, 'Honour
is for the King',[14] say the Souls of Ōn; they provide you with life and
dominion.

If he[15] lives among the living, then will Sokar live among the living; if he
§ 1290 lives among the living, then will the King live among the living.¦ O King,
come, live your life here from season to season[16] in these years when you
are content and your desire is at ease.

1. As Sethe remarks, this is an interpolation which in fact makes no sense.

2. Cf. Utt. 532, n. 3.

3. *Wnt·ṯ* is a puzzle I am unable to solve. Sethe, *Komm.* v, 196, favours the view that we have here a form of *wnn* 'be', *rm sn·ṯ* following as predicate, and translates the passage as 'Bist du es, bist du es, die deinen Bruder beweint hat', but there are objections to such an interpretation. Leaving aside the fact that such a use of the *sḏmt·f* form is unparalleled, a construction of that nature would require the *m* of predication and the feminine participle *rmt.* In fact *rm* here is almost certainly an imperative, which Sethe admits to be an alternative possibility. There seems to be a remote chance that the repeated *wnt·ṯ* before an imperative may have interjectional or ejaculatory force, but I can quote no similar usage.

4. Jackal-fashion; as Sethe has seen, *ỉnp* is a verb.

5. Possibly to be understood as 'he of the tomb' (*ḥꜣt*), cf. *Komm.* v, 199.

6. Quite obscure.

7. On this enigmatic passage cf. ibid. 200 f.; the pronoun 'your' is in the plural, which lends colour to Sethe's suggestion that 'three' may possibly refer to the three funerary deities Osiris, Anubis, and Wepwawet. *Ndny* lacks a subject, possibly as a result of confusion between the knife-determinative [hieroglyph] and the suffix [hieroglyph].

8. In § 1180*b* described as 'daughter of Anubis'; cf. Utt. 515, n. 2.

9. i.e. the dead king's son succeeds him.

10. The kings who were the predecessors of the newly dead.

11. A jingle on *nmḥ*; the second *nmḥ* is probably old perfective and the third possibly a 'complementary infinitive', lit. 'orphans are orphaned for you an orphaning'. What exactly this means remains obscure.

12. Cf. § 1089*b*. *Šṯ* with the determinative [hieroglyph] and meaning 'satchel' or the like, *CT* i, 71*h*, is doubtless a secondary use of the same word. For the verb *šṯ* 'gird' see also §§ 1373*b*; 1507*a*.

13. For this sense of *tp* cf. §§ 609*b*; 1523*c*; *JEA* 17, 59 (39).

14. Sethe translates differently, but in rendering *wtwty* 'first-born' as 'Erbe' he is rather stretching a point. My own version, which itself is open to question, regards *wtwty* as an ejaculation by an officiant to the king, followed by the comment of the Souls of Ōn as quoted by the officiant.

15. Presumably Osiris.

16. Cf. *r tr r tr·f* 'from season to season', *Urk.* iv, 1198, 7. Sethe, *Komm.* v, 209, would read *rr* rather than *tr*, but the sense is not affected. For my part, I have a suspicion that hieroglyphic *rr* 'season' originated in a misreading of hieratic *tr* and that the error was perpetuated in the written language.

## Utterance 536

*A 'resurrection' text*

Your water is yours, your flood is yours, your efflux which issued from Osiris § 1291
is yours. The doors of the sky are opened for you, the doors of Nūt are thrown open for you; the doors of the sky are opened for you, the doors of the
firmament are thrown open for you.[1] 'Endure!'[1] says Isis; 'In peace!' says § 1292
Nephthys, when they see their brother. Raise yourself, loose your bonds,
throw off your dust,[1] sit on this your iron throne, be purified with your four § 1293
*nmst*-jars and your four *ꜥbt*-jars which have come forth to you from the Castle of the God that you may be divine, they being filled to the brim from
the Canal of the God, which Horus of Nekhen gave to you.[1] He has given § 1294
you his jackal-spirits as Horus who is in his house, as the pre-eminent one who is foremost of the Powers; how enduring is what has been done for you![1]
Anubis who presides over the God's Booth has commanded that you go § 1295
down as a star, as the Morning Star. May you traverse the Mound of Horus of the Southerners, may you traverse the Mound of Horus of the Northerners,[1]
may the honoured ones(?) clap their hands at the stairway of your throne. § 1296

He[2] has come to you his father, he has come to you, O Gēb;[1] do for him § 1297
this which you did for his brother Osiris on that day of your complete fishing out of the water[3] for the putting of bones in order and for the making firm of soles and the cleansing of his upper and lower nails,[4] so that the Southern Conclave and the Northern Conclave may come to him bowing [. . .].

1. Cf. § 256*d*.
2. Presumably the king.
3. Of the corpse of Osiris; cf. *Komm.* v, 222 f.
4. i.e. of fingers and toes.

## Utterance 537

*As last*

O King, stand up and sit on the throne of Osiris! Your entire flesh is that § 1298
of Atum, your face is that of a jackal,[1] you turn your mouth to Rēꜥ that he § 1299
may smite down for you the impediment against what you would say and that he may favour your speech.

Stand up! You shall not perish, you shall not be destroyed, but live, O § 1300
King! Your mother Nūt lays hold of you that she may enfold you, and Gēb takes your hand; 'Welcome!' say your forefathers. May you have power in

§ 1301 your body, may your body be clothed;[1] may you go up as Horus of the Netherworld who is at the head of the Imperishable Stars, may you sit on your iron throne at your pool of cool water. May you live as a living scarabaeus, may you be long-lasting as the *ḏd*-pillar for ever and ever.

## Utterance 538

*A protective spell*

§ 1302 Get back, you needy long-horn! Your head is in the hand of Horus, your tail is in the hand of Isis, and the fingers of Atum are on your horns.

## Utterance 539

*An 'ascension' text*

§ 1303 My[1] head is a vulture;
I will ascend and rise up to the sky.[2]
The sides of my head are the starry sky of the god;
I will ascend [and rise up to the sky].
§ 1304 [My vertex is . . .] and Nu;
I will ascend and rise up to the sky.
My face is Wepwawet;
I will ascend and rise up to the sky.
§ 1305 My eyes are the Great One[3] at the head of the Souls of Ōn;
I will ascend and rise up to the sky.
My nose is Thoth;
[I] will ascend [and rise up to the sky].
§ 1306 [My mouth] is *Ḫns* the Great;
I will ascend and rise up to the sky.[4]
My tongue is the pilot in charge of the Bark of Righteousness;
I will ascend and rise up to the sky.
§ 1307 My teeth are the Souls ⟨of Pe(?)⟩;[5]
I will ascend and rise up to the sky.
My lips [. . .];
[I will ascend and rise up] to the sky.
§ 1308 My chin is Kherty, foremost in Khem;
I will ascend and rise up to the sky.
My spine is the Wild Bull;[6]
I will ascend and rise up to the sky.

My shoulders are Seth; § 1309
I will ascend and rise up [to the sky].
[My hands(?) are . . .];
[I will ascend and rise up to the sky].
[My fingers(?)][7] are Babi; § 1310
I will ascend and rise up to the sky.
My heart is Bastet;
I will ascend and rise up to the sky.
My belly is Nūt; § 1311
I will ascend and rise up [to the sky].
[My back(?) is Gēb(?)];[8]
[I will ascend and rise up to the sky].
[My vertebrae(?)][9] are the Two Enneads; § 1312
I will ascend and rise up to the sky.
My hinder-parts are Ḥeḳet;
I will ascend and rise up to the sky.
My buttocks are the Night-bark and the Day-bark; § 1313
I will ascend and rise up to the sky.
My phallus is Apis;[10]
I will ascend and rise up to the sky.
My thighs are Neith and Selḳet; § 1314
I will ascend and rise up to the sky.
The calves of my legs are the two Souls who preside over the Field of *Ḏr*;
I will ascend and rise up to the sky.
The soles of my feet are the two Barks of Righteousness; § 1315
I will ascend and rise up to the sky.
My toes are the Souls of Ōn;
I will ascend and rise up to the sky.
I am the companion of a god, the son of a god; § 1316
I will ascend and rise up to the sky.
I am the well-beloved son of Rēʿ;
I will ascend and rise up to the sky.
I was begotten for Rēʿ; § 1317
I will ascend and rise up to the sky.
I was conceived for Rēʿ;
I will ascend and rise up to the sky.
I was born for Rēʿ; § 1318

I will ascend and rise up to the sky.
The magic which appertains to me is that which is in my belly;
I will ascend and rise up to the sky.
§ 1319 I am the Great Power in the Great Tribunal in Ōn;
I will ascend and rise up to the sky.
§ 1320 Uproar![11]
I will ascend and rise up to the sky.
Horus the young child;
I will ascend and rise up to the sky.
§ 1321 Nūt: she can neither copulate nor use her arms;
I will ascend and rise up to the sky.
Gēb: he cannot overleap his path(?);[12]
I will ascend and rise up to the sky.
§ 1322 As for any god who will not set up a stairway for me—
I will ascend and rise up to the sky—
He shall have no loaf,
He shall have no fan,
He shall not wash himself in a bowl.
§ 1323 He shall not smell the foreleg,
He shall not devour the hind-leg,
The earth shall not be ploughed for him,
No offering shall be presented to him,[13]
But I will ascend and rise up to the sky.
§ 1324 It is not I who says this to you, you gods,
It is Magic who says this to you, you gods.
I am bound for the Lower *Ỉꜣt* of Magic,
I will ascend and rise up to the sky.
§ 1325 But as for any god who will set up a stairway for me—
I will ascend and rise up to the sky—
And as for any god who will provide my seat in his bark—
I will ascend and rise up to the sky—
§ 1326 The earth shall be ploughed for him,
An offering shall be presented to him,
A *nmtt*-bowl shall be prepared for him,
He shall smell the foreleg,
He shall devour the hind-leg,
And I will ascend and rise up to the sky.
§ 1327 As for any god who shall take my hand in the sky,

And shall betake himself to the Mansion of Horus which is in the firmament,
His double shall be vindicated before Gēb.

1. For the 1st person cf. *Komm.* v, 235.
2. Here the text reads *pr·f rf šwy·f rf*, but in nearly all other cases the reading is *pry·f rf šwy·f rf*. The ending *-y* indicates the prospective *sḏm·f*, as in *iry·i m* 'What shall I do?', *Adm.* 2, 9; *iry⟨·i⟩ mrt·k* 'I will do what you wish', *D. el B.* 107.
3. Feminine.
4. The text shows a dittograph of *šwy·f rf*.
5. The *m* of predication is omitted after *ibḥw P. pn* and a place-name (Pe, Ōn, or Nekhen) after *bw*.
6. So Sethe, surely rightly, despite the absence of the bull-determinative.
7. Cf. *Komm.* v, 239.
8. Cf. loc. cit.
9. Cf. ibid. 239 f.
10. So rather than Ḥapy son of Horus; the association with the phallus suggests the bull.
11. Cf. ibid. 243 f. The trouble affects the gods named hereafter.
12. Cf. Utt. 307, n. 5.
13. Cf. Utt. 441, n. 1.

*A series of spells from the funerary ritual*

## Utterance 540

I have come to you, my father, I have come to you, Osiris,[1] I have brought to § 1328
you this double of yours, which is . . .[2] O you ornament(?)[3] of your mother
Nūt, shining on her vertex,¦ she who provides(?)[4] has raised you up, your § 1329
mouth is split open by *Šsꜣ* foremost in *Snꜥt*, your mouth is split open by
*Dwꜣ-wr* in the Mansion of Gold, [your mouth] is split open by the two images
which are foremost in the Mansion of Natron,¦ your mouth is split open by § 1330
Horus with this little finger of his with which [he] split open the mouth of his
father, with which he split open the mouth of Osiris.¦ I am your son, I am § 1331
Horus, I am a 'loving-son' priest of my father in this my name of 'Loving
son';¦ you are pure, you are wiped over, your clothing is presented, (also) § 1332
your thousand of alabaster and your thousand of clothing which I have
brought to you and for which I make you firm.

1. Read *iy·n⟨·i⟩ ḫr·k it⟨·i⟩, iy·n⟨·i⟩ ḫr·k Wsir* with Nt, 836. The dead king's son is speaking to his father, but the sense has been obscured in P by the insertion of the cartouche.
2. *Ibꜣy*, meaning unknown. Sethe, *Komm.* v, 250 f., conjecturally suggests 'frisch (oder lebenswahr) gebildet'.
3. On *izzni* or *izz ni* cf. ibid. 251.
4. Cf. Utt. 307, n. 7.

## Utterance 541

§ 1333 O you children of Horus, Ḥapy, Duamūtef, Imsety, Ḳebḥsenuf, spread the protection of life over your father Osiris the King, since[1] he was caused to be
§ 1334 restored by the gods.| Smite Seth, protect this Osiris the King from him at dawn. Mighty is Horus, he of himself protects his father Osiris the King. Whoever shall act on behalf of the King,[2] you[3] shall worship him.

1. Cf. *Komm.* v, 257.
2. 𓇋𓏏 stands here for 'king'; 'father' would require a suffix, either *·f* or *·ṯn*.
3. Plural, presumably addressed to all the company present at the burial.

## Utterance 542

§ 1335 This is Horus who has come that he may recognize his father Osiris the King. It is dangerous to him that the King's death should be proclaimed(?)[1] in the
§ 1336 establishments of Anubis,[2] and no one who hears this shall live.| O Thoth, have no pity on anyone who hates the King. O Thoth, go and see if[3] the King is proclaimed as dead(?), for it is dangerous to him.

1. Cf. *Komm.* v, 261 f. In § 2100*c*, in another text concerning embalming, *nꜥ* is certainly a transitive-passive sense of *nꜥi* 'travel'—so also § 1423*a*—but such a meaning is impossible here; the word seems to refer to news which has to be kept under the rose. The person so endangered seems to be the dead king and not his successor (= Horus).
2. The place of embalming.
3. Cf. ibid. 264; Utt. 440, n. 1. Here the subject follows *in* in anticipatory emphasis.

## Utterance 543

§ 1337 Go to this Osiris the King. O Osiris the King, I bring to you him who would kill you; do not let him escape from your hand. O Osiris the King, I bring to you him who would kill you, and a knife is made ready for him.[1] O Osiris the King, I bring to you him who would kill you, he having been cut three times.[2]

1. Lit. 'his knife is made'.
2. i.e. quartered.

## Utterance 544

§ 1338 O Children of Horus, go to this Osiris the King; O Children of Horus, go, put yourselves under this Osiris the King, let there be none of you who shall turn away, but lift him up.

## Utterance 545

O Osiris the King, I bring to you him who would kill you, he being cut up § 1339
and a knife made ready for him. O Children of Horus, Ḥapy, Duamūtef,
Imsety, Ḳebḥsenuf,[1] lift up your father this Osiris the King and guide him. § 1340
O Osiris the King, it is caused that you be restored and that your mouth be
split open, so stand up!

## Utterance 546

I am Nūt who will cause this Osiris the King to mount up to me; give him to § 1341
me, that I may embrace him.

## Utterance 547

O my father Osiris the King, raise yourself up to me. O Osiris the King, betake § 1342
yourself to me.

## Utterance 548

*A 'resurrection' text*

The mouth of the earth is split open for this King, Gēb has spoken to him. § 1343
This King is great like a king and kingly(?)[1] like Rēᶜ. 'Be welcome!' to the
King say the Two Enneads.[2] There is opened for him the eastern door of the
sky by[3] Him whose powers endure.[1] Nūt the Great puts her hands on him, § 1344
(even) she the long-horned, the pendulous of breast. She suckles this King
and does not wean him,[1] she takes him to ⟨herself⟩[4] at the sky, she does not § 1345
drop him to the earth, she prepares this King's station at the head of the Two
Conclaves.

He goes aboard the bark like Rēᶜ at the banks of the Winding Waterway,[1]
this King rows in the Bark of Lightning, he navigates therein to the Field of § 1346
the Lower Skies at this south of the Field of Rushes.[1] His hand is taken by § 1347
Rēᶜ, his head is lifted up by Atum, the end(?) of his bow-warp is taken by Isis,
his stern-warp is coiled(?) by Nephthys,[1] the Celestial Serpent[5] has placed § 1348
him at her side, she drops him down among the *ḫntyw-š* as calf-herds.

1. Sethe takes a different view, *Komm.* v, 272. I suggest that *swty* is a nisba of *swt*, emblem of Upper Egypt; the old perfective *swt·t(y)* of a denominative verb from the same stem occurs in the parallel text § 2169*a*.

2. There is some uncertainty as to the translation of this sentence; I have adopted Sethe's alternative rendering as being the more probable. The meaning of *sḏ3 m ḥtp* is shown unmistakably in § 1362*a*.

3. *N* here is certainly a writing of *in* 'by', cf. § 2170*c*; in § 1343*c* it appears to stand for *in* 'so says'.

4. Read *šd·s n(·s) sw* with Sethe.

5. Cf. Utt. 515, n. 3.

## Utterance 549

*A protective spell*

§ 1349 Get back, Babi, red of ear and purple of hindquarters! You have taken the thigh-joint[1] of your goddess to your mouth!

1. Not the goddess's own thigh, but the portion allotted to her to eat, which apparently Babi has stolen.

## Utterance 550

*A protective spell*

§ 1350 Get back, great Black One! Crawl away into *Ḫr-ʿḥ3*, into that place where they[1] crawled!

1. Horus and Seth, cf. *Komm.* v, 279.

## Utterance 551

*A protective spell*

§ 1351 . . .[1] the she-jackal[2] as(?) one who transgresses(?) her boundary. Get back, you forepart of a lion! retreat, you hindquarters! You shall miss(?)[3] the passing of the god.

1. *Wnḏr*, meaning unknown.
2. Shown to be feminine by the suffix in *t3š·s*.
3. Lit. 'pass' in the sense of 'overlook', 'disregard'.

## Utterance 552

§ 1352 May you live for me, O King, for ever!

## Utterance 553

*A 'resurrection' text*

Gēb raises you, he awakens this your spirit for you.[1] Your water-jar is firm, § 1353
your water-jar is firm,[2] you are raised aloft on the hands of Shu and Tefēnet[3]
in the Mansion of Her who provides(?),[4] O King,| because you are a spirit § 1354
whom Nephthys suckled with her left breast. Osiris has given you the spirits,
you have taken the Eye of Horus. These four paths of yours are those which
are in front of the tomb of Horus,| on which the god has walked since the § 1355
going down of Rēʿ.| He has grasped your hand, Sokar who presides over § 1356
*Pḏw-š* has cleansed you on your throne which is in the firmament.

Raise yourself,[5] O spirit of this King, sit down and eat; may your double § 1357
sit down and eat bread and beer with you without cessation for ever and
ever.| This going of yours is like that of the successor of Osiris;[6] your feet § 1358
step out their dance(?)[7] for you, they bring your festivals to you, because
your white teeth are the claws of Her of the Cerastes Mountain.| May you § 1359
cross over, O Great Bull, to the green fields, to the pure places of Rēʿ.

Raise yourself, O spirit of this King! Your water is yours, your flood is § 1360
yours, your efflux which issued from the putrefaction of Osiris is yours.| The § 1361
doors of the sky are opened for you, the doors of the firmament are thrown
open for you, the doors of the tomb are opened for you, the doors of Nūt are
unbolted for you.| 'Greeting, O King!' says Isis; 'Be welcome, O King!' says § 1362
Nephthys, for they[8] saw your father Osiris on that day of fowling with a
throw-stick.[9] May the chapels which your soul founded be exalted.

Raise yourself, throw off your dust, remove the mask(?) which is on your § 1363
face, loosen your bonds, for they are not bonds, they are the tresses of
Nephthys.| May you traverse the Southern Mounds, may you traverse the § 1364
Northern Mounds, being seated on your iron throne. Anubis who presides
over the God's Booth commands that your spirit be behind you and your
power within you, you being established at the head of the Powers;| may you § 1365
be purified with these four *nmst*-jars, a *špnt*-jar and a *ʿ3bt*-jar,[10] which have
been issued for you from the God's Booth, that you may become divine.| The § 1366
sky weeps for you, the earth quakes at you, the Mourning-Woman[11] calls to
you, the Great Mooring-Post[12] cries out to you; your feet stamp, your arms
wave,[13] and you ascend to the sky as a star, as the Morning Star.

The King has come to you his father, he has come to you, O Gēb, he has § 1367
joined your *ḫrmt*,[14] you gods; may he sit on the great throne on the thighs of
his father *Ḫnt-irty*,| for his mouth is cleansed with *nṯr*-natron and *ḥzmn*- § 1368

natron, his upper and lower nails are cleansed; there has been done for him what was done for his father Osiris on that day of re-uniting the bones, of making good the soles, and of extending the feet.

§ 1369 The . . . go down to you bent (in obeisance);[15] those who belong to the Conclave of Upper Egypt go down to you, the Conclave of Lower Egypt comes to you bowing, you being everlasting at the head of the Powers.

1. Read *ỉs ṯw Gb srs·f n·k ỉḫ·k pw*, cf. *Komm.* v, 285 f., though I disagree with Sethe's view that Gēb is addressed in the vocative; what follows is addressed to the king, and the same must apply to the present passage, which is a statement to the deceased.

2. Cf. JPII, 1308+27.

3. Emend into *ḏsr·t(y) ỉr ꜥwy Šw ḥnꜥ Tfnt*, cf. *Komm.* v, 286.

4. Cf. Utt. 307, n. 7.

5. Here begins a partial variant of Utt. 436.

6. Cf. Utt. 436, n. 2.

7. Sethe: 'Deine Füsse sie schlagen dir ihr Hände', but this makes no sense. I suggest that [hieroglyphs] is intended for [hieroglyphs] 'dance', cf. § 863*a*, and that the sentence should be translated as 'your feet step out their dance for you'; for *sḳr* in the sense of 'step out', 'stamp', cf. §§ 791*b*; 1366*b*.

8. For *·s* read *·sny*, cf. § 1292*a*.

9. [hieroglyphs] may be a corruption of *ꜥmꜥꜣt* 'throw-stick', *Concise Dict.* 42.

10. Sethe translates *ỉpnt ꜥbt* as 'die dickbäuchig wie ein *ꜥbt*-Krug sind', but this would require *mỉ* 'like' between the two words. I have taken *ỉpnt* to be the word for a full-bodied jar, cf. e.g. *Urk.* iv, 821, 7.

11. For the *smntt*-woman cf. §§ 726*a*; 1997; 2013*b*. Here the word is curiously determined with a bag, and is translated by Sethe as 'der *smnt*-Sack'.

12. Cf. §§ 794*c*; 2013*b*.

13. In a ritual dance; cf. Utt. 419, n. 2 and *Komm.* v, 296.

14. Cf. § 2015*b*, where *ḥrmt* is determined with two 'causeway' signs.

15. Read *hꜣw* ⟨*n*·⟩*k*; § 2017*a* has *hꜣw n·k*. Possibly *hꜣw* should be read here also, in which case *hꜣ* will have been an anticipation of the next sentence. Who the *sꜣtw* are remains obscure.

## Utterance 554

*The king is reborn and becomes a star*

§ 1370 You[1] are a son of the Great Wild Cow. She conceives you, she bears you, she puts you[2] within her wing (*sic*). She crosses the lake with you,[3] she traverses

§ 1371 the *Šlw*-waterway with you, | your cognizance which is in front of the Mansion is behind you, your papyrus-sceptre[4] is in your hand. May you smite and

§ 1372 govern at your translation to the possessors of honour,[5] | for you belong to those who surround Rēꜥ, who are about the Morning Star. You shall have no evil and your name which is on earth shall have no evil.

1. For the translation in the 2nd person cf. *Komm.* v, 301 f. For the interpretation of this sentence as a statement rather than as a question, cf. *Syntax*, 60 (8); in this case the archetype will have read *ṯwt zꜣ*, etc. The affirmative fits the context better than the interrogative.

2. Read *dỉ·s n(·s) sw* with Sethe, emending *sw* into *ṯw*.

3. From here on the original 2nd person remains unaltered.

4. In *ʿbꜣ·k mnḥy* the second word is a nisba of *mnḥ* 'papyrus-plant', *Concise Dict.* 109.

5. See Utt. 438, n. 3.

## Utterance 555

### *The king is crowned in Pe*

I[1] have gone up in Pe to the gods of Pe. I am girded as Horus, I am adorned § 1373
as the Two Enneads,[1] I appear as King, I am on high as Wepwawet, I have § 1374
assumed the White Crown and the Green Crown,[2] my mace is in my hand,
my sceptre is in my fist.[1] My mother is Isis, my nurse is Nephthys, she who § 1375
suckled me is the *Sḫꜣt-Ḥr* cow, Neith is behind me, and Selḳet is before me.

### *A funerary text*

My ropes are knotted,[3] my ferry-boats are made ready[4] for the son of Atum,[5] § 1376
who is hungry and thirsty, thirsty and hungry on this southern side of the
Winding Waterway.[1] O Thoth, you who are in the region of the shade of your § 1377
bush, put me on the tip of your wing on yonder northern side of the Winding
Waterway.[1] I am hale and my flesh is hale; I am hale and my garment is § 1378
intact, I have gone up to the sky as Montju, I have gone down as a soul which
he[6] entraps, as a soul which he makes divine.[7]

1. For the 1st person cf. the N-text and Utt. 505, n. 1, in reference to the parallel passage §§ 1089 f.

2. Cf. *JEA* 35, 73.

3. In the first sentence both P and N retain the original 1st person.

4. Cf. *Komm.* v, 310; *CT* ii, 191*b*; 198*a*.

5. Sethe has 'meinen Sohn, sagt Atum', presumably regarding  after *zꜣ* as the suffix 1st sing., but it yields a better sense to take the sign in question as a determinative and to read *n zꜣ n Ỉtm* 'for the son of Atum' = the king, who thus refers to himself, as in § 1742*c*.

6. i.e. Thoth, who takes the king's bird-soul into his care and custody.

7. Cf. Utt. 506, n. 9.

## Utterance 556

### *A 'resurrection' text*

Someone goes [. . .][1] the Great Ones to the thrones of the gods. Be exalted, O § 1379
my father Osiris the King, as Wepwawet[1] [. . .] my father Osiris the King, and § 1380
Anubis of the Baldachin raises him.[2]

Your feet are those of a jackal,[3] so stand up! Your arms are those of a
§ 1381 jackal, so stand up!¹ [. . .] to him who rows(?) on his behalf(?) that he may bring to you the Unique One, the Double Crown;[4] [he will] ferry [you . . .¹
§ 1382 . . .] my father Osiris the King; the Winding Waterway is flooded. Call, O my father Osiris the King, to *Ḥm* and *Smt*, that they may ferry my father the King. Awake,[5] [stand up(?) at yonder] eastern [side] of the sky at this place [where the gods] are born,[6] [when there comes this time of tomorrow
§ 1383 and this time of the third day;¹ my father the King] will be born [on] yonder eastern side of [the sky] where the gods are born,[7] when there comes this
§ 1384 time of tomorrow and this time of the third day.¹ [Lo, my father the King arises] as the Lone Star[8] [which is on the underpart of the sky . . .] like Ḥarakhti.[9]

§ 1385 [O you four gods who stand at the supports] of the sky,[10] my father Osiris the King has not died the death,[11] for my father Osiris the King
§ 1386 possesses a spirit ⟨in⟩ the horizon.[12] ¹ [My father the King] has come to you [. . .].

1. Sethe: 'gegangen sind die grossen . . .', but not enough is preserved before *wrw* to warrant a restoration.

2. Sethe, *Komm*, v, 316, thinks that *ṯz sw* should be emended into the 2nd person, cf. § 1380*c*. He may well be right, but in view of the damaged state of the text it is safer to accept it as it stands.

3. The king is addressed by his son.

4. Sethe: 'er dir eine von den beiden Mächtigen Kronen bringe', but *sḫmty* is the name of the Double Crown as a unity, cf. § 805, and surely the combined crown is to be brought rather than one of its elements. I have thus translated *wrt* as 'Unique One', as an epithet of the Double Crown as a whole.

5. JPII, 1301 has 𓇋𓂋N𓇋𓂋▨𓋴▨ . . . in place of Sethe's restoration *ḏrwt*, which must be discarded. The restoration 𓇋𓂋[𓋴]𓋴 'awake!' (imperative) seems certain, followed possibly by the further imperatives *ꜥḥꜥ* 'stand up!' or *ṯz ṯw* 'raise yourself!'.

6. JPII, 1302 preserves *ir bw pf mss* . . . at the beginning of this lacuna.

7. In place of Sethe's restoration read *msw* [*it N ir*] *gs pf iꜣby n* [*pt*] *mssw nṯrw im*, cf. JPII, 1303.

8. For Sethe's *m sbꜣ* [*pw*] read *m sbꜣ wꜥty* . . . with JPII, 1305.

9. After *Ḥr-ꜣḫty* JPII, 1306 has 𓇋𓄿𓋴𓂝▨ . . ., which casts a doubt on Sethe's restoration of § 1385*a*, though it is not impossible that the signs in question may have stood on a misplaced fragment.

10. See n. 9 above. The 'staffs of the sky' represent its supports at the four cardinal points; one is reminded of those stelae which above the main scene display 𓇯 supported by two 𓌀.

11. *N mt·n is it N* confirmed by JPII, 1307.

12. Supplying *m* before *ꜣḫt*, cf. § 350*c*. *ꜣḫt* cannot be a 'complementary infinitive' as Sethe appears to have thought, because the preceding *ꜣḫ* is not a verb but a noun.

## Utterance 557

*The king is addressed*

. . . Turn yourself to your house, turn yourself about,[!] for your heir who is §§ 1387–8
on your throne will cultivate [barley for you[!] . . .]. § 1389

## Utterance 558

*As last*

O King, Hail to you, you Chaos-god![1] The travelling of the Great Black One § 1390
is travelled for you, you stop (with) the stopping[2] of the Eldest God, there is
censed for you the censing of *Ḳꜣi-smk* in Ōn.[!] Be alive, alive! Have dominion, § 1391
dominion! Life is raised up behind you, so live!

1. i.e. god of the primeval Chaos before the Creation, cf. *Amun*, §§ 128. 147. 148. 200; *Ex Oriente Lux*, 18 (1965), 268 f.

2. Lit. 'you stop a stopping'. In this context *ḥni* surely means 'alight', 'stop' rather than 'dance' as Sethe.

## Utterance 559

*As before*

O King, come in peace to Osiris! Welcome to Osiris! The fields are filled for § 1392
you, the banks are inundated for you as a boon which the King grants.[!] The § 1393
Foremost of the Westerners takes your hand on the edge of the *Ḥbt*-mountain.
Osiris makes presentation and gives to you what is upon the *sšrw*-cloth.

## Utterance 560

*A burial text*

The earth is hacked up by the hoe, the offering is presented, the earth of *Tbi* § 1394
is presented, the two nomes of the god shout before [the King] when he goes
down into the earth.[!] O Gēb, open your mouth for your son Osiris, for what is § 1395
behind him belongs to food, what is before him belongs to the catch.

## Utterance 561

*Destroyed except for a few scattered words* §§ 1396–1404

## Utterance 562

*The king joins the gods*

§ 1405 The earth is raised on high under the sky by your arms, O Tefēnet, and you have taken the hands of Rēʿ; take the King's hand and set him as [a noble one(?)][1] among the nobles that the King may sit at the head of the Two
§ 1406 Enneads[1] and govern the gods as a king, as the representative of Horus[2] who protects his father Osiris. Your body is this King, O god; so also(?)[3] your
§ 1407 bodies are the King, you gods.[1] This King has come safely to you, O Horus; the Eye of Horus belongs(?) to you,[4] it will not be given over to the rage of Seth.

1. Restoring either *sr* (so Sethe) or *špsw* in the lacuna.
2. Read *ỉt ỉs sty Ḥr ỉs*. In P (*ỉ*)*s* after *st*(*y*) is superfluous.
3. Cf. *Komm.* v, 329; Edel, § 858*a*.
4. Plural, in reference to the gods.

## Utterance 563

*A variant of Utterance* 325

§ 1408 The doors of the sky are opened,
The doors of the firmament are thrown open for Horus of the Gods,
That he may ascend[1] and bathe in the Field of Rushes.
The doors of the sky are opened for me,
The doors of the firmament are thrown open for me,[2]
That I may ascend and bathe in the Field of Rushes.
§ 1409 The doors of the sky are opened,
The doors of the firmament are thrown open for Horus of Shezmet,
That he may ascend and bathe in the Field of Rushes.
The doors of the sky are opened for me,
The doors of the firmament are thrown open for me,
That I may ascend and bathe in the Field of Rushes.
§ 1410 The doors of the sky are opened,
The doors of the firmament are thrown open for Horus of the East,
That he may ascend and bathe in the Field of Rushes.
The doors of the sky are opened for me,
The doors of the firmament are thrown open for me,
That I may ascend and bathe in the Field of Rushes.
§ 1411 The doors of the sky are opened,
The doors of the firmament are thrown open for Ḥarakhti,

That he may ascend and bathe in the Field of Rushes.
The doors of the sky are opened for me,
The doors of the firmament are thrown open for me,
That I may ascend and bathe in the Field of Rushes.
Horus of the Gods will indeed ascend § 1412
That he may bathe in the Field of Rushes;
I will indeed ascend
That I may bathe in the Field of Rushes.
Horus of Shezmet will indeed ascend § 1413
That he may bathe in the Field of Rushes;
I will indeed ascend
That I may bathe in the Field of Rushes.
Horus of the East will indeed ascend § 1414
That he may bathe in the Field of Rushes;
I will indeed ascend
That I may bathe in the Field of Rushes.
Ḥarakhti will indeed ascend § 1415
That he may bathe in the Field of Rushes;
I will indeed ascend
That I may bathe in the Field of Rushes.

I am pure, I have taken the golden kilt, I ascend to the sky, and the earth § 1416
remains behind. Pressure is in your womb, O Nūt, through the seed of the
god which is in you;[3] | it is I who am the seed of the god which is in you. O § 1417
Nūt, receive[4] me as you would receive the son of a god.

O *Hpꜣt, Hpꜣt*! O *Hnny, Hnny*! Take me with you, and I will remain with you. § 1418

O *Ḥftnt*, mother of the gods! Give me your hand, take my hand and take § 1419
me to the sky, just as[5] you took Osiris to the sky.

O *Hnny, Hnny*! O *Hpꜣt, Hpꜣt*! Take me with you, and I will remain with § 1420
you.

1. The frequent writing of the *sḏm·f* form *prỉ* with final *ỉ*, §§ 1409 ff., points to the prospective *sḏm·f* form **peryáf*; the prefixing of the imperfective *sḏm·f* form *prr* before *prỉ* in §§ 1412 ff. is, as Sethe points out in *Komm.* v, 335, for the purpose of emphasis. That the *ỉ* of *prỉ* is not merely an unerased suffix 1st sing. is shown by the fact that it occurs also with original nominal subject and so must be a verbal ending; the verb-form must be the same whether followed by a noun or a suffix.

2. For the 1st person see the dependent pronoun *ỉw* (*wỉ*) in § 1419*c* (P).

3. Cf. § 532*a*.

4. Var. M. N: *ꜥm* 'swallow', 'absorb'.

5. *Mỉ nw* is an early equivalent of *mỉ nꜣ*, on which see *Ḥeḳanakhte*, pp. 111 f.

## Utterance 564

*A variant of Utterance 253*

§ 1421 Someone bathes in the Lake of Rushes.
Rēʿ bathes in the Lake of Rushes,
And I myself[1] bathe in the Lake of Rushes.
Shu bathes in the Lake of Rushes,
And I myself bathe in the Lake of Rushes.
§ 1422 O Shu, Shu, lift me up to the sky;
O Nūt, put your hands on me.
. . .[2]

1. For the 1st person cf. *Komm.* v, 339.
2. Untranslatable. A bungled version of §§ 1418*a*; 1420*a*; similarly § 1430*e*.

## Utterance 565

*An 'ascension' text*

§ 1423 I am[1] pure, I am conveyed to[2] the sky thereby, I remain more than human,[3]
I appear in glory for the gods. I have appeared with Rēʿ at his appearing, |
§ 1424 I have made the third of those two who are with me,[4] one behind me and one
§ 1425 before me; one gives water and one gives sand. | I have leant on your arm, O
Shu, just as Rēʿ has leant on your arm. These two have found me, having sat
§ 1426 down opposite me, even the two spirits, the Ladies of this land. | O Nūt, be
joyful at meeting me, for there has received me the hem of her petticoat
§ 1427 which is under her dress.[5] | He whom they have fashioned for themselves is
myself,[6] and evil has rejected me. Selḳet[7] has set her hands on me, she has
§ 1428 extended her breast to my mouth; | *Dwꜣ-wr* has shaved[8] me, Sothis has
washed my hands. It is my rebirth today, you gods; I do not (now) know my
first mother whom (once) I knew, it is Nūt who has borne me and also Osiris.[9]

1. For the 1st person cf. *Komm.* v, 343.
2. On *nr* cf. Utt. 542, n. 1.
3. Sethe: 'N. bleibt (in Erinnerung als furchtbar für) die Menschen', but to me it seems that we have here a straightforward comparison between the king and the ruck of humanity.
4. Read probably *ḫmt·n·ì sny nty ḥnʿ·ì*, lit. 'I have thirded the two who are with me'. Both P and N appear to be corrupt; M has *ḫmt·n⟨·ì⟩ sny* and then is lost. Who the 'two' are is explained in § 1425*c*.
5. Sethe, *Komm.* v, 347 f., sees in this passage an indication of sexual intercourse between king and goddess. The *mʿḳ* is clearly an undergarment of the nature of a petticoat or slip.
6. A somewhat complicated instance of a sentence with adverbial predicate expressing identity with the *m* of predication; the subject is the relative form *ms(w)·n·sn* with reflexive dative

and the predicate refers to the king himself. The suffix after *iw* appears to be due to the presence of the enclitic particle *ḥm*, cf. *i·f wnnt ik·n·f w⟨i⟩ . . . i·f wnnt sʿḥ·n·f w⟨i⟩* 'he has attacked me . . . he has kicked me', § 959*a. c.* When the enclitic is followed by a noun, *iw* does not take the anticipatory suffix: *iw ḥm ḥm⟨·i⟩ rḫ mrr·k dd ḫt nb mrrt ḥm⟨·i⟩* 'My Majesty knows that you always wish to say everything that my Majesty desires', *Urk.* i, 180, 1.

7. Var. 'Nephthys'.
8. Var. N: 'I am adorned by *Dwɜ-wr*'.
9. The king disowns his earthly parents.

## Utterance 566

*An 'ascension' text*

Take me[1] with you, O Horus; ferry me over, O Thoth, on the tip of your § 1429
wing as Sokar who presides over the Bark of Righteousness. Horus is not asleep behind the canal, Thoth is not boatless; nor am I boatless, for I possess the Eye of Horus.

1. For the 1st person cf. *Komm.* v, 352.

## Utterance 567

*A variant of Utterance* 564

Rēʿ has bathed in the Field of Rushes; § 1430
Horus has bathed in the Field of Rushes;
I have bathed in the Field of Rushes.
O Shu, lift me up;[1]
O Nūt, give me your hand.
. . .[2]

1. Emending the text into *fɜ iw* (= *wi*), cf. *Komm.* v, 356.
2. Untranslatable; compare § 1422*c*.

## Utterance 568

*An 'ascension' text*

Someone goes to his double, *Mḫnt-irty* goes to his double, and this King goes § 1431
to his double, to the sky. A ladder is set up for him that he may ascend on
it in its name of 'Ascent to the sky';[1] its ferryboat is ferried across for him § 1432
by the staffs of the Imperishable Stars. The Bull of the sky has bent down his
horn that he[1] may pass over thereby to the Lakes of the Netherworld:[1] 'O § 1433
King, you shall not fall to the ground!'[2]

This King has grasped for himself the two sycamores which are in yonder side of the sky: 'Ferry me over!'[3] And they set him on yonder eastern side of the sky.

1. i.e. the king.
2. According to Sethe this is a speech by the Bull to the king.
3. The king speaks; cf. *Komm.* v, 359.

## Utterance 569

*An address to the sun-god*

§ 1434 I know[1] your name, I am not ignorant of your name; your name is 'Limitless', your father's name is 'You-are-great', your mother's name is 'Peace', (even) she who bears you on the path of the dawn(?), the path of the dawn(?).[2]

§ 1435 The birth of Limitless in the horizon will be prevented
If you prevent me from coming to the place where you are.[3]
The birth of Selḳet will be prevented
If you prevent me from coming to the place where you are.
§ 1436 The Two Banks will be held back from Horus
If you prevent me from coming to the place where you are.
The birth of Orion will be prevented
If you prevent me from coming to the place where you are.
§ 1437 The birth of Sothis will be prevented
If you prevent me from coming to the place where you are.
The Two Apes, his beloved sons, will be held off from Rēʿ
If you prevent me from coming to the place where you are.
§ 1438 The birth of Wepwawet in the *Pr-nw* will be prevented
If you prevent me from coming to the place where you are.
Men will be held back from the King,[4] the son of the god,
If you prevent me from coming to the place where you are.
§ 1439 Your crew of the Imperishable Stars will be prevented from rowing you,
If you prevent them from allowing me to go aboard this bark of yours.
Men will be prevented from dying
If you prevent me from going aboard this bark of yours.
§ 1440 Men will be held back from food
If you prevent me from going aboard this bark of yours.

I am *Sksn*, envoy of Rēʿ,[5] and I will not be held back from the sky; the *mꜣṯt*-tree has laid her hands on me, (even she) the door-keeper of the sky;[1]
§ 1441 *Ḥr·f-ḥꜣ·f* has made ready for me,[6] (even he) the ferryman of the Winding

Waterway. I will not be held back, nor will obstacles be set against me, for I am one of you, you gods.

I have come to you, O Rēʿ, I have come to you, O Limitless, and I will row you, I will escort you, I will love you with my body, I will love you with my heart. § 1442

1. *Ỉ·rḫ·k(ỉ)* is old perfective 1st sing., overlooked by the ancient editor when he transposed this text into the 3rd person; cf. also *ỉnk* (P¹) in § 1440*c*.

2. 'Accusative of respect'? Despite *Komm.* v, 365, I believe that *dwt* in P¹ and M (*dwȝt* in P²) is merely an emphatic repetition of the preceding *dwȝt* in a shorter writing. The translation of the word remains uncertain, but it appears to be a noun derived from *dwȝw* 'dawn', 'morning'.

3. Following P² and M. Edel, §§ 820, 2; 1101, is inclined to regard *ȝ* in these two texts as a variant of the negative particle *w*, but, with Sethe, I take it to be the well-known enclitic. In § 1435*a* (P². M) the *w* is most probably the ending of the passive *sḏm·f* before a nominal subject, for the clause is a threat that if (§ 1435*b*) the king is hindered—a virtual conditional clause—the birth of Limitless will be prevented (§ 1435*a*). The editor of P¹ seems to have taken the *w* in § 1435*a* as the negation and in § 1435*b* has changed the enclitic *ȝ* of the other two texts into the negation *w*, so that his version runs: 'the birth of Limitless will not be prevented if you do not prevent this P from coming to the place where you are.' The text of P² and M is the more forcible and thus more likely to be the original; P¹ has watered the threat down.

4. i.e. the reigning king as distinct from the deceased one who is speaking.

5. Cf. *Komm.* v, 372 f. Note the pronoun of the 1st person in P¹.

6. Cf. Utt. 555, n. 4.

## Utterance 570

*The sun rises*

The face of the sky is washed, the celestial expanse is bright, the god is given birth by the sky upon the arms of Shu and Tefēnet, upon my arms.[1] § 1443

*The king announces himself*

'The Great One rises' is what the gods say;[2] § 1444
Hear it, this word which I say to you;
Be informed[3] concerning me, that I am a great one, the son of a great one.
I am with you; take me with you.
O Khoprer, hear it, this word which I say to you; § 1445
Be informed concerning me, that I am a great one, the son of a great one;
I am with you; take me with you.
O Nu, hear it, this word which I say to you; § 1446
Be informed concerning me, that I am a great one, the son of a great one;
I am with you; take me with you.
O Atum, hear it, this word which I say to you; § 1447

Be informed concerning me, that I am a great one, the son of a great one;
I am with you, take me with you.

§ 1448 O Strong One, son of Gēb; O Mighty One, son of Osiris,
Hear it, this word which I say to you;[4]
Be informed concerning me, that I am a great one, the son of a great one;
I am with you, take me with you.

*The king summons the sun-god*

§ 1449 Mount up[5] to me in your name of Rēʿ, that you may dispel the cloudiness of the sky until[6] Ḥarakhti shows himself that he may hear my fame and my
§ 1450 praise in the mouths of the Two Enneads.| 'How beautiful you are!' is what my mother says; 'My heir!' is what Osiris says.

*The king is protected and served*

I will never swallow the Eye of Horus so that men may say: 'He[7] is dead because of it.' I will never swallow[8] a limb of Osiris so that men may say:
§ 1451 'He[9] is dead because of it.'| I live by grace of(?) my father Atum; protect me, O Nekhbet. You have protected me, O Nekhbet, dwelling in the Prince-
§ 1452 Mansion which is in Ōn,| you have commended me to Him who is in his[10] service that I may be served. He who is in his service has commended me to Him who is in his litter that I may be served.

*The king is immortal*

§ 1453 I escape my day of death just as Seth escaped his day of death.
I escape my half-months of death just as Seth escaped his half-months of death.
I escape my months of death just as Seth escaped his months of death.
I escape my year of death just as Seth escaped his year of death.

*The king becomes a star*

§ 1454 Do not break up the ground, O you arms of mine which lift up the sky as Shu; my bones are iron and my limbs are the Imperishable Stars.

§ 1455 I am a star which illumines the sky, I mount up to the god[11] that I may be protected, for the sky will not be devoid of me and this earth will not be devoid of me for ever.

§ 1456 I live beside you, you gods of the Lower Sky, the Imperishable Stars, who traverse the land of Libya, who lean on your *ḏʿm*-staffs; I lean with you on
§ 1457 a *wꜣs*-staff and a *ḏʿm*-staff,| for I am your fourth.[12]

O you gods of the Lower Sky, the Imperishable Stars, who traverse the land of Libya and lean on your *ḏꜥm*-staffs; I lean with you on a *wꜣs*-staff and a *ḏꜥm*-staff,[1] for I am your fourth. § 1458

O you gods of the Lower Sky, the Imperishable Stars, who traverse the land of Libya and lean on your *ḏꜥm*-staffs; I lean with you on a *wꜣs*-staff and a *ḏꜥm*-staff by command of Horus the patrician, King of the Gods.

*The king wears the crowns of Egypt*

I am he who grasps the White Crown, Master of the curl of the Green Crown, § 1459
I am the uraeus which went forth from Seth, which moves incessantly.[13] Take me and nourish me.

I am he who takes care of(?) the Red One which came out of . . .,[14] I am the § 1460
Eye of Horus which was not chewed nor spat out,[15] and I am not chewed nor spat out.

*The king is one with the sun-god*

Hear it, O Rēꜥ, this word which I say to you; your nature is in me, O Rēꜥ, § 1461
and your nature is nourished in me, O Rēꜥ.[1] The baboons are slain by the § 1462
leopard(?) and the leopard(?) is slain by the baboons. O you eunuch(?), O you male, one of you two runs, (even) this one who belongs to the first generation for punishment(?)[16] and for vindication[1] which was born before § 1463
anger came into being; which was born before noise came into being; which was born before strife came into being; which was born before tumult came into being; which was born before the Eye of Horus was gouged out(?), before the testicles of Seth were torn off.

I am the redness which came forth from Isis, I am the blood which issued § 1464
from Nephthys; I am firmly bound up(?) at the waist(?), and there is nothing which the gods can do to me,[17] for I am the representative of Rēꜥ, and I do not die.[1] Hear, O Gēb, chiefest of the gods, and equip me with my shape; § 1465
hear, O Thoth, in whom is the peace of the gods. Open, O Horus; stand guard, O Seth, that I may rise in the eastern side of the sky like Rēꜥ who rises in the eastern side of the sky.

1. Unmistakable traces of the 1st person in this long Utterance, see also *Komm.* v, 384.

2. This sentence appears to be in effect a sentence with nominal predicate, *wbn wrr* being the subject and *ḏdw nṯrw* the predicate, *ḏdw* being the relative form: 'He-who-is-great-rises is what-the-gods-say.'

3. *Wḏꜣ n ib·k*, lit. 'haleness for your heart', is clearly related to *wḏꜣ ib·k* 'may it please you' introducing an announcement of news, *Sh. S.* 1–2, and to *swḏꜣ ib* 'inform', *Peas.* B1, 36–7. 213, as well as to *swḏꜣ ib pw n nb·i* 'it is a communication to my lord', the well-known epistolary

formula. Sethe in *Komm.* v, 386 has seen this, but has not realized that the following *ḫr* is simply the preposition 'as to', 'concerning', and so has missed the point of the passage.

4. Singular suffix, probably only by force of habit; the dual *·ṯny* is needed.

5. Hortative old perfective.

6. *R (r)dit*, preposition *r* before *sḏmt·f* form. Sethe in his translation 'damit . . .' or 'sodass . . .' does not account for the ending *-t* of the verb, nor does his comparison (*Komm.* v, 389) with *iry·i r ḥzt·k* hold good, since *ḥzt·k* is infinitive with objective suffix, 'I will act so as to please you', and the infinitive is out of the question here.

7. i.e. Horus.

8. Var. *wnm* 'eat'.

9. Osiris.

10. Atum's?

11. So $P^2$. M; $P^1$ has less probably 'you shall mount up to this King, O God'.

12. Var. 'third', perhaps in error.

13. On *it in* cf. *JEA* 24, 124 f. In § 1459*c* the $P^1$-text is to be preferred.

14. *Nwnw*, meaning unknown. Cf. *Komm*, v, 402 f.

15. So $P^2$; $P^1$ and M are in the affirmative.

16. Cf. *idryt* 'punishment', *Concise Dict.* 36.

17. For the translation of *ins* as 'redness', i.e. blood, despite the determinative in $P^2$, cf. Sethe in *Komm.* v, 409 and Alliot in *Rev. d'Ég.* 10, 4; but the latter's version of § 1464*b*—'il se détache de son sein (maternel), les dieux n'agiront pas contre ce Pepi'—cannot be accepted. I believe that *dḥr* here means not 'lasso' but 'bind firmly together', and for *bnw* I suggest 'waist' or 'buttocks', cf. *wbnw* 'root of tail(?)', § 547*b*; Utt. 336, n. 3, perhaps here with loss of initial *w*. I take it that the meaning of the sentence is that no harm can come to the king because his body is firmly bound up. *Irty* in the next clause is prospective relative form.

## Utterance 571

### *The king is the son of Atum and is a star*

§ 1466 The King's mother was pregnant with him, (even he) who was in the Lower
Sky, the King was fashioned by his father Atum before the sky existed,
before earth existed, before men existed, before the gods were born, before
§ 1467 death existed;| the King escapes his day of death just as Seth escaped his day
§ 1468 of death, this King is bound for your . . .[1] O you gods of the Lower Sky,| who
suffer no harm from your foes,[2] this King will suffer no harm from his foes;
O you who die not[3] because of a king, this King will not die because of a
king; O you who die not because of any dead, the King will not die because of
§ 1469 any dead,| for the King is an Imperishable Star, son[4] of the sky-goddess who
dwells in the Mansion of Selḳet. Rēʿ has taken this King to himself to the
sky so that this King may live, just as he who enters into the west of the sky
§ 1470 lives when he goes up in the east of the sky;| He who is in his service has

commended this King to Him who is in his litter that they may serve the King, for the King is a star. The protection of Rēʿ is over this King and the protection of Rēʿ will not be removed from over this King;| Horus has offered § 1471 this King his arms[5] on his own account and allots this King to Shu, whose arms which are under the sky are upraised. O Rēʿ, give this King your hand; O great god, give this King your staff that he may live for ever.

1. *Wdrw*, meaning unknown.
2. Read *iḫmw nk n ḫftyw·sn*, lit. 'who know no injury of their foes'. Sethe, *Komm.* v, 417, would emend *nk* into *sk*, but this seems needless; I take *nk* to be the simplex of the partial reduplication *nkn* 'harm', *Concise Dict.* 141.
3. Read *tmiw mt*, referring back to the gods of the Lower Sky. Sethe, loc. cit., is surely right in regarding ⏜ as the determinative of *tmiw*, despite its abnormal position.
4. On the reading of the broken sign as *zꜣ* 'son' cf. loc. cit. and JPII, 1350+84. *Pt wrt* 'great sky' is here a personification of the sky as goddess.
5. Read simple *rmnwy* here; the absence of a preposition speaks against Sethe's '(an) seine Seite'. He also translates *wdn* as 'ernennen', which does not suit the context; as I see it, Horus is offering a helping hand to the king. *N* has been omitted before the cartouche.

## Utterance 572

### *An 'ascension' text*

'How lovely to see, how pleasing to behold!' says Isis, when you[1] ascend to § 1472 the sky, your power upon you, your terror about you, your magic at your feet;| you are helped[2] by Atum just as he used to do, the gods who are in the § 1473 sky are brought to you,[3] the gods who are on earth assemble for you,| they § 1474 place their hands under you, they make a ladder for you that you may ascend on it to the sky, the doors of the sky are opened for you, the doors of the starry firmament are thrown open for you,[4]| Atum has assembled the nomes for you, § 1475 he has given the cities of Gēb to you, having spoken about it, (even) the Mounds, the Mounds of Horus, the Mounds of Seth, and the Field of Rushes.| You are *Rꜣhs*[5] who presides over Upper Egypt, you are *Ddwn* who presides § 1476 over Nubia, you are Sopd who is under his *ksbt*-trees.| Have they killed you § 1477 or said that you shall die?[6] You shall not die, but shall live for ever.[7] You shall be effective against them as[8] the Enduring Bull of the wild bulls, that you may be superior to them, living and enduring(?)[9] for ever.

1. The 2nd person is original here, cf. *Komm.* v, 422 and n. 3 below. The king is addressed.
2. Reading *irw* with M.
3. At this point the M-text reverts to the original 2nd person.
4. P only.

5. Var. *Ṭḥs.*

6. Following M, cf. *Komm.* v, 424 f. The persons referred to are the murderers of Osiris = the King. P strangely addresses them in the 2nd person: 'Have you harmed him or said that he shall die?'

7. P only.

8. Sethe strangely translates *m* with 'zum Trotz zum'; not only is it questionable whether *m* can bear this meaning, but its function here seems simply to express identity or similarity.

9. Cf. Utt. 422, n. 2.

## Utterance 573

*The morning hymn to the sun*

§ 1478 May you wake in peace, O Purified, in peace!
May you wake in peace, O Horus of the East, in peace!
May you wake in peace, O Soul of the East, in peace!
May you wake in peace, O Ḥarakhti, in peace!
§ 1479 May you sleep in the Night-bark,
May you wake in the Day-bark,
For you are he who oversees the gods,
There is no god who oversees you!

*The king wishes to join the sun-god*

§ 1480 O my[1] father, take me with you to your mother Nūt,| that the doors of the sky may be opened for me and that the doors of the firmament may be thrown open for me. I am on my way to you that you may nourish me;[2] command that I shall sit beside you, beside Him who at morning-tide is on the horizon.|
§ 1481 O my father, give command to this *Msḫntt*[3] who is at your side that she may cause a place to be cleared for me at the causeway beneath the firmament;|
§ 1482 give command to Him who has life, the son of Sothis, that he may speak on my behalf and establish my seat in the sky. Commend me to him who is greatly noble, the beloved[4] of Ptaḥ, the son of Ptaḥ, that he may speak on my behalf and that he may provide supplies for my jar-stands(?) which are on
§ 1483 earth,| because I am one of these four gods, Imsety, Ḥapy, Duamūtef, Ḳebḥsenuf, who live by right-doing, who lean on their staffs and watch over Upper Egypt.

*The king flies up to the sky*

§ 1484 Someone flies up from you, O men, as do ducks,
He wrests his hands from you as does a falcon,[5]

He has removed himself from you as does a kite,
The King is saved from him who was obstructive on earth,
The King is loosed from him who attacked him.[6]

1. For the 1st person cf. *Komm.* v, 428. P shows that Rēʿ is addressed.
2. The 'nourishing' clause only in P.
3. Compare *msḫȝt*, name of a sacred beetle, Cairo 20328.
4. Var. 'who pleases Ptaḥ'.
5. Var. *smn* 'goose'. The allusion is to the Egyptian habit of carrying live birds by their wings; the king is envisaged as a bird escaping from the hand of the fowler.
6. For the sense of *ỉmy* in *ỉmy-rd*, lit. 'in whom is a foot', and *ỉmy-ʿwy*, lit. 'in whom are hands', cf. *JEA* 28, 66 f. In translating § 1484*d–e* I have followed the P-text; M and N have undergone some corruption.

## Utterance 574

*Address to a sacred tree*

Hail to you, you tree which encloses the god, under which the gods of the § 1485
Lower Sky stand, the end of which is cooked, the inside of which is burnt,
which sends out the pains of death:[1] ⌉ may you gather together those who are § 1486
in the Abyss, may you assemble those who are in the celestial expanses. Your
top is beside you[2] for Osiris when the *ḏd*-pillar of the Great One is loosed,
like her who presides over *Ḥtpt* who bows to(?)[3] the Lord of the East.⌉ Your § 1487
tomb(?), O Osiris,[4] your shade which is over you, O Osiris, which repels your
striking-power, O Seth; the peaceful(?)[5] maiden who helped this spirit of
*Gḥsty*; your shadow, O Osiris.

The dread of you[6] is on those who are in the sky, the fear of you is on § 1488
those who are on earth, you have thrust(?)[7] the terror of you into the hearts
of the Kings of Lower Egypt who were in Pe.

I have come[8] [to you], O Horus, the heir of Gēb of whom Atum spoke; to § 1489
you belongs all, of whom the Two Enneads spoke; to you belongs all, as you
say.⌉ I will be in their company, (even) the gods who are in the sky. Those § 1490
who are in the celestial expanses assemble for you, those who are among the
Imperishable Stars flash[9] for you.

Turn about, O King![10] Turn about, O King! Shout! Shout! Day by day, § 1491
night by night, day after day, [so long as . . . exists], he[11] shall exist for ever.

1. Cf. *Komm.* v, 442 f.
2. i.e. bent over horizontally in obeisance to Osiris.
3. Read *dh[nt(?) n] nb ỉȝbt.*
4. § 1487 is composed of epithets of the tree.

5. Sethe: 'die Jungfrau (oder: die Lieferin) des Mahles'.

6. The pronoun is feminine and therefore must refer to the tree, which apparently is addressed by the king.

7. *Nd* may well be a niph'al formation from *d(w)* 'place', etc.

8. The king appears still to be speaking.

9. Cf. Utt. 488, n. 1.

10. Sethe: 'munter soll N sein', but *inn* means 'turn about', cf. §§ *222a*; *705b*; *1786a*, *CT* i, *306a*, here in the sense of 'turn back to life' as an imperative addressed to the king. The following summons to 'shout' means in effect 'let us hear that you are alive again'.

11. The king?

## Utterance 575

*The king arrives in the Beyond*

§ 1492 'Behold, he has come; behold, he has come', says *Zḥpw*.
'Behold, the son of Rēʿ has come; behold,[1] the beloved of Rēʿ has come', says *Zḥpw*.
'I caused him to come; I caused him to come', says Horus.

§ 1493 'Behold, he has come; behold,[2] he has come', says *Zḥpw*.
'Behold, the son of Rēʿ has come; behold, the beloved of Rēʿ has come', says *Zḥpw*.
'I caused him to come; I caused him to come', says Seth.

§ 1494 'Behold, he[3] has come; behold, he has come', says *Zḥpw*.
'Behold, the son of Rēʿ has come; behold, the beloved of Rēʿ has come', says *Zḥpw*.
'I caused him to come; I caused him to come', says Gēb.

§ 1495 'Behold, he has come; behold, he has come', says *Zḥpw*.
'Behold, the son of Rēʿ has come; behold, the beloved of Rēʿ has come', says *Zḥpw*.
'I caused him to come; I caused him to come', say the Souls of Ōn and the Souls of Pe.

§ 1496 O Rēʿ, thus men say,[4] when they stand beside this King on earth: 'When you have appeared in the east of the sky, give your hand to the King, take him with you to the eastern side of the sky.'

§ 1497 O Rēʿ, thus men say, when they stand beside the King on earth: 'When you have appeared in the southern side of the sky, give your hand to the King, take him with you to the southern side of the sky.'

§ 1498 O Rēʿ, thus men say, when they stand beside this King on earth: 'When you have appeared in the middle of the sky, give your hand to the King, take him with you to the middle of the sky.'

What is brought is your tribute, the couriers who come are your attendants. § 1499

1. Read probably ⟨*m*⟩ *mry* with the two *m*'s merged by haplography.
2. The second 𓇋 is a dittograph, as again in § 1495*a*.
3. 𓇋[hieroglyph] is an error for [hieroglyph].
4. Cf. *JEA* 21, 183(*e*); Sethe regards *in* as interrogative.

## Utterance 576

### *A 'resurrection' text*

Osiris was laid low by his brother Seth, but He who is in Nedit moves, his § 1500
head is raised by Rēᶜ; he detests sleep and hates inertness,| so the King will § 1501
not putrefy, he will not rot, this King will not be cursed[1] by your anger, you gods.

May you wake in peace, may you wake, Osiris, in peace, may you wake, O § 1502
you who are in Nedit, in peace.| His head is raised by Rēᶜ, his savour [is that § 1503
of *Iḫt-*]*wtt*; the King's head is indeed raised by Rēᶜ, the King's savour is
that of *Iḫt-wtt*,| and he will not rot, he will not putrefy, this King will not be § 1504
cursed by your anger, you gods.

The King is your seed, O Osiris, you being potent[2] in your name of Horus § 1505
who is in the sea, Horus at the head of the spirits;| the King will not rot, he § 1506
will not putrefy, he will not be cursed by your anger, you gods.

The King [has gone out] from his house girded as Horus and adorned as § 1507
Thoth; the King's mother is your Ōnite, you god; the King's father is an
Ōnite, and the King himself is your Ōnite, you god.| The King is conceived § 1508
for Rēᶜ, he is born for Rēᶜ; the King is your seed, O Rēᶜ, you being potent
in this your name of 'Horus at the head of the spirits, Star which crosses| the § 1509
sea'. The King will not rot, he will not putrefy, he will not be cursed by your anger, you gods.

The King is one of these four gods whom Gēb fashioned, who traverse § 1510
Upper Egypt, who traverse Lower Egypt, who stand with their staffs,| who § 1511
smear on unguent, who are clad in red linen, who live on figs and drink wine;|
the King is anointed with that wherewith you are anointed, the King is clad § 1512
with that wherewith you are clad, the King lives on that whereon you live, the
King drinks of that whereof you drink.| This King is hale in your company, § 1513
he lives on that whereon you live, you give his meal from this which your father Gēb has given to you, possessing which you will not be hungry,

§ 1514 possessing which you will not rot.[1] You shall hold this King's hand for life, (even) the chief pleasant of savour, this King's bones shall be reassembled, his members shall be gathered together, this King shall sit on his throne,[1]
§ 1515 and he will not rot, he will not putrefy, the King will not be cursed by your wrath, you gods.

§ 1516 The King has come to you, O mother of the King, he has come to Nūt, that you may bring the sky to the King and hang up the stars for him, for his savour is the savour of your son who issued from you, the King's savour is that of Osiris your son who issued from you.

§ 1517 O Nu, raise the King's arm to the sky that he may support the earth which he has given to you. He will indeed ascend and rise to the sky, he will act
§ 1518 as escort to Rēʿ,[1] (even) Horus at the head of the spirits, the chief pleasant of savour. May you awake in peace, may Rēʿ awake in peace; may you awake
§ 1519 in peace, may *Mdl* wake in peace.[1] He will put a writing in his register for this King, the chief pleasant of savour.

1. For *šn* in the sense of 'curse' the king cf. *Sin.* B74.

2. i.e. 'effective' in a sexual sense; *spd·t(y)* is old perfective 2nd sing. The fem. suffix in the following *m rn·ṯ* here and in § 1508*c* is due to misunderstanding *spd·t(y)* as referring to *mtwt* 'seed'; in fact it refers to the dead Osiris who becomes the living Horus.

## Utterance 577

*Osiris and the king are associated*

§ 1520 Osiris appears, the Sceptre is pure, the Lord of Right is exalted at the First of the Year, (even he) the Lord of the Year.

§ 1521 Content is Atum, father of the gods;
Content are Shu and Tefēnet;
Content are Gēb and Nūt;
Content are Osiris and [Isis];
Content are Seth and Neith;[1]
§ 1522 Content are all the gods who are in the sky;
Content are all the gods who are on earth, who are in the flat-lands:
Content are all the southern and northern gods;
Content are all the western and eastern gods;
Content are all the gods of the nomes;
Content are all the gods of the towns
§ 1523 With this great and mighty word
Which issued from the mouth of Thoth for Osiris,
(Even he) the Treasurer of Life, Seal-bearer of the gods.

Anubis who claims hearts, he claims Osiris the King from the gods who are on earth for the gods who are in the sky.

The Lord of wine in flood, his seasons have recognized him, his times have remembered him, and the King is recognized by his seasons with him, his times with him have remembered him. § 1524

'Here comes the Dweller in the Abyss', says Atum. 'We have come', say § 1525
they, say the gods to you, O Osiris.[1] 'Here comes the brother of the Oldest § 1526
One, the first-born of his father, the eldest of his mother', say they, say the
gods.[1] The sky has conceived him,[2] the dawn has borne him, and this King § 1527
is conceived with him by the sky, this King is borne with him by the dawn.

You bear up the sky with your right side, possessing life; you live because the gods have ordered that you shall live; (so also) the King bears up the sky with his right side, possessing life; he lives, he lives, because the gods have ordered that he shall live. § 1528

You support the earth with your left side, possessing dominion; you live, you live, because the gods have ordered that you shall live; (so also) the King supports the earth[3] with his left side, possessing dominion;[4] he lives, he lives, because ⟨the gods⟩ have ordered that he shall live. § 1529

The King has gone up from the east side of the sky, he descends as a green duck, the Lord of the Lakes of the Netherworld descends to him,[5] and this King has bathed in the Goose-lakes. § 1530

1. So Sethe's published text; we would have expected 'Nephthys' here.

2.  is almost certainly an error for . Sethe's alternative explanation, *Komm.* v, 480, seems improbable.

3. Making the obvious emendation of *pt* into *tꜣ*, see n. 4 below.

4. *ꜥnḫ* 'life' is to be emended into *wꜣs* 'dominion' as § 1529*a*; clearly the scribe has repeated § 1528*c* in error.

5. Restore as *ḥꜣ r[f r·]f*, where the first *rf* is the enclitic particle. Sethe, ibid. 482, would restore the preposition as *ẖr*, but there seems hardly room for ● in the lacuna as shown in the published text.

## Utterance 578

### *A 'resurrection' text*

O Osiris the King, you shall not go into these eastern lands, you shall go § 1531
into those western lands by the road of the Followers of Rēꜥ;[1] your porters § 1532
hasten, your couriers run, those who stand before you hurry, that they may
announce you to Rēꜥ as one whose left arm is raised.

§ 1533 You do not know them,[1] you are astonished at them, but you take them
§ 1534 into your embrace as the herdsmen of your calves.| You it is who prevent them from becoming inert in your embrace; you go up to them empowered, effective, as all my children, as all my children,[2] in this your name of Sopd.|
§ 1535 Your flail is in your hand, your sceptre is at your hand, the slayers fall on
§ 1536 their faces at you, the Imperishable Stars kneel to you.| You it is who prevent them from slipping[3] from your embrace; come to them in this your name of
§ 1537 *Mḥyt.*| They recognize you in this your name of Anubis; the gods will not
§ 1538 descend against you in this your name of Milk-goddess.| Stand up in front of the gods, O eldest son, as heir, as one upon the throne of Gēb.

1. The pronoun must refer to beings who had been named in an omitted portion of text; cf. *Komm.* v, 485 f.

2. Read *msw(·i) t⟨w⟩t*, cf. ibid. 487.

3. Cf. Utt. 484, n. 4.

## Utterance 579

*As last*

§ 1539 This ascent of yours from your house, O Osiris this King, is the ascent of Horus seeking you, O Osiris this King. Your porters hasten, your couriers
§ 1540 run, your heralds hurry;| they tell Rēʿ that you have come, O King, as the
§ 1541 son of Gēb upon the throne of Amūn.| May you cross the Winding Waterway, may you traverse the Canal of Kenzet, may you fall in the eastern side of the sky, may you sit in the Two Conclaves of the horizon, may you put your
§ 1542 hand on them,| may you put your hand on the gods, may they give you praise when they come to you bowing just as they give praise to Rēʿ when they come to him bowing.

## Utterance 580

*An offering text in which the sacrificial ox represents Seth*

*Address to the ox by the priest impersonating Horus*

§ 1543 O you who smote my father, who killed one greater than you, you have smitten my father, you have killed one greater than you.

*Address to the dead king*

§ 1544 O my father Osiris this King, I have smitten for you him who smote you as an ox; I have killed for you him who killed you as a wild bull; I have broken for you him who broke you as a long-horn on whose back you were, as a

subjected bull.[1] | He who stretched you out is a stretched bull; he who shot(?) § 1545
you is a bull to be shot(?);[2] he who made you deaf is a deaf bull. I have cut off its head, I have cut off its tail, I have cut off its arms (*sic*), I have cut off its legs.| Its upper foreleg is on Khopr(er?), its lower foreleg [belongs to § 1546
Atum],[3] father of the gods, its haunches belong to Shu and Tefēnet, its *mid3* belong to Gēb and Nūt,| its thighs belong to Isis and Nephthys, its § 1547
shanks belong to *Ḫnt-irty* and Kherty, its back belongs to Neith and Selḳet, its heart belongs to Sakhmet the Great,| the contents of its udder (*sic*)[4] belong § 1548
to these four gods the children of Horus whom he loves, Ḥapy, Imsety, Duamūtef, Ḳebḥsenuf.| Its head, its tail, its arms, and its legs belong to Anubis § 1549
who is on the mountain and Osiris *Ḫnty-mnwt·f*. What of it the gods have left over belongs to the Souls of Nekhen and the Souls of Pe.| May we eat, § 1550
may we eat the red ox for the passage of the lake which Horus made for his father Osiris this King.

1. Lit. 'on-the-back bull', i.e. a subjected animal on whose back the king stands. For a group embodying this notion, but with a leopard instead of a bull, see Fox, *Tutankhamun's Treasure*, pl. 56.

2. I suggest that *isr* may be a denominative verb from *isr* 'arrow'; it seems to make better sense as 'shoot' than Sethe's 'melken', even in the latter's secondary sense of 'impoverish'.

3. Sethe: 'sein oberer Vorderschenkel, der sein unterer Vorderschenkel geworden ist, gehört dem [Atum]'. Apart from its obscurity, this translation is ruled out of court by the absence of *m* after *ḫpr*. By analogy with what follows, it would seem that *ḫpr* is a shortened form of the god's name *Ḫprr*.

4. The determinative makes the meaning of *mpḥ* clear beyond a doubt; the original compiler of this text has forgotten that he is writing about a bull, but Sethe has missed this point. The word looks like a derivative in *m* from *pḥwy* 'hinder-parts'; so also Sethe.

## Utterance 581

### *The king is identified with Osiris*

This is this cavern of yours,[1] the Broad Hall, O Osiris this King, which brings § 1551
the wind that it may strengthen(?)[2] the north-wind and lift you up as Osiris this King.| The Winepress-god comes to you bearing grape-juice, and § 1552
*Ḫnty-mnwt·f* bearing the bowls of those who preside over the Conclaves. May you stand and sit as Anubis who presides over the Sacred Land,| for § 1553
the Earth-god attends on you, Shu rages(?)[3] for you, those who see the Nile when it surges tremble,| the meadows laugh, and the river-banks are inun- § 1554
dated. The god's-offerings descend, the faces of men are bright, the hearts of the gods rejoice.

§ 1555 'May you save this King from the knot which holds back(?) the living and
hinders the gods' (is said) in the mouths of those who have gone to them on
§ 1556 that happy day of running.| 'Seth is offered up,[4] Osiris is in the right' (is said)
in the mouths of the gods on that happy day of going up on the mountain,|
§ 1557 and those who are on earth have abundance. O you who run in your power
hence(?)[5] to your cavern, may you go after your spirit in order to catch the
winds like the hand of Kherty who is pre-eminent in *N*[*z*]*ɜt*.

1. *In* has been taken to be the emphasizing particle before a sentence with nominal predicate, cf. Edel, § 845; to regard this sentence as a question, as Sethe does, yields a poorer sense, for no answer to the question is forthcoming.

2. For *sɜkh* see also § 701*b* and *Komm.* iii, 284 f.

3. Perhaps a reference to high winds, Shu being the air-god.

4. i.e. killed; on Seth's role as sacrificial bull see Utt. 580.

5. For *i nw* read probably *ir nw*.

## Utterance 582

*An 'ascension' text*

§ 1558 I have come[1] to you, O Horus, that you may utter to me this great and goodly
word which you gave to Osiris, that I may be great by means of it, that I may
§ 1559 be mighty by means of it,| that I may have power within myself, that my
soul may be behind me, that my effectiveness may be upon me, (even that)
which Horus gave to Osiris, that I may endure in the sky like a mountain,
§ 1560 like a support.| May I soar cloudwards to the sky like a heron, may I surpass
the side-locked ones of the sky, the plumes on my shoulders being like
§ 1561 spines.[2] | May Orion give me his hand, for Sothis has taken my hand. The
earth is hacked up for me, offerings are presented to me, (even I) for whom
§ 1562 the Two Districts shout.[3] | I am more pre-eminent than he who presides
over the Two Enneads, I sit on my iron throne, my iron sceptre in my hand;|
§ 1563 I lift up my hand to the children of their fathers and they stand up; I lay my
§ 1564 hand down toward them and they sit down.| My face is that of a jackal, my
middle is that of the Celestial Serpent,[4] I govern as Sobk who is in Shedet
§ 1565 and as Anubis who is in *Tɜbt*.[5] | I summon a thousand, and the sun-folk come
to me bowing. If they say to me: 'Who has done this for you?', (I reply):|
§ 1566 'It is my mother the great Wild Cow, long of plumes, bright of head-cloth,
pendulous of breasts, who has lifted me up to the sky, not having left me
§ 1567 on earth, among the gods who have power.'| I see that they are powerful,
and I am powerful likewise. I [am saved(?)] by my father Osiris, the sun-folk
have guarded me.[6]

1. For the 1st person cf. e.g. the cognate Utt. 467. 471. 484. 509.
2. Cf. Utt. 674, n. 13.
3. Var. 'the Two Districts of the god come down to me'.
4. Cf. § 1749*a*.
5. Cf. *Dict. géogr.* vi, 14.
6. Sethe's translation and commentary end here.

## Utterance 583

*The sun-god's attention is called to the king*

O Rēʿ, turn yourself about and see this King [. . .] this King; she (*sic*) whom § 1568
you should redden[1] is this King [. . .] is the King, O Rēʿ, the uraeus which is
on the vertex of Rēʿ.

*The king himself is addressed*

You are he who is lifted up, you are she who is lifted up;[2] you are he who § 1569
is . . ., you are she who is . . .,[3] you are [. . .| . . .]. The arm of Horus is § 1570
about you, the arm of Thoth [is about you(?)],| the two great gods have § 1571
supported you and they prepare your place which is in [. . .| . . .] you who § 1572
are lifted up, you who are lifted up by means of your legs [. . .].

1. i. e. supply with blood to restore the corpse to life. The fem. gender of the relative form may be due to the king being equated with some goddess named in the lacuna, as in § 1568*c* with the uraeus on the head of Rēʿ; in § 1569*a*–*b* the personal pronoun as subject remains masculine but the participial predicates are alternately masculine and feminine.
2. *Šwyt* in P has one 𓇋 too many.
3. *Nšz*, *Nšzzt*, meaning unknown.

## Utterance 584

*A variant of Utterance* 469

I have [occupied] my seat, [I have taken my] oar, [I sit in the bow] of the bark § 1573
of the Two Enneads,| [I row Rēʿ to the West and he inscribes me at the head § 1574
of the living], he makes firm my seat [at the head of the owners of doubles, he
sets me over the banks of the Winding Waterway], he sets me at the head of
the Elders,[1] | [the doors of *Bꜣ-kꜣ* which are in the firmament are opened for § 1575
me, the doors] of iron which are in the starry sky [are thrown open for] me,
[. . . and it is well with me] and with my name [. . .].

1. Or: 'the *nḫḫw*-stars'.

## Utterance 585

§§ 1576–81 *This Utterance is almost entirely lost. According to Jéquier, Nt, p. 26, Sethe suggested that Nt, 9–14 might belong here, but this supposition is ruled out because Nt, 9 ff. correspond to Utt. 736–40, see the Supplement, pp. 80–1.*

## Utterance 586[1]

*The king is urged to be like Rēʿ*

§ 1582 May you shine[2] as Rēʿ; repress wrongdoing, cause Māʿet to stand behind
§ 1583 Rēʿ, shine every day for him who is in[3] the horizon of the sky.| Open the gates which are in the Abyss.[4]

1. Supplement, p. 11.
2. The imperatives which follow point to the interpretation of *psḏ·k* as an optative.
3. 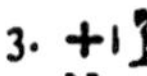 of Nt, 14 is certainly to be read as *imy*.
4. Nt, 15 has a stanza-sign here, which marks what follows as a separate Utterance (586A).

## Utterance 586A[1]

*The king is a star*

(§ 1583) O Great One of Atum, son of a great one of Atum, the King is a star in the
§ 1584 sky among the gods.| Tell your mother, O *Ssꜣ*, that it is the King who weeps
§ 1585 for you, it is the King who mourns[2] you [. . .]| give a hand to the King when he comes. O *Ḥꜣ·f* and *Mḥꜣ·f*,[3] bring to the King [the ladder][4] which Khnum
§ 1586 made that the King may ascend on it to the sky| and escort Rēʿ in the sky.

1. Supplement, pp. 11–12.
2. *Ḥꜣ* Nt, 16; P inexplicably .
3. So Nt, 17; P has *Nḥꜣ·f*.
4. Nt, 17 , but the determinative and context are decisive as to the reading *mꜣḳt*.

## Utterance 587

*An address to the sun-god*

§ 1587 Hail to you, Atum!
Hail to you, [Khoprer] the Self-created!
May you be high in this your name of 'Height',
May you come into being in this your name of Khoprer.

*An address to the Eye of Horus = Egypt*

Hail to you, Eye of Horus, which he has restored with both his hands! § 1588
He will not permit you to obey the Westerners,
He will not permit you to obey the Easterners,
He will not permit you to obey the Southerners,
He will not permit you to obey the Northerners,
He will not permit you to obey those who are in the middle of the earth,
But you shall obey Horus. § 1589
It is he who has restored you,
It is he who has built you up,
It is he who has set you in order,
That you may do for him everything which he says to you § 1590
Wherever he goes.
You shall lift up to him all the waters[1] which are in you,
You shall lift up to him all the waters which shall be in you.
You shall lift up to him all the trees[2] which are in you, § 1591
You shall lift up to him all the trees which shall be in you.
You shall lift up to him the bread and beer which are in you,
You shall lift up to him the bread and beer which shall be in you.
You shall lift up to him the offerings which are in you, § 1592
You shall lift up to him the offerings which shall be in you.
You shall lift up to him everything which is in you,
You shall lift up to him everything which shall be in you,
Which you shall take to him at any place
Which his heart desires.[3]
The doors which are on you stand like *Iwn-mwt·f*: § 1593
They will not open to the Westerners,
They will not open to the Easterners,
They will not open to the Northerners,
They will not open to the Southerners,
They will not open to those who are in the middle of the earth,
But they will open to Horus. § 1594
It is he who made them,
It is he who erected them,
It is he who saved them from every ill
Which Seth did to them.
It is he who sets you in order[4] § 1595
In this your name of 'Settlement';

It is he who comes and goes behind you
In this your name of 'City';
It is he who saved you from every ill[5]
Which Seth did to you.
§ 1596 Turn back, turn back, O Nūt;
Gēb has commanded that you turn back
In this your name of 'City'.

*The king speaks*

I am[6] Horus who restored his Eye with both his hands:
§ 1597 I restore you,[7] O you who should be restored;
I set you in order, O you settlements of mine;
I build you, O you city of mine;[8]
You shall do for me every good thing which I [desire];
You shall act on my behalf wherever I go.
§ 1598 You shall not obey the Westerners,
You shall not obey the Easterners,
You shall not obey the Northerners,
You shall not obey the Southerners,
You shall not obey those who are in the middle of the earth,
§ 1599 But you shall obey me.
It is I who restored you,
It is I who built you up,
It is I who set you in order,
§ 1600 And you shall do for me everything which I say to you
Wherever I go.
You shall lift up to me all the waters which are in you;
You shall lift up to me all the waters which shall be in you;
§ 1601 You shall lift up to me all the trees which are in you;
You shall lift up to me all the trees which shall be in you;
You shall lift up to me ⟨all⟩[9] the bread and beer which are in you;
You shall lift up to me all the bread and beer which shall be in you;
§ 1602 You shall lift up to me the offerings which are in you;
You shall lift up to me the offerings which shall be in you;
You shall lift up to me everything which is in you,
Which you shall take to me at any place
Which my heart desires.
§ 1603 [The doors which are in you] stand like *Ỉwn-mwt·f*;

They will not open to the Westerners,
They will not open to the Easterners,
They will not open to the Northerners,
They will not open to the Southerners,
They will not open to those who are in the middle of the earth,
[But they will open to] me. § 1604
It is I who made them,
It is I who erected them,
It was I who saved them from every ill
Which men did against them.
It is I [who set you in order] § 1605
In this your name of 'Settlements';
It is I who come and go behind you
In this your name of 'City';
It is I who saved you from every [ill]
[Which men did] against you.
Obey me alone, § 1606
For it is I who made you;
You shall not obey Him of the sharp knife.

1. Read *mw iwnw*, lit. 'the waters altogether'; for *iwnw* cf. § 575*c*.
2. For *ḫt·k* read *ḫt nb* as § 1591*b*.
3. The fragment in P at the end of § 1592*e* is surely out of place.
4. Here and in § 1595*c* P inserts the preposition *n* 'because' before *swt*, but it seems not strictly necessary, and N omits it.
5. Var. P: *wꜣḏt* 'fresh' in error for *mrt* 'harmful'; [hieroglyph] is an error for [hieroglyph].
6. The 1st person is original here, cf. *niwt⟨·i⟩* in § 1597*c*.
7. The realm of Egypt, as also above in § 1588*a* as 'Eye of Horus'.
8. Var. N: 'into my city'.
9. Supply *nb* 'all', cf. § 1601*d*.

## Utterance 588

### *Nūt assists the king*

O Osiris the King, your mother Nūt has spread herself over you in her name § 1607
of *St-pt*; she has caused you to be as a god to your foe in your name of 'God';[1]
she has protected you from everything evil in her name of 'Great Protec- § 1608
tress', for you are the eldest among her children.

## Utterance 589

*The king is the divine essence*

§ 1609 O King, you are the essence of all the gods, and Horus has protected you, you having become the essence of him.

## Utterance 590

*The king is free to come and go*

§ 1610 O Osiris the King, behold you are protected and alive, so that you may go to
§ 1611 and fro daily, and none will interfere with you.[1] That which appertains to a king is set in order for you, a king is caused to resemble you(?),[1] *Ꞽsnrt*[2] is fallen upon her son.

1. In § 1611*a*, *n·k* after *grg* and *ꞽszn* seems to me to be the dative rather than the ending of *sḏm·n·f* forms (Mercer), nor in this context can I accept his non-enclitic particle *ꞽs*. *Ꞽszn* (N) = *szn* (M) I take to be a *sḏm·f* form with (in N) a prothetic *ꞽ*. We may have here a reference to the dead king's successor.

2. Apparently a designation of the goddess Nūt, cf. § 1629*a*.

## Utterance 591

*The king assumes the šzmt-apron*

§ 1612 Horus has adorned himself with his *šzmt*-apron
Which has travelled over his land completely(?).[1]
Seth has adorned himself with his *šzmt*-apron
Which has travelled over his land completely(?).
§ 1613 Thoth has adorned himself with his *šzmt*-apron
Which has travelled over his land completely(?).
*Dwn-ˁnwy* has adorned himself with his *šzmt*-apron
Which has travelled over his land completely(?).
§ 1614 This King also has adorned himself with his *šzmt*-apron
Which has travelled over his land completely(?).
O Horus, take your Eye which was recognized for you
In the Prince-Mansion which is in Ōn.
O King, your double recognizes you from your foes.

1. *Nmtt* appears to be a feminine participle referring to the *šzmt*-apron. *Mtl-wtl* is completely obscure; I have guessed it to be a bungled writing of *m twt* 'in completeness', but with all reservations.

## Utterance 592

*Gēb is invoked on the king's behalf*

O Gēb, son of Shu, this is Osiris the King;[1] may your mother's heart quiver § 1615
over you in your name of Gēb, for you are the eldest son of Shu, his first-born.

O Gēb, this is Osiris the King; care for him, make complete(?)[2] [what § 1616
appertains to him], for you are the sole great god.| Atum has given you his § 1617
heritage, he has given to you the assembled Ennead, and Atum himself is
with them, whom his eldest twin children joined to you;| he sees you power- § 1618
ful, with your heart proud and yourself able(?) in your name of 'Clever(?)
Mouth', chiefest of the gods,| you standing on the earth that you may govern § 1619
at the head of the Ennead. Your fathers and your mothers are pre-eminent
among them, for you are mightier than any god. You shall come to Osiris the
King that you may protect him from his foe.[3]

O Gēb, clever(?) mouth, chiefest of the gods, Osiris the King is your son; § 1620
may you nourish your son with it,[4] may your son be made hale by means of it,|
for you are lord of the entire land. § 1621

May you have power over the Ennead and all the gods,| may you have § 1622
power and drive away all ill from this Osiris the King; may you not allow it to
come again against him in your name of Horus who does not repeat his work,|
for you are the essence of all the gods. Fetch them to yourself, take them, § 1623
nourish them, nourish [Osiris] the King, | for you are a god having power § 1624
over all the gods. The eye has issued from your head as the Upper Egyptian
crown Great-of-magic; the eye has issued from your head as the Lower
Egyptian crown Great-of-magic;| Horus has served you and has loved you,| §§ 1625–6
you having appeared as King of Upper and Lower Egypt and having power
over all the gods and their spirits.

1. Most abnormal word-order. Perhaps *zꜣ·k* 'your son' has been omitted before *pw*, cf. §§ 1620*a*; 1810*a*.
2. I have taken *ỉtm* to be the imperative of *tm* 'be complete', assuming a possible transitive sense; 'cease' seems to make no sense here, *pace* Mercer, who would connect the word with the stem *ỉtm* 'suffocate'.
3. Read *ḥw·k sw m-ꜥ ḫfty·f*, cf. JPII, 709+47; Nt, 380.
4. The sonship; cf. also § 1810*b*.

## Utterance 593

*A variant of Utterance* 366

Stand up, give your hand to Horus, that he may help you up.| Gēb has wiped § 1627
your mouth for you,| the Great Ennead has protected you, they have put Seth § 1628

under you on your behalf that he may be burdened with you, they have warded
§ 1629 off his evil influence[2] which he spat out against you. | Nūt has fallen upon
her son, namely you, that she may protect you; she enfolds you, she embraces
§ 1630 you, she lifts you up, for you are the eldest among her children. | Your sisters
Isis and Nephthys come to you, they have sat down[3] there in the place where
you are. Your sister Isis has laid hold of you, and she has found you complete
§ 1631 and great in your name of 'Bitter Lakes'.[4] | May you enclose[5] everything in
your embrace in your name of 'Surrounder of the Islanders', you being great
§ 1632 in your name of *ꜥꜣ-sk*.[6] | Horus brings Seth to you, he has given him to you,
bowed down under you, for your strength is greater than his. Horus has
§ 1633 caused that you enclose for yourself all the gods within your embrace, | for
Horus has loved his father in you, Horus will not allow you to be troubled(?),
Horus will not be far removed from you, Horus has protected his father in
you, you being alive as a living beetle, that you may be permanent in Mendes. |
§ 1634 Isis and Nephthys have waited for you in Asyūṭ because their Lord is in you
in your name of 'Lord of Asyūṭ'; because their god is in you in your name of
§ 1635 'Canal of the God'; | they worship you, do not be far from them. Isis comes
§ 1636 to you rejoicing through love of you; | your seed issues into her, she being
ready as Sothis. Ḥar-Sopd has issued from you in his name of 'Horus who
§ 1637 is in Sothis'; | you have power through him in his name of 'Spirit who is in
the *Ḏndrw*-bark'. Horus has protected you in his name of 'Horus the son who
protects his father'.

1. Lit. 'that he may cause you to stand'.
2. On *ꜥꜣꜥ* cf. *JEA* 21, 39 f. (with det. [hieroglyph]).
3. Read probably *ḥm⟨s⟩*.
4. *Km wr*; this peculiar epithet is due solely to the desire for a pun on *kmt wrt*.
5. *Sḏm·f* in N; imperative with reflexive dative in M.
6. Var. § 629*c*: *Šn-ꜥꜣ-sk*.

## Utterance 594

*An 'ascension' text*

§ 1638 You have ascended to the portal, having appeared as King and gone on high
as Wepwawet;[1] he will give support[2] and will not tire.

1. N puts all this into the 3rd person.
2. P has *rmn·k* as against *rmn·f* of N. Here the N-text is surely correct; in this and the next clause the suffixes must refer to Wepwawet as supporter of the king, though the wording is a little obscure; in this context the king requires external support. The change of person in P from the 2nd in *rmn·k* to the 3rd in *n wrḏ·n·f* is evidence of confusion, since both verbs must refer to the same person.

## Utterance 595

*The king becomes immortal*

Hail to you, O King! I have come to you on this day of yours at night,[1] § 1639
I have given to you *Nwt·k-nw*.[2] | I bring to you your heart and place it in § 1640
your body for you, just as Horus brought the heart of his mother Isis and just
as ⟨Isis⟩[3] brought the heart of her son Horus.

1. Read *ḏr ḫw* with M; N has a dittograph of *ḏr ḫ* . . . The sense given to *ḏr* is confirmed by *CT* i, 80*i*, which has *m* instead of *ḏr* in an otherwise identical sentence.
2. See Utt. 455, n. 1. Note the variants in *CT* i, 80*k*.
3. Omitted in our text by inadvertence and supplied from *CT* i, 80*n*.

## Utterance 596

*A 'resurrection' text*

They have indeed raised up for themselves those who are in the tombs, whose § 1641
seats are hidden. Awake! Raise yourself! Your hands on your possessions!

## Utterance 597

*The king is robed*

O King, come, don the intact Eye of Horus which is in Weaving-town. § 1642

## Utterance 598

*The king is censed*

This is this Eye of Horus which he gave to Osiris; give[1] it to him that he § 1643
may provide his face with it. This indeed is[2] something pleasant of odour
about which Horus spoke to Gēb—Incense of the fire.

1. Read *imi n·k*, imperative with reinforcing dative.
2. *Tn ḥm tw*; an unusual independent use of the demonstrative *tn*, probably an archaic and obsolete usage. That this Utterance is very old is shown by the use of the fem. *tw* as copula instead of the invariable *pw*. On the construction in general see Edel, § 840.

*The headings of Utterances quoted by Sethe in* § 1644 *have been translated above as headings to their respective Utterances*

## Utterance 599

*The king is identified with Gēb*

The King is Gēb, the clever(?) mouth, chiefest of the gods, whom Atum § 1645
placed at the head of the Ennead, with whose utterance the gods were pleased.

All the gods are pleased with everything which this King says, by means
§ 1646 of which it goes well with him for ever and ever.[1] Atum said of the King: 'See the clever(?) mouth who is among us; he summons us; let us go and join[1] him.'

§ 1647 Ho all you gods! Come all together, come assembled, just as[2] you came
§ 1648 together and assembled for Atum in Ōn.[1] He summons you that you may come and do everything good there for this King for ever.

*A prayer for pyramid and offerings*

§ 1649 A boon which the king grants and Gēb grants of these choice joints, invocation offerings for all gods who shall bring into being all good things for the King and who shall cause to endure this construction and this pyramid of the King, in accordance with what the King wishes in the matter, for ever and ever.

§ 1650 O all you gods who shall cause this pyramid and this construction of the King to be fair and endure: You[3] shall be effective, you shall be strong, you
§ 1651 shall have your souls, you shall have power,[1] you shall have given[4] to you a boon which the king grants of bread and beer, oxen and fowl, clothing and alabaster; you shall receive your god's-offerings, you shall choose for yourselves your choice joints, you shall have your oblations made to you, you shall take possession of the *Wrrt*-crown in the midst of the Two Enneads.

1. ○ in [hieroglyphs] is apparently a writing of the suffix 1st plur., *išm·n* and *iꜥḥ·n* being optative *sḏm·f* forms.

2. *Mi nw*; see Utt. 563, n. 5.

3. Following on the vocative *hꜣ nṯrw nb* in § 1650*a*, the translation of the Egyptian pronouns of the 3rd person into the English 2nd person is inevitable.

4. A participial statement with a passive participle as predicate; so also *intišn irw* in § 1651*d*.

## Utterance 600

*A prayer for the king and his pyramid*

§ 1652 O Atum-Khoprer, you became high on the height, you rose up as the *bnbn*-stone in the Mansion of the 'Phoenix' in Ōn, you spat out Shu,[1] you
§ 1653 expectorated Tefēnet,[1] and you set your arms about them as the arms of a *ka*-symbol, that your essence might be in them.[2] O Atum, set[3] your arms about the King, about this construction, and about this pyramid as the arms of a *ka*-symbol, that the King's essence may be in it, enduring for ever.

§ 1654 O Atum, set your protection[4] over this King, over this pyramid of his, and over this construction of the King, prevent anything from happening evilly[5] against it for ever, just as your protection was set over Shu and Tefēnet.

O you Great Ennead which is on Ōn, (namely) Atum, Shu, Tefēnet, Gēb, § 1655
Nūt, Osiris, Isis, Seth, and Nephthys; O you children of Atum, extend his goodwill(?)[6] to his child in your name of Nine Bows.[1] Let his back be turned(?)[7] § 1656
from you toward Atum, that he may protect this King, that he may protect this pyramid of the King and protect this construction of his from all the gods and from all the dead and prevent anything from happening evilly against it for ever.

O Horus, this King is Osiris, this pyramid of the King is Osiris, this § 1657
construction of his is Osiris; betake yourself to it, do not be far from it in its name of 'Pyramid',[1] you being complete and great in your name of 'Mansion § 1658
of the Bitter Lakes'.[8] Thoth has set the gods under you, hale and true(?) in *Ḏḏꜣ* and in *Dmꜣꜥ*,[9] O Horus, as your father Osiris in his name of 'Mansion of the Monarch'. Horus has given the gods to you,[1] he has made them mount § 1659
up to you with reed-pens(?) that they may make your face bright in the Castles of the Mace.

1. *M* before the object of a transitive verb looks like an early instance of Coptic ⲛ in this position, cf. Till, *Koptische Grammatik*, § 258(*a*).

2. The first *kꜣ* is a reference to the actual ⊔-sign with its upraised open arms; the second has here the meaning 'essence' or the like, referring to the divine nature passed on by Atum to his offspring.

3. Imperative with reinforcing dative.

4. A reduplicated form of *nḫ* 'protect'.

5. The position of *ḏw* in the sentence, as well as the absence of the fem. ending, shows that it is the adverb and not the adjective.

6. Lit. 'heart'. The translation of this passage is not certain, but it seems to be an appeal to the Ennead to extend Atum's goodwill to his other offspring the king.

7. Reading *ỉm(ỉ) psḏ·t(w)·f*, lit 'cause that he be back-turned' to the protecting god, who stands behind him. Mercer's rendering 'no one among you separates himself from Atum' is grammatically impossible; it would require *n psḏ·tw sw ỉm·ṯn r Ỉtm*. On *psḏ* 'turn the back' cf. also Utt. 613, n. 2.

8. *Km wr*; cf. Utt. 593, n. 3.

9. Names of places or of buildings; *Ḏḏꜣ* and *Dmꜣꜥ* are puns on (*w*)*ḏꜣw mꜣꜥw* preceding; so also *ỉt*(*y*) 'father' and *ỉt*(*y*) 'monarch' next below.

## Utterance 601

*As last*

O you Great Ennead which is in Ōn, make the King's ⟨name⟩ endure, make § 1660
this pyramid of this King and this construction of his endure for ever, just

§ 1661 as the name of Atum who presides over the Great Ennead endures. | As the name of Shu, Lord of Upper *Mnst*[1] in Ōn, endures, so may the King's name endure, and so may this pyramid of his and this construction of his endure likewise for ever.

*This stock formula is repeated many times, each time for a different deity, their names being as follows:*

§ 1662. Tefēnet, Mistress of Lower *Mnst* in Ōn.
§ 1663. Gēb who is at *B-t*.[2]
§ 1664. Nūt in the *Šnít*-mansion in Ōn.[3]
§ 1665. Osiris in the Thinite nome.
§ 1666. Osiris as Foremost of the Westerners.
§ 1667. Seth in Nūbet.[4]
§ 1668. Horus in Djebʿat.[5]
§ 1669. Rēʿ who is at the horizon.
§ 1670. *Ḫnt-írty* at Khem.[6]
§ 1671. Wedjōyet in Dep.[7]

1. On the Upper and the Lower *Mnst* cf. *Dict. géogr.* iii, 41.
2. Unknown locality.
3. See Utt. 7, n. 2.
4. Cf. *AEO* ii, 28*.
5. Cf. Utt. 413, n. 2.
6. Cf. *AEO* ii, 161*.
7. Cf. *AEO* ii, 188*.

## Utterance 602

*An incantation on behalf of the king*

§ 1672 To Earth! To Gēb! To Osiris! To Anubis! To the Master of Festival! Make[1] the King festal in the festival of Horus; may he who is among the falcons
§ 1673 run for the double of the King . . .[2] | May you[3] open his eyes for the King, may you break open his nostrils for him, may you split open his mouth for the King, may you unstop his ears for him and firmly plant his plumes for
§ 1674 him. | May you cause the King to surpass the god, filled with the power(?)[4] of the winds. When you have eaten this,[5] the King will find the remainder with you, and you shall give the King the remainder, for he has come.

1. *Dì·k*; the suffix shows that it is the *wr-ḥb* alone who is addressed here, whereas the plural suffix *·ṯn* which appears in §§ 1673–4 must be addressed to all the beings named.

2. *Ḥmmi* is quite obscure. Mercer, connecting it with *ḥmmyt* in *Wb.* iii, 95, 13, thinks it is the name of a magician, which seems to me most unlikely.

3. Plural, see n. 1 above.

4. Cf. *Wb.* iv, 50, 3.

5. Apparently a reference to a food-offering to the gods which accompanied the incantation.

## Utterance 603

*A 'resurrection' text*

Raise yourself,[1] O my father the King, knit on your head, gather together § 1675
your members, lift yourself up on your feet, that your will may guide you.
Your porters run, your heralds hurry,[1] your reporter comes to [you from](?) § 1676
the horizon,[2] Anubis comes to meet you, *Ḥtp* has given you his hand, [for which(?)] the gods have prayed [. . .]. 'Here comes the ibis as his spirit,' say the
Two Enneads,[1] 'he has crossed the lake, he has traversed the Netherworld, § 1677
[. . .] does not oppose his feet, [. . .] does not accuse [him][3] to this Power who
endures every day,[1] he has come that he may rule towns and govern settle- § 1678
ments, and give orders to those who are in the Abyss.' Be seated[4] [. . .[1]. . . he § 1679
rests] in life in the West among the Followers of Rēʿ who approach the sky at dawn.

1. The lacunae have been completed from JPII, 709+40 ff.; see the Supplement, pp. 12–13.

2. JPII, 709+41 reads ; before *ꜣḫt* is a trace restored in the facsimile as . This is improbable; *m* 'in' is more likely. The passage has thus been restored as *ỉy smy·k n*[*·k m*] *ꜣḫt*; admittedly the position of the dative is abnormal, but it is not unique, and the trace of *n* recorded in Sethe has to be accounted for. The proposed restoration fits the space, and a reasonable sense is obtained.

3. For §§ 1676*c*–7*b* cf. JPII, 709+41–2.

4. Read *ḥms rk*, imperative, cf. JPII, 709+42.

## Utterance 604

*As last*

Raise yourself, O my father, great King, that you may sit in front of them;[1] § 1680
the aperture of the sky-window is opened for you and your sunshine-stride is extensive.[2] I say this to you, O my father the King; I call out 'Oho!'

1. Presumably the gods and spirits of the blessed dead.

2. The king steps out skyward on a path of sunbeams.

## Utterance 605

*The king is offered eye-paint by his son*

§ 1681 O my father the King, I have come and I bring[1] to you green eye-paint;
§ 1682 I bring to you the green eye-paint which Horus gave to Osiris.| I give you[2]
to my father the King just as Horus gave you to his father Osiris; Horus has
filled his empty Eye[3] with his full Eye.[4]

1. Var. 'behold, I bring'.
2. The eye-paint is addressed.
3. The eye torn out by Seth.
4. The eye-paint.

## Utterance 606

*His son reconstitutes the dead king*

§ 1683 Stand up for me, O my father; stand up for me, O Osiris the King, for I
§ 1684 indeed am your son, I am Horus.| I have come for you that I may cleanse you
and purify you, that I may bring you to life and collect your bones for you,
that I may gather together your soft parts[1] for you and collect your dismem-
§ 1685 bered parts for you,| for I am Horus who protected his father, I have smitten
him who smote you, I have protected you, O my father Osiris the King,
§ 1686 from him who would do ill to you;| I have come for you as a messenger[2] of
Horus, for he has installed you, O my father Osiris the King, upon the throne
of Rēʿ-Atum, that you may lead the sun-folk.

*The king is assimilated to the sun-god*

§ 1687 Go aboard this bark of Rēʿ to which the gods desire to draw near, aboard
which the gods desire to go, in which Rēʿ rows to the horizon, that you[3]
§ 1688 may go aboard it as Rēʿ;| sit on this throne of Rēʿ that you may give orders
to the gods, because you are Rēʿ who came forth from Nūt who bears Rēʿ
§ 1689 daily, and you are born daily like Rēʿ;| take possession of the heritage of your
father Gēb in the presence of the company of the Ennead in Ōn. 'Who
is like him?' say the two great and mighty Enneads who preside over the
§ 1690 Souls of Ōn.| These two great and mighty gods who preside over the Field
§ 1691 of Rushes install you upon the throne of Horus as their first-born;| they set
Shu for you on your east side and Tefēnet on your west side, Nu on your
§ 1692 south side and Nēnet on your north side;| they guide you to[4] these fair and
pure seats of theirs which they made for Rēʿ when they set him on their
§ 1693 thrones.| O King, they make you live and resemble the seasons of Ḥarakhti[5]

when they made his name. Do not be far removed from the gods,| so that § 1694
they may make for you this utterance which they made for Rēʿ-Atum who shines every day. They will install you upon their thrones at the head of all
the Ennead(s) as Rēʿ and as his representative.| They will bring you into § 1695
being like Rēʿ in this his name of Khoprer; you will draw near to them like Rēʿ in this his name of Rēʿ; you will turn aside from their faces like Rēʿ in this his name of Atum.

The Two Enneads are indeed joyous, O my father, at meeting you, O my § 1696
father Osiris the King, and they say: 'Our brother comes to us'[6] say the
Two Enneads about Osiris the King, my father Osiris the King.| 'One of us § 1697
comes to us' say the Two Enneads about you, O my father Osiris the King.|
'The eldest son of his father comes to us' say the Two Enneads about you, § 1698
O my father Osiris the King. 'First-born of his mother' say the Two Enneads
about you, O my father Osiris the King.| 'He to whom ill was done by his § 1699
brother Seth comes to us' say the Two Enneads. 'It will never be permitted that Seth be free of bearing you aloft for ever', O my father Osiris the King,
say the Two Enneads about you, O my father Osiris the King.| Raise yourself, § 1700
O my father Osiris the King, for you are alive.

1. Cf. *Wb.* ii, 236, 13; lit. apparently 'your swimming parts' as distinct from the rigid bones.

2. The determinative in N points to the reading *wpwtyw* 'messenger' rather than *wpt* 'message'.

3. In reference to the king, this text vacillates between the 2nd person and the 3rd, but the former is certainly original, and the text has been translated accordingly.

4. For *lrt* read the preposition *ir*.

5. i.e. reign as long as he; for *nḥr* 'resemble' cf. *nḥr·n·s ḥrt mi s(y)* 'it resembled the sky when one looked at it', *Urk.* iv, 860, 3.

6. Read *iy n·n sn·n.*

## Utterance 607

*Even as a child the king was protected*

The King was fashioned by Nu[1] at his left hand when he was a child who had § 1701
no wisdom;[2] he has saved the King from inimical(?)[3] gods, and he will not give the King over to inimical(?) gods.

1. Var. 'Nu fashioned the King'.

2. Cf. *JEA* 34, 28.

3. Read *tḥtḫ*; the related verb means 'make disturbance', § 392*d*; 'disorder' hair, *Urk.* v, 87, 4; *Herdsm.* 25; 'crumple' papers, *CT* iv, 385*d*.

## Utterance 608

*The king is called on to greet his divine relatives*

§ 1702 O King, stand up for your father the Great One, sit down for your mother Nūt, give your hand to your son Horus, for behold he has come to meet you.

## Utterance 609

*The king is heaven-born and crosses to the horizon*

§ 1703 O King, your mother Nūt has borne you in the West; go down to the West as a possessor of honour. Your mother Isis has borne you in Chemmis; extend your hands which belong to[1] the north-wind, that your field(?) may be in-
§ 1704 undated[2] behind the north-wind, O my father the King.| The Lake of Rushes is filled, the Winding Waterway is flooded, the Nurse-canal is opened for you;[3] you cross thereon to the horizon, to the place where the gods were born, and you were born there with them.

§ 1705 The reed-floats of the sky are set down for Rēʿ
That he may cross thereon to the horizon,
To the place where the gods were born,
Where he was born with them.

§ 1706 The reed-floats of the sky are set down for this King
That he may cross on them to the horizon,
To the place where ⟨the gods⟩[4] were born,
Where he was born with them.

§ 1707 Your sister is Sothis, your offspring is the Morning Star, and you shall sit between them on the great throne which is in the presence of the Two
§ 1708 Enneads.| 'Pray bring'[5] say those four regional spirits who sit by their staffs[6] and who ascend from the eastern side of the sky. They will raise up this good utterance of yours to *Nḥbw-kꜣw* when your daughter[7] has spoken to you, and *Nḥbw-kꜣw* will raise up this good utterance of yours to the Two Enneads.|
§ 1709 It is *Ḥnnty* who will grasp[8] your hand when you go aboard the bark of Rēʿ. Go aboard with a boon which the King gives; go aboard and ferry across.

1. *Nty* is the fem. dual genitival adjective, therefore the dual *ḏꜣty* 'hands' is to be read.

2. N reads 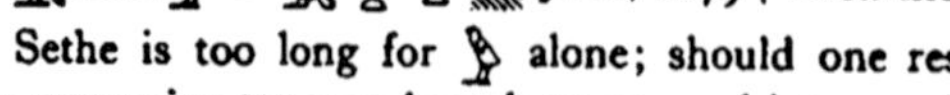 JPII, 1079+1. In the M-text the lacuna after  as indicated by Sethe is too long for  alone; should one restore M as 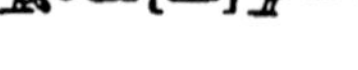 ? In N the two successive  may have been merged into one in error.

3. There is a confusion of persons in this Utterance as in Utt. 606; sometimes the king is spoken of in the 3rd person instead of the 2nd.

4. *Nṯrw* omitted in error.

5. I read this passage as *in m in fdw ipw ḥtyw*; Edel, § 615, however, seems to have understood it as *in my n*, etc., 'Bring to these four regional spirits'. Either view is grammatically possible. The object of *in* is not stated: the king?

6. *Dʿb* is a (dialectical?) var. of *dʿm* 'staff'.

7. Lit. 'your female daughter'.

8. *Ndrw·f* is a *sḏm·f* form in the future construction *in* + noun + *sḏm·f*; the writing out of the weak final radical here, as in *ḥmsw·k* in § 1707*b*, indicates that the precise verb-form used is the prospective *sḏm·f*.

## Utterance 610

### *A variant of Utterance* 437

Awake for Horus! Stand up for Seth! Raise yourself, you eldest son of Gēb, § 1710
at whom the Two Enneads tremble!¹ Stand up, O Herdsman, for whom the § 1711
three-day festival is celebrated! May you appear for the monthly festival,
may you be pure for the New Moon festival. The Great Mooring-post calls
out, because you are he who stands and will never tire in the midst of Abydos.¹
O earth, hear this which the gods have said, which Horus said when he made § 1712
a spirit of his father as Ḥa, as Min, and as Sokar who presides over *Pḏw-š*.¹
[The earth (*tₐ*)] speaks to you, the gate of the earth-god¹ is opened for you, § 1713
the doors of Gēb are thrown open for you that you may go forth at the
voice and spiritualize yourself,² O King, as Thoth and as Anubis, magistrate
of the Tribunal.

May you give orders when you are beside the Two Enneads between the § 1714
Two Wands in this spirit-form of yours which the gods commanded to
belong to you.¹ May you walk with the gait of Horus, [may you] speak [with] § 1715
the speech of Seth, may the limit of your foot be the limit of the feet of the
gods.¹ Betake yourself to the waterway, fare upstream to the Thinite nome, § 1716
travel about Abydos in this spirit-form of yours which the gods commanded
to belong to you;¹ may a stairway to³ the Netherworld be set up for you to the § 1717
place where Orion is, may the Bull of the sky take your hand, may you eat
of the food of the gods.¹ The savour of *Ddwn*, the youth of Upper Egypt who § 1718
issued from Nubia, is on you; may he give you the incense wherewith the gods
are fumigated.

The twin children of the King of Lower Egypt who are upon the Lord of § 1719
the *Wrrt*-crown have fashioned you; Rēʿ summons you into the zenith(?) of
the sky as the Jackal, the Governor of the Two Enneads, and as Horus *Ḥnty-
mnit·f*; may he set you as the Morning Star in the midst of the Field of Rushes.¹
The door of the sky at the horizon opens to you, the gods are glad at meeting § 1720

you as the star which crosses the sea below the under-part of the sky in this
§ 1721 dignity of yours which issued from the mouth of Rēʿ.| May you sit on this iron throne of yours as the Great One who is in Ōn, may you lead the spirits
§ 1722 and propitiate the Imperishable Stars.| May you have abundance of that herbage whereof the gods have abundance, whereof the spirits eat; your eyes are opened by the earth, your severed parts are raised up by the Lord of
§ 1723 Rebellion(?);| He who presides over Khem raises you and has given a *t-wr* loaf and this grape-juice; the *ỉmꜣ*-trees serve you, the zizyphus-tree bows its head to you, a king's boon is what is given to you, being what Anubis made for you.

1. The — after *ꜣkr* is a miswriting of — as determinative.

2. *Sꜣḫ ṯw* (N) is probably to be emended into *sꜣḫ·k ṯw*, in accord with what precedes and follows. The M-text is damaged. Compare § 796.

3. Emending as *ỉ(r) dꜣt*.

## Utterance 611

*The king is summoned to live again*

§ 1724 Live! May you live,[1] O my father, whoever you may be,[2] with the gods.
§ 1725 May you appear as *Wpỉw*, a soul at the head of the living;| have power here at the head of the spirits. O Great One of the Castle of the Mace,[3] O my father, may you both be at the head of the spirits. O Great Power, O my father, may you both be at the head of the spirits. My father the King is Thoth in your midst, you gods.

§ 1726 The bolt is opened for you[4] in the double Ram-gate which keeps out the plebs; may you number the slaughterers,[5] may you take the hands of the
§ 1727 Imperishable Stars.| Open your eyes, unstop your ears, enter into the House
§ 1728 of Protection, for your father Gēb has protected you.[6] | The great waters are joined together for you, the hoed lands(?)[7] are united for you and for Horus who protected his father and for my father this King who has protected
§ 1729 himself.| Worship is on you, the Great Vulture is on you, for you are worshipped and your nostrils are (bent) over the savour of *Ỉḫt-wtt*.

1. *ʿnḫ* is imperative and *ʿnḫ·ty* is hortative old perfective, as also *ḫʿ·ty* in § 1724*b*.

2. Cf. Utt. 249, n. 2. The doubt here expressed apparently refers to uncertainty as to which god the dead king has become.

3. *Pw* is certainly vocative here, for in the next clause the 'great one' and the king are referred to by the 2nd person (dual), as also in § 1725*b*. Note that *ʿḥ-ḥḏ* has lost the *ʿḥ*-sign in M.

4. The king.

5. i.e. the armed celestial door-keepers. On this text and its variants see *ZÄS* 79, 36 ff.

6. M appears to have a vocative: 'O you whom Gēb protects'.

7. The determinatives of *mrw* in M seem to represent land rather than water, so that the word may be from the same stem as *mrı* in *Tı-mrı* 'the hoed land', i.e. Egypt. A contrast to 'great waters' seems required here.

## Utterance 612

### *A continuation of the foregoing*

Indeed[1] this journey of yours, O my father the King, is as when Horus went to § 1730
his father Osiris so that he might be a spirit thereby, that he might be a soul thereby, that he might have strength thereby, and that he might have power thereby;| your spirit is behind you [. . .] ⟨your⟩ son's ears [hear] your utter- § 1731
ance, O my father the King.[2]| Gather together your bones, take your members, § 1732
cast off the earth which is upon your flesh,| take [these four *nmst*-jars of yours § 1733
which are filled to the brim from the Canal of the God in Iseion, which possesses the breath of Horus, and Isis the Great will dry you][3] as Horus.|
Rise up to the Eye of Rēʿ for this name of yours which the gods made for § 1734
Horus of the Netherworld, for Horus *Sksn*,[4] for Horus [. . .].| Raise your- § 1735
self and sit on this iron throne of yours, for your nails have wrecked(?)[5] the Mansion. May you circumambulate the Mounds of Horus, may [you] circumambulate [the Mounds of Seth . . .].

1. A writing of the non-enclitic particle *iwsw*, cf. Edel, § 858*b*.

2. Before *ıt N* in § 1731*b*, JPII, 1331 has .

3. Mercer, probably rightly, restores the long lacuna from § 1140*a–c*, and I have followed him in this. In place of *Ḥr ıs* in M at the end of § 1733*b*, JPII, 1332 at the end of the line has 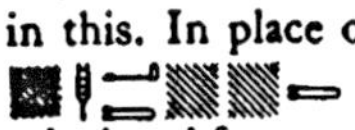 and then continues as M in § 1734*a*; these signs are almost certainly on misplaced fragments.

4. Meaning unknown; cf. § 1440*c* and *Komm.* v, 372.

5. Lit. probably 'your nails are what has destroyed the Mansion', with *ḥbıt ḥwt* as nominal predicate of *ʿnwt·k*; it is difficult otherwise to account for the fem. ending *-t*. The boat-determinative remains unaccounted for; possibly 'wreck' may be the best translation. Mercer's comments on this passage are far-fetched.

## Utterance 613

### *The king is ferried to the Beyond*

[. . .[1] *H*]*ḏhḏ* [. . .] to the Field of Offerings. *Hḏhḏ* the ferryman of the Winding §§ 1736–7
Waterway [comes] for him [. . .| . . .] the King on the western side of the § 1738

Field of Offerings behind the two great gods and the King hears what [they]
§ 1739 say [. . .[1] . . .]. Tefēnet seizes you, Shu grips you; the Majesty of Rēʿ will not turn back[2] in the horizon, for every god sees him.

1. Some fragments of this Utterance are said to be recorded in JPII, 1350+72–5, but except for the top of 1350+75, these odd sentences and parts of sentences cannot be linked with Sethe's text.

2. Hardly 'shine', since the verb is negatived; I take it to be a denominative verb from *psḏ* 'back', cf. also Utt. 600, n. 7. The sense is that Rēʿ will continue to shine.

## Utterance 614

*The king receives his subjects*

§ 1740 [. . .] at the gateway of the Mansion of the Soul; may you extend your hand
§ 1741 to them when they come to you bowing,[1] may you smite them [. . .] if you are translated to the possessors of honour.[1]

1. Cf. Utt. 438, n. 3.

## Utterance 615

*The king crosses to the Beyond*

§ 1742 The Eye of Horus is placed on the wing of his brother Seth, the ropes are tied, the ferry-boats are made ready[1] for the son of Atum, for the son of Atum is not boatless. This King is bound for the son of Atum, and the son of Atum is not boatless.

1. Cf. Utt. 555, n. 4.

## Utterance 616

*A summons to the ferryman's oar*

§ 1743 O you who are in the grasp of the ferryman of the Field of Rushes, bring me this[1] and ferry me over.

1. 'This' refers to the boat. As always in this class of text, the king himself is speaking.

## Utterance 617

§ 1744 Hasten,[1] punish[2] [. . .] O Osiris, hasten[3] [. . .] may you be united with the gods in Ōn.

A boon which the king grants wherever you may be, a boon which the § 1745
king grants in all your dignities, that you may walk in [your sandals] at the
side of Him who is in his swamp(?).[4]

1. *M* after *iz* is probably the particle *m*(*y*) which reinforces the imperative.
2. For *zz*(*i*) 'punish' cf. §§ 271*a*; 643*c* (with prothetic *i*).
3. Cf. JPII, 1314, which reads . . . 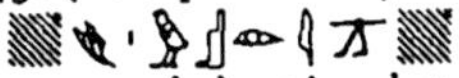 . . .
4. After the restored *wḫꜣty·k* JPII, 1315 reads *ir gs imy ḥnt·f*.

## Utterance 618

Be silent, O men, hear [. . .] to the Foremost of the Westerners. § 1746

## Utterance 619

*A 'resurrection' text*

Raise yourself, O King, raise yourself for the Great Adze,[1] raise yourself § 1747
upon your left side, place yourself upon your right side,| wash [your hands § 1748
in this] fresh [water] which your father Osiris[2] has given to you.[3] I have
cultivated barley, I have reaped emmer, I have acted on behalf of your
festival-supplies thereof which the Foremost of the Westerners has made for
you.| Your face is that of a jackal, your middle is that of the Celestial Serpent, § 1749
your hinder-parts are a broad hall;[4] a stairway has been set up to the sky that
you may ascend| and give judgement between the two great gods, (even) you § 1750
whom the Two Enneads support. Isis cries out to you, Nephthys calls to you,|
She of Imet[5] will sit on the steps of your throne; take your two oars, the one of § 1751
*wꜥn*-wood and the other of *sḏd*-wood,| so that you may cross the waterway to § 1752
your house the sea and protect yourself from him who would harm you.[6]
Oho! Beware of the Great Lake!

1. A ceremonial adze used in the rite of 'Opening the Mouth', cf. § 13*c* and Blackman, *Meir*, iii, p. 28, n. 2. Read ⟨*n*⟩ *nwi wr*.
2. *Wsir* written defectively without .
3. Gunn, *Syntax*, 73, tentatively suggests 'is giving', but this suits less well.
4. i.e. pointed of face, slim of body, and broad of hindquarters. Cf. § 1564*a*.
5. Tell el-Farꜥun (Nebeshah), *AEO* ii, 170* f.
6. Read *ir nn ir·k*, lit. 'who would do this against you', with 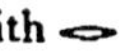 in error for .

## Utterance 620

*The king is summoned to rise*

I am Horus, O Osiris the King, I will not let you suffer. Go forth, wake up § 1753
for me and guard yourself!

## Utterance 621

*Perfume is offered to the king*

§ 1754 O Osiris the King, take the perfume of the Eye of Horus to yourself, even the Eye of Horus which he has diffused abroad by means of its perfume.[1]

1. Cf. § 19.

## Utterance 622

*The king is clothed*

§ 1755 O Osiris the King, I have clad you in the Eye of Horus, this Ernūtet-garment[1] of which the gods are afraid, so that the gods may fear you just as they fear the Eye of Horus.

1. Cf. Utt. 256, n. 2. Here Ernūtet embodies the royal robe.

## Utterance 623

§ 1756 O Osiris the King, take the Eye of Horus which I have made, for he has poured it out(?).[1]

1. The translation rests on a possible identity of *st*(?) with *stì* 'pour out'. It may be that a libation is in mind. Mercer has translated the relative form *ìrt·n*(·*ì*) as if it were a participle.

## Utterance 624[1]

*An 'ascension' text*

§§ 1757–8 I have gone up[2] on Shu, I have climbed on the wing of Khoprer,⁽ it is Nūt who takes my hand, it is Nūt who makes a way for me. Hail to you, you two
§ 1759 falcons⁽ who are in this [bark] of Rēᶜ which conveys Rēᶜ to the East: may you
§ 1760 lift me and raise me up to the Winding Waterway,⁽ may you set me among those gods the Imperishable Stars that I may fall among them; I will never
§ 1761 perish nor be destroyed,⁽ but I will sit between the two great gods who give judgement among the gods . . .[3] for(?) his brother [. . .] me. He acts as(?) [Min(?)][4] who goes forth by day, and I am Osiris who goes forth by night.

1. Supplement, pp. 14–15.

2. For the 1st person cf. *ḫr·ì m-m·sn* 'that I may fall among them', § 1760*b*, left unaltered by the original editor.

3. The use of the suffix 3rd masc. sing. in *smḥw·f* and *sn·f* without an antecedent points to an ancient textual omission. The meaning of *smḥw* is not known; its double occurrence in N is probably a dittograph.

4. See the textual note.

## Utterance 625[1]

*As last*

I have gone up by means of[2] the staff which is in *Grgw-bꜣ·f*, I have descended § 1762
upon the *hpwty*-pole;[3] I have gone up among the great ones,| I have descended § 1763
among the *šꜣsw*;[4] I have gone up upon the ladder with my foot on Orion and
my arm uplifted,| I have laid hold of the lashing[5] of *Ḫnty-mnwt·f*, and my § 1764
hand is taken to the Great Place, I take my seat which is in the God's Bark, so|
do not . . . me; I occupy for myself my seat which is in the God's Bark, so do § 1765
not . . . me.[6] [. . .] me as an official of the sky, my mansion is there among the
owners of names [. . .| . . .] the sun-folk,[7] and his two boats. My name is there § 1766
in the horizon, and the holy images fear me| [. . .] tremble(?)[8] in the presence § 1767
of *Ỉmy-nhd·f.*| Every god who shall give me his power shall take possession § 1768
[. . .] Mā‘et; I create peace from fighting in the presence of *Sd-bs*;| it is I [. . .] § 1769
*Mꜣ-ḥꜣ·f* who brings to me the range(?) of offerings(?)[9] which Khnum made,
and I go up [. . .].

1. Supplement, pp. 15–16. The text of Nt, which is in the 1st person, ends at § 1765*b*.
2. Sethe's restoration *N pw* is to be discarded; the trace of a bird's legs before *ḏ‘m* in N is shown by Nt to belong to *m*.
3. Only here; in Nt, 806 the word reads *hwty*.
4. *Šꜣsw* of Nt, 806 is hardly to be connected with the Bedawi tribes of that name. Mercer's 'Field of the royal women' is fantasy.
5. Presumably of the ladder.
6. The meaning of *sḥmꜣ* in Nt, 808 is not known. The Nt-text ends here.
7. JPII, 152 shows [*ḥ*]*nmmt*.
8. JPII, 153 shows .
9. *Ḳd ḥtp* could be the name of a ferry-boat; compare § 445*a*.

## Utterance 626

*The king flies like a bird*

The king has gone up as a swallow,[1] the King has alighted as a falcon; this § 1770
King's face [. . .] islands(?),[2] his tower(?) is the islands(?), the two districts of
the god are given to him.

1. *Wr* is written with a determinative as though it meant 'great one', but the association with *bik* 'falcon' makes it certain that 'swallow' is meant. For *wr* 'swallow' see also § 1216.
2. JPII, 158 shows , etc.

## Utterance 627

*The king is reborn*

§ 1771 The King is an equipped spirit who demands existence, and the sky thunders,
§ 1772 the earth quakes [. . .].[1] | The King was [born][2] in the month, he was conceived
in the half-month, he has ascended in the body[3] of a locust among these
§ 1773 children of the hornet(?),[4] | the wings [. . .] serpents. The King passes the
night, having daily mounted up to Rēʿ, and the shrine is opened for him when
§ 1774 Rēʿ shines.[5] | The King has ascended on a cloud, he has descended [. . .]
Māʿet in the presence of Rēʿ on that day of the Festival of the First of the
§ 1775 Year.| The sky is at peace, the earth is in joy, for they have heard that the
§ 1776 King will set right [in the place of wrong| . . .] the King [is vindicated(?)] in
his tribunal[6] on account of the just sentence which issued from his mouth,
the King has demanded what he needs as ruler, (namely) two arourae [. . .|
§ 1777 the King is a] great falcon who demands existence, the King crosses the sky
over its four quarters(?).[7]

The King has ascended on a cloud, he has descended [. . . equipped . . .].[8]|
§ 1778 The King is a great falcon which is on the battlements[9] of Him whose name
is hidden, taking what belongs to Atum to Him who separates the sky from
the earth and the Abyss; the King's eye(?) is the Lady of(?) the Sunshine,[10]|
§ 1779 his lips[11] are the Bull of the Holy Images, his neck is the Mistress of Flame,
§ 1780 his claws[12] are the Bull of the Evening,| his wings are *Ḫnty-mnw[t·f]* who
dwells in the pool (*sic*) of his chapel,[13] authority[14] is given to the king from(?)[15]
Him whose face suffers greatly[16] in the presence of Him who is in the Abyss;
§ 1781 the King ranks as First-born[17] to the extent of eternity| [. . .] the King
[goes(?)] to the Field of Sunshine, his hands have fallen on Him whose horns
are curved[18] north of the island of Elephantine, who sowed the earth in his
§ 1782 first holy image| beside[19] [. . . the uraeus] was [guide] at his first birth; He who
is on the eyelashes(?)[20] serves him,[21] and it goes well with the King in his
§ 1783 bird-shape| [. . .]-tree which is beside the *nfrs*-tree. The King's name is made
§ 1784 out as 'Divine Falcon', of whose face he who passes by him[22] is afraid,| because
the King is the successor(?) of the Oldest One who is at . . .[23] [. . .] the King
is bound for his throne of malachite,[24] his food is in the Fields of Offerings in
§ 1785 the Lakes of Turquoise [. . .] for him, a million within . . .[25]| [. . .]. The King
guides Rēʿ in his two Barks of Truth on that day of bringing the year to an end.

1. JPII, 159 ff. preserves a few fragments of the lacunae, but they are mostly isolated and too small to be of use. Only in ll. 170 and 171 (§§ 1784–5) are there any appreciable remains not recorded by Sethe.

2. Read [*ms·*]*tw*; the ending is preserved in JPII, 159.

3. *Bkśw* is lit. 'spine', but the reference here is to the articulated body of an insect. The determinative of *bkśw* here may be intended to represent a single vertebra.

4. Or 'wasp', but of the two the hornet is the more vicious; *tkkt* probably means 'attacker'.

5. Or 'he has opened'; but the translation as a passive is to be preferred. *Psḏ* here must mean 'shine'.

6. The court of justice over which Rēʿ presides; it is to him that the suffix *·f* refers.

7. The exact reading and meaning of *fdw·s rw* or *fdw srw* are doubtful, but the general sense seems clear.

8. Somewhere in the lacuna JPII, 164 has *ʿpr*.

9. *Znbw*; cf. also *CT* ii, 221*e*. Aba, 625 ff. comes in at § 1778*a*.

10. Supplied from Aba, 626–7, which reads: *tw brt*(?) *A pn m nb*[*t*](?) *ỉꜣḫw*.

11. Sethe's restoration *tw* is to be deleted, cf. Aba, 627.

12. In Aba, 628 *ỉꜣft* is determined with a single hoof-sign.

13. *Dmꜣt(y)·f m Ḫnt-mnw*[*t·f*] *ḥr-ỉb š kꜣr·f*, Aba, 628–9.

14. Sethe's restoration *tw* before *ḥw* is to be deleted in favour of *rdỉ*, Aba, 629.

15. Or 'as'.

16. Lit. perhaps 'him who suffers in his face greatly'; for verbs of suffering pain with direct object of the part affected cf. *mn*, *Concise Dict.* 107; *šn*, ibid. 268. Aba, 629 has *zp* for *znw* and at l. 630 passes to another text.

17. Lit. 'first-born-ness belongs to the King'.

18. Khnum appears to be meant.

19. JPII, 168 has preserved *ỉr-gs* at the beginning of the lacuna, but nothing else that is helpful.

20. *Spdw nwꜣt*; the translation 'eyelashes' was tentatively suggested by Gunn. Lit. perhaps 'the points of the eye'.

21. Cf. Utt. 456, n. 2.

22. Lit. 'his passer-by'.

23. JPII, 170 reads *ỉswt(y) smsw ỉr(y) nhdw* or alternatively *ỉs wt*, etc., in which case *ỉs* would be a particle and *wt* a writing of *wtw* 'eldest', cf. *Dram. Texte*, 29.

24. *Šzmt*; cf. *Stud. Griff.* 320.

25. JPII, 171: 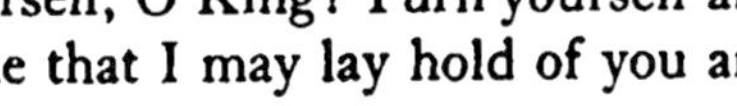; *ḥḥ* is represented by a female head and *ḥfnn* may be either the numeral or the word for 'tadpole'; in neither case is the meaning clear.

## Utterance 628

*Nephthys restores the king to life*

Rouse[1] yourself, O King! Turn yourself about, O King! I am Nephthys, and § 1786
I have come that I may lay hold of you and give to you your heart for your body.[2]

1. Read *wḥ* 'rouse up', cf. §§ 214*a*; 218*c*; 222*a*.

2. Cf. Utt. 5.

## Utterance 629

*Nephthys rejoices over the king*

§ 1787 O Osiris the King, I have come rejoicing[1] for love of you, O King.

1. Old perfective 1st sing.

## Utterance 630

*Restoration of the circulation of the blood(?)*

§ 1788 O Osiris the King, a current(?) courses round(?) in you, surging(?) and dripping(?).[1]

1. A very doubtful translation. *Nn* has been tentatively identified with *nni* 'go to and fro', § 310c; *ꜥrꜥr*, normally 'pool', appears here to be something which flows; on *ḥrpy* see Sethe, *Dram. Texte*, 178; and for the meaning 'drip' given to *nšfšf* cf. the determinative and *nšf* 'fangs(?)' of a snake dripping poison, § 230a.

## Utterance 631

*The king's body is restored*

§ 1789 I have put my brother together,[1] I have reassembled his members.

1. It is probably Isis who is speaking.

## Utterance 632

*An address to the decaying corpse(?)*

§ 1790 O you who trust in(?)[1] the place where you are, how bad[2] is your smell! How offensive is your smell! How great is your smell!

1. The exact significance of *mḥ ib* is not clear, but the implication of this text seems to be that if the corpse is content to remain in the tomb, its condition will go from bad to worse. This may be a very ancient Utterance referring to a time when embalming had only just been invented.
2. On *sw* 'bad' cf. Utt. 23, n. 2; here we should read *sw w(y)*.

## Utterance 633

§ 1791 It is you[1] who mourn over him.

1. Feminine, probably referring to Isis. The use of the obsolete pronoun *ṯmt* points to the great age of this brief Utterance.

## Utterance 634[1]

O Osiris the King, I bring to you [the Eye] of Horus(?), that the spirits may § 1792
[. . .] you by means of it.| O Osiris the King, I bring it to you in(?) [. . .] § 1793
thereby(?), that you may live thereby [. . .] by means of it.

1. Supplement, p. 16.

## Utterance 635

*The king is robed*

O Osiris the King, I bring to you the Eye of Horus which is in Weaving- § 1794
town,[1] this Ernūtet-garment of which the gods are afraid,[2] so that the gods may fear you just as they fear Horus.| O Osiris the King, Horus has put his § 1795
Eye on your brow in its name of Great-of-Magic. O Osiris the King, appear[3] as King of Upper and Lower Egypt.

1. *Tʒit*, location unknown.
2. Cf. § 1755*b* and JPII, 476.
3. Hortative old perfective.

## Utterance 636

*A spell for the king's protection*

Wake, O Great One! Give me your hand that I may help you up.| I have §§ 1796–7
come [that I may embrace you], I have [come] that I may guard you; it is I who protect you and I will never fail to protect you.[1] Live, live,[2] | because you § 1798
are [. . .], you being more hale than they. Live, O my father Osiris the King, for I set for you the Eye of Horus on you.

1. See Utt. 357, n. 10; for *in nḏ* read *ink nḏ*.
2. Hortative old perfectives + *ʿnḫ* as a noun: 'live, live the life'.

## Utterance 637

*The king is anointed*

Horus comes filled with unguent; he sought for his father Osiris and he § 1799
found him on his side in *Gḥsty*;| Osiris has filled himself with the Eye of § 1800
Him whom he begot.

O King, I also[1] have come to you, I fill[2] you with the ointment which went forth from the Eye of Horus,| I fill you with it. It will raise up your bones, § 1801
it will reassemble your members for you, it will gather together your flesh

§ 1802 for you; it will let your bad sweat drop to the ground.[1] Take its perfume to yourself, that your odour may be as pleasant as that of Rēʿ when he ascends from the horizon and the gods of the horizon are delighted with him.

§ 1803 O King, may the perfume of the Eye of Horus be on you, may the gods
§ 1804 who follow Osiris be delighted with you.[1] Take possession of their *Wrrt*-crown, being equipped with the shape of Osiris, that you may have more power thereby than the spirits by the command of Horus himself, the Lord of Patricians.

1. Cf. Edel, §§ 111. 180.

2. *Ἰ·mḥ* appears to be *sḏm·f* form 1st sing. rather than imperative; it is the officiant who applies the unguent so as to restore the king to life.

## Utterance 638

*The king's power of sight is restored*

§ 1805 O Osiris the King, the gods have knit together your face for you and Horus
§ 1806 has given you his Eye, [that you may see with it].[1] O Osiris the King, Horus has split open your eye for you that you may see with it in its name of 'She who opens the ways of the god'.

## Utterance 639

*As last*

§ 1807 [O Osiris] the King, take the Eye of the living Horus that you may see with it.

O Osiris the King, may your vision be cleared by means of the light.

O Osiris the King, [may] your [vision be brightened] by the dawn.

§ 1808 O Osiris the King, I give to you the Eye of Horus when Rēʿ gives it.[1]

O Osiris the King, [I put for you the Eye] of Horus on you that you may see with it.

§ 1809 O Osiris the King, I have split open your eye that you may see with it.

O Osiris the King, [I have given you(?)] the ointment.

1. i.e. the dawn (*hḏ-tꜣ*), which is masculine; the pronoun *sw* cannot refer to the Eye of Horus, which is always feminine. I take the construction here to be *m sḏmt·f* in a clause of time.

## Utterance 640

*The king is commended to the care of Gēb*

§ 1810 O Gēb, this is your son Osiris the King; nourish your son by means of it,[1] [may your son be] made hale [by means of it]. Let him not die and he will not

die;[1] if he lives, you will live; if he is hale, you will be hale; you will have § 1811
effectiveness, O Gēb; you will have strength, O Gēb; [you will have a soul,
O Gēb;] you will have power, O Gēb.[1] Be strong and drive out everything § 1812
evil which is on this Osiris the King, [cast] your [protection] of life about
this Osiris the King, and he will not die, nor will his name perish.

1. The sonship, cf. also § 1620*b*.

## Utterance 641

### *Horus champions the king as Osiris*

O Osiris the King, I have come in [search of][1] you, for I am Horus. I have § 1813
come that I may speak on your behalf, for I am your son.[1] O Osiris the King, § 1814
you are the eldest son of Gēb, his first-born and his heir. O Osiris the King,
you are he who succeeded him,[1] and the heritage was given to you by the § 1815
Ennead, for you have power over the Ennead and every god.[1] [I give you the § 1816
crown of Upper Egypt, the Eye which went up from your head; I give you
the crown of Lower Egypt, the Eye][2] which went up from your head [. . .].

1. Restore *m* [*zḥn*]·*k* as § 11*a*.
2. Restoring tentatively as [*di·i n·k wrt-ḥkɜw šmʿt, irt prt m tp·k; di·i n·k wrt-ḥkɜw mḥt, irt*] *prt m tp·k*, cf. § 1624.

## Utterance 642

### *Shu is prayed to protect the king*

O Shu, you enclose for yourself all things within your embrace [. . .] this § 1817
Osiris the King; may you prevent him from escaping [from you[1] . . .] of Atum, § 1818
whose phallus is on you(?),[1] that you may be [. . .] his double; may you
protect him from [. . .].

1. Translation uncertain. If it be correct, it implies that the dead king is endowed with the masculine power of the primeval god. Both Breasted, *Development*, 11, n. 3, and Mercer in his translation of this passage, see in it an allusion to Atum's act of creation by masturbation, but there seems no real evidence for this view.

## Utterance 643

O Osiris the King [. . .] that he may(?) live.[1] You are a god [having power § 1819
over the gods,[1] and the eye has gone up from your head as] the *wrt-ḥkɜw* § 1820
crown of Upper Egypt [. . .][2] the meal(?) which went forth from him[1] [. . .]. § 1821

§ 1822 May your double stand among [the gods . . .] him who survives you.[1] O King, [. . .].[2] A double is raised up behind you, [life[3] is raised up behind you], dominion[4] is raised up behind you. O Osiris the King, [. . .].

1. For ○ read ●.
2. A long lacuna with only a few remnants preserved.
3. Or: 'an *ꜥnḫ*-symbol'.
4. Or: 'a *wꜣs*-staff'.

## Utterance 644[1]

*The Children of Horus carry the king*

§ 1823 [O you Children of] Horus, betake yourselves beneath the King [that you may carry him]. Let there be none of you who shall turn away, but you [shall carry] Osiris the King.

1. Supplement, p. 16; Sethe's restoration in § 1823*c* is to be discarded.

## Utterance 645[1]

*The king is placed in the bark of Sokar*

§ 1824 O Osiris the King,[2] Horus has lifted you into the *Ḥnw*-bark, he raises you into the Bark of Sokar, for he is a son who raises up his father, O Osiris the King, in your name of Sokar.[3] May you be mighty in Upper Egypt as this Horus through whom you are mighty; may you be mighty[4] in Lower Egypt as this Horus through whom you are mighty, that you may be mighty and protect yourself from your foe.

1. Supplement, p. 17.
2. So N; Nt, 360 reads: *twt nṯr ꜥꜣ*.
3. § 1824*d* is omitted in Nt.
4. From here onward in Nt only; in N a variant of this appears in Utt. 647.

## Utterance 645A[1]

*The Children of Horus raise the king up*

(§ 1824) O Osiris the King, you are a god powerful and unique, and Horus has given you his children that they may raise you up. Be mighty through them when they go to you, for not one of them shall turn away. Gēb has given you all the gods of Upper and Lower Egypt that they may raise you up; be mighty through them.

1. Supplement, pp. 17–18.

## Utterance 646[1]

*The king is endowed with magic*

O Osiris the King, Horus has granted[2] that your magic be great in your name § 1825
of Great-of-Magic.

1. Supplement, p. 18.
2. For *dỉ·n Ḥr* of Nt, N (Sethe) has *ꜥnḫ·n Ḥr*; Nt yields the better sense.

## Utterance 647[1]

*Horus carries the king*

[O Osiris] the King, [Horus] has carried you [that he may raise you into the § 1826
Bark of Sokar] in your name of Sokar[1] [. . .] that you may be [provided] with § 1827
it, having power [over Lower Egypt as this Horus. May you have power] through it.

1. A variant of Utt. 645.

## Utterance 648[1]

*The Children of Horus carry the king*

O Osiris the King, [Horus has given you these four children of his] that you § 1828
may have power over them.[1] [He has said to them: 'Betake yourselves] be- § 1829
neath the King and carry [him; let none of you turn away.'][2] They shall betake themselves[3] to you and shall carry [you; none of them will turn away].

1. Cf. Utt. 644.
2. *In the restoration of* § *1829b. d* delete [hieroglyphs], cf. §§ *637c; 1823b.*
3. Read *ỉmꜣ·sn* ⟨*sn*⟩.

## Utterance 649

*Gēb and Horus take the King under their protection*

O Osiris the King, Gēb has given you all the gods of Upper and Lower § 1830
Egypt,[1] and they bear you up[2] so that you may have power over them; they are your brothers in their name of '*Snwt*-shrine';[3] they will never reject you
in their name of ['the Two Conclaves'].[4] [1] [O Osiris] the King, Horus the § 1831
Uniter has assigned them to you.[5] O Osiris the King, [behold, you are protected] and alive, you daily move to and fro. O Osiris the King, no one will

interfere [with you. O Osiris] the King, you are the essence of all the gods.|
§ 1832 Horus has protected you, for [you] have become [his double], and the Eye went up from your head as the crown of Upper Egypt Great-of-Magic.

1. See Nt, 365.
2. Read *wṯz·sn kw* with loc. cit.; Sethe's [*dmḏ*] is to be discarded.
3. Read *smw·k pw m rn·sn n smwt* with Nt, 366; on the *smwt* see *Dram. Texte*, 234.
4. Nt omits this sentence. For *twr* 'reject' cf. §§ 127*c*; 128*b*; 577*d*.
5. At this point Nt, 366 continues with a different text.

## Utterance 650

*The king assumes authority*

§ 1833 [. . .] This King is Osiris, whom [Nūt] bore, and [she has caused] him [to appear] as King of Upper and Lower Egypt in all his dignities [. . . as(?)] Anubis Foremost of the Westerners, as Osiris the son of Gēb [. . .] the gods
§ 1834 as *ʿnḏty* who presides over the eastern nomes.| [He who begot] the land is the King, so that he might be at the head of the gods [who are in] the sky
§ 1835 as Gēb who presides over the Ennead.| His mother the sky bears him alive every day like Rēʿ, and he appears with him in the East, he goes to rest with
§ 1836 him in the West, and his mother Nūt is not free from him any day.| His son provides this King with life, he makes him glad, he gives him pleasure,|
§ 1837 he sets Upper Egypt in order for him, he sets Lower Egypt in order for him, he hacks up the fortresses of Asia for him, he quells[1] for him all the hostile[2] plebs under his fingers.

1. Read *wḫı*.
2. *Znṯt* is a fem. adjective or participle qualifying *rḫyt*. Mercer (his p. 846) ignores the fem. ending and equates the word with *znṯw* 'foreign enemies'. Although he is in error in this respect, the two words are clearly derived from a common stem *znṯ* which appears to have the meaning 'hostile'. *Wb.* iii, 462, 2, suggests 'rebellisch', which is not far removed from my own translation.

## Utterance 651

§ 1838 O Osiris the King, take the Eye of Horus [to your brow . . .].

## Utterance 652

§ 1839 O Osiris the King, take the Eye of Horus which I rescued from Seth when he had snatched it [. . .].

## Utterance 653

O Osiris the King, take the Eye of Horus [. . . making] libation. § 1840

## Utterance 654[1]

O King, [. . .] open the mouth[2] . . .[3] [. . .] those with braided hair. Come to § 1841
him, come to him![4]

1. Supplement, p. 18.
2. *Ḥpḏ r*; cf. *CT* iii, 57*e*; *Wb.* iii, 72, 12.
3. *Ḳdn*(?), meaning unknown.
4. See Nt, 574. Sethe has a somewhat different text.

## Utterance 655[1]

*The king flies to the sky*

The King [. . .] the thighs of the gods are firm [. . .] the King by Shezmētet.[1] § 1842
The King is the falcon which issued from the Eye of Horus, the uraeus § 1843
which issued from the falcon [. . .][1] Horus(?) [. . .] . . .[2] to the sky, . . . to the § 1844
earth.[1] The King's plumage is that of a duck, he attains the sky as do divine § 1845
falcons, at the Field of Rushes,[1] [as(?)] a star which crosses the sea.[3] § 1846

1. Supplement, pp. 18–19.
2. , meaning unknown. Mercer has guessed 'birds'.
3. In JPII, 577 there is a stanza mark at this point, so that Sethe's § 1847 must belong to a fresh Utterance, here numbered 655A.

## Utterance 655A[1]

*The king travels in the Beyond*

[. . .] the King's *gsp*-trees are the *gsp*-trees of the *Ḥnw*-bark, his movements § 1847
[are toward] the Jackal-lakes, the King travels(?) to you.[2]

1. Supplement, p. 19.
2. Plural, referring to beings who presumably were named in the lacuna at the beginning of this Utterance.

## Utterance 656

*Almost entirely destroyed* §§ 1848–9

## Utterance 657[1]

§§ 1850–1 The King has come [. . .]| the King will never pluck out [the Foremost of the
§ 1852 Westerners] from his place| [. . .].

1. Supplement, p. 19.

## Utterance 658[1]

§§ 1853–4 [. . .]| the gods have made you hale, for they love you; the gods who exist(?)
crown(?) you in your name of 'He of Elephantine(?)';[2] [the gods who exist(?)]
§ 1855 have made you into(?) [. . .].[3] | [He[4] trembles under you] as the earth trembles;
do not let him escape[5] from you. Descend, being holier than he; ascend and
§ 1856 confront him, drive him back,| leap on him [. . .] . . .[6] [. . .] Thoth [. . . do
§ 1857 not let go] of him, do not let him escape from you.| Horus has placed your
foes under you, they being truly opposed(?); [. . .] has reckoned up for you
[. . .] he has felled for [you . . .] this [sweet(?)] Eye of his [has given] it to you
§ 1858 [. . .]| Horus [has] filled you completely with his Eye in its name of Horus-
§ 1859 offering;| Horus has rescued his Eye from Seth and has given [it] to [you . . .
Seth(?)] is driven back for you [. . .] in your name of Plenty [. . .] Horus in you
[. . .] Horus has [. . .] you [. . .] you; may you have power over them [. . .]
Horus for you [. . .] they serve [you . . .] Horus in [his(?)] name of [. . .].

1. Supplement, pp. 20–1.
2. *Sbn* may be the verb 'crown', cf. § 409*a*; *ntyw* apparently has its rare absolute sense of 'those who are existing'; *ỉbw* has lost its determinative. Mercer has strangely translated *ỉbw* as 'ceaseless', ignoring the absence of the negation.
3. Reading [*nṯrw n*]*tyw* as before; Mercer 'translates' *ỉr·n ṯw* as 'thou hast done'!
4. Seth.
5. For the construction with the negation *m* before *sḏm·f* in the 3rd person see Edel, § 1104.
6. *Bḫh*, meaning unknown.

## Utterance 659

*The king is announced to Rēʿ*

§ 1860 Indeed[1] this journey of yours, indeed these journeys of yours are the journeys
§ 1861 of Horus in search of his father Osiris.| Go,[2] you messengers of his! Run,
§ 1862 you couriers of his! Hurry, you heralds of his!| Go to Rēʿ and tell Rēʿ that
an arm is upraised in the east when he[3] has come as a god. Stand up, O King,
§ 1863 in the Conclaves of the Horizon,| that you may hear the word of Rēʿ as
a god, as Horus the Shooter(?),[4] for I am your brother as Sopdu.

Behold, he has come, behold, he has come, behold, your brother has come, § 1864
behold, *Mḫnt-irty* has come.| If you do not know him, in order to stop your § 1865
efflux lie in his embrace[5] as your calf, for he is your herdsman.| Take these § 1866
white teeth of yours in a bowl, go round about them with an arrow in this
their name of 'Arrow'.| Your foreleg[6] is in the Thinite nome, your[7] hind-leg § 1867
is in Nubia, you have descended as a jackal of Upper Egypt, as Anubis upon
the baldachin.| May you stand up at the causeway [as Gēb] who presides § 1868
over his Ennead.| You have your heart, you have your double.[8] Provide, O § 1869
King, your house; maintain, O King, your gate.[9]

1. On the non-enclitic particle *iwsw* cf. Edel, § 858*b*.
2. A series of imperatives, cf. § 1862*a*.
3. The dead king as Osiris.
4. *Mst*(*i*), possibly a nominal formation in *m* from *sti* 'shoot'.
5. In order to read better, the translation of § 1865*b* has been placed before *sḏr·k*, etc.
6. Of beef.
7. Emending *·f* into *·k*.
8. Emending *kꜣ·k n N* into *kꜣ·k n·k*.
9. Or 'courtyard'.

## Utterance 660

*The king is the son of Atum*

'O Shu, I am[1] the son of Atum.' § 1870

'You are[2] the eldest son of Atum, his first-born;| Atum has spat you out § 1871
from his mouth in your name of Shu. He[3] has said . . .[4] in your name of
"Upper *Mnst*" '.[5]

'O Shu,[6] this one here is Osiris the King whom you have caused to be § 1872
restored[7] that he may live. If you live, he will live, for you are lord of the
entire land.'

1. In § 1870*b* the king is addressed in the 2nd person, so that in § 1870*a* he himself must be speaking.
2. Shu replies.
3. Presumably Atum.
4. *Tn msw ir·k* defeats me; it has evoked such different translations as 'Count my children', *ZÄS* 54, 18 and 'Where born?' verbally by Gardiner. Neither seems to fit the context.
5. Cf. Utt. 601, n. 1.
6. *Hꜣ nn* as it stands is meaningless; as Gunn once suggested, [hieroglyph] is probably a sculptor's error for [hieroglyph]. We appear now to have a third speaker, perhaps a funerary priest.
7. Cf. § 167*a* ff. The suffix *·k* after *sḏb* is to be discarded.

## Utterance 661

*The king is nursed by Isis and Nephthys*

§ 1873 O my father the King, take this milky fluid of yours which is in the breasts of your mother Isis; O Nephthys, give him your hand.

## Utterance 662

*The rising sun is addressed*

§ 1874 O shining one! O shining one! O Khoprer! O Khoprer! You are for the King and the King is for you; you live for the King and the King lives for you.

*The papyrus plant of the North is invoked*

§ 1875 O Papyrus-plant which issued from Wedjōyet, you have gone forth in the King, and the King has gone forth in you, the King is powerful through your strength.

*The king is supplied with food*

§ 1876 Sustenance belongs to the King's morning meal, Plenty belongs to the King's
evening meal, famine[1] will not have power over the King's life, conflagration
§ 1877 will be far removed from the King.⌉ The King lives on your[2] bounty, he has
daily abundance of your abundance, O Rēʿ.

*The king is summoned to return from the dead*

O my father the King, arise! Take this first cold water of yours which came
§ 1878 from Chemmis!⌉ Arise, you who are in your tombs![3] Cast off your bonds,
throw off the sand which is on your face, raise yourself upon your left side,
§ 1879 support yourself upon your right side,⌉ lift up your face that you may see
§ 1880 this which I have done for you; I am your son, I am your heir,⌉ I have hoed
emmer for you, I have cultivated barley for you, barley for your *wꜣg*-festival
§ 1881 and emmer for your yearly sustenance;⌉ I offer to you the Eye of Horus and
it belongs(?) to you, it travels from afar to you. O Lord of the House, your
hand be on your goods!

1. *Ḥddwt*, cf. *Wb.* ii, 506, 10.
2. The sun-god's, see below.
3. *Sic* plural. From the reversion to the singular in the next sentence but one it looks as if the plural were original and that the text was edited into the singular to suit the particular occasion.

## Utterance 663[1]

*The king is provided with food*

[. . .] O King, your bread is due every day of which you said: 'Be!'[2] The § 1882
*imy-iz*[3] has said to you [. . .] your arm is before you, O Osiris, your ox [. . .] red; your thousand of figs, your thousand of wine, your thousand of zizyphus-
bread, your thousand of *ḥb[nnt]*-bread, your thousand of ⸢*gt*⸣ which Gēb has § 1883
fashioned for you. You have ⟨your⟩ name [. . .]. Hail to you, my father the King! You have your water, you have your flood, you have your milk which is in the [breast] of your mother Isis.

1. Supplement, pp. 21–2.
2. Taking *wnn* to be an imperative, object of the relative form *i·ḏd·n·k*.
3. For this title cf. e.g. *Urk.* i, 98, 8; *Beni Hasan*, i, 44, 1. In § 1930*a* we have the full expression *imy iz ḏr ḥr·ṯn*, but its meaning escapes me.

## Utterance 664[1]

*Isis gives the king his heart*

Rouse yourself, turn yourself over, O King, for I am Isis;⸣ I have come that §§ 1884–5
I may lay hold of you and give you your heart for your body.[2]

1. According to JPII, 583+4 ff., Sethe's Utt. 664 consists of three short Utterances and one longer, here numbered 664–4C. See the Supplement, pp. 22–4.
2. Cf. Utt. 4.

## Utterance 664A[1]

*Isis comes to the king*

O Osiris the King, I am Isis; I have come into the middle of this earth, into § 1886
the place where you are; I have come[2] and have laid hold of you.

1. Supplement, pp. 22–3.
2. Read *iw·n(·i)*; there is one *n* too many.

## Utterance 664B[1]

*Horus protects the king*

Horus is [. . .] within your arms and he protects you; it goes well with him, § 1887
he being kind(?)[2] to you in your name of 'Horizon from which Rēʿ ascends'.[3]⸣
Close your arms about him, about him,⸣ and he will not escape from you §§ 1888–9
[. . .].

1. Supplement, p. 23.
2. For this sense of *ʿn* cf. *Prisse*, 15, 7, but with *n* instead of *ḥr* as here.
3. The suffix in *im·k* is superfluous.

## Utterance 664C[1]

§ 1890 O Osiris the King, knit together [your] limbs, reassemble your members,|
§§ 1891–2 set your heart in its place! O Osiris the King, do not be lacking [. . .| O
Osiris] the King, I have brought for you your heart into your body, I have
§ 1893 set it in its place for you. What it asks from you is protection [. . .| O Osiris]
the King, I am Horus, I have come that I may guard you [. . .] because of
§§ 1894–5 what he[2] did to you.| O Osiris the King, command [. . .]| she [raises] you.
§ 1896 O Osiris the King, I have come that Nūt may protect you,| for Nūt has
§ 1897 embraced [you]| and the Children of Horus raise [you . . .]. O Osiris the
King, I am Nūt, I have fashioned . . .[3] and the mouth of Osiris the King is
wiped [. . .].

1. Supplement, pp. 23–4.
2. Seth.
3. 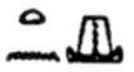 is quite obscure.

## Utterance 665[1]

*The dead king is summoned to rise again*

§ 1898 Wake up, wake up, O King, wake up for me! I am your son; wake up for
§ 1899 me, for I am Horus who wakes you.| Live, be alive, O King, in this name of
yours which is with the spirits, you appearing as *Wpiw*, as a soul at the head
of the living, as a Power at the head of the spirits, as the Lone Star who has
eaten his enemy.

§ 1900 O King, you are Thoth who is in his Castle of the Mace in your name
which is with Osiris . . .[2] is in your hand and also mud; to me belong sweet
spices(?),[3] and you shall take your hand to the Imperishable Stars.

§ 1901 O King, go up, you sleeper! Be ready, you drowsy one![4] The Great Ones
stand up for you, the Watchers sit down for you as Horus, protector of his
father. If the perfume of ⟨*Iḫt-*⟩*wtt* be pleasing to the nose, then will the
perfume of the King be pleasing to the nose(?).[5]

§ 1902 Raise yourself, O King! Take these four *nmst*-jars of yours which are
§ 1903 filled for you from the Canal of the God;| take this lotus-bud sceptre of yours
which your mother *Ḥdbtt* has given to you, for its . . . shall not be removed(?).[6]

§ 1904 Raise yourself, O King, that you may see your Horite mounds and their

tombs, that you may see your Sethite mounds and their tombs. Loose your bonds, O Horus who is in his house; get rid[7] of your fetters, O Seth who is in *Ḫnt*.| I have saved you from *Ḫrty* who lives on the hearts of men, I have not § 1905
given you[8] to *Nwt·k-nw* when I say this to you.| Beware, you two ⟨. . .⟩[9] as § 1906
Isis, the Mourning-Woman calls to you as Nephthys, the earth quakes at you, an offering is presented to you, the dancer dances for you, Thoth comes to you with the knife which came forth from Seth, he finds you seated on your throne of ebony as Rēʿ at the head of the Ennead,| you give orders to the § 1907
spirits, their heads bow(?)[10] to you, their couriers fetch for you, and you live on their hearts, standing on [your] feet [by] the sea. I give to you your name of Jackal; take your name of *Wpiw*. O King, your arms are in front of you.[11]

1. Supplement, pp. 24–8.
2. A lacuna in N; Nt has corruptly , which is meaningless.
3. Cf. possibly *Wb*. iii, 221, 8–10; Mercer's 'thousands' is ruled out by the writing *ḫꜣꜣ* of N.
4. For *bꜣn*, usually with prothetic *i*, cf. §§ 735*a*; 894*a*; JPII, 709+4.
5. § 1901*c–d* is clearly corrupt. The perfume of *Iḫt-wtt* is mentioned in §§ 791*a*; 1915*h* (Supplement, p. 31) and one might perhaps emend here as *sṯ Iḫt-wtt pw imꜣ n šrt, sṯ Nt pw imꜣ n šrt*.
6. Another obscure sentence; the form *drrt* is inexplicable, as also is *mšws ir·s*.
7. *Sšm* with this meaning is not recorded, but the sense is clear. In these two clauses 'Horus' and 'Seth' both refer to the king.
8. On 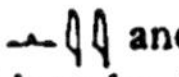 and  see Edel, §§ 1092 ff. The circular sign before *m mdw* in JPII is superfluous and is to be discarded.
9. *Zꜣ·tiwny ꜣst is* is certainly corrupt, for it makes no sense; evidently there has been an omission after *zꜣ·tiwny*, probably the names of the beings addressed, and also a clause ending with *ꜣst is* parallel to the following one ending in *Nbt-ḥwt is*.
10. *Izm* is not recorded, and its translation rests on the context.
11. Read *rmnwy·k ḫnt·k*.

## Utterance 665A[1]

### *A 'resurrection' text*

Raise yourself, O King, gather your bones together, resume your members! § 1908
Your water issues from Elephantine, you are god-like in the Castle of the God, standing at the head of the Two Conclaves, at the head of the Jackal-gods.| May you smite your arm against your foes, whom Anubis who presides § 1909
over the God's Booth gave over to you when he placed you, O King, at the head of the Westerners. The tomb is opened for you, the doors of the tomb-chamber are thrown open for you, and you find your abundance meeting you.

§ 1910 Raise yourself, O King, to your thousand of bread, your thousand of beer, your thousand of oxen, your thousand of poultry, your thousand of clothing,
§ 1911 your thousand of alabaster.[1] I have gone forth for you from the house, O King, that you may inherit the leadership of the Lord of the Gods and give orders to the Westerners, because you are a great and mighty spirit, and those
§ 1912 who have suffered death(?)[2] are united for you wherever you wish to be.[1] O King, may you have power thereby, for the gods have commanded that you guard yourself from those who speak against you, O King, because you are he whom Osiris installed on his throne that you may lead the Westerners and be a spirit at the head of the gods.[3]

1. Supplement, pp. 28–30.

2. Reading *ḫr(yw) mt* with Nt, 733, though the version of JPII, 719+27 with determinative ‹ looks like an unknown word *ḫrmt*; cf. § 1367.

3. The last two sentences (§ 1912*d*) are confined to Nt, 733–4 and apparently never stood in the parallel texts.

## Utterance 665B[1]

*As last*

§ 1913 O King, live the life! Live the life by means of this name of yours which is
§ 1914 with the gods, you having appeared as *Wpiw*,[1] as a soul at the head of the living, as a Power at the head of the spirits. The King is Thoth; assemble, O you gods who are in this Castle of the Mace;[2] this King is with you, O Osiris.

1. Supplement, p. 30.

2. Of the two successive *pw*, the first may be masc. sing. qualifying *ʿḥ ḥḏ* and the second masc. plur. (*i*)*pw* used as a vocative for the whole phrase *nṯrw imyw ʿḥ ḥḏ*.

## Utterance 665C[1]

*A variant of Utterance* 611

§ 1915 The six door-bolts,[2] which keep Libya out, are opened for you; your iron sceptre is in your hand that you may number the slayers,[3] control the Nine Bows, and take the hand of the Imperishable Stars. The Great Ones will care for you and the Watchers will wait on you as on Horus, protector of his father. O King, the Great One is sound asleep, this Great One is lying down, He who is greater than you is drowsy.[4] The perfume of the Great One on you is pleasing to the nose, (even) the perfume of *Iḫt-wtt*.[5]

1. Supplement, p. 31.
2. The only recorded full spelling of the word for door-bolt, showing that the original reading was *zȝ*.
3. Cf. Utt. 611, n. 5.
4. Cf. § 1901*a* (Supplement, p. 25). The function of *tȝ* in § 1915*g* (see also Aba, 542) is not clear; it appears to be an enclitic particle.
5. Compare §§ 791*a*; 1901*c–d*.

## Utterance 666[1]

*A 'resurrection' text*

O King, collect your bones, assemble your members, whiten your teeth, take § 1916
your bodily heart, throw off this earth which is on your flesh,ꜝ take this § 1917
purification of yours,ꜝ these four *ʿȝbt*-jars of yoursꜝ which are filled full from §§ 1918–19
the Canal of the God, cleanse yourself with them as a god and go forth thence as the Eye of Rēʿ, having appeared in front of them as Gēb who
is at the head of the company of the Ennead of Ōnꜝ when he governs the § 1920
gods and speaks in the session of the living god. Assume the *Wrrt*-crown as the Lone Star who destroys foes; indeed,[2] this going of yours, O King, is that of which Horus spoke to his father Osiris.

O King, come, you also,[3] tell of this going of yours that you may become § 1921
a spirit thereby, that you may be great thereby, that you may be strong thereby, that you may be a soul thereby, that you may have power thereby.

O King, may you have a spirit within you, may you have your soul behind you, may you have your bodily heart! Sever your bonds as Horus who is in
his house, throw away your fetters as Seth who is in *Ḥnbt*,[4] ꜝ having entered § 1922
into protection, for your father Gēb has protected you. As for him who would exclude you,[5] he shall not live; as for him who calls to you 'Something behind me', that is not your name.[6]

O King, may the Eye of Horus belong(?) ⟨to you⟩, for your hand is on § 1923
your bread.

O King, I present you with your bread just as Horus presented him[7] with
his Eye,ꜝ and this . . .[8] here is my presentation; I provide you with this § 1924
bread of yours just as Horus provided him with his Eye, and this . . . here is your *wȝg*-offering.

Lift yourself to the sky in company with the stars which are in the sky. § 1925
Those who are in front of you go into hiding because of you, those who are behind you are afraid of you because of this name of yours which your father Osiris made for you, which Horus of the Netherworld made, because they

are smitten, because they are drowned,[9] because they are destroyed when you smite them, when you drown them, when you destroy them on land and
§ 1926 sea.[1] May you stand at the head of the Imperishable Stars, may you sit on
§ 1927 your iron throne from which the dead are far removed,[1] your adzes having hacked up[10] the Mansion of *Nwt·k-nw*.[11]

1. Supplement, pp. 31–5.
2. On *lst* cf. Edel, § 858*b*.
3. Reading *ml m ḏdṯ*, *m* being the enclitic particle *m(y)*.
4. Cf. § 1904*d–e*, where Seth is in *Ḥnt*, varr. *Ḥnbt* as here and *Ḥnḥnt*, § 734*d*.
5. For *ḫm* in its sense of 'exclude', 'debar' cf. *CT* i, 212*c*; *BD* 292, 13.
6. For the construction of *n rn·k ls* cf. Gardiner, § 134, third example.
7. Osiris.
8. 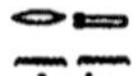 is quite obscure; in a similar context in § 2230*b* (Supplement, p. 66) we have *rn ṯn pw n ḥnkt*, where it is equally obscure.
9. Cf. § 2186*b*, determined with , as in § 692*c*; the star-determinative is borrowed from *zbš* 'be clear', of sky, § 458*a*, with which *ʿbš* is confused in § 2231*b*. *c* (Supplement, p. 67). The error clearly arises through the similarity of  and  in hieratic, combined with the identity of the other two consonants in the two words.
10. *Bıt* can be only an active-transitive old perfective; to translate it as a participle leaves the whole clause in the air.
11. Between Utt. 666 and 666A Nt inserts a short Utterance here numbered 759 (Supplement, p. 88).

## Utterance 666A[1]

*As last*

(§ 1927) Rise up,[2] O Sleeper! The doors of the sky are opened for you, the doors of the firmament are thrown open for you that you may go forth from them as *Wpiw*. The *mizwt*-crown which is on your shoulders is Thoth with the knife which went forth from Seth. Thoth has implanted an obstacle for you against
§ 1928 what he[3] would do to[4] you. The Mooring-post summons you as Isis,[1] the Mourning Woman calls to you [as Nephthys, you appearing] upon the causeway; may you travel around your Horite Mounds, may you travel around your Sethite Mounds as Min at the head of the company of the Ennead, may the gate of *Ḫnty-mnwt·f* be opened for you.

§ 1929 O King, behold this which I have done for you; you have a spirit, you have no dilapidation. Guard yourself, for your jar-stand and your bread are made to flourish; your bread is ⟨in⟩ its due time, your bread of worship(?) is ⟨in⟩ its due time,[5] your warm[6] bread is with this King every day.

O King, I know this,[7] the *ỉmy-ỉz* does not know . . .[8] I say(?): 'You have § 1930
an arm(?) in front of you, O Osiris.'

1. Supplement, pp. 35–6.
2. For this sense of *ṯn* cf. *CT* ii, 224*c*.
3. Seth.
4. Surely so, though we would expect *r·k* rather than *n·k* after *ỉrt·f*.
5. Cf. § 113*b*.
6. Making the obvious emendation of *stf* into *srf*; cf. also § 1937.
7. Read *ỉrḫ·k(ỉ) ỉr⟨·ỉ⟩ nw*.
8. Cf. Utt. 663, n. 3. I can make nothing of this nor of what follows in § 1930*b*.

## Utterance 666B[1]

*The king crosses to the Beyond*

O King, [pass over(?)][2] this Great Lake to the spirits and this *Ḫns*-water[3] (§ 1930)
to the dead. Beware of those people of yonder House of the Soul[4] who are
terrible and hostile | in this their name of 'Female Opponents'.[5] Do not let § 1931
them lay hold of your hand at yonder House of the Soul; it is dangerous, it is
painful, it is nasty(?),[6] it is foul-smelling,[7] | but you shall out-nasty(?) it, § 1932
you shall out-stink it.[8] | [You] will find the Two Enneads seated, and you § 1933
shall sit with them.

1. Supplement, p. 37.
2. Lost except for a final *-w*. Exactly what verb stood in the lacuna is uncertain.
3. Cf. *Wb.* iii, 300, 8–9.
4. Cf. § 1931*b*.
5. Note that in § 1930*e* *rmṯ* is determined with the heads of women.
6. For *sw* 'dangerous' cf. Utt. 23, n. 2. The translation of *nh* as 'nasty' is based solely on the context, but cf. *Komm.* ii, 18.
7. For *ḥb* with this meaning cf. § 1790*b*.
8. Here *nh* and *ḥb* are used as transitive verbs, extra force being given to them by the use of 'complementary infinitives'; the king is to make himself so foul that even the denizens of the House of the Soul will avoid him. Nt comes to an end here, but N continues with § 1933*a–b*, which looks like a later addition, as it seems to have little connection with what has gone before.

## Utterance 667[1]

*The king goes to the sky*

Go to Him who is glad, that you may worship[2] the *Ḥnw*-bark, O you beloved (§ 1933)
of his.[3] May he give you a road with those who are in it,[4] may you eat bread
with those who are in it, may you row in the Green Boat with those who are
in it. Heaven trembles at you, the earth quakes at you, the Imperishable

§ 1934 Stars come to you bowing,[1] *Nḥbw-kꜣw* grasps your hand at(?) . . .[5] Sit upon your iron throne and govern in company with the Two Enneads.

O King, take your head, for your teeth are yours and your hair is yours; open the doors which keep out the plebs, you enduring for ever and ever.

§ 1935 O King, may you ascend, your face[6] being that of the Seth-animal;[7] may you sit at the head of those who are greater than you. The sky reels at you,
§ 1936 the earth quakes at you, the Imperishable Stars are afraid of you.[1] I have come to you, O you whose seats are hidden, that I may embrace you in the sky. Hidden is he, and I cannot find(?) him since the sky became at peace, since the earth became at peace. The Two Lords are at peace, those who raise peace on high(?)[8] are at peace. I have reaped barley for your *wꜣg*-festival and . . .[9] to be your annual supply, your white bread of Anubis, your *pꜣḳ*-bread, dough(?)-cakes,[10] and *fnnt*-cakes,[11] O Foremost of the Westerners;[1]
§ 1937 your bread is warm, O King, in front of the gods.

§ 1938 O King, raise yourself, push yourself off on your left side, sit up (*sic*) on your right side, sit on the pure thrones of Rēʿ, separate your back from the
§ 1939 wall(?), your hand being[12] on your altar:[1] Your thousand of bread, your thousand of beer, your thousand of oxen, your thousand of fowl, your thousand of clothing and alabaster(?), your thousand of everything which a god eats; your thousand of *t-wr*-loaves is with me(?) in the middle of the Broad Hall. May you eat the foreleg, may you devour the (hind-)leg, may you catch hold of the two ribs upon the slaughter-block of Horus[13] for ever and ever.

§ 1940 O King, they will ask your name from you, but you shall not tell them your name. 'Who acts for you?', they will say. 'It is my successor who makes for you . . .[14] his tomb(?); his brick is installed(?)', you shall say . . .[15]

§ 1941 O King, eat this alone, and do not give to those men who are beside you.

O King, there comes this time of tomorrow and this time of three days; a stairway to the sky is [set up] for you among the Imperishable Stars.

§ 1942 O King, hail to you in peace! May it go very well with you![1] I prepare for you a place as Foremost of the Westerners, I make for ⟨you⟩ a kingly successor; spread your protection over those who survive you, that they may celebrate your festivals.

1. Supplement, pp. 38–41.

2. *Snz* may be an early writing of *snsy* 'worship', not otherwise known before the Eighteenth Dynasty, though *Wb.* iv, 171 does not record the construction with following *r*.

3. The suffix in *mry·f* presumably refers to Sokar, the owner of the *Ḥnw*-bark. It can hardly refer to the bark itself, which in § 1933*d–f* takes a feminine suffix, apparently because the

generic term *dpt* 'boat' is feminine; compare the feminine gender of place-names following on *ni̓wt* 'town' or *ḫꜣst* 'foreign land'.

4. Read *ḥnꜥ·sn i̓myw·s* here and in the next two sentences. The plural suffix must refer to the gods on board the boat, but strictly speaking is superfluous.

5. After *nḏr*, emend *n·f* into *n·k*; for *Nḥm-kꜣw* read *Nḥb(w)-kꜣw*. The meaning of *šꜣrw* is obscure; it may be a mythological place-name.

6. Despite the writing with *r*, 'face' is surely meant.

7. On *šꜣ* cf. *Wb*. iv, 401, 6; *JEA* 14, 217.

8. *Ḫi̓w ḥtpt*; the translation is by no means certain.

9. Apparently a crop of some kind, but I can neither read nor translate it.

10. Apparently so, though one would expect *ḥzꜣt* rather than *ḥsꜣt*.

11. The suffix after *fnnt* covers also *pḳ* and *ḥsꜣt*.

12. Or possibly 'standing at'; it may be that [hieroglyph] has been omitted by confusion with the preceding sign.

13. Following JPII, 733.

14. Untranslatable.

15. Again untranslatable.

## Utterance 667A[1]

### *An 'ascension' text*

How good it is for those who see, how comforting it is for those who hear § 1943
when Osiris the overseer of the gods arises! You have your tomb, O King, which belongs to the heart of Him whose seats are hidden; he opens for you the doors of the sky, he throws open for you the doors of the firmament(?), he makes a road for you that you may ascend[2] by means of it into the company of the gods, you being alive in your bird-shape.

O King, you have not died the death; live among them, the Imperishable § 1944
Spirits. When the season of Inundation comes, provide the efflux which issued from Osiris, that Horus may be cleansed from what his brother Seth
did to him,[l] that Seth may be cleansed from what his brother Horus did to § 1945
him, that this King may be cleansed from every evil thing on him, and that there may be cleansed those who watched for Horus when he sought his father Osiris. He has appeared upon the Stone(?), upon his throne, he has sharpened the iron by means of his spirit. I have begged him from *Ḫrty* and I will never give him to Osiris; I open for him the gate which keeps out ⟨the plebs⟩;[3] I have done for him what should be done as the Lone Star who has
no fellow among them, the gods.[l] Be seated on your great throne; your bread § 1946
is the *t-wr*-loaf, your bread is in the Broad Hall.[l] The Watchers dance for § 1947
you and the Mourning-Woman calls to you as Isis.[4] Raise yourself, O King, gather together your bones, take your head, for the Ennead have commanded

that you be seated at your *ṯ-wr*-loaf and that you cut up the foreleg upon the great slaughtering-block, for the joints have been placed for you on the slaughtering-block of Osiris.

§ 1948 O King, raise yourself as Min; fly up to the sky and live with them,[5] cause your wings to grow with your feathers on your head and your feathers on your arms. Make the sky clear and shine on them as a god; may you be enduring at the head of the sky as Horus of the Netherworld.

1. Supplement, pp. 42–4.
2. So Nt; N (Sethe) has *bꜣ* 'be a soul'.
3. *Rḫyt* omitted, cf. §§ 1726*b*; 1934*e* (Supplement, p. 39).
4. For *Wsỉr* read *ꜣst*.
5. The gods.

## Utterance 667B[1]

### *A food-spell*

§ 1949 Hail to you, O King, whose seats are hidden! May your herald ascend
§ 1950 happily to the firmament.[1] I have threshed barley, I have reaped emmer, I have made your yearly sustenance therefrom. Go up, seat yourself,[2] O King, and empower(?)[3] me; I cannot see you, but you can see me.

'How great are those whom my face has seen, how mighty are those whom my eyes have seen!'[4]

§ 1951 Horus comes with bound hair[5] as the protector of his father, he stands as Horus upon the river-bank with his sisters Isis and Nephthys beside him.[6]

1. Supplement, p. 45.
2. Read *ḥms*, see the textual note on § 1950*c*.
3. *Sḫmḫm* is a hapax, a partly reduplicated transitive derivative of *sḫm*. The lacuna before the suffix in the facsimile of Nt, 784 looks rather large for a determinative, but it is hard to see what else could have stood there; *sḫmḫm·k wỉ* is what one would expect.
4. The king speaks.
5. *Ỉw* 'comes' is followed by ; presumably 'Horus' is intended. *Snḫ* is old perfective 3rd masc. sing.
6. There has been confusion between Horus, i.e. the king's son, and Osiris the brother of Isis and Nephthys, i.e. the dead king.

## Utterance 667C[1]

### *A 'resurrection' text*

§ 1952 Raise yourself, O King, collect your bones, gather your members together. Raise yourself, O King, take your head [. . .] your face at the birth-stool(?)

which Meskhēnet your mother has made,[2] even she who has made you content(?), for you are in the jaws(?)[3] of . . .| . . . Shu . . .[4] He overthrows the § 1953
ramparts, he removes the ramparts.[5] | Turn yourself about, O King, whose § 1954
seats are hidden. Will you[6] not overthrow ⟨the ramparts⟩ nor remove ⟨the ramparts⟩?[7] [. . .]| the three(?) *ḥmwst* and the four [. . .]. They overthrow § 1955
the ramparts, they remove the ramparts. Turn yourself about, O King, whose seats are hidden.

1. Supplement, pp. 46–7.
2. The mention of the birth-goddess Meskhēnet suggests that the doubtful object which she is said to have made may be a birth-stool, in which case we will have here an allusion to the rebirth of the dead king. In this passage in Nt, 786 there are two obvious errors, see the textual notes on § 1952*d*.
3. So JPII, 741. I can make nothing of the rest of this passage.
4. § 1953*a* is unintelligible.
5. So N (Sethe); similarly in § 1955*b*. The Nt-text is obviously defective here; for *dr·f* it has *ir·f* 'he makes' and it omits the second clause.
6. Plural; apparently in reference to the beings mentioned in § 1955*a*.
7. See the textual note on § 1954*b*. At this point Nt leaves this spell, but it is continued in JPII, 742 + Sethe (§ 1955).

## Utterance 667D[1]

*A formula of offering*

[. . . your thousand] of *fnnwt*, your thousand of [. . .| your thousand] of all §§ 1956–7
kinds of stone vessels, your thousand of all kinds of clothing, your thousand of oxen, your thousand of fowl, your thousand of all kinds of sweet things.|
I equip you as a god [. . .][2] to *Pḏw-š*. § 1958

1. Supplement, p. 47.
2. About half a column lost except for a group  in the middle of the lacuna.

## Utterance 668[1]

*The king becomes a falcon*

The King is a screeching falcon who flies around the Eye of Horus who dwells § 1959
in the Netherworld; the King is a falcon who is censed with [. . .], and you[2] have censed(?) the King with it.| The King is bound for the eastern side of § 1960
the sky, for the King was conceived there and the King was born there.

1. Supplement, pp. 47–8. The passage which was not available to Sethe is § 1959*b*.
2. Plural.

## Utterance 669[1]

*An 'ascension' and 'rebirth' text*

§ 1961 The prince(?) ascends in a great storm[2] from the inner horizon; he sees the preparation for the festival, the making of the braziers, the birth of the gods before you in the five epagomenal days, and(?) the great-breasted one who
§ 1962 is at the head of the . . .[3] [. . .]| the King by his mother. Yours is rebirth in the nest [of] Thoth within the Field of Tamarisk in the protection of the
§ 1963 gods,| because the King is my brother who issued from the leg, who judged the rivals, who parted the combatants, and who will split your heads, you
§ 1964 gods| [. . .]; she provides the King with a fillet[4] as the ferryman who travels(?),[5] the great one who is among you, you gods, for whom you . . .,[6] you gods, when Isis spoke to Nu.

§ 1965 'You[7] have borne him,[8] you have shaped him,[9] you have spat him out,[10] but he has no legs, he has no arms; wherewith can he be knit together?'

§ 1966 'This iron shall be brought for him,[11] the *Ḥnw*-bark [shall be brought(?)][12] that he may be [lifted up(?)][13] into it.'

'. . . who was brought up in it within your[14] arms', say the gods.

'Behold, he is born; behold, he is knit together; behold, he is in being.'[15]

§ 1967 'Wherewith shall we break[16] his egg?', say the gods.

§ 1968 'Sokar of *Pḏw*⟨-*š*⟩ shall come for him, for he has fashioned his harpoon-points and has cut out his barbs [. . .]; it is he who will break [the egg and
§ 1969 split(?)] the iron.[17] | The god will make his arms hale, for sharp are the teeth and long are the claws of the two guides[18] of the gods. Behold, the King is in being; behold, the King is knit together; behold, the King has broken the egg.'

§ 1970 'Wherewith can the King be made to fly up?'

'There shall be brought to you[19] [. . .] the *Ḥnw*-bark and the . . .[20] of the *ḥn*-bird(?). You shall fly up therewith, you shall fly up therewith; the [south]-wind shall be your wet-nurse and the north-wind shall be your dry-nurse;|
§ 1971 you[21] shall fly up and alight on account of the plumes of your father Gēb.'

1. Supplement, pp. 48–51.

2. The text as shown in JPII is quite different from Sethe's restoration. §§ 1961–4 show the pronouns of the 2nd masc. sing. interspersed with those of the 3rd in reference to the king; either the text has had its pronouns partly changed in ancient times, or else there have been textual omissions. In the circumstances the text has been translated exactly as it stands, without attempting to disentangle the confusion of pronouns.

3. *Bꜣtww*, meaning unknown.

4. For the transitive use of *sšd* cf. *Urk.* iv, 1439, 6.

5. For *nwrw* cf. *Wb.* ii, 223, 3; *ḥpw* may be a participle of *ḥp* 'travel'.
6. *nwṯw* appears to be the relative form of a verb otherwise unknown.
7. i.e. Isis; the suffix is feminine. What follows in § 1966 shows that the gods are speaking; this is the first of a series of questions which the gods ask and Isis answers.
8. The 3rd person is used rightly in what follows, since the king is being spoken of by a third party.
9. A metaphorical use of *dn* 'knead' dough, *Ikhekhi*, p. 70.
10. For *nḫ* 'spit out', 'eject', cf. *CT* iii, 98*o*; cf. also *nḫ* 'venom' of snake, § 686*b*.
11. Isis replies to the gods' question.
12. A conjectural restoration.
13. Restore as *ṯ*[*z*]·*f*.
14. Plural; apparently an error for the 2nd fem. sing. ·*ṯ*, influenced by the following plural *nṯrw*. The pronoun must surely refer to Isis.
15. Isis speaks again.
16. See the textual note.
17. A metaphorical reference to the hard shell of the egg containing the new-born king. Again Isis is speaking.
18. *Sic!*
19. Singular; Isis is now addressing the king.
20. *Ḳdmw*, meaning unknown.
21. Here the 2nd person must certainly have been original; the king's name is a later substitution.

## Utterance 670[1]

### *In part a variant of Utterance* 482

The doors of the sky are opened, the doors of the celestial expanses are § 1972
thrown open;| the gods who are in Pe are full of sorrow, and they come to § 1973
Osiris the King at the sound of the weeping[2] of Isis, at the cry of Nephthys,
at the wailing of these two spirits[3] [over this great one who has come forth]
from the Netherworld.[4] | The Souls of Pe clash sticks(?)[5] for you, they smite § 1974
⟨their⟩ flesh for you, they clap their hands for you, they tug[6] [their] side-
locks for you, they [smack] their thighs for you,| and they say to you: 'O § 1975
Osiris the King, you have gone, but you will return,[7] you have slept, [but
you will awake], you have died,[8] but you will live.| Stand up and see what your § 1976
son has done for you, wake up and hear [what] Horus [has done for] you.[9] |
He has smitten for you him who smote you as [an ox],[10] he has slain for you § 1977
him who slew you as a wild bull, he has bound for you him who bound
you and has set him under your eldest daughter who is in *Ḳdm*,[11] | that § 1978
mourning may cease in the Two Conclaves of the gods.'

Osiris speaks to Horus, for he[12] has removed the evil [which was on the
King] on his fourth day, he has nullified what was done to him[13] on his
§ 1979 eighth [day,| and you have come forth] from the Lake of Life,[14] having been
cleansed[15] [in the Lake] of Cool Water and having become Wepwawet. Your
son Horus guides you, he has given you the gods who are your foes, and
§ 1980 Thoth brings them to you.| How happy are those who see, how content are
those who behold, even they who see Horus when he gives life to his father
§ 1981 [and extends the *wꜣs*-staff] to Osiris in the face of the western gods!| A
libation for you is poured out by Isis, [Nephthys has cleansed you, even your
two] great and mighty sisters[16] who gathered your flesh together, who raised
up your members, and who caused your eyes to appear in your head,|
§ 1982 (namely) the Night-bark and the Day-bark. I[17] have given Atum to you,
§ 1983 I have made the Two Enneads for you,| your children's children together[18]
have raised you up, (namely) Ḥapy, [Imsety,] Duamūtef, and Ḳebḥsenuf,
[whose] names you have [wholly] made. [Your face is washed,] your tears
§ 1984 are wiped away,[19] your mouth is split open with their iron fingers,| and you
go forth that you may go up to the broad hall of Atum, travel to the Field of
§ 1985 Rushes, and traverse the places of the great god.| The sky is given to you,
the earth is given to you, the Field of Rushes is given to you; [it is] the two
great gods who row you, (even) Shu and Tefēnet, the two great gods of Ōn.[20]|
§ 1986 [The god][21] wakes, [the god stands up because of this spirit which came
forth from] the Netherworld, (even) Osiris the King who came forth from
Gēb.

1. Lacunae partly completed from JPII, 760–5.
2. Delete brackets and hatching in Sethe.
3. Delete the restoration and substitute *ỉptw*.
4. Delete hatching and brackets from *-r m dꜣt*.
5. Delete brackets and hatching; for *rtw* read *rtỉ*, var. of *rwỉ* Cf. Utt. 482, n. 2.
6. Read *nwn·sn* with § 1005*c*; the initial *n* has been merged with preceding *·sn*.
7. Prospective *sḏm·f*.
8. 𓇋 of *mnỉ* 'die' is preserved.
9. *Sḏm* and *·k Ḥr* preserved.
10. Delete brackets and hatching except for *tḥ*.
11. Cf. *Komm.* iv, 291 f.
12. Horus.
13. Osiris = the King.
14. *M š n ꜥnḫ* preserved; for ☥ read ☥𓈖𓏏.
15. *Wꜥb·ty* partly preserved.
16. *-t·k wrt ꜥꜣt* preserved.
17. The officiant, representing Horus.

18. At end read *twt*, old perfective used adverbially; first pointed out by Gunn. Cf. *Komm.* v, 33.
19. *ꜥḥ* of [ꜥ]*ꜥḥw* preserved in JPII.
20. Delete brackets and cross-hatching.
21. Osiris = the dead king. *Rs* 'wakes' is preserved.

## Utterance 671

*The king is summoned to occupy his throne*

O King, you are the son of a great one; bathe in the Lake of the Netherworld § 1987
and take your seat in the Field of Rushes.

## Utterance 672

*The king succeeds to his throne*

It is she who once led[1] Horus who leads this King. O King, you have gone, § 1988
O King, clothed, and you return dressed.| This King has inherited, and § 1989
sorrow ceases, laughter comes into being. I greet you, O King, be welcome!

1. *Mꜣꜥt* is a fem. participle of *mꜣꜥ* 'lead', 'guide', 'direct', *Concise Dict.* 102, and has nothing to do with *mꜣꜥt* 'truth' as Mercer thinks. The same verb occurs in § 2099*b*.

## Utterance 673

*An 'ascension' text*

O my father the King, such is your going when you have gone as a god, your § 1990
travelling is as a celestial being.| Your porters hurry, your couriers run, they § 1991
ascend to the sky and tell Rēꜥ| that you stand in the Conclaves of the horizon § 1992
upon the void of the sky,[1] and sit on the throne of your father Gēb in front
of the Conclave upon this throne of iron at which the gods marvel.| The Two § 1993
Enneads come to you bowing, you give orders to the sun-folk as Min who is
in his house, as Horus of Djebꜥat,[2] and Seth will not be free from bearing the
burden of you.

1. Emending [hieroglyph] into [hieroglyph] as does Mercer, though *šw* and *nwt* are interpreted as the void of air and as the sky respectively rather than as their deified embodiments.
2. Cf. Utt. 413, n. 2.

## Utterance 674

*The king assumes royal state in the Beyond*

I come to you, for I am your son; I come to you, for I am Horus.[1] I set your § 1994
staff for you at the head of the spirits and your sceptre at the head of the

§ 1995 Imperishable Stars.| [I have found you knit together, your face][2] is that of a jackal, your hinder-parts are the Celestial Serpent; she freshens your heart
§ 1996 in your body in the house of her father[3] Anubis.| Be purified and sit at the head of those who are greater than you, sit on your iron throne,[4] on the seat
§ 1997 of the Foremost of the Westerners . . .[5] | The Mourning-Woman calls to
§ 1998 you as Isis, the Joyful One rejoices over you as Nephthys,[6] | you stand before the *snwt*-shrines as Min, you stand at the head of the people of Athribis(?)[7]
§ 1999 as Apis,[8] you stand in *Pdw-Š* as[9] Sokar,| you stand at the great causeway[10] (with)[11] your sceptre, your *nwḏt*,[12] your nails which are on your fingers, the spines[13] which are on the arms of Thoth, and the sharp knife which came forth from Seth. You shall extend your hand[14] to the dead and to the spirits who shall grasp your hand for the Foremost of the Westerners.

1. So Nt, 601–2.
2. Lacuna in Nt, 602 also. For *ḥr·f* read *ḥr·k* as Mercer; so also for *pḥwy·f* read *pḥwy·k*; the king is being addressed directly.
3. For *it·k* read *it·s* with Mercer; *Ḳbḥwt* is daughter of Anubis in § 1180*b*.
4. Preserved in Nt, 603.
5. § 1996*c* is untranslatable.
6. Cf. Nt, 604.
7. Cf. *Dict. géogr.* v, 199 f.
8. Surely so, despite the absence of the bull-determinative. The alternative would be *Ḥpy* a son of Horus, who is not likely to be the tutelary deity of a town.
9. *Is* is preserved in Nt, 605.
10. Cf. loc. cit.
11. Despite the absence of any nexus with what has gone before, the list of the king's possessions which follows can hardly be other than a description of his equipment when he stands at the causeway.
12. Only here, meaning unknown. Mercer suggests that it may refer to the curl on the Red Crown, usually called *ḥsbt*, which appears to have been deemed a potent object in its own right.
13. For *msꜣw*, fuller writing *mlsꜣw*, cf. 1560*c*; *CT* i, 289*c*. Possibly the word may refer to the shafts of the feathers on the wing of Thoth; in § 1560*c* they are identified with plumes.
14. Sethe's restoration in § 1999*d* is to be discarded; according to Nt, 606 the text reads *ḥw·k ᶜ·k ir mtw ir ꜣḫw*. For the meaning given to *ḥw ᶜ* cf. *Urk.* iv, 870, 16; *JEA* 7, 125.

## Utterance 675

*The king is welcomed into the Beyond*

§ 2000 O King, come in peace[1] to Osiris! O messenger[2] of the great god, come in
§ 2001 peace to the great god!| The doors of the sky are opened for you, the starry sky is thrown open for you,[3] the Jackal of Upper Egypt comes down to you[4]

as Anubis at your[5] side, as the *ḥpìw*-snake[6] which presides over Ōn;| the § 2002
Great Maiden has laid her hands on you, (even) she who dwells in Ōn.
O King, you have no[7] human father who could beget you, you have no
human mother who could bear you;| your mother is the Great Wild Cow who § 2003
dwells in Nekheb, white of head-cloth, long of hair, and pendulous of breasts,
she suckles[8] you and does not wean you.
Raise yourself, O King, clothe yourself in this cloak of yours which is out § 2004
of the Mansion, with your mace on your arm and your sceptre in your hand,
your sceptre[9] on your arm and your mace in your hand,| standing at the head § 2005
of the Two Conclaves that you may judge the gods.
O King, you belong to the *nḫḫw*-stars which shine in the train of the Morn-
ing Star,| and indeed no god will be absent,[10] because of what has been said § 2006
to him; he will offer to you your thousand of bread, your thousand of beer,
your thousand of oxen, your thousand of fowl, and your thousand of everything on which a god lives.

1. *Ír·k* here and in § 2000*b* is the enclitic particle reinforcing the imperative *m* 'come'.
2. The repeated imperative shows that, despite the writing, we have to read *wpwt(y)* 'messenger', which here is apparently an epithet of the dead king.
3. Preserved in Nt, 608 as corrected in *Neit*, p. 26.
4. Var. Nt, 608 *hꜣ n·k m rd zꜣb šmꜥ*.
5. Emending *gs·f* (so also Nt) into *gs·k*.
6. Cf. § 662*c*.
7. The negation is preserved in Nt, 609.
8. *Mnḏwy* and *snk* preserved in loc. cit.
9. Sethe's restorations are confirmed by Nt, 611, which, however, is somewhat corrupt at this point.
10. In the lacuna in § 2006*a*, Nt, 612 has 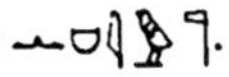.

## Utterance 676[1]

*A 'resurrection' text*

You have your water, you have your flood, you have your efflux which issued § 2007
from Osiris;| gather together your bones, make ready[2] your members, throw § 2008
off your dust, loosen your bonds.| The tomb is opened for you, the doors of § 2009
the coffin are drawn back for you,[3] the doors of the sky are thrown open for
you; 'Greeting', says Isis; 'In peace', says Nephthys, when they see their
brother in the Festival of Atum.| This cold water of yours, O Osiris, is what § 2010
is in Busiris and what is in *Grgw-bꜣ·f*,[4] your soul is within you and your power
is about you, it having been established at the head of all[5] the Powers.
Raise yourself, O King; may you traverse the Southern Mounds, may you § 2011

traverse the Northern Mounds,[6] may you have power ⟨by means of⟩ the powers which are in you. There have been given to you your spirits, the jackals which Horus of Nekhen has given to you.[7]

§ 2012 Raise yourself, O King; may you sit on your iron throne, for Anubis who presides over the God's Booth has commanded that you be purified with your eight *nmst*-jars and your eight *ꜥꜣbt*-jars which came forth from the
§ 2013 Castle of the God.| You are indeed god-like, for ⟨you⟩[8] have shouldered the sky, you have raised up the earth. The Mourning-Woman cries out to you,
§ 2014 the Great Mooring-post calls to you,| hands are clapped for you, feet are stamped[9] for you, you ascend here as a star, as the Morning Star.

§ 2015 He[10] comes to you his father, he comes to you, O Gēb;| take his hand and let him sit on the great throne that he may join the two . . .[11] of the sky; his mouth is cleansed with natron, he is purified on the thighs of *Ḫnt-irty*, his
§ 2016 upper and lower nails[12] are cleansed.| Do for him what you did for his brother Osiris on that day of putting the bones in order, of making good the soles, and of travelling the causeway.[13]

§ 2017 The . . .[14] come to you[15] bent (in obeisance), you summon the Upper Egyptian Conclave, and the Lower Egyptian Conclave comes to you bowing.

1. Lacunae completed from Nt, 613 ff.
2. Cf. *ZÄS* 79, 89.
3. Cf. Nt, 615.
4. Read *imyw Ḏdw imyw Grgw-bꜣ·f* with Nt, 616; compare § 719*a*. Sethe's restoration is to be discarded.
5. For [hieroglyph] read [hieroglyph].
6. Cf. Nt, 617.
7. The 'jackals' in question are the 'Souls of Nekhen', cf. *Urgeschichte*, §§ 191 f.
8. The suffix ·*k* omitted, cf. Nt, 619.
9. *Ḏꜣm* of stamping feet only here; of waving hands and arms in §§ 743*d*; 1366*b*; *CT* i, 272*d*.
10. The king; a change of person.
11. *Ḫrmt*, meaning unknown, occurs also in § 1367*b* with det. [hieroglyph].
12. Of fingers and toes.
13. Cf. § 1368.
14. *Sꜣtw*, meaning unknown; see also Nt, 622.
15. The king; another change of person. Cf. Utt. 553, n. 15.

## Utterance 677

*The king dies and rises again*

§ 2018 The Great One has fallen on his side, (even) he who stood as a god with his
§ 2019 power with him and his *Wrrt*-crown on his head.| The King has fallen on his

side, (even) the King who stood as a god with his power with[1] him and his *Wrrt*-crown on his head, like the *Wrrt*-crown of Rēʿ. He ascends from the horizon, he is greeted by[2] Horus in the horizon.

O King, raise yourself, receive your dignity which the Two Enneads have § 2020
made for you| that you may be on the throne of Osiris as successor to the § 2021
Foremost of the Westerners. [Take his power, receive] his [*Wrrt*-crown].

O King, how good is this, how great is this which your father Osiris has § 2022
done for you! He has given his throne to you,| and you give orders to those § 2023
whose seats are hidden, you lead their august ones, and [all] the spirits follow you [whoever they may be(?)].[3]

[O King, be happy] and proud, because you belong to him from whose § 2024
action you will not be far removed.[4]| Rēʿ summons you in this your name of § 2025
'Him of whom all the spirits are afraid', and the dread of you is in hearts like [the dread of Rēʿ when he ascends from the horizon].

[O] King, your[5] shape is hidden like that of Anubis on his belly; receive § 2026
your jackal-face and raise yourself, stand up| and sit down to your thousand § 2027
of bread, your thousand of beer, your thousand [of oxen, your thousand of fowl, your thousand of everything on which a god lives].

O King, be pure, that Rēʿ may find you standing with your mother Nūt,[6] § 2028
that she may lead you[7] on the ways of the horizon, and that you may make your abode there happily in the company of your double for ever and ever.

1. *Ḥn* is an obvious slip for *ḥnʿ*.
2. The restoration [𓇋𓈖] at the beginning of l. 816 in § 2019*c* is to be deleted, see *Pyr.* iii, 109.
3. Or 'the spirits [and the dead]', or even 'the spirits [whose seats are hidden]', cf. ibid. 109–10.
4. *Tm* is a relative form; for the exceptional position of the suffix after the main verb cf. Edel, §§ 1104–5. A later example is *im mꜣꜣ·i* 'may I not see', *CT* iii, 33*b* (B5C, emending 𓇋𓄿𓂜 into 𓇋𓅓𓂜). Mercer interprets *tm* as the name of Atum, despite the determinative 𓂜.
5. Emending *irw·f* into *irw·k*.
6. Emending ○ into ○.
7. Read *sšm·s i*⟨*w*⟩.

## Utterance 678

*The king is not to be deprived of his magic power*

O *Iḥmty*,[1] O *Smty*,[2] do not oppose(?)[3] the King, do not examine[4] the King, § 2029
do not guard against the magic in the King's hand, do not ask for the King's
magic from the King;| you have your magic and the King's magic is his. May § 2030

the King not break your pen nor shatter your ink-shell,[5] for it is the King who possesses a meal.

1. See also § 1102*a*.
2. Probably so to be read rather than *Sḏmty*, cf. *Wb.* iv, 144, 9.
3. *Ḥmm*, otherwise unknown. The meaning 'oppose(?)' assigned to it is a guess.
4. 'Verhören', *Wb.* iv, 144, 8.
5. The determinative appears to represent a mussel-shell used as an ink-well; cf. *wḏryt* 'mussel', *JEA* 18, 158.

## Utterance 679

*The king possesses his bodily fluids*

§ 2031 You have your water, you have your efflux, you have your flood which issued
§ 2032 from Osiris.[1] May you . . .[1] them as Horus, may you divide them as Wepwawet, because you are a great one, the son of a great one.

1. *Ḫsd*, meaning unknown.

## Utterance 680

§ 2033 O Osiris the King, take the Eye of Horus, for it is yours.

## Utterance 681

*The king assumes his kingship in the Beyond*

§ 2034 O Great Sky, give your hand to the King; O Great Nūt, give your hand to the
§ 2035 King, for the King is this divine falcon of yours.[1] The King has come that he may ascend to the sky and explore the firmament; the King greets his
§ 2036 father Rēʿ,[1] and he[1] has crowned him as Horus from whom the King has come, so that he may give the King a new accession and set in place for the
§ 2037 King his two divine eyes.[1] The King ascends to him, Horus grasps(?)[2] Nūt by the top-knot, even he who smote the *Nt*-crowns and gave orders to the
§ 2038 *Wtnw*.[3][1] The King is followed by the Brewers(?), the chiefs of sky and earth come to him bowing, even the two Guide-serpents, the jackals, and the Spirits
§ 2039 of Seth who are above and below,[1] who smear on ointment, who are clad in
§ 2040 fine linen,[4] who live on offerings.[1] The King gives orders, the King bestows dignities, the King assigns places, the King gives offerings, the King directs
§ 2041 oblations,[1] for such indeed is the King; the King is the Sole One of the sky, a potentate at the head of the heavens.

1. Rēʿ.
2. Cf. Allen, n. 100.
3. *Wtmw* occurs again in *CT* v, 220*b* with  as determinative; the context here suggests that the word may refer to the nobles who supported the Delta king in the War of Unification, and who as a result of it became subjects of the king of Upper Egypt.
4. *Pꜣt* appears to be an error for *pꜣḳt* 'fine linen'.

## Utterance 682

### *An 'ascension' text*

You are greeted by Sokar, O King, your face is washed by *Dwꜣ-wr*. The § 2042
King soars as a divine falcon, the King flies heavenward like a heron, the
King flies up as a goose,| the King's wings are those of a divine falcon, § 2043
the King's wing-feathers are those of a divine falcon. The bones of the em-
balmed King are raised up, for the King is pure;| the King's cloak is on his § 2044
back, the King's *ḳnỉ*-garment is upon him, even his *nšdw* which belongs to the
*šnp*.[1]| The King embarks with Rēʿ in this great bark of his, he navigates in it to § 2045
the horizon in order to rule the gods in it,| and Horus navigates in it to the § 2046
horizon with him, the King rules the gods in it with him in the horizon, for
the King is one of them.

1. On this passage, cf. *Dram. Texte*, 211 f.

## Utterance 683

### *The king is greeted by the gods*

Behold this which they said concerning the King, which the gods said con- § 2047
cerning the King; now the gods speak concerning the King: 'This is Horus
who came forth from the Nile, this is the long-horn which came forth from
the stockade, this is the viper which came forth from Rēʿ, this is the uraeus
which came forth from Seth.'| As for everything which she[1] brings about § 2048
for the King, the like will come about for her who does the will of[2] the
monarch, even the daughter of Rēʿ who is on his lap; as for everything which
she brings about for the King, the like will come about for *Mḏꜣ*,[3] even the
daughter of Rēʿ who is on his lap,| because the King is a hale one, son of § 2049
a hale one, who came forth from a hale one.[4]| The King is hale, the King is § 2050
hale, and hale is the Eye of Horus which is in Ōn. The King lives, the King
lives, and lives the Eye of Horus which is in Ōn.

1. The two serpents considered as one being.

2. Cf. *mḏd* 'obey', *Urk.* iv, 484, 5.

3. Masculine, despite the feminine context. The meaning is obscure, for *mdnw* 'adversary', § 1237*b*, can hardly be intended here.

4. Feminine.

## Utterance 684

### *An 'ascension' text*

§ 2051 This King ascended when you ascended, O Osiris; his word and his double
are bound for the sky, the King's bones are iron and the King's members
§ 2052 are the Imperishable Stars.| If the King be caused to be embalmed, the
§ 2053 Great One[1] will fall before the King, for the King's mother is Nūt,| the
King's (grand)father is Shu, the King's (grand)mother is Tefēnet,[2] they take
§ 2054 the King to the sky, to the sky, on the smoke of the incense.| The King is
§ 2055 pure, the King is alive, the King will take his place as Osiris.| The King will
sit beside you, O Osiris, the King will spit on your scalp, O Osiris.[3] He will
not let it be ill, the King will not let it be bald, according to the King's
daily speech at the half-monthly festivals and at the monthly festivals.

§ 2056 The King will sit beside you, O Horus, the King will spit on your scalp, O
Horus, the King will not let it be ill, the King will not let it be bald, according
to the King's daily speech at the half-monthly festivals and at the monthly
festivals.

§ 2057 The King is one of these four beings whom Atum begot and Nūt bore,|
§ 2058 who will never become corrupt, therefore the King will not become corrupt;
who will never decay, therefore the King will not decay; who will never fall
to the earth from the sky, therefore the King will not fall to the earth from the
§ 2059 sky.| The King is sought out, the King is found for them,[4] the King is one of
§ 2060 them, even those who are favoured by the Bull of the Sky.| The King lifts his
§ 2061 double aloft, the King turns about, the King . . ..[5]| O you good companion,[6]
lift the double aloft, turn about, . . .; be firm,[7] O King, on the underside of
the sky with the beautiful star[8] upon the bends of the Winding Waterway.|
§ 2062 The King ascends to the sky and the King gives it to you,[9] (even) this spell,
so that Rēʿ may be happy every day. The King places himself upon your
path, O Horus of Shezmet, by means of which you guide the gods to the
fair paths of the sky and of the Field of Offerings.

1. Feminine.

2. 'Father' and 'mother' here signify 'grandparents', since the King's mother is stated already to be Nūt, herself the daughter of Shu and Tefēnet.

3. With intent to cure scalp trouble, see also § 521; spittle is a known remedy in folk-medicine.

4. The triliteral verb *zḫn* is in the passive *sḏmm·f*, while the tertiae infirmae verb *gmỉ* is in the passive *sḏmw·f*, apparently because the weak final radical of tertiae infirmae verbs does not double in the former 'tense', cf. Edel, § 558, where no tertiae infirmae verbs are recorded. In the case of the quartae infirmae *nḏrỉ* (Edel, loc. cit.) the weak final radical has been assimilated to the preceding consonant.

5. *Wꜣḥwꜣḥ*, meaning unknown. Mercer's 'stride' seems no more than a guess.

6. *Ỉry nfr*. Is this the king or a being with him?

7. The particle *ỉr·k* shows that *mn* is imperative.

8. Feminine; possibly Sothis may be meant. For the sense given to *m* cf. *JEA* 25, 166; 39, 20. 31; the feminine gender of the star precludes the translation of *m* as 'as'.

9. To whom? Perhaps Horus of Shezmet, who is named in § 2062*b*.

## Utterance 685

*The king is reborn*

The waters of life which are in the sky come, the waters of life which are in § 2063
the earth come, the sky is aflame for you, the earth quakes at you before the
god's birth;[1] the two mountains are split apart, the god comes into being, the § 2064
god has power in his body; (so) the two mountains are split apart, this King
comes into being, this King has power in his body.

Behold this King, his feet are kissed by the pure waters which exist through § 2065
Atum, which the phallus of Shu makes and which the vagina of Tefēnet
creates.[1] They have come and have brought to you the pure waters with their § 2066
father; they cleanse you and make you divine, O King.[1] You shall support the § 2067
sky with your hand, you shall lay down the earth with your foot, a libation
shall be poured out at this King's gate. When the face of every god is washed,[1]
you shall wash your hands, O Osiris, you shall wash your hands, O King, § 2068
you shall be young (again), O god; your[1] third is he who orders offerings.
The perfume of *Ỉḫt-wtt* is on this King,[1] a *bnbn*-loaf is in the Mansion of § 2069
Sokar, a foreleg is in the House of Anubis. This King is hale, the Herdsman
stands up, the month is born,[2] *Sp*[3] lives.[1] I have prepared arourae so that you § 2070
may cultivate barley, you may cultivate emmer; this King will be presented
therewith for ever.

1. Plural, referring apparently to Shu and Tefēnet.
2. The rising of the new moon?
3. Either a place-name or an epithet derived therefrom. Not *spꜣt* 'nome', for the feminine ending is lacking.

## Utterance 686

*The king is anointed*

§ 2071 O Ointment of Horus! O Ointment of Seth! Horus has taken possession of
§ 2072 his Eye and has saved it from his foes, and Seth has no rights over it.[1] | Horus
has filled himself with unguent, and Horus is pleased with what he has done,
Horus is equipped with what is his.[2] The Eye of Horus cleaves to him,[3] its
§ 2073 perfume is on him, its wrath falls upon his foes.| Ointment belongs to this
King, this King fills himself with it, its perfume is joined to him,[4] and its
wrath falls upon his foes.

1. So Gunn; lit. 'there is nothing appertaining-to-property of Seth in it'.
2. *Swt·f* is the independent pronoun *swt* in its possessive sense, construed as a noun and provided with a possessive suffix.
3. For this sense of *dmi* (here with prothetic *i*) cf. *Eb.* 91, 14; *Leb.* 150, where, however, the preposition is *ḥr* instead of *im* as here.
4. Here *dmi* is written as *dmr* and takes *r* instead of *im* after it.

## Utterance 687

*The king is perfumed*

§ 2074 O King, I have come and I bring to you the Eye of Horus which is in its
§ 2075 container(?),[1] and its perfume is on you, O King.| Its perfume is on you,
the perfume of the Eye of Horus is on you, O King, and you will have a soul[2]
by means of it, you will have power by means of it, you will be strong by
means of it, and by means of it you will assume the *Wrrt*-crown among the
§ 2076 gods.| Horus comes, joyful at meeting you and joyful at meeting his Eye
which is on you. Behold, the King is at the head of the gods and is provided
§ 2077 as a god, his bones are knit together as Osiris;| the gods do obeisance when
meeting the King just as the gods do obeisance when meeting the rising of
Rēʿ when he ascends from the horizon.

1. The literal sense of *tꜣ* as 'kiln' is obviously unsuitable here, and probably the jar containing the perfume is meant.
2. Reading *ibꜣ·k*.

## Utterance 688

*An 'ascension' text*

§ 2078 These four gods, friends of the King, attend on this King, (namely) Imsety,
§ 2079 Ḥapy, Duamūtef, and Ḳebḥsenuf, the children of Horus of Khem;| they tie

the rope-ladder for this King, they make firm the wooden ladder for this
King, they cause the King to mount up to Khoprer when he comes into being
in the eastern side of the sky.| Its[1] timbers have been hewn by[2] *Šsꜣ*; the § 2080
lashings which are on it have been drawn tight with sinews of *Gꜣswty*, Bull of
the sky, the rungs have been fastened to its sides with leather of *Ỉmy-wt*,[3]
born of the Cow-goddess; the Supporter-of-the-Great-One has been set
under it by Him who lassoed the Great One.

Lift up this King's double to the god, lead him to the Double Lion-god, § 2081
cause him to mount up to Atum,| for Atum has done what he said he would § 2082
do for this King; he ties the rope-ladder for him, he makes firm the wooden
ladder for this King, for this King is far removed from what men detest,
this King's hands are not on what the gods detest.| The King could not eat § 2083
. . .,[4] the King could not chew the monthly . . .,[5] he could not sleep by night,
he could not pass the day, he swooned in one of the two seasons of Khoprer,[6]|
but those who are in the Netherworld have recovered their wits, they have § 2084
unstopped their ears at this King's voice, for he descends among them,| and § 2085
He whose power is heavy tells them that this King is one of them, for this
King is recorded among them as a great recorded one who has been con-
ducted to the West.| The King's rank is high in the Mansion of the Double § 2086
Lion-god, the hindering arms[7] which were on this King have been removed
by the Repeller of Wrong in the presence of *Ḫnt-ỉrty* in Khem.

1. The wooden ladder.
2. Read *ỉn* 'by'; the *n* has been omitted.
3. So read by Mercer.
4. *Ḏꜣs*, a plant of unpleasant taste, *Wb.* v, 520, 12–15.
5. In § 2083*b* read *nn* (*sic*) *wsꜥ·n Nt pn bḏꜣ n ꜣbdw* with Nt, 28; the meaning of *bḏꜣ* with head-determinative remains obscure.
6. Day and night?
7. Cf. *ṯwꜣ* 'hindrance', *CT* i, 309*a*.

## Utterance 689

*Concerning the Eye of Horus*

Gēb has raised on high the potent(?)[1] Eye of Horus which is on the hands of § 2087
his great souls and upon his ordinary souls.[2] | Turn your head that you may § 2088
see Horus,[3] for he has sat down [. . .] and judgement comes to pass.| Isis § 2089
comes, having grasped her breasts because of her vindicated son, and the
King has found the Eye of Horus,| this one finds the Eye of Horus, to whom § 2090
her head has been given,[4] and she has acted as a frontal on the brow of

Rēʿ,[5] who is as aggressive as a crocodile(?);[6] follow[7] the Eye of Horus to the sky, to the stars of the sky, . . .[8] who shall beseech(?) Horus because of his
§ 2091 Eye.[1] O Shu, supporter of Nūt, raise[9] the Eye of Horus to the sky, to the stars of the sky, since Horus sits on this iron throne of his . . . who shall beseech(?) Horus because of his Eye.

1. The meaning of *kꜣꜣt* is uncertain; the word occurs again in an 'eye' context in *CT* iv, 8*e*.
2. 'Souls' seems the only possible translation for *kꜣw* in this context. There is a play on words between *kꜣw* and *kꜣꜣt*.
3. The feminine suffixes show that this instruction is addressed to the Eye of Horus.
4. Regarding *rdy* as perfective passive participle.
5. The Eye is regarded here as a uraeus.
6. The damaged sign looks like a mummified crocodile.
7. Imperative with reflexive dative addressed to the dead king.
8. *Z m* here and in § 2091*d* defeats me. Mercer translates it as 'go thou', taking — to be a writing of [hieroglyph] and 𓅓 as the particle reinforcing the imperative, but he has taken no account of the negation-sign 𓂜 in § 2091*d*. *Sꜣrwt·f* appears to be a *sḏmty·fy* form, guessed to be of *sꜣꜣ* 'beseech', though this is followed usually by the dative of the person addressed.
9. Read *wṯz n·k*, imperative with dative.

## Utterance 690[1]

*A miscellany of short Utterances*

§ 2092 Osiris awakes, the languid god wakes up, the god stands up, the god has
§ 2093 power in his body.[1] The King awakes, the languid god wakes up, the god
§ 2094 stands up, the god has power in his body.[1] Horus stands up and clothes this King in the woven fabric which went forth from him. This King is provided as a god, the Herdsman stands up, the Two Enneads sit down.

§ 2095 O King, stand up and come in peace to Rēʿ, you messenger of the great
§ 2096 god;[2] go to the sky, come forth from the gate of the horizon.[1] May Gēb guide you, you having a soul as a god, you being strong [as a god], and having power in your body as a god,[3] as a soul at the head of the living, as a Power at the head of the spirits.

§ 2097 This King comes provided as a god, his bones are knit together as Osiris,[4] having followed after [him].[5] This King comes(?)[6] to you[7] in Ōn, you being
§ 2098 protected, and your heart being placed in your body for you.[1] Your face is that of a jackal, your flesh is that of Atum, your soul is within you, your
§ 2099 power is about you, Isis is before you and Nephthys is behind you,[1] you encompass the Horite Mounds and you go round about the Sethite Mounds, it is Shu and Tefēnet who guide you when you go forth from Ōn.

O King, Horus has woven his booth on your behalf, Seth has spread out § 2100
your awnings. Be covered, my father, by the God's Booth, that you may be conveyed[8] therein to your seats which you desire.| O King, Horus comes to § 2101
you provided with his souls,[9] namely Ḥapy, Duamūtef, Imsety, and Ḳebḥ-senuf;| they bring to you this name of yours of 'Imperishable Star', and you § 2102
will never perish nor be destroyed.

O King, your sister the Celestial Serpent has cleansed you[10] upon the § 2103
causeway in the meadow,[11] you having appeared to them[12] as a jackal, as Horus at the head of the living, as Gēb at the head of the Ennead, and as Osiris at the head of the spirits.| May you govern the spirits, may you control § 2104
the Imperishable Stars.[13] | If Osiris be in evil case, then will the King be in § 2105
evil case, and the Bull of the Two Enneads will be in evil case, but the god is released, the god has power in his body, (so therefore) the King is released, the King has power in his body.

O King, stand up for Horus, that he may make you a spirit and guide you § 2106
when you ascend to the sky.| May your mother Nūt receive you, may she § 2107
take your hand; may you not languish, may you not groan, may you live as the Beetle, being stable as a *ḏd*-pillar.[14]

O King,[15] you are clad as a god, your face is that of a jackal as Osiris, this § 2108
soul who is in Nedit, this Power who is in the Great City.| The sky trembles, § 2109
the earth quakes at the feet of the god, at the feet of this King;| if this King § 2110
be not cursed[16] by the earth, then will *Iḫt-wtt* not be cursed by the earth. Your power is that of Rēʿ, you make (men) tremble[17] in the night as does a god, lord of terror; govern[18] the gods as a Power at the head of the Powers.[19]

O Osiris, the inundation comes, the flood hastens, Gēb engenders(?).| § 2111
I have mourned you at the tomb, I have smitten him who harmed you with § 2112
scourges(?).[20] May you come to life, may you raise yourself because of your strength.| O King, the inundation comes, the flood hastens, Gēb engenders(?);[21]| § 2113
provide the efflux[22] of the god which is in you, that your heart may live, that § 2114
your body may be revived(?),[23] O god, and that your sinews[24] may be loosed.|
Horus comes to you, O King, that he may do for you what he did for his § 2115
father Osiris so that you may live as those who are in the sky live[25], that you may be more extant than those who exist on earth.| Raise yourself because of your § 2116
strength, may you ascend to the sky, may the sky give birth to you like Orion, may you have power in your body, and may you protect yourself from your foe.

O King, [I have] wept [for you],[26] I have mourned you,| and I will not § 2117–18

forget you, I will not be inert until the voice comes forth for you every day, in the monthly festival, in the half-monthly festival, at the Setting down of the Brazier, at the Festival of Thoth, at the *Wꜣg*-festival, and at the Festival of Carving(?) as your yearly sustenance which you fashioned for your monthly
§ 2119 festivals,[27] that you may live as a god.[1] O King, may your body be clothed so that you may come to me.

1. Lacunae restored from Nt, 582 ff.; cf. also Nt, 655–7 and JPII, 984 ff.
2. So N; Nt, 584 has 'Rēꜥ the great (*ꜥꜣ*) god'.
3. Cf. Nt, 584–5.
4. 'Osiris' from Nt, 586.
5. Reading *zb m-ḫ[t·f]* without Sethe's *ꜣḫt*; in Nt, 586 there is room only for in the lacuna.
6. The reading of Nt, 586 must surely have been , though the traces in Jéquier appear more suited to a large than to , which is what is needed at that point.
7. Presumably Osiris.
8. See above, Utt. 542, n. 1.
9. Cf. Nt, 589.
10. Cf. Nt, 590.
11. Cf. in § 279*d*.
12. Presumably the gods.
13. Cf. Nt, 591.
14. Read with Nt, 593; Sethe's restoration is to be discarded.
15. Cf. Nt, 594.
16. Cf. Nt, 595.
17. *Sdꜣ* must have its original causative sense here; for the simplex *dꜣ* cf. *ZÄS* 57, 116.
18. Interpreting *wḏ·ty* as a hortative old perfective.
19. For Sethe's [*ꜥnḫw*] read *sḫmw* with Nt, 596.
20. Cf. *nwḏ* 'suffer(?)', § 829*e*. The determinative may be a plant; since here it is used for chastisement, it could be either a stinging plant like a nettle or a flexible stem which could be used like a schoolmaster's cane. The sign shows no indication of thorns.
21. Cf. Nt, 597, which writes *bꜥḥ ꜣỉ* as , running two words into one.
22. For *ḳwꜣg rḏw* cf. § 1944*c* (Supplement, p. 42).
23. *Nkꜣkꜣ* is rendered as 'gutes Zustand des Fleisches' in *Wb.* ii, 345, 15.
24. Cf. *Šsmy*, *Dream-book*, 11, 4; *Ch. B.* Text, 20, n. 6.
25. Cf. Nt, 598; for Sethe's *ꜥnḫ[·k ỉr* . . .] read *ꜥnḫ·k mr* . . .
26. Cf. Nt, 599.
27. Read *m ḥnṯt m rnpwt·k ms·k ỉr tpw ꜣbdw*, Nt, 600–1. With *ḥnṯt* compare *ḥnṯỉ* 'carve' and *ḥnṯtyw* 'carvers', § 966*e*.

## Utterance 691[1]

### *A variant of Utterance* 467

§ 2120 O my father, O Rēꜥ, this is what you have said: 'O for a son, glorious, shining,
§ 2121 besouled, strong, mighty, far-reaching, far-striding!'[1] Here am I,[2] I am your

son; here am I, I am the King. I am glorious, shining, besouled, strong, mighty, far-reaching, and far-striding.[1] I go aboard,[3] for I am pure; I receive § 2122
the oar, I take[4] my seat in the rowing-side[5] of the sky, I row in the rowing-side of the sky, I ply[6] my oar in the rowing-side of the sky.

O my father, O Rēʿ, this is what you have said: 'O for a son glorious, § 2123
shining, besouled, strong, mighty, far-reaching, far-striding!'[1] Here am I, § 2124
I am your son; here am I, I am the King. I am glorious, shining, besouled, strong, mighty.[1] I go aboard, for I am pure; I receive the oar, I take my seat § 2125
in the Ennead, I row in the Ennead, I ply my oar in the Ennead.

1. Supplement, pp. 51–3.
2. *Mk w⟨i⟩ ir⟨·i⟩*.
3. Into the solar bark.
4. *Sḥḏ*, lit. 'illumine', used metaphorically.
5. Cf. *rmn* 'side' of rowers, *Westc.* 5, 18; 6, 4.
6. Cf. *sḫ't* 'Art des Fahrens', *Wb.* iv, 268, 2.

## Utterance 691A[1]

### *A 'reed-float' Utterance*

The reed-floats of the sky are set in place for Rēʿ, § 2126
The reed-floats of the sky are set in place for Rēʿ,
That he may be on high from the East to the West
In company with his brethren the gods.
His brother is Orion, his sister is Sothis,
And he sits between [them] in this land for ever.
The reed-floats of the sky are set in place for this King,
The reed-floats of the sky are set in place for this King,
That he may be on high from the east to the west
In company with his brethren the gods.
His brother is Orion, his sister is Sothis,
And he sits between them in this land for ever.

1. Supplement, p. 53.

## Utterance 691B[1]

### *The king as Horus calls on Osiris to wake*

Wake, wake, O my father Osiris, for I am your son who loves you, I am ⟨your⟩ § 2127
son Horus who loves you. Behold, I have come[2] that I may bring to you what he[3] took from you. Has he rejoiced over you? Has ⟨he⟩ drunk (blood)[4] from

you? Has Seth drunk (blood) from you in the presence of your two sisters? The two sisters who love you are Isis and Nephthys, and they will support you. Do not pass me by, for I have provided(?) you; may you not suffer(?),[5]
§ 2128 may your wisdom judge Horus who is in his house.| Quell[6] Seth as Gēb, as the being[7] who devours entrails, for your front is that of a jackal, your hinder-parts are the Celestial Serpent, your spine is the door-bolt of the god. I have cultivated barley, I have reaped emmer, which I have prepared for your yearly sustenance, so wake, wake, O my father, for this bread of yours.

1. Supplement, pp. 54–5.
2. [hieroglyphs] of Nt, 831 is an obvious error; read [hieroglyphs]?
3. Seth.
4. Cf. *Wb.* i, 447, 1–4, with the object 'blood' understood. Nt has omitted the suffix of *bꜥbꜥ·n*.
5. For *nsnsn* 'suffer' cf. § 903*a*.
6. Imperative with enclitic *m*.
7. *Rpw*, masculine counterpart of *rpwt* > *rpyt* 'presiding goddess', etc., *Concise Dict.* 148; the masculine form apparently only here.

*Utt.* 691C; 692; 692A; *and* 692B *are recorded in the Supplement, pp.* 55–8, *but are too fragmentary to yield an intelligible text.*

## Utterance 692C[1]

(§ 2138) Hail to you, Unique One who endures every day! Here comes Horus the Far-Strider, here comes He who has power in the horizon, who has power [. . .].

Hail to you, Soul who is in his blood, Unique One who says to(?) [. . .] Wise One who says to(?) [. . .] who occupies[2] his seat [. . .] with which he is content, who crosses the sky [. . .].[3]

1. Supplement, p. 58.
2. Restore perhaps [*ḥt*]*p st·f*.
3. The rest of the Utterance is fragmentary.

## Utterance 693[1]

§§ 2139–41 Wake [. . .]| the Bows bow [their heads] to you [. . .]| the gods rejoice, [. . .] are
§ 2142 joyful [. . . Gēb], chiefest of the gods;| he has taken possession of the heritage
§ 2143 which was saved from [. . .]| may you provide yourself with his *Wrrt*-crown, may you eat bread [. . .] as(?) a food-offering [. . .].

1. Supplement, p. 59.

## Utterance 694[1]

### *A 'resurrection' text*

[. . .] says Isis; 'I have found', says Nephthys, for they have seen Osiris on § 2144
his side on the bank [. . .].| Arise[2] [. . .] my brother, for I have sought you. § 2145
'Raise yourself, O spirit, and speak', says Gēb; I(?) have smitten [. . .] the
Ennead[3] [. . .| . . .] so says(?) your father Atum; he causes you to be well- § 2146
provided(?) among the gods as the Great One who presides over [. . .].| Those § 2147
who are in the Abyss come to you, the sun-folk go to and fro for you, that
you may be Horus [. . .| . . .] with him at your due time and who prepares § 2148
your yearly sustenance with him at your due season, by the command
[. . .| . . .]. The King's road is opened for the King, a road is made ready § 2149
for the King,| for the King [. . .] in authority over the Two Lands, the King § 2150
is Thoth in authority over the sky, the King is Anubis in authority over the
house.| There are brought [. . .] to the King before the King,| for he is §§ 2151–2
the Egret which went up from the cultivation [. . .| . . .] who is(?)[4] one of the § 2153
four wardens of the border(?);[5] be far from the King;| the King [. . .] and § 2154
pure is the tongue which is in the King's mouth.| The King is protected § 2155
[. . .] the King[6] [. . .], the King will not be hanged head downwards.| The § 2156
King is a bull [. . .] the King is a bull[7] [. . .], a trio in the sky and a pair on
earth.

1. Reconstructed in part from JPII, 1029 ff.
2. *Wṯz*, JPII, 1029.
3. JPII, 1030.
4. *Imy* of equivalence?
5. Lit. 'a *ṯnw* of the four *ṯnww*'; for the meaning allotted to this word see *Ann. Serv.* 42, 108, with n. 6, though its precise significance here is obscure, see also Utt. 701, n. 1. Possibly the four *ṯnww* may be the guardians of the four cardinal points.
6. JPII, 1038.
7. *N pw kꜣ*, JPII, 1039.

## Utterance 695[1]

The fillet has come into being, [. . .] are flooded.| [. . .] I sit upon the throne §§ 2157–8
of Rēʿ, I have driven off Horus from the south of the sky, I have driven off
[Seth[2] from the north of the sky(?)], the arms of [Seth(?)] are loosed[3] [. . .]
I have driven off[4] the hidden ones of the Nine,| I sit [. . .] I have found the § 2159
Lord of [. . .][5] I who am over the sky, my hands are on the pillar(?) [. . .]
feet [. . .| . . .][6] at(?) it. My head is in the upper part, my feet are [in the lower § 2160

§§ 2161-2 part¹ . . .] the King⁷ [. . .] length to length. Behold, I am [. . .]⁸ ¹ guide⁹ [. . .] just as she guides Seth, just as [she] guides . . .¹⁰

1. Partly reconstructed from JPII, 1041 ff.
2. *Ḥsr·n(·ỉ) S[tš(?) . . .]*, JPII, 1041; restore as *S[tš m mḥt pt]*?
3. *Fḫ rwy S[tš(?) . . .]*, loc. cit.
4. Here the ancient editor starts to alter the text to the 3rd person.
5. Read *gm·n·f nb* [. . .], JPII, 1042.
6. Discard the restoration *nfryt* and read *ỉwnw* [. . .] *rdwy* [. . .], JPII, 1043.
7. JPII, 1044.
8. Discard the restoration and read *mk N swt* [. . .], JPII, 1045.
9. *Sšm*, loc. cit.
10. Read *mr sšm* [. . .] *m* [. . .] *ỉ* [. . .], JPII, 1046.

## Utterance 696¹

### A 'ferryman' text

§ 2163 O Jackal-breaker, O *Dḳḳ*, bring me this² [. . .] pray bring me this [. . .] the
§ 2164 messenger of Atum. I possess a *szf*-cloth [and(?)]³ a *nnỉt*-cloth [. . .].¹ O
§ 2165 *Hhỉw, Hhỉw*, bring me this, pray bring me [this . . .]¹ who approaches him [. . .] the messenger of Atum. I possess a *szf*-cloth [and(?)] your (*sic*) *nnỉt*-cloth¹
§ 2166 [. . .] the Eye of Horus there, who runs against the fingers of Seth [. . .].¹
§§ 2167-8 The land is at peace, and my arms [. . .] to(?) the heart.¹ I have arisen, [I have(?)] arisen [by day(?)]⁴ . . .], I have arisen by night [. . .]. Bring me this [. . .] son of the Cow-goddess [. . .].⁵

1. Supplement, pp. 59-60.
2. The regular formula for this class of text, in which the 1st person is original. The dead king is calling for the ferry-boat.
3. There is room for a co-ordinating preposition in the lacuna. For *szf* cf. *Urk.* iv, 1867, 9; perhaps the cloths (or garments?) are the ferryman's fare for the crossing.
4. Restore *m hrw*? Cf. § 2168*b*.
5. The rest of the Utterance is in lacuna except for isolated fragments.

## Utterance 697

### A 'resurrection' text

§ 2169 O King, the mouth of the earth is split open for you, Gēb speaks to you. Be
§ 2170 great like a King, be kingly(?)¹ like Rēꜥ!¹ May you be cleansed in the Jackal Lake, may you be purified in the Lake of the Netherworld. Come in peace to the Two Enneads! The eastern door of the sky is opened for you by Him
§ 2171 whose powers endure;¹ Nūt has laid her hands on you, O King, even she whose hair is long and whose breasts hang down; she carries you for herself

to the sky, she will never cast the King down to earth.| She bears you, O § 2172
King, like Orion, she makes your abode at the head of the Conclaves. The
King shall go aboard the bark like Rēʿ on the banks of the Winding Water-
way,| the King shall be rowed by the Unwearying Stars and shall give orders § 2173
to the Imperishable Stars, the King shall be rowed as a swamp-dweller,[2] the
King shall proceed by boat to the Fields of *Ḫ3ḫ3*.| Your messengers run, your § 2174
couriers hurry, and they say to Rēʿ: 'Behold, the King has come, behold,
the King has come in peace.'

Do not travel [on] those western waterways, for those who travel thereon § 2175
do not return, but travel on these eastern waterways among the Followers of
[Rēʿ . . .] an arm [is upraised] in the East [. . .].

1. Cf. Utt. 548, n. 1; both *wrt* and *swtt* appear to be hortative old perfectives addressed to the king.
2. For *ḫnty*, regarded as a nisba-form of *ḫnt* 'swamp', see also §§ 871*b*; 1169*a*.

## Utterance 698[1]

[. . .] your whip(?) to the ground; the King is cleansed [. . .] the King is § 2176
Thoth(?) [. . .] knife; the gods are(?) [. . .| . . .] flesh; hold still(?), be far distant § 2177
behind the King.

1. Supplement, pp. 60–1.

## Utterance 699

### *An 'ascension' text*

[. . .] Anubis will take your arm and Nūt will give you your heart.| May you §§ 2178–9
soar like a falcon, may you fly aloft like a heron, may you travel ⟨to⟩ the
West [. . .| . . .]. [Live,] be alive! Be young, be young beside your father, § 2180
beside Orion in the sky.| May you live the life [. . .]. § 2181

## Utterance 700

### *A 'resurrection' text*

O my father the King, raise yourself on your right side, lift[1] yourself upon § 2182
your left side, gather your flesh together [. . .| . . .] that you may be pure § 2183
thereby as a god. Go up as do the messengers of Rēʿ, for your hand will be
taken by the Imperishable stars and [you] shall not [perish . . .| . . . as Anubis] § 2184
who is in *T3ḫbt*.[2] | You are provided with bread just as Horus provided his § 2185

§ 2186 Eye in this ⟨your⟩ name of '*Wꜣg*-festival', you are offered [. . .| . . .] your foes perish, and they *will* perish; drown them, put them in the lake, put them
§ 2187 in the sea.| The sun-folk shall come to you [. . .].

1. Read *sdꜣrw*.
2. Unknown locality.

## Utterance 701

*As last*

§ 2188 The Great One has fallen in Nedit, the throne is released by its occupant(?).[1]
§ 2189 She who is in Iseion raises you [. . .] raises you [. . .| . . .] the god is released,|
§ 2190 Horus comes forth from Chemmis; Pe attends on Horus and he is purified
§§ 2191–2 there.| Horus comes pure that [he] may protect [his father . . .| . . . 'I am your sister] who loves you' say[2] Isis and Nephthys; they lament you, they arouse
§§ 2193–4 you.| O King, raise [yourself . . .| . . . your thousand of bread, your thousand of beer], your thousand of oxen, your thousand of fowl, roast meat of the two ribs from the slaughter-block of the god, a *t-wr*-loaf and a *ỉtḥ*-loaf from the
§§ 2195–6 Broad Hall;| provide yourself, O King [. . .].| You have your *Wrrt*-crown, your *Wrrt*-crown is upon you, and you shall assume the *Wrrt*-crown before
§ 2197 the Two Enneads. May you have power among [your] brethren [. . .| . . .]
§ 2198 spirits.| O King, stand up and sit down at your desire as Anubis the Foremost
§ 2199 of the Westerners,| having come to [your former] condition [. . .].

1. *Ṯnw*; cf. Utt. 694, n. 5. However, 'warden of the border' makes no sense whatever here, and I have guessed 'occupant' of the throne.
2. *N* is for *ỉn* 'says'.

## Utterance 702

§ 2200 The King has come to you two, you great and mighty companions who are in the eastern side of the sky; lift the King and set him at the eastern side of the sky.

## Utterance 703

*A 'resurrection' text*

§ 2201 O King, you have your soul with you [. . .] as Osiris. O King, live, for you
§ 2202 are not dead.| Horus will come to you that he may cut your cords and throw off your bonds; Horus has removed your hindrance and the earth-gods shall not lay hold of you.

O King, [your] double is mighty [. . .] you have no human father and you § 2203
have no human mother,[1] for this mother of yours is the great *ḥwrt*-serpent, § 2204
white of head-cloth, who dwells in Nekheb, whose wings are open, whose breasts are pendulous;[1] the King will not be laid hold of by [. . .]. § 2205

## Utterance 704[1]

This King is the [. . .][2] which went forth from Rēʿ, this King has come forth § 2206
from between the thighs of the Two Enneads; he[3] was conceived by Sakhmet, the King was borne by Shezmētet. This King is the falcon which came forth [from Rēʿ] and the uraeus which came forth from the Eye of Rēʿ;[4] the King has flown up and alighted on the vertex of the Beetle in the bow of the bark which is in the Abyss.

1. An almost complete text is in Nt, 7–8, see the Supplement, p. 61; this is an older text than that of Cairo 28083, which Sethe used in his restoration of the Utterance, and is therefore to be preferred. The original text of N is nearly all lost.
2. Both N and Nt are in lacuna at this point; Sethe restores as , but the determinative preserved in Nt does not suit.
3. Nt for once employs the feminine suffix.
4. Nt is corrupt here; read *ỉrt prt m ỉrt Rʿ*.

*The remaining Utterances in Sethe's edition, Nos. 705–14, are too badly damaged to furnish a translation, apart from one or two isolated sentences, and are therefore omitted here. The Utterances translated below, the texts of which will be found in the Supplement, pp. 62 ff., are additional to Sethe's text, having been taken from JPII and Nt. No attempt has been made to deal with Utterances which are in too fragmentary a state to yield a connected sense. The texts in Aba, which are later in date and appear to have undergone some measure of editing, have been utilized only to supplement Utterance 716.*

## Utterance 715[1]

[. . .] Seth took it [. . .] that you may be nourished [. . .] which happened § 2218
to you through the strength of [. . .] this King, you prevent him from dying.[1]
Come into being as the essence of every god, appear[2] [. . .] Shu the son of § 2219
Atum. O Osiris, this one here is the King; if he lives, you will live[1] [. . .].
O Shu, have power! O Shu, spread your protection of life about Osiris the § 2220
King, your protection about [. . .]. O King, Horus has split open your mouth for you,[1] he has split open your eyes with the God's-Castle adze, with the Great-of-Magic adze, the mouth of [. . .] is split open [. . .] Horus and his

§ 2222 children [. . .]. Do not be languish, do not groan[1] [. . .] Horus . . . [. . .] it for you with his members [. . .] yourself. Fill [. . .] . . . filled with strength(?), that she may be with you, for you are [the foremost of(?)] your spirits of your desire.

1. Supplement, pp. 62–3.
2. These imperatives are addressed to the king.

## Utterance 716[1]

### *A variant of Utterances* 611. 665C

§ 2223 Your sceptre is laid in your hand that you may open the bolt in the double Ram-gate which keeps out [the Fenkhu. May you number the slayers, may] you [control] the Nine Bows, and take the hand of the Imperishable Stars.[1]
§ 2224 The Great Ones will care for you and the Watchers [of Horus Protector of his Father] will wait on ⟨you⟩. [O King, the Great One is] sound [asleep], this Great One is lying down, ⟨He who is greater than you⟩ is drowsy. Wake, raise yourself [. . . the perfume of the Great One on you is pleasing] to your nose, even the perfume of *Ỉḫt-wtt*.

1. Supplement, pp. 63–4.

## Utterance 717[1]

### *A variant of Utterance* 666

§ 2225 Wash yourself, take these four *ꜥbt*-jars of yours, [which are filled to the brim from the Canal of the God; cleanse yourself] with them as a god, go forth by means of them as the Eye of Rēꜥ. [Stand up] at the head of the Imperishable
§ 2226 [Stars,[1] having appeared in front of them as Gēb who is at the head of the company of] the Ennead of Ōn when he gives [orders to the gods, having spoken in the session of the living god. Assume] the *Wrrt*-crown [as the
§ 2227 Lone Star who destroys foes;[1] indeed this going of yours, O King, is] that of which Horus [spoke] to his father Osiris. [May you become a spirit] thereby,
§ 2228 [may you be great thereby, may you be strong thereby . . .[1] may you have your soul] behind you, may you have your spirit within you, [may you have your] bodily [heart]. Sever your bonds [as] Horus [who is in his house,
§ 2229 throw away] your fetters as Seth who is in *Ḥnḫnt*,[1] [you having entered into] the House of Protection, for [your] father [Gēb] has protected you; [as for him who would exclude you], he shall not live, and as for him who calls out behind you [. . .]. May [the Eye of Horus] belong(?) to you, [. . . for your

hand is on(?)] this bread of yours,[1] even as Horus presented himself [with] § 2230
his Eye, and this . . .[2] is for the presentation; provide [yourself with this bread of yours, just as Horus provided himself with his Eye];[1] this [. . .] is for the § 2231
*Wꜣg*-festival.

Lift yourself to the sky in company with the gods because of your name of [. . .] they are destroyed and drowned.[3] Smite them, destroy them, drown them on [land] and sea [. . .] *Nwt·k-nw*.

1. Supplement, pp. 64–7.
2. Cf. Utt. 666, n. 8.
3. Cf. ibid., n. 9; *zbỉ* here is a miswriting of *ʿbỉ*.

## Utterance 718[1]

### *A partial duplicate of Utterance* 666A

Behold this which I have done for you, O my father the King; I have saved § 2232
you from him who would obstruct you [. . .] your faces, you spirits. The doors of the sky are opened for you, [the bolts] are drawn back for you [. . .]. The Mourning-Woman [summons you] as Isis, the Mooring-post calls to you as Nephthys,[1] you having appeared upon the causeway; may you travel § 2233
around [your Horite Mounds, may you travel around your] Sethite [Mounds]. You have your spirit, O my father the King, you have no dilapidation; make yourself into a spirit, for your gate is strengthened.

1. Supplement, pp. 67–8.

## Utterance 719[1]

### *An 'ascension' text*

The sky thunders, the earth quakes, [. . .] O King, Gēb has given you up § 2234
and Nūt has accepted you; ascend to the sky, for the doors of the sky are opened for you, the earth is hacked up for you, and an offering is presented to you[1] [. . .] the sun-folk give to you and Seth ferries you over the Winding § 2235
Waterway. O you who are in the tomb(?) [. . .] your horizon-dwelling spirit(?).[2] Stand up,[3] that they may replace what should be on [you(?) . . .] at your throat.[1] They commend you ⟨to⟩ Him who presides over the Enneads as lord § 2236
of the heritage of Gēb which Nu places under your feet for you [. . .] as [Lord(?)] of the sky.

1. Supplement, pp. 68–9.
2. Probably a nisba-form rather than a dual.
3. Hortative old perfective.

## Utterance 720[1]

*As last*

§ 2237 The firmament and the Castle of the God grant [. . .] wash your face, O Osiris. Your second is *Dwn-ʿnwy*, your third is *Wḏ-mrwt* [. . .]. The monthly festivals [are celebrated for you(?)], the half-monthly festivals accrue to you, the sixth-day festival is celebrated so that you may come into being, O Lord of [. . .] the Great One(?) who presides over Ōn.

§ 2238 The sky trembles, the earth quakes before the Great One when he arises; he has [opened] the doors of the sky, he throws open the doors of the firmament; the earth is hacked up for you,[2] an offering is presented to you, the
§ 2239 hands of Horus are given to you, the dancer ⟨dances⟩ for you,[1] the Great Mooring-Post speaks to you as Isis, the West calls to you ⟨as⟩ Nephthys, as (to) Horus the Protector of his father Osiris.

1. Supplement, pp. 69–70.
2. From here on the King is addressed directly.

## Utterance 721[1]

§ 2240 [. . .] which(?) all the gods have given to you. They serve you, and you have power over them; Horus has raised you aloft in his name of [. . .] you in your name of Sokar, you being alive [. . .] the East, being drowsy.

§ 2241 O King, raise yourself against those who are greater than you, that you may eat figs and drink wine; your face is that of a jackal, as Anubis girded
§ 2242 [. . .] nomes, those who are in the realm of the dead serve you,[1] the chamberlains make purification for you, the Great Mooring-Post calls to you, your two mothers the two White Crowns caress you, your two mothers the two White Crowns kiss you [. . .] mourning, your gate which is on earth is strengthened for ever and ever.

1. Supplement, pp. 70–1.

## Utterance 722[1]

§ 2243 The Pillar of the *Zḥzḥ*-bird[2] is the Horn of *ʿnḥ·f*, and happy is she who sees.[3] Tell[4] Rēʿ that the King comes. O King, go, go[5] and meet Rēʿ and tell him a true thing; the *ḳni*-garment is high.[6] Do not oppose him.[7]

1. Supplement, pp. 71–2. Nt exceptionally has feminine suffixes.
2. Cf. *ḏw zḥzḥ* 'mountain of the *zḥzḥ*-bird', §§ 389*a*; 1118*d* (written *sḥsḥ*).

3. So JPII; Nt appears to be slightly corrupt. There is no indication as to who this female person can be.
4. So Nt; JPII has *sr* 'prophesy'.
5. Hortative old perfective.
6. Reading *ḏd·k n·f ḫt mꜣꜥ ḳꜣꜣ ḳnỉ* with JPII, frag. 28, l. 6.
7. *Scil.* the king.

## Utterance 723[1]

### *A 'resurrection' text*

O King, raise yourself upon your iron bones and golden members, for this § 2244
body of yours belongs to a god; it will not grow mouldy, it will not be
destroyed, it will not putrefy. The warmth which is on your mouth is the
breath which issued from the nostrils of Seth,| and the winds of the sky will § 2245
be destroyed if the warmth which is on your mouth be destroyed; the sky
will be deprived of its stars if the warmth which is on your mouth be lacking.[2]
May your flesh be born to life, and may your life be more than the life of the
stars when they live.[3]

1. Supplement, p. 72.
2. Cf. *Komm.* v, 77 f.; *ZÄS* 90, 23.
3. Var. JPII: 'more than (that of) the stars in their season of life'.

## Utterance 724[1]

### *A variant of Utterance* 524[2]

The King has purified himself with the purity of the Pure One which Horus § 2246
made for [his] Eye [. . .] as(?) the King, Seth [. . . there are opened for] the
King the doors of the firmament which keep out the plebs. The King has
come bearing the great and mighty Eye of Horus [at which] the gods rejoice
and the Two Enneads rejoice. [The King wears the White Crown, wherewith
the Eye of Horus is powerful and fulfilled . . .]| the King's [arms] are those § 2247
of falcons, the King's wing-feathers are those of Thoth, Gēb causes the King
to fly up among his brethren the gods; [. . . who overleaps] your[3] landmarks,
the obstructions which are under the hand of Osiris. The King is a power
who demands his place, (even) Thoth, ⟨the mightiest of the gods⟩,[4]| whom § 2248
Atum summoned to the sky that the King might take [the Eye of Horus
to him . . .] these souls who preside over Ōn, the cloak[5]—your face turns to
Rēꜥ. Hear, O Bull of the Two Enneads,| open the King's path, [make the § 2249
King's place spacious at the head of the gods . . . who grants], O King, that

you may see with both your entire eyes. The enemies among you are hunted down,[6] because Horus has taken possession of his Eye, the perfume of which
§ 2250 he has granted.[1] The perfume of the god, the perfume of the Eye of Horus, is on him, and the King is pre-eminent [. . . the King is he who prevents] the gods [from becoming weary] when seeking the Eye of Horus, which the King found in Pe, which the King sought in Ōn; the King saved it from the mouth of Seth in that place [where they fought . . .].

1. Supplement, pp. 73–5.

2. Utt. 524 appears to have been originally in the 1st person, but there is nothing to show whether the same holds good of this text.

3.  for , cf. Utt. 524, n. 4.

4. Supplied from the fragment at the bottom of JPII, pl. 13; cf. also § 1237c.

5. Read *ḥꜣt(y)*, cf. § 737a. Following this, there appears to be a textual omission, for the relevance of this word to the context is obscure; § 1238b reads *rw mdw pn ḏr ḥr·k Rꜥ*.

6. Cf. *Wb.* iii, 434, 4. The suffix in *ḥm·ṯn* is in the 2nd person plural, which points to some corruption or omission in the text.

## Utterance 725[1]

§ 2251 [. . .] the cavern is opened for the King, the chapel is thrown open for the King when(?) Rēꜥ is on high and Nubti appears. Make a road for the King [that he may] pass [on it . . .] Horus, Lord of the Egret.[2]

1. Supplement, p. 75.

2. Or: 'of trembling'.

## Utterance 726[1]

*A garbled version of Utterance* 440

§ 2252 If you wish to live, O Horus, chiefest of ꜥAnut,[2] do not seal up the doors of the sky, do not slam shut its door-leaves when the King's double ascends to the sky for him whom the god knows, for him whom the god loves, the eater of
§ 2253 figs, who burns incense and dons clothing of red linen,[1] who escorts the great god, for the King's double escorts the great god; it causes the King to mount up to the great god, because he is one of them.[3] The King will not die because of a king, the King will not die because of men; there shall not come into being nor exist anything evil which they may say evilly against the King by day or by(?)[4] night, in his monthly festivals, in his half-monthly festivals, or in his yearly festivals.

1. Supplement, pp. 75–6.

2. Unknown locality, possibly to be identified with *ꜥmwꜣt*, itself unlocated, *Dict. géogr.* i, 146. JPII, 1055+44 reads *ꜥmw*.

3. Here the resemblance to Utt. 440 ends.

4. *Tpt n ḏr*, obscure to me.

*A series of spells against snakes and other dangers*

## Utterance 727[1]

The bull-snake falls to the *sḏḥ*-snake and the *sḏḥ*-snake falls to the bull-snake,[2] which has been put a stop to because of what it has seen; the son-of-earth snake falls with its head beneath it,[3] the flame goes out against the Earth-god,[4] | *Nḥbw-kꜣw* burns with the poison. O monster, die![5] § 2254 § 2255

1. Supplement, pp. 76–7.
2. Cf. § 430*a*.
3. Reading *ḏꜣḏꜣ·f ḥr·f* with JPII; *ṯz* of Nt, despite the determinative 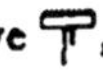, apparently stands for 'spine'. In either case 'upside down' is what is meant.
4. The snake injects its poison harmlessly into the earth.
5. Read *mt·ty*, hortative old perfective.

## Utterance 728

*Supplement, p. 77. The text is untranslatable.* § 2256

## Utterance 729[1]

[. . .] his neck; O monster, lie down! O *hpn*-snake, crawl away! O you who are on your *nꜣwt*-bush, crawl away because of Nu! § 2257

1. Supplement, p. 77.

## Utterance 730[1]

Down on your face, you crocodile, you herdsman of [. . .]! § 2258

1. Supplement, p. 77.

## Utterance 731[1]

O Starer,[2] go out into the night, for the smell of earth is on you! § 2259

1. Supplement, p. 78.
2. An allusion to the fixed unblinking stare of a snake.

## Utterance 732[1]

§ 2260 O you whom the vulture tramples, O *hpnw*-snake, O *hipty*-snake, O snake of the West, your name is [. . .].

1. Supplement, p. 78.

## Utterance 733[1]

§ 2261 Get back, snake which attacks in the night[2] . . .[3] O Thoth,[4] the night-snake! the night-snake!

1. Supplement, p. 78. Compare Utt. 279.
2. Probably a derivative of *tkk* 'attack', with determinatives of 'night' and 'snake'.
3. Untranslatable.
4. So JPII; Nt has *ıḫ*, which makes no sense here. The text reads like a panic appeal to Thoth for protection.

## Utterance 734[1]

*A 'resurrection' text*

§ 2262 Your face which has been knit on is that of a jackal like Wepwawet; take this papyrus-plant sceptre of yours which is over the Great Ones; the Lord of the Nine controls [. . .] the Great Ones like Horus who protects his father. O
§ 2263 King, raise yourself upon your left side,[1] put yourself upon your right side, raise your lid,[2] strengthen your court, save your children from mourning [. . . as Horus] who is in his house and as Seth who is in [*Ḥnḥnt*]. Libate, libate! Dance,
§ 2264 dance! Be quiet, be quiet![1] Hear, hear the word which Horus said to his father Osiris, so that you may be a spirit thereby, so that you may be great thereby; sit on the throne [. . .] the altar [. . .] and lead the Imperishable Stars. O King, your thousand of bread, your thousand of beer, your thousand of *r*-geese, your thousand of *s*(*r*)-geese, your thousand of *ṯrp*-geese, your thousand [. . .].

1. Supplement, pp. 78–9.
2. Lit, 'door' of the coffin; read *sꜥḥꜥ ꜥꜣ*.

## Utterance 735[1]

*An 'ascension' text*

§ 2265 The King has gone up from [. . .] as a falcon, the King's face is among the coils of *Šzꜣw*. The lords of its[2] boundary-wall divide it, the ladies of [. . .] the two districts of the god's hands.

1. Supplement, p. 80.
2. Feminine, but apparently not referring to Queen Neit.

## Utterance 736[1]

The King is the Great One who issued from the vertex of Thoth [. . .] the spirits who are among those who open a road for the Great One who belongs to Gēb.[2] § 2266

1. Supplement, p. 80.
2. i.e. the buried king.

## Utterance 737[1]

The King is the son of Atum, second to *Nfr-mrt*; it was the King who climbed to the House of [. . .], who adjudged the Enneads. § 2267

1. Supplement, p. 80.

## Utterance 738[1]

*The king joins the gods*

The King has come to you, you gods, the third of those who protect the Great One, who stand at the junction[2] of the Two Lands, the third of Shu [. . .]; the King will never pull down the High One from his seat. The King is the fourth of these four gods who issue from the vertex of Gēb [. . .] the King because of what he[3] has seen [. . .] the stars which are near Orion. § 2268

1. Supplement, pp. 80–1.
2. *Ḥtrt*, lit. 'the yoking' of the Two Lands, i.e. the point where they meet.
3. In the original the suffix is exceptionally feminine to agree with the name of Neit.

## Utterance 739[1]

The King is your fifth, you Imperishable Stars; a record[2] of [. . .] is made. § 2269

1. Supplement, p. 81.
2. For *gnt* 'record' cf. § 1160*a*.

## Utterance 740[1]

O Rēʿ, the King does not know the . . .[2] of the Lord of Khmun; [the King] is the eighth of [. . .]. § 2270

1. Supplement, p. 81.
2. *Šḳ*, meaning unknown.

## Utterance 741[1]

*The king is censed*

§ 2271 O Osiris the King, take the Eye of Horus with which I provide you, for Horus has censed himself with his Eye. O King, I cense you with the Eye of Horus, I make you divine because of the Eye of Horus, I provide you with the Eye of Horus, I provide you with [. . .].[2]

1. Supplement, p. 82.
2. The group ⌉—▒ might refer to *nṯr* 'natron' or possibly be a miswriting of *snṯr* 'incense'.

*Presentation of insignia*

## Utterance 742[1]

§ 2272 Horus has placed gold[2] on his Eye—a gold collar.

1. For Utt. 742–56 see the Supplement, pp. 82–6.
2. Cf. *nbi* 'gild', etc., *Concise Dict.* 129.

## Utterance 743

§ 2273 *Lost*

## Utterance 744

§ 2274 O Osiris the King, I make firm the Eye of Horus on your head—a head-band.[1]

1. Cf. *Frises*, 6.

## Utterance 745

§ 2275 O Horus who is Osiris the King . . . .

## Utterance 746

§ 2276 O Osiris the King, take the sole(?) Eye of Horus that you may see with it, which belongs to his body, a collar[1] [. . .] in the road, that your throat may breathe by means of it—a uraeus-serpent.

1. Cf. *ḥ3t* 'collar', *BH* ii, 7.

## Utterance 747

§ 2277 [. . .] she provides support and makes your brow to live. O King [. . .]—a *ḏt*-serpent.

## Utterance 748

O Osiris the King, I give to you the pupils which are in[1] the Eye of Horus § 2278
[. . .]. O Osiris the King, I put them on you and they shall be with you [. . .] they shall guide you—two uraei.

1. *Ỉm(y)t* is preceded in the facsimile by 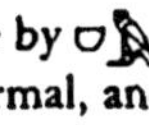; this has been regarded as the enclitic particle, but its position in the sentence is abnormal, and raises the question as to whether it is not on a misplaced fragment.

## Utterance 749

O Osiris the King, these Eyes of Horus [. . .] for you as your two doubles. § 2279
O Osiris the King, they shall be upon you [. . .] upon you as the two crowns Great-of-Magic [. . .] its magic is [great] on me[1]—a 'Great-of-Magic' serpent.

1. Cf. § 2285 (Utt. 755) below.

## Utterances 750–1

O Osiris the King, take the Eye of Horus [. . .] that you [may see] with it.[1] § 2280
O my father, take the Eye ⟨of Horus⟩ that you may see with it. I split open § 2281
your eye for you that you may see with it—a *st*-loaf.[1]

1. This offering of bread, which is common to both Utterances, seems out of place in a long list of items of insignia.

## Utterance 752

O Osiris the King, take the Eye of Horus which Seth had hidden—a *ỉmnt*- § 2282
vulture.[1]

1. Cf. *Frises*, 15.

## Utterance 753

Which he has reassembled[1]—a *dmḏt*-vulture. Extend(?)[2] it, . . .[3] it from him § 2283
—a . . .[4]-*pḏt*-vulture; a 'god-of-Upper-Egypt' vulture.

1. A continuation of the preceding Utterance; 'he' presumably is Horus.
2. *Ỉspḏ* is apparently a causative of *pḏ* 'stretch' in the imperative with prothetic *ỉ*; the feminine object-pronoun refers to the Eye of Horus.
3. *Dȝm*, a verb of unknown meaning, likewise in the imperative with prothetic *ỉ*.
4. The reading of the first sign is obscure; hardly *bnr*.

## Utterance 754

§ 2284 I do not overawe(?) it[1]—a *nrt*-vulture.

1. For *nr* used transitively with this meaning cf. *Urk.* iv, 2081, 19.

## Utterance 755

§ 2285 O Osiris the King, take the Eye of Horus about which you spoke, for its magic is great on me. O Osiris the King, take the Eye of Horus, great of magic—a 'Great-of-Magic' vulture.

## Utterance 756

§ 2286 O Osiris the King, take the intact Eye of Horus—a razor-case.[1]

1. Cf. *Frises*, 127.

## Utterance 757[1]

*Presentation of perfume*

§ 2287 This is this Eye of Horus which he gave to Osiris; I give it to you that you may provide your face with it [. . .] the perfume about which Horus spoke to Gēb.

1. Supplement, p. 87.

## Utterance 758[1]

*The king is given breath and food*

§ 2288 O Lord of the horizon, Foremost of the gods, to whom worship(?)[2] is done at dawn, who lives on food and quenches[3] his thirst with the water(?)[4] of life, who will never perish: Behold, the King has come[5] to you, this King is this one, the lord of witness regarding the Just One. The King was conceived in
§ 2289 the nose, the King was born in the nostril,[6] the King lies down in your coil, the King sits in your circle, the King lives on your life, the King is provided with your peace.

The King has come to you, the King eats of the provisions of the double, the King feeds(?)[7] on food, the King receives an offering from the god's
§ 2290 hand.[1] It is the King (*sic*)[8] who makes *pꜣt*-cakes, who gives supplies(?)[9] to the King on the day of the *Sꜣd*-festival. Collect[10] what belongs to truth, for truth is what the King says.

1. Supplement, pp. 87–8.
2. *Snw*, a *hapax* of doubtful meaning.
3. For this sense of *ḫtm* cf. *CT* i, 90c.
4. is obscure, but it must refer to a life-giving drink. I would suggest that may be an error for (drinking-bowl) and that *ḥw* may be connected with *ḥy* 'flood of water', *Wb.* iii, 48, 24.
5. Here again the original is in the feminine.
6. Compare the creation of Shu by exhalation from the nostrils of Atum, *Ex Oriente Lux*, no. 18 (1964), 266 ff.
7. *Twnb*, otherwise unknown.
8. Surely an error for *nṯr* or the like, for the King has to be supplied by an external agency, cf. the clause which follows. Presumably the 'Lord of the horizon' is still being addressed, so that some term referring to him should be substituted for the royal name.
9. Cf. *ḥt* 'food', *Concise Dict.* 160. Another possibility is the *ṯḥ*-cake.
10. Regarded as imperative with reinforcing dative, since that seems to give better sense here than a *sḏm·n·f* form.

## Utterance 759[1]

### *A protective spell*

O King, behold this which I have done for you; I have saved you from your § 2291
obstructor, I will never give you over to your attacker,[2] I have protected you from *Nwt·k-nw* by means of the power of repulsion(?) which is on my face.[3]

1. Supplement, p. 88.
2. Cf. Utt. 573, n. 6.
3. Reading *m šnʿt irt ḥr·i*; the sign following may have been derived from the hieratic form of *šnʿ*. The speaker apparently frightens the enemy away by making a fierce grimace.

# INDEXES

## I. DIVINITIES

*The references are to section-numbers of the hieroglyphic text*

## II. LOCALITIES

*Nisba derivatives are included under the basic name*

*The references are to section-numbers of the hieroglyphic text*

## III. SELECTED MODERN PROPER NAMES

*The references are to the pages of the preceding index*

## IV. SELECTED WORDS DISCUSSED IN NOTES

*The references are to Utterances*

# THE
# ANCIENT EGYPTIAN PYRAMID TEXTS

TRANSLATED INTO ENGLISH

BY

R. O. FAULKNER
D. LIT., F.S.A.

## SUPPLEMENT OF HIEROGLYPHIC TEXTS

# PREFACE

THIS Supplement to my volume of translations of the Pyramid Texts contains those Utterances preserved in Jéquier's publications *Le monument funeraire de Pepi II*, hereinafter cited as JPII; *Les pyramides des reines Neit et Apouit* (Nt); and *La pyramide d'Aba* (Aba) which in Sethe's edition of the Pyramid Texts are damaged too badly to be adequately completed in footnotes to the translations, and also other Utterances which were not included in Sethe's publication because in 1910 they had not yet been discovered. It cannot be too strongly stressed, however, that it has not been my purpose to provide an edition with full *apparatus criticus*, but only to show the foundation on which I have based my translation so that scholars can judge the latter, at the same time keeping the bulk of this volume, and therefore the cost, down to the minimum. It will be noticed, therefore, that where there is more than one new source for a text, with but two exceptions (Utt. 502 and 733) I have not set out the texts in parallel, but have copied only the more complete version (usually Nt), so far as possible completing lacunae with the help of the alternative texts, any significant variants being shown in textual notes. This procedure, though perhaps unorthodox, is the less unsatisfactory in that JPII is often so imperfect that copies of some Utterances extant in both JPII and Nt would, if set out in full, consist largely of blanks so far as JPII is concerned; the texts from Aba are later in date than the others, and are not strictly in accord with the original canon, so that they have been utilized only when all other sources fail. Nor have I devoted space to additional fragments which are too piecemeal to yield an intelligible sense; these will be best dealt with in a critical re-edition of the whole of the Pyramid Texts which I am glad to learn is in course of preparation by Professor Leclant. The present copies have been made solely as a practical convenience.

In the pages of hieroglyphic text which follow, square brackets without cross-hatching indicate that the text has been completed from a parallel text of the same Utterance in Sethe or Jéquier; restorations with cross-hatching are from a source of similar but not identical content.

**Utt. 57A.**

Nt 283

§40+1  N.B. The formal rubric [rubric sign] has been regularly omitted.

**Utt. 57B.**

Nt 284

§40+2 

**Utt. 57C.**

Nt 285

§40+3 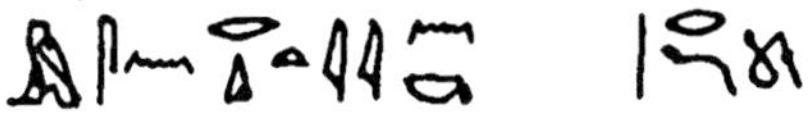

**Utt. 57D.**

Nt 286

§40+4 

**Utt. 57E.**

Nt 287

§40+5  a. For the reading cf. Jéquier, Neit, p. 26.

**Utt. 57F.**

Nt 288

§40+6 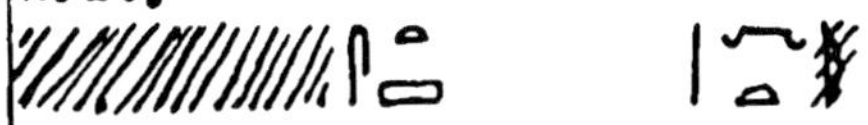

**Utt. 57G.**

Nt 289

§40+7 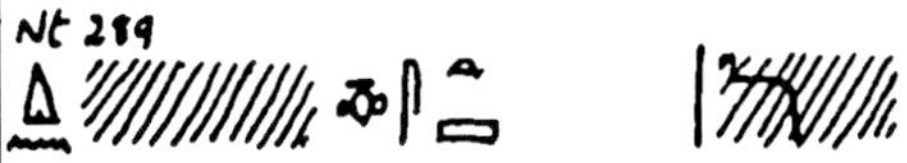

Utt. 57H.

Nt 290

§40+8 

?

Utt. 57I.

Nt 291

§40+9 

Utt. 57J.

Nt 292

§40+10 

Utt. 57K.

Nt 293

sic

§40+11 

Utt. 57L

Nt 294

§40+12 

Utt. 57M.

Nt 295

§40+13 

Utt. 57N.

Nt 296

§40+14 

## Utt. 57 O.

Nt, 297

§40+15 

a-b. Sic; read nḥmt.n.f.

## Utt. 57 P.

Nt, 298

§40+16 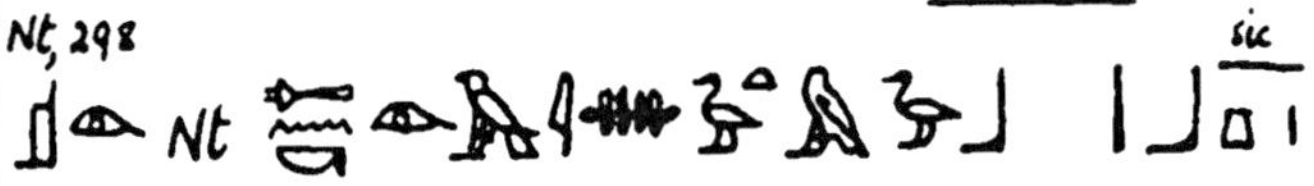

## Utt. 57 Q.

Nt, 299

§40+17 

a. Perhaps a ⌓ after [sign], Neit, p. 26.

## Utt. 57 R.

Nt, 300

§40+18 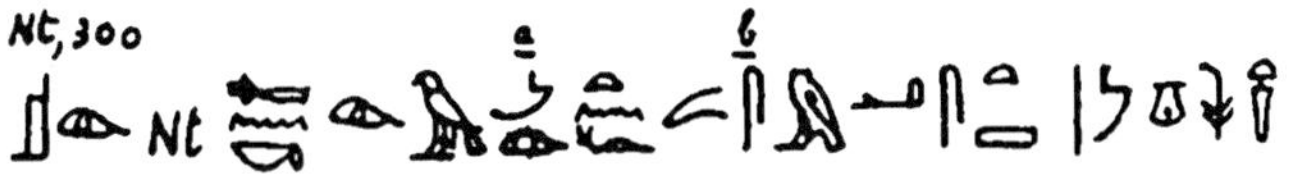

a-b. Sic; read m3gst.n.f.

## Utt. 57 S.

Nt, 301

§40+19 

a. Read nḥm.
b. Read ḥnp.n.f sic.

## Utt. 58.

Nt, 302

§41a 

a-b. Inserted in error.

## Utt. 59.

Nt, 303

§41b 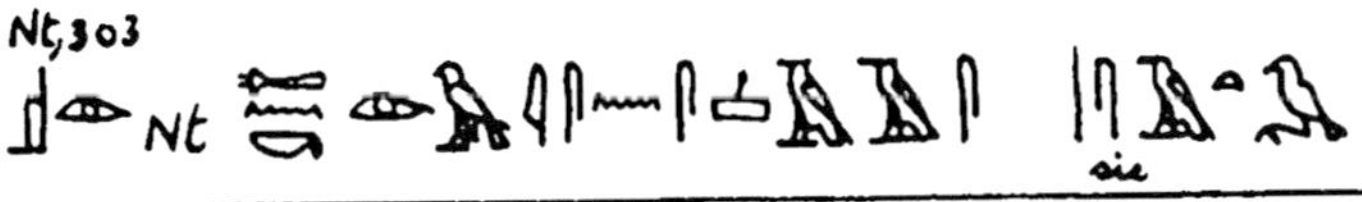

## Utt. 59A

| | | |
|---|---|---|
| §41c | Nt, 304  | Repetition of Utt. 57 O.S, not in N. |

## Utt. 60.

| | | |
|---|---|---|
| §42 a-b | Nt, 305  | An entirely different main text from N §42 a-b. |

## Utt. 61.

| | |
|---|---|
| §42 c | Nt, 306 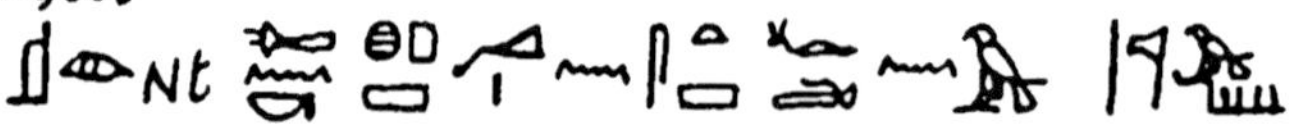 |

## Utt. 62.

| | |
|---|---|
| §43 a | Nt, 307  |

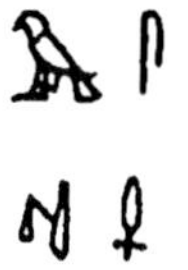

## Utt. 62A.

| | |
|---|---|
| §43 b | Nt, 308 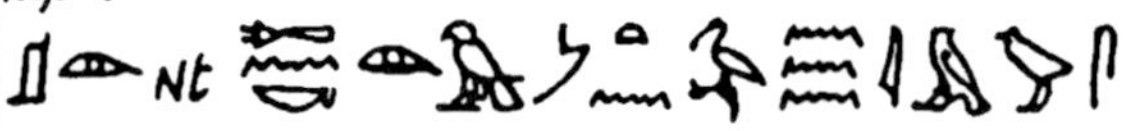 |

## Utt. 63.

| | |
|---|---|
| §44 a-c | Not in Nt. |

## Utt. 64.

Nt, 309

§45a-b 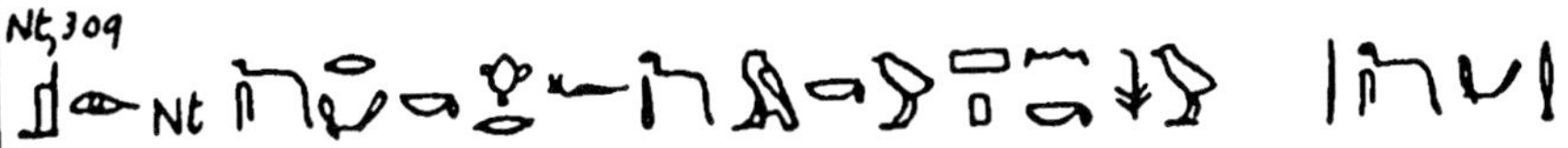

## Utt. 65.

Nt, 310

§45c  a-b. Read mr·k <sw> swt.

## Utt. 66.

Nt, 311

§46a  a-b. Read sḫt;  is an error.

## Utt. 67.

Nt, 312

§46b 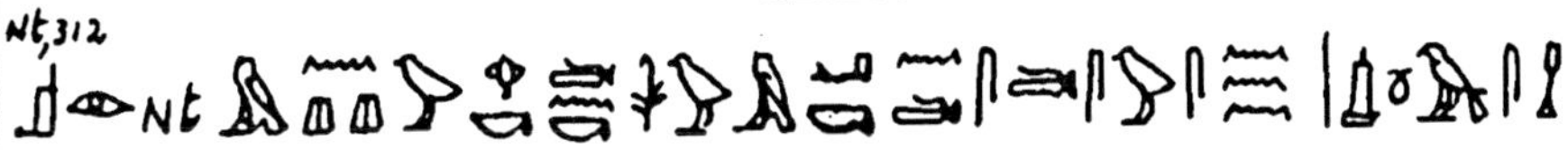

## Utt. 68.

Nt, 313

§47a 

Nt, 314

§47b 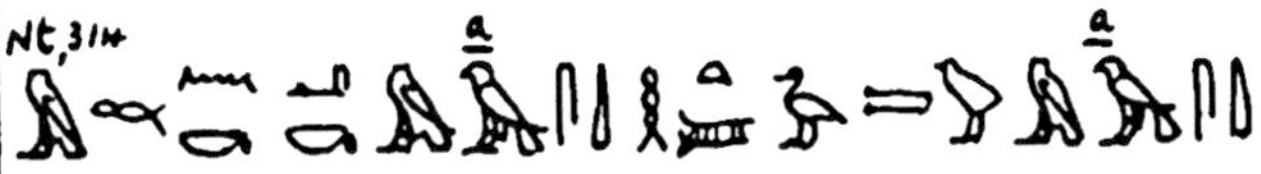 a. Written like ; the copyist frequently confuses  and .

Nt, 315

§47c 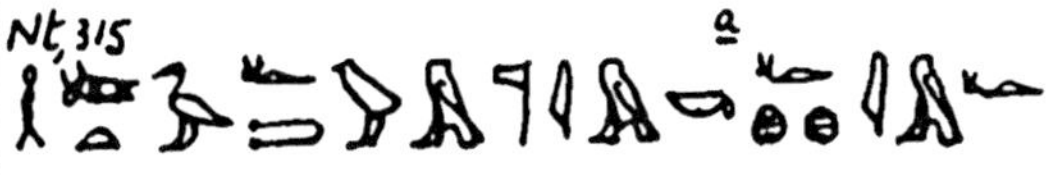 a. Causative s omitted.

(Nt, 315)

§47d 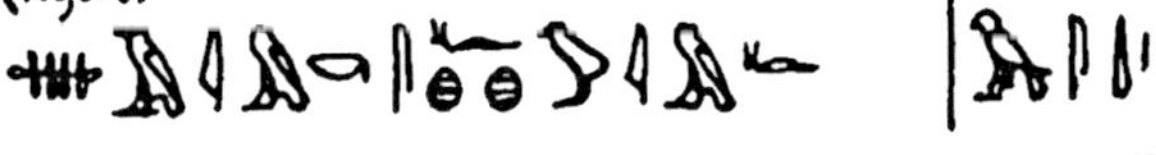

Utt. 69.

Nt, 316

§48a 

Utt. 70.

Nt, 317

§48b 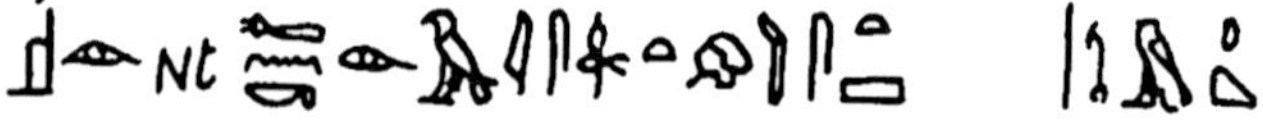

Utt. 71.

Nt, 318

§49 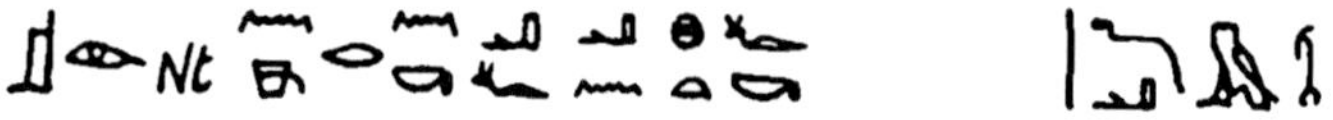

Utt. 71A.

Nt, 319

§49+1 

a. Corrected out of , Neit, p. 26.

Utt. 71B.

Nt, 320

§49+2 

Utt. 71C.

Nt, 321

§49+3 

Utt. 71D.

Nt, 322

§49+4 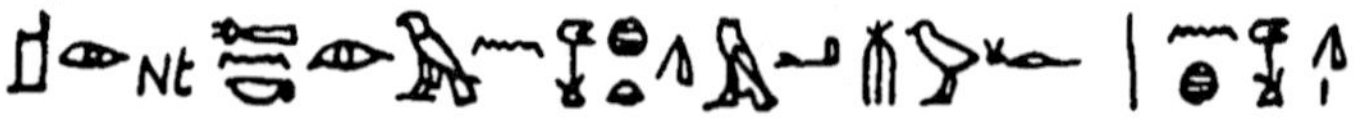

## Utt. 71 E.

Nt, 323

§49+5 

## Utt. 71 F.

Nt, 324

§49+6 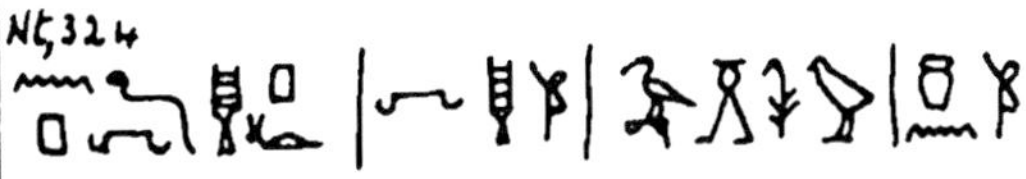

## Utt. 71 G.

Nt, 325

§49+7a 

Nt, 326

§49+7b 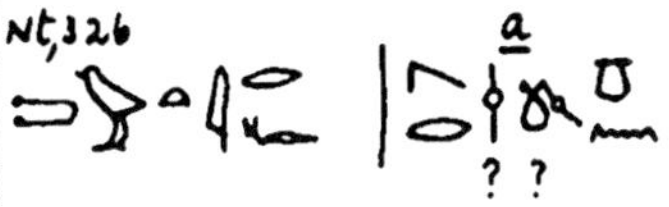

a. Cf. Neit, p. 26.

## Utt. 71 H.

(Nt, 326)

§49+8a 

Nt, 327

§49+8b 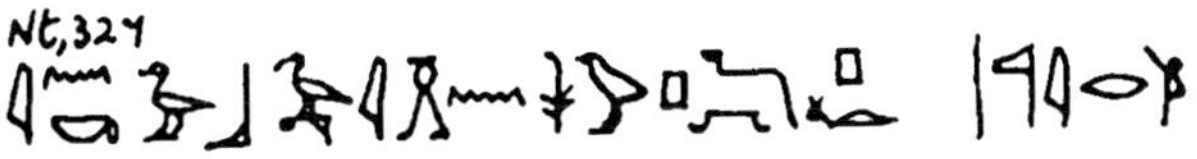

## Utt. 71 I.

Nt, 328

§49+9 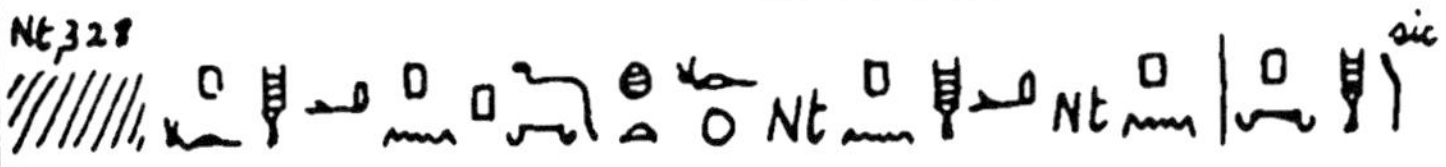

## Utt. 493.

Nt, 700 ff.; JP II, 1055 + 47 ff.; P, 214 ff.

(Nt, 700)

§1059a 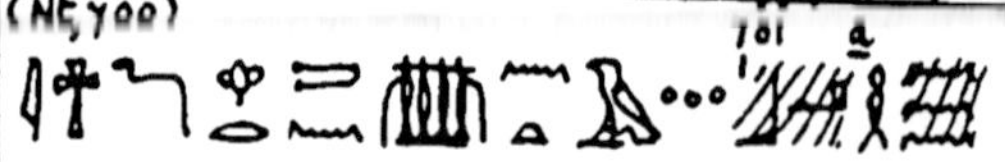 a. Cf. Neit, p. 27.

(701)

§1059b  a-b. Cf. loc. cit. and JP II, 1055 + 47.

(701)

§1059c 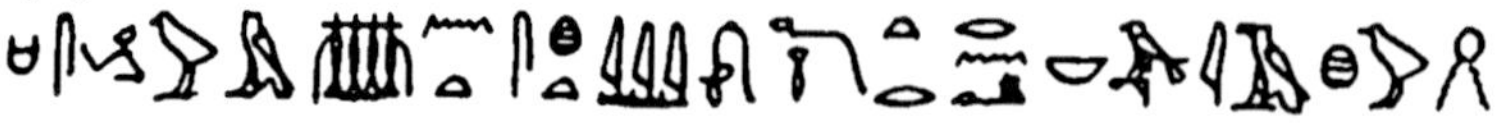

(701)

§1059d 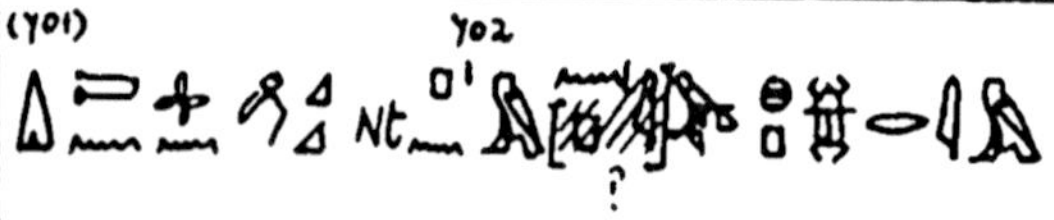

(702)

§1059e  a. Restored from JP II, 1055 + 48. b. Det.  loc. cit.

(702)

§1059f 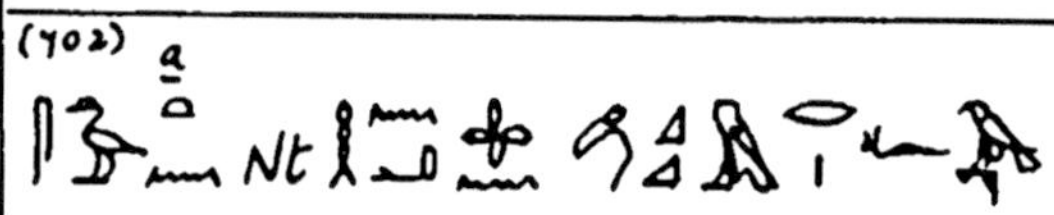 a.  loc. cit.

(702)

§1059g  a-b. So P215; JP II, loc. cit. 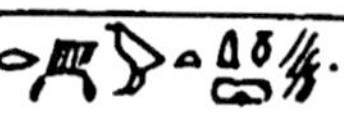 c. P215 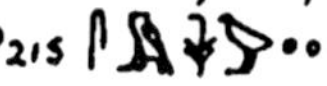

(703)

§1060a 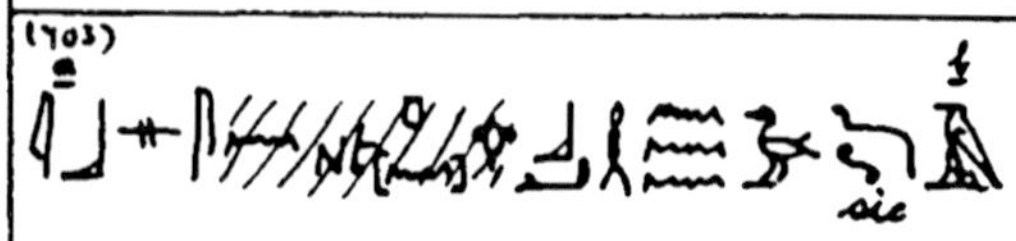 a-b P215: ꜥbz·sn wi hr bꜥḥ, ꜥbz·sn [wi] [hr df3w]; JP II, 1055+49 has preserved df3 only.

(703)

§1060b 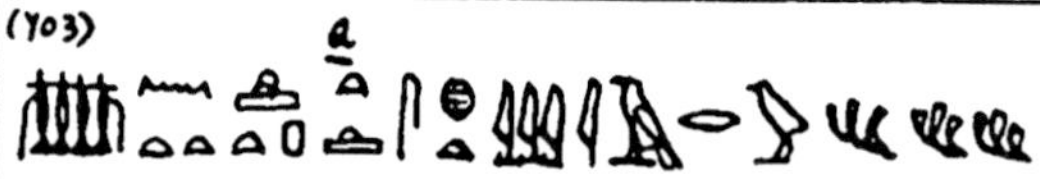 a. Cf. Neit, p. 27; JP II, loc. cit. has 

§1060c  a-b. Cf. locc. cit.

§1061a (704) 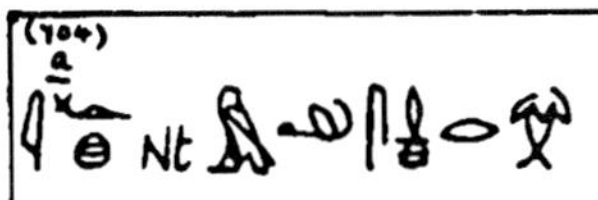 a. Read sfh with JPII, 1055+49.

§1061b (704) 

a-b. Cf. JPII, 1055+50.

§1061c 705 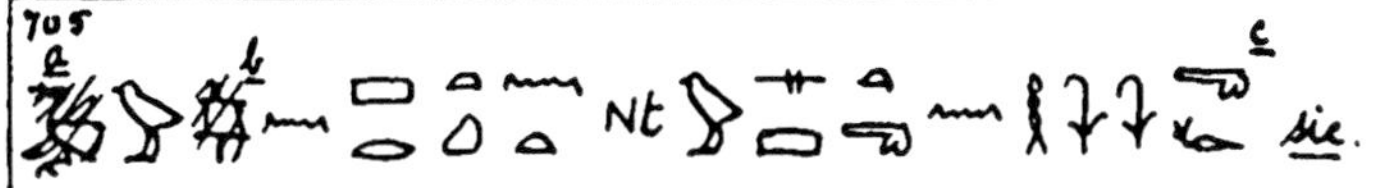 sic.

a-b. Misread in facsimile as [hieroglyphs]; the present reading confirmed by loc. cit.
a-c. The text of P216 is to be preferred: t3w m fnd·i mtwt m hnn·i.

§1061d (705) 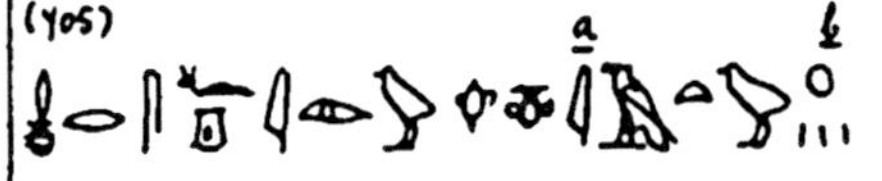 a-b. Read [hieroglyphs] with P216; JPII, 1055+51.

§1062a (706)  a-b. Read m3·n Nt Nw with JPII, 1055+51.
c. Cf. loc. cit.

§1062b (706)  a. Facsimile [hieroglyph], but cf. loc. cit.

§1062c (706) 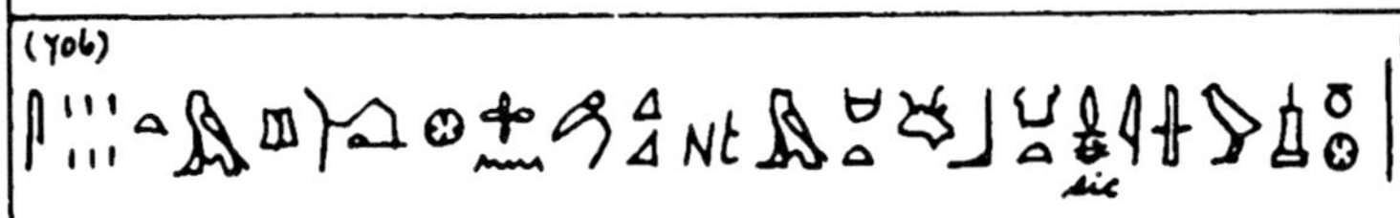 a. Foot of column.

## Utt. 502

JPII, 1055+64.68.

(JPII)
(1055+64)

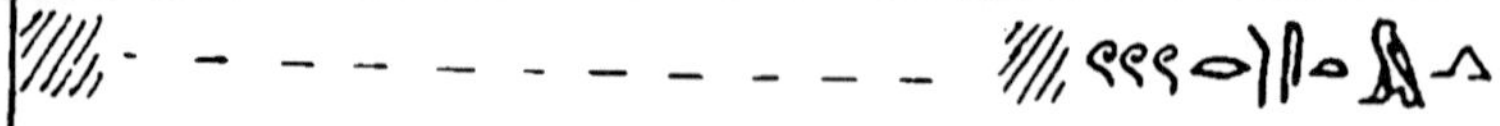

§1073a

(1055+64)

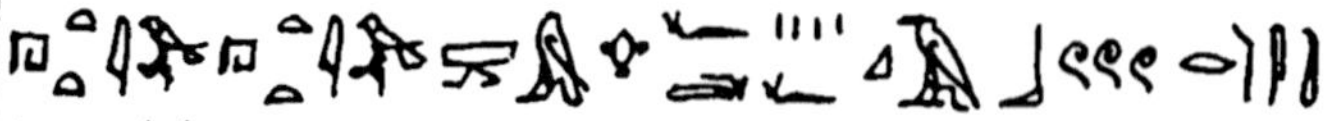

(1055+68) 1055+69

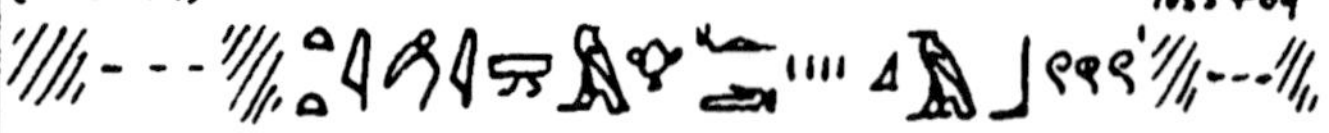

§1073b

(1055+64)

(1055+69)

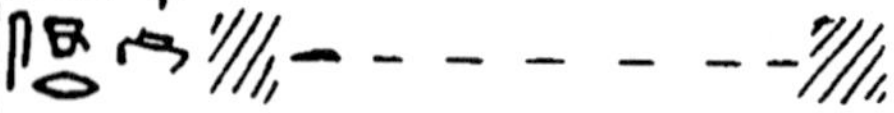

## Utt. 502A.

Nt, 418-9; JPII, 1055+65.

§1074a

(Nt, 418)

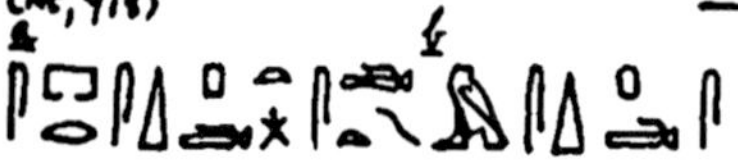

a. JPII, 1055+65. b. Loc. cit. det.

§1074b

(418)

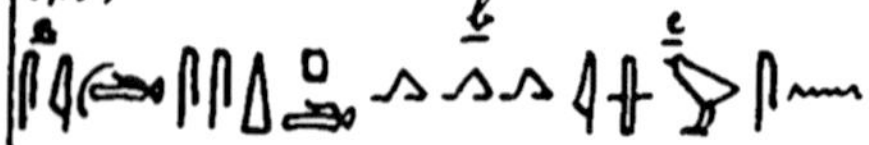

a Loc. cit. b. Loc. cit. c. JPII breaks off in lacuna.

§1074c

(418)

§1074d

(418) 419

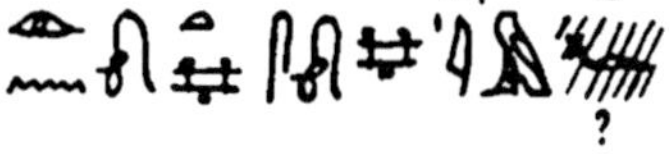

a. An obscure trace, certainly not

§1074e

(419)

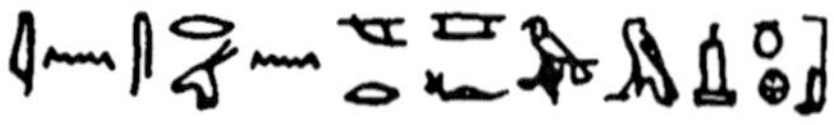

## Utt. 502B.

JP II, 1055+66.

(JP II, 1055+66)

§1075 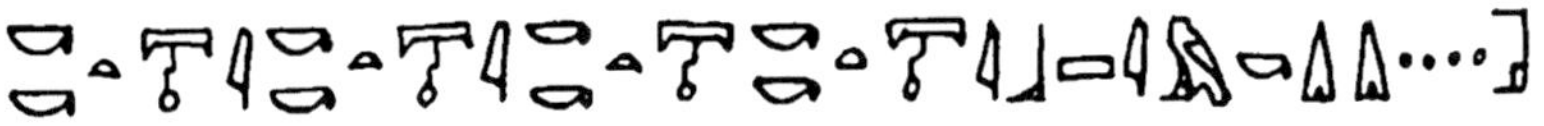

## Utt. 502C.

JP II, 1055+67.

(JP II, 1055+67)

§1076a  a. [glyph] omitted.

(1055+67)

§1076b 

(1055+67)

§1076c 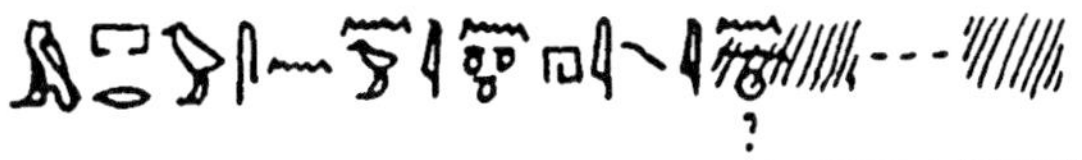

## Utt. 586.

Nt, 14-15.

(Nt, 14) a

§1582a  a. [glyph] restored from N.

(14)

§1582b 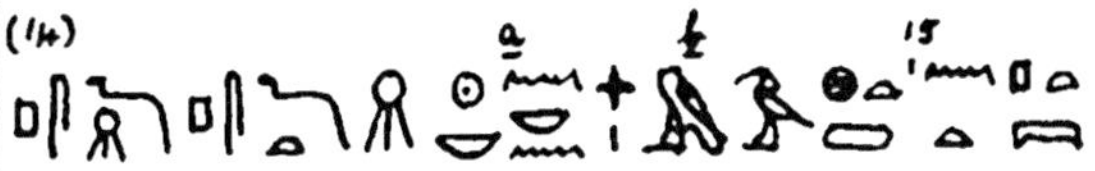 a-b. Sic; dittograph of [glyph] and [glyph] for [glyph]; read r' nb n imy.

(15)

§1583a 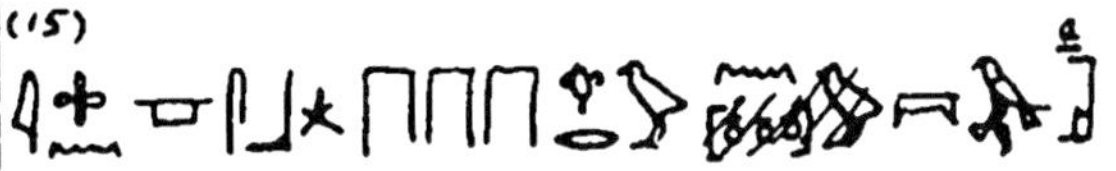 a The stanza-sign in Nt shows that §1583b begins a new Utterance.

## Utt. 586A

Nt, 15-17.

(Nt, 15)

§1583b 

§1584a 

§1584b 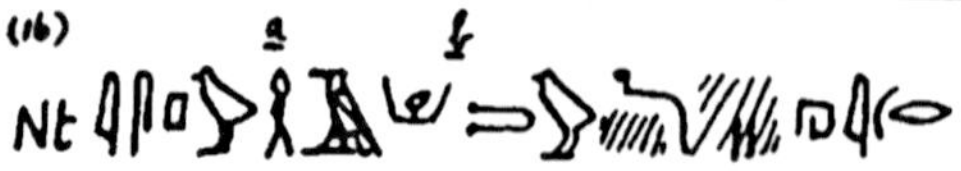

a-b. Var. P .

§1585a 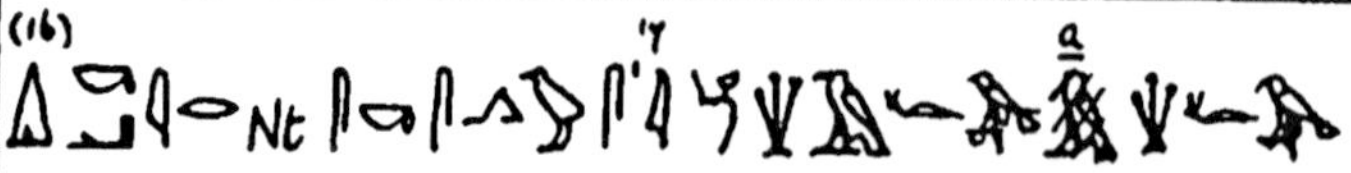

a. Var. P .

§1585b 

a. Restoration certain; trace of 𓆓 visible.

§1586 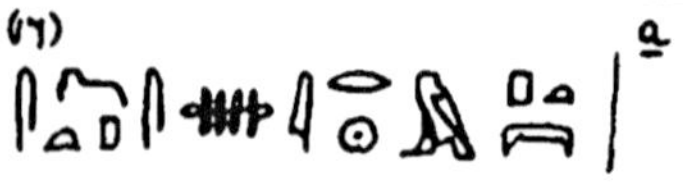

a. Foot of column.

## Utt. 603.

### JP II, 709+40-43.

§1675a 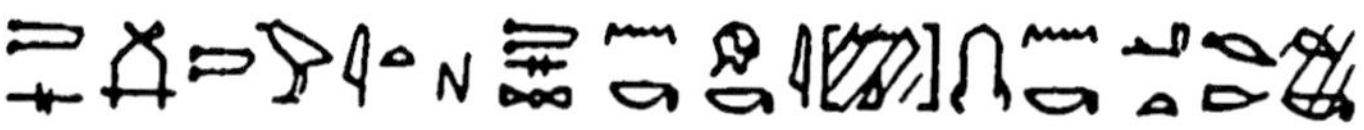

§1675b 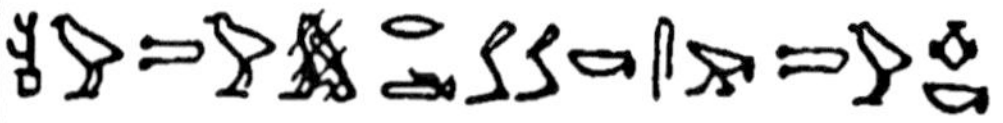

§1675c 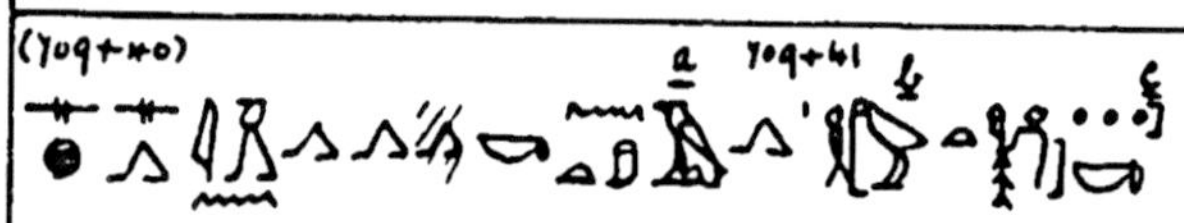

a. As M; JP II wrongly 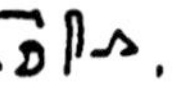.

b-c. Restored from M.

§1676a 

a-b. So M; JP II 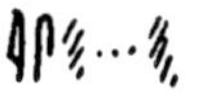. c. So JP II. d. *Ỉm.k* is from M; traces only in JP. II.

§1676 b (709+41)

a. [hieroglyphs] restored from M.
b. M [hieroglyph].

§1676 c (709+41)
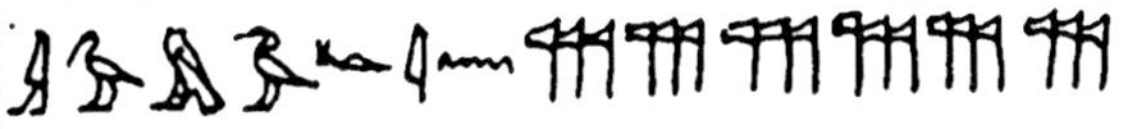

§1677 a 709+42

§1677 b (709+42)
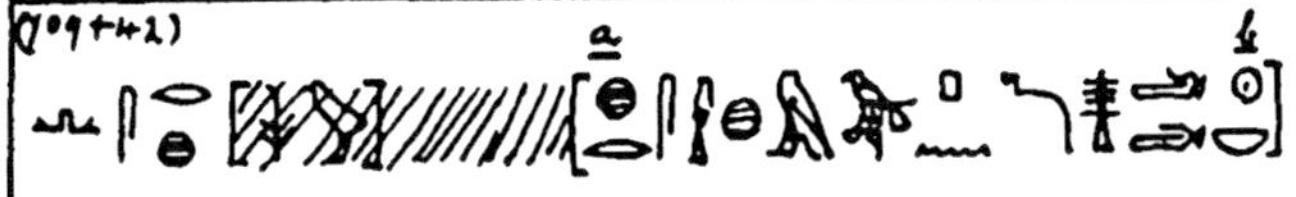
a-b. Restored from M; traces of [hieroglyphs] in JPII.

§1678 a (709+42)
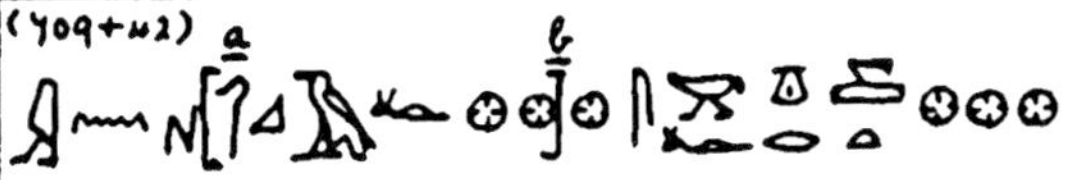
a-b. Restored from M

§1678 b (709+42)

§1678 c 709+43
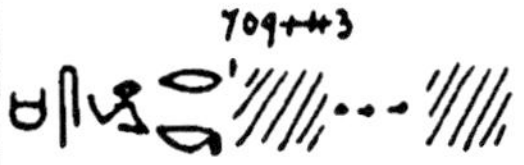

§1679 a (709+43)
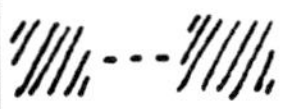

§1679 b (709+43)

a-b. Restored from M.

§1679 c (709+43)
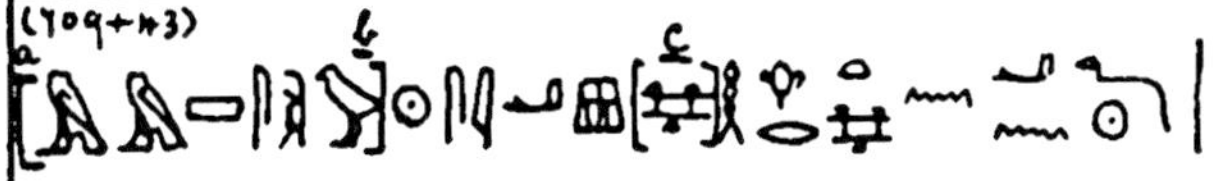
a-b. Restored from M.
c. Restored from M.

Utt. 624.
Nt, 1-4.

§1757a 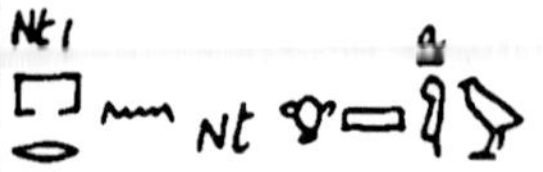
a. Cf. Neit, p. 26.

§1757b 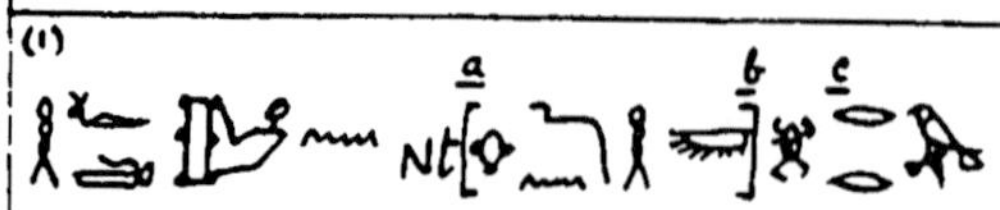
a-b. Restored from N.
c. Var. N

§1758a 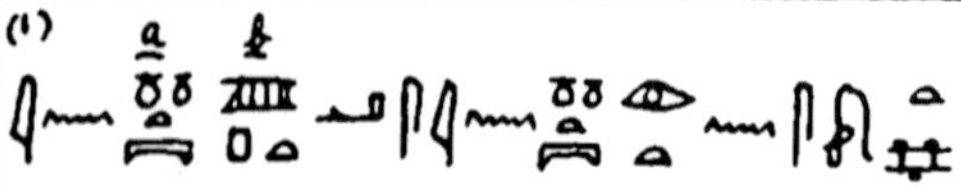
a. So N; Nt
b. Misread in facsimile of Nt as

§1758b 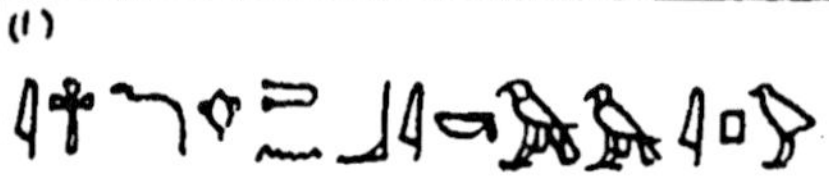

§1759a 
a-b. According to N; only the greater part of shddw preserved in Nt.

§1759b 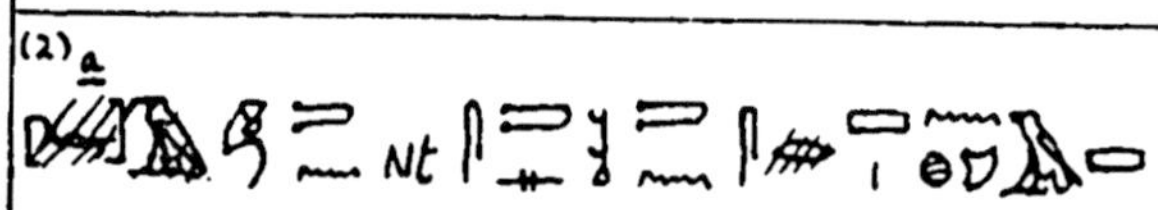
a. N

§1760a 

§1760b 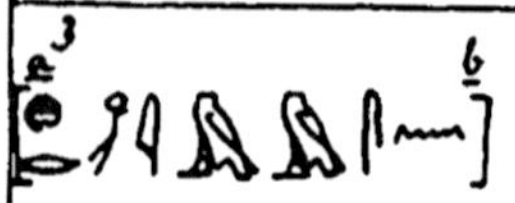
a-b. Restored from N.

§1760c 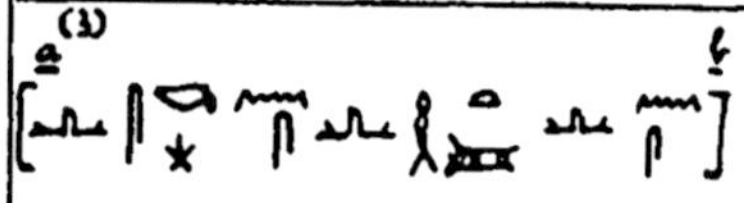
a-b. Restored from N with fem. suffixes.

§1761a 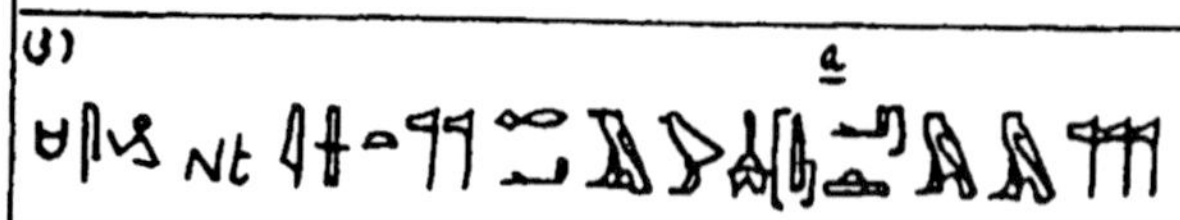
a. Cf. Neit, p. 26 and N.

§1761 b (3)
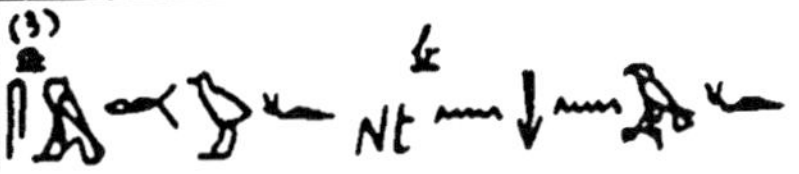
a-b. N smh·f N smh·f N.

§1761 c 4

a. A low horizontal sign; ━ ?

§1761 d (4)
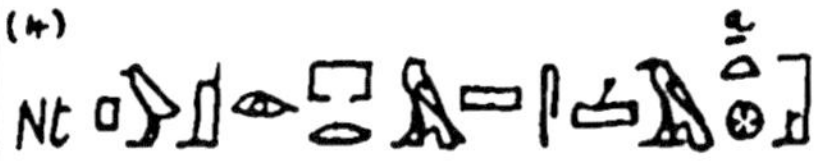
a. Sic facsimile; misreading of ⊙̂ ?

## Utt. 625.

Nt, 805-8; then N.

§1762 a (Nt 805)
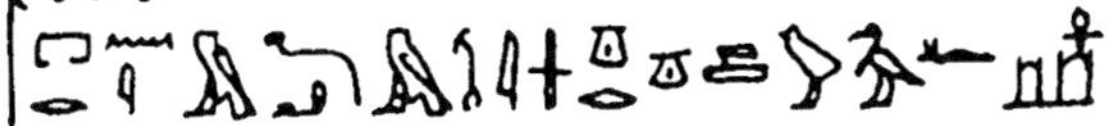

§1762 b 806
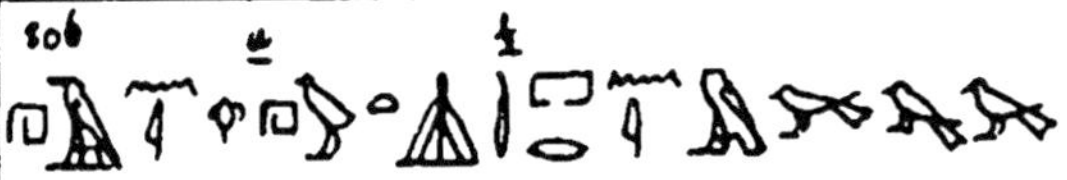
a-b. Sethe hpwty.

§1763 a (806)

§1763 b (806)
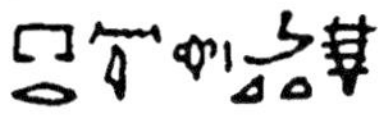

§1763 c 807
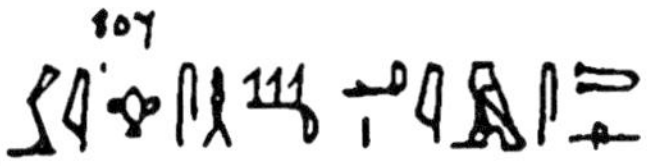

§1764 a (807)

§1764 b (807)

a. Restored from N.

808

§1764c 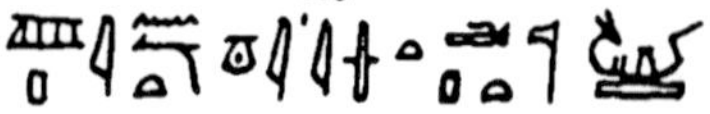

(808)

§1765a 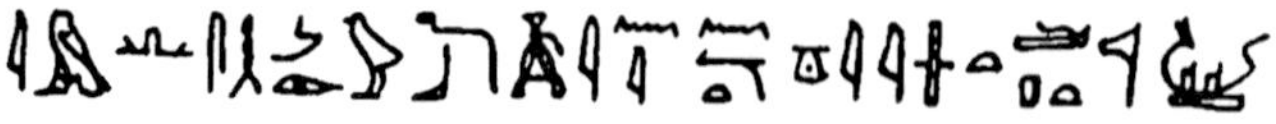

(808)

§1765b 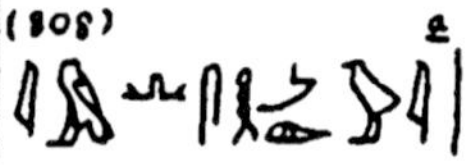

a. Foot of the column. The Nt-version of Utt. 625 ends here; for the rest of the Utterance see the N-text in Sethe.

## Utt. 634.

JP II, 474-6.

(JP II, 474)

475 a b

§1792 

a-b. Traces only.

(475)

476

§1793 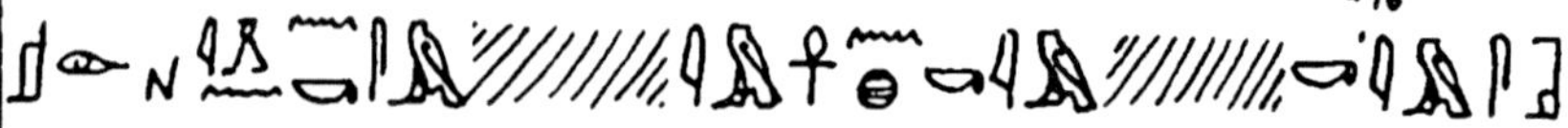

## Utt. 644.

JP II, 552+14-16 (p. 19, fig. 11).

(JP II, 552+14)

552+15

§1823a 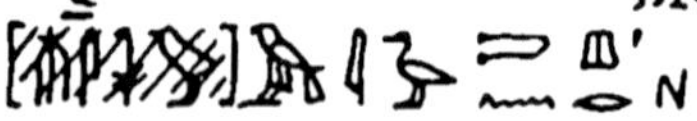

a. Sethe's restoration.

(552+15)

§1823b 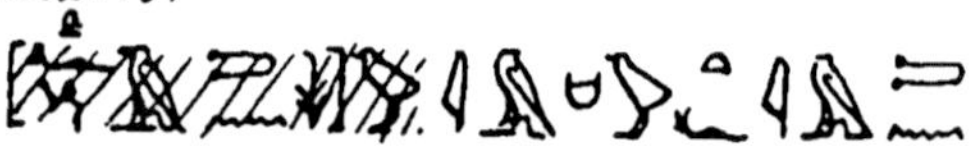

a. Sethe's restoration.

552+16

§1823c 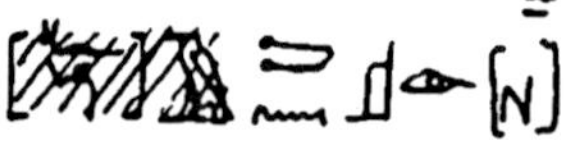

a. End of Utterance; delete Sethe's restoration.

## Utt. 645.

Nt, 360-3; JP II, 552+16-19 (p. 19, fig. 11).

§1824 a  a-b. So N (Sethe); Nt, 360 reads ṯwt nṯr 13. c. JP II, 552+17 has … instead of ….

§1824 b  a. So Sethe; Nt …. b. Sethe … for ….

§1824 c 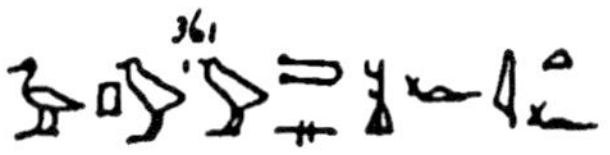

§1824 d  a-b. Supplied from JP II, 552, 18-19; not in Nt.

§1824 e 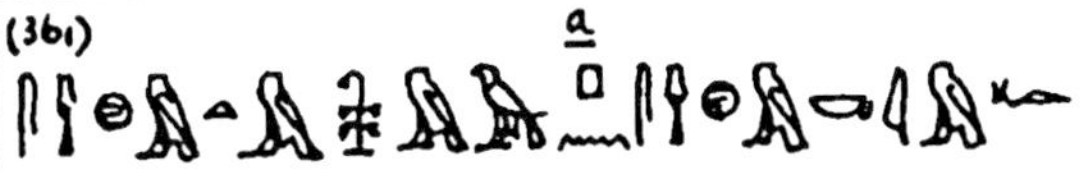 a. So JP II, 552+19; Nt facsimile ….

§1824 f  a. From here on only in Nt; not in Sethe or JP II.

§1824 g 

## Utt. 645A.

Nt, 363-5.

§1824 h 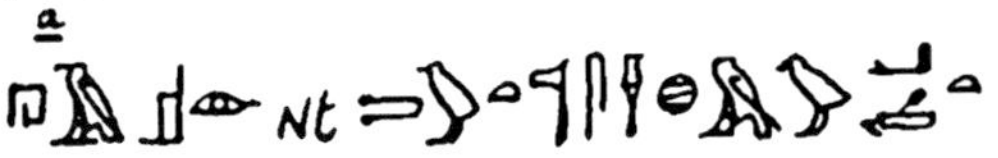 a. Continues Utt. 645 without division.

§1824 i 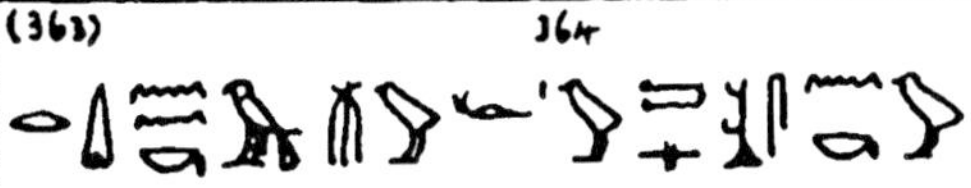

(364)

§1824 j 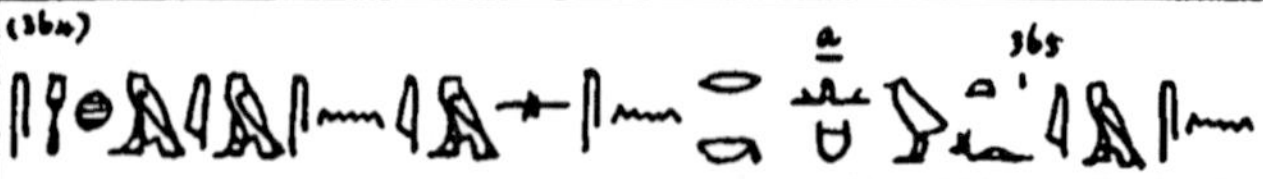

a. Facsimile ; for the confusion of □ and ∀ see §§ 40 + 15.19; 415.

(365)

§1824 k 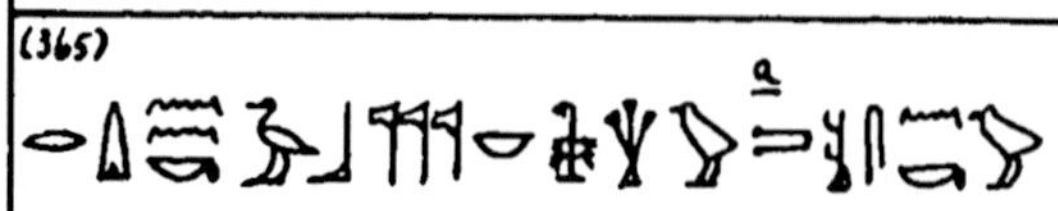

a. Sic, miswriting of wtz.

(365)

§1824 l 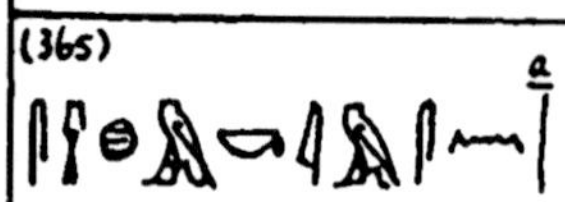

a. Foot of column.

## Utt. 646.

## Nt. 359.

(Nt 359)

§1825 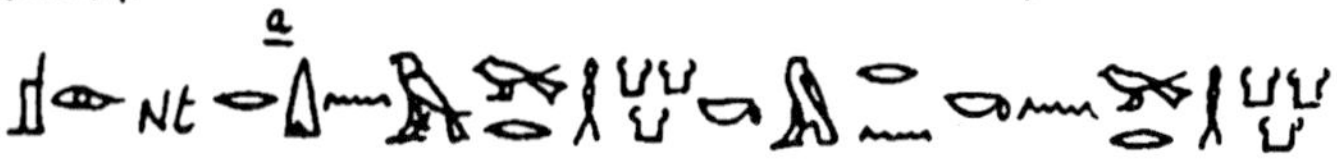

a. For rdi, N (Sethe) has ////.

## Utt. 654.

## JP II, 574.

(JP II, 574)

§1841 a 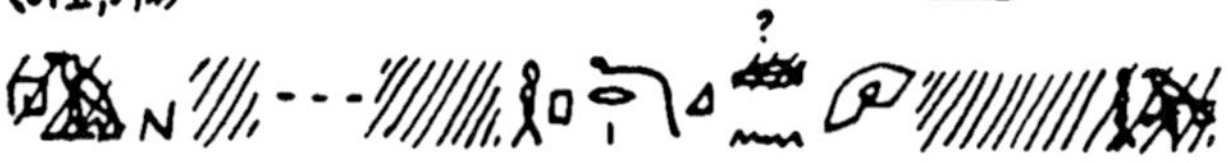

(574)

§1841 b 

a. Sethe . b. Sethe .

## Utt. 655.

## JP II, 574-7.

(JP II, 574)

§1842 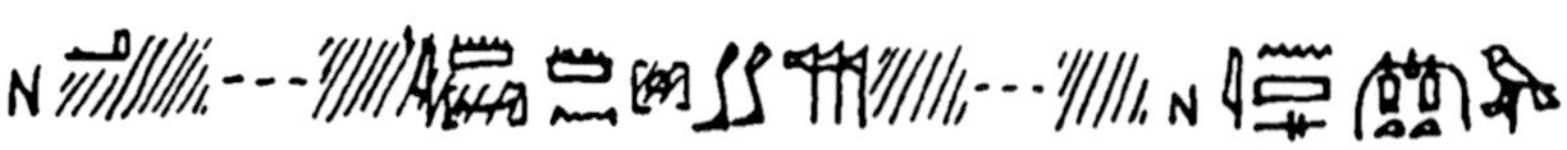

575

§1843 

a-b. Sethe omits prt.

§1844 (576)

§1845a (576)

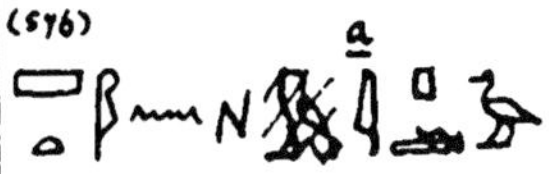

a. So Sethe; facsimile has

§1845b (576)

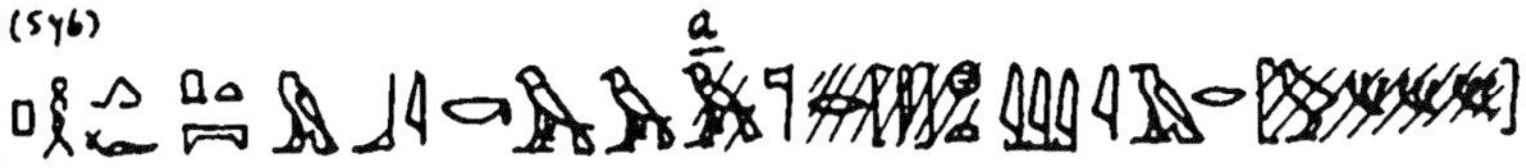

a. The facsimile of JPII has

§1846 (577)

a. The stanza-sign in JPII marks off §1847 as a separate Utterance 655 A.

## Utt. 655A.

### JPII, 577.

§1847a (JPII, 577)

§1847b (577)

a. As Sethe.

## Utt. 657.

### JPII, 578-579+6.

§1850 (JPII, 578) 579

§1851 (579)

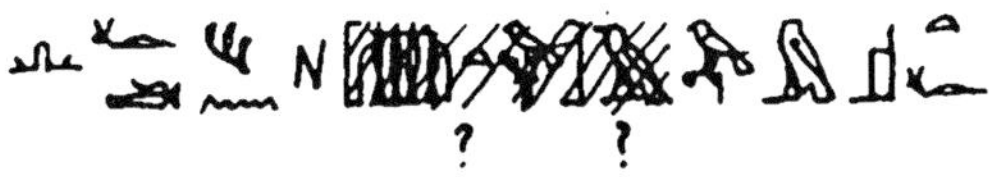

§1852 579+1

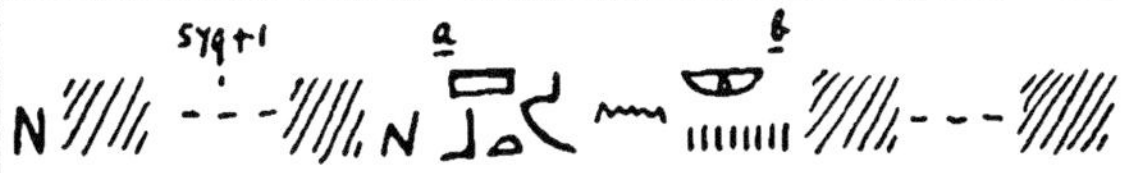

a-b. This fragment may belong to another Utterance.

## Utt. 658.

JP II, 580-583+2.

JP II, 580

§1853 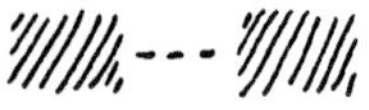

(580)

§1854a 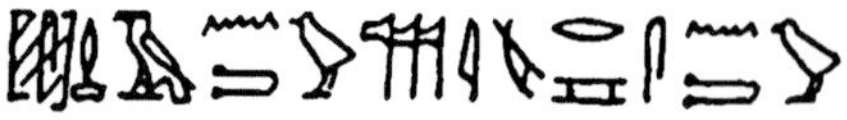

(580)

§1854b 

(580)

§1854c 

a. Restoration suggested by the preceding clauses, but the space and trace in the facsimile do not fit.

(581)

§1855a 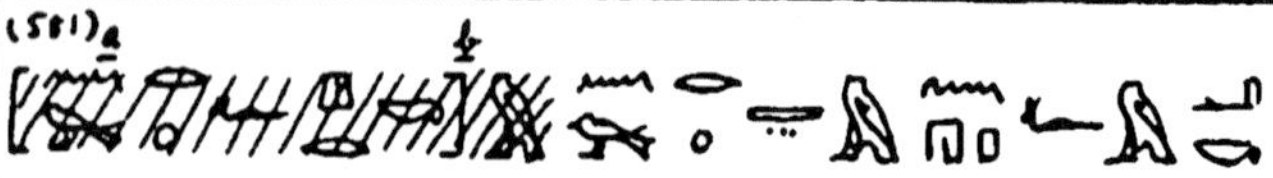 a-b. Sethe's restoration.

(581)

§1855b 

(581)

§1855c 

(582)

§1856a 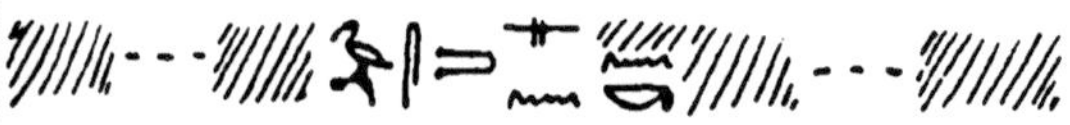

(582)

§1856b  a-b. Sethe's restoration.

(582)

§1857a 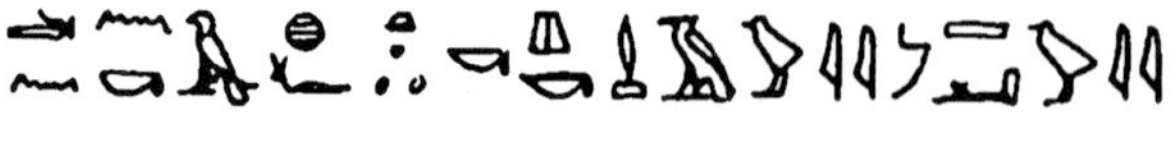

§1857 b (582) 583

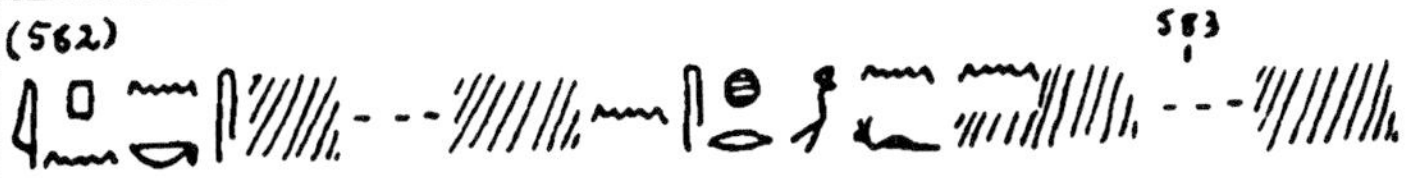

§1858 a (583)

§1858 b (583) a b

a. So Sethe rightly; JP II has . b. So Sethe.

§1859 a (583)

§1859 b (583)

§1859 c 583+1

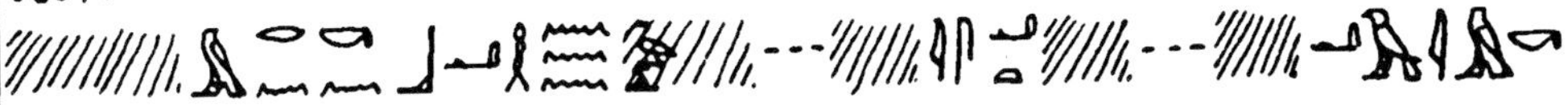

§1859 d (583+1) 583+2

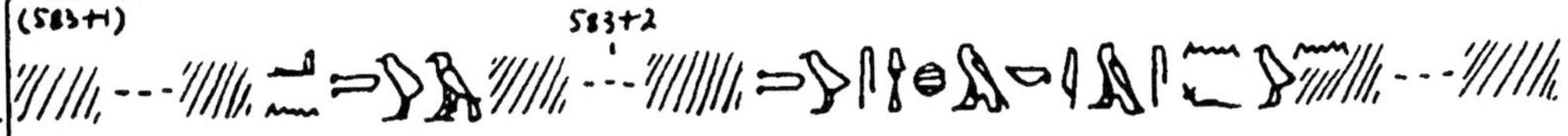

§1859 e (583+2)

## Utt. 663.

### JP II, 709+20–22.

§1882 a (JP II, 709+20)

§1882 b (709+20)

(709+20)

§1882 c 

709+21

§1882 d 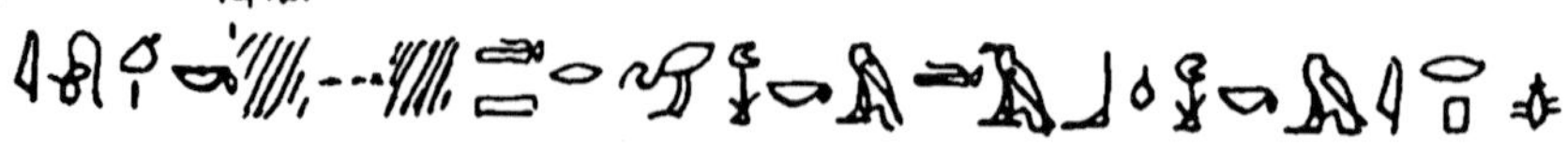

(709+21)

§1882 e 

(709+21) 709+22

§1883 a 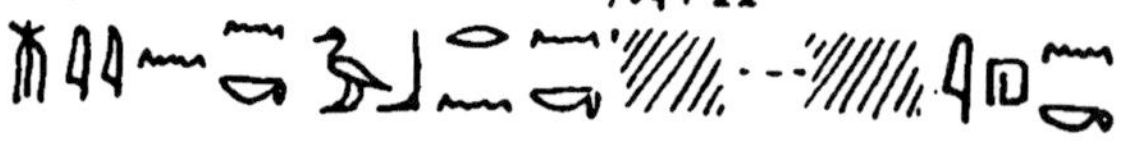

(709+22)

§1883 b 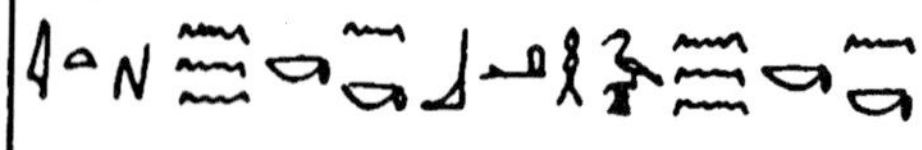

(709+22)

§1883 c 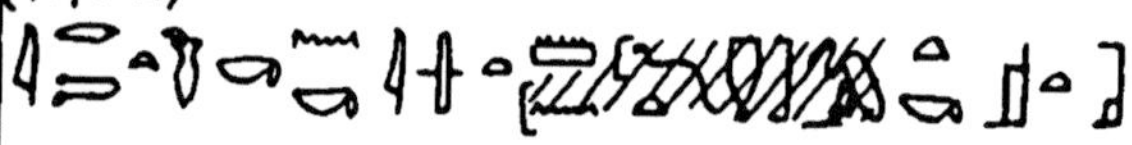

## Utt. 664.

JP II, 583+4.

JP II, 583+4

§1884 

(583+4)

§1885 

## Utt. 664A.

JP II, 583+4-5.

§1886 a 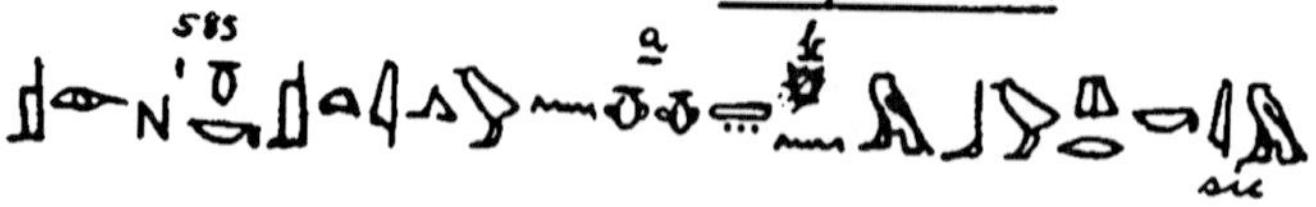

a. Sic Sethe, read ḥr ỉb.

b. Sic Sethe, read pn.

(583+5)

§1886b 

## Utt. 664B.

JP II, 583+5-6.

(583+5)

§1887a 

(583+5) 583+6

§1887b 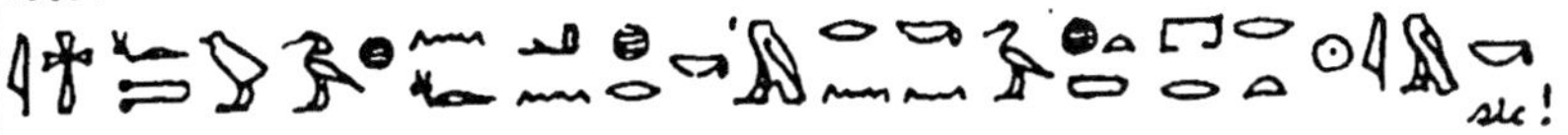

(583+6)

§1888 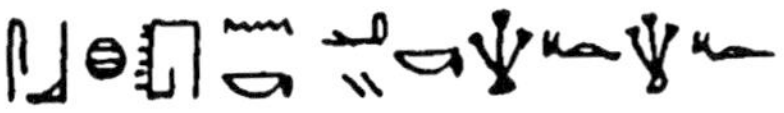

(583+6)

§1889 

## Utt. 664C.

JP II, 583+6-10.

(583+6) 583+7

§1890 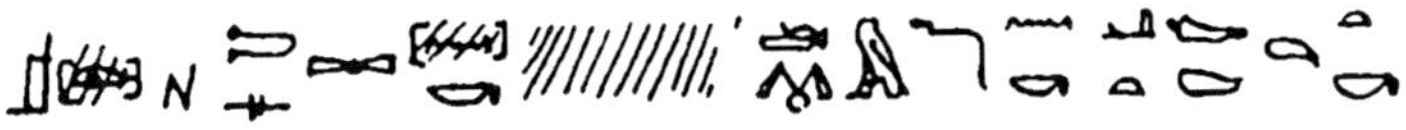

(583+7)

§1891 

583+8

§1892a 

(583+8)

§1892b 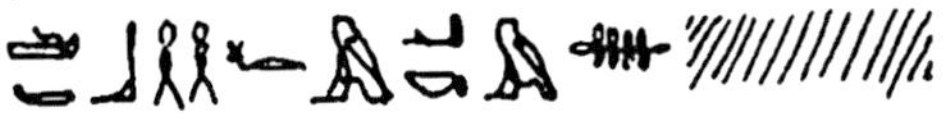

(583+8) 583+9

§1893 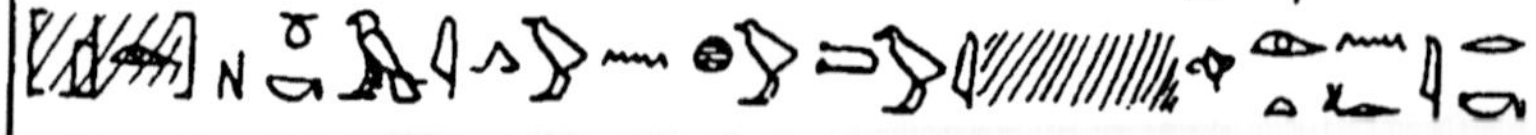

(583+9)

§1894 

(583+9)

§1895 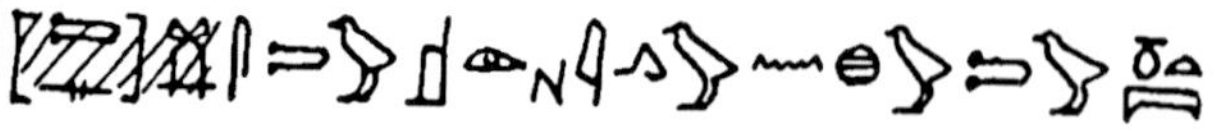

(583+9) 583+10

§1896 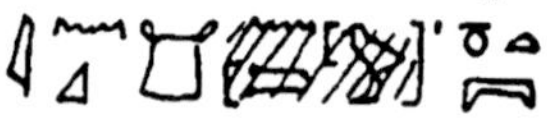

(583+10)

§1897a 

(583+10)

§1897b 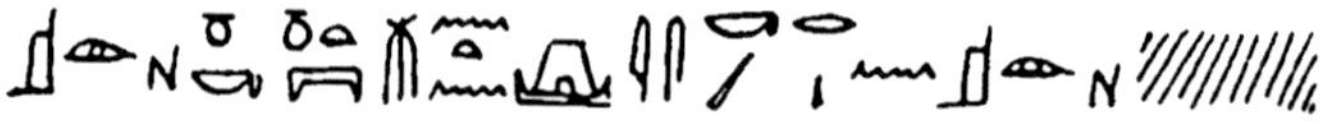

## Utt. 665.

Nt, 658-69; JP II, 719+20-25.

Nt 658

§1898a 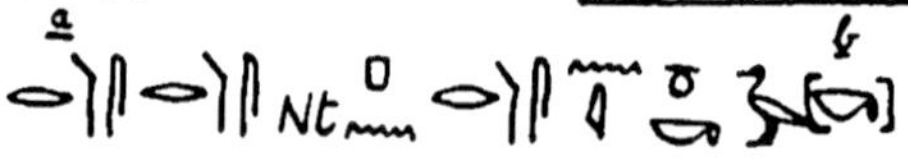 a. JP II, 719+20 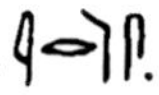. b. Restored from JP II.

(658)

§1898b 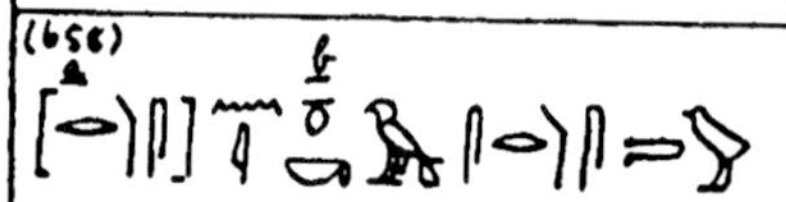 a. Restored from JP II, 719+20, which reads 'irs. b. As JP II; the facsimile of Nt has 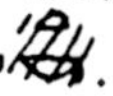.

(658)

§1899a 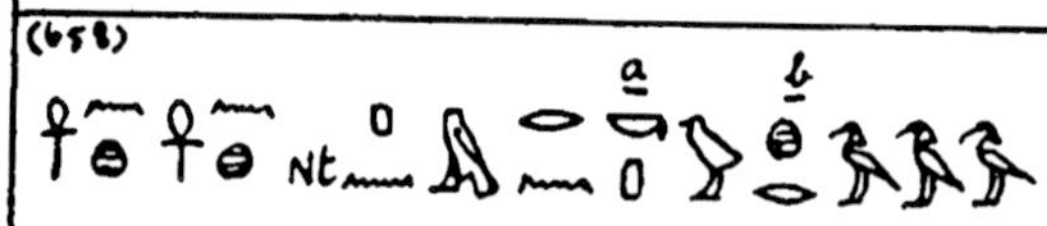 a. In the facsimile  looks like . b. N (Sethe) 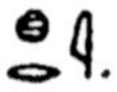.

659

§1899b 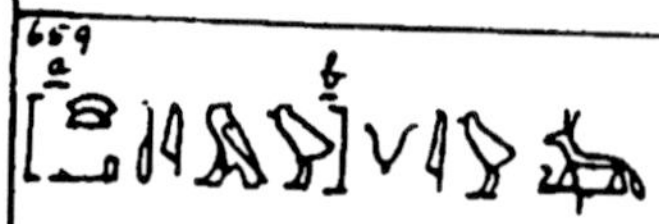 a-b. Restored from Sethe.

| § | Text | Notes |
|---|---|---|
| §1899 c | (659) 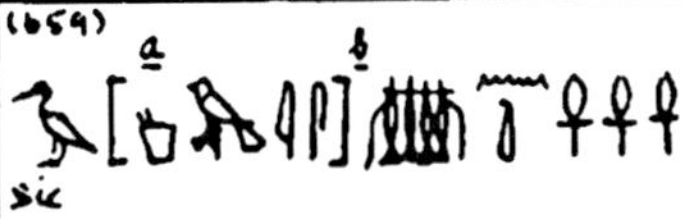 | a-b. Restored from JPII, 719+20. |
| §1899 d | (659) 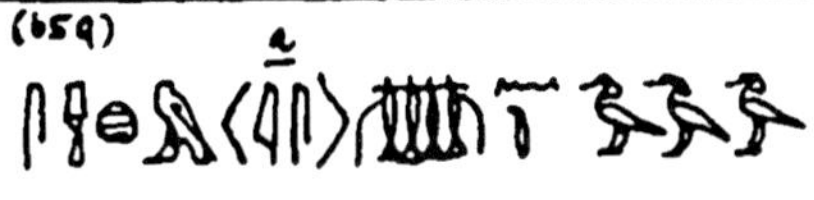 | a. [hieroglyph] almost certainly omitted in error; cf. §1899 c. e. |
| §1899 e | (659) 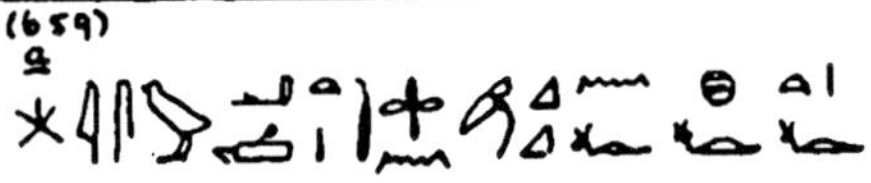 | a. JPII, 719+20 [hieroglyphs] *. |
| §1900 a | 660 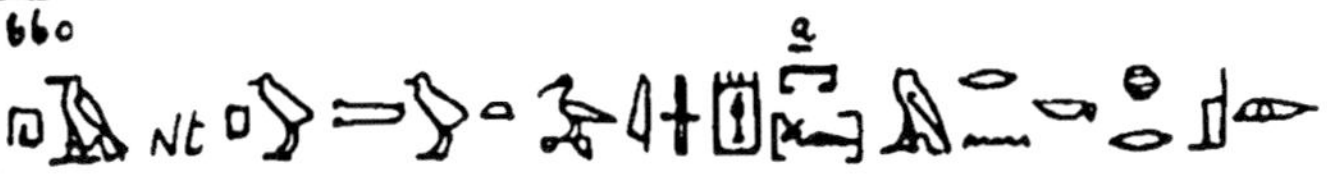 | a. Suffix f from JPII, 719+21. |
| §1900 b | (660) 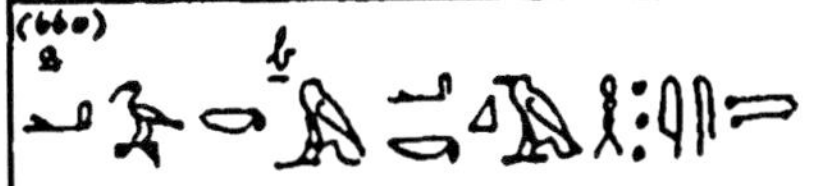 | a-b. Sic Nt. |
| §1900 c | (660) 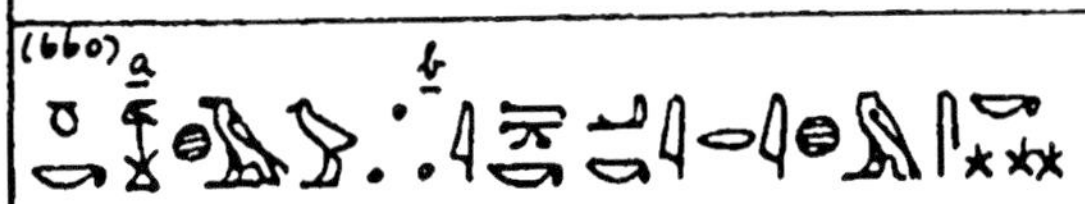 | a-b. JPII, 719+21 [hieroglyphs]. |
| §1901 a | 661 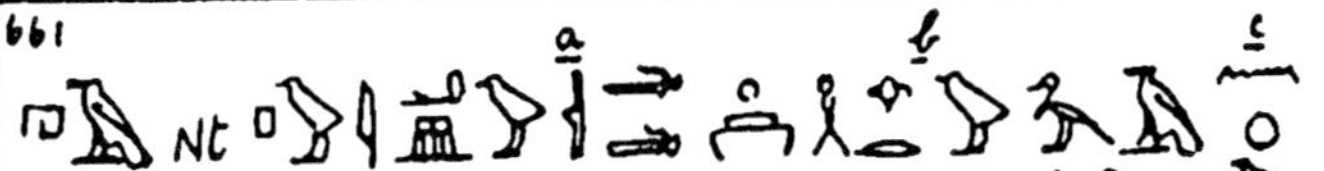 | a. Nt facsimile [hieroglyph]. b. JPII, 719+21 [hieroglyphs]. c. JPII [hieroglyphs]. |
| §1901 b | (661) 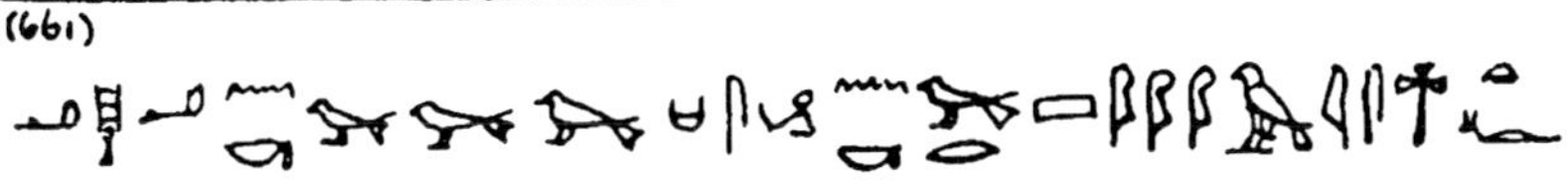 | |
| §1901 c | (661)  | |
| §1901 d | (662)  | |
| §1902 a | (662) 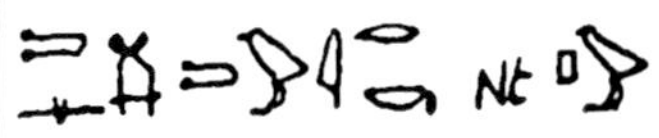 | |

(662)

§1902 b    [hieroglyphs]    a-b. Restored from JP II, 719+22.

(662)

§1902 c    [hieroglyphs]

(663)

§1903 a    [hieroglyphs]

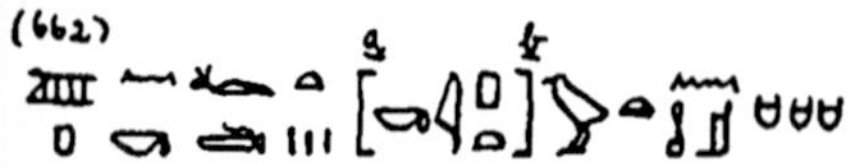

a-b. Supplied from Sethe; omitted in Nt in passing from column to column.

c-d. JP II, 719+22 [hieroglyphs].

(663)

§1903 b    [hieroglyphs]    a. sic Nt and JP II.

(663)

§1904 a    [hieroglyphs] Nt [hieroglyphs]

(663)

§1904 b    [hieroglyphs]    664

(664)

§1904 c    [hieroglyphs]

(664)

§1904 d    [hieroglyphs]    a-b. JP II, 719+23 [hieroglyphs] alone.

§1904 e    665 [hieroglyphs]

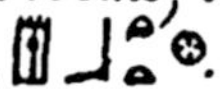

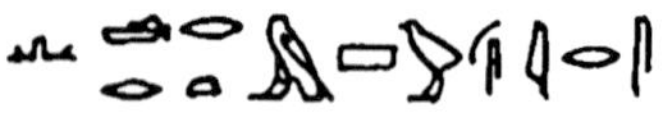

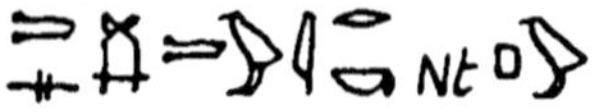

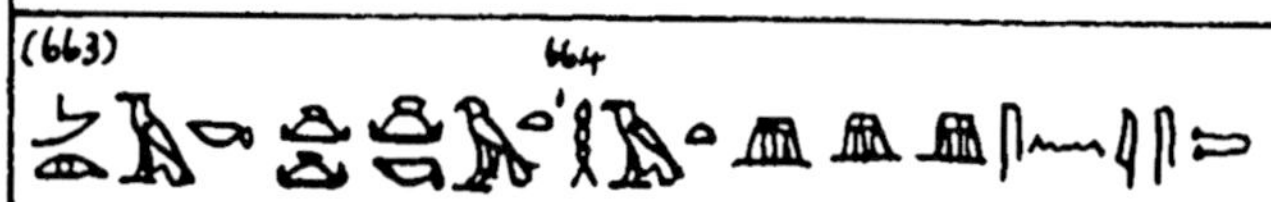

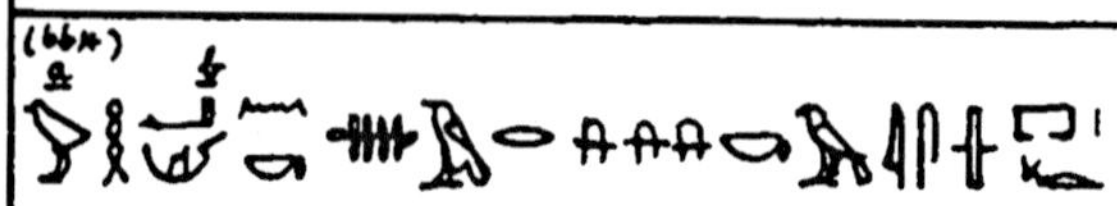

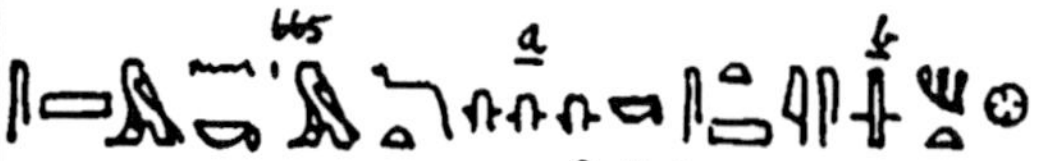

a. Sethe (his §1904 b) has [hieroglyphs], surely a misreading.

b. Nt facsimile [sign], but certainly [sign] is to be read, as in Sethe, loc. cit

(665)

§1905 a    [hieroglyphs]    a. Cf. Neit, p. 27 and Sethe.

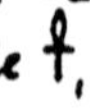

§1905b (665) 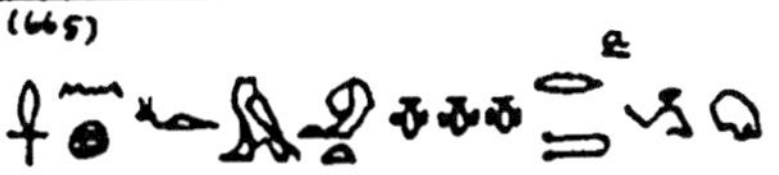 a. JP II, 719+23 .

§1905c (665) 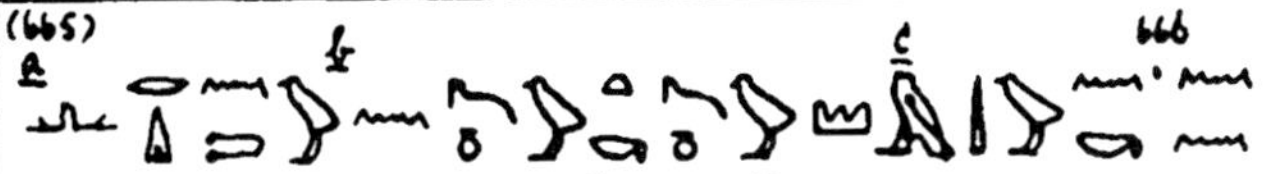

a-b JP II, 719+23 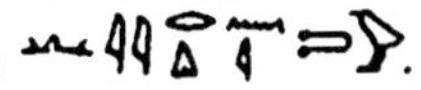. c-d. Loc. cit. 

§1906a (666) 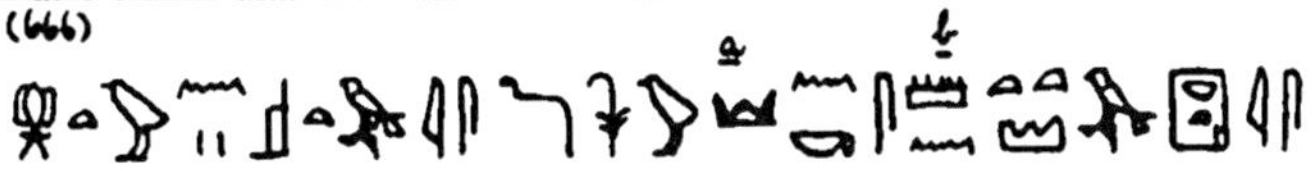

a. Sic facsimile, perhaps a misreading of . b. Facsimile .

§1906b (666) 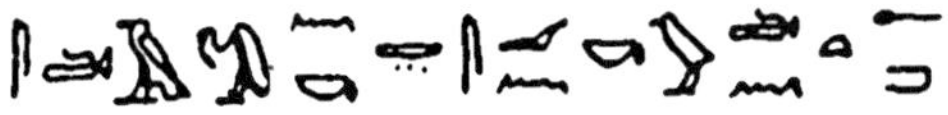

§1906c (666) 

§1906d 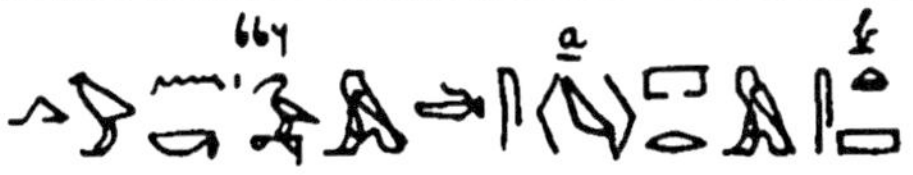 a.  supplied from JP II, 719+24. b. So JP II correctly; the Nt facsimile has .

§1906e (667) 

§1906f (667) 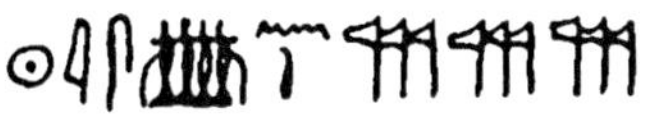

§1907a (667)  a. JP II, 719+24 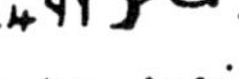 rightly. b. JP II thw·sn, again rightly.

§1907b 668 

(668)

§1907c 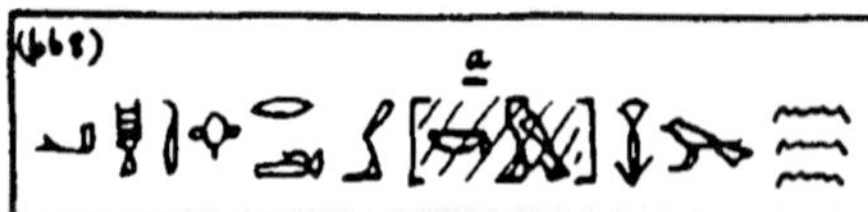

a. The lacuna as shown in the facsimile of Nt has room only for , but the sense demands that be restored.

(668)

§1907d 

(668)

§1907e 

a. Nt facsimile .

§1907f 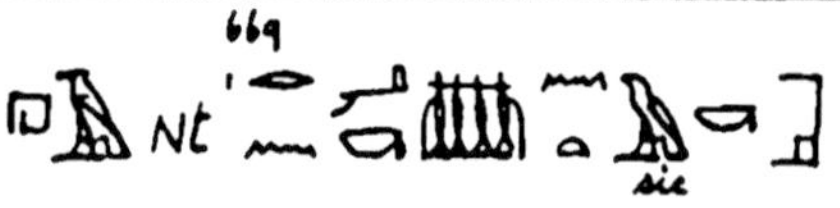

## Utt. 665A.

Nt, 729-34; 479-83; JP II, 719+25-7.

(Nt 729)

§1908a 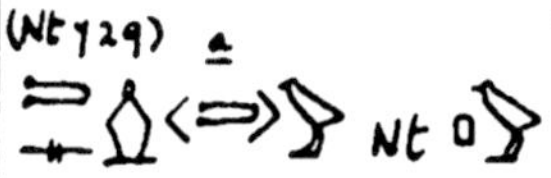

a. supplied from N (Sethe); Nt facsimile omits.

(729)

§1908b 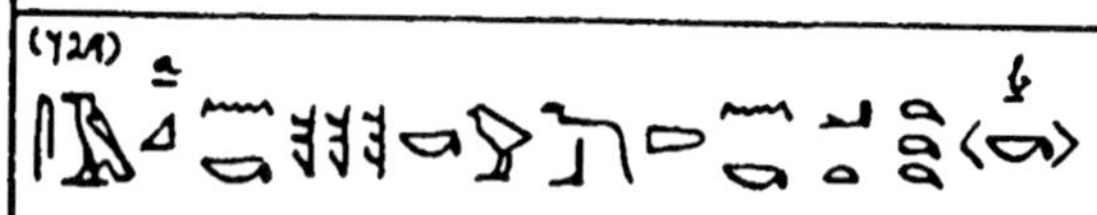

a. So Sethe and Nt 479 rightly; Nt 729 .
b. Supplied from Nt 479.

(729)

§1908c 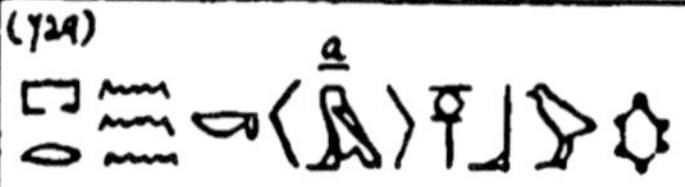

a. Supplied from Sethe.

§1908d 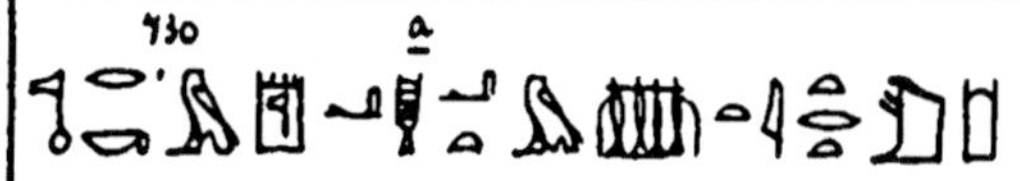

a. JP II, 719+25 .

(730)

§1908e 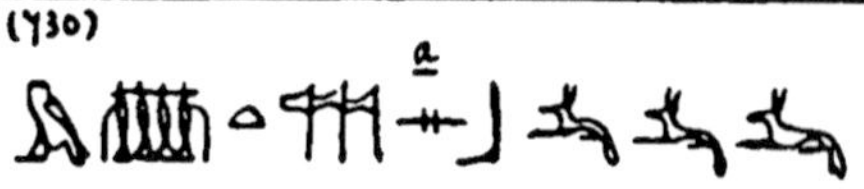

a. Facsimile Nt 730 .

§1909a (730) 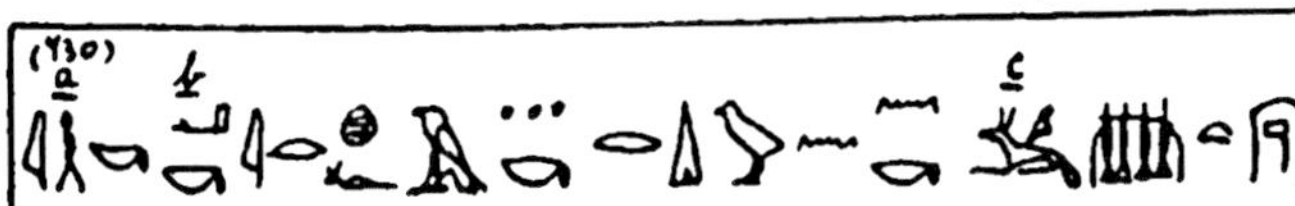

a. Nt, 480. b. Loc. cit. omits. c. Loc. cit. without feather.

§1909b (730) 

§1909c 731 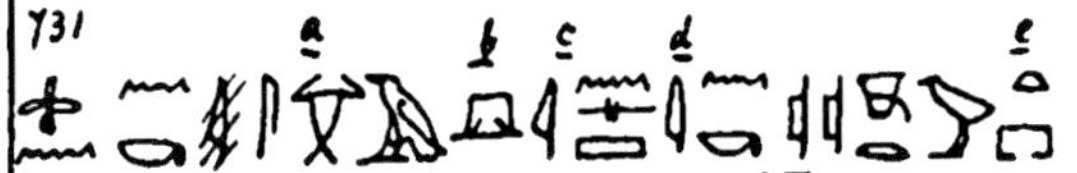

a-b. Apparently a misreading of ; a word for 'tomb' must stand here.
c-d. Read i͗zn.i e. For Sethe (his §1909b) has .

§1909d (731) 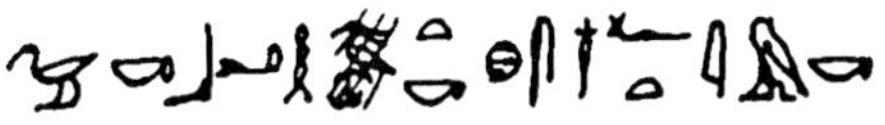

§1910a (731) 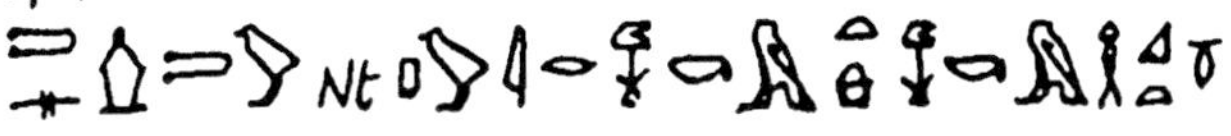

§1910b 732  a-b. A dittograph.

§1911a (732) 

a. sic; read or .
b. sic; read as Nt, 462.

§1911b (732) 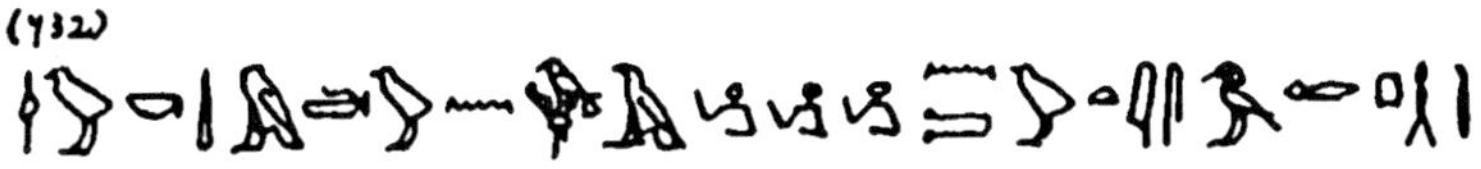

§1911c 733 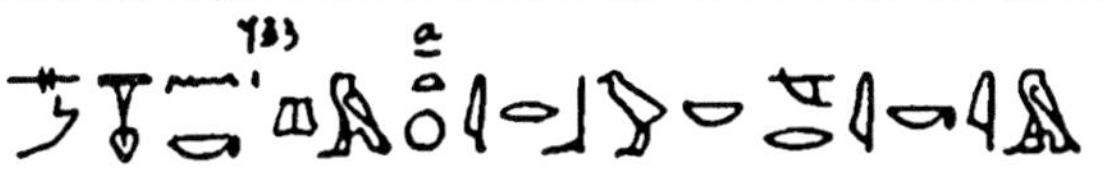 a. For JPII, 719+27 has .

§1912a (733) 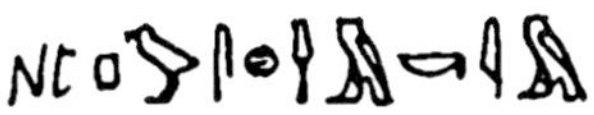

§1912 b [hieroglyphs] Nt

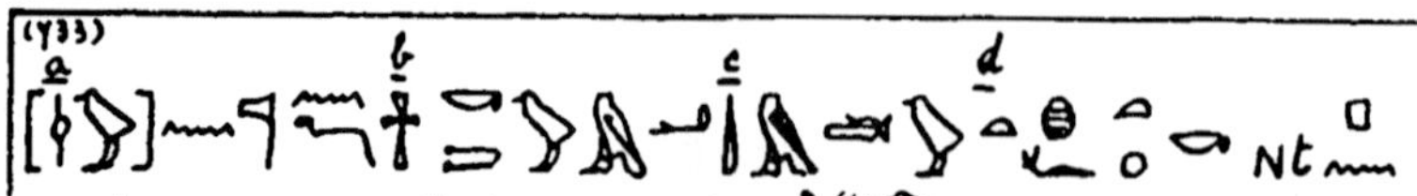

a. Restored from Sethe; Nt, 483 has [hieroglyphs]. JPII, 719+27 has the *sḏm.f* form *wḏ*, but both the Nt-texts clearly were intended to read *wḏ·n*. b. For [sign] Nt, 733 has [sign]; JPII and Nt, 483 have the normal form. c-d. JPII, 719+27 has [hieroglyphs] (masc.); Nt, 483 reads [hieroglyphs] (*sic*), presumably a misreading of [sign].

(733)

§1912 c [hieroglyphs] a. The *n* which is required here has been merged by haplography with the preceding *n* of *ḥn*; in Nt, 483 the *n* has been preserved by *pw* preceding instead of *ḥn*.

§1912 d 734 [hieroglyphs] a. Facsimile Nt, 734 [sign].
    b. For [sign], stanza-mark.

## Utt. 665 B.

Nt, 734-5; 624-5; JPII, 719+28.

(Nt 734)

§1913 a [hieroglyphs] a-b. Nt, 624 [hieroglyphs].

(734)

§1913 b [hieroglyphs]

§1914 a 735 [hieroglyphs] a. Supplied from JPII, 719+28.

(735)

§1914 b [hieroglyphs] a-b. *sic* all texts. c. Nt, 625 has [sign] here.

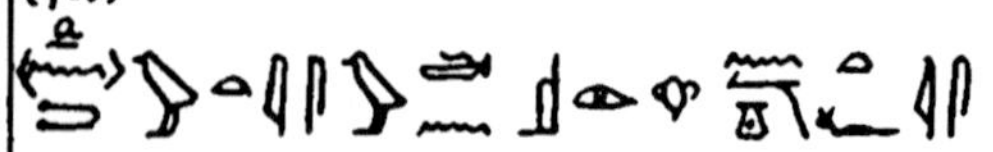

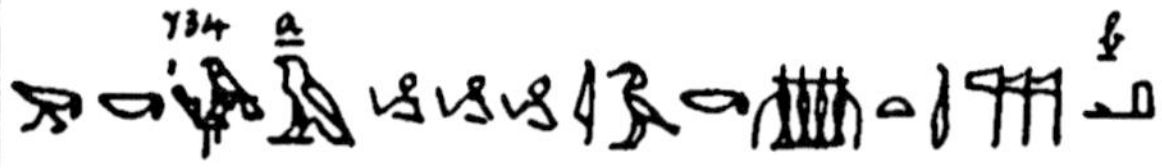

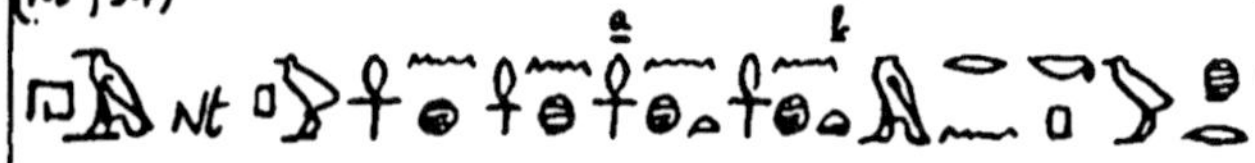

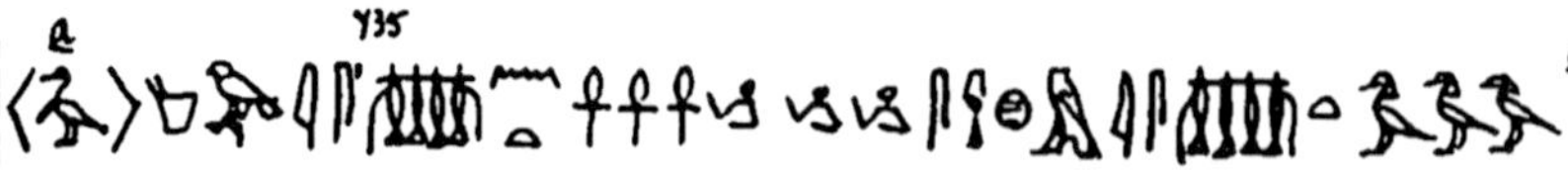

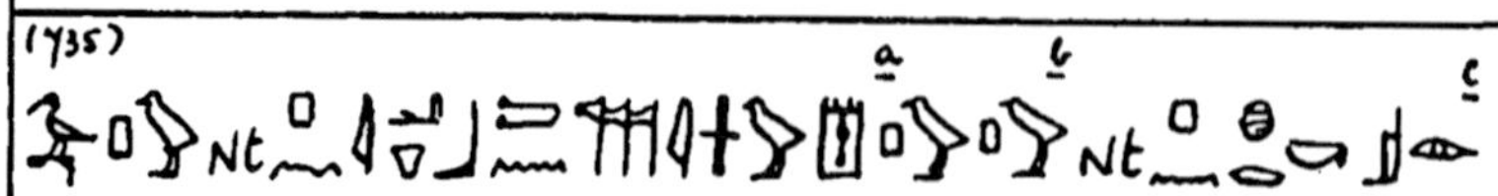

## Utt. 665C.

Nt, 735-8; JPII, 719+29-30.

(Nt 735) 736

§1915a 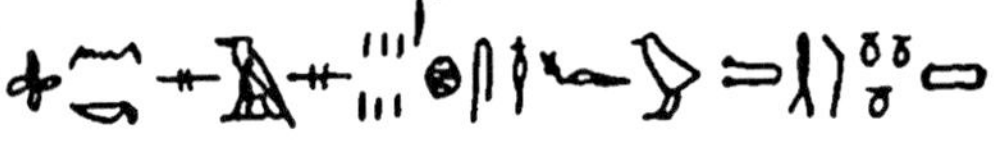

(736)

§1915b 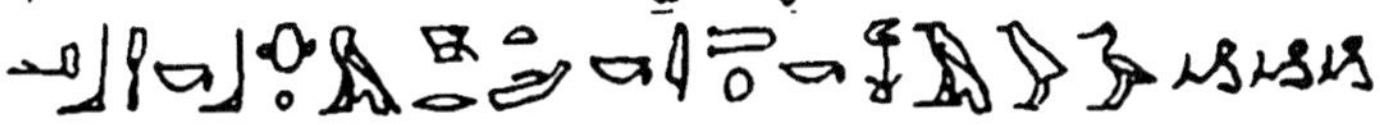 a-b. Read [illegible], cf. §1426c.

(736)

§1915c 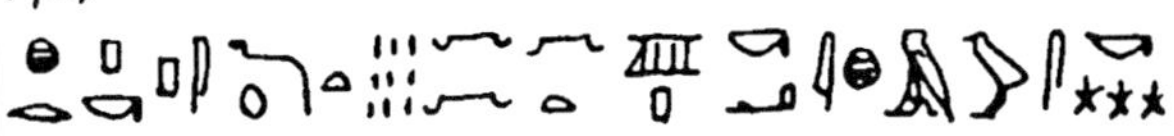

737

§1915d  a. Supplied from N (Sethe, his §1915b).

(737)

§1915e 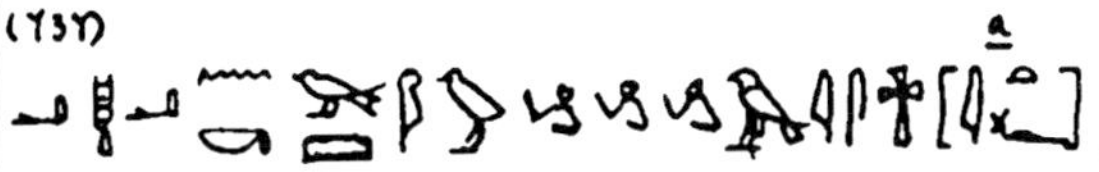 a. Restored from JPII, 719+29; Nt 737 may have had [illegible] only.

(737)

§1915f 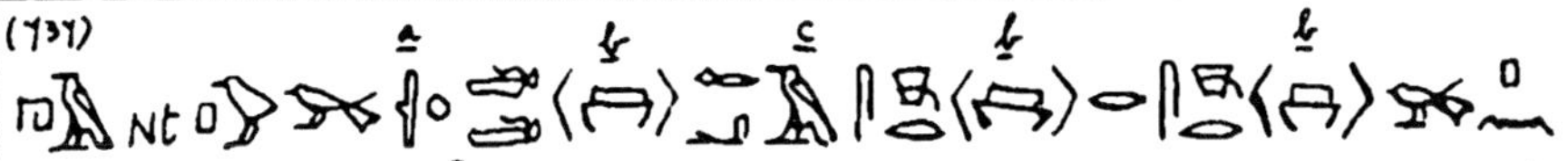
a. Facsimile Nt, 737 [illegible]. b. Supplied from JPII, 719+29. c. For ꜥ3w (adverb), cf. §2224c.

(737)

§1915g 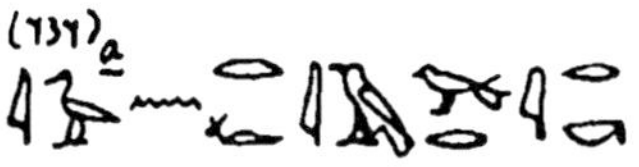 a. B3-bird without breast-tuft.

738

§1915h 

## Utt. 666.

Nt, 738-49; JPII, 719+30-724.

This Utterance begins at §1916a, placed in Utt. 665 by Sethe.

(Nt, 738)

§1916a 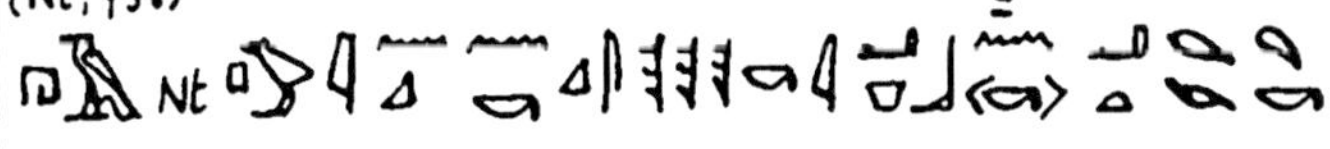 a. [illegible] supplied from JPII, 719+30.

| | |
|---|---|
| §1916 b | (738) 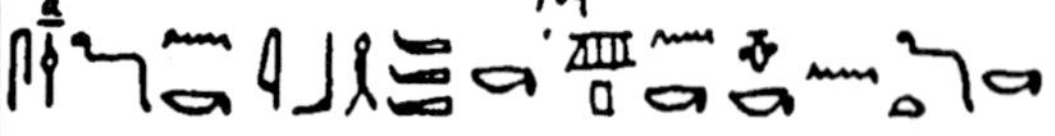 a. Read *shd* as JP II, 719+30. |
| §1916 c | (739)  |
| §1917 | (739)  |
| §1918 | (739) 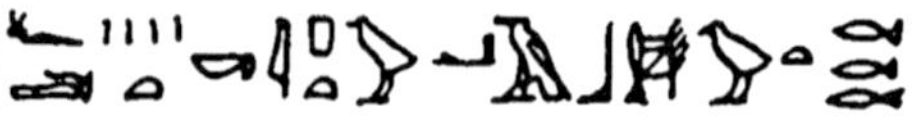 |
| §1919 a | (739)  a-b. Read *ˁbḫ* 'fill up', Pyr. §§1140.1902; CT I, 298. |
| §1919 b | 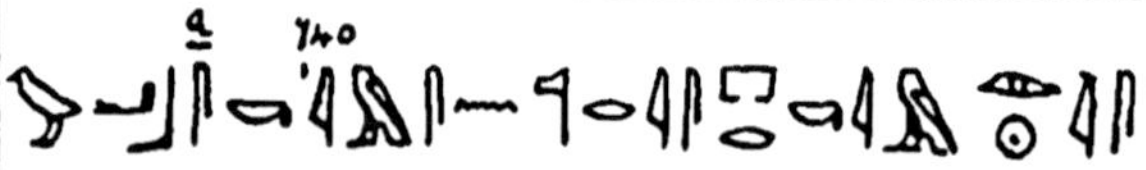 a. *Sic*; perhaps intended for a 'folded napkin' determinative. |
| §1919 c | (740) 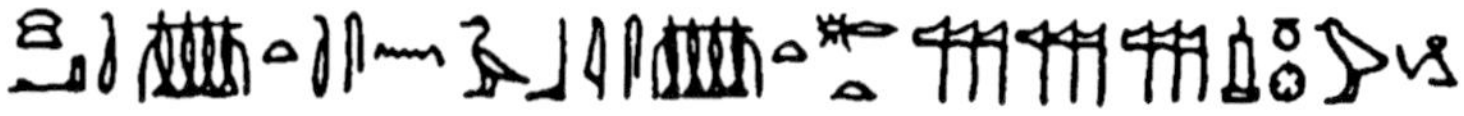 |
| §1920 a | (740)  a. Read 'to'. |
| §1920 b | (740) 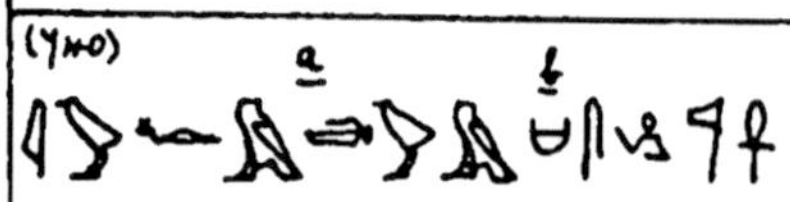 a JP II, 720. b. Nt facsimile has for as often. |
| §1920 c | 741 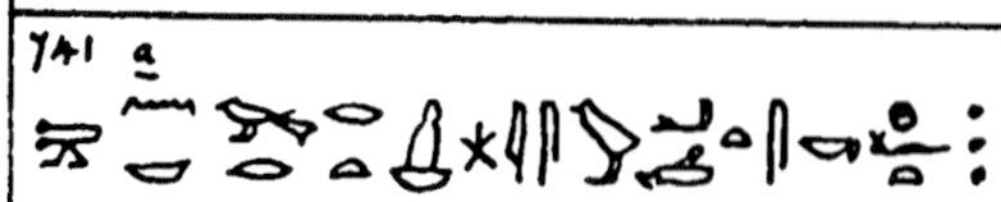 a. Read with JP II, 720. |
| §1920 d | (741) 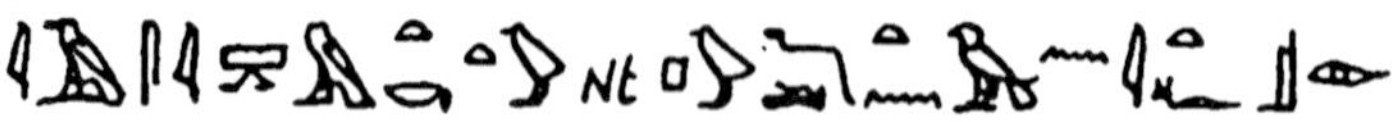 |

§ 1921a  

(742)

§ 1921b  

(742)

§ 1921c  

(742)

§ 1921d      *a. Dittograph.*

(742)

§ 1921e  

(743)

§ 1921f  

(743)

§ 1921g  

(743)

§ 1922a  

(744)

§ 1922b      *a. Cf. Neit, p. 27.*

(744)

§ 1922c  

(744)

§ 1923a

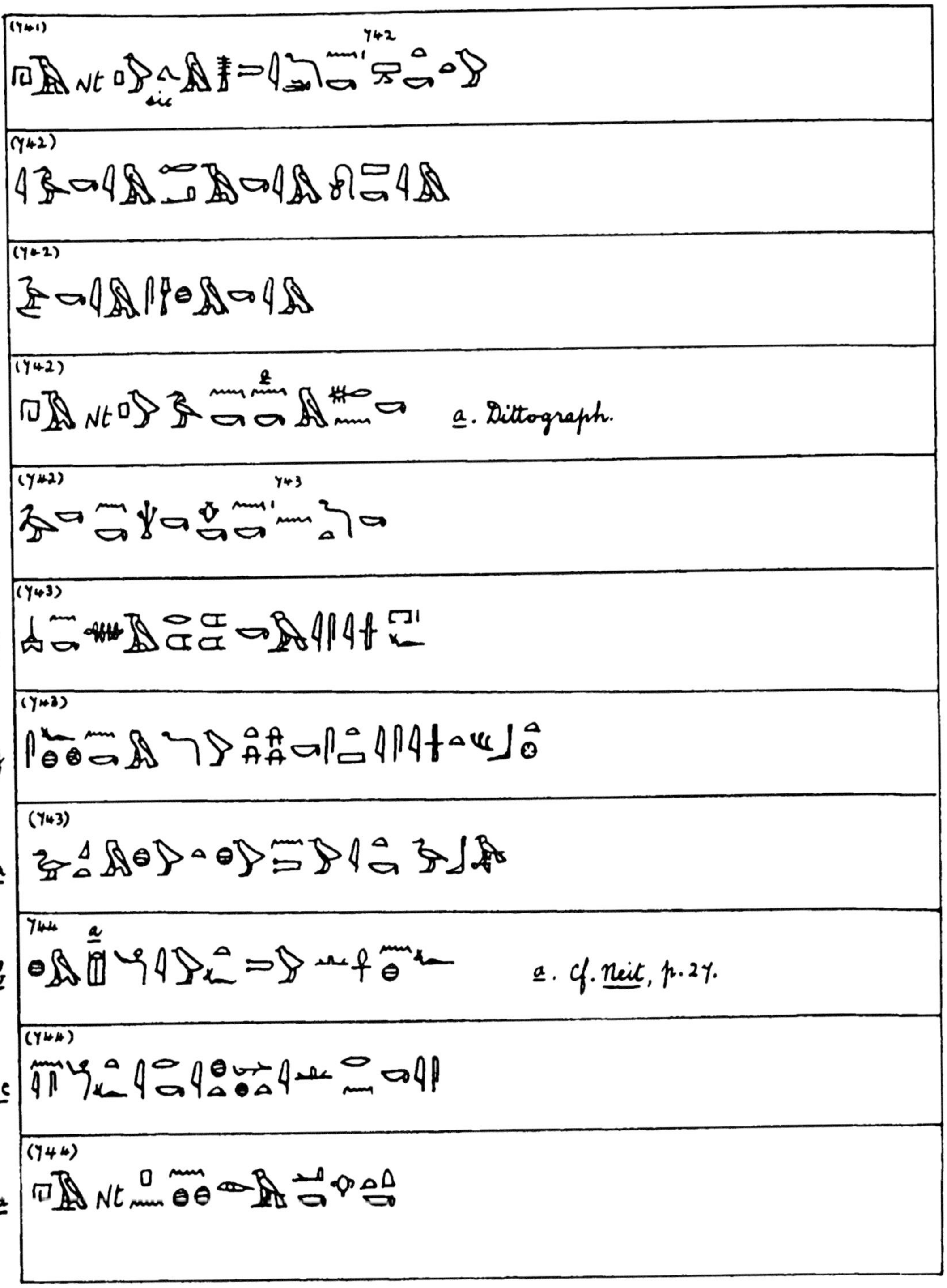

§1923 b — (744)

§1923 c — 745

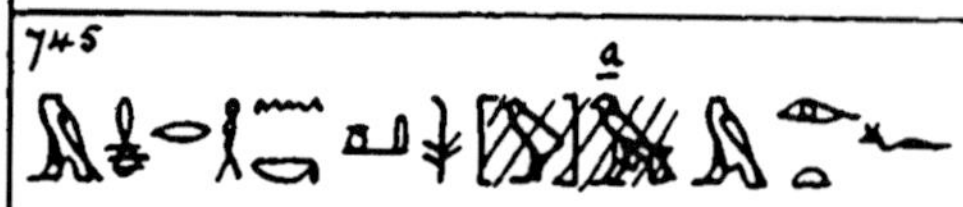

a. Trace of feet; cf. §1924 b.

§1924 a — (745)

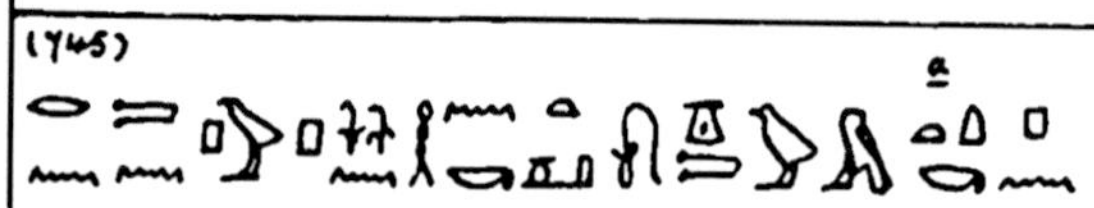

a. Nt facsimile ⌓ for ⌓.

§1924 b — (745)

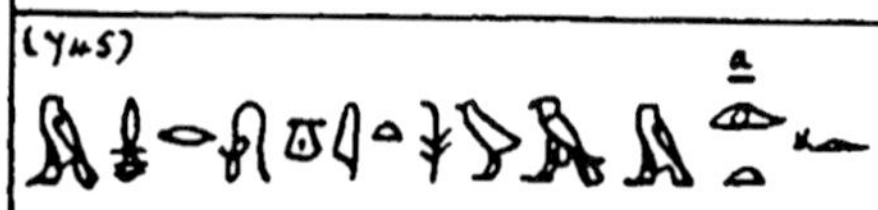

a Nt facsimile shows no pupil in the eye.

§1924 c — (745)

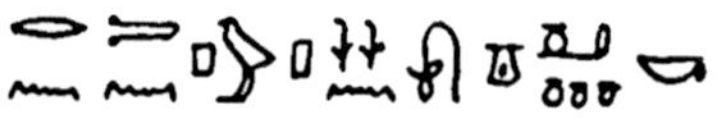

§1925 a — 746

§1925 b — (746)

§1925 c — (746)

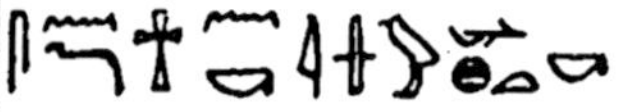

§1925 d — (746)

§1925 e — (746)

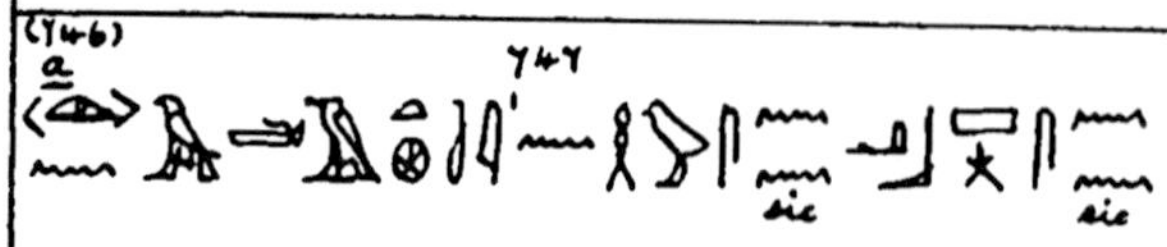

a ⌓ omitted by haplography.

§1925 f — (747)

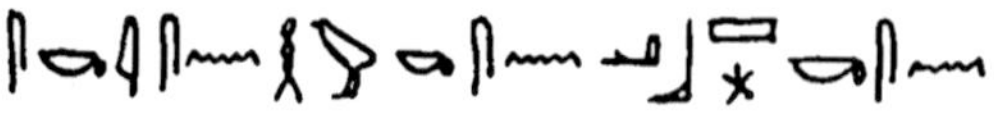

§1925 g (747)
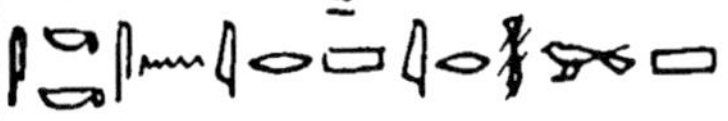
a. Error for .

§1926 a (747)
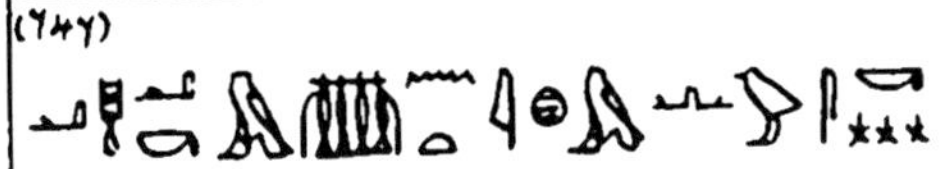

§1926 b 748

§1927 a (748) 749
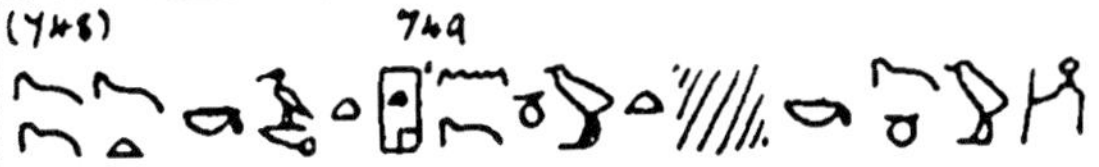

## Utt. 666 A.

Nt, 751–61; JP II, 724–6.

§1927 b (Nt 751) 752
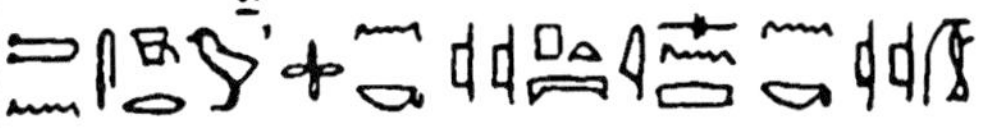
a. In N (Sethe) determined with three .

§1927 c (752)

a. Cf. Neit, p. 27.

§1927 d 753

a. Nt facsimile
b. Cf. Neit, p. 28.

§1927 e (753) 754
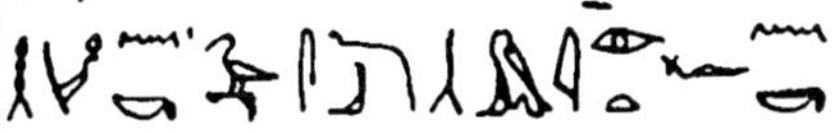
a. Cf. Neit, p. 28.

§1927 f (754)

§1928 a 755
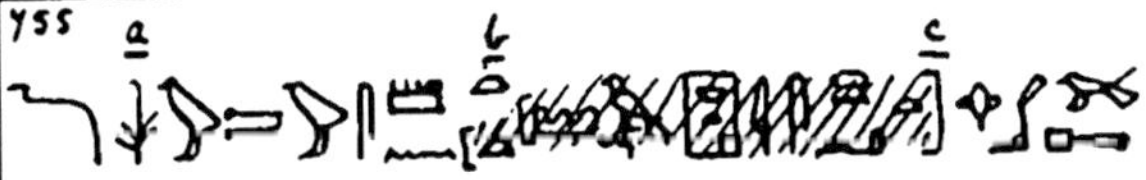
a. Cf. Neit, p. 28.
b–c. Cf. §§ 2232 d – 2233 a.

§1928 b
756

§1928 c
(756)
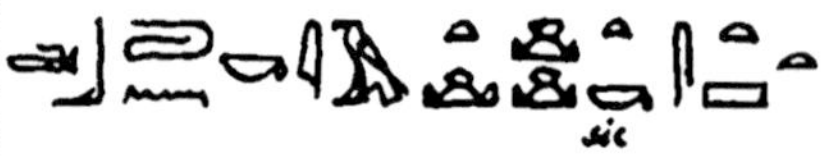
sic

§1928 d
757
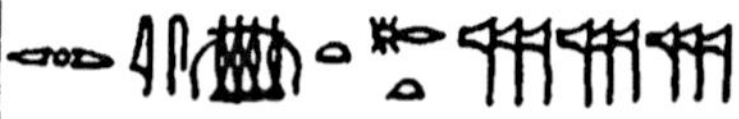

§1928 e
(757)
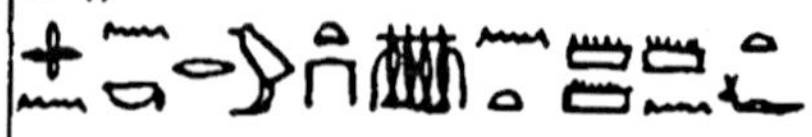

§1929 a
758
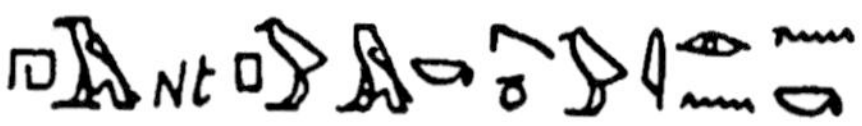

§1929 b
(758)
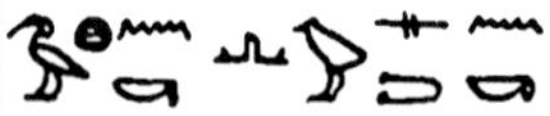

§1929 c
759
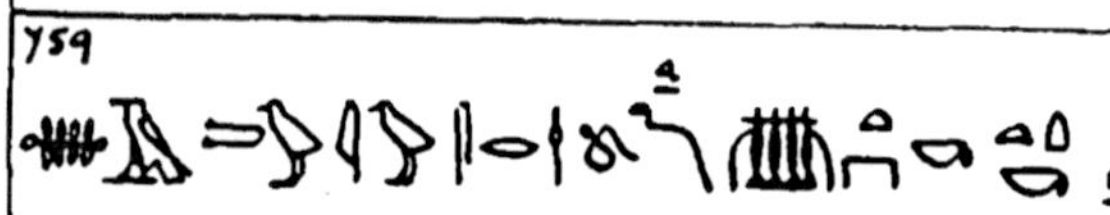
a. Nt facsimile ⌒.

§1929 d
760
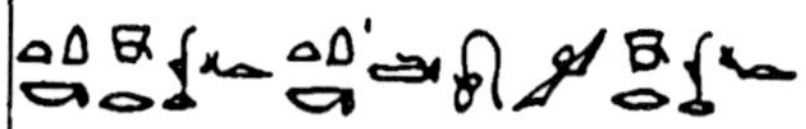

§1929 e
(760)
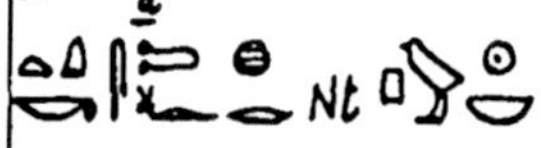
a. Read srf 'warm'.

§1930 a
761
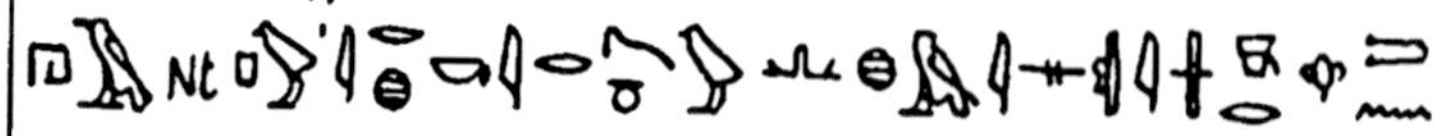

§1930 b
(761)
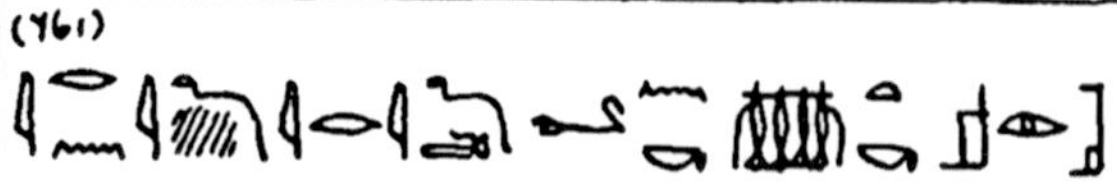

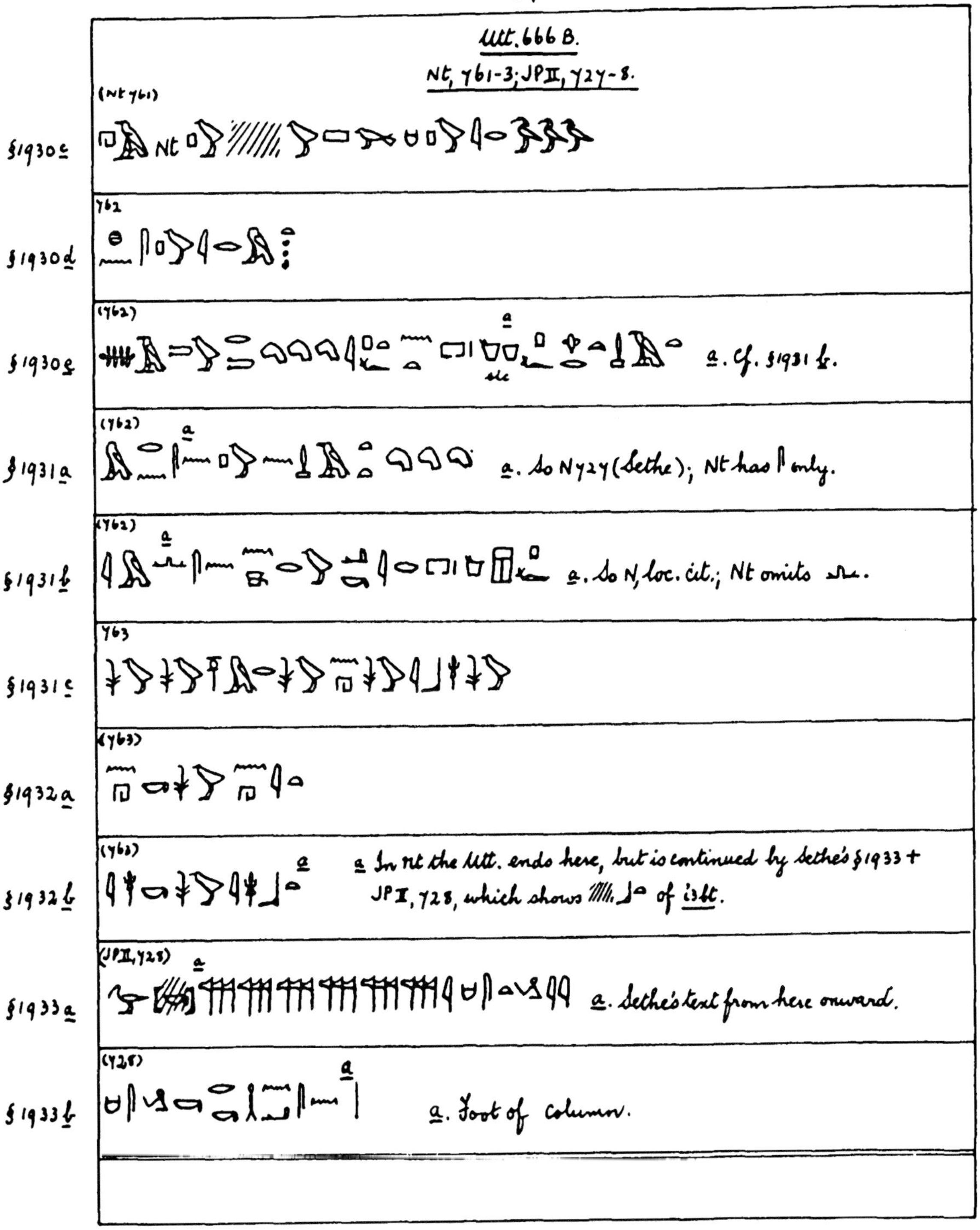

Utt. 666 B.
Nt, 761-3; JP II, 727-8.
(Nt 761)
§1930c
762
§1930d
(762)
§1930e
a. Cf. §1931 b.
(762)
§1931a
a. So N 727 (Sethe); Nt has only.
(762)
§1931b
a. So N, loc. cit.; Nt omits.
763
§1931c
(763)
§1932a
(763)
§1932b
a. In Nt the Utt. ends here, but is continued by Sethe's §1933 + JP II, 728, which shows of isbt.
(JP II, 728)
§1933a
a. Sethe's text from here onward.
(728)
§1933b
a. Foot of column.

## Utt. 667.

Nt, 763-75; JP II, 729-34.

(Nt, 763)

§1933c 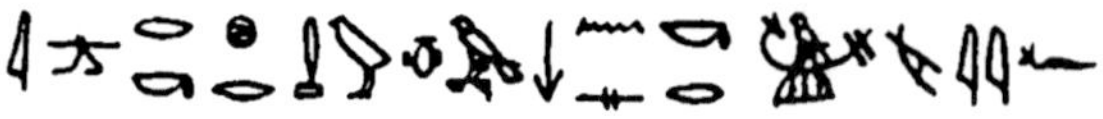

764

§1933d 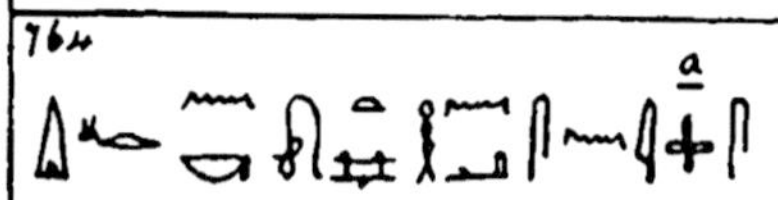

a *sic* Nt facsimile; JP II, 729, apparently starting the Utt. at this point.

(764)

§1933e 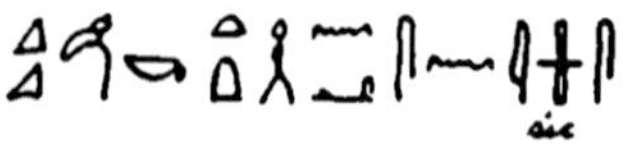

(764)

§1933f 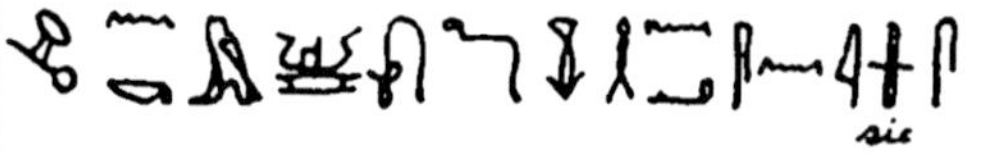

(764)

§1933g 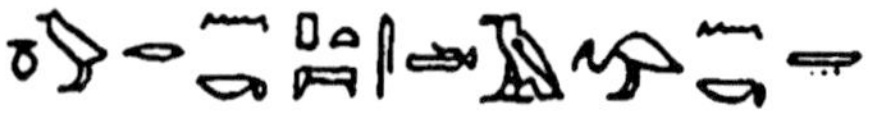

765

§1933h 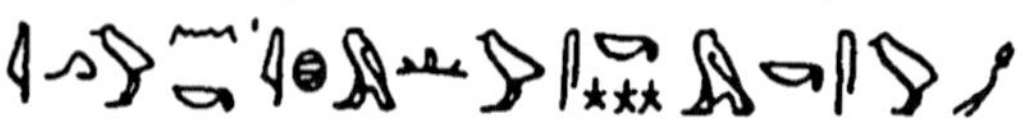

(765)

§1934a 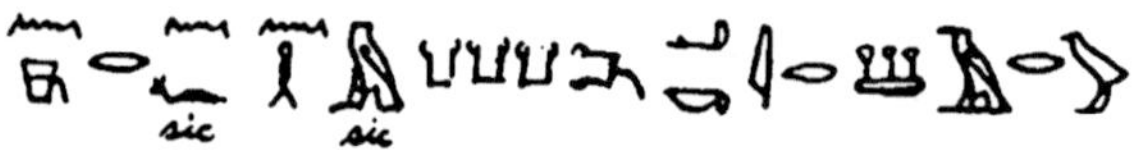

(765)

§1934b 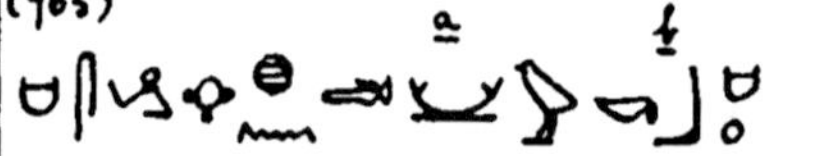

a. *sic* Nt facsimile; N (Sethe) has.
b. N (Sethe) inserts *fw*.

(765)

§1934c 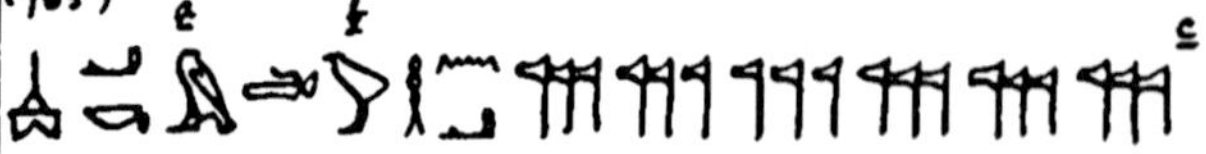

a-b. N (Sethe). c. At the end of N 729 (Sethe, §1934d) appears, superfluous and apparently partly erased.

766

§1934d 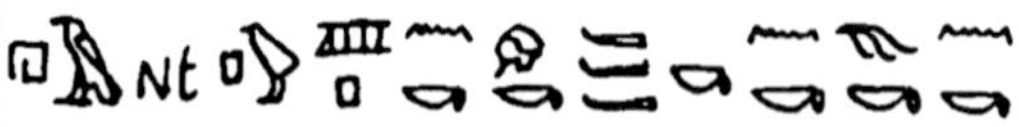

| | |
|---|---|
| §1934e | (766) [hieroglyphs] |
| §1935a | (766) [hieroglyphs] Nt [hieroglyphs] |
| §1935b | (766) [hieroglyphs] |
| §1935c | 767 [hieroglyphs] sic [hieroglyphs] xxx |
| §1936a | (767) [hieroglyphs] |
| §1936b | (767) [hieroglyphs] a. [hieroglyphs] 768 [hieroglyphs]    a. For [hieroglyphs] gm? |
| §1936c | (768) [hieroglyphs] |
| §1936d | (768) [hieroglyphs] |
| §1936e | (768) [hieroglyphs] sic [hieroglyphs] |
| §1936f | [hieroglyphs] 769 [hieroglyphs] |
| §1937 | (769) [hieroglyphs] Nt [hieroglyphs] |

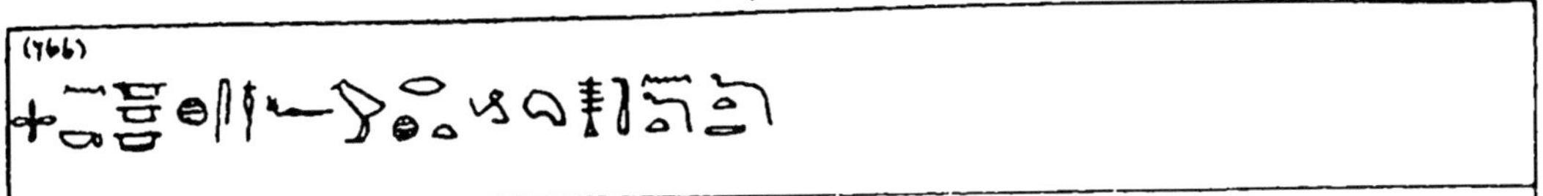

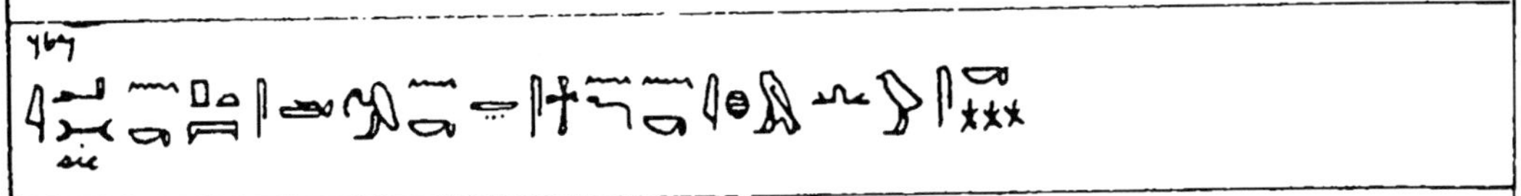

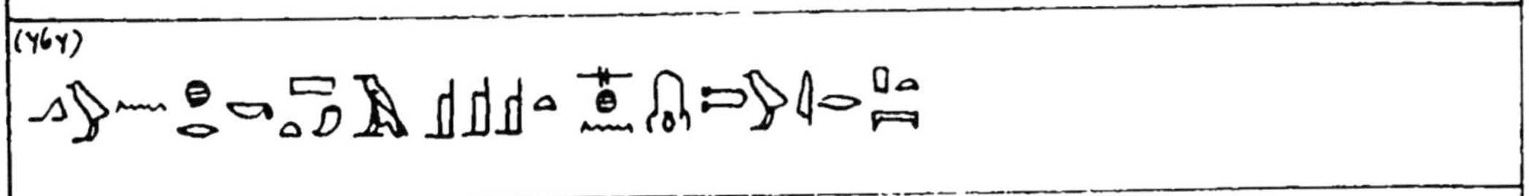

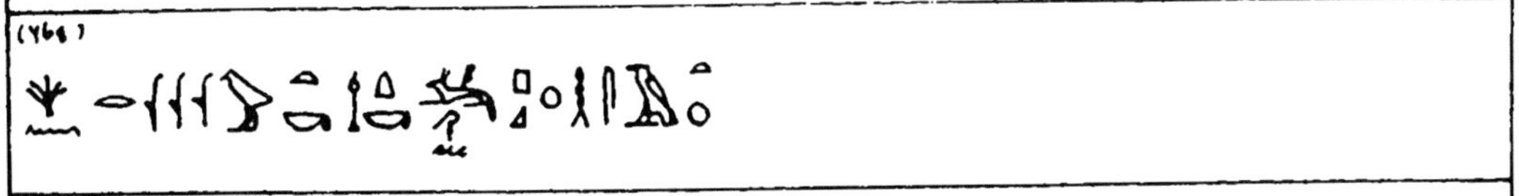

| | | |
|---|---|---|
| §1938a | (769) 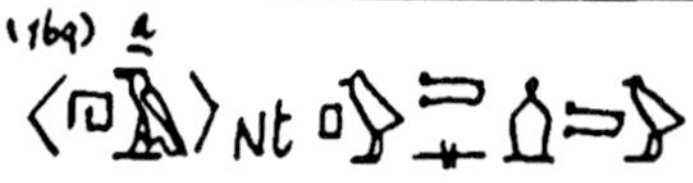 | a. Ḥ3 supplied from N (Sethe). |
| §1938b | (769) 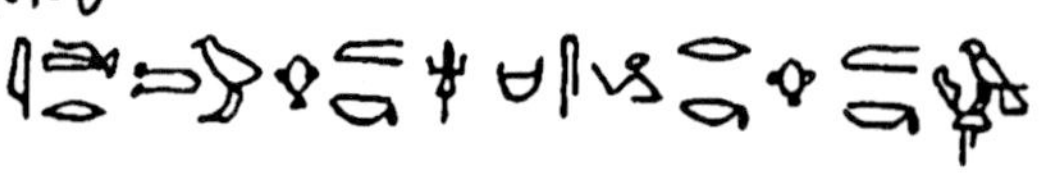 | |
| §1938c | (769)  | a. Nt facsimile □ as often. |
| §1938d | 770 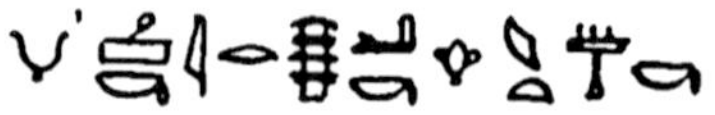 | |
| §1939a | (770) 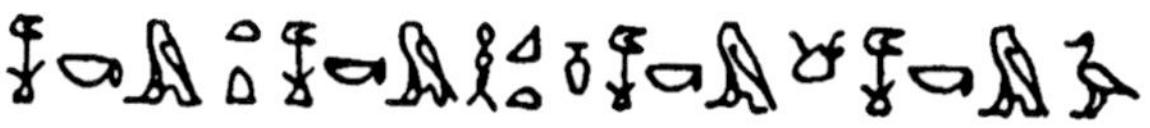 | |
| §1939b | (770) 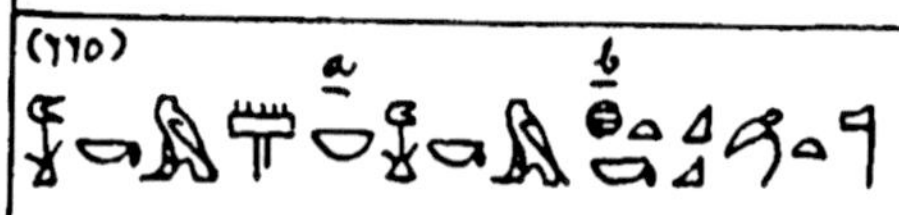 | a Read šs 'alabaster'? b. Read ḫt nb(t). |
| §1939c | (770) 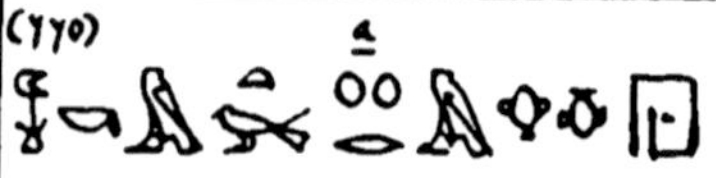 | a. Read twr (det. o) ḥr<·i>? |
| §1939d | 771 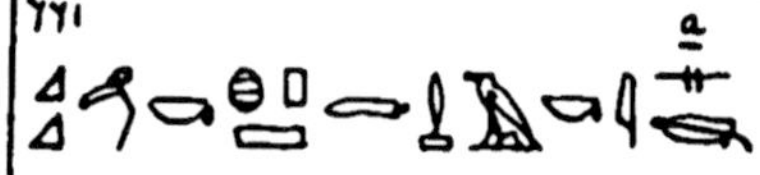 | a. Sic; N (Sethe) has 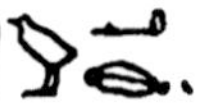. |
| §1939e | (771) 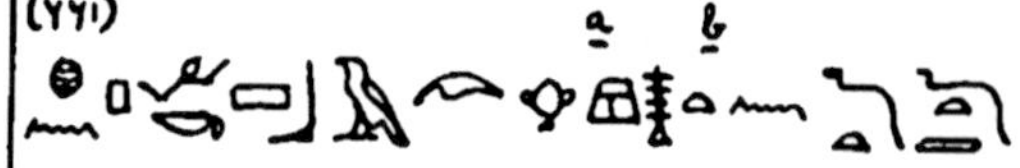 | a-b. Sic; JP II, 733 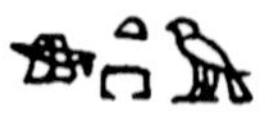. |
| §1940a | (771)  | a. ·k supplied from JP II, 733. |
| §1940b | (771)  | a. Cf. Neit, p. 28, but ·k in m.k should be retained. |

§1940c (772)
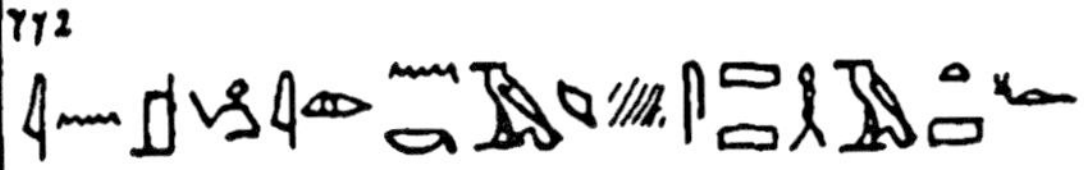

§1940d (772)
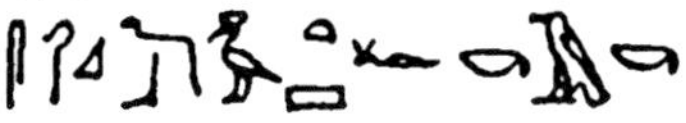

§1940e (772)

a. Cf. Neit, p. 28.

§1941a (772) 773

§1941b (773)
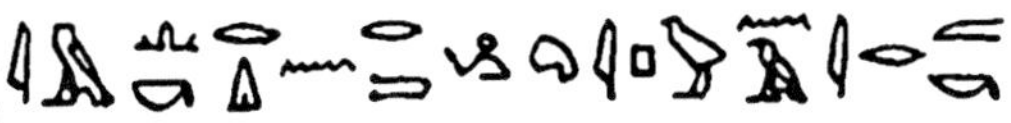

§1941c (773)

a. Cf. Neit, p. 28

§1941d (773) 774

a. Cf. Neit, p. 28.

§1941e (774)

§1942a (774)

§1942b 775
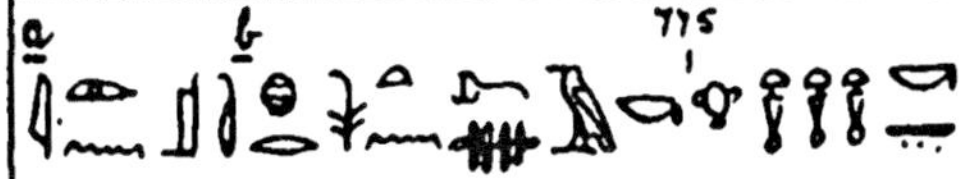
a-b. N(Sethe): ir-n N sti·f; read ir‹·i› n‹·k› sti.

§1942c (775)

## Utt. 667A.

Nt, 775-82; 485-91; JPII, 735-9.

(Nt, 775)

§1943 a 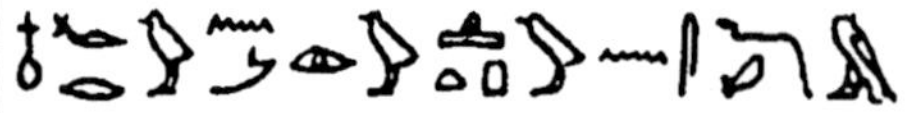

(775)

§1943 b 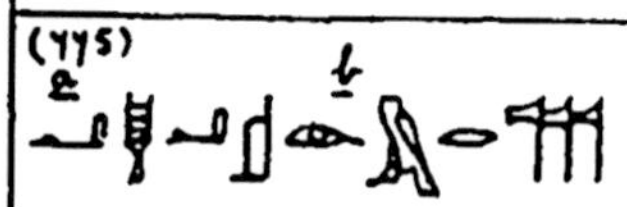 a-b. JPII, 735 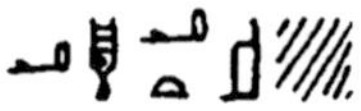

(775)

§1943 c 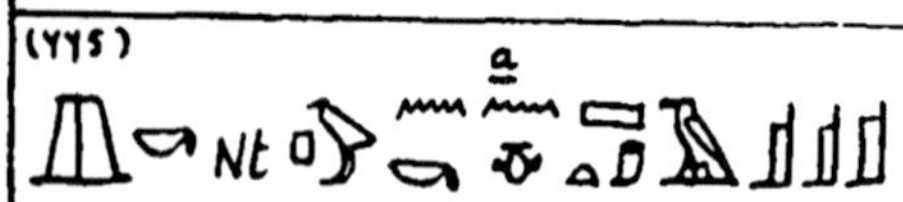 a. Reading confirmed by Nt, 485.

776

§1943 d 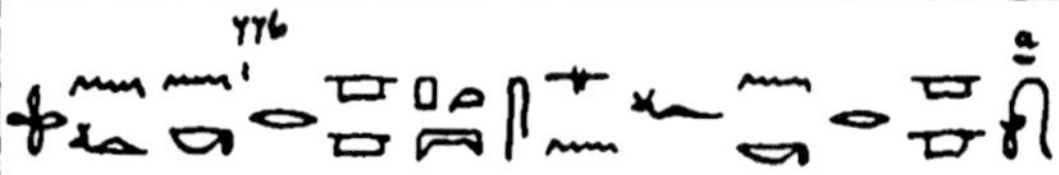 a. Sic; perhaps an error for . The parallel texts are lost.

(776)

§1943 e 

(776)

§1943 f 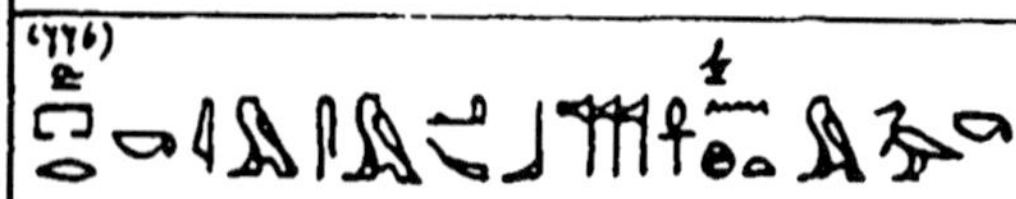 a Sethe (his §1943 f) 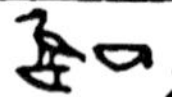. b. Neit, p. 28, Sethe; Nt, 485 .

(776)

§1944 a  a. Nt, 486 omits is.

(776) 777

§1944 b 

(777)

§1944 c 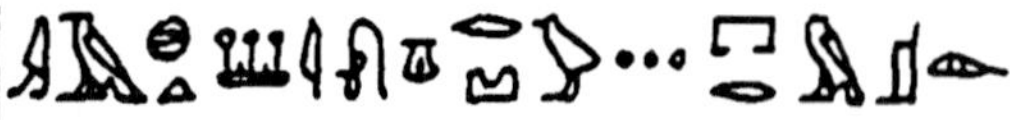

(777)

§1944 d 

(777) 778

§1945a 

(778)

§1945b 

(778)

§1945c 

(778) 779

§1945d 

a. Nt, 487.
b. Loc. cit.
c. loc. cit., JP II, 737.

(779)

§1945e 

a. Cf. Neit, p. 28.

(779)

§1945f 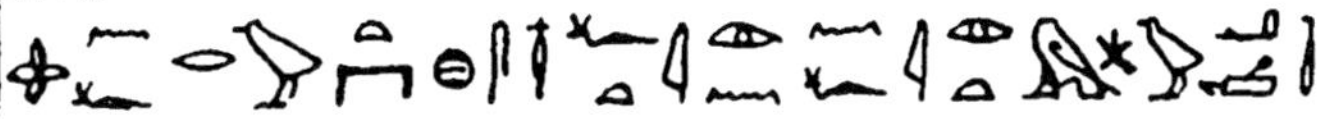

(779)

§1945g 

a-b. JP II, 737.
c. A dot, probably fortuitous, after in facsimile of Nt, 779.

780

§1946a 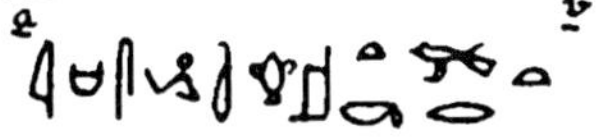

a-b. JP II, 737 ---; Sethe seems to have taken to be the base of . Nt, 488-9 has sic! sic.

(780)

§1946b 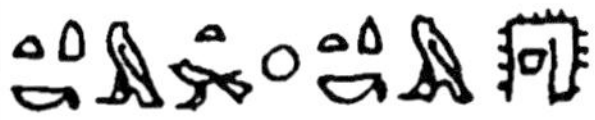

(780)

§1947a 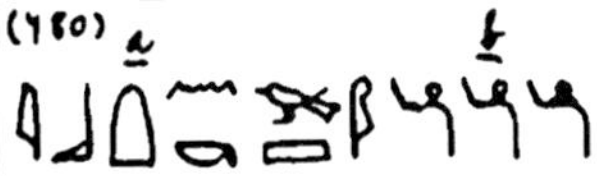

a. Nt, 489 dets. ; N (Sethe) dets. .
b. N (Sethe) dets. .

| § | Text | Notes |
|---|---|---|
| §1947 b | (780) | a. Sic Nt, 780 facsimile; emend into [hieroglyphs]. |
| §1947 c | (780) Nt | a-b. Cf. Neit, p. 28. |
| §1947 d | 781 | a-b. Nt, 490 has the meaningless [hieroglyphs]. |
| §1947 e | (781) sic | |
| §1947 f | (781) | a. Nt, 490 [hieroglyphs].<br>b. Loc. cit. det. [hieroglyphs].<br>c. Sic; JP II, 738 [hieroglyphs]. |
| §1948 a | (781) Nt | a-b. Reading and det. supplied from N (Sethe) and Nt, 490. |
| §1948 b | (781) 782 | a. Facsimile Nt, 782 [hieroglyphs]; Sethe [hieroglyphs]; Nt, 490 [hieroglyphs]. |
| §1948 c | (782) | a. N (Sethe) det. [hieroglyphs]; Nt, 491 [hieroglyphs].<br>b-c. N (Sethe) [hieroglyphs]; Nt, 491 [hieroglyphs]. |
| §1948 d | (782) | a. Sic; Nt, 491 [hieroglyphs]; JP II, 739 [hieroglyphs]. |
| §1948 e | (782) | a-b. Nt, 491 [hieroglyphs] sic. |
| §1948 f | (782) | a. Nt, 491 adds the epithet [hieroglyphs]. There is no [hieroglyphs]. |

## Utt. 667B.

Nt, 783-5; JP II, 739-40

| § | Text | Notes |
|---|---|---|
| §1949 a | Nt, 783 | a-b. Sic facsimile; read ŝt3 as JP II, 739. |
| §1949 b | (783) | a-b. N (Sethe) |
| §1950 a | (783) | a. Sic facsimile; N (Sethe) |
| §1950 b | (783) | |
| §1950 c | (783) Nt 784 | a-b. Sic facsimile; read probably … for hms. c. … = wi. |
| §1950 d | (784) | |
| §1950 e | (784) | |
| §1950 f | (784) sic | a-b. JP II, 740 |
| §1951 a | 785 | a. Sic facsimile, read …: JP II, 740. b. N (Sethe) |
| §1951 b | (785) | a. No stanza mark, but a different topic follows. |

Utt. 667C.

Nt, 785-7; JPII, 740-2.

(Nt, 785)

§1952a    [hieroglyphs] Nt [hieroglyphs]    a. N (Sethe) inserts [hieroglyphs].

§1952b    [hieroglyphs] sic   786 Nt [hieroglyphs]

(786)

§1952c    [hieroglyphs] ?    a-b. JPII, 741 [hieroglyphs].

(786)

§1952d    sic [hieroglyphs]    a. Nt facsimile [hieroglyphs].   b. Facsimile [hieroglyphs].

(786)

§1952e    [hieroglyphs]    a-b. JPII, 741 [hieroglyphs].

§1953a    787 [hieroglyphs] sic [hieroglyphs] ? ?   d [hieroglyphs]

a-b. JPII, 741 + Sethe: [hieroglyphs].    c-d. Not in JPII.

(787)

§1953b    [hieroglyphs]   a-b. N (Sethe) [hieroglyphs]; cf. §1955.

(787)

§1954a    [hieroglyphs] Nt [hieroglyphs]

(787)

§1954b    a [hieroglyphs] sic [hieroglyphs] sic [hieroglyphs] b

a-b. Read ỉn ỉf n dr·n·ṯn n shr·n·ṯn, cf. §1953b (N); §1955b. The object znbwt of the verbs has been omitted; Neit, p. 23 notes that the end is indistinct.

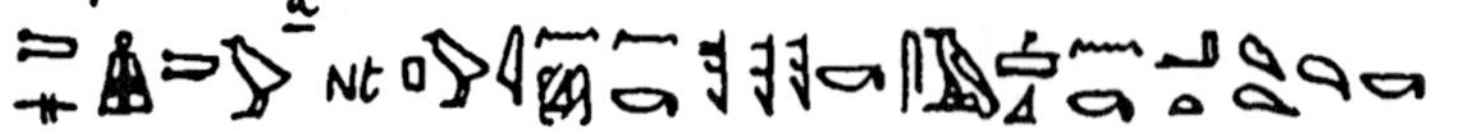

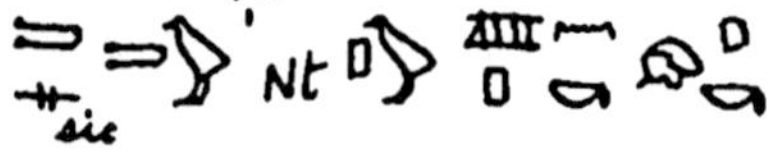

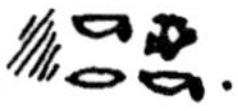

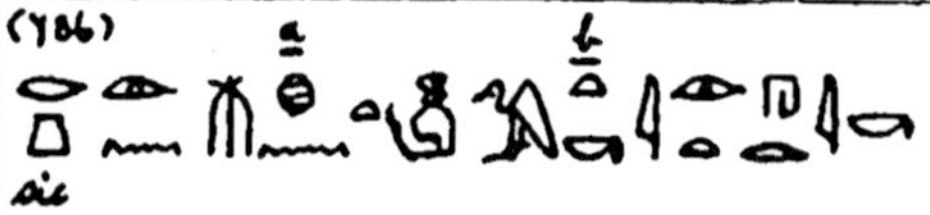

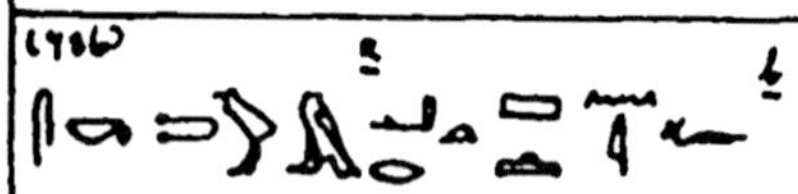

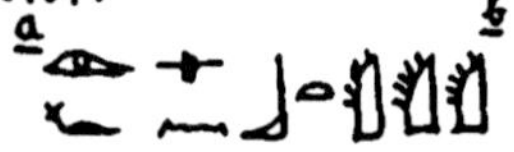

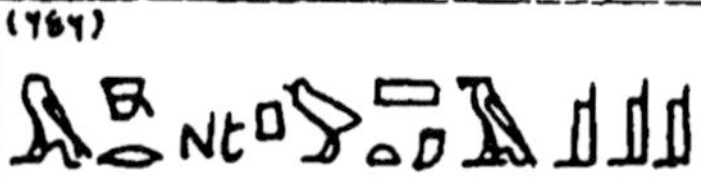

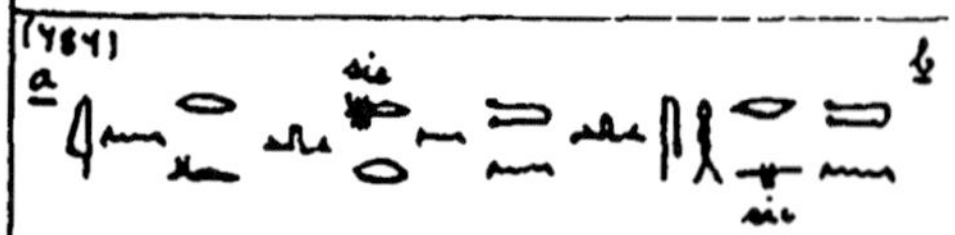

§1955a JPII, 742 [a]
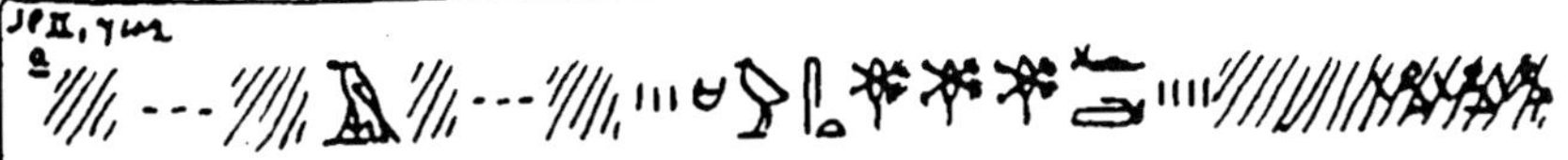
a. From here on only in N+JPII.

§1955b (742)
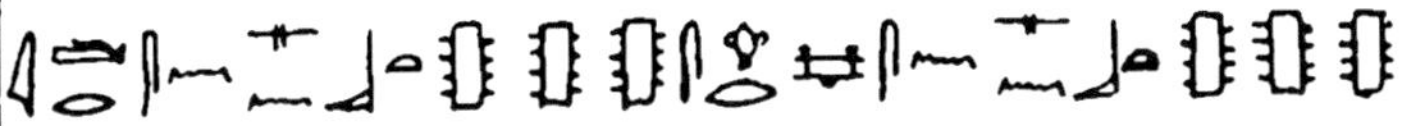

§1955c (742)
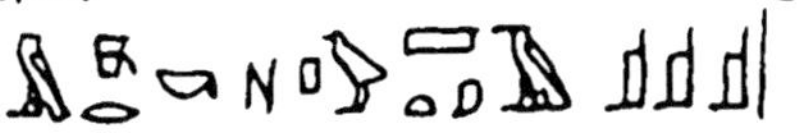
a. Foot of column. Utt. 667C may have ended; after the lacuna of half a column in JPII, 742 is a different text, see Utt. 667D.

## Utt. 667D.
### JPII, 743-4.

§§1956-57a (JPII, 743)

§1957a (743)

§1957c (743)

§1958a 744

§1958b (744)
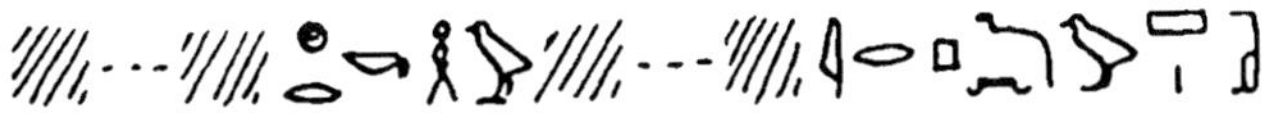

## Utt. 668.
### JPII, 749-50

§1959a (JPII, 749) 750

sic

§1959 b (750)

§1960 a (750)

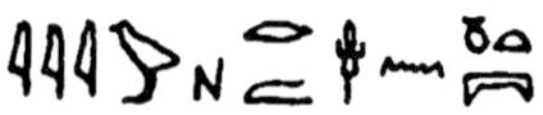

§1960 b (750)

## Utt. 669.

JP II, 754-9.

§1961 a (754)

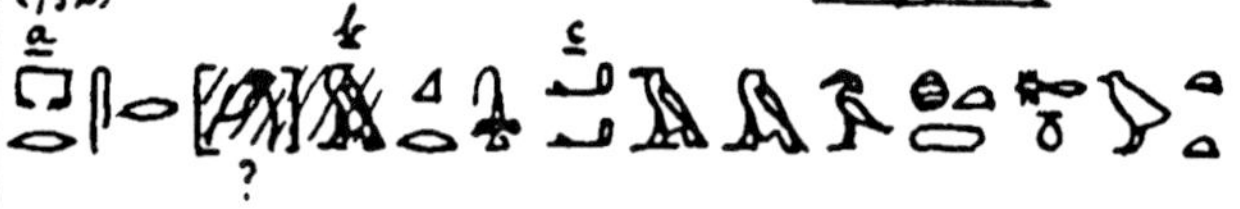

a. Sethe's restoration is to be discarded. b. Facsimile …, but only the legs and the lower part of the body are preserved. c. Sic facsimile; read … or ….

§1961 b (754)

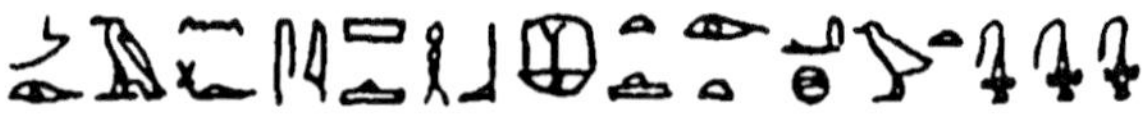

§1961 c (754)

§1961 d (754)

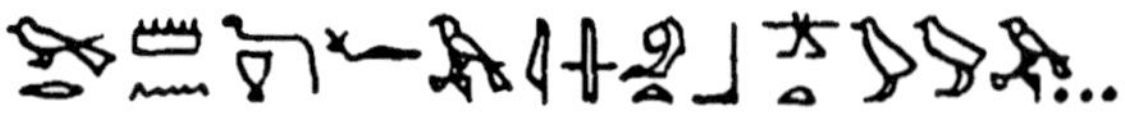

§1962 a (755)

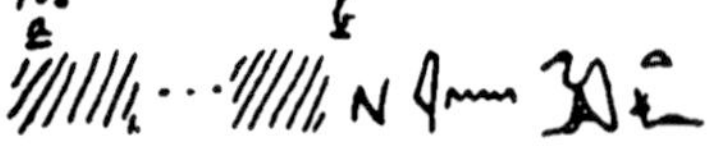

a-b. About 1/4 column is lost.

§1962 b (755)

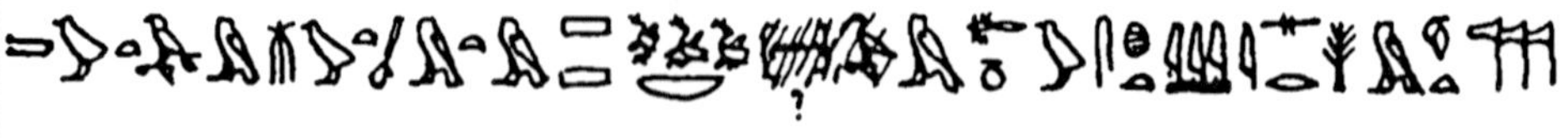

§1963a (455)

§1963b (455)

§1964a 456 a ... b

a-b. 1/4 column. Sethe has placed in the lacuna a fragment with nt N, but nt is not in JP II.

§1964b (456)

§1964c (456)
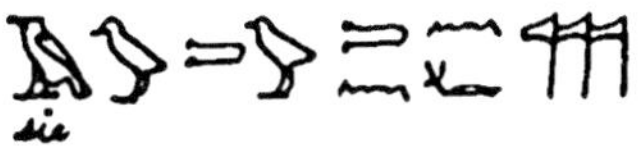

§1964d (456)
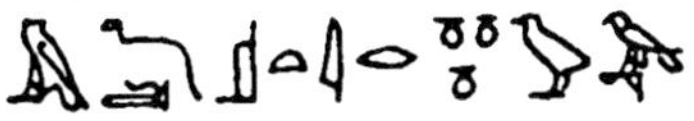

§1965a (456)

§1965b (456)

§1965c (456)

§1966a 457

§1966b (457)

(Y57)
§1966c 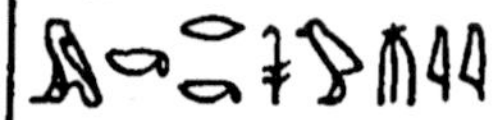

(Y57)
§1966d 

(Y57)
§1967 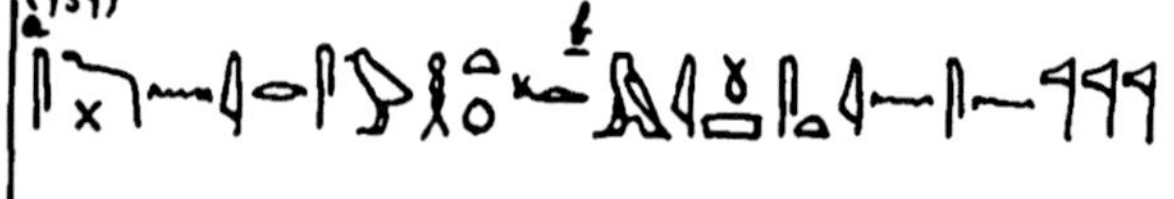 a-b. Read sḏ·n ỉr⟨·n⟩ swḥt·f

(Y57)
§1968a 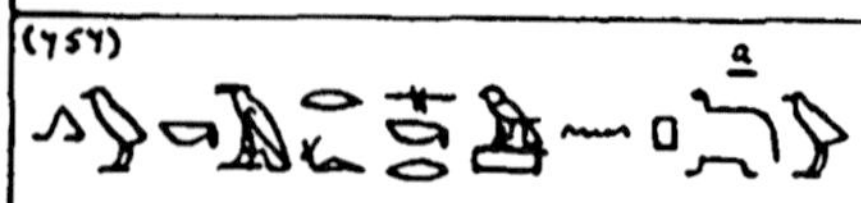 a. Read pḏw-{š} cult-centre of Sokar.

(Y57)
§1968b 

758
§1968c 

(Y58)
§1968d 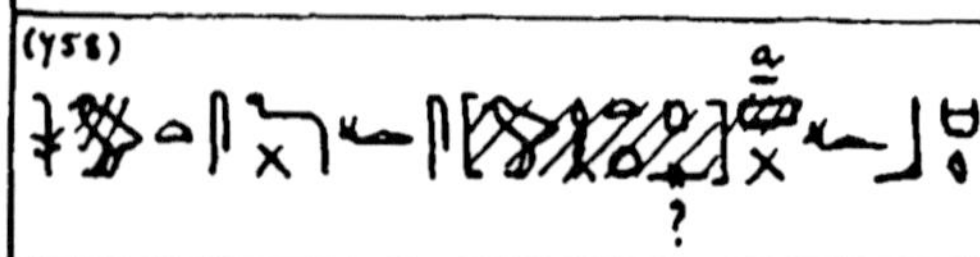 a. Sethe , which seems unlikely.

(Y58)
§1969a 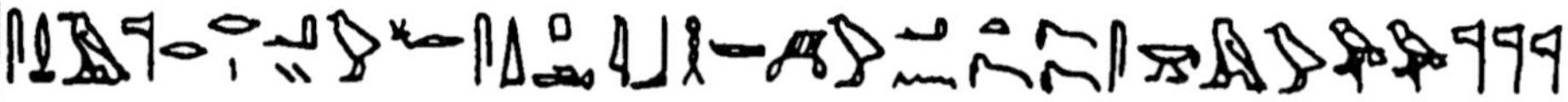

(Y58)
§1969b 

(Y58)
§1969c 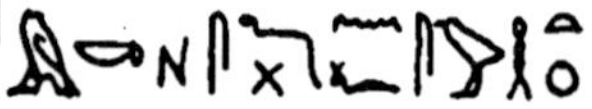

(Y58)
§1970a 

759

§1970b  a. Facsimile ////.

(759)

§1970c 

(759)

§1970d 

(759)

§1971 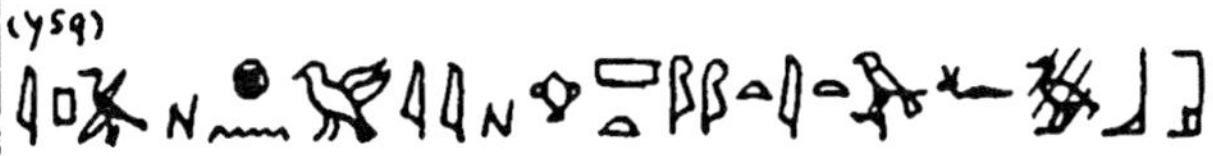

Utt. 691.

Nt, 819-26; JP II, 1002-7.

Nt, 819

§2120a 

(819) a b

§2120b  a-b. N (Sethe) .

820 a

§2120c  a. N (Sethe) .

(820)

§2121a  Nt

821

§2121b 

(821)

§2121c 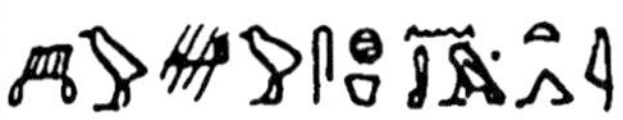

| § | Text |
| --- | --- |
| §2122a | (821)  |
| §2122b | 822 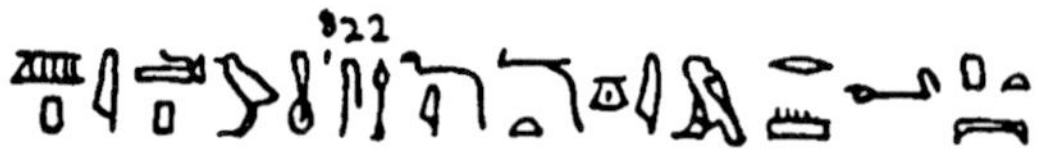 |
| §2122c | (822)  |
| §2122d | (822) a b 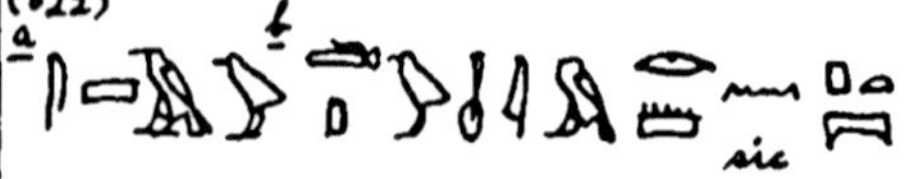 sic a-b. N(Sethe) . |
| §2123a | 823 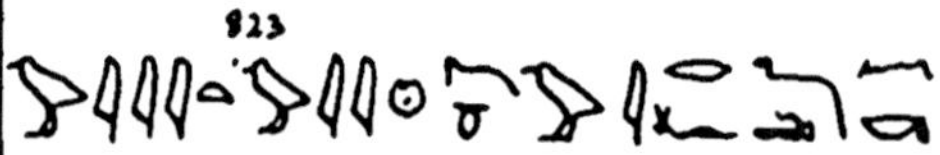 |
| §2123b | (823) a  a. b3-bird without breast-tuft. |
| §2123c | (823) 824 a 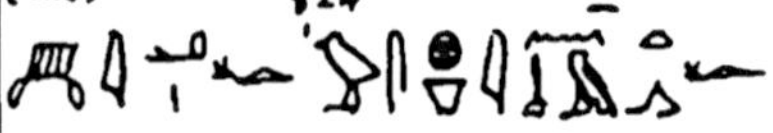 a. N(Sethe) 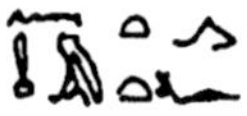 |
| §2124a | (824)  Nt |
| §2124b | (824) a 825 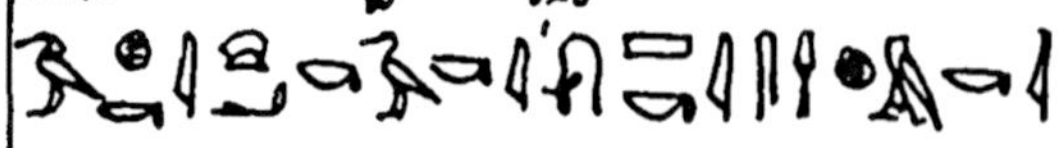 a. b3-bird without breast-tuft. |
| §2125a | (825)  |
| §2125b | (825) 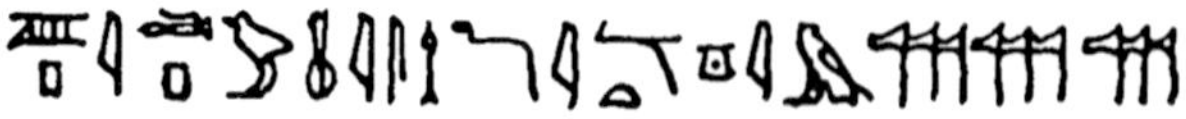 |

§2125c 826
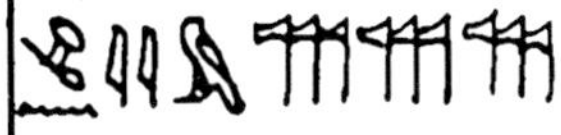

§2125d (826)
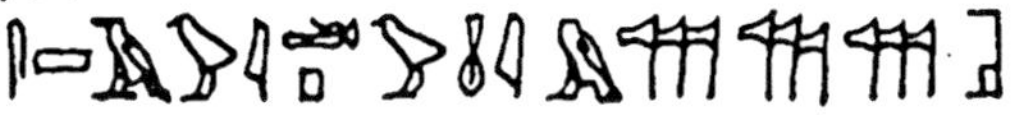

## Utt. 691A.

Nt, 826-30; JP II, 1008-9.

§2126a (Nt, 826) 827

sic

§2126b (827)
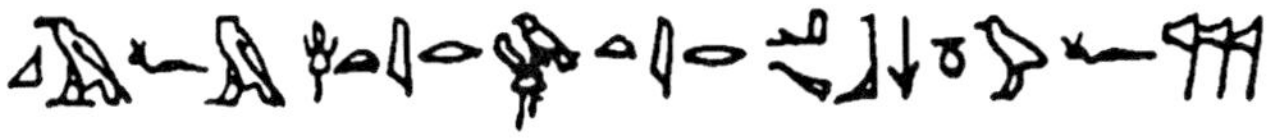

§2126c (827) 828
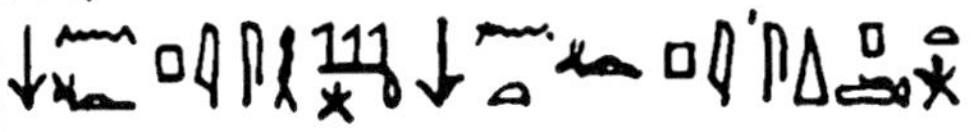

§2126d (828)

a. cf. §2126h.

§2126e (828) 829
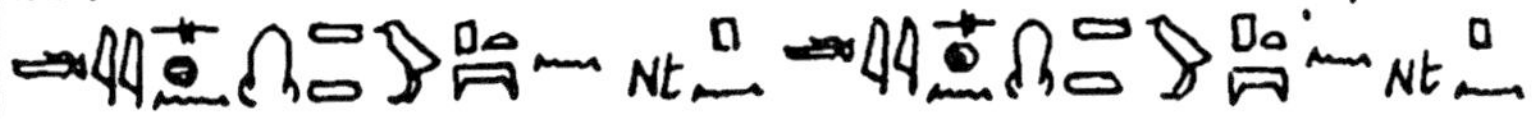

§2126f (829)
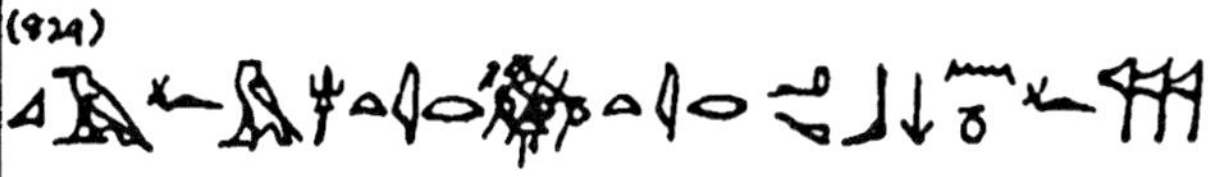

§2126g (829)
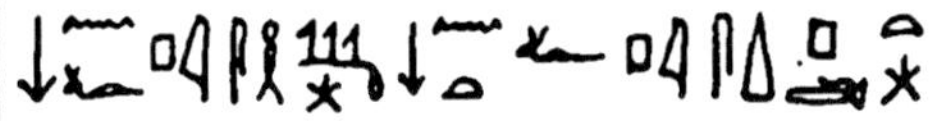

§2126h 830

a. Nt facsimile ].

Utt. 691B.

Nt, 830-5; JP II, 1009-11.

(Nt, 830)

§2127a 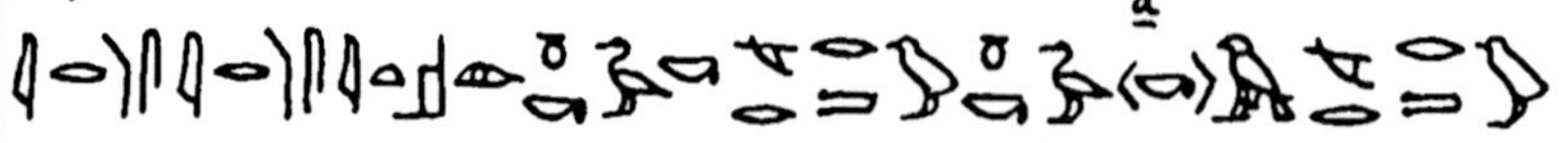 a. (·k) omitted.

831

§2127b 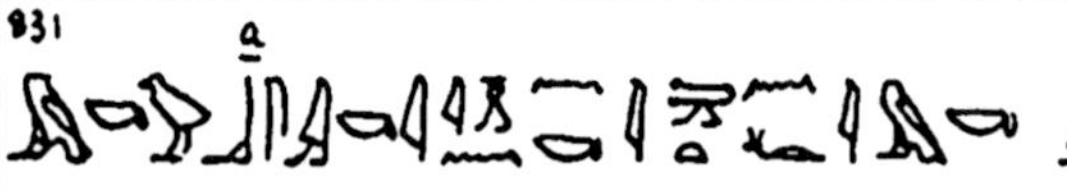 a. Sic Nt facsimile; read is?

(831)

§2127c 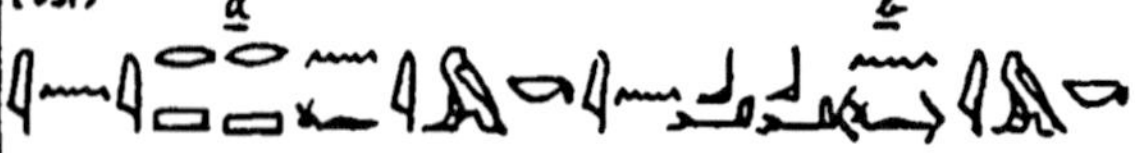

a. For ršrš cf. N (Sethe, his §2127b); Nt facsimile [hieroglyphs]. b. (·f) omitted.

832

§2127d 

(832)

§2127e  a. Sic Nt facsimile; read snty.

833

§2127f 

(833)

§2127g 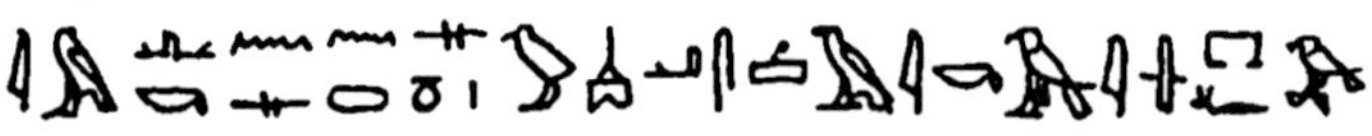

834

§2128a 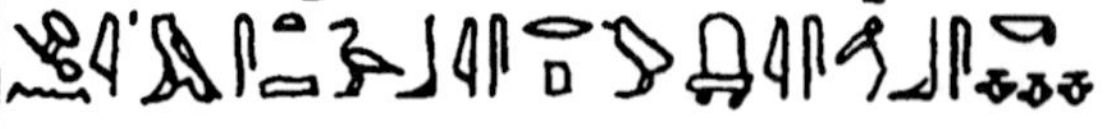 a. Sic Nt. b. Sic; read wnm as JP II, 1010 ([hieroglyphs]).

(834)

§2128b 

835

§2128c 

(835)

§2128b 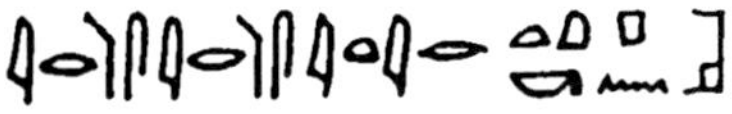

## Utt. 691C

### JP II, 1011–1016 + 2.

a very fragmentary text; there remains a doubt whether all the fragments are correctly placed.

(JP II, 1011) ? 1012

§2129a 

(1012)

§2129b 

(1012) 1013

§2130a 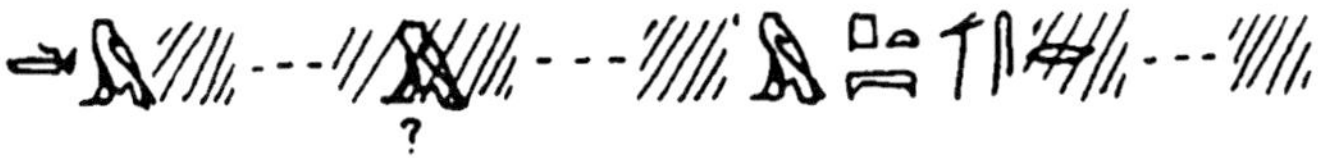

(1013)

§2130b 

(1013)

§2131a 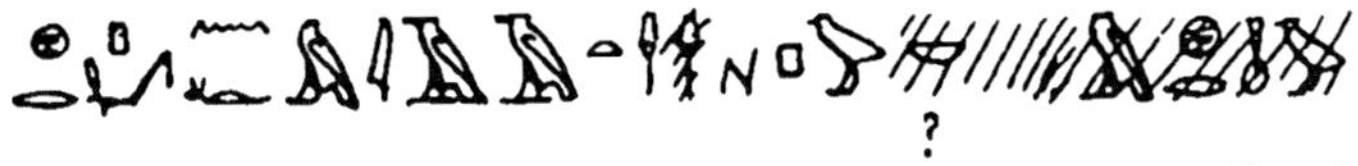

(1013) 1014

§2131b 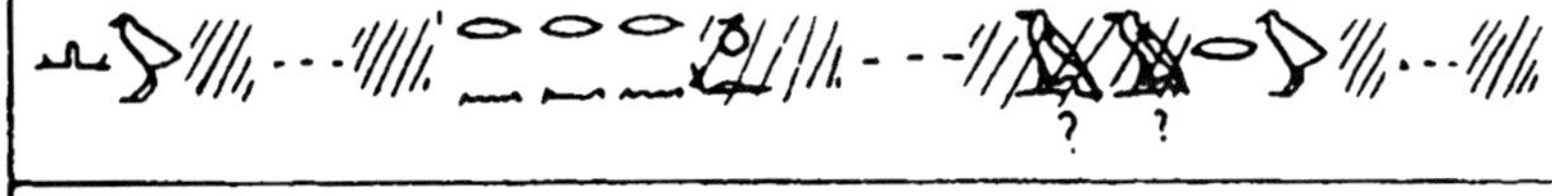

(1014)

§2132a 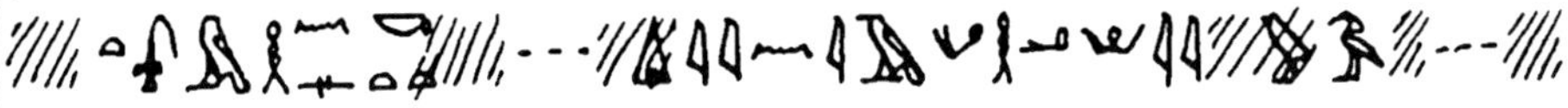

1015

§2132b 

§2133 a
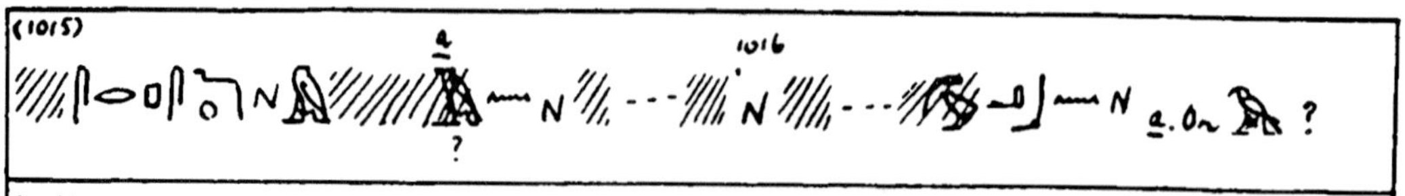


§2133 b

§2134 a
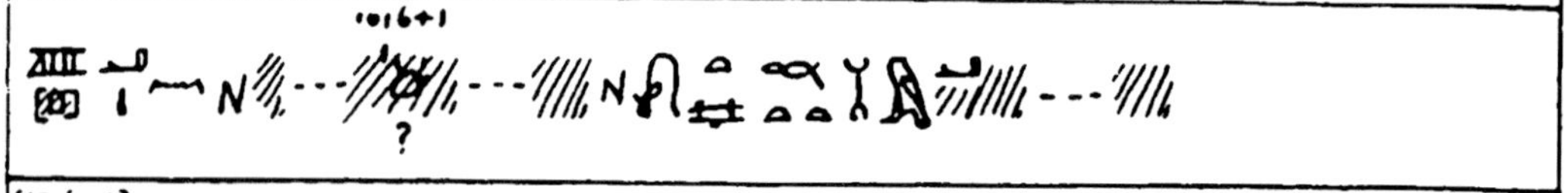


§2134 b
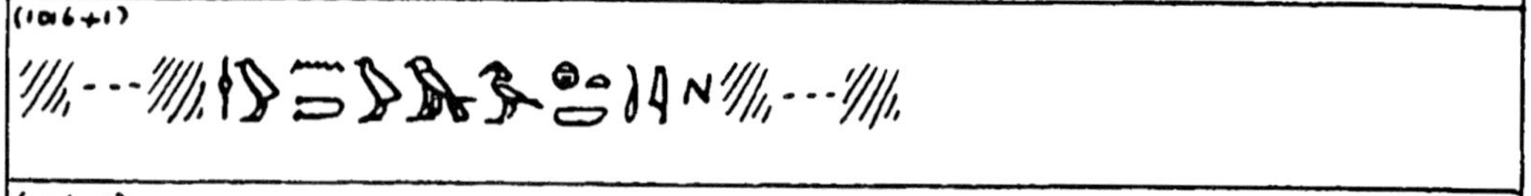


§2135 a

§2135 b
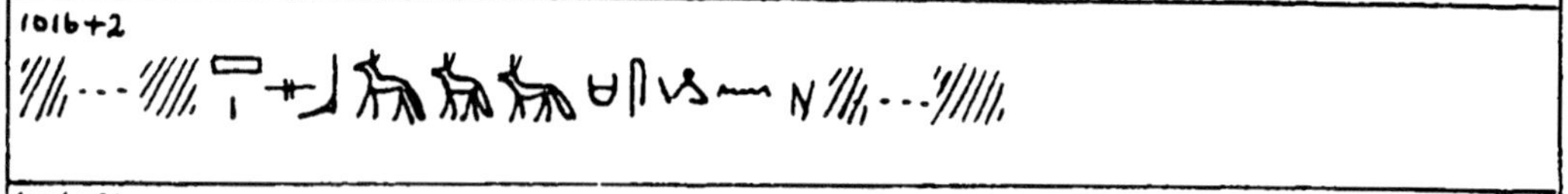


§2135 c

## Utt. 692.

JP II, 1016+2-5.

§2136 a
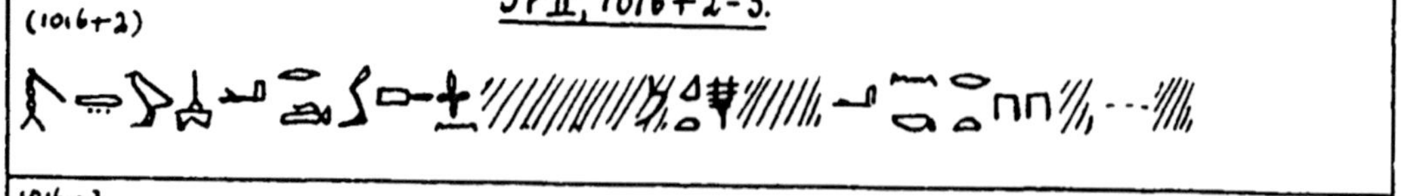


§2136 b
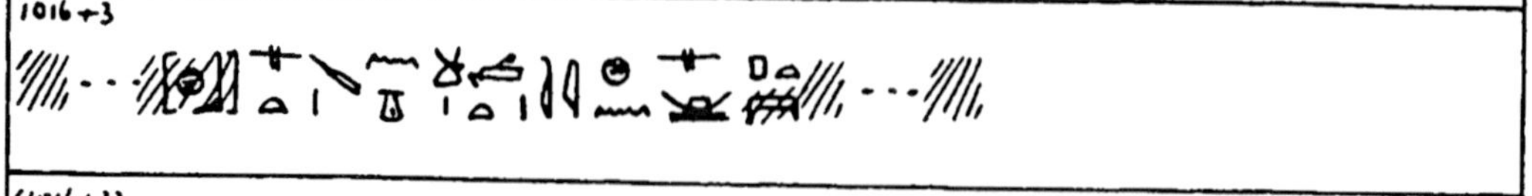


§2136 c
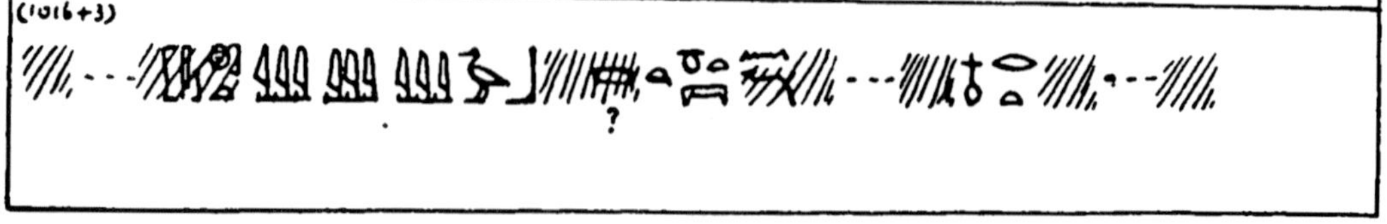

(1016+3)

§2136d 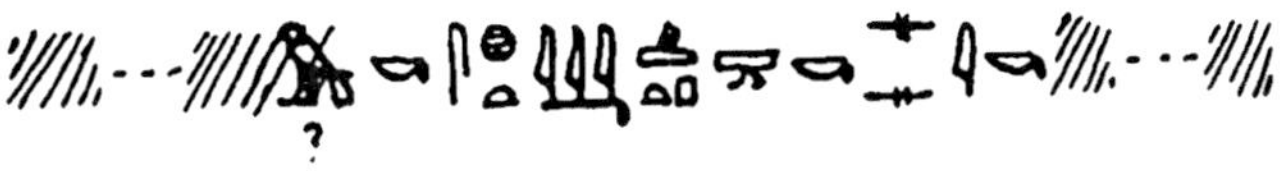

1016+4

§2136e 

(1016+4)

§2136f 

1016+5

§2137a 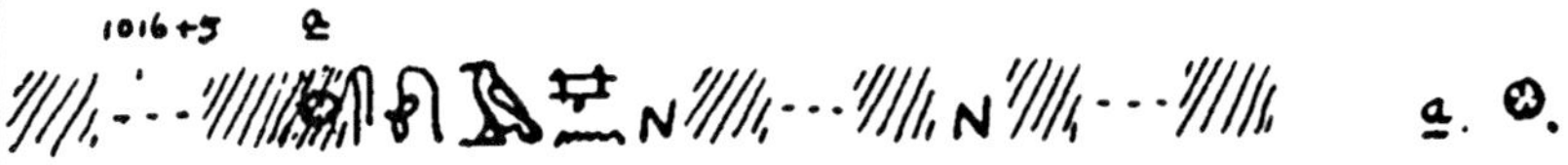

(1016+5)

§2137b 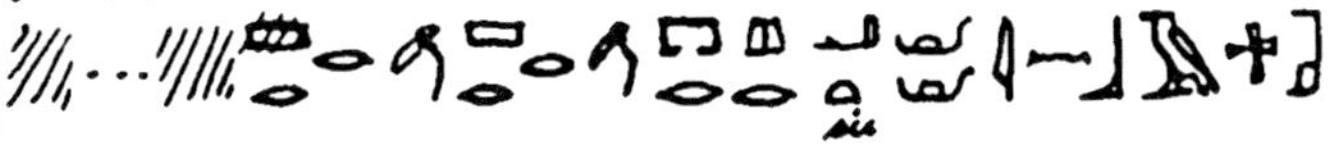

## Utt. 692A.
JP II, 1016+5-7.

(JP II, 1016+5) 1016+6

§2137c 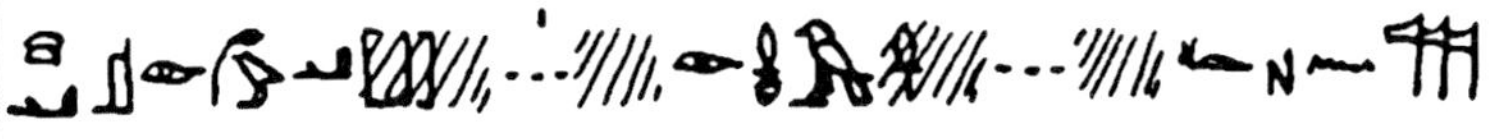

(1016+6) 1016+7

§2137d 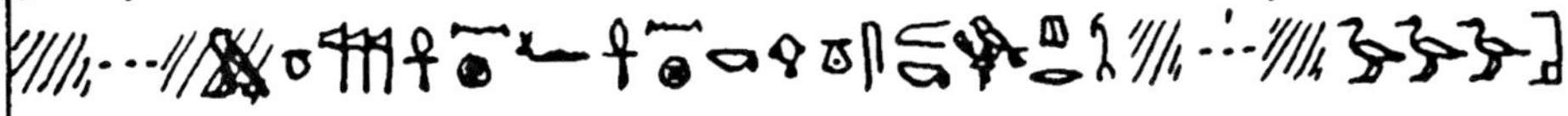

## Utt. 692B.
JP II, 1016+7-13.

(JP II, 1016+7)

§2138a 

1016+8

§2138b 

§2138c 1016+9

§2138d 1016+10-12 1016+13
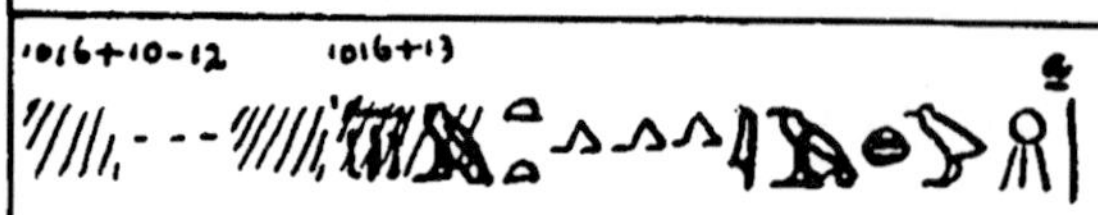
a. Foot of column.

## Utt. 692 C.

JPII, 1016+14-1021.

§2138e JPII, 1016+14
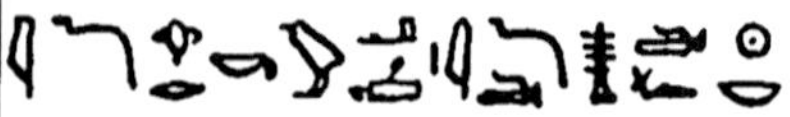

§2138f 1016+15 1016+16
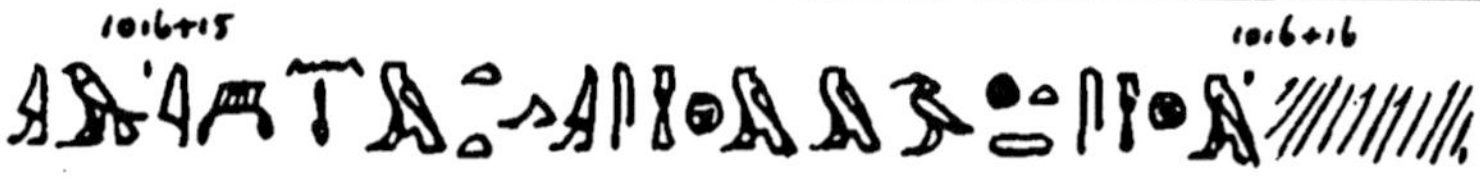

§2138g (1016+16) 1016+17

§2138h (1016+17) 1016+18
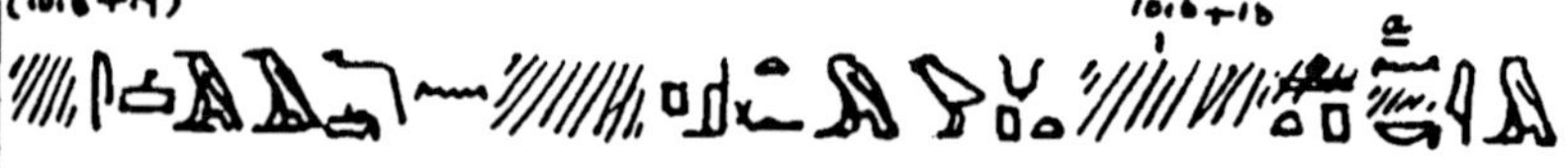
a. Perhaps nothing lost.

§2138i (1016+18) 1016+19

§2138j 1016+20.21.22 1017 1018
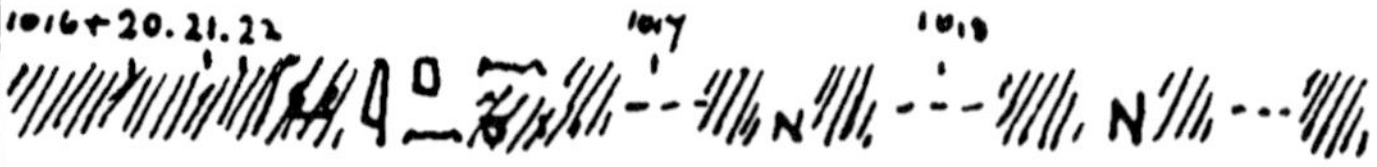

§2139k 1019
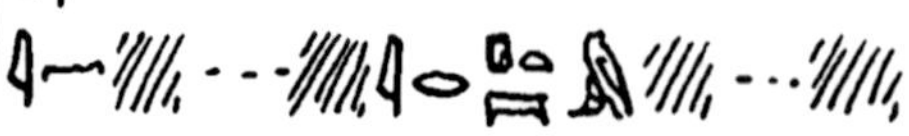

§2139l 1020 1021
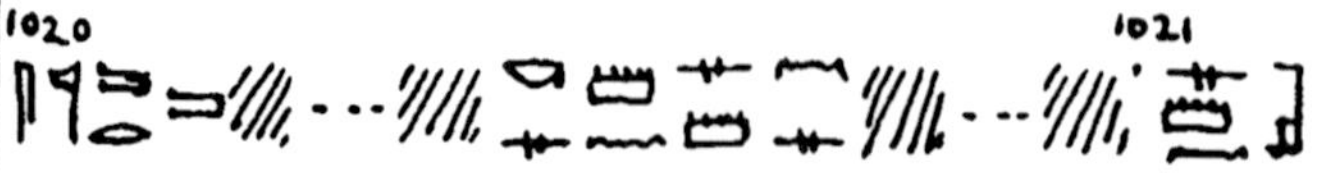

## Utt. 693.
### JPII, 1021-5.

JPII, 1021

§2139 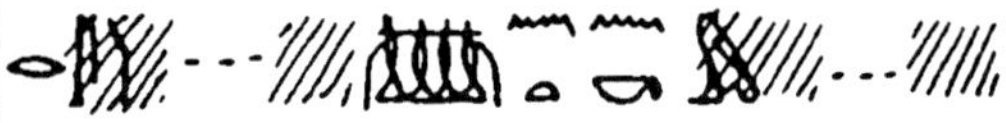

1022

§2140 

1023 … 1024

§2141 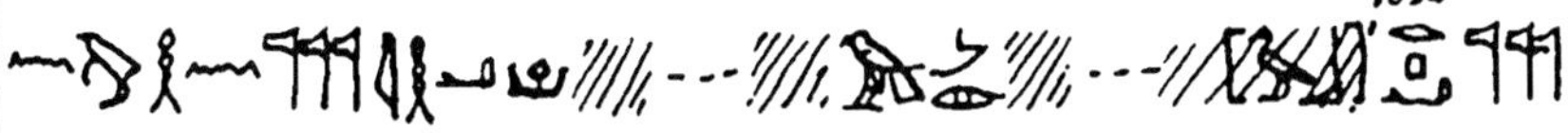

(1024)

§2142 

1025

§2143 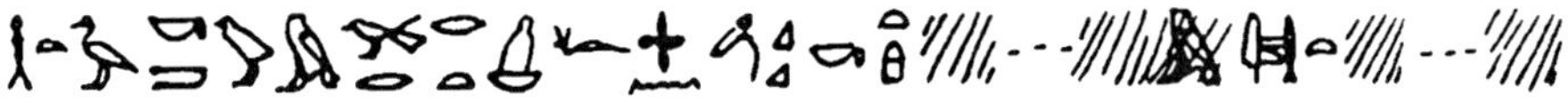

## Utt. 696.
### JPII, 1047-54.

JPII, 1047 a

§2163a  a. sic facsimile; read .

(1047)

§2163b 

1048

§2163c 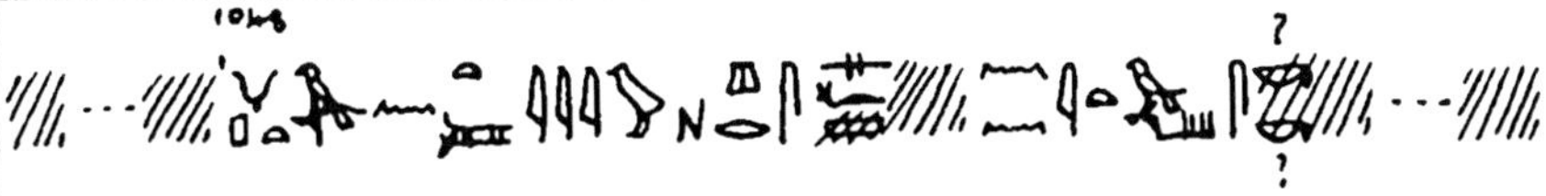

1049 … 1050

§2164 

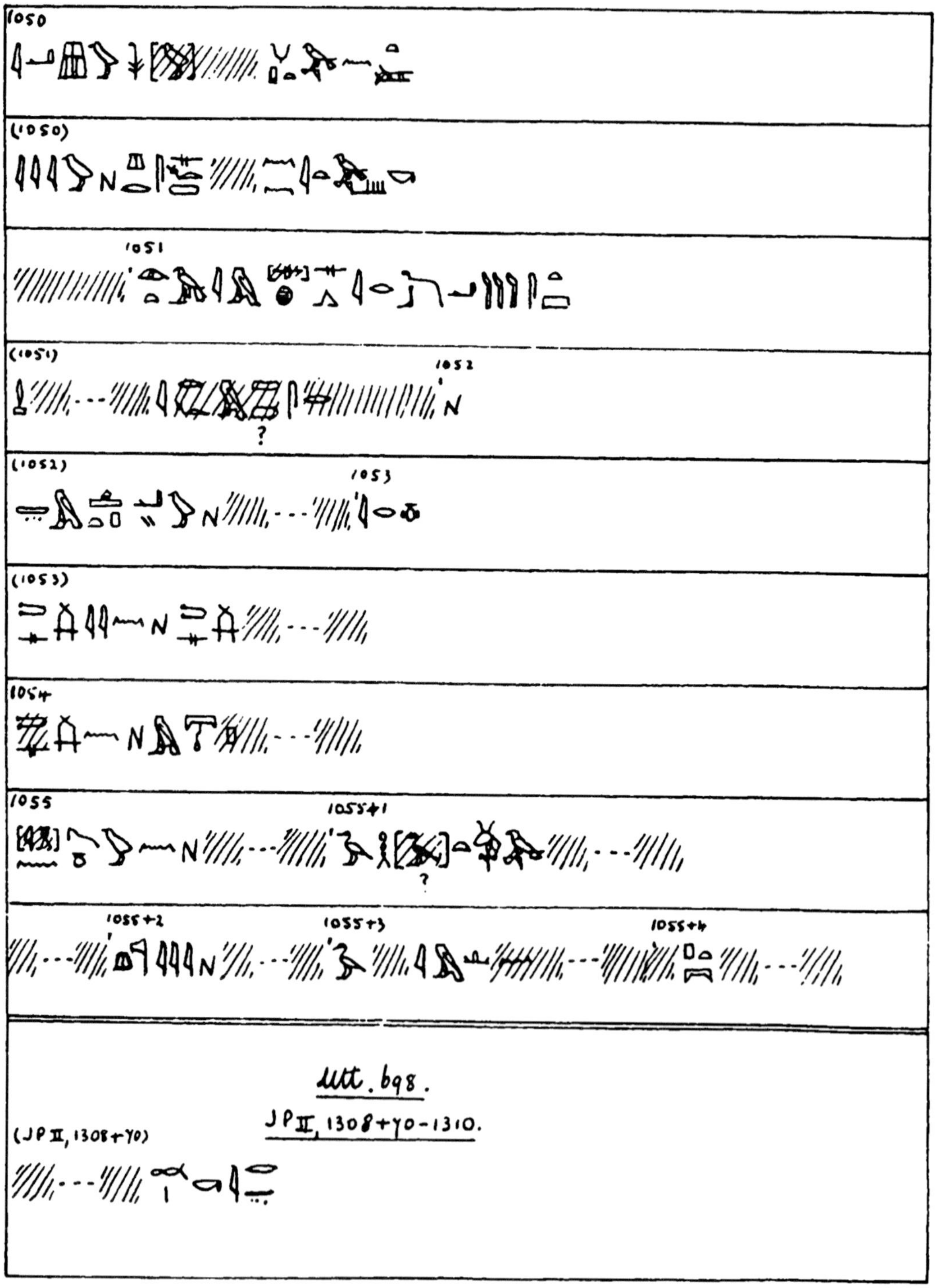


§2165a

§2165b

§2166a

§2166b

§2167

§2168a

§2168b

§2168c

§2168d

§2176a

§2176b 1309 

§2177a (1309) 

§2177b 1310 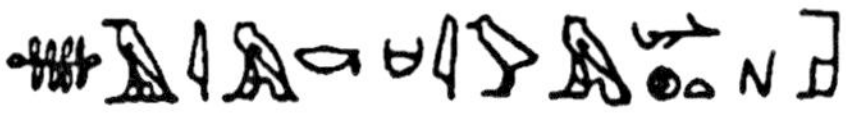

## Utt. 704
## Nt, 7-8.

§2206a Nt. 7 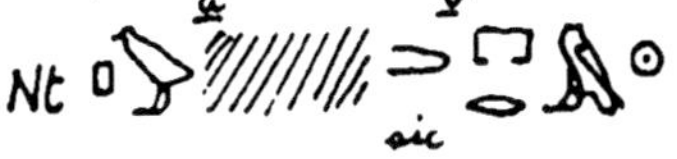 a-b. Sethe, following Cairo 28083, restores  here.

§2206b (7) 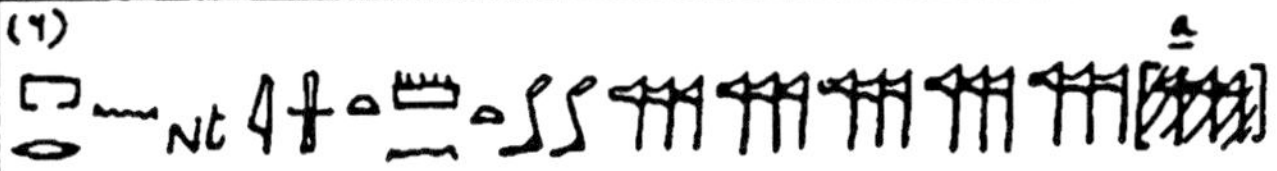 a. The lacuna as shown in the facsimile is a little too small.

§2206c (7) 

§2206d (8)  a Cf. §2206a and Sethe.

§2206e (8) 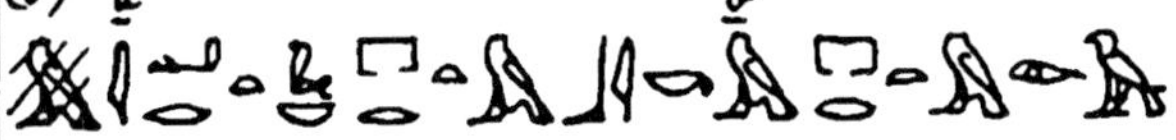

a-c. Read i'rt prt m irt Ḥr; the passage contains a partial dittograph of §2206d.

b. Error for , det. of bik.

§2206f (8) 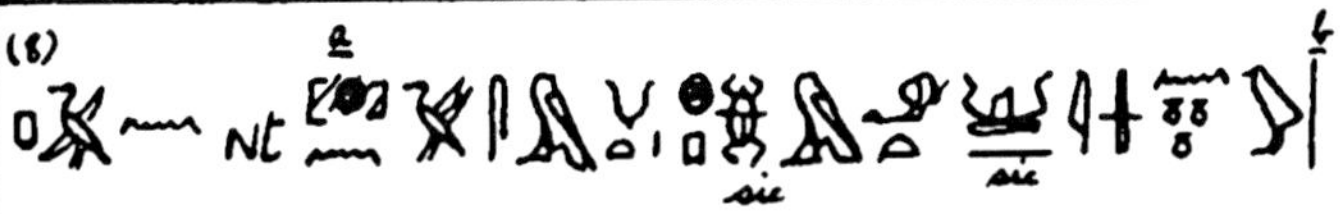 a. No room for a second  in the facsimile. b. Foot of column.

The following Utterances were not available to Sethe for his edition of the Pyramid Texts, which appeared in 1910; they have been collected from the later publications of Jéquier's excavations at the pyramids of Pepi II and Neit.

Utt. 715.

JPII, 473+1-10.

The beginnings of all lines have been lost except 473+9-10.

JPII, 473+1

§2218a 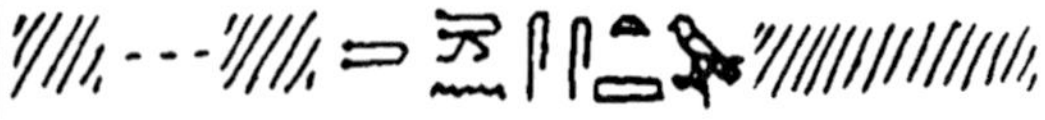

473+2

§2218b 

473+3

§2218c 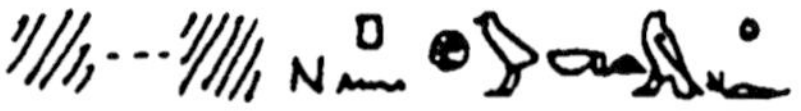

(473+3)

§2219a 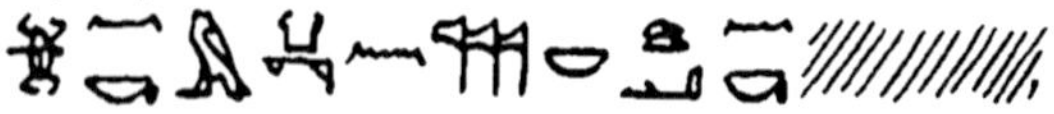

473+4

§2219b 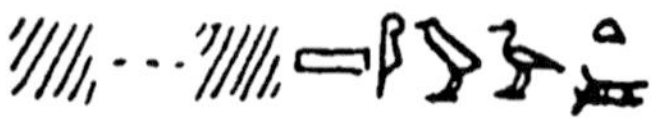

(473+4)

§2219c 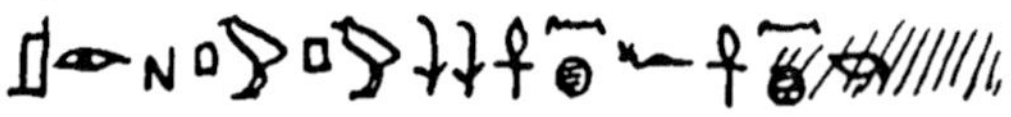

473+5

§2220a 

(473+5) 473+6

§2220b 

(473+6)

§2220c 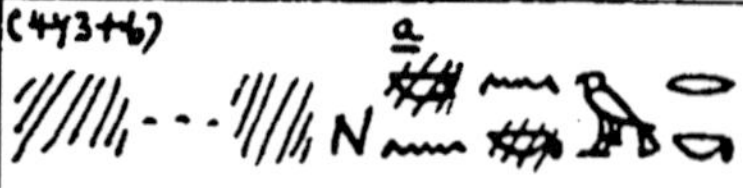

a. sic facsimile; read 

(473+6)

§2221a 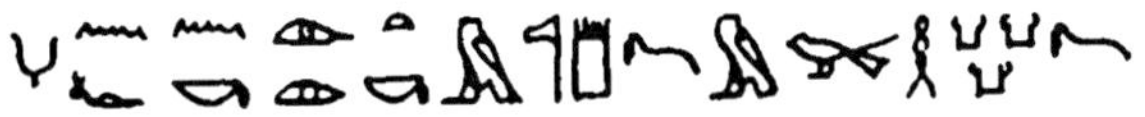

473+7

§2221b 

(473+7)

§2221c 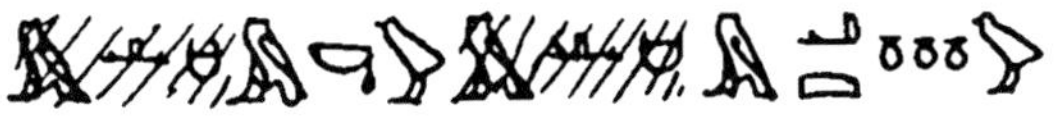

473+8 473+9

§2222a 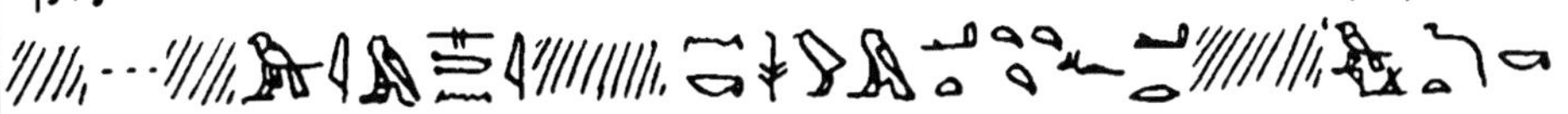

(473+9)

§2222b 

(473+9) 473+10

§2222c 

## Utt. 716.

JP II, 709+2-5; Aba, 537-42.

Variant of Utt. 665C.

(JP II, 709+2)

a

§2223a  a. Read ʿb3·k, cf. Aba, 537.

(709+2) a 709+3 b

§2223b 

a-b. Restored from Aba, 538; §1915a has Ihnw for Inhw.

(709+3) a b

§2223c 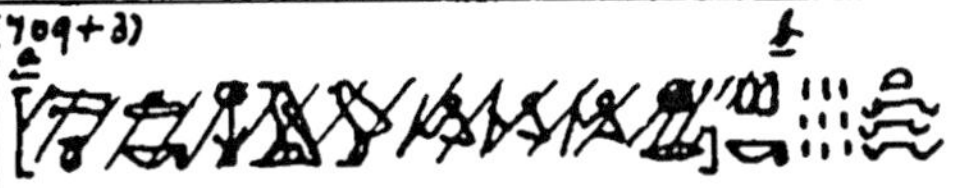 a-b. Restored from §1915 b-c

§2223d (709+3)
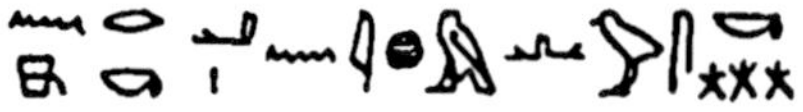

§2224a (709+3)

§2224b (709+3)

a. ⊂ supplied from Aba, 540. b-c. Restored from §1915e; Aba, 540 reads wršw n tḥr nd it.f.

§2224c (709+4)

a-b. Cf. §1915f.

§2224d (709+4)
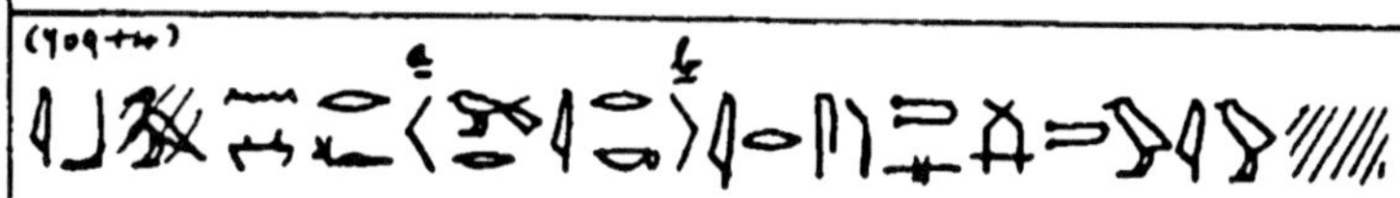
a-b. Supplied from §1915g.

§2224e 709+5
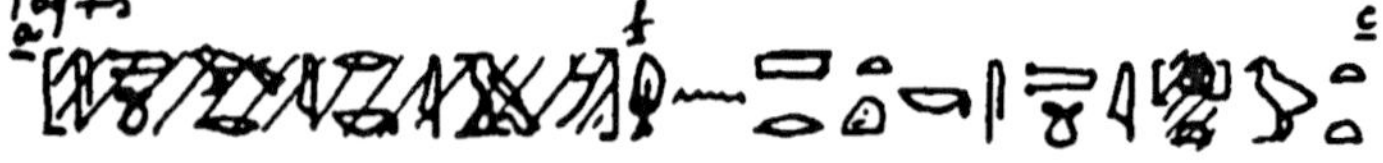
a-b. Cf. §1915h.
c. No stanza mark.

## Utt. 717.

JP II, 709+5-16.

Variant of Utt. 666.

§2225a (709+5)
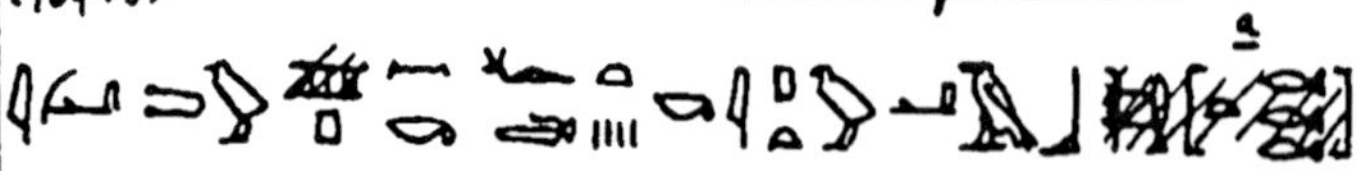
a. Cf. §1918.

§2225b 709+6

a-b. Cf. §1919a = Nt, 739.

§2225c (709+6)
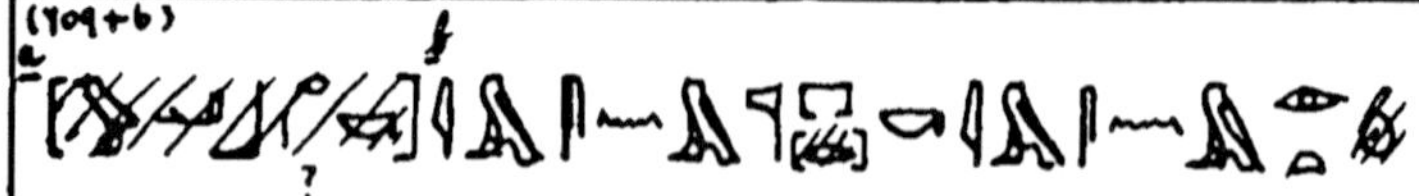
a-b. Cf. §1919b.

§2225d 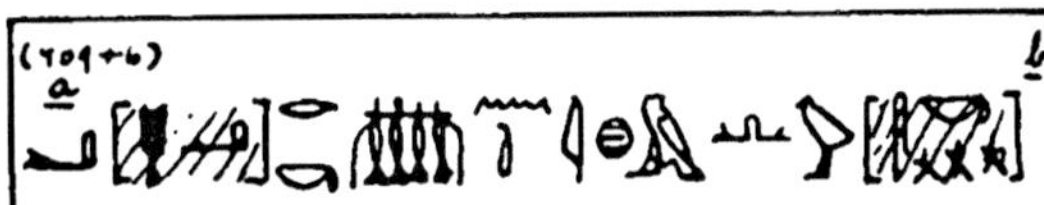 a-b. Cf. §1926a.

§2226a 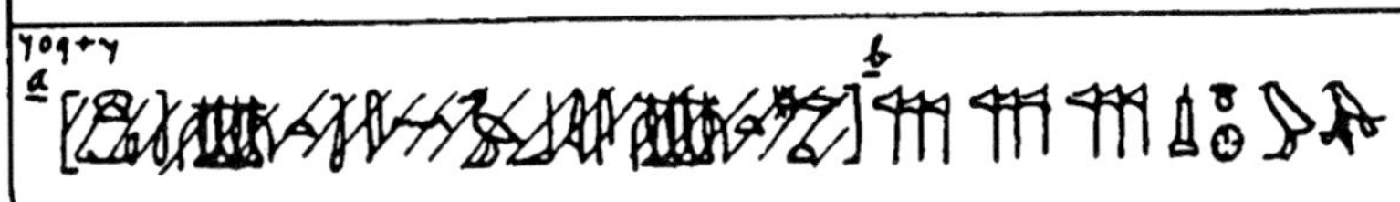 a-b. Cf. §1919c.

§2226b  a-b. Cf. §1920a.

§2226c  a-b. Cf. §1920b.

§2226d  a-b. Cf. §1920c.

§2227a 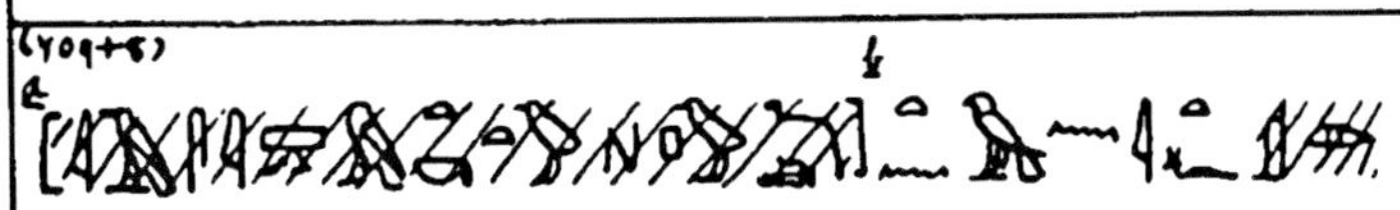 a-b. Cf. §1920d.

§2227b 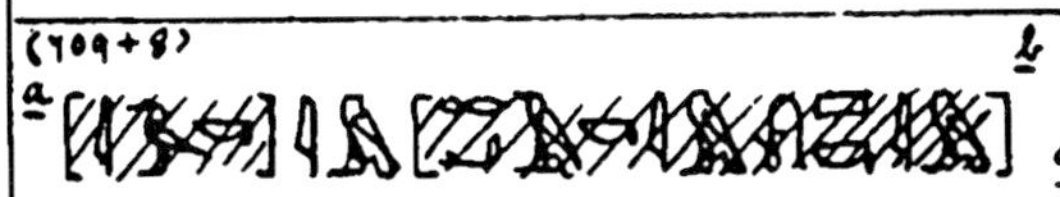 a-b. Cf. §1921b. If the fragment with  is rightly placed in the facsimile, there is no space for a duplicate §1921a.

§2227c 
a-b. From the few signs preserved, it would appear that the text here differed from §1921c-d.

§2228a 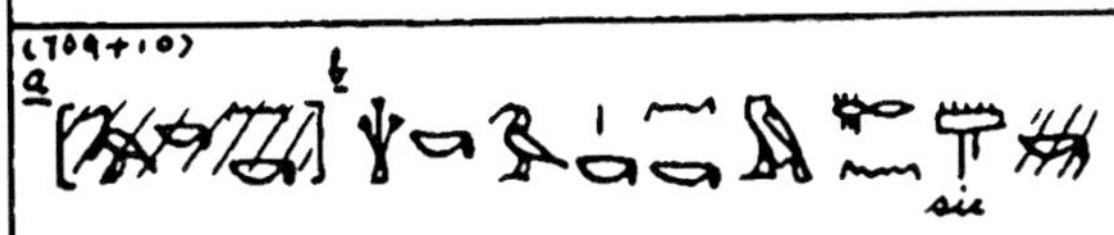 a-b. Cf. §1921e.

§2228b 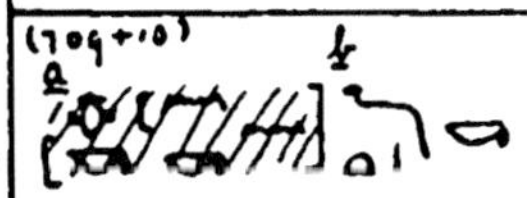 a-b. Cf. §1921e.

§2228c (709+10) 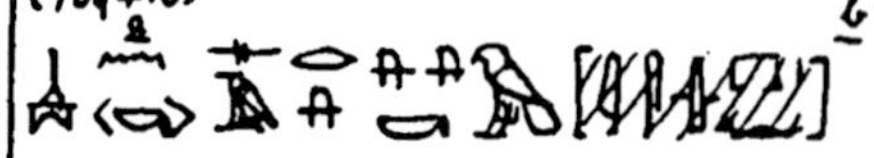 a-b. Cf. §1921 f.

§2228d 709+11 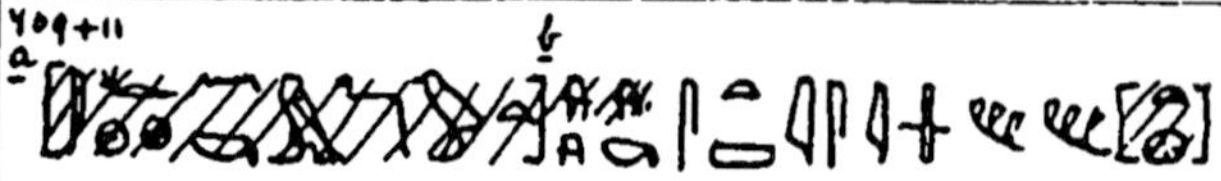 a-b. Cf. §1921 g.

§2229a (709+11)  a-c. Cf. §1922 a. b. [sign] misread in facsimile as the top of [sign]

§2229b (709+12) 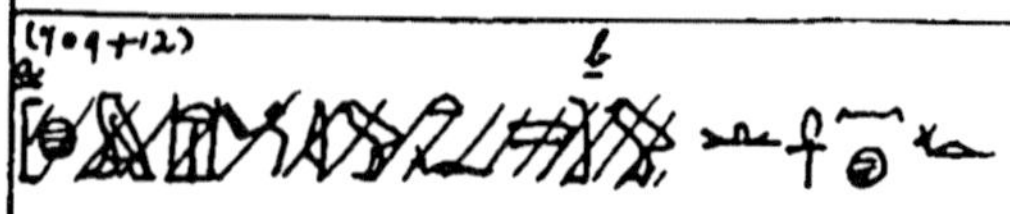 a-b. Cf. 1922 b.

§2229c (709+12) 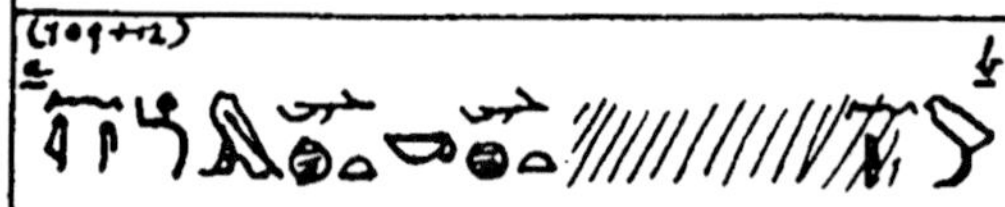 a-b. Varies considerably from §1922 c.

§2229d (709+12) 709+13  a-b. Cf. §1923 a, but the size of the lacuna shows that an addition was inserted between irt ṯḥ and tk.

§2230a (709+13)  a. Cf. §1923 b, but in the facsimile the space is insufficient for [sign].

§2230b (709+13) 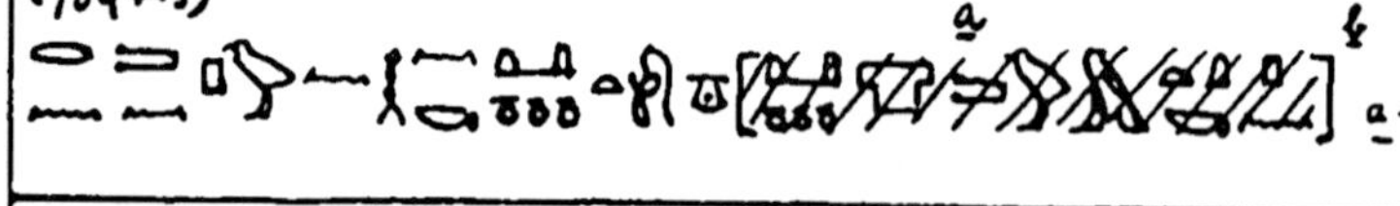 a-b. Cf. §1924 a.

§2230c 709+14  a-b. Cf. §1924 b.

§2230d (709+14)  a-b. Cf. §1924 c.

§2231a (709+14)  a-b. Cf. §1925 a.

709+15

§2231b 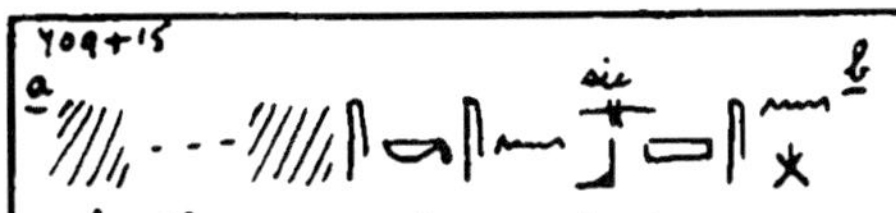

a-b. Cf. §1925b-c, which requires more space than is available here. For *zbš* read presumably *ʿbš* as in §1925a.

(709+15)

§2231c 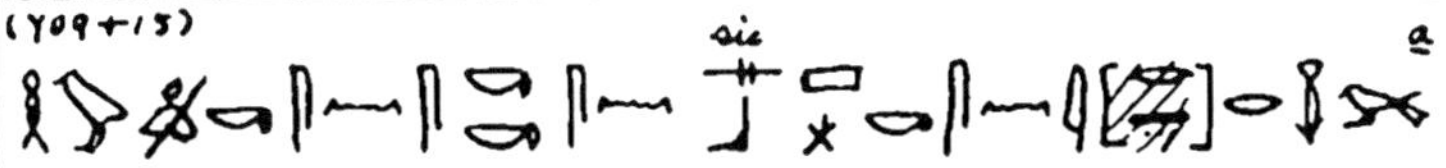 a. Cf. §1925e-g.

709+16

§2231d 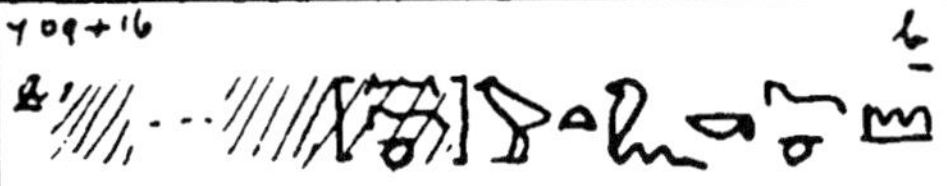 a-b. Cf. §§1926a-1927a, which requires more space than is available here.

## Utt. 718.

### JP II, 709+16-19.

(JP II, 709+16)

§2232a 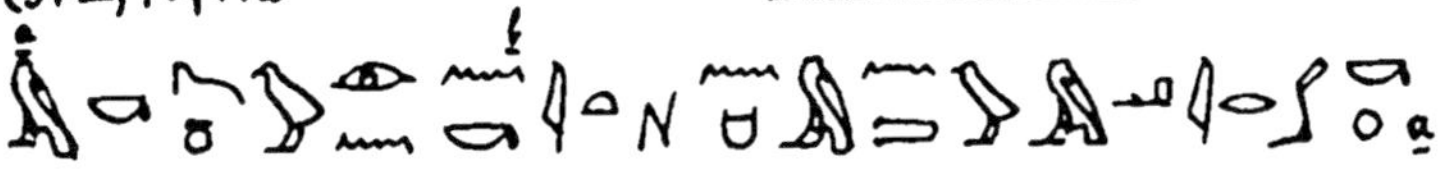 a-b. Cf. §1929a.

709+17

§2232b 

(709+17)

§2232c 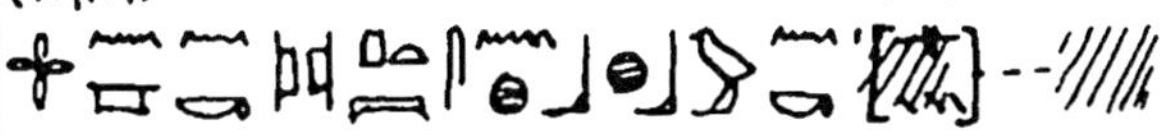

(709+18)

§2232d 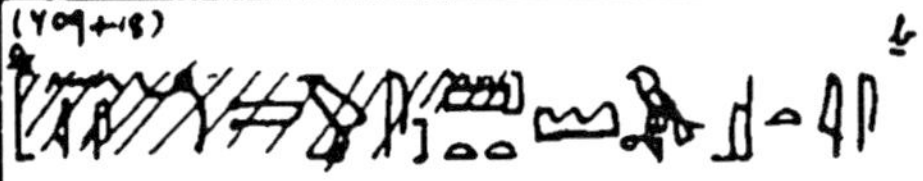 a-b. Cf. §1927f.

(709+18)

§2232e 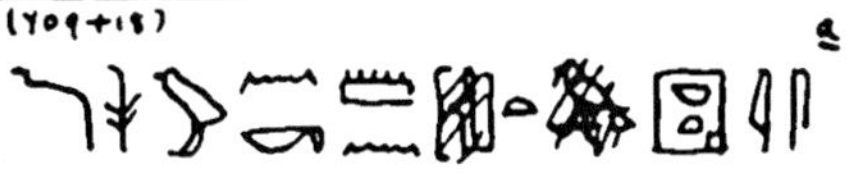 a. Cf. §1928a.

(709+18)

§2233a  a. Cf. §1928a.

§2233b 709+19

a-b. Cf. §1928b.

§2233c (709+19)

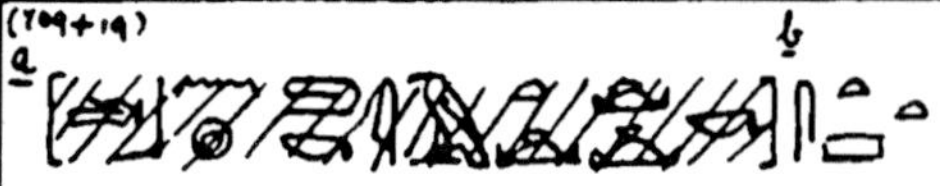

a-b. Cf. §1928c.

§2233d (709+19)

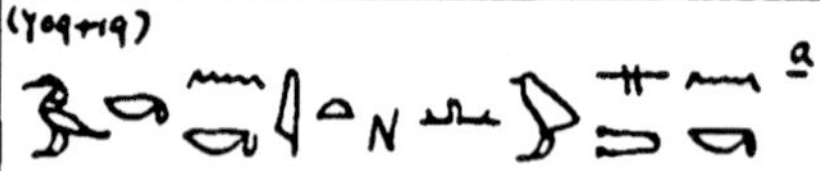

a. Cf. §1929b.

§2233e (709+19)

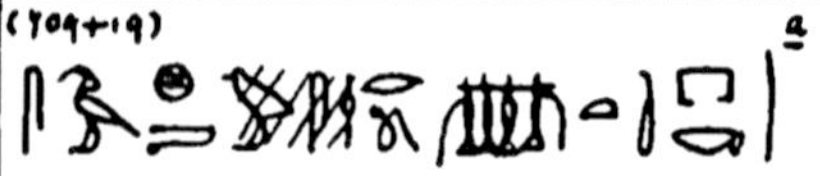

a. Cf. §1929c. Col. 709+19 ends here; the text following the lacuna in 709+20 is another Utt.

## Utt. 719.

JP II, 709+22-6.

§2234a (709+22)

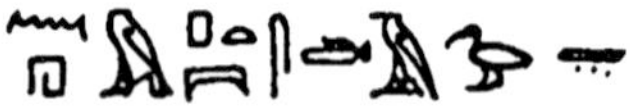

§2234b 709+23

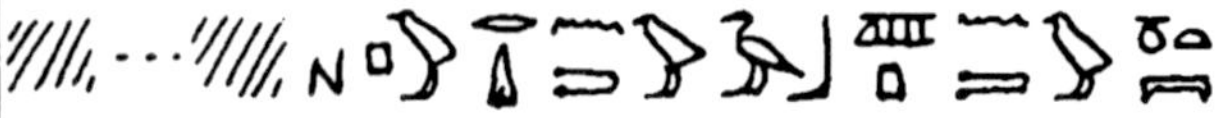

§2234c (709+23)

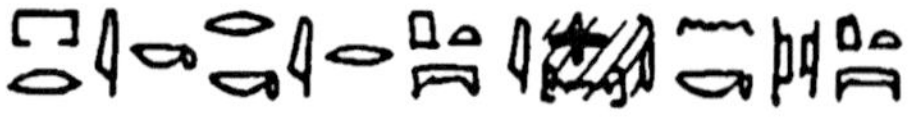

§2234d (709+23)

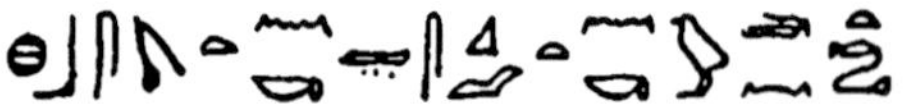

§2235a 709+24

§2235b (709+24)

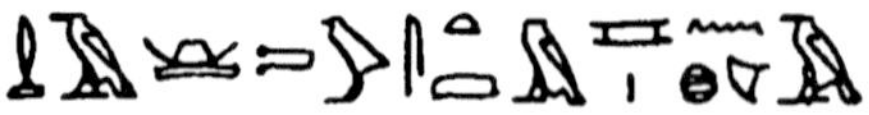

§2235c (709+24)

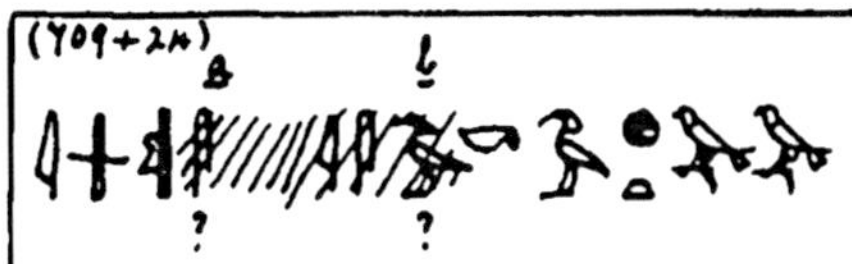

a. Facsimile [glyph], b. Or [glyph] z3 ?

§2235d (709+24) … 709+25

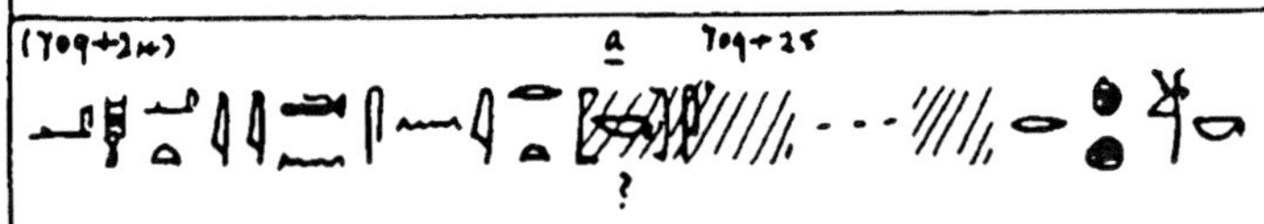

a. A trace only; in the facsimile it does not suit the expected [glyph].

§2236a (709+25)

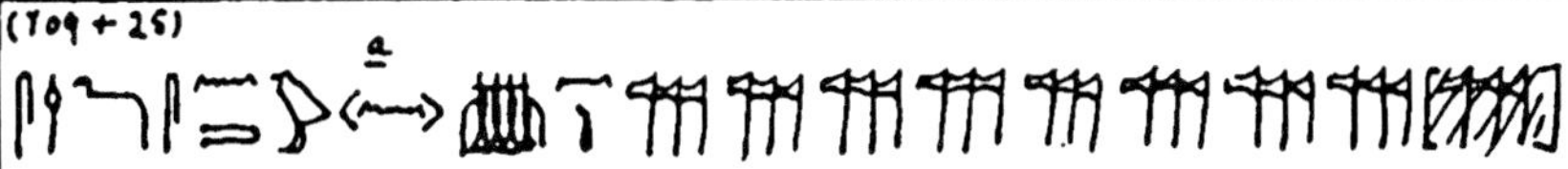

a. n omitted.

§2236b (709+25)

§2236c 709+26

## Utt. 720.

JP II, 709+37-40.

§2237a (709+37)

§2237b (709+37)

§2237c 709+38

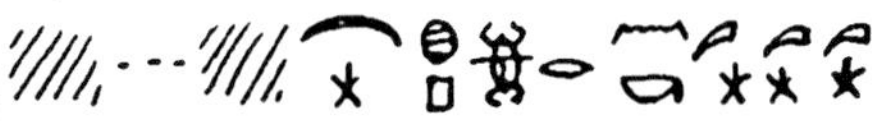

§2237d (709+38)

§2238a (709+38)

709+39

§2238b 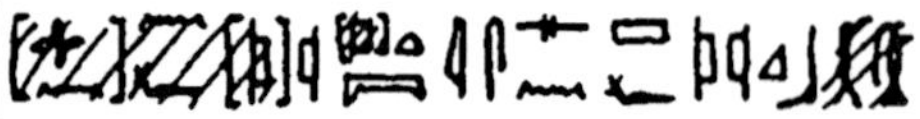

(709+39)

§2238c 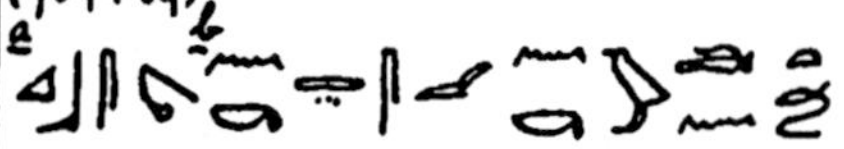 a-b. Sic facsimile, read 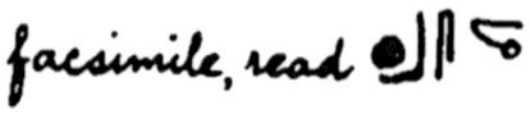 as §2234d.

(709+39)

§2238d 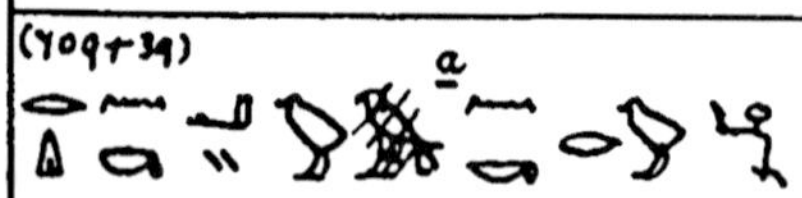 a. Rwi 'dance' omitted in facsimile.

(709+39)

§2239a 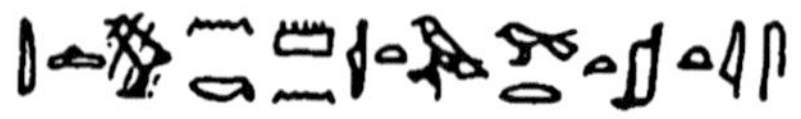

709+40

§2239b 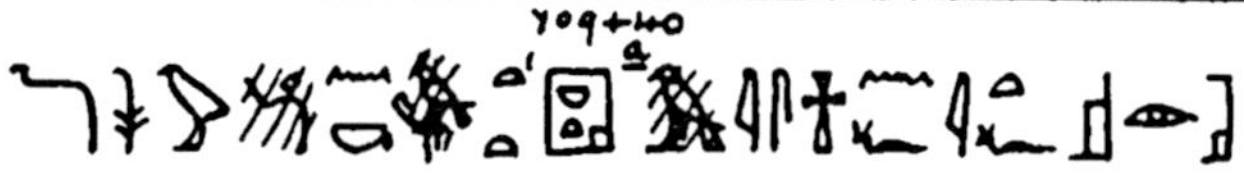 a. The particle is omitted; there is no space for it.

## Utt. 721.

JP II, 1055+27-30.

JP II, 1055+27

§2240a 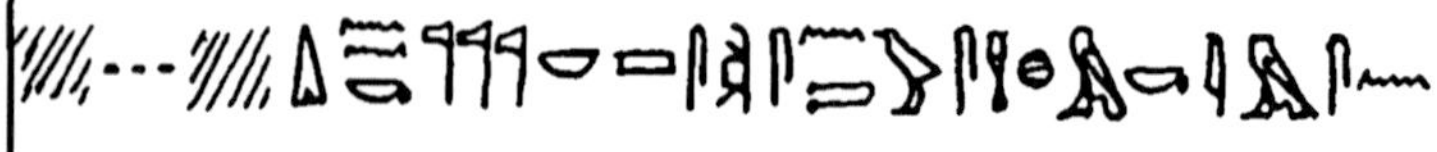

(1055+27)

§2240b 

1055+28

§2240c 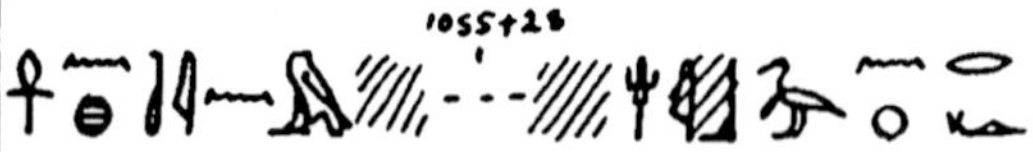

(1055+28)

§2241a 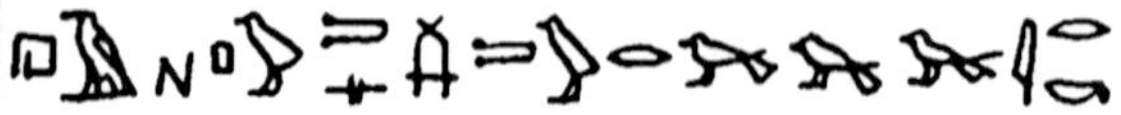

(1055+28)

§2241b 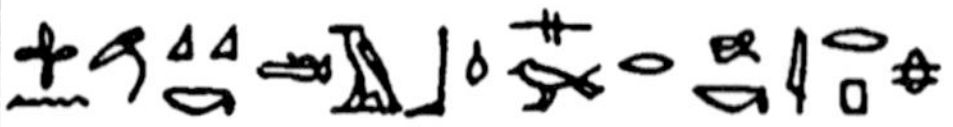

§2241c (1055+28) 1055+29

§2242a (1055+29)

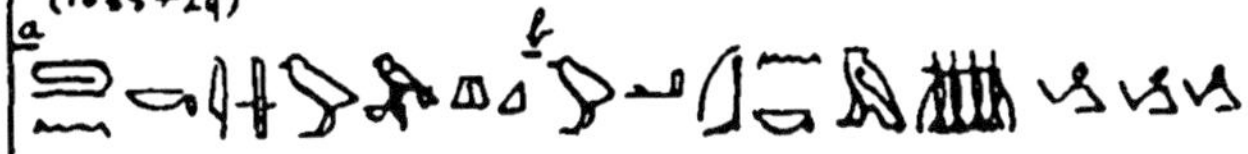

a-b. pḥr n·k imyw ḫrt-nṯr; [hieroglyph] has been dismembered.

§2242b (1055+29)

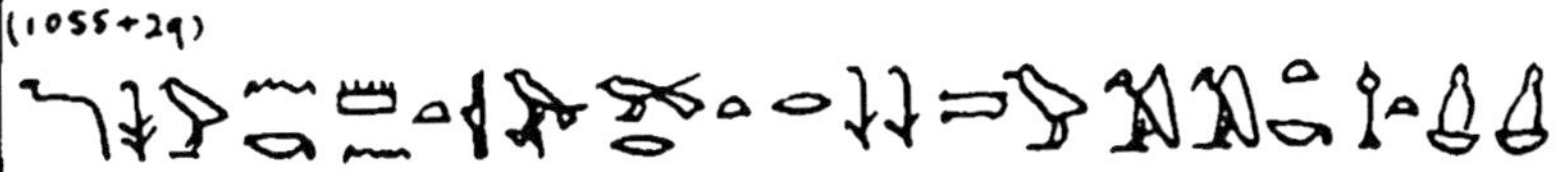

§2242c (1055+29)

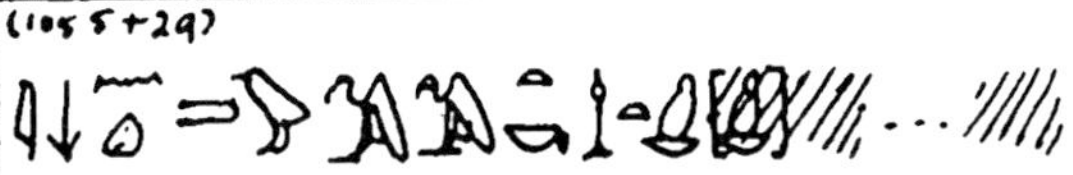

§2242d 1055+30

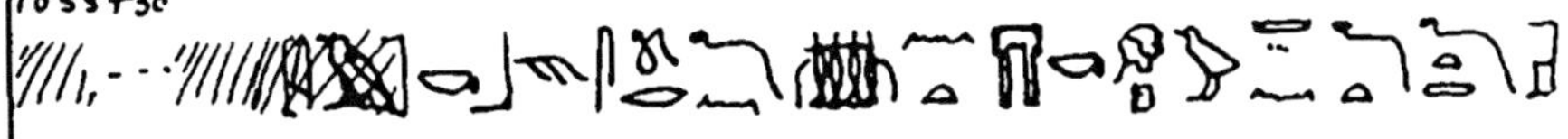

## Utt. 722.

Nt, 40-41; JPII, 1055+30; frag. 28 (pl. 15).

§2243a (Nt, 40)

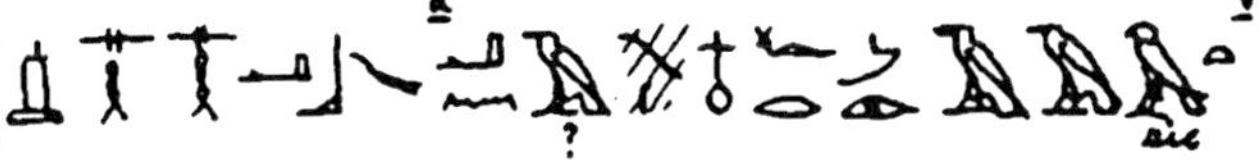

a-b. Var. JPII, 1055+30 

§2243b (40) 41

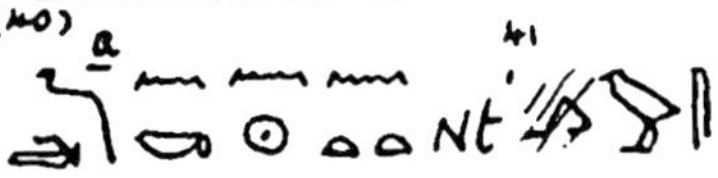

a. JPII, 1055+30 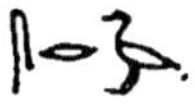

§2243c (41)

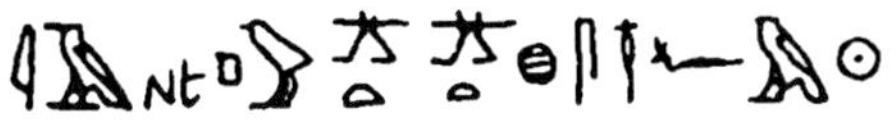

§2243d (41)

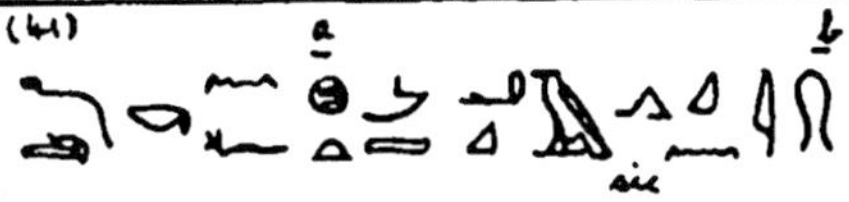

a-b. JPII, frag. 28, l. 6:  On the position of this fragment see n. on §2246f.

§2243e (Nt) a-b. Not preserved in JP II.

## Utt. 723.

Nt, 652-5; JP II, 1055+31-2; frag. 28, l. 7.

§2244a (Nt, 652) Nt 653

§2244b (653)

§2244c (653)

§2244d 654

§2245a (654)

§2245b (654) a-b. JP II, frag. 28, 7 .

§2245c. 655 sic

§2245d (655) a-b. JP II, 1055+32 .

## Utt. 724.

JP II, 1055+32–8; frag. 28, 8–12.

JP II, 1055+32

§2246a  a. Cf. §1233a.

(1055+32) frag. 28, 8 b (1055+33)

§2246b 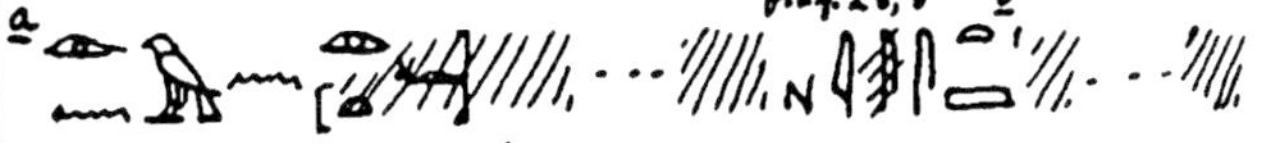

a–b. Cf. §1233a–b. Frag. 28, 8–9 contains a portion of a partial duplicate of Utt. 724; on its position see note on §2246f.

(1055+33)

§2246c 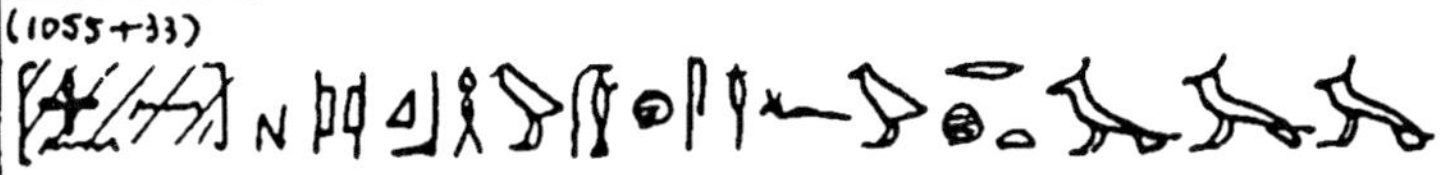

(1055+33)

§2246d 

(1055+33)

§2246e  a–b. Cf. §1233c.

(1055+33)

§2246f 

a–b. Cf. §1234b + frag. 28, l. 9 + the frag. at the bottom of JP II, pl. 13, which is out of place here, see n. on §2247d. Both these fragments partly duplicate the main text. Frag. 28, l. 9 has  for ḥdt.

1055+34

§2247a  a. Cf. §1235a.b.

(1055+34)

§2247b  a. Cf. §1235c.

1055+35

§2247c 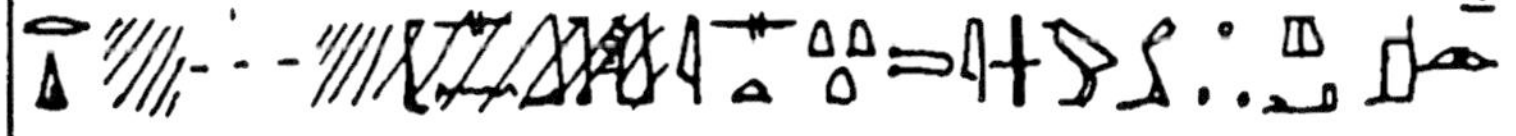 a–b. Cf. §1236b.

| | | |
|---|---|---|
| §2247d | (1055+35)  a. The fragment placed in the lacuna at the bottom of JP II, 1055+32-6 cannot belong there, since at this point it overlaps the main text at, as also in 1055+36 (wp.k w3t) (§2249a). | |
| §2248a | (1055+35) 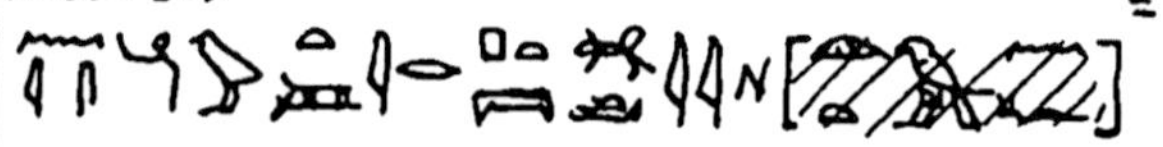 | a. Cf. §1237d-e. |
| §2248b | 1055+36  | |
| §2248c | (1055+36)  | a. Cf. §1238b. |
| §2248d | (1055+36) 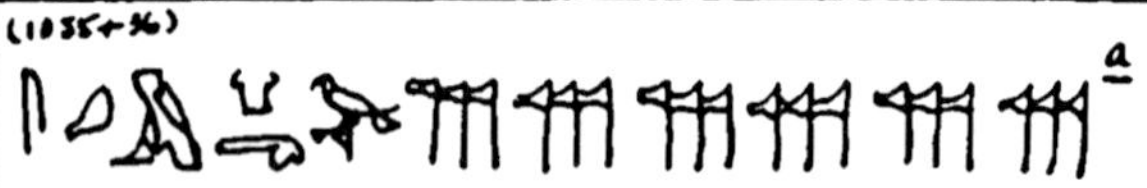 | a. Cf. §1238a. |
| §2249a | (1055+36) 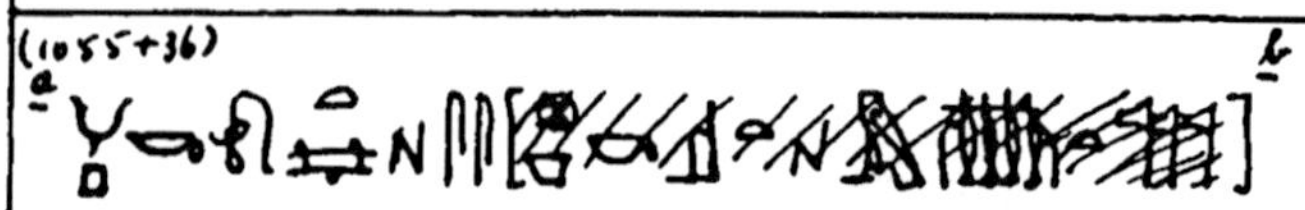 | a-b. Cf. §1239a |
| §2249b | (1055+37)  a-b. Cf. §1240a. The lacunae at the bottom of 1055+36 and at the top of 1055+37 between them must have contained a longer text than §1239b. | |
| §2249c | (1055+37) 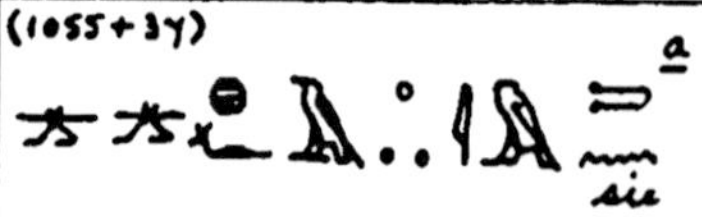 | a. Cf. §1240b. |
| §2249d | (1055+37) 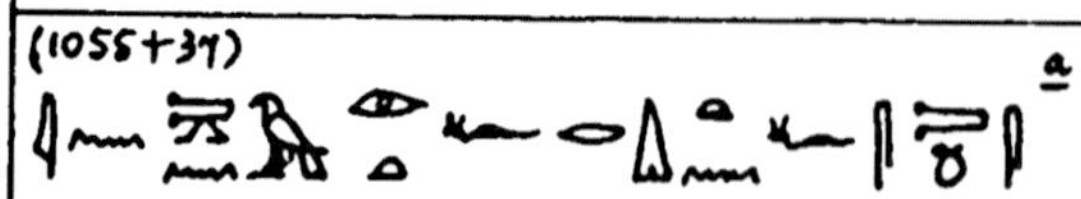 | a. Cf. §1240c. |

§2250a (1055+37)  a. Cf. §1241a.

§2250b 1055+38 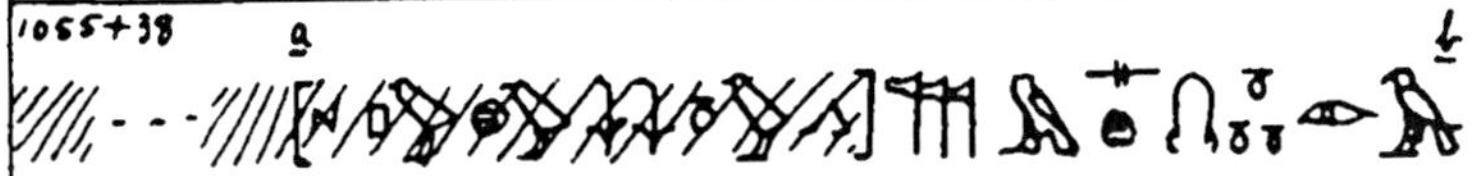 a-b. Cf. §1242a.

§2250c (1055+38)  a. Cf. §1242b.

§2250d (1055+38) 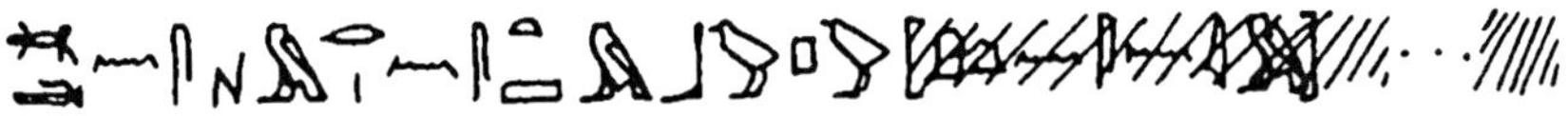 a. Cf. §1242c

## Utt. 725.

JP II, 1055+39-40.

§2251a JP II, 1055+39 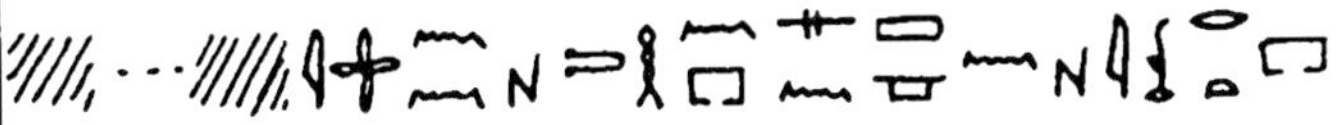

§2251b (1055+39) 

§2251c (1055+39) 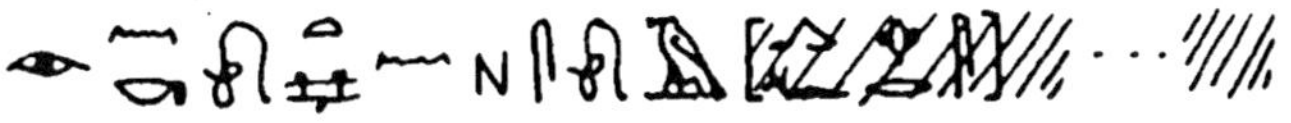

§2251d 1055+40 

## Utt. 726.

Nt, 692-5; JP II, 1055+44-7.

§2252a Nt, 692  a-d. Cf. §815a. b. JP II, 1055+44 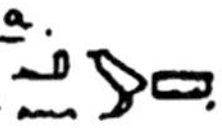

c.  is the negation; JP II, loc. cit. wrongly inserts  before ḥtm.k w.

(692)

§2252b 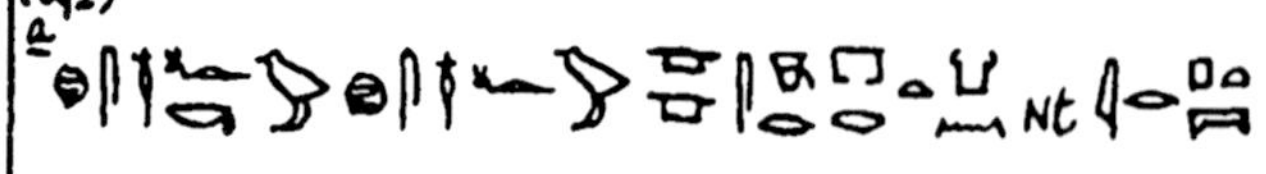 a. JPII, 1055+44 again inserts a superfluous [hieroglyph] before ḥȝf.k

§2252c 

a-b. Sic Nt facsimile; read [hieroglyphs]. Only [hieroglyphs] preserved in JPII, 1055+45.

(693)

§2252d 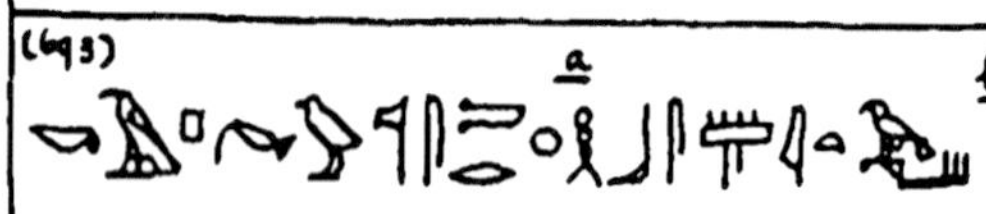 a-b. JPII, 1055+45 [hieroglyphs].

(693)

§2253a 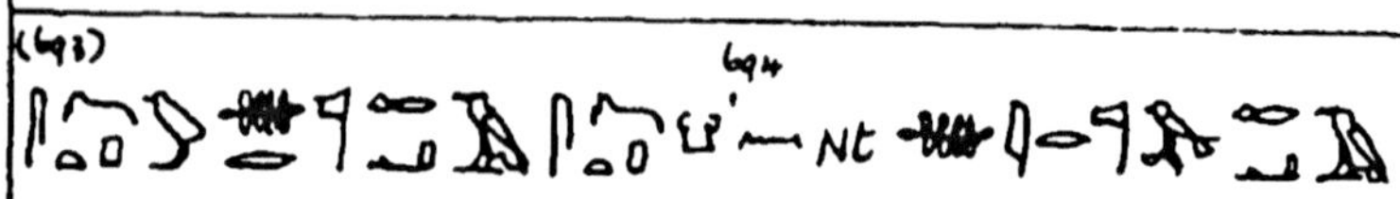

(694)

§2253b 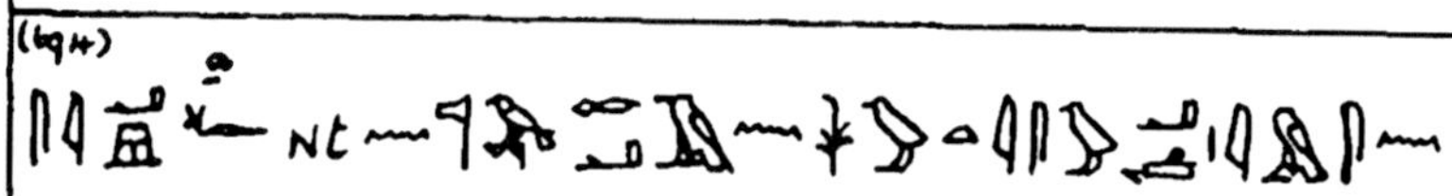 a. A fortuitous dot over [hieroglyph].

(694)

§2253c 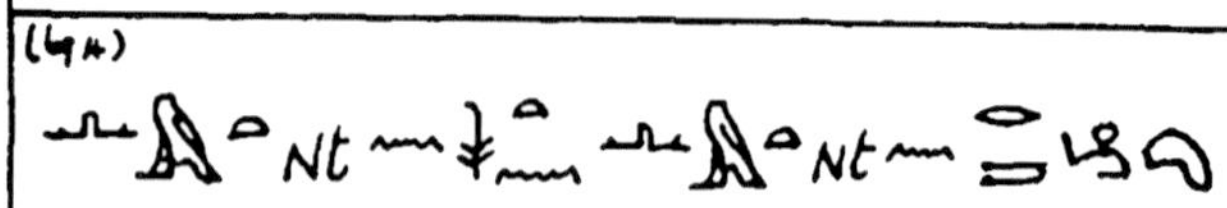

695

§2253d 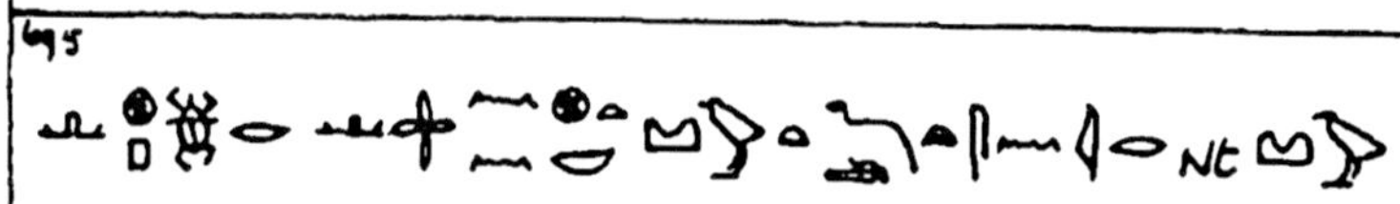

(695)

§2253e 

## Utt. 727.

Nt, 716-7; JPII, 1055+56.

(Nt, 716)

§2254a  a. Cf. §430a

§2254b 

§2254c (727)
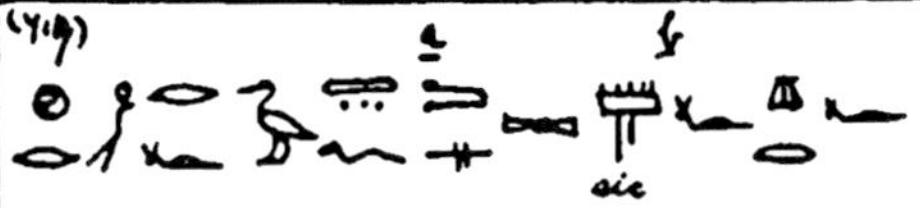
a-b. JPII, 1055+56 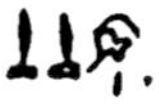.

§2254d (727)
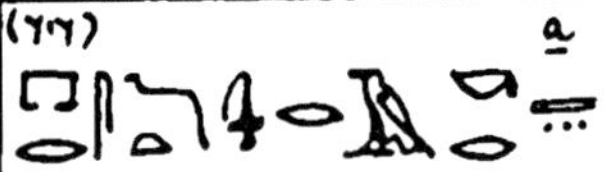
a. JPII, 1055+56 .

§2255a (727)
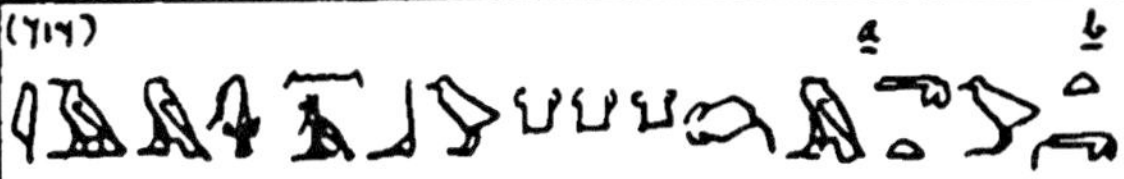
a-b. JPII, 1055+56 .

§2255b (727)

a-b. JPII, 1055+56 . Foot of column and end of Utt.

## Utt. 728.

JPII, 1055+60.

§2256 (JPII, 1055+60)
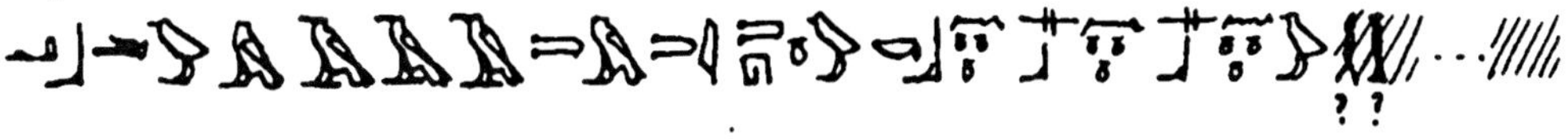

## Utt. 729.

JPII, 1055+62.

§2257a (JPII, 1055+62)
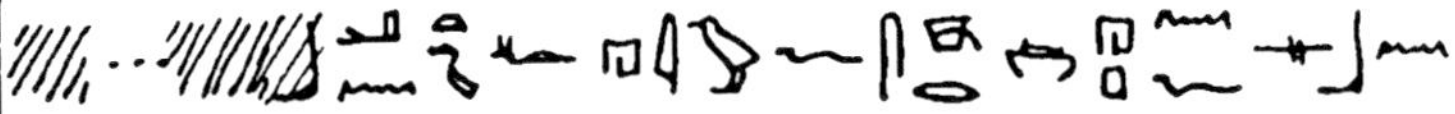

§2257b (1055+62)
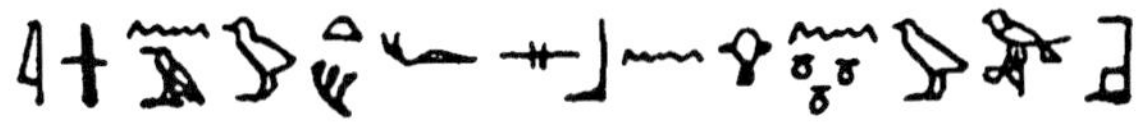

## Utt. 730.

JPII, 1055+63.

§2258 JPII, 1055+63

## Utt. 731.

JP II, 1055+65; Nt, 720.

(JP II, 1055+65)

§2259 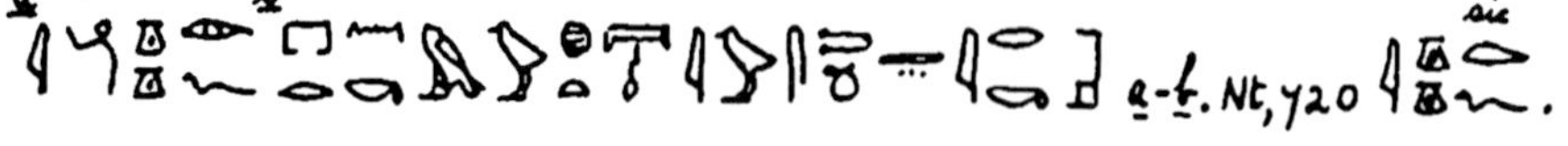

a-b. Nt, 720

## Utt. 732.

JP II, 1055+66.

(JP II, 1055+66)

§2260 

## Utt. 733

Nt, 722; JP II, 1055+69.70.

(Nt, 722)

Nt 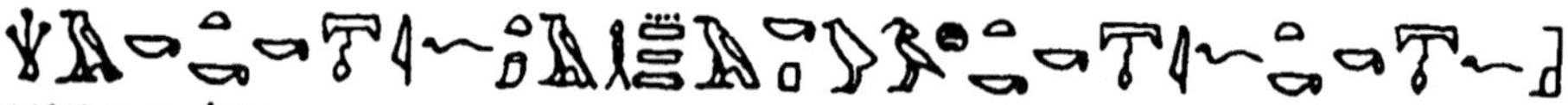

(JP II, 1055+69)

§2261 N 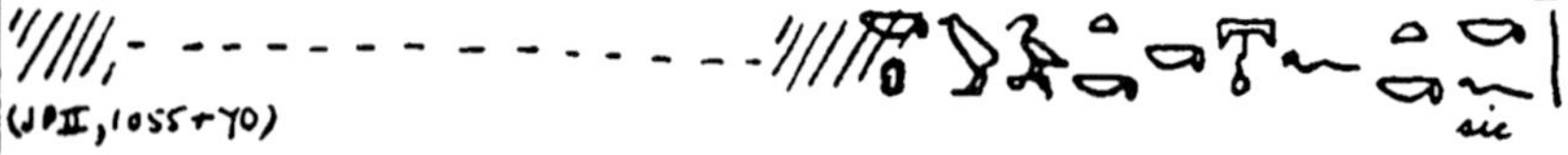

a. Foot of column.

(JP II, 1055+70)

N 

## Utt. 734.

JP II, 1055+74-7.

(JP II, 1055+74)

§2262a 

(1055+74)

§2262b 

§2262c 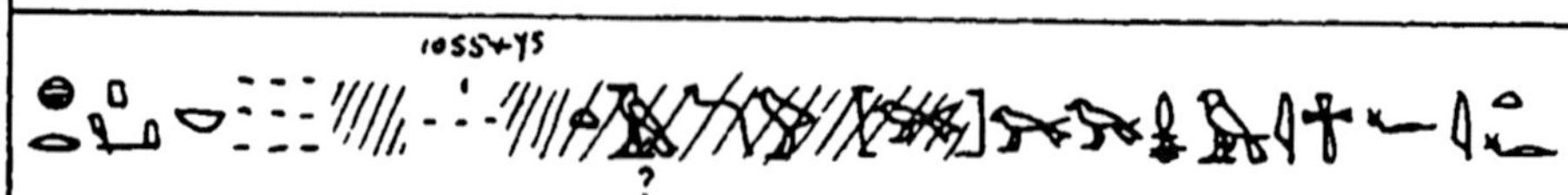

1055+75

§2262*d* (1055+75)

§2263*a* (1055+75)

a. Read *sꜥḥꜥ*.

§2263*b* (1055+75)

a. *sic*; read *nḥm*.

§2263*c* 1055+76

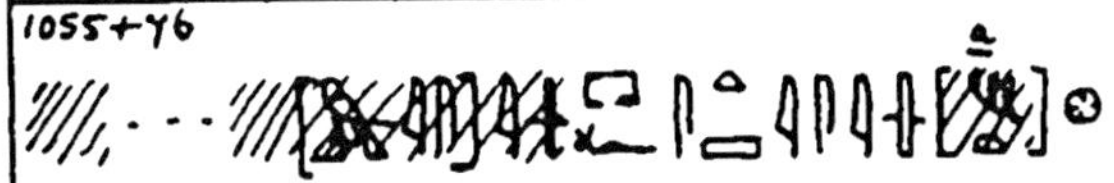

a. Or  ?

§2263*d* (1055+76)

a.  omitted in facsimile.

§2264*a* (1055+76

§2264*b* (1055+76)

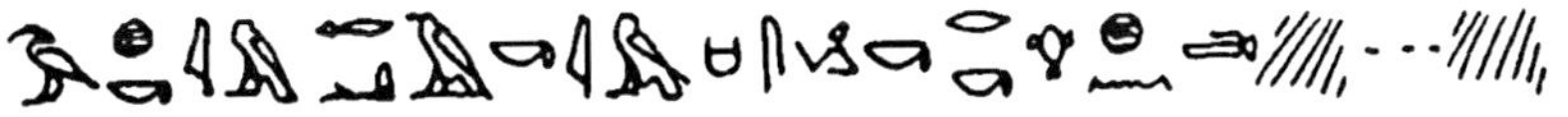

§2264*c* (1055+77)

§2264*d* (1055+77)

§2264*e* (1055+77)

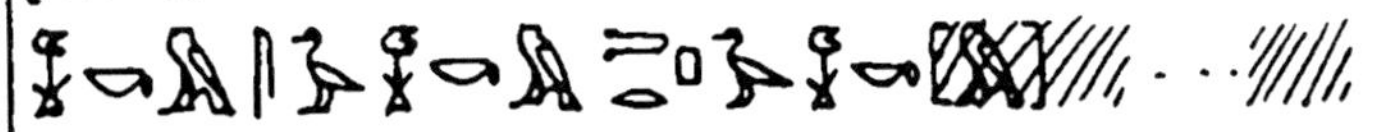

## Utt. 735.
## Nt, 6-7.

(Nt, 6)

2265 a 

(6)

2265 b 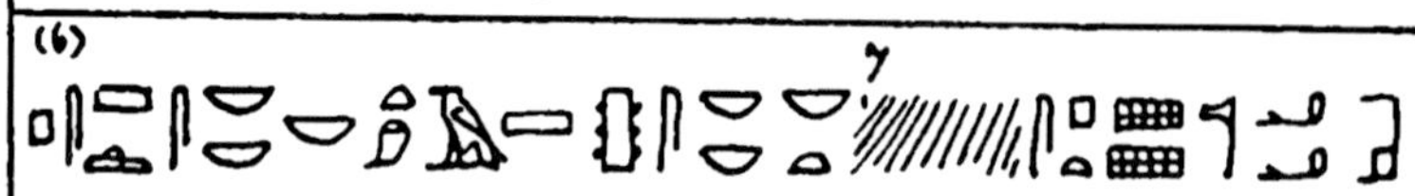

## Utt. 736.
## Nt, 9.

Nt, 9

§2266 a 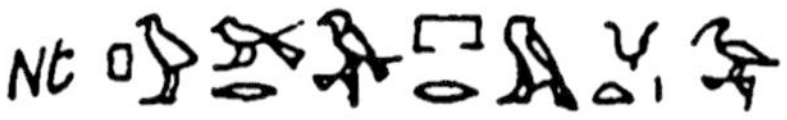

(9)

§2266 b 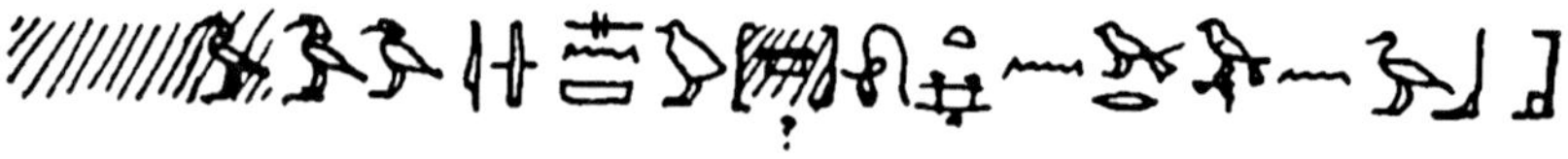

## Utt. 737.
## Nt, 9-10.

(Nt, 9)

§2267 a 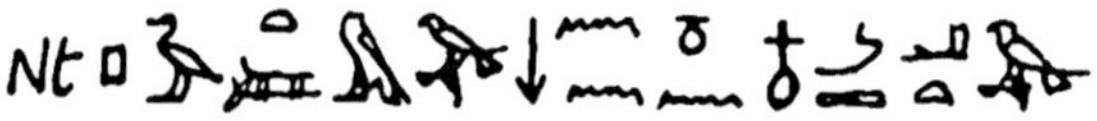

10

§2267 b 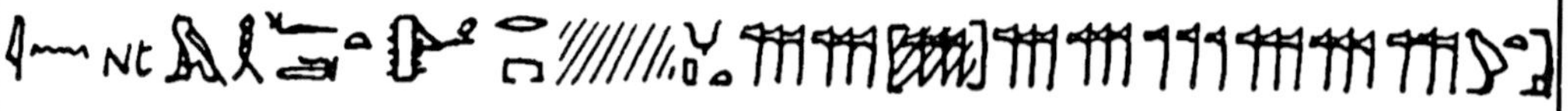

## Utt. 738.
## Nt, 10-12.

(Nt, 10)

§2268 a 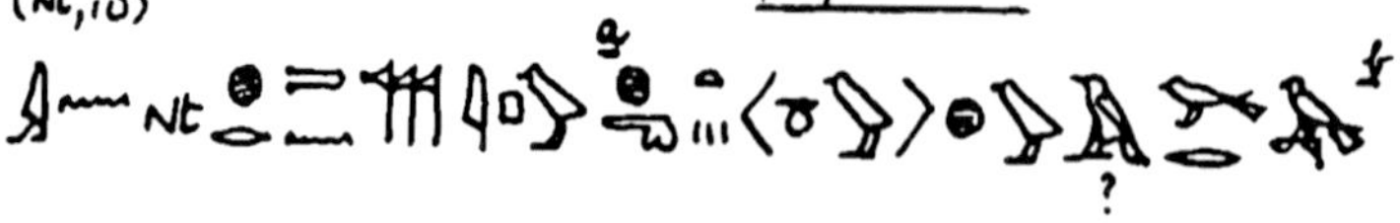

a-b. Read ḥmt·⟨nw⟩ ḥwtyw (?) wr;  omitted by confusion with following .

§2268b. 

(11)
§2268c 

(11)
§2268d 

12
§2268e 

## Utt. 439.
## Nt, 12-13.

Nt, 12
§2269a 

(12) 13 a
§2269b 

a. The text of Nt 13 between Utt. 439 and 440 is too badly damaged to be usable.

## Utt. 440.
## Nt, 13-14.

(Nt, 13) a
§2270a 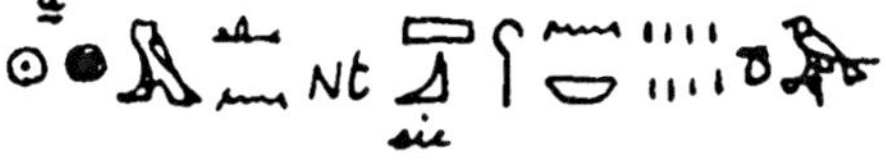

a ⊙⊖ shown in facsimile as OO.

14
§2270b 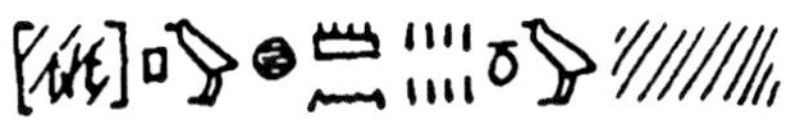

Utt. 741.
Nt, 41-2.

(Nt, 41)

§2271a [hieroglyphs]

42

§2271b [hieroglyphs]  a-b. sic facsimile; read [hieroglyphs].

(42)

§2271c [hieroglyphs]  a. Facsimile [hieroglyphs].

(42)

§2271d [hieroglyphs]  a-b. sic facsimile, read [hieroglyphs] or [hieroglyphs].

(42)

§2271e [hieroglyphs]
a. Facsimile [hieroglyphs].  b. Cf. Neit, p.26.  c. Foot of column.

Utt. 742.
Nt, 43.

§2272 [hieroglyphs] ?

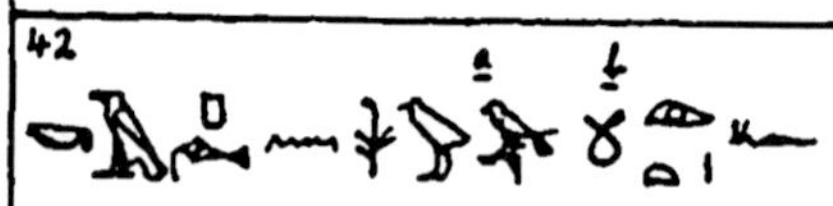

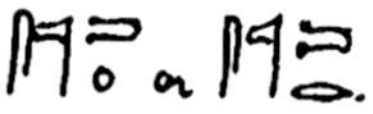

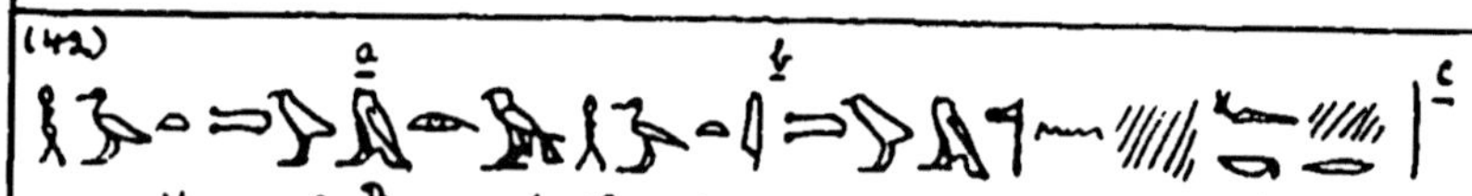

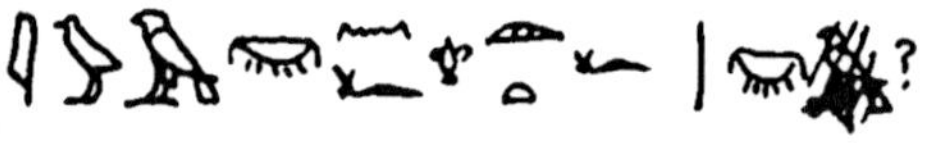

Utt. 743.
Nt, 43.

§2273  Lost.

## Utt. 744.
### Nt, 43.

§2274 

## Utt. 745.
### Nt, 44.

§2275 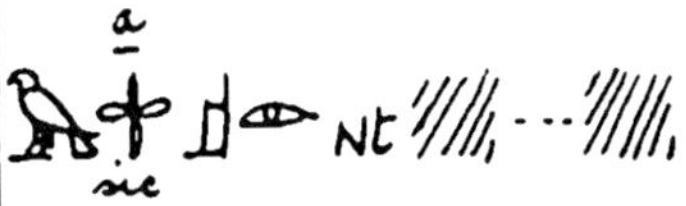

a. Read .

## Utt. 746.
### Nt, 44-5.

(Nt, 44)

§2276 a 

a Read  ? b. Facsimile .

45

§2276 b 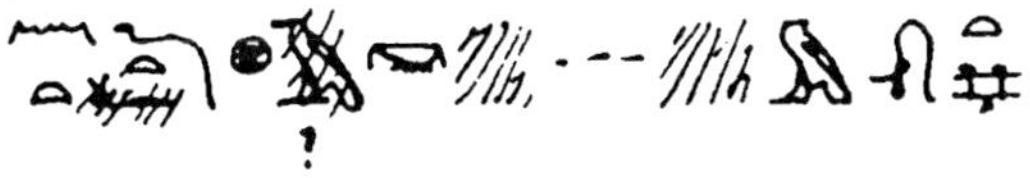

(45)

§2276 c 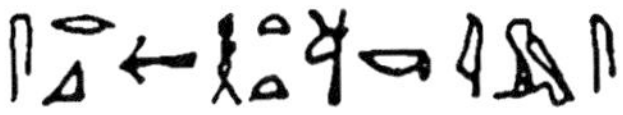

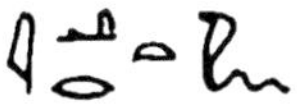

Continued over.

**Utt. 747.**
**Nt, 46-7.**

Nt, 46

§2277a 

(46)

§2277b 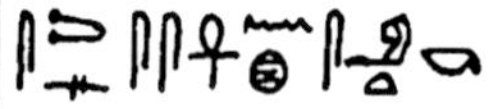

47

§2277c 

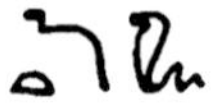

**Utt. 748**
**Nt, 47-9.**

(Nt, 47)

§2278a  a. Read .

48

§2278b 

(48)

§2278c  a-b. Read 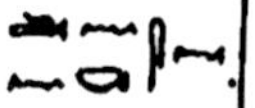.

49

§2278d 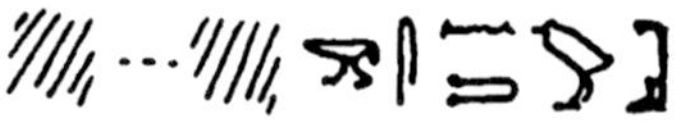

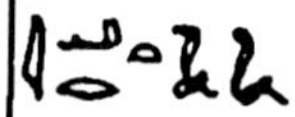

Utt. 749.

Nt, 49-52.

§2279a (49)  a-b. Read 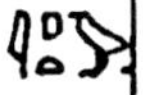

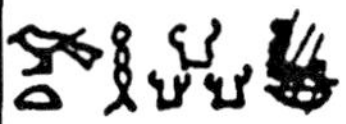

§2279b (50) 

§2279c 51 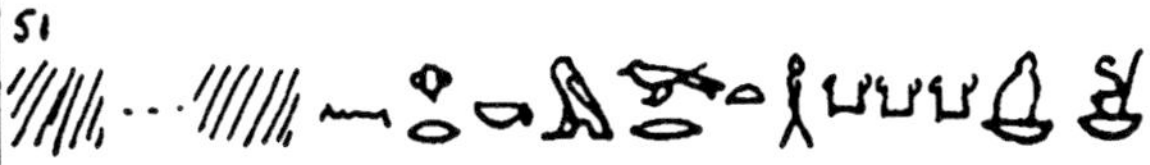

§2279d 52 

Utt. 750.

Nt, 52-3.

§2280 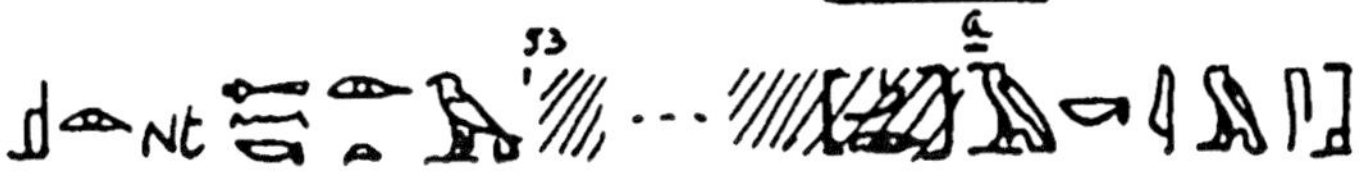 a. Facsimile 

Utt. 751.

Nt, 53.

§2281 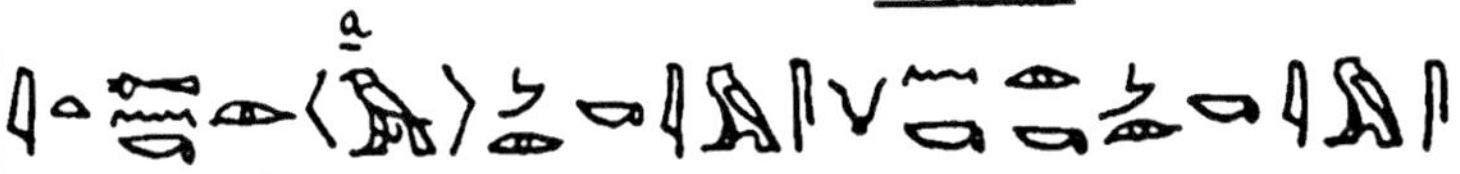

a. A clear textual omission.

## Utt. 752.

Nt, 54-5; JPII, 216+47-8.

Nt, 54 — 55 — a

§2282 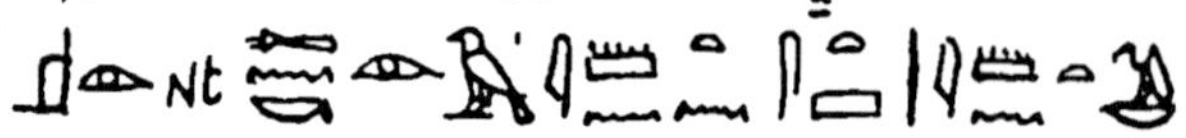

a. JPII, 216+48 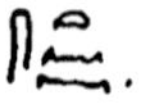.

## Utt. 753.

Nt, 56-7; JPII, 216+49.

Nt, 56 — 57 — a — b

§2283 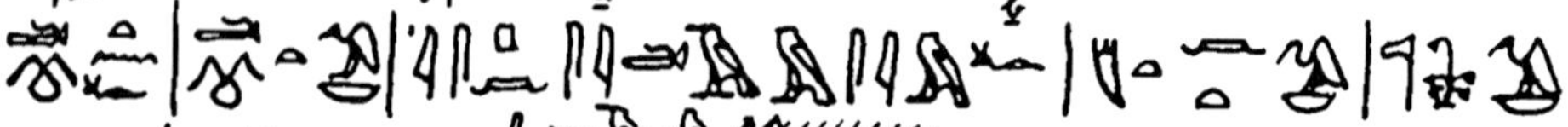

a-b. JPII, 216+49 .

## Utt. 754.

Nt, 58.

§2284 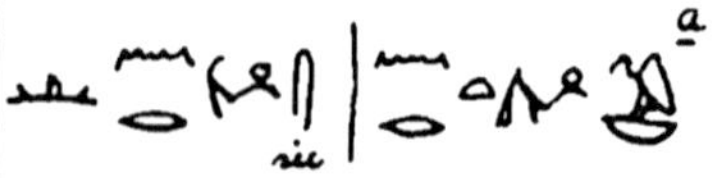 a

a. JPII omits this Utt.

## Utt. 755.

Nt, 59-63; JPII, 216+50-53.

Nt, 59 — 60 — 61

§2285a 

Nt, 62 — 63

§2285b 

## Utt. 756.

Nt, 64; JPII, 216+54.

§2286  a

a. This offering-list is continued in JPII, 216+55-64, but only fragments remain.

## Utt. 757.

Nt, 492.

§2287a 

§2287b 

§2287c 

## Utt. 758.

Nt, 696-700.

Nt, 696

§2288a 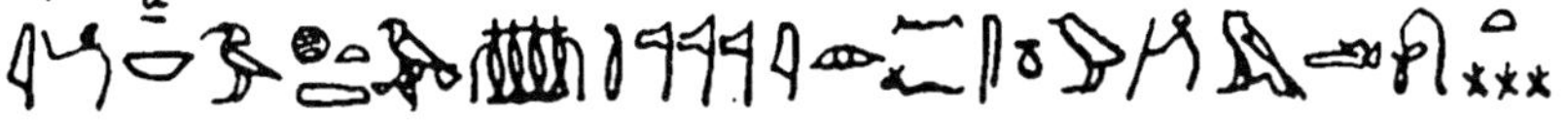 a. Cf. Neit, p. 27.

(696)  697

§2288b 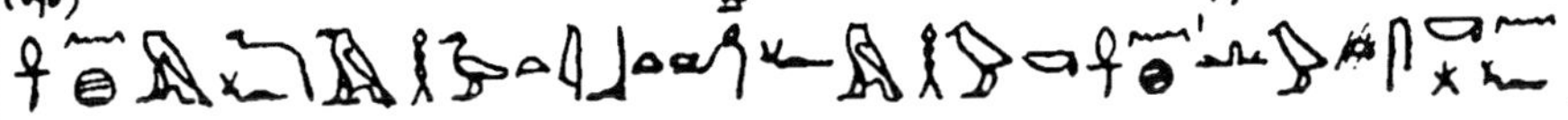 a. Cf. loc. cit.

(697)

§2288c 

(697) 698

§2288d 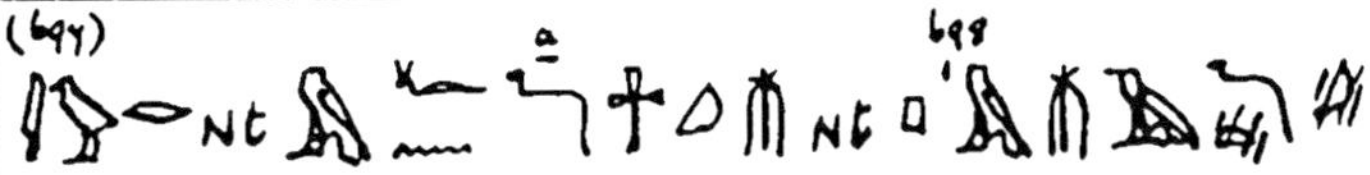 a. Cf. loc. cit

(698)

§2289a 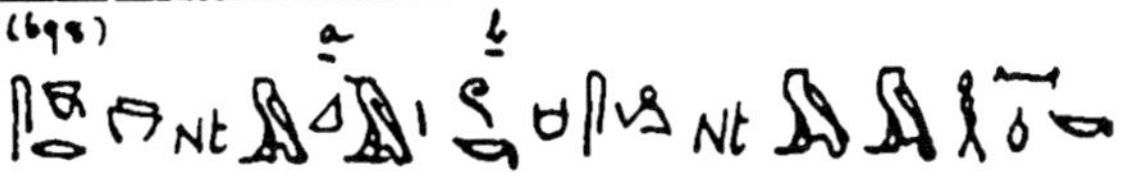 a-b. Read ḥ3bt.k.

(698)

§2289b 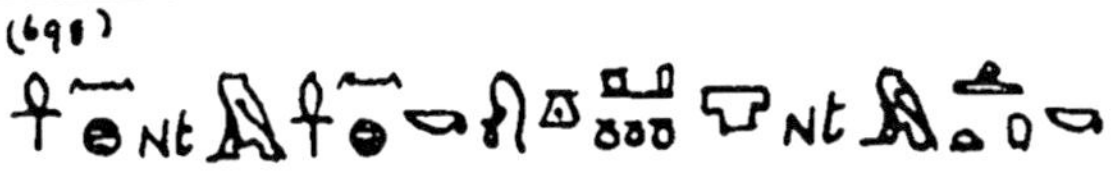

699

§2289c 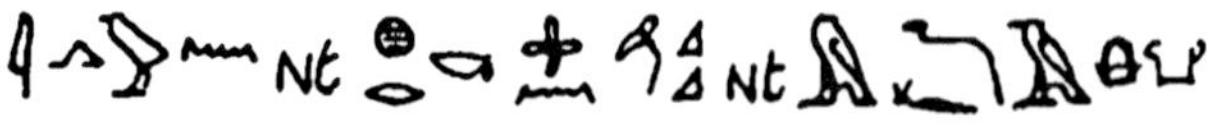

(699)

§2289d 

(699)

§2290a  a-b. Cf. Neit, p. 27.

(700)

§2290b 

## Utt. 759.

### Nt, 749-51.

(Nt, 749)

§2291a  a. Cf. Neit, p. 27. b. Read .

750

§2291b  a. Facsimile .

(750)

§2291c 

§2291d 

(751)

§2291e 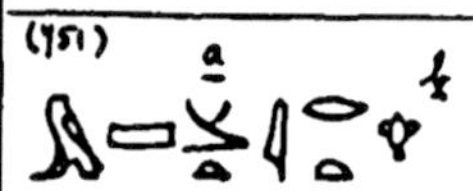 a. Sic facsimile; read 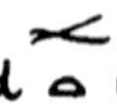 (ỉnct)? b. No stanza mark.

CPSIA information can be obtained
at www.ICGtesting.com
Printed in the USA
BVOW00s1359131116
467348BV00009B/15/P

9 781420 929348